John Costa

A History of Rock & Roll

Seventh Edition

Custom Edition for the University of Utah

Pearson Learning Solutions, 501 Boylston Street, Suite 900, Boston, MA 02116
A Pearson Education Company
www.pearsoned.com

Printed in the United States of America

2 3 4 5 6 7 8 9 10 V202 17 16 15 14 13 12

000200010271292591

CT/CK

PEARSON   ISBN 10: 1-256-52280-5
ISBN 13: 978-1-256-52280-5

Table of Contents

CHAPTER I: ROCK 'n' ROLL'S FIRST GOLDEN AGE

I. MUSIC THROUGH THE NIGHT

    A.) <u>Eclecticism</u>: and the question of rhythmically based music.

        1.) Different varieties that hovered beneath the mainstream radar screen.

            - Blues, boogie-woogie, barrelhouse blues, honky-tonk, country, and rhythm & blues (R&B).

                * The average African American musician at that time, could play all of these styles because to them, it was all the same.

                    a.) Stylistic labels did not carry much weight.

                * <u>Concept</u>: the eclecticism of mixing different rhythmic styles together, would be crucial to the originality of early rock and roll artists.

                    a.) Because, by mixing various rhythmic styles together, an original, individual sound would result.

            - These rhythmic styles that were hovering in the fringes would eventually progress into mainstream success.

                * Country music was one such style.

Dixie Cannonball
  Gene Autry

                    a.) <u>Gene Autry</u>: the first of the "singing cowboys" who started off on the fringe...

                        - ...would eventually become mainstream partly as a result of his TV show in the mid 50's.

    B.) <u>Filling in the vacuum</u>: the gap — no adolescent music.

        1.) Adult Music: "Tin Pan Alley" – pop music of the late 1940's/early 50's.

            - <u>Main Focus</u>: the published song.

                * Tin Pan Alley, a side street in lower Manhattan, was home to a number of music publishing houses.

                    a.) These publishing houses had their own songwriters.

                      - <u>Goal for a Publishing House</u>: to get as many artists as possible to record the same exact published song.

                          * this was how they made their profit.

            - Three defining elements of the Tin Pan Alley style:

                * Crooning, melodic focus.

                * Slow to moderate tempos.

                * Cool, easy jazz or Broadway type of sound.

            - Examples of Tin Pan Alley Composers:

                * Cole Porter, Irving Berlin, George & Ira Gershwin, Jerome Kern, etc.

            - 50's pop performers/crooners inspired by the Tin Pan Alley tradition:

*I've Got You
Under My Skin*
  Frank Sinatra

                * Frank Sinatra, Jo Stafford, Patti Page, Perry Como, Peggy Lee, Dinah Shore, etc.

                    a.) Recorded on major corporate record labels such as:

                      - Decca, RCA Victor, MGM, Capitol, Mercury, and Columbia (CBS) Records.

        2.) Children's music.

            - from children's TV shows such as Buffalo Bob & Howdy Doody or The Disney Mouseketeers.

        3.) <u>Filling In The Gap</u>: music for white teen adolescents.

            - Rock and roll would eventually fill in that gap.

                * Resulting from a rise of teenage consumerism: and with it, disposable income.

                    a.) <u>Causes</u>: Baby Boom, flight to suburbia, and a new post-war prosperity.

    C.) <u>From The Fringes To The Mainstream</u>:

        1.) The main vehicle of bringing rock and roll to the mainstream: independent radio and independent record labels.

            * The process begins with new music hovering in the fringes.

a.) Through a long, step by step process, this fringe sound eventually progresses into the mainstream.

D.) <u>WLAC (Nashville):</u> The beginning of Black Rhythm and Blues from the fringes to the mainstream – a power station with a 50,000 watt transmitter.

    1.) At night, WLAC's signal could reach as far southeast as Miami, FL and Havana, Cuba.

        - As far north as New York, Boston, Cleveland, Chicago.

        * As far west as the Rockies.

            a.) With short wave radio, WLAC could be heard from the European continent.

        - WLAC's tentacles spread far and wide.

    1.) <u>Gene Nobles:</u> first white DJ to play black R&B music on the air at WLAC.

        - 1946: African American students from a black college called Fisk University, brought in a number of rhythm & blues 78 rpm vinyl records.

        * And requested to have this music played on the air.

            a.) Music by artists such as Wynonie Harris, Amos Milburn, Louis Jordan & The Timpany Five, Arthur "Big Boy" Crudup, etc.

        - Gene Nobles started playing these R&B records on his nightly radio show.

        * There was an immediate response from white listeners throughout the South.

            a.) They were interested in that new sound: "What was it? Where did it come from? How can I get these records?"

    2.) <u>Nobles and Randy Wood:</u> first massive R&B record sales pitch on the air.

        - Offering several "78's" (78 RPM) for a low price.

        * Resulting in a massive positive public response.

    3.) <u>William "Hoss" Allen (Nobles' protégé):</u> was the prototype white DJ to both use and excel at using, black street jive lingo on the air – he was the first to inspire a hip attitude that accompanied black R&B.

        - the practice in which a host of other white DJ's would emulate. (even to the point of being coached by African Americans).

        * DJ's such as Hunter Hancock in LA, Hound Dog Lorenz in Buffalo, Wolfman Jack in Chicago...

            a.) ...emulated the use of inner-city street jive in order to become hip.

        - <u>RESULT</u>: A growing number of white teenagers were tuning in.

E.) But what exactly was this music and where did it come from?

    1.) <u>Rhythm and Blues</u> (originally referred to as "Race Music"): the term "Rhythm & Blues" was an expression first coined by Jerry Wexler in 1949 as a writer for Billboard Magazine.

        - Definition: "Music made by and for Black Americans".

    2.) <u>The Genesis of R&B</u>: Louis Jordan, the father of rhythm & blues.

        - Former big band performer who founded a group called The Timpany Five even though there were 6 to 7 members in the group).

        * He was the first to develop the blueprint of what would be known as rhythm & blues in the following manner:

            a.) The first R&B band prototype.

                - By pairing the number of instruments down to 6 or 7 (from 12 to 20 in Big Band), the beat would become considerably, more accentuated.

            b.) Mixing of Jazz and Blues together creating a style known as "Jump Blues".

                - Perky jazz rhythms mixed with a bluesy beat and blues-styled vocalizing.

            c.) Humor: by adding a sense of humor, Louis Jordan made his jump blues style fun.

Saturday Night Fish Fry

Louis Jordan & The Timpany Five

- He was a humorous and adept story teller.
* <u>NOTE</u>: These combined elements created the first template for rhythm & blues.

F.) Two occurrences in 1951 charted the way in giving black rhythm & blues a national notoriety (up to this point, it had been gaining notoriety mostly throughout the South).

    1.) <u>Alan Freed (Cleveland, 1951)</u>: a white DJ who would only play black records.

        - He, more than anyone else at the time, did the most to promote black R&B music to white America.

            * <u>Example</u>: March 21, 1952 – Alan Freed and his radio station WJW, sponsored Freed's "Moondog Coronation Ball" at the Cleveland Arena.

                a.) This was a major concert for rhythm & blues.

                    - 25,000 people showed up for this event (which gave testimony to Freed's influence and popularity as a DJ).

        - As a DJ for WJW in Cleveland, he was the first to use the term "Rock and Roll" as a label for R&B in 1951.

            * This was the reason why Cleveland was chosen to house the Rock and Roll Hall of Fame (even though the induction ceremonies take place in New York City).

                a.) <u>"Rock and Roll"</u>: black slang term for sexual activity.

                    - Freed used this term for marketing purposes.

      - <u>Freed's "Rock and Roll Parties"</u>: hated by Police and older, conservative white America.

            * White and black teenagers intermingled at these gatherings (sometimes intimately).

            * At first, they were called his "Moondog Parties", but at the suggestion of his manager Morris Levy, he changed the name to "Rock n' Roll Parties".

                a.) The beginnings of the gradual disintegration of racial and socio-economic boundaries.

                    - In some ways, mirroring the beginnings of the Civil Rights struggle.

      - The term "Rock n' Roll" would carry a black rhythm & blues connotation until the rise of Elvis Presley's popularity.

            * the term would take on a strictly white connotation thereafter.

Rocket 88
Jackie Brensten
& His Delta Cats

    2.) "<u>Rocket 88</u>"(1951): the first record to introduce rhythm & blues to national audience in a singles format. Written and recorded by Jackie Brenston & His Delta Cats featuring Ike Turner.

        - It was also, the first true rock and roll record. A hybrid of various aesthetic styles blended together to create a new sound (the hallmark of rock 'n' roll's originality).

            * The synthesis of the following stylistic elements gave this record an R&B feel:

                a.) Boogie-woogie piano.

                b.) Jazzy saxophone choruses.

                c.) Blues-derived singing.

                d.) A jump blues type of beat.

            * <u>NOTE</u>: This record established the saxophone as rock and roll's primary solo instrument.

G.) As the 1950's progressed, independent record labels would record the important artists of rock and roll's first golden age.

    1.) There were many labels in many different cities throughout the US.

        - But of all the areas, there are three cities where the most influential artists of this period were both discovered and recorded:

            * New Orleans, Memphis, and Chicago.

II. THE THREE CRADLES OF ROCK AND ROLL CIVILIZATION: NEW ORLEANS, MEMPHIS, & CHICAGO - The Triumph of Independent American Entrepreneurship.

    A.) <u>Cosimo Matassa</u>: J&M Studios

        1.) <u>Goal</u>: to record black music and target a white mainstream audience.

            - The seeds for this idea came from his observations in his father's juke joint in New Orleans. Because segregation was coded into law back then, there were two sides: one for whites and one for "coloreds".

                * Each side had their own unique jukebox: the white side was country music and the black side was R&B.

                    a.) He noticed the white patrons going to the black side to play R&B…

                        -…and the black patrons visiting the Caucasian side to hear Country music.

        2.) <u>J&M Studios</u>: a first in the following ways:

            - The model session band.

                * <u>Dave Bartholemew</u>: established the first rock and roll band prototype along with the rock and roll signature sound (featuring Earl Palmer: the first great rock and roll drummer who was also the first to establish the conventional rock and roll drumming sound).

                    a.) Putting the recording focus on making the drums and bass sounds as the most prominent.

                        - situating them in closest proximity to the studio microphones.

            - <u>NOTE</u>: These two elements — rock and roll studio session band and recording techniques – provided the structure from which other pioneering studios would utilize.

        3.) <u>Antoine "Fats" Domino</u> (b. 2/26/28; New Orleans, LA): rock and roll's first crossover sensation.

            - From a musical family: began playing at the age of 9.

                * At 10, began playing for petty change at various honky-tonk bars such as The Hideaway Club.

                    a.) A local bandleader named Bill Diamond dubbed him "Fats".

            - In his mid-teens, he began playing alongside two important blues influences:

                * <u>Professor Longhair</u> (a New Orleans blues legend) and <u>Amos Milburn</u>.

            - In addition, his boogie-woogie/stride music influences were:

                * <u>Fats Waller</u> and <u>Albert Ammons</u>.

                    a.) Their influences behind Domino's solid piano technique.

                        - Left Hand rhythmic patterns supporting arpeggiations in the right hand.

            - His vocal influences: country and western music.

            - <u>RESULT</u>: a stylistically multi-faceted style.

                * A synthesis of the following:

                    a.) <u>Boogie-woogie/stride piano</u> (the Waller/Ammons influences).

                    b.) <u>Blues-derived beat</u> (the Prof. Longhair/Amos Milburn influences).

                    c.) <u>Country styled singing</u>: featuring his country vocal twang.

            - Mid 1940's: he joined trumpeter <u>Dave Bartholemew</u>.

                * He [Bartholemew] helped arrange Domino's contract with the *Imperial* label.

                    a.) He also became Domino's manager, arranger, and producer.

                * In addition to Fats Domino's blues, boogie-woogie/stride, and country western influences...

The Fat Man
Fats Domino

a.) Dave Bartholemew's session band arrangements provided a *rhythm and blues styled feel*.

   - He and Domino co-wrote most of Domino's singles.
- 1949: "The Fat Man" – his first successful single which eventually sold 1,000,000 copies.
   * produced by Dave Bartholemew.
      a.) the single that introduced the "New Orleans Sound".
- The 1950's: early 50's R&B hits included:
   * "Goin Home" (1952) and "Going To The River" (1953).
   * 1955: "Ain't That A Shame": his first breakthrough hit which made the top ten on the pop charts.
      a.) His already well-established, blues/boogie woogie/country/ R&B style easily fit into the new rock and roll paradigm.
   * Next three years: hits (on pop charts) included...
      a.) 1956: "I'm In Love Again" (#3), "Blueberry Hill" (#2), and "Blue Monday" (#5)
      b.) 1957: "I'm Walkin' " (#4)
      c.) 1958: "Whole Lotta Loving" (#6)
      d.) 1960: "Walkin' To New Orleans"
         - his last million seller.

Ain't That A Shame
Fats Domino

Blueberry Hill
Fats Domino

I'm Walkin'
Fats Domino

- Television Appearances: he also had an easy going/non-threatening demeanor which mainstream audiences found to be pleasant.
   * his African American visage was the first to be widely accepted into the TV living rooms of white homes all over America.
      a.) He made this initial exposure of black music to white teenagers very easy.
         - He would also open the door for other black musicians to make their way into suburban white households.
- RESULT: 30,000,000 singles sold in the decade of the 50's alone including 23 gold singles.
   * Whereas the mainstream viewed Fats Domino as pleasant and unthreatening, the next performer out of J & M Studios would convey a completely different image.

4.) Little Richard (b. Richard Penniman, Macon, GA. 1932): the artist who injected a new sense of rebelliousness and overt sexuality into rock and roll thereby becoming the first true rock star.

- Earliest musical experience: the Fountain Temple AME church where gospel played an important part of his youth.
   * As he mentioned in an interview: "there was no organ or piano playing, just people singing and stomping their feet."
      a.) This was where Penniman first learned to play piano and sing gospel.
- At the age of 13, he was thrown out of his house allegedly for homosexuality and moved in with a white couple – Ann & Johnny Johnson – who ran the Tick Tock Club in Macon, GA.
   * Penniman's first performance venue outside of the church.
- In his teens, he joined a traveling circus doing different types of musical performances under different names.
   * This is where he eventually discovered boogie-woogie (one of his greatest musical inspirations).
- 1951: he signed a contract with RCA.
   * Resulting from an Atlanta audition on radio.
      a.) He basically played conventional jump blues.
- 1953: recorded on the Houston-based Duke-Peacock label (owned by Don Robey: the first successful African American entrepreneur in black music).

* He [Little Richard] recorded with back-up groups such as the Deuces of Rhythm and the Tempo Toppers.
- <u>1955</u>: after performing as frontman for Johnny Otis' Orchestra:
     * He started gigging in New Orleans with a band called The Upsetters.
         a.) they basically played (and he sung) the blues.
             - His rocking tunes were not appreciated at that time.
- Art Rupe, owner of Los Angeles-based *Specialty Records* reviewed a demo tape he received from Little Richard.
     * Rupe was looking for the type of hard-edged voice that Little Richard had to offer.
         a.) At the suggestion of R&B singer Lloyd Price, Little Richard signed with the Specialty label and recorded in Matassa's studio.
             - This was the point where his hard, rocking style would finally become appreciated.
- <u>RESULT</u>: a style built on the bedrock of gospel and blues which was energized by the jump rhythms of boogie-woogie. This combination would create a new and highly aggressive style that captured the free spirit of a frenzied performer like Little Richard.
     * Complete with screaming, hollering, and performances which exhibited all-out, sexually explicit energy (complete with hip gyrations) along with wild, heavy-banging piano playing.
         - Again, a synthesis of the following:
             * Gospel-derived singing.
             * Jump rhythms of boogie woogie.
             * Blues influenced, musical foundation.
     * <u>Little Richard and his Upsetters</u>: were also among the first in rock and roll to develop a "groupie" culture.
- <u>September 14, 1955</u>: Little Richard's entered J&M Studios to record "Tutti Frutti".
     * The original lyrics were very sexually explicit so, Dorothy La Bostrie was hired to clean up the lyrics into something more palatable for a mainstream audience.
         a.) "<u>Tutti Frutti</u>" became one of the first major blueprints of the free-spirited, frenzied style of no-holds-barred rock and roll.
- Among his many gold records (on pop charts):
     * <u>1956</u>; "Tutti Frutti" (#17), "Long Tall Sally" (#6), and "Rip It Up" (#17).
     * <u>1957</u>: "Lucille" (#21), "Jenny, Jenny" (#10), "Keep A Knockin' " (#8).
     * <u>1958</u>: "Good Golly Miss Molly" (#10).
- <u>Conservative/Parental Adult White America</u>: despised him and considered him a threat to the moral well being of their children. Especially given the fact that white girls were crazy about him (a definite no-no at the time).
     * Parents exercised a de facto censorship by confiscating Little Richard recordings from their kids.
- <u>BACKLASH</u>: the beginning of white, tin-pan-alley type performers doing covers of black R&B tunes – especially those of Little Richard.
     * <u>Pat Boone</u> (b. Charles Eugene Boone, 6/1/34, Jacksonville, FL): One of the most successful pop teen idols of the 1950's.
         a.) He recorded 38 hit singles that reached the top 40 category.
             - Including a number of R&B covers which parents felt were cleaner, safer versions of the original black recordings.

Tuttti Frutti
Little Richard

Lucille
Little Richard

Good Golly Miss Molly
Little Richard

                           * Songs like "Tutti Frutti", "Long Tall
                               Sally", "Ain't That A Shame", etc.
                  - As a teen pop star, he became the alternative to
                  renegade artists like Little Richard, and Elvis one that
                  parents and older white conservative America could
                  easily accept.
            * White artists such as Pat Boone would reap large financial rewards at
            the expense of the original black artists.
                  a.) We will see this scenario played out repeatedly through the
                  course of rock and roll's development.
        - <u>Little Richard</u>: was the first aggressive, high-flying, free spirit ever to appear
        on the rock and roll scene and the first to be appreciated by a mainstream
        teenage audience.

     B.) <u>MEMPHIS</u>: Sam Phillips (b. 1/5/23; d. 7/30/03):
        1.) founded the "<u>Memphis Recording Service</u>" in 1950.
            - originally inspired by the blues clubs on Beale Street.

Moanin' At
Midnight
Howlin' Wolf
            - as an experienced radio engineer, he started out recording local black R&B
            talents such as B.B. King, Howlin' Wolf (Chester Burnett), Memphis DJ: Rufus
            Thomas, etc.
        2.) "<u>Rocket 88</u>" (1951): by Jackie Brensten and His Delta Cats featuring Ike Turner.

Rocket 88
Jackie Brensten
& His Delta Cats
            - Sam Phillips' first recording success: "Rocket 88" would make it to #1 on the
            R&B charts.
                  * A mixture of rhythm and blues, boogie-woogie along with a
                  bluesy vocal twang.
            - first R&B record to become a crossover success with the white mainstream
            teenage population.
                  * Primarily achieved because of the jump rhythms of boogie-woogie –
                  the first ingredient in black music that would become a deliberate tool
                  for the engineering of crossover appeal.
                      a.) It would also give white teenage America, their first full-
                      fledged introduction to the sound of black music. In Sam
                      Phillips' words, Rocket 88, "broadened the base for white
                      males and females to appreciate black music or rhythm and
                      blues".
            - Written on the drive from Clarksdale, Miss. to Memphis. (Ike Turner's friend,
            B.B. King, set up the appointment with Sam Phillips.
                  * Sometimes, as in this case, last minute pressure can inspire one to be
                  creative very quickly and produce an original product. This is where
                  having strong stylistic foundations, can kick in and support this instant
                  creativity.
            - The success of "Rocket 88" inspired and afforded Sam Phillips an opportunity
            to reinvent his amateur operation into a professional studio.
                  * the result: the legendary <u>Sun Records</u> (1953).
       3.) He continued to record local R&B/blues talents as he had done before. But in spite of
his great success with "Rocket 88", he continually kept running into barriers that
inhibited the acceptance of black music in white America (mainly in the South).
            - <u>IDEA</u>: Sam Phillips thought that if he could only find a young white male who
            could perform black rhythm and blues with an air of authenticity (i.e. with a true
            African American feel)…
                  *…he [Phillips] might be able to crack those racial barriers standing in
                  his way.
                      a.) Southerners would be quick to accept a white substitute as
                      opposed to an authentic black artist.
                          - <u>NOTE</u>: this idea – putting a white face on an
                          African American art form and reaping the financial

rewards at the expense of the original black artists – would have major implications throughout rock and roll's development.
> > > * It is a scenario that will be played out time and time again.

III. <u>Elvis Aaron Presley</u> (b. Tupelo, MS: 1/8/35 - d. Memphis, TN: 8/16/77):
    A.) Early Years: He developed a love for a wide, eclectic variety of music at an early age.
        1.) He played his guitar and sung in private or in small intimate settings at the Lauderdale Courts – a housing project near downtown Memphis where Elvis' family lived during his teen years.
            - <u>Songs</u>: mostly ballads by Tin Pan Alley singers such as: Kay Starr, Bing Crosby, Eddie Fisher, and Perry Como.
                * <u>Country</u>: songs by Eddie Arnold and Hank Williams.
        2.) <u>Gospel Music</u>: was perhaps his favorite at that time (with its emotional and spiritual catharsis).
            - Gospel Influences: <u>The Blackwood Brothers</u> – members of Elvis' Assembly of God church.
                * They [Blackwood Brothers] were influenced by black gospel groups such as The Soul Stirrers and The Original Gospel Harmonettes of Birmingham.
            - <u>The Statesmen</u>: was Elvis' favorite gospel group.
                * Combination of high tenor voices capped by the virtuosic falsetto of Jake Hess plus the steady bass voice of Big Chief (Jim Weatherington).
                    a.) In Elvis' view, The Statesmen took the raw emotion and flamboyant showmanship of gospel to the limit.
            - Elvis at one time auditioned for a Gospel group in his church known as The Songfellows but was rejected.
        3.) <u>His Rhythm & Blues Influences</u>: Ivory Joe Hunter, Wynonie Harris, Eddie Vinson, Rufus Thomas, Little Junior Parker, and Arthur "Big Boy" Crudup.
            - He oftentimes, listened to these artists on Dewey Phillips' radio show on WHBQ in Memphis.
        4.) <u>April 4, 1953</u>: his first public performance on a real stage: The Humes High School "Annual Minstrel Show".
            - Elvis performed "Till I Waltz Again With You" by Teresa Brewer.
    B.) <u>Sun Records</u>: August of 1953.
        1.) <u>Marion Keisker</u>: Sam Phillips' assistant at Sun Records first met Elvis after he walked into the studio carrying an old worn-out acoustic guitar. (At this time, he was a very shy, eighteen-year-old truck driver working for Crown Electric Company).
            - He paid $3.98 to record a two-sided acetate.

My Happiness
Elvis Presley

                * Side A: "<u>My Happiness</u>", a 1948 pop hit recorded by Jon & Sandra Steele.
                * Side B: "<u>That's When Your Heartaches Begin</u>" - 1941: The Ink Spots with lead singer Bill Kenny (another influence on Elvis).
                * Legend has it, as a birthday gift for his mother Gladys Love Presley (b. Gladys Love Smith 4/25/1912)
                    a.) However, because of his mother's April birthday, it was more likely that he just wanted to hear himself on tape, (As opposed to the birthday present legend)…
                        - He immediately caught the attention of Sam Phillips for he [Phillips] thought that this might be the person he was looking for.
            - <u>Elvis at Sun Records</u>: a gradual progression from shyness/insecurity to the confidence/free-spirit of flamboyant showmanship.
                * From someone with little experience in front of large audiences to a unique, accomplished performer.

a.) He would inspire countless others to follow in his footsteps emulating his style and individuality.

    * From an artist who sang mostly Tin Pan Alley and country songs…

        a.) … to one who created a trans-racial fusion of blues, gospel, R&B, and Country which transformed rock 'n' roll into a Caucasian, hard-rocking connotation.

            - Up to this point, the term "rock 'n' roll" was used to denote black R&B.

2.) <u>The Audition</u>: Sam Phillips solicited guitarist Scotty Moore to audition Elvis (at that time, Moore was a member of a country/hillbilly group called The Starlight Wranglers).

    - Scotty Moore's influences:

        * <u>Jazz Influence</u>: Barney Kessell

        * <u>Country Influence</u>: Chet Atkins

    - <u>July 4, 1954</u>: Elvis auditioned at Scotty Moore's house (bass player, Bill Black, another Starlight Wrangler member - was also in attendance).

        * Elvis played songs by: The Ink Spots, Billy Eckstein, Eddie Arnold, and Hank Snow.

            a.) Scotty thought that Elvis was nothing special, just average (Phillips decoded that he wanted to hear for himself).

    - <u>Elvis' First Recording Session</u>:

Harbor Lights
Elvis Presley

        * The following night: Elvis, Scotty, and Bill met for a recording session at Sun Records. They started out working on ballads.

            a.) The first was <u>Harbor Lights</u>, a Bing Crosby hit.

                - Sam Phillips did not initially record it (he did eventually record "Harbor Lights" but it was never released – it would be released in 1976 as part of a compilation *Elvis – A Legendary Performer Vol. 2*).

I Love You Because
Elvis Presley

            b.) "I <u>Love You Because</u>": a 1949 hit by Leon Payne. This rendition captured Sam Phillips' attention enough to press the record button.

                - For the first time, Phillips had heard a true emotional, expressive mood out of Elvis' voice that he [Phillips] wanted to capture on tape.

            c.) This discovery notwithstanding, Sam Phillips became disappointed because he was hoping for something more along the lines of black R&B jump rhythms – something wild instead of subdued.

    - <u>The Breakthrough</u>: in one spontaneous moment during a coffee break that followed the recording of "I Love You Because", Elvis, Scottie, and Bill were joking and jumping around in the studio playing a fast, fun version of an R&B tune called: "<u>That's All Right (Mama)</u>".

That's All Right (Mama)
Elvis Presley

        * Written and first recorded in 1946 by an early rhythm and blues artist Arthur "Big Boy" Crudup.

            a.) It originally had a jumpy, upbeat tempo.

        * Elvis' "interpretation" immediately caught Phillips' attention.

            a.) Reason: because Elvis took this upbeat, perked-up R&B tune and added a new sense of energy and flamboyance while maintaining an authentic black sound. In other words, he rocked it.

                - Sam Phillips recorded this rendition of "That's All Right (Mama)" immediately on the spot (and made a one-sided acetate for radio DJ Dewey Phillips).

                    * For the first time, he discovered originality in Elvis' sound.

- <u>NOTE</u>: the concept of "rocking out" a cover song thereby basically reinventing it, would be one of Elvis' signature trademarks throughout his early career.

* Such an achievement was possible because Elvis — like many other rhythm-based artists — was highly adept at appreciating and playing a fusion of various styles because to him (as well as them), these styles were all under the same "umbrella"…

    a.) … styles such as gospel, country-western, rhythm and blues, traditional blues, rockabilly, etc. were synthesized into a unique, energetic hybrid.

      - This allowed him to approach any cover song in any style and basically reinvent it in his own original way.

* Black Influences: during his Sun Records years, Elvis' Presley immersed himself in black culture by hanging out at black clubs, shopping at black retail outlets (such as Lansky Bros. on Beale Street) emulating the African American style of dress.

    a.) He emulated black music to the point of sounding like an African American singer.

      - Complete with the heart, soul, feel, and raw vitality that characterized black R&B artists.

        * His emulation of black artists (especially Arthur "Big Boy" Crudup) along with gospel in an authentic manner was another trademark of Elvis' style while at Sun Records.

    b.) In addition, Elvis' originality of evoking a trans-racial fusion, fulfilled Sam Phillips' vision of a Caucasian substitute for the real thing [black artists] that white southerners can openly embrace.

C.) The Birth of Elvis Presley's Legend

    1.) July 8, 1954: "That's All Right (Mama)" was introduced to the general public on WHBQ's "Red, Hot, and Blue Show" hosted by DJ Dewey Phillips (no relation to Sam)…

      - …to an overwhelming favorable response throughout the Memphis area (the radio station phone was ringing off the hook).

        * He played two acetates simultaneously on two turntables (giving a quasi-stereo sound).

        a.) He repeated the record on the air multiple times.

      - There was no doubt, that this record would be a big success (at least in the Memphis area).

        * What was needed, was a Side B in order to create a two-sided vinyl record for distribution.

    2.) "Blue Moon of Kentucky": written and first recorded in 1947 by country/bluegrass legend, Bill Monroe.

Blue Moon Of Kentucky
Bill Monroe

      - Originally, a slow country ballad in waltz time.

        * Elvis greatly increased the tempo, rocked it out, and transformed it into a completely different and original piece.

        a.) But it did not start out that way.

      - They began by recording it at a slow tempo and going through many different takes (they had a difficult time getting it right).

Blue Moon Of Kentucky
Elvis Presley

        * But once again, in a serendipitous moment, Bill Black started jumping and goofing around with it (he was the first to start goofing around when they recorded "That's All Right (Mama)").

        a.) Then, Elvis and then Scotty Moore, followed suit.

          As a result, another original, rocking-out sound was born.

      - "Slapback": Sam Phillips used a technique known as "tape deck echo" (he called it "Slapback") to record *Blue Moon of Kentucky*.

* <u>Definition of Tape Deck Echo</u>: recording from the primary reel-to-reel tape deck directly to a secondary tape deck thereby creating a slight, echoed delay (while simultaneously recording the artists in the studio).

      a.) <u>Example</u>: from the microphones – to the primary tape deck —- to the secondary tape deck = tape deck echo (slight, echoed delay).

        - This added more audio depth to an otherwise anemic-sounding acoustic trio setup.

          * It also accentuated Bill Black's combination of melodic and percussive sounds on the acoustic bass.

- <u>July 19, 1954</u>: the actual record – catalogued as #209 – was released.

    * Side A: "That's All Right (Mama)"

    * Side B: "Blue Moon of Kentucky"

      a.) There were already thousands of orders for this record before its release.

3.) <u>His First Important Public Performance</u>:

- Later that month on July 30th, Elvis, Scottie, and Bill performed before a large audience for the first time on the Slim Whitman Package Show – an outdoor concert at Overton Park in Memphis. (organized by radio DJ, Bob Neal).

    * Elvis, Scottie, and Bill performed "That's All Right (Mama)" and "Blue Moon of Kentucky" (the latter was played again for an encore).

      a.) The audience response was overwhelmingly enthusiastic.

- <u>His first important regular performance venue</u>: "The Louisiana Hayride" (Shreveport, LA) – the Grand Ole Opry's archrival.

    * Broadcasted on KWKH radio.

      a.) It was through his exposure on KWKH with The Louisiana Hayride, that Elvis began achieving notoricty outside of the Memphis area.

        - In addition to Louisiana, this new notoriety had spread to southern states such as Texas, Arkansas, Alabama, Mississippi, and Missouri.

- <u>Additional Singles</u>: that Elvis would interpret in his own original manner.

    * <u>Good Rockin' Tonight</u> (recorded on 9/22/54): written by Roy Brown and recorded by Wynonie Harris in 1948.

      a.) A hard-rockin', gospel-driven single.

    * <u>Baby Let's Play House</u> (Side A), <u>I'm Left, You're Right, She's Gone</u> (Side B).

      a.) Elvis' first single to chart nationally in July of 1955.

        - In this case, the country charts.

    * <u>Mystery Train</u> (recorded on 7/11/55): Elvis' last recording at Sun records.

      a.) Originally recorded on Sun Records by Little Juniors Blue Flames.

- <u>The Big Change</u>: Although Elvis was becoming a Southern sensation; his limited rise in popularity did not go unnoticed by the corporate record industry who began to see his potential for stardom.

    * These corporate labels were offering Sam Phillips huge sums of money to buy out Elvis' contract with Sun Records.

      a.) Among the front runners was Colonel Tom Parker representing RCA Victor.

        - "Colonel Parker and Hank Snow Enterprises" had served as Elvis' management team beginning in June of 1955.

Good Rockin'
Tonight
Elvis Presley

Baby Let's
Play House
Elvis Presley

Mystery Train
Elvis Presley

Mystery Train
Little Junior's
Blue Flames

He crafted a buy-out package that combined his management team, Hill & Range music Publishing, and RCA Victor.

* After extensive negotiations, Sam Phillips agreed to sell Elvis' contract to the Colonel Parker, Hill & Range, and RCA consortium for $35,000 – a large amount in those days.

    a.) Sam Phillips desperately needed this cash to pay back - royalties, and the money he owed to his brother Jud (to buyout his brother's share of Sun Records).

        - He also needed the cash to produce other white artists along with promoting a hit single written and originally recorded by one of those new artists…

D.) <u>Carl Perkins</u> (b. 4/9/32, Tiptonville, TN; d. 1/19/98, Jackson, TN): although he was multi-faceted stylistically like most rhythm-based artists of his period…

    - … Country and Honky-Tonk would always remain a highly prominent trait in his musical personality that he could never shed or water-down for the sake of consistent, mass-market appeal.

      * This became the reason of his failure to maintain a successful career as a bona fide pop icon.

- Influences:

      * <u>John Westbrook</u>: a porch-pounding, African American sharecropper known as "Uncle John" who introduced [a very young] Carl Perkins to the art of the blues.

        a.) He sang the blues with a lot of heart and soul that would be influential to Perkins' vocalizing.

          - And the bending of notes on the blues guitar for expressive purposes.

      * <u>The Grand Ole Opry</u>: listening to country-styled guitar picking on WSM radio broadcasts.

        a.) <u>"Butterball" Page</u>: was one such influence.

          - Who, along with Ernest Tubb, was adept at playing lead melodic lines on the guitar.

        b.) <u>Arthur Smith</u>: wrote and recorded "Guitar Boogie" in 1946.

          - Helped popularize a new standard for guitar-playing dexterity which inspired a whole new generation of guitar players.

      * <u>Resulting Style</u>: developing his style in mostly honky-tonk bars, Perkins' musical personality was a combination of the following:

        a.) A honky-tonk/hillbilly style.

          - Especially with a country guitar-picking approach.

          - Faster tempos.

        b.) Black Music (mainly the blues):

          - The raw emotion, the phrasing/harmonic structure, and the focus on rhythm (especially the backbeat).

            * This was why, in a time where no country artists used drummers, Carl Perkins did in order to accentuate the rhythm.

          - He also sped up the tempo of his blues influences.

        c.) RESULT: <u>Rockabilly</u> – a fusion of country/hillbilly and black music (mainly blues and/or R&B).

          - *Billboard Magazine* called it "mongrel music".

- <u>His Breakthrough Single</u>: "Blue Suede Shoes" – written and first recorded in late 1955.

* Sun Records' first major hit on the national pop charts.
    a.) …and in the process, became Sun Records' first single to sell 1,000,000 copies.
* "Blue Suede Shoes" would also become the first single to sit atop of 3 major charts: country, R&B, and pop.
    a.) <u>Reason</u>: a synthesis of country, R&B, and a hip, pop tune sensibility that crossed all of the lines.
        - Blues-influenced phrasing and harmonic structure.
        - Country-styled beat.
        - Country-styled guitar fill-ins.
        - Blues-influenced emotional singing and melodic style.

Blue Suede Shoes
Carl Perkins

* Inspired by Johnny Cash's suggestion to write a tune about words he overheard while waiting in a line: "Don't step on my blue suede shoes".
    a.) Carl Perkins burned the midnight oil after waking up at the wee hours with the idea for the song.
        - According to Colin Escott, Perkins wrote the song on the surface of an empty potato bag.
* Released on January 1, 1956 after circulating acetates of the single to various radio stations to test the response.
    a.) By April of 1956, "Blue Suede Shoes" had reached the top echelons of all three major charts.
        - The first single to do so.
- <u>Aftermath</u>: Carl Perkins would never come up with a follow-up hit to solidify his star status.
    * Although "Boppin' The Blues" , "Dixie Fried", and "Matchbox" became hits on the country charts…
        a.) Perkins would never again score big on the pop charts.
            - <u>Reason</u>: he was too hillbilly/country/honky-tonk in nature.
               * He was never meant to succeed as a teen pop poet/idol.

Matchbox
Carl Perkins

Dixie Fried
Carl Perkins

- Sam Phillips however, would discover an even greater talent who would in many ways, would not only reach teen idol status with a string of hits, but also, would become Elvis' de facto successor at Sun Records.

6.) <u>Jerry Lee Lewis</u> (b. 1935 in Ferriday, LA): grew up listening to an eclectic mix of musical styles that would become influential to his musical development.
    - These influences consisted of the following:
        * <u>Radio</u>:
            a.) The music of jazz singer <u>Al Jolson</u>.
            b.) Country and Western artists: <u>Jimmy Rodgers</u>, <u>Hank Williams</u>, and <u>Gene Autry</u>.
               - These artists [Jolson included] had the talent to take any song of any style and make it conform to their own individual characteristics. In other words, they molded these songs to fit their own personalities (rather than the other way around).
                  * This particular talent would become Lewis' trademark, too.
        * <u>Carl McVoy</u> (Lewis' cousin): was the first to teach Jerry Lee to play the piano and the art of boogie-woogie while Jerry Lee was visiting him one summer in Pine Bluff, Arkansas.
            a.) At age 8: he began playing his aunt's piano back home.

* <u>Haney's Big House</u>: A black roadhouse on the outskirts of Ferriday where he [Lewis] received his first "education" in hard-driving black music styles such as honky-tonk, blues, and R&B.

> a.) Jerry Lee Lewis was only about 9 years of age when he started sneaking in through a window to watch these influential black performers such as B.B King.
>
> > - He usually hid behind the bar.

* <u>Gospel Hymns</u>: of his local Assembly of God church.
* <u>Swing Era</u>: Big Band music.

- <u>His first public performance</u>: at age 14 was with a local country & western band at a Ford auto dealer in June of 1949.

> * At 16, he enrolled in Southwest Bible College in Waxahachie, Texas and was soon expelled for playing a boogie-woogie styled interpretation of a gospel hymn, "My God is Real" during a service.

- He returned to Ferriday, LA and back to playing the bars doing honky-tonk and boogie-woogie music – until he heard about Sun Records…

> * He and his father sold in Lewis' words: "39 dozen eggs to get some gas"…
>
> > a.) …and made the trip to Memphis.
>
> * <u>1956</u>: he auditioned for Jack Clement, Sam Phillips' assistant at Sun Records (Phillips was away on vacation).
>
> > a.) Clement had suggested to Lewis that he [Lewis] adopt a more rock 'n' roll approach in the spirit of Elvis (who had recently signed with RCA).
> >
> > > - Clement proceeded to cut a demo tape for Sam Phillips on November 14, 1956.
> > >
> > > > * In that demo session, Lewis then recorded a Ray Price country tune called "Crazy Arms" in a rock and roll style.
> >
> > b.) Clements then contacted Phillips and spoke favorably of Lewis (partly because of Lewis' persistence but mostly, because of his talent).

Crazy Arms
Jerry Lee Lewis

> * Phillips was immediately convinced when he heard Lewis' first recording: "<u>Crazy Arms</u>".
>
> > a.) Sun Records released "Crazy Arms" (Side A) with "End Of The Road" (Side B) on December 1, 1956.
> >
> > > - It was Jerry Lee Lewis' debut release.

- Signing with Sun Records was one of the most important breaks for Lewis.

> * The other, was the discovery of a song that would become his first major hit.

Whole Lotta
Shakin' Going On
Jerry Lee Lewis

> > a.) It happened one night when he attended a bar called "The Wagon Wheel" in Natchez, MS. (across the Mississippi River from Ferriday, LA).
> >
> > > - It was there that he happened by chance to hear the band play a song called: "<u>Whole Lotta Shakin' Going On</u>".
> > >
> > > > * Performed by Roy Hall.
> > >
> > > - He immediately recognized the song's hit potential and learned the tune.
>
> * He recorded "Whole Lotta Shakin' Going On "in February of 1957.
>
> > a.) It became his breakthrough hit that launched him into rock 'n' roll stardom.
> >
> > > - It sold 100,000 copies throughout the south initially due to Memphis DJ Dewey Phillips' promotional efforts.
> >
> > b.) <u>Sunday, July 28, 1957</u>: his first national exposure.

- Jerry Lee Lewis performed "Whole Lotta Shakin' "
on one of the top variety shows in the country, The
Steve Allen Show.
> * It was an unforgettable performance full of
> wild, free-spirited frenzy including his
> signature piano acrobatics of slides up &
> down the keyboard, kicking back the piano
> bench, and hammering the chords with an
> overall sense of fury.
>> a.) RESULT: an additional
>> 6,000,000 copies were sold
>> reaching to #3 on the pop charts.
> c.) The success of this recording made Jerry Lee Lewis, Sun
> Records' biggest star to date (remember that Elvis did not
> become the great international sensation until he signed with
> RCA).

- For all practical purposes, Jerry Lee Lewis became Elvis' successor at Sun
Records because like Elvis, Lewis performed with a straight-ahead, all-out
frenzy and injected an aura of a "no holds barred" free spirit.
> * Pounding, banging of chords on the piano.
> * Flashy showmanship.
> * Massive use of sliding up and down the keyboard (i.e. glissandi).
> * Onstage Acrobatics: especially when he kicked away the piano
> bench.
>> a.) He developed this signature, free-spirited performance
>> style during a tour with Carl Perkins and Johnny Cash (from
>> March 31st to May 5th of 1957).

Great Balls Of Fire
Jerry Lee Lewis

- His legend was solidified by his next hit: "Great Balls of Fire".
> * This follow-up hit was released on November 15, 1957.
> * Sold 5,000,000 copies and rose to #2 on the pop charts.
>> a.) Along with "Whole Lotta Shakin' ", "Great Balls of Fire"
>> reached the top five in the pop, R&B, and country charts at the
>> same time.

High School Confidential
Jerry Lee Lewis

> * 1958: other hits included "Breathless" which rose to # 7 on the pop
> charts and "High School Confidential" (#21).
> a.) He would never again, have another major hit within the top 25.
>> - Unlike Elvis' slew of hit records, hit albums, and
>> movie appearances while at RCA…
>>> * Jerry Lee Lewis had relatively fewer
>>> commercial successes for an artist of such
>>> legendary status.
>>>> a.) His Sun Records recordings up
>>>> to 1958 are his only important
>>>> benchmarks up to date.

- A Change of Fortune: in 1958, Lewis was booked for several tours including
the Alan Freed Tour (March 28th – May 10th) and a brief international tour,
which took him to the UK.
> * By this time, his fame had reached rock 'n' roll icon status…
>> a.) During his visit, the British press had caught on to
>> something controversial and scandalous with a girl named
>> Myra Gale Brown (daughter of J.W. Brown: Lewis' bass
>> player) that would cause Lewis to be heckled off the stage
>> during a performance.
>>> - Lewis abandoned the tour to be replaced by a
>>> teenage UK artist who was squeaky clean: Terry
>>> Wayne.

15

b.) This controversial scandal would lead to the blacklisting of Jerry Lee Lewis for the next decade.

- The reasons will be presented later on in this chapter when the demise of rock 'n' roll's first golden age is discussed.

7.) <u>Elvis with RCA</u>: January of 1958 marked his first nationally televised appearance.

- there would be about a dozen more by the year's end.

* The highlight was the Fall of 1956 on The Ed Sullivan Show.

a.) Where legend has it, that they would not show him from waist down.

- his other achievements, due in great part from the heavy promotional campaign that a major label like RCA can afford to embark on…

* 2, number one albums.

* a hit movie.

* several number one singles.

- In addition, as earlier mentioned, Elvis' mainstream popularity changed the meaning of the term "rock 'n' roll".

* What was once a term synonymous with black R&B, "rock 'n' roll" was now (due to his popularity)...

a.) ... a white, rhythm-based, musical label.

- but all of this sudden popularity did not come without a price.

8.) <u>CONCEPT</u>: whenever any artist attempts to reach as wide an audience as possible, several adjustments must be made:

I Want You,
I Need You,
I Love You
Elvis Presley

Don't Be Cruel
Elvis Presley

- the sound must be polished up and devoid of any type of rawness.

- the delivery cannot be too rough, it has to be molded and in some cases, carefully choreographed.

- also in many cases, background vocal harmonizations are needed to "sweeten up" an already subdued or sometimes deficient lead voice.

- in other words, a performer's sound, look, and delivery cannot be threatening in any way.

* <u>Reason</u>: in order to cross all the lines and be acceptable to practically everyone thereby insuring commercial success.

- <u>RESULT</u>: Elvis had given up his black influences once he moved to RCA. In order to appeal to that wide, mainstream audience.

8.) <u>The price for going mainstream</u>: one has to give up much of their uniqueness and raw intensity that started them off in the first place...

- and settle for elevated mediocrity in order to fit a particular mold…

a.)…and avoid any risk-taking (which is the basic element in artistic invention and integrity).

- <u>FALLOUT</u>: this is exactly what happened to Elvis under the watchful eyes of both RCA and Colonel Tom Parker.

* He would never again sing and perform with the raw intensity and free spirit abandonment as he did during his tenure at Sun Records.

* While Elvis gained immense popularity on one hand…

a.) …on the other, he gave up much of himself and his black influences (the bedrock of his early artistry) in order to be appealing to everyone…

- …as a result, something was lost.

C.) <u>CHICAGO</u>: Phil and Leonard Chess emigrated from Poland to escape Nazi persecution of the Jews.

1.) They brought with them, a business acumen.

- which they applied to several businesses on Chicago's South Side, African American section.

2.) Black migration from the South:

- Millions of African Americans moved to Northern industrial cities from the South.

*Most of whom grew up in and worked in Southern plantations as sharecroppers.
- They migrated to in order to find better paying factory jobs which were prevalent in Northern cities such as Detroit; Chicago; Gary, IN, and Buffalo.
* Many of these factories were part of the military industrial complex, which was seeing rapid growth beginning in the 1920's.
- They brought with them, their culture and their music.
* In Chicago, they primarily settled in both the South and West sides of that city.
- NOTE: Both the Chess brothers and the Southern blacks migrated in search of a better life. These two forces: the entrepreneurship of the Chess brothers and the great artistry of the black southern blues musicians…
*…would come together and redefine the genre of blues honing in a new style called Chicago (or Electric) Blues.
a.) The catalyst for recording this new style would be Chess Records.

3.) One of businesses the Chess brothers were operating in the South Side of Chicago: The Mocambo: a nightclub devoted primarily to jazz and blues music.
- In nightclubs such as The Mocambo, blues artists who were primarily from the South, played acoustic instruments.
* The Problem: they could not be heard over the noisy atmosphere inherent in most inner city establishments (like The Mocambo).
a.) The Solution: amplification.
- The Result: electric blues which eventually became known as Chicago Blues.

4.) 1946: Phil and Leonard Chess founded Aristocrat Records.
- Primarily, to record jazz artists.
* but jazz records did not sell well.
a.) 1950: the label's name was changed to Chess records.

*Got My Mojo
Working*
Muddy Waters

- They began recording electric blues artists such as Muddy Waters (McKinley Morganfield), Howlin' Wolf (Chester Burnett), Sonny Boy Williamson (Rice Miller), and Willie Dixon.
* in fact, Willie Dixon would eventually become Chess' de facto "A&R Man" (meaning artist & repertoire) not only discovering new talent…
a.) …but also having an important hand in writing arrangements for various artists.
* NOTE: These artists will be covered in greater detail in Chapter 5 which will focus on the British blues based guitarists such as Eric Clapton, Jeff Beck, etc.
a.) Because the discussion of blues history will be more pertinent due to the tremendous influence it had on these British artists.
- Although Chicago Blues sold well within the confines of the black community, mainstream white America was almost completely unaware of it's existence.
* There would be two artists however, who, being influenced by this genre, would mix it up with more pop rhythms and blues flavor.
a.) thereby introducing the Chess sound to the mainstream pop charts and audience.

5.) Bo Diddley (b. Ellas McDaniel in McComb, MS, December 28, 1928)
- Moved to Chicago when he was 8 years old with his mother's first cousin, Mama Gussie McDaniel.

Boogie Chillen
John Lee Hooker

* In Chicago, he grew up around church music, spirituals.
a.) The first blues record that caught his attention was "Boogie Chillen" by John Lee Hooker.

Walkin' The Boogie (Alternate Take)
John Lee Hooker

Pretty Thing
Bo Diddley

* At the age of 15, he started taking boxing lessons to defend himself against the bullies who were harassing him (he boxed for about seven years).

    a.) Once he mastered the schoolyard brawl where no one could beat him, kids started calling him Bo Diddley.

    - "Man, you're a Bo Diddley!"

- <u>Musical Education</u>: he began taking classical violin lessons at the age of 8 from Professor O.W. Frederick at the Ebenezer Missionary Baptist in Chicago.

    * He continued to play violin for about 14 years.

    * It was through the violin, that inspired Bo Diddley to take a different approach to guitar playing namely, a purely rhythmic approach.

        a.) "The rhythm guitar sound that I started (on "Pretty Thing", "I Can Tell", and others) I call the muted sound. I learned that from playing the classical violin. I taught myself how to play it on the guitar..."

    * He got his first guitar at age 13 as a Christmas present from his sister Lucille.

- Radio broadcasts of blues guitarist <u>John Lee Hooker</u> became Diddley's first guitar playing inspiration thereby, becoming his first blues influence.

    * Hooker's musical trademarks that influenced Bo Diddley were the following (these are the trademarks he first heard in "Boogie Chillin'"):

        a.) no chord changes (for the most part).

        b.) a foot stomping beat.

        c.) guitar amplification.

        d.) chant-like singing.

        e.) African-styled polyrhythms derived from the Ring Shout tradition.

    * There would be other Chicago Blues influences such as Muddy Waters and Sonny Boy Williamson.

        a.) He was also influenced by country rhythms.

- His main lyric influence came from <u>Cab Calloway</u> who encouraged Diddley to look for song subjects in the "street corner".

    * Calloway had some old Chicago-style classics of his own like "Reefer Man" and "Minnie The Moocher".

        a.) Calloway also encouraged Diddley to utilize the street corner "jive".

        b.) This jive/slang lingo would open a creative door by allowing Diddley to write highly rhythmic word passages which changed his voice into a rhythmic instrument.

            - He also used the flexibility of jive to create twisted nursery rhymes and contorted lyrics (... "I used a cobra snake for a necktie"...).

- In addition to his voice being a rhythmic instrument, Bo Diddley was the first artist in rock and roll to treat the electric guitar – an up-to-this-point, melodic instrument – as a purely <u>rhythmic instrument</u>.

    * his signature "shave-and-a-haircut, shave-and-a-haircut" rhythms along with "boom...boom...ch-boom..." (moderately fast)...or clave rhythms: ...tick ... tick ...tick,   tick, tick.

        a.) ...are major staples in rock and roll.

- <u>African-Derived Influences</u>: The Ring Shout (aka "The Shout"), the first important body of African American music.

    * A sanctified rhythmic music (derived from the West African polyrhythmic tradition).

        a.) The original backbone of the Spiritual and Gospel.

    * A polyrhythmic groove:

a.) In the case of The Shout, crossrhythms between people stomping their feet on a wooden floor and syncopated hand clapping.

- Definition of African-Derived Polyrhythms: superimposed layers of various repetitive rhythms that result in an underlying groove.

* In addition to the polyrhythmic influence, The Shout also provided Bo Diddley's music with a sense of emotion and feel.

- RESULT: Bo Diddley became the first artist to introduce the concept of African-derived polyrhythms into rock and roll.

* His first recording at the age of 26 on the Chess label: "Bo Diddley".

a.) A complete reinvention of the concept of rhythm in early rock and roll...

- ...through the focus on clavé rhythms (an African-derived polyrhythmic scheme that originated in Cuba).

- CONCEPT: once again, originality in this period was the result of artists who were stylistically, multi-faceted in rhythm-based music. He once said in an interview that, "I play the guitar like a drummer would play the drums".

* for Diddley, it was blues and country with some street corner jive added in.

a.) Bo Diddley's rhythmic originality (guitar as rhythm instrument) was way ahead of his time and was influential to rock and roll guitarists for each generation since.

- Diddley took the African-based concept of multi-rhythmic layerings, and applied it to his band in the following manner...

* First, his guitar: like the standard guitar setup, the 6 strings were arranged so that the top string was the lowest register, the second string was a slightly higher register and so on...

a.) ...until you get to the bottom string which is the highest register of them all.

b.) Diddley would use the upper three strings (lower register) and the lower three strings (higher register) like two distinct drumheads.

c.) RESULT: a polyrhythmic interchange between the upper and lower strings. That is how he approached the electric guitar as a drum-like instrument.

* Secondly, his drummer: played polyrhythms in the lower register drums: the Tom-Tom (drum connected to the top of the base drum), the Floor Tom, and the Base Drum.

a.) The maracas player, Jerome Green, would play a variant of an Afro-Cuban clave rhythm. This would serve as the high-register percussion instrument.

* NOTE: in his early days at Chess, the bass player was optional.

a.) At that time, Diddley let his upper three strings (lowest register strings), serve that [bass] function.

* Finally, his voice: as mentioned before, also a rhythmic instrument.

a.) in addition to twisted nursery rhymes, he also indulged in a street corner tradition called, "dozens".

- Basically, a competitive exchange of insults between two people.

- For example: "Your girlfriend was so ugly, she had to sneak up behind a glass to get a drink." "Oh yeah? Well your girlfriend was so ugly, the wind blew her hair in the street".

Say Man
Bo Diddley

- RESULT: dozens would give his voice along with his sparring partner's a sharp rhythmic edge.
- "Say Man": was an example (paraphrased above) of Bo Diddley and that sparring partner, Jerome Green exchanging rhythmic jabs.
  * While the accompanying music is molded in the polyrhythmic layering (in the African tradition) with no chord changes.
  * It's as if every instrument could be a drum of some sort and work.
  * Ironically, this was his only Chess release that became a big hit.
- SUMMARY: It was the above mentioned elements…
  *… massive polyrhythmic activities superimposed over one another resulting in an overall, underlying groove (the basis of African-based polyrhythms). The first time this concept was attached to rock and roll.
    a.)… plus, the rhythmic focus on a traditionally melodic instrument – the electric guitar.
      -… in addition, pioneering the art of noise and feedback on the electric guitar (one example is a piece entitled: "Cracklin").
  * RESULT: These aspects made Bo Diddley one of the most important pioneers in the early developments of rock and roll with a tremendous legacy to follow.
- As important a rock and roll innovator as Bo Diddley was, there would be another Chess artist who would do some innovating of his own and completely redefine the role of rock heroism.

6.) Chuck Berry: (b. Charles Edward Anderson Berry; San Jose, CA - 10/18/26)
  - Rock and Roll's first guitar hero.

Johnny B. Goode
Chuck Berry

  * He was the first to standardize the solo the electric guitar twang thereby, transferring the electric guitar into rock and roll's new signature, solo instrumental sound (replacing the solo saxophone).
    a.) Noted for his extended guitar intros (Johnny B. Goode) and extended guitar solos (Maybelline) which were unprecedented in rock and roll.
  * Another aspect that qualified him as the first guitar hero:
    a.) He would be the first to gain a following of emulators and would be an inspiration to future artists like John Lennon, Keith Richards, and southern rhythm ace, Jimmy Johnson.
      - As well as several generations of garage bands.
        * Inspiring teens with basic, rudimentary skills a chance at rock and roll success.
  - His Talent: a great storyteller, gift of humor, and catchy, twangy riffs on the electric guitar.
    * Sources:
      a.) Humor and storytelling: inspired by Louis Jordan's approach.
      b.) Musical foundation: blues.
      c.) Musical surface: country
        - Country rhythms and the guitar twang.
      d.) Subject matter: white/mainstream teenage concerns.
        - Cars, High School, Sexual Liberation, Repression from Adults, and love.

        * The basic nomenclature of teen-oriented
        pop music that became standard in pop
        music.
- He also had a very flashy performance style – especially with his famous duck
walk.
    * Stylistically: musically intense synthesis of blues, country, and white
    teen concerns.
        a.) Extremely influential to countless artists who followed.
- Background: growing up in St. Louis, MO, he began playing guitar as a
teenager.
    * 1944-47: he was sent to reform school for an armed robbery
    conviction.
        a.) After his release: he worked at a General Motors body
        plant by day while attending night school studying hair
        dressing and cosmetology.
- He first started performing in St. Louis' local clubs.
    * He started adding country music to his Tin Pan Alley repertoire (such
    as Nat king Cole) and blues covers…
        a.) …when he realized that black audiences appreciated a wide
        variety of music including country.
    * He performed his own interpretations of various covers that were
    popular…
        a.)…and became a hit with the St. Louis club circuit.
- 1952: He joined Johnny Johnson's Blues Trio who, up to then was playing
straight blues.
    * after Berry had joined them, they added country music to their
    repertoire,
- 1955: they became the top St. Louis club act rivaled by only two other artists:
    * Ike Turner & The Kings of Rhythm and blues guitarist Albert King.
        a.) He [Berry] still maintained his day job in cosmetology.

- Chuck Berry moved to Chicago and, at the suggestion of Muddy Waters
(whom Berry had a two minute conversation with) delivered a demo tape to
Chess Records featuring a blues tune called "Wee Wee Hours" and another
called "Ida Red" (later named "Maybelline").
    * May, 1955: Muddy Waters introduced Berry to Leonard Chess.
        a.) After signing with Chess, he cut a record that would
        become Chess' first top ten hit:

Maybelline
Chuck Berry

- "Maybelline": (recorded on May 21, 1955)
    * Originally called, "Ida Red" but was changed during a recording
    session at the suggestion of Leonard Chess.
        a.) featuring that original electric guitar country twang that
        separated Berry's sound from the rest…
          -…and the ever present country beat/rhythms.
    * "Maybelline" would reach up to #5 on the pop charts in 1955 and was
    heavily promoted by DJ Alan Freed.
        a.) Chess Records sent "Maybelline" to Alan Freed to
        specifically promote this single.
          - In return for that promotion, Allen Freed was given
          co-writing credit (even though he never wrote a thing
          on that record).
            * The Reason? Payola. The royalties that he
            [Freed] received from the record's
            commercial success was a form of financial
            compensation.

- <u>To Summarize:</u> Chuck Berry came up with his own formula for massive crossover success.
  * Inspired by his early experiences in St. Louis where he first developed a keen sense of what most people wanted in music.
    a.) He would also inject that essential ingredient for pop supremacy: catchy melodic tunes that were easily memorable
      - and perked up rhythms.
  * <u>RESULT:</u> a series of anthems such as: "School Days", "Sweet Little Sixteen", "Johnny B. Goode", "No Particular Place To Go".
    a.) In essence, Chuck Berry's music crossed all of the boundaries giving everyone, something in his music to appreciate.
  * Like other great rhythm artists of his time, Chuck Berry created a synthesis of various styles which resulted in an original sound:
    a.) <u>Musically:</u> a solid blues foundation.
      - with slashing country rhythms on the electric guitar.
      - jazzy elements on the drums.
      - boogie-woogie on the piano.
      - catchy, easily memorable tunes.
      - electric guitar twang as the main instrumental focus.
    b.) <u>Lyrics:</u> that were easy for white teens to relate with.
      - with a good dose of humor added in.
      - and excellent storytelling.
- Along with his up-front focus on the electric guitar twang, Chuck Berry's music gained wide mainstream appeal which as mentioned earlier, would serve as an inspiration for other important guitarists in rock and roll to follow.

School Days
Chuck Berry

III. <u>THE CONCLUSION OF ROCK AND ROLL'S FIRST GOLDEN AGE.</u>
  A.) As if by one big sweep, rock and roll's first guilded age (1955-1958) was coming to an abrupt end for the following reasons:
    1.) <u>Elvis Presley:</u> enlisted in the Army.
    2.) <u>Little Richard:</u> left secular music to preach the gospel for the Seventh Day Adventist Church.
    3.) <u>Jerry Lee Lewis:</u> was snubbed by the public for marrying his 13-year-old cousin, Myra Gale Brown.
      - His 3rd marriage. As a result, he had to abandon his world tour because of heckling spectators and negative press coverage in Britain.
    4.) <u>Chuck Berry:</u> arrested and eventually convicted for violation of the Mann Act by transporting an underage teenage prostitute across state lines.
      - Charges in the first trial were dropped.
      - He was convicted in the second trial: 2 years in a federal prison.
        * He was released in 1964 (during the British invasion spearheaded by The Beatles).
    5.) <u>Eddie Cochran:</u> died in an automobile accident.
    6.) <u>Buddy Holly, Ritchie Valens, and The Big Bopper:</u> killed in a plane crash in northern Iowa.
  B.). <u>RESULT:</u> a large vacuum ensued and when that happens…
    1.) Someone or something is always bound to step in and in this case, it was the corporate record industry.
      - which was spearheaded by Dick Clark.
    2.) <u>Dick Clark</u> (b. 1929 as Richard Augustus Clark II): started hosting American Bandstand in 1956.
      - By 1958, he was one of the most powerful forces in the pop music industry.

- Starting in 1958 from Philadelphia (where his show aired at that time), he introduced a virtual army of clean-cut, non-threatening Philadelphia born-and-bread, pop teen idols.

    * <u>Fabian</u> (Fabian Forte), <u>Frankie Avalon</u> (Francis Avallone), <u>Bobby Rydell</u> (Robert Ridarelli), and <u>Chubby Checker</u> (Ernest Evans).

        a.) Their music was basically the watered-down Elvis/RCA formula:

            - catchy pop tunes with background vocals to sweeten-up their sound and a very contained delivery.

        b.) But, unlike Elvis, Clark molded these stars to be completely safe for teenage consumption thereby giving his pop idols, for the first time,

            - …conservative America's imprimatur.

Tiger
Fabian

- Clark owned his first corporation called: "Click" – basically, a record distribution company.

    * Inspired by his growing popularity of DJ-ing on the side (outside of "Bandstand") at various dances or record hops.

        a.) Somewhat similar to what Alan Freed pioneered only he became Freed's antithesis: playing to a completely mainstream, white crowd playing white records.

- He also carried financial interests in the following record labels:

    * "<u>Chancellor</u>" (Fabian, Frankie Avalon)

    "<u>Cameo-Parkway</u>" (Bobby Rydell and Chubby Checker)

    "<u>Swan</u>" and "<u>Jamie</u>" Record Companies in Philadelphia.

        a.) He also owned copyrights for over 160 songs.

- By the end of the 1950's, Dick Clark became the most powerful force in popular music.

    * He could get an unknown artist national attention and recognition in just one day.

        a.) One of those artists, was a group called The Teddy Bears.

            - Because of Dick Clark's power, their single entitled "To Know Him Is To Love Him" would become a #1 hit.

        b.) The band member who wrote the tune happened to be a very gifted guitarist, songwriter, and eventually a great producer.

            - His name was Phil Spector…

CHAPTER I: REVIEW

What type of pop music was prominent in the late 40's/early 50's? Its emphasis was on the "song" and the style was in the tradition of Cole Porter, George & Ira Gershwin, and Irving Berlin (among others).

What were the three defining elements of this style?
1.)
2.)
3.)

Name several recording artists from this era:

Who is credited for creating the blueprint of what would be known as rhythm & blues?

List three elements of this blueprint:
1.)
2.)
3.)

Which DJ was the first to coin the term "Rock and Roll" in 1951?

What was his main mission?

What was the significance of the 1951 single, "Rocket 88"? Jackie Brenston & His Delta Cats recorded it.

Was this the first true rock and roll single?

List 4 elements that were synthesized to give his record an R&B feel.
1.)
2.)
3.)
4.)

Name the most important radio station in the early rock and roll era. It was responsible for exposing most of the continental United States to black R&B:

Name the first DJ on this station to play R&B records.

In the 1950's, who were the two primary acts to come out of New Orleans?
    1.)
    2.)

        In addition to New Orleans, what were the two other important cities of rock and roll's early development?
            1.)
            2.)

Who became rock and roll's first crossover sensation?

    Name his main influences:

        1.) Blues Influences:
        2.) Boogie Woogie Influences:
        3.) Singing Influence:

Name the first great drummer in rock and roll. He was a member of Dave Bartholemew's session group for Cossimo Matassa's J&M Studios in New Orleans:

Name the artist first true "Rock Star". What elements did he inject into R&B that would forever be associated with rock and roll?

    Name his band:

        List his three musical influences:
            1.)
            2.)
            3.)

    Name his 1955 breakthrough single that became the blueprint of the free-spirited, frenzied performance style in rock 'n' roll.

Who became the most successful white, less-threatening alternative to renegades such as Little Richard and Elvis that parents could easily accept?

Which record company did Sam Phillips establish in 1953?

What was this company's original name in 1950?

What was his first recording success in 1951?

Name the first song ever recorded by Elvis Presley in the summer of 1953:

What were Elvis Presley's three stages of development?
    1.)
    2.)
    3.)

Which single (1954) became Elvis Presley's breakthrough? It was written and recorded by Arthur "Big Boy" Crudup in 1946.

    What was Elvis' "Side B" single that accompanied his first breakthrough single?

    What date was this two-sided single first unveiled to the local Memphis public?

    Name the radio station and DJ:

What was Elvis' first regular performance venue that gained him widespread exposure throughout the South?

    Name the radio station that regularly broadcasted this show.

Name three of his additional singles including his last recording with Sun Records.
    1.)
    2.)
    3.)

Which consortium bought out Elvis' contract and for how much?

What was the genius of Elvis Presley during his time at Sun Records? In other words, what was his signature trademark for interpreting cover songs?

Which artist wrote and first recorded "Blue Suede Shoes"?

    What was the significance of *Blue Suede Shoes* in regard to simultaneous chart successes?

What were Carl Perkins' two main influences?
    1.)
    2.)

    What specific style resulted from the synthesis of these influences?

Name Jerry Lee Lewis' four main radio influences:
1.)
2.)
3.)
4.)

What was his first studio recording?

Name the single that made Jerry Lee Lewis into a star.

Name his follow-up hit.

What were the elements of his "no holds barred" free-spirited performance style?
1.)
2.)
3.)
4.)

How did Elvis Presley's style change after he signed with RCA Records?

What changed in his sound?

What changed in his delivery?

Why were background vocals used?

What was Elvis' fallout for going mainstream with RCA?

What important independent record label was founded in Chicago? (Hint: it was the important record label of Chicago Blues):

In clubs such as The Macambo, blues artists playing acoustic instruments could not be heard over the noisy atmosphere of the club. What was the solution?

Name the new style of blues that resulted:

Who was the first artist in rock and roll to play the electric guitar as a purely rhythmic instrument? He also introduced the concept of African-derived polyrhythms into rock and roll.

Name the first blues record that first caught his attention:

What were this record's (and artist who recorded it) musical trademarks?
     1.)
     2.)
     3.)
     4.)
     5.)

Who was Bo Diddley's main lyric influence?

How did Bo Diddley incorporate African-derived polyrhythms into rock 'n' roll for the following instruments?
     1.) His Guitar:
     2.) The Drums:
     3.) His Voice:

Who was rock and roll's first guitar hero?

List two reasons as to why he became the first guitar hero:
     1.)
     2.)

Name the influential sources of the following:
     1.) Humor and Storytelling:
     2.) Musical Foundation:
     3.) Musical Surface:
     4.) Subject Matter:

Name the subjects dealing with teenage concerns:
     1.)
     2.)
     3.)
     4.)
     5.)

Stylistically, what 3 elements did he synthesize to create his original sound?
Name his first big hit:

Which DJ received payola in exchange for promoting this record?

Name three of his other teen anthems:
       1.)
       2.)
       3.)

What happened to the following artists starting in 1958?
       1.) Elvis Presley:
       2.) Little Richard:
       3.) Jerry Lee Lewis:
       4.) Chuck Berry:

Which hit TV show did Dick Clark nationally syndicate?

Name at least three squeaky-clean teen idols that Dick Clark promoted on this nationally syndicated show:
       1.)
       2.)
       3.)

       How would you describe their musical style?

CHAPTER II: 1958 TO FEBRUARY 7, 1964

I. 1958 TO FEBRUARY 7, 1964

    A.) In most cases, a period that gets glossed over in regard to important musical developments.

        1.) Usually, the Dick Clark/American Bandstand phenomena receives a lot of coverage.

            - along with other subjects dealing mostly with the record industry and the clean-cut teen idols that they promoted.

        2.) Or, Don Kirshner, whose publishing company wrestled control of pop music from the primacy of Tin Pan Alley.

            - Tin Pan Alley had, up to then, cornered the teen market.

            - Kirshner's (and Al Nevins') Aldon Music:

                * hired new writers who would compose an array of chart-friendly, rock and roll influenced, melodic pop tunes.

                    a.) Like Tin Pan Alley, Aldon Music was a publishing company that focused strictly on *the song*.

                        - Only in this case, they adapted their musical focus to rock inspired pop music.

                            * As opposed to easy jazz/Broadway influenced tradition (i.e. Tin Pan Alley).

                    b.) Their success would enable Aldon Music to outperform their Tin Pan Alley rivals and in turn, become the new kings of the pop music domain.

                        - Thus bringing the primacy of music publishing under the rock and roll umbrella.

        3.) But all and all, it was this pop domain that usually received the main focus…

    B.) But there were other things happening that made this era, a very ripe period for rock and roll.

Baby Workout
Jackie Wilson

        1.) The great black male voices: perhaps at no other time in rock and roll were there so many great voices assembled in one era…

            - Usually, they would perform in venues throughout the "Chitlin Circuit".

Wonderful World
Sam Cooke

                * Now that corporate record companies have once again taken over in the wake of the demise of rock and roll's first "Golden Age"…

                    a.) Black performers (whom corporate labels were not interested in signing), were once again relegated to this touring circuit.

Goin' Out Of My Head
Little Anthony
& The Imperials

            - Voices included: Jackie Wilson, Sam Cooke, Little Anthony, Hank Ballard, and Jesse Belvin.

                * They not only were great singers but were all terrific performers…

                    a.) …especially when it came to dancing.

        2.) Dance Crazes: Perhaps at no other time (with the exception of the Disco era) has America seen so many different dancing styles.

            - The Twist, The Hully-Gully, The Jerk, The Mashed Potatoes, The Watusi, etc.

                * These dances along with other dance styles, had at least one accompanying single that popularized each of them.

                    a.) Usually, a particular dance was determined by the beat and the tempo of the song.

                      - Most popular among them, was The Twist.

Twist & Shout
The Isley Brothers

                        * "Twist and Shout" - The Isley Brothers

                          "Do The Twist" - Chubby Checker

                          "Do You Love Me" - The Contours

                    - Others included:

                      * "Do The Mashed Potatoes" - Nat Kendrick & The Swans (featuring James Brown)

                      * "The Watusi"

3.) <u>The Girl-Group Sound</u>: Perhaps no other sound captures the essence of this era (especially in the early 60's) than the Girl-Group sound.

He's So Fine
The Chiffons

Chapel Of Love
The Dixie Cups

    - A massive proliferation of these groups with the overwhelming majority being black girl groups:

        * The Shirelles, The Chiffons, The Chantals, The Cookies, The Ronettes, The Dixie Cups, The Crystals, The Marvalettes, etc.

          - Among the few white girl groups/artists included:

        * The Angels, Leslie Gore, and The Shangri-Las.

    - They would release hit after hit.

        * Which were written and arranged for them by a new team setup that would become Tin Pan Alley's legacy…

4.) <u>Songwriting Teams</u>: some of whom had their offices/studios at the legendary Brill Building on 1619 Broadway.

    - Where great Tin Pan Alley writers like Cole Porter, Irving Berlin, George & Ira Gershwin, and Rodgers & Hart wrote one great tune after another.

        * Now home to such songwriting teams as:

          a.) Ellie Greenwich and Jeff Barry

          b.) Barry Mann and Cynthia Weill

          c.) Neil Sadaka and Howard Greenfield

        * And, in another building close by:

          a.) Carole King and Gerry Goffin

        * Usually, the setup was: one person wrote the lyrics and the other, composed the music.

          a.) As in the Tin Pan Alley tradition, the emphasis for the Brill Building writers,was strictly on the *published song*…

    - <u>The Brill Building</u>: was in essence, a song writing factory churning out hit after hit. As a result, it became *the* symbol of outstanding songwriting craftsmanship during this period.

        * Especially with the Girl-Groups. Some of many hits included:

          a.) "<u>Chapel Of Love</u>" - The Dixie Cups

          b.) "<u>Da Do Ron Ron</u>" - The Crystals

            - Both written by Jeff Barry & Ellie Greenwich.

          c.) "<u>Will You Love Me Tomorrow</u>" - The Shirelles

          d.) "<u>Chains</u>" - The Cookies

            - Written by Carole King & Gerry Goffin

        * <u>NOTE</u>: The primacy of Brill Building writers was another example of the Tin Pan Alley tradition evolving into the rock and roll domain.

5.) <u>The Rise of The Record Producer</u>: Rock and roll's new geniuses — the most important development of this period.

    - They did the following:

        * They either wrote or co-wrote the songs.

        * Supervised recording sessions.

        * Wrote the arrangements.

        * Chose the session musicians.

        * Chose the featured recording artists.

          a.) In other words, they were all-encompassing. They practically did it all.

    - It was these record producers who set the standard of musical development in rock and roll right up to February 7, 1964.

        * including the use of studio techniques (or magic) to greatly elevate the quality of a song.

    - <u>NOTE</u>: They were responsible for transforming the three-and-a-half-minute single, into a highly crafted work of art.

        * The term they used for such a single: the "<u>Record</u>".

          a.) Again, the focus being on *the song*.

    - <u>Record Producers</u> to be covered include:

* Jerry Lieber & Mike Stoller
* George "Shadow" Morton
* Phil Spector
* Brian Wilson

- They set the structure and foundation for many other record producers to follow.

II. THE RECORD PRODUCER

A.) <u>Lieber and Stoller</u>: the first to create the blueprint for the rise of the great record producers.

1.) They would synthesize the Tin Pan Alley tradition of melodic, tuneful writing with the raw, emotional vitality of black rhythm & blues. And in the process, elevate the level of sophistication of R&B thereby, adding a touch of elegance never before seen in this [R&B] tradition.

- Their success – two white Jewish men writing black R&B – paved the way for other white artists to make their impacts on the direction of R&B. Especially when it came to "Blue-Eyed Soul".

* Unlike other white artists as Elvis (at Sun Records) who approached R&B in an authentic manner, Lieber and Stoller presented their brand of R&B from a strictly black perspective in terms of humor, social commentary, and everyday life.

a.) The secret behind this success? Their massive exposure to black culture starting at a very young age.

2.) <u>Jerry Lieber</u> (b. 1933, Baltimore, MD): son of Polish Jewish immigrants, grew up in Baltimore where his widowed mother owned a neighborhood grocery store on the edge of a black, inner city section.

- Through his experience as a delivery boy for his mother's store, he was exposed to many aspects of black culture. Especially, hearing R&B on radios in these African American households.

* According to Lieber, their radios were always on. He gradually acquired a keen interest in black culture.

a.) <u>RESULT</u>: he started living it [black culture].

- <u>1945</u>: his family moved to Los Angeles. Some of his inspirations to become a lyricist were:

* His older sister's marriage to a songwriter named Lew Porter, who became an inspiration for his younger brother-in-law in the art of songwriting.

* His love of Blues and R&B: especially the lone, hard-driving-beat artists such as Amos Milburn and Wynonie Harris.

* He also became interested in Bebop Jazz (which in the mid to late 40's, was starting to generate interest in the black community). His interests expanded to back alley blues (a blues offshoot of jazz).

- He thereafter, became a total hipster complete with speaking the black lingo, dating black women, and hanging out in black clubs,

3.) <u>The Lester Sill Connection</u>: Jerry Lieber met Lester Sill in 1950 when Sill was working as a sales manager for Modern Records (founded by Jules, Joe, and Saul Bihari in 1943) – an independent label specializing in black, R&B music.

- <u>Lieber</u>: at the time was attending Fairfax High School in Los Angeles and working in a record store, called Norty's, that specialized in selling recordings of Jewish traditional music.

* One day, while Lieber was working at Norty's, Lester Sill walked in. As Sill was trying to sell a John Lee Hooker record to the Norty's catalog, they discovered that they both had a mutual love for blues and black music in general.

a.) It was through this connection that he [Lieber] and his eventual partner, Mike Stoller, were signed to Modern

Records in 1951 as staff writers.

4.) <u>Mike Stoller</u>: (b. 1933, Belle Harbor, Long Island): grew up in New York City where his mother played a role in George Gershwin's "Funny Face" on Broadway.

- She encouraged Mike to take classical piano lessons (which he did). <u>At age 11</u>: he took an interest in boogie-woogie, stride, and bebop jazz. He learned these styles from a teacher named James P. Johnson in Harlem. In 1949, his family moved to LA.

* He attended UCLA as a music composition major where he learned to write for symphonic orchestra under Arthur Lange. He also learned to compose in the dissonant 12-tone style (which was in vogue in music academia at the time). He wrote an orchestral piece in that particular style that the LA Symphony premiered.

a.) <u>NOTE</u>: His classical background of orchestral writing would be crucial to the development of the Lieber and Stoller style in the late 1950's.

- He was also playing boogie-woogie, blues and bebop and frequenting jazz and blues clubs. It was through the jazz club musician network, that Mike Stoller first heard about Jerry Lieber.

* They eventually crossed paths and agreed to collaborate (after some initial skepticism from Stoller). Mike Stoller initially felt that song writing was not for him. After some persistence from Lieber, he agreed to collaborate.

a.) Two aspects of Lieber's approach to lyrics captured Stoller's interest: Lieber's use of traditional blues narratives, and his effective use of catchy refrains that bordered sets of verses.

* Their personalities differed. Lieber was the outgoing hipster. Stoller was soft-spoken and introverted.

5.) <u>Their early influences</u>: the lone, post Louis Jordan blues singers/songwriters of the late 40's such as: <u>Amos Milburn</u> (honky-tonk piano) - bluesy on one hand, but with a hard-driving, rhythmic focus on the other.

Good Rockin' Tonight
Wynonie Harris

- <u>Wynonie Harris</u>: "Good Rockin' Tonight" and "All She Wants To Do Is Rock" - another blues influence with a hard rocking beat.

* <u>Their original creative goal</u>: to write straight blues influenced rhythmic music in the tradition of their various influences.

6.) <u>Their first professional gig</u>: They were hired by Lester Sill as staff writers for the Modern Records label in 1951.

Smokey Joe's Café
The Robins

- Lieber and Stoller's first collaboration at Modern Records: "That's What The Good Book Says" (1951). Written for a black vocal group called: <u>The Robins</u> (they would later be revamped as The Coasters). Other songs they wrote for The Robins included "Smokey Joe's Café" and "Riot in Cell Block #9".

Kansas City
Wilbert Harrison

* Other artists that Lieber and Stoller would write for included: <u>Wilbert Harrison</u> ("Kansas City"), <u>Wynonie Harris</u>, <u>Little Esther</u>, <u>Joe Turner</u>, <u>Ruth Brown</u>, and <u>The Isley Brothers</u>.

- Their first collaborative success: "<u>Hound Dog</u>" (1953), originally written for Willie Mae "Big Mama" Thornton and released on the Duke label (owned by Johnny Otis). It reached to #1 on the black, Rhythm & Blues charts. Musical features included:

Hound Dog
Willie Mae
"Big Mama"
Thornton

* I, IV, V blues chord progression (standard blues progression).
* Funky "Urban Bluesy" beat.
* Instrumental breaks (in this case, a solo electric guitar) in between sung verses (again, a blues standard).
* catchy easily singable melodies (not usually, a blues standard).
(All items mentioned were Mike Stoller musical properties).

- Jerry Lieber's early approach to writing lyrics.

* <u>Social commentary</u>: Mostly dealing with racial conflict between

African Americans and mainstream culture.
> * <u>Satire</u>: Flavoring of social commentary with humor in a "poking fun" sort of manner (mainly at racial politics).
> * <u>Theatre</u>: Presented in a theatrical framework which could be acted out on stage as if it was a miniature musical theatre production. Complete with minimal props.

- <u>Resulting Style</u>: of the Lieber and Stoller combination:
> *<u>Playlets</u>: the single as a three-and-a-half minute story being played out on stage. Presenting urbane, everyday life from a uniquely black perspective.
>> a.) Utilizing black humor told in the black vernacular.
> * <u>Debut of a new concept – the "Record"</u>: the three-and-a-half minute recorded single presented as a *highly crafted work of art*. It was in this context, that the term: "The Record" was born (as Lieber and Stoller once said: "We didn't write songs, we wrote records").
>> a.) <u>Record</u>: the overall finished product. Not just the song, but also the quality of the finished recording — the result of the producer's overall creative vision…
>>> - …where all aspects behind the making of the record would fit together perfectly like a mosaic.

- As mentioned before, Lieber and Stoller wrote and produced primarily for black singers.
> * <u>Exception</u>: they wrote "Jailhouse Rock" and "Kid Creole" for Elvis Presley. Otherwise on a consistent basis, they would regularly use the same black artists.

7.) <u>Atlantic Records</u>: it was through the R&B network, that Atlantic Records first became aware of Lieber and Stoller's work in LA.
- <u>1955</u>: They were signed with Atlantic Records as writers and producers (the first time in the rock 'n' roll recording industry that the term, "producer" was accredited with to writers instead of the traditional financial backers).
> * <u>Atlantic Records</u>: an independent label in New York City founded by Herb Abramson and Ahmet Ertegun in 1947 — they specialized in recording black music.

- <u>The Coasters</u>: first black vocal group that Lieber and Stoller consistently wrote for and produced at Atlantic Records. This was where they [Lieber and Stoller] honed in their signature "playlet" style.
> * Originally, the lyrics dealt with racial conflicts peppered with humor and the music was written and produced with a black audience in mind.
>> a.) Mike Stoller's music was written in a gritty R&B style with a hard-driving beat and saxophone solos/breaks in between sung verses.

- <u>1957</u>: white audiences took interest in Lieber and Stoller's black music for the first time with a double-sided hit: "<u>Searchin'</u> " (Side A) and "<u>Youngblood</u>" (Side B).
> * It was at this time, that Jerry Lieber began writing lyrics that targeted a broader, white teenage audience. And in the process, expanded his subject matter to areas that were more universal: conflicts between teens and their parents (the growing generation gap) and commentary on other mainstream issues.
>> a.) <u>Example</u>: "<u>Yakety Yak</u>", pokes fun of the new generational conflict between teens with independent attitudes and their parents.
>>> - Another example: "<u>Along Came Jones</u>" – a humorous commentary on the new culture surrounding the mainstream's new obsession with TV.

Searchin'
The Coasters

Young Blood
The Coasters

Yakety Yak
The Coasters

Along Came Jones
The Coasters

- <u>Choosing The Repertoire</u>: The Coasters would not record a tune unless they liked it first. Lieber and Stoller would audition the new song themselves and The Coasters would listen.

     * If they didn't like the music or were uncomfortable with the subject matter, they'd refused to record it.

          a.) The Coasters would act out these playlets as if they were a Vaudeville act complete with some minimal props and a healthy dose of humor.

- <u>NOTE</u>: Lieber and Stoller's music for The Coasters starting in 1957 and with The Drifters two years later, kept the white mainstream's interest in black pop music alive during the time when corporate record companies were saturating TV and radio with these white teenie-bopper idols.

     * This was important because in the early 1960's, the rock 'n' roll pop sound will be dominated by black music influenced by Lieber and Stoller.

8.) <u>The Drifters</u>: with this group, Lieber and Stoller's musical sound would turn in a new direction which would set the style of black pop music for the early 60's until 2/7/64.

- The elements of this new sound:

     * A lush black pop melodic sound — melody lines which were catchy, fluid, and elegant (well beyond the conventional blues format).

     * Studio technology such as reverberation (i.e. reverb) that gave the record a polished, glossy finish.

This Magic Moment
The Drifters

     * Orchestral strings and percussion (this was where Mike Stoller's classical music background became a crucial element).

          a.) <u>Orchestral Strings</u> (i.e. violins, violas, cellos, and double basses) and orchestral percussion (timpani drums, etc.) would be introduced into the three-and-a-half minute "single" format.

               - Thereby elevating the sophistication of their sound.

There Goes
My Baby
The Drifters

- "<u>There Goes My Baby</u>"(1959): the first Lieber and Stoller record to introduce this new and elegant symphonic black pop sound.

     * Written for <u>The Drifters</u>, who started out as a street corner, a capella vocal group type known as Doo-Wap. These groups were adept at four-part harmonization with a nice sense of rhythmic ease.

          a.) The drifters had a gifted lead singer named: <u>Ben E. King</u> who Lieber and Stoller eventually produced as a solo artist.

9.) <u>Ben E. King</u>: for whom Lieber and Stoller wrote their most sophisticated music to date. <u>EXAMPLE</u>: "Spanish Harlem" (1961) reached up to #10 on the pop charts. Music written by Phil Spector and arrangement finished by Mike Stoller.

Spanish Harlem
by Ben E. King
reprinted from *The Very*
Best of Ben E. King,
Rhino R272970: 1998, by
permission of Hal Leonard
Corporation.

- <u>Lieber</u>: His writing transcended traditional lyrics to a poet's tradition featuring sophisticated word-play with meanings hidden beneath the surface. In every stanza, the poetic rhythm is constantly shifting (again, in the poet tradition). In the example below, the poetic rhythmic stresses are underlined…

     * "There is a <u>rose</u> in Spanish Harlem,
       A red rose <u>up</u> in Spanish Harlem,
       It is a <u>special</u> one, it's never <u>seen</u> the sun,
       It only <u>comes</u> out when <u>the</u> moon is <u>on</u> the run <u>and</u> all the <u>stars</u>,
       Are <u>gleaming</u>.
       It's growing <u>in</u> the street,
       right up <u>through</u> the concrete but <u>soft</u> and sweet,
       and <u>dreamin'</u> "

- <u>Stoller</u>: glossy, sophisticated classical styled arrangement that builds in intensity with the development of the stanza.

     * He uses the vibraphone, another percussion orchestral instrument to carry the main instrumental theme, with catchy, easily memorable melodies in the voice.

10.) The Lieber and Stoller songwriting techniques exhibited in songs like "Spanish Harlem", would become a major inspiration and influence for various songwriting teams that would rule pop music in the early 60's.

    - OVERALL CONCEPT: blueprint created by Lieber and Stoller for this era:

        * Tin Pan Alley influence + Rock and Roll = 3-and-a half minute single as a highly crafted work of art = The Record = the Record Producer's artistic vision.

B.) The Songwriting Teams: a part of the Lieber and Stoller legacy.

    1.) The top teams:

        - Carole King and Gerry Goffin
        - Barry Mann and Cynthia Weil
        - Neil Sedaka and Howard Greenfield
        - Ellie Greenwich and Jeff Barry

            * As earlier mentioned, their professional culture was rooted in the Brill Building tradition. Their main focus was *the song* (consistent with the Tin Pan Alley influence).

    2.) Carole King and Gerry Goffin: Lieber and Stoller was a major inspiration upon them.

        - They adopted the following Lieber and Stoller trademarks:

            * Splitting of specific responsibilities: King wrote the music, Goffin wrote the lyrics.
            * The glossy, orchestral strings and percussion sound.
            * Tuneful, easily singable melodies.
            * The sturdy, meaningful lyric writing inspired by Lieber.

        - In a blues sense, they too, wrote for black voices but in this case:

            * They wrote for black women's voices.

        - "Will You Love Me Tomorrow" (1961) - recorded by The Shirelles.— King and Goffin's first major hit as songwriters.

            * Carole King adopted the Stoller musical properties (i.e. strings, percussion, etc.).
            * Gerry Goffin wrote lyrics that had a deeper meaning than what the "surface" conveyed, yet written in a simple format (a Lieber trademark).

                a.) Lyrics addressed for the first time, thoughts on the sexual revolution (which began in the early 50's in tandem with spread of R&B to white America) from a female perspective.

                b.) Before this, the sexual revolution in rock and roll was expressed exclusively from a male (yee-haa!) point of view.

                    - Lyrics like Little Richard's "Lucille" that say:
                        * "Lucille, Baby satisfy my heart".
                    - As well as other songs which take on a free-spiriting "propositioning" stance toward women.

                c.) Instead, "Will You Love Me Tomorrow" expressed the sexual revolution in a more cautious, more emotional manner.

                    - the female viewpoint was basically a "Will you still respect me after the fact" perspective.
                        * In other words: a "Let's stop and really think about this" scenario.
                    - these lyrics spoke to and for many women in this sexual revolutionary age of uncertainty (it was something any woman could relate to).

        - "Will You Love Me Tomorrow" was the first song of the new "Girl-Group" genre to reach #1 on the pop charts.

* <u>RESULT</u>: The success of The Shirelles opened the door for many other black girl-groups to follow…

        a). …making the girl-group sound, the standard for rock and roll in the early 60's.

3.) <u>Ellie Greenwich and Jeff Barry</u>: also writing girl-group hits and also caught the Lieber and Stoller influence.

- in one particular case, the theatrical influence.

- in collaboration with producer George "Shadow" Morton…

        * they would write their own "playlet"…

- "<u>Leader Of The Pack</u>" (1963): does the traditional playlet one better by introducing the song with spoken dialogue.

Leader Of The Pack
The Shangri-Las

        * Recorded by one of the few white girl-groups: The Shangri-Las.

        a.) the only prominent girl-group that George "Shadow" Morton produced.

        b.) This song greatly fitted the Shangri-La's "renegade" characteristics.

        - This song was also released at a time where the lone "biker" or the bike "Gang Leader/Renegade" was becoming an integral part of 60's romantic folklore.

C.) <u>George "Shadow" Morton</u> (b. 1942): more of an uncharacteristic example of the record producer.

1.) He was not a musician by any means.

- He had no knowledge of musical fundamentals like pitch or rhythm (in a schooled sense).

2.) He did however, hear original, unorthodox ideas/sounds in his head.

- Which were not musical in a traditional sense.

Remember
(Walkin' In The Sand)
The Shangri-Las

        * Sounds of: seagulls, motorcycles, and spoken dialogue to name a few.

        a.) Seagull sounds are featured in another Shangri-la's recording he produced: "<u>Remember (Walkin' In The Sand)</u>".

- Also because of his removal from the traditional musical experience…

        * His arrangements did not conform to traditional song-structure.

3.) <u>RESULT</u>: Morton's musical "deficiency" allowed him the room to experiment with sounds and structures that traditionally trained writers/arrangers would probably not think of.

- He was a prime example in rock and roll, of one who turned disadvantage into advantage (a concept that we will see more of in the course rock and roll development).

4.) Morton, in the context of the great record producers, would turn out to be the exception rather than the rule in regard to musicianship (i.e. lack of it) of this period.

- The next producer, would also be an exception but in an entirely different manner.

        * in this case, he would be the epitome of what the record producer was all about musically and would raise the bar in this art-form to a new level:

        a.) the record producer as an eccentric genius…

III. <u>PHIL SPECTOR</u> (b. Harvey Philip Spector, 12/26/39, The Bronx, NY):

A.) <u>Early Career</u>: a gifted guitarist. His greatest influence – jazz guitar legend, <u>Barney Kessell</u>.

1.) He began studying the art of arranging and songwriting as a student at Fairfax High School in Los Angeles.

2.) <u>His First Recording</u>: Gold Star Studios (founded in 1950 by San Ross and Dave Gold).

- He paid $40 for a two-hour session.

        * "<u>Don't Worry My Little Pet</u>" was the song he recorded along with Annette Kleinbard (vocals), Marshall Lieb (bass), and Harvey Goldstein (drums). They became known as <u>The Teddy Bears</u>.

a.) A perky tune reminiscent of Buddy Holly and The Everly Brothers.
- This demo caught the attention of Lew Bedell and Herb Newman of Era Records. They had a subsidiary label: Dore Records.
* Spector's group signed with the Dore label.

3.) "To Know Him Is To Love Him" (1958): the Side B to "Don't Worry My Little Pet" was garnering more radio airplay than the Side A ("Don't Worry...").

To Know Him Is To Love Him
The Teddy Bears

- The title was an inscription on his father's gravestone.
* This single was slowly climbing its way up the pop charts.
- The Big Break: Lew Bedell contacted his friend Dick Clark of *American Bandstand* to arrange the "To Know Him Is To Love Him" and eventually, The Teddy Bears to appear on the show.
* RESULT: Due to their debut performance on November 28, 1958, "To Know Him..." reached to #1 on the pop charts.

4.) Career Change: After the eventual breakup of The Teddy Bears, Spector decided that a career in performing was not for him. Instead, he wanted to make his career in the background albeit, an important background person.
- Needed: networking with the right people.
* Solution: Lester Sill – sales manager for Modern Records (an independent R&B label based in LA).
a.) RESULT: Sill hired Spector as a staff writer and producer.
- Apprenticeship: Lester Sill arranged Spector to observe his business partner, Lee Hazelwood working in the recording studio producing records. This was the beginning of Phil Spector's education.
* The Lieber & Stoller Connection: Lester Sill felt that Spector needed an education in learning the music business and solicited his former protégés, Jerry Lieber & Mike Stoller to take him [Spector] under their wing and show him the ropes.
a.) This meant that Phil Spector would work under Lieber & Stoller at Atlantic records in New York City.

B.) Atlantic Records/NYC Connection: In addition to following Lieber & Stoller around the studio and learning their production techniques, Spector also played session guitar for their recordings of The Drifters (which included singles such as, "On Broadway").
1.) Networking: he also connected with other prominent figures in the music industry such as Ahmet Ertegun (founder and president of Atlantic records), Paul Case (A&R head at Hill & Range Music Publishers), and Don Kirshner (Owner of Aldon Music).
- These connections would become vital to his further career development.

Corrine, Corrina
Ray Peterson

* Reason: They would supply him the songs he would need to achieve career success as a producer.
2.) Spector's First Production: "Corinne, Corinna" recorded by Ray Peterson.
- This marked the first time that Spector used orchestral strings (a la Lieber & Stoller).
3.) His First Success: "Spanish Harlem" (1961) which he co-wrote with Jerry Lieber.
- Reached #10 on the pop in January of 1961.

C.) Rise Of The Record Producer: Although he was influenced by the great Tin Pan Alley writers such as George and Ira Gershwin, Jerome Kern, and Irving Berlin (among others), he realized that songwriting would not be his forte.
1.) Priority #1: find a source of great songs.
- Answer: Don Kirshner who (along with Al Nevins), founded Aldon Music located on 1650 Broadway (one block south of the Brill Building).
* He had a virtual array of great songwriting teams that included:
a.) Barry Mann & Cynthia Weil, Neil Sedaka & Howard Greenfield, Ellie Greenwich & Jeff Barry, and Carol King & Gerry Goffin
- These writers had a run on the burgeoning teen market.

I Know How
You Love Me
The Paris Sisters

- First Production in Los Angeles: "I Know How You Love Me" written by Barry Mann & Cynthia Weil and recorded by The Paris Sisters.
   * Hank Levine, who composed the arrangement, used lush strings.
      a.) This marked the first harbinger of what would later be known as "The Wall of Sound".

2.) New Label: Phil Spector and Lester Sill founded their own independent label called "Philles" ("Phil" + "Les"). Spector also created his own music publishing company called, "Mother Bertha" (after his mother) both based in Los Angeles.
   - Gold Star Studios: became his home studio where he would exercise complete artistic control and where his legend as a producer would be made.

3.) His First Success As A Producer: The Crystals – Philles Records' first signing. They were originally called, The Blossoms with Darlene Love (b. Darlene Wright) as lead singer (they would also be known as Bob B. Soxx & The Blue Jeans).
   - Among their early Philles recordings:
      * "Uptown" (Mann/Weil) reached to #13.
      * "There's No Other (Like My Baby)" – Leroy Bates (#20).

He's A Rebel
The Crystals

   - "He's A Rebel": written by Gene Pitney – one of Phil Spector's protégés.
      * His first important record made at Gold Star Studios.
         a.) It also began a long collaboration with his arranger: Jack Nitzsche.
      * November/1962: "He's A Rebel" became Spector's first, #1 single that he produced.
         a.) Unlike the rich textures of his previous productions, this single was recorded in a straightforward, gritty gospel-driven manner (utilizing the gospel-singing talent of Darlene Love).

D.) The Wall Of Sound: Phil Spector's signature trademark sound.
   1.) End of 1962: The Wrecking Crew, Phil Spector's session group consisted of over 25 players. They constituted the backbone of his signature sound at Gold Star Studios.
      - Up to 5 guitarists, 3 Basses, 3 pianos, 2 drummers, orchestral strings, and percussion (if you were there as a guest, you would be recruited to play a percussion instrument). He also had a chorus of backup singers.
         * These multiple instrumental groups (i.e. multiple guitars, etc.) would be playing their own melodic line in unison.
   2.) Goal: an imposing, huge sound carrying a wealth of presence. Partly inspired by the music of a Romantic era/operatic composer from Germany: Richard Wagner (1813-1883).

Prelude:
Tristan und Isolde
Richard Wagner

      - One of Wagner's signature sounds was his thickly textured, orchestral compositional style that conveyed a huge, imposing sound.
         * This huge, imposing sound, that would be influential to Spector's signature style, was ironically recorded in a small studio 22'x31' – "Studio A" at Gold Star.
            a.) Spector's goal was to realize the sound he was hearing in his head (and wouldn't stop until he got it right).
      - Standard Working Sequence: usually beginning at 8:00 pm and lasting through the early morning hours.

Then He
Kissed Me
The Crystals

         * The foundation was the Guitar line: either playing the same identical melody line in unison or eighth-note chords (again in unison) repeated throughout the entire record.
            a.) Since the guitars constituted the foundation, everything else was blended into them.
      * Next, the Pianos were added: playing their own distinct unison line.
            a.) Then the Basses and then the Horns.
      * Finally, the Drums: brought in with a slamming backbeat played only on the low-registered Tom-Toms.

a.) After that, the rest of the percussion instruments which included maracas, tambourines, castanets, etc. (adding that finishing touch).
- RESULT: Once everything was finally balanced and in place (which took approximately 3 hours), the group would record the arrangement together.
* It usually took only one run-through, two at the most.
a.) Vocal Lines: the final addition. They were recorded separately in a different session.
* Recording: the instrumental arrangement would be recorded on 1 track. The vocal lines were recorded on another [track].
a.) Both tracks, on a two-track machine would be mixed down to mono with lots of reverb added in. (It was during this last process that Spector would call, "Back To Mono").
- RESULT: Phil Spector's signature "Wall of Sound" trademark: a huge, thickly textured, imposing mono mix where the instruments blurred into one another (to the point where one could not tell them apart).
* "Zip-a-Dee Doo Dah": recorded by The Crystals was when this process became honed in.
3.) The Crystals and The Ronettes were the two girl-groups that Spector wrote (or co-wrote) and produced for.
- They each had a lead singer who could hold her own, and cut through the wall of sound.
* For The Crystals, it was Darlene Love and Lala Brooks.

Da Do Ron Ron
The Crystals

* For The Ronettes, it was Veronica (Ronnie) Bennett.
- The Crystals: "He's A Rebel" (Darlene Love), "Then He Kissed Me", and "Da Do Ron Ron" (Lala Brooks).
* The Ronettes: "Walkin' In The Rain", "The Best Part Of Breaking Up", and "Be My Baby".
4.) Ronnie Bennett: Spector's most featured female singer (who would later become his wife). Spector was first sold on Ronnie Bennett's voice when, during an audition, she sounded like Frankie Lymon (of Frankie Lymon & the Teenagers fame).
- In fact, it was after her rendition of a Frankie Lymon hit, "Why Do Fools Fall In Love", that Spector was sold.

Be My Baby
The Ronettes

* "Be My Baby" (1963): a song he co-wrote with the songwriting team of Ellie Greenwich and Jeff Barry (b. Joel Adelberg).
a.) Recorded at Gold Star Studios with a full contingent of The Wrecking Crew plus orchestral strings and a virtual choir of backup singers. The arrangement was written by Jack Nitzsche.
- It took an additional three days to record Ronnie Bennett's vocal line.
* "Be My Baby" (released in August, 1963): which peaked at #2 on the pop charts, became the embodiment of the girl-group era (that one song which would capture the girl-group era essence above all others).
a.) In the process, Ronnie Bennett became rock and roll's first female sex symbol.
E.) Spector's Greatest Achievement: "You've Lost That Lovin' Feelin'" – composed by the Brill Building writing team of Barry Mann and Cynthia Weil. Spector's greatest example of what he called his "Little Symphony for the Kids" concept.
1.) Background: Throughout 1964, it became evident that the girl-group sound was gradually falling out of fashion. This was due primarily, to the new wave of Beatlemania and the British invasion bands that followed in their wake. Their new sound rapidly inundated the airwaves.

- Spector's New Lifeline: <u>The Righteous Brothers</u> (Bill Medley b. 9/19/40, Santa Anna, CA) and Bobby Hatfield) b. 8/10/40, Beaver Dam, WI, d. 11/06/03, Kalamazoo, MI).

(You're My)
Soul And Inspiration
The Righteous Brothers

         * Medley was the low-voiced bass/baritone; Hatfield was the sharp-edged, high-voiced tenor.

            a.) They sang in a rough-edged, soulful, and authentic black style that became a natural part of their performance artistry. They were greatly admired by black audiences especially at one of their regular performance venues — the El Toro Marine Base in San Diego.

         * They recorded their first three singles at Gold Star Studios under Stan Ross. These records, all released on the Moonglow label were commercial failures.

            a.) It was through the Stan Ross/Gold Star connection that Spector first heard of the Righteous Brothers.

2.) <u>Opportunity</u>: Although the Righteous Bothers sounded "very black" (to quote Bill Medley), Spector believed that they would be an easier sell to pop mainstream audiences entranced by The Beatles et al.

    - Although Barry Mann and Cynthia Weil wrote, "You've Lost That Lovin' Feelin' " (initially inspired by a 4-Tops single released by Motown called "Baby I Need Your Loving"), It was Spector who molded it to fit the natural style of the Righteous Brothers (i.e. lowering the key, slowing the tempo, etc.).

You've Lost That
Lovin' Feeling
The Righteous Brothers

         * The symphonically-oriented Wall of Sound arrangement was written by Gene Page.

            a.) It would be the Wall of Sound at its most symphonic with musical ebbs & flows, peaks and valleys (like that of a real symphony).

3.) <u>His Crowning Achievement</u>: released in early November of 1964, this record reached to #1 on the pop charts by late December (it would also reach #1 in the UK).

    - in the record industry as well as Spector himself believed that this record marked the apex of his artistic career – his greatest triumph that transcended the test of time.

         * The recordings of the Righteous Brothers would be the last great recordings under the Philles label.

F.) <u>The Beatles/Spector Connection</u>: Phil Spector's career would be resurrected in the early 70's with his new collaborators: The Beatles.

1.) <u>Allen Klein</u> (b. 1931), became a noted accountant with a reputation for unearthing back royalties that his clients were previously unaware of.

    - <u>Among them</u>: Bobby Darin, Sam Cooke, The Dave Clark Five, Herman's Hermits, and eventually, The Beatles. After Klein was hired to represent The Beatles, he started sifting through Apple Records in search of potential revenue sources.

         * He found an unfinished Beatles album called: *Get Back*. Tapes from these sessions were lying around waiting to be edited and mixed. However, due to the acrimony now existing between them, The Beatles had no desire to finish the project.

            a.) Klein came up with a solution that would bring this record to a successful conclusion: he called on Phil Specter to finish the album (he arrived in London in January, 1970).

         * After a considerable amount of tape editing, mixing, and adding in his signature string arrangements, the album, now known as *Let It Be*, was released in May of 1970.

2.) <u>Aftermath</u>: Spector was also instrumental in producing solo albums of two former Beatles: <u>George Harrison</u> and <u>John Lennon</u>.

- George Harrison's *All Things Must Pass* (released November, 1970): became Harrison's landmark solo statement. In addition, this album topped the American charts making George Harrison the first ex-Beatle to do so.
> * "My Sweet Lord", the most well-known single of the album, remained at #1 for several straight weeks.

- For John Lennon, Spector produced his first three albums:
> * *John Lennon/Plastic Ono Band* (1970).
> * *Imagine* (1971)
> * *Some Time In New York City* (1972)

- also produced an album in 1979 for The Ramones entitled, *End Of The Century*.
> * Some of which was featured in a 1982 film, *Rock and Roll High School.*

- NOTE: As accomplished as these projects were, they would never achieve the artistic level comparable to his apex in the early 60's.
> * It does not mean, however, that his influence had died out without a legacy. On the contrary, his influence would resonate with the next major producer.

IV. BRIAN WILSON (b. 6/20/42, Hawthorne, CA): a Phil Spector protégé. Of the influences that impacted his musical development, there are three that stand out. The first to be discussed is surf music.

A.) But first, the Southern California Surf Culture focusing on San Diego.
1.) In existence since the 1930's.
2.) They had their own culture:
- their own lingo.
- their own clothing fashion.
- their own music.
> * They were in culture in and of themselves.
3.) But there was one man who's music would greatly reflect the essence of this culture...
- while laying down the groundwork that would standardize the surf music sound.

B.) Dick Dale (b. Richard Monsour, 5/4/37, Boston, MA): in the early 60's would become that symbol.

1.) Three Most Important Influences: his original last name was Monsour (of Lebanese decent).
- The OUD: a mandolin-type of instrument of middle-eastern origin.
> * As a child, he grew up listening to his uncle playing it.
>> a.) This instrument requires a large pick in order to play rapid-fire, repeated staccato picking on the same string.
>> b.) Also, the melodies played on the Oud featured middle east styled, chromatic inflections.
- Gene Krupa: Big Band/Swing Era drummer for bandleaders such as Harry James and Benny Goodman.
> * Dick Dale used to listen to his parents records of Gene Krupa in action with these legendary band leaders.
>> a.) Dale was captivated by the tight rhythmic style of Krupa and eventually, tried to emulate his [Krupa's] influence on his style of guitar playing.
- Latin-Styled Music: primarily, Latin-influenced chord progressions.
> * Other Latin flavors including a Mariachi-influenced trumpet solo in "Misirlou".
- RESULT: The electric guitar-driven, Southern California surf sound.
> * Influence of the Oud: mid-east melodic, chromatic inflections.
> * Influence of Gene Krupa: tight, rhythmic picking where the guitar is played as a rhythmic instrument (as opposed to melodic).

a.) Supported by <u>Latin-styled chord progressions</u>.
- Dick Dale was said that he played the guitar as if he were playing drums.

2.) Through his tight rhythmic picking, mid-east inflected melodies, and sliding chords up and down the guitar neck…
- he would present a musical illustration of various surfing situations.
3.) It is within this context that he was known then, now known, and known forever more as "<u>The King Of The Surf Guitar</u>".
- whose rapid-picking style in middle to low registers on the electric guitar. His became the standard which gave surf music, it's own distinct identity.
4.) He also developed a substantial local following of both surfers and non-surfers alike.
- as a regional icon, over a thousand people crowded into the Balboa Ballroom on Saturday nights to watch Dick Dale & The Del-Tones.
* He would release regional hits on his own independent regional label called: "The Del-Tone" label.
a.) An early example of the D.I.Y. (Do-It-Yourself) concept which would grow in scope and in scale as rock and develops into the late 60's and early to mid 70's.
5.) At the height of his popularity, Dick Dale became the absolute epitome of the Southern California surfing lifestyle.
C.) <u>The Four Freshmen</u>: Brian Wilson's vocal harmonization influence.
1.) Thy were founded in the late 40's by four students – all freshmen at the time (hence, the name) – at the Arthur Jordan Conservatory of Music in Indianapolis, IN.
- Original Personnel:
* <u>Ross Barbour</u> (trumpet), his brother <u>Don Barbour</u> (guitar), a cousin <u>Bob Flanigan</u> (Trombone), and a friend <u>Hal Kratzsch</u> (trumpet, bass).
* In the course of the 50's, some personnel changes:
a.) Hal Kratzsch replaced by <u>Ken Errain</u> in 1953.
b.) He in turn, was replaced by <u>Ken Albers</u> (1955).
2.) For Brian Wilson, it was the Four Freshmen's signature four-part vocal harmonization style that captivated him the most.

- the song that initially captured Wilson's interest was: "<u>Day By Day</u>".
* Hearing it at the age of 14 for the time, he immediately fell in love with sound.
- He would compose arrangements that imitated the four-part vocal harmonic style of The Four Freshmen.
* <u>NOTE</u>: This case of imitating another style inadvertently led to an original sound.
a.) Because Wilson's group – The Beach Boys — were not The Four Freshmen, they [Beach Boys] sounded somewhat like them vocally, but not exactly…
- they sounded like the Beach Boys.
3.) In addition to both The Four Freshmen and the southern California surf sound standardized by Dick Dale…
- There is one more influence to discuss…
D.) <u>Chuck Berry</u>: lyrics.
1.) <u>Mainstream Teenage Concerns</u>: as mentioned in Chapter 1, Chuck Berry's lyrics dealt mainly with teenage concerns such as cars, love, sexual liberation, and adult repression.
- <u>Brian Wilson</u>: took the Chuck Berry lyric template and transformed it into a beach context.
* Fun-in-the-sun, surf waves, and wide sandy beaches would be joined with cars. love, sexual liberation, adult repression (and other Chuck Berry lyrical trademarks).
a.) creating an entirely new approach to mainstream teenage concerns.
E.) <u>Phil Spector</u>: Brian Wilson's mentor. Wilson once referred to Spector as: "The biggest

inspiration in my life".

Surfin' USA
The Beach Boys

1.) Spector's production techniques (i.e. the wall of sound) would be highly influential.
- Wilson would create his own version of the wall of sound with background vocal harmonies (al a, The Four Freshmen).
2.) Spector's approach to the three-and-a-half minute single as a highly crafted work of art was another touchstone for Wilson.
- He [Wilson] would approach his crafting of the "record" with the same intent.
F.) The Beach Boys: originally called, The Pendletones.
1.) Brian Wilson would combine all three influences discussed earlier to create a new, original sound. A summarization:
- The surf music sound: the Dick Dale standard style.
- Vocal harmonization: The Four Freshmen
- Lyrics: Chuck Berry
- Phil Spector: the wall of sound and "record" approach.
2.) Personnel:
- Brian Wilson (bass, vocals [falsetto] producer, writer, arranger), his two brothers; Dennis (drums) and Carl (guitar and background vocals), their cousin Mike Love (lead singer), and Al Jardine (guitar and background vocals), a high school friend.
3.) "Surfer Girl"(1963): according to Brian Wilson, their first true creation.

Surfer Girl
The Beach Boys

- of this new combination of influences.
* The first Beach Boys single that Brian Wilson produced.
4.) Brian Wilson: wrote or co-wrote the songs, wrote the arrangements, supervised the recording sessions, and produced all of the Beach Boys' records.
- making him a first-rate record producer in the Lieber and Stoller/Phil Spector tradition.
5.) Another point of interest regarding the Spector influence:

Don't Worry Baby
The Beach Boys

- Brian Wilson would use The Wrecking Crew, Spector's studio session band, to accompany Beach Boy's recordings.
* The Beach Boys would sing on the vocal tracks.
G.) In January of 1964, a paradigm was firmly in place in the rock and roll domain:
1.) The Beach Boys had become a "hit after hit" sensation.
The great black male voices like Jackie Wilson, Sam Cooke, and Ben E. King.
The Girl-Group sound.
The songwriting teams churning out many hits.
The producer with a controlling hand in every step of the creative process.
- Where the finished record fulfilled his artistic vision.
The music crossed all of the racial lines. In other words, a "people's music".
2.) It seemed to everyone involved in this paradigm that the juggernaut was set in motion.
- that the possibilities for them were endless.
- that their successes and strengths were unquestionable.
- that their dominance in the pop field would last indefinitely.
- that the concept of a "people's music" would allow black artists to become stronger than they ever were in the past.
3.) All signs of continued, unabated dominance and success were firmly set in place for as far as the eye could see.
- until all of sudden, the members of this structure [paradigm] were blind-sided and caught completely off guard. In other words, disaster struck…
H.) February 7, 1964: the day that would live in rock and roll infamy.
1.) On Pan Am flight 101, The Beatles arrived in America for the first time and at that exact moment — 1:30 pm — at New York's Idlewild (now JFK) International Airport:
- the entire paradigm and it's rules, changed immediately.

V. THE BEATLES

(<u>NOTE</u>: The following is a brief overview of The Beatles. A more highly detailed survey will be presented in the next chapter).

A.) Began as a rag-tag skiffle group out of Quarry Bank High School in Liverpool who named themselves, <u>The Quarrymen</u>.

    1.) of which John Lennon was an original member (the only one of The Beatles to be an original member).

    2.) The Quarrymen played at weddings, parties, and church dances.

        - As original members left the group one by one, <u>Paul McCartney</u> and <u>George Harrison</u> – both attending the Liverpool Institute – eventually joined the group.

    3.) After performing in a talent show in Manchester, they landed their first professional gig.

        - a minor touring gig in the remote villages in northern Scotland as a back-up band for the main act: Johnny Gentle.

        - It was just before this tour that they named themselves: <u>The Silver Beatles</u>.

            * consisting at that time, of John, Paul, and George.

    4.) By the time they played their next important professional gig – in Hamburg, Germany – <u>The Beatles</u> (as they were now called) consisted of two more members:

        - <u>Pete Best</u> (drums) and <u>Stuart Sutcliffe</u> (neophyte bass player).

    5.) <u>Brian Epstein</u> (b. 9/19/34, Liverpool; d. 8/27/67, London): son of a furniture store owner and manager of two record stores his father established for him called NEMS (North End Music Stores).

        - By the time he took an interest in The Beatles, Sutcliffe had quit the band to remain in Hamburg after marrying Astrid Kirchherr (more on the importance of her in the next chapter).

        - Soon after Epstein became The Beatles' manager in early 1962…

            * He would sack Pete Best and replace him with <u>Ringo Star</u>.

    6.) Another one of Epstein's accomplishments, was to secure a recording contract with Parlophone Records, a subsidiary of EMI.

        - thereby transforming The Beatles from a bar/nightclub band, into a recording group.

            * <u>George Martin</u> (b. 1/3/26, Highbury, North London): who became their producer at Parlophone, would transform them from cover group, to a group writing their own original songs.

    7.) Epstein also spearheaded a massive PR campaign in America.

        - The Beatles first several singles were not released by the Capitol label (EMI's American affiliate).

            * They were released instead by <u>Vee-Jay Records</u>: an independent black-owned company in Chicago.

                a.) They were Chess' rival label. Their most notable artist was <u>Jimmy Reed</u>.

                b.) The early Beatles singles they released were only nominally successful.

        - Epstein (on his first trip to New York City) convinced Capitol to release the Beatles' fifth single, "<u>I Wanna Hold Your Hand</u>" (which would become their first #1 hit in the US).

            * He also convinced Capitol to launch a $50,000 advertisement campaign to promote the Beatles in America.

                a.) Posting their images literally across the US.

        - these two major deals that Epstein struck with Capitol along with a cover story on America's most popular magazine at the time, "<u>LIFE Magazine</u>":

            * The Beatles became a sensation before their maiden voyage to America.

    8.) <u>RESULT</u>: By the time they arrived in the US on that infamous day of 2/7/64…

- they were already immensely popular.
- On that day, the American paradigm already in place was shattered.

VI. AFTERMATH
    A.) Summary:

Old Paradigm	New Paradigm
1.) Songwriting Teams were the norm. (with the exception of The Beach Boys).	The Beatles wrote their own music. They standardized the concept of recording artists writing their own music.
2.) Black male voices, surf music, and the girl-group sound.	The self-contained, white electric guitar quartet became the new model.
3.) Record producer had complete control. Where the record fulfilled his creative vision.	The Beatles had total control over their own creative destinies. The record would now be the artistic vision of the recording artists themselves.
4.) A "people's" music for whites and blacks alike.	White mainstream America's music. Mainstream America would ignore black music (with the exception of Motown).

B.) The British Invasion: In the wake of The Beatles' first appearance in America, other British pop bands would follow.
    1.) The Moody Blues, The Dave Clark Five, Chad and Jeremy, Manfred Mann, and Jerry and The Pacemakers were some of the best known examples.
        * They would cover songs originally written for, recorded, and released by black artists.
            a.) Radio DJ's all over America would play the British cover versions instead of the original black versions.
            b.) RESULT: the disenfranchisement of black recording artists in regard to mainstream audiences.
                - all of a sudden most black artists faced unemployment.
        * Because white America could directly relate to the Beatles by means of race:
            a.) They wanted to emulate the look (i.e. the hairstyle) and sound of The Beatles.
                - hence the beginning of the garage bands in every suburban neighborhood.
            b.) Which again, further alienated black artists from the mainstream.
        * So once again, because of this new paradigm:
            a.) segregation has made it's way back into the rock and roll domain.
C.) But on the other hand, the negative racial results notwithstanding, this new paradigm would eventually lead rock and roll into many new directions at once.
    1.) The Beatles would be one of the catalysts.
        - The other, would begin his career as a folk singer hailing from a northern Minnesota town called, Hibbing.

CHAPTER II: REVIEW

Name the publishing company founded by Don Kirshner that wrestled control of pop music from the primacy of Tin Pan Alley.

Between 1958 and February 7, 1964, there were five aspects that made this era a very ripe period in rock and roll. Name the five aspects:
  1.)
  2.)
  3.)
  4.)
  5.)

Name at least four great black male singers from this era:
  1.)
  2.)
  3.)
  4.)

Of all the dance crazes of this period, which dance became the most popular?

Which sound captured the essence of this era in the early 60's?

  Name at least five of these groups:
  1.)
  2.)
  3.)
  4.)
  5.)

Name four songwriting teams that were prominent in the early 60's. They personified the Brill Building concept of great songwriting craftsmanship.
  1.)
  2.)
  3.)
  4.)

  As in the Tin Pan Alley tradition, what was their main emphasis?

The late 50's/early 60's marked the rise of the new genius in rock 'n' roll, which was arguably, the most important development of this period. What was this new genius?

Name five things that they did:
1.)
2.)
3.)
4.)
5.)

Name the four that will be covered in this chapter:
1.)
2.)
3.)
4.)

What term was used to denote the three-and-a-half minute single as a highly crafted work of art?

Who created the model and structure for the rise of the record producer?

Which melodic/pop-influenced tradition did they mix with rhythm & blues?

What was the result of this synthesis?

In addition to classical music, what were Mike Stoller's 3 other musical influences?
1.)
2.)
3.)

Name two of Lieber & Stoller's early R&B influences:
1.)
2.)

What was their first professional gig in 1951?

What was their first collaboration on this gig and who recorded it?

Name their first collaborative success in 1953 and the artist who recorded it:

    Name four musical features in this single:
        1.)
        2.)
        3.)
        4.)

List three aspects of Jerry Lieber's approach to writing lyrics:
        1.)
        2.)
        3.)

What were "playlets" and what did they present?

    Which vocal group did Lieber and Stoller consistently write these playlets for?

What independent label hired Lieber & Stoller as writer/producers in 1955?

    Originally, what subject matter did their "playlets" (written for The Coasters) deal with?

    What was their target audience for these "playlets"?

Name Lieber and Stoller's first "crossover" hit in 1957 (hint: it was a double-sided hit):
    1.) Side A:
    2.) Side B:

    Jerry Lieber expanded his subject matter to areas that were more universal. Name two:
        1.)
        2.)

What was the significance of Lieber and Stoller's music in the late 1950's during the era when the squeaky-clean teen idols ruled mainstream pop? In other words, what did they accomplish with black music vis-à-vis a mainstream audience?

What changed in Mike Stoller's songwriting approach with The Drifters? In other words, what were the three new elements of his music?
        1.)
        2.)
        3.)

Name the first single from 1959 that marked the beginning of this new direction:

How did this new Lieber and Stoller sound — orchestral strings/percussion, reverb, and lush black pop melodies — significantly influence the signature sound of rock and roll in the early 60's?

Name four Lieber & Stoller trademarks that the songwriting team of Carole King & Jerry Goffin adopted:
     1.)
     2.)
     3.)
     4.)

Name the first girl-group hit written by Carole King and Gerry Goffin in 1961:

     Which girl group recorded it?

     What was the significance of this first girl-group hit?

     What did the lyrics of Gerry Goffin's address for the first time?

What was producer George "Shadow" Morton's limitation?

     How did he turn this disadvantage into advantage?

     Which girl-group did he produce?

     Name one of their hit singles that he produced.

How did Phil Spector begin his professional career?

     Name his first 1959 hit single that he wrote?

Who were Phil Spector's arranger/producer mentors in New York while he [Spector] worked at Atlantic Records?

     What did he learn under his mentors?

Which Romantic Era composer – with a thick orchestral sound – greatly influenced Phil Spector?

Phil Spector adapted this composer's sound to fit his environment at Gold Star Studios and as a result, created a new signature sound. What was this sound called?

What was the instrumentation behind this signature sound?

Which studio technique did he use to saturate this big sound?

What type of mix would he meld this big blurry, impressive sound into?

Name two girl groups that Phil Spector co-wrote for and produced:
    1.)
    2.)

Who was the lead singer for The Crystals?

Who became rock and roll's first female sex symbol?

Which 1963 single that Phil Spector produced for The Ronettes became the embodiment of the girl-group era sound?

What was unique about the "blue-eyed soul" of The Righteous Brothers? In other words, what style of music could they deliver/perform in a highly authentic manner?

Name their greatest hit that made Spector's "Wall of Sound" the most symphonic (it was written by Brill Building writers Barry Mann and Cynthia Weil):

What did Phil Spector call these types of singles?

Who was the original architect of the Southern California Surf Sound?

List three of his most important influences:
    1.)
    2.)
    3.)

Name the record producer of The Beach Boys:

What were his four most important influences?
1.)
2.)
3.)
4.)

What influence did The Four Freshmen have upon Brian Wilson?

What influence did Chuck Berry have upon Brian Wilson in regard to lyrics?

Which single was The Beach Boys first "true creation" in 1963?

What influence did Phil Spector have upon Brian Wilson?

What was Brian Wilson's version of the "Wall of Sound"?

What significant event happened on February 7, 1964?

What did this significant event change in rock 'n' roll?

Compare the four properties of the "Old Paradigm" with the "New Paradigm" (list them below):

OLD:	NEW:
1.)	1.)
2.)	2.)
3.)	3.)
4.)	4.)

What became the resulting fallout of the British invasion in regard to black recording artists?

CHAPTER III: THE BIG SPREAD – BOB DYLAN AND THE BEATLES

I. INTRODUCTION

A.) In addition to the items attributed to the old paradigm of the early '60's (pre-Beatles), there are two more:

    1.) Songs that were very adult in medium: very highly crafted. Some would appeal to a more mature type of listener.

        - as opposed to those with more simplistic tastes.

    2.) Lyrics containing hidden meanings (like "Spanish Harlem").

        - submersed within the deep poetics.

B.) But big changes were about to be unleashed that would dismantle this one paradigm and replace it, with a vast array of other different paradigms that artists themselves (rather than producers) would have complete control over.

    1.) In other words, rock and roll was about to split into many simultaneous directions.

        - mainly because of the influences of two artists: <u>Bob Dylan</u> and <u>The Beatles</u>.

            * Their legacies would set various structures in motion that would allow an infinite number of artists to pursue their own individual creative destinies.

II. BOB DYLAN (b. Robert Zimmerman, May 24, 1941 in Duluth, MN)

A.) <u>Background</u>: At the age of 6, his family moved to Hibbing, MN.

    1.) Where he grew up and came of age.

        - He learned to play guitar and harmonica during his childhood.

        - Throughout high school, he was a rock and roll enthusiast.

            * During this time, he started a band called "The Golden Chords".

    2.) In 1959, he enrolled at the University of Minnesota majoring in art and living in an area called "Dinkytown".

        - While there, he performed folk music in various local coffeehouses…

            * …and was also listening to the blues.

                a.) During a summer gig (1960) in Denver, he was inspired by blues artist, Jesse Fuller.

                    - This was one of his blues inspirations that would manifest itself later in his [Zimmerman's] musical development beginning in 1965.

    3.) His most important folk influence: <u>Woody Guthrie</u> (b. 7/4/12, Okemah, OK; d. 10/3/ 67, Queens, NY): Dust bowl poet and troubadour who sang with an Okie twang and played folk guitar and harmonica at the same time (the harmonic rested stationary on a shoulder rack).

        - Zimmerman would adopt these characteristics and in the act of imitating Woody Guthrie (in both the Okie twang and in the folk guitar/harmonica on the shoulder rack),

            * He would achieve his own sound.

        - <u>NOTE</u>: Sometimes, originality is spawned by an artist attempting to sound like somebody else…

            * .. but winding up sounding completely different.

                a.) Such was the case for Zimmerman: in attempting to sound like Guthrie, he sounded like something else: Bob Zimmerman.

    4.) During his time at the University of Minnesota, a dancer-friend and her boyfriend invited him over and introduced him to the music of Woody Guthrie.

        - They played for Dylan, the classic Guthrie album: *Dust Bowl Ballads.*

            * Dylan immediately became a Woody Guthrie fanatic.

                a.) He learned as many Guthrie songs as possible and read Guthrie's autobiography: *Bound For Glory.*

        - Woody Guthrie's primary musical influence: <u>The Carter Family</u>.

            * <u>Alvin Pleasant Carter</u> (1891-1960), vocals; <u>Sara Dougherty Carter</u> (1898-1979), vocals, guitar, autoharp; <u>Maybelle Addington Carter</u> (1909-1978), vocals, guitar, autoharp, banjo.

Single Girl, Married Girl
The Carter Family

The Boll Weevil
Woody Guthrie

Oregon Trail
Woody Guthrie

Dirty Overhalls
Woody Guthrie

Talkin'
New York
Bob Dylan

a.) Pioneering of country/folk music
    - Presented in a rapid-tempo'd, string band setting.
b.) Began recording in 1927 via the Bristol Sessions headed by Ralph Sylvester Peer.
    - He was sent to Bristol, Tennessee by RCA Victor to scope out the local artists/talent there.
        * This was how the country legend Jimmie Rodgers was discovered (also in 1927).
* Guthrie: would borrow melodies from Carter family songs and set them to his own lyrics.
    a.) As well as emulate the Carter family style.
        - Thus contributing to his originality.
- Woody Guthrie's primary lyrics influence: Will Rogers (1879-1935).
    * Legendary Oklahoman satirist, movie star, personality, philosopher, columnist, Ziegfeld Follies star, and trick roper.
        a.) His anecdotes of humor masqueraded as political and social commentary, became an inspiration to Guthrie.
    * He emulated Will Rogers' in his lyrics and in his day-to-day interactions with people by turning on his Okie accent and demeanor.
        a.) His lyrics engaged in social commentary within the context of anecdotes (but without the humor).
            - In "Oregon Trail", he uses an anecdote of the failed farm to inspire a move to a new land of plenty and the hope of a better life.
        b.) He also established the use of metaphor in order to get his message across.
            - An example is a song called "Dirty Overhalls" where he uses metaphors of war to depict the struggle of working the farmland.
- The Birth of Modern Folk Music: Woody Guthrie inspired folk artists to write their own music.
    * In addition, he provided a new blueprint for folk music.
        a.) A vehicle for social commentary, social consciousness, and protest on behalf of the struggling working class poor and disadvantaged.
            - He made folk music into a voice of national consciousness -- a folk version of John Steinbeck.
5.) Bob Dylan: became inspired by what he felt, was Guthrie's ability to compose simple songs with complexed social themes.
    - The Guthrie songwriting blueprint, would become Dylan's blueprint as well.
        * He would also imitate Guthrie's Okie twang in his singing voice.
            a.) In the act of emulating Guthrie, Bob Dylan acquired an original sound at the age of 20.
B.) 1961: Bob Dylan dropped out of school and in January, he hitchhiked to New York City and headed to the Greenwich Village folk scene.
    1.) NOTE: When he left Minnesota, he was Robert Zimmerman, after he arrived in New York, he reinvented himself as Bob Dylan, folksinger (named after Dylan Thomas).
        - He began performing at the Cafe Wha?, a club presenting various acts (i.e. singers, jugglers, comedians, etc.) owned by Freddie Neil.
            * He [Dylan] was also performing in various coffeehouses throughout the area.
    2.) Although Woody Guthrie was his primary musical influence, another performance inspiration was Dave Van Ronk.
        - He [Van Ronk] performed regularly at the Gaslight: a club that Dylan aspired to perform in (performers there were paid weekly instead of the normal passing-of-the-hat solicitations as in other clubs/coffeehouses).

* Dylan first heard Van Ronk before he arrived in New York.

    a.) He liked Van Ronk enough to copy his style "phrase for phrase".

      - Dylan once wrote that Van Ronk could "turn the blues into ballads and ballads into blues".

    b.) Dylan loved Van Ronk's approach to performance and felt that he [Van Ronk] ruled the folk scene in Greenwich Village.

3.) <u>Bob Dylan</u>: developed a sizeable repertoire of folk songs and performed them with loud, aggressive guitar strumming.

    - To him, folk songs were about exploration.

      * He felt it most important to transcend the song's full expressive force to the listener. In other words, the performances were not about himself but rather, about the song.

        a.) He would begin to gather a following.

4.) In October of 1961, critic Robert Shelton of the New York Times reviewed him favorably.

    - This caught the attention of the legendary Columbia (CBS) Records A&R man: <u>John Hammond</u>.

      * He discovered among others: Billie Holiday, Teddy Wilson, Cab Calloway, Charlie Christian, Count Basie, Benny Goodman, and Lionel Hampton. He would also discover Aretha Franklin.

        a.) He once said that when it came to finding talent, he understood sincerity. He saw that sincerity in Bob Dylan.

          - He also felt that Dylan was part of the American tradition of folk, blues, and jazz.

      * Hammond signed Bob Dylan to a five-year contract.

5.) Dylan's debut album, *Bob Dylan* was released in March of 1962 with only two original singles:

Song To Woody
Bob Dylan

    - "Talking New York" and "Song to Woody" (At the time, Dylan was regularly visiting Woody Guthrie at a psychiatric institution where Guthrie was dying of Huntington's disease).

      *The remaining songs were all covers.

        a.) The album itself, sold poorly and Bob Dylan became known as "Hammond's Folly".

6.) Bob Dylan would not achieve wide-scale notoriety on his own persona. He would need some help.

    - He would gain initial fame by other, more famous artists covering his music.

      * <u>Peter, Paul, and Mary</u> would be the first.

        a.) Personnel: <u>Peter Yarrow</u> (b. 5/31/38, New York): vocals, guitar, <u>Noel Paul Stookey</u> (b. 11/3/37, Baltimore, MD): vocals, guitar, <u>Mary Travers</u> (b. 11/7/37, Louisville, KY): vocals.

C.) <u>The American Folk Music Scene</u>: was not popular with the mainstream.

    1.) Followers and musicians of the folk scene felt that they were part of an idealistic movement.

    - They all shared a vision of the world becoming a better place for humanity.

      * especially for the disadvantaged.

        a.) A sort of utopian vision that was turning into a political movement.

    - This movement became a conscience for social change in the early 60's.

      * <u>Peter Yarrow</u> (of Peter, Paul, & Mary) once said that folk music,

        a.) "Became the liturgy for change in America".

2.) The folk movement's direct activism in Civil Rights protests afforded them national exposure for the first time.

    - In 1962, mainstream America would have its first introduction to folk music.

     * <u>Peter, Paul, and Mary</u>: became the first folk artists to achieve a top
ten song on the pop charts.
       a.) "<u>If I Had A Hammer</u>" reached to number 10.
       b.) This song not only introduced the masses to folk music…

If I Had A Hammer
(The Hammer Song)
Peter, Paul, & Mary

         - …but it also injected <u>social commentary</u> into rock
         and roll for the first time.
  - <u>Dylan's first major breakthrough</u>: occurred when Peter Yarrow heard him
[Dylan] doing a performance of "<u>Blowin' In The Wind</u>"…
    *…and immediately decided to cover it.
    * "Blowin' In The Wind" was a part of Dylan's second album: "<u>The
Freewheelin' Bob Dylan</u>" (1962).

Blowin' In The Wind
Bob Dylan

       a.) Peter, Paul, and Mary would release their own cover of
"<u>Blowin' in The Wind</u>" in 1963.
        - It became Dylan's first major hit that catapulted him
        to folk icon status.

Blowin' In The Wind
Peter, Paul, & Mary

  - "<u>Blowin' In The Wind</u>": also became an anthem for the Civil Rights
Movement.
    * It would become a regular fixture at outdoor civil rights rallies and
marches.

D.) <u>Bob Dylan</u>: would had a new level of depth to lyricism in folk music.
  1.) Rather than the traditional lyric writing of a conventional songwriter, he approached
the words from a poet's perspective.
    - Highly crafted "wordsmith-ism" with deeper meanings below the surface.
      * which made the listener think and ponder.
  2.) For "Blowin' In The Wind", this song asks questions that do not have a clear answer.
    "How many times can a man look up
    Before he can see the sky?
    Yes, 'n' how many ears must one man have

Blowin' In The Wind

by Bob Dylan, reprinted
from *Bob Dylan's Greatest
Hits*, CBS Records CK
9463: 1987, by permission
of Special Rider Music.

    Before he can hear people cry?
    Yes, 'n' how many deaths will it take till he knows
    That too many people have died?
    The answer, my friend, is blowin' in the wind,
    The answer is blowin' in the wind."
      * In hearing these "unanswerable" questions, the listener cannot only
      imagine what the possible answers may be, but also:
        a.)… what the possible solutions are (to the lingering,
        problems these questions address).
        b.) In this sense, the thoughts these lyrics provoke, can inspire
        one to become sympathetic to a world vision…
          - that could lead to the benefit of all humanity.
          - due to the profound thought that the lyrics challenge
          in the listener.
  - This is what a poet's perspective does. It causes one to think beyond the box in
ways that conventional lyrics do not.
    * And also, to look beneath the surface for answers that are not so
    readily apparent.
  3.) <u>Bob Dylan</u>: had significantly raised the level of poetics in the lyric domain.
    - And with it, the level of folk artistry as a whole.
      * <u>RESULT</u>: Dylan was developing a major following in both the US
      and Britain.
E.) "<u>Finger-Pointing Songs</u>": the term Dylan used to describe his folk music.
  1.) "<u>Talkin' John Birch Society Blues</u>", "<u>A Hard Rain's Gonna Fall</u>", "<u>Masters Of War</u>",
and "<u>The Times They Are A-Changin'</u>".
    - Significance: for example, in "<u>The Times They Are A-Changin'</u>", the poetry
    is applicable today as it was back in 1964. Injecting a sense of timelessness into
    folk poetics.

The Times They Are A-Changin' by Bob Dylan, reprinted from *Bob Dylan's Greatest Hits*, CBS Records CK 9463; 1987, by permission of Special Rider Music.

* "Come senators, congressmen,
Please heed the call
Don't stand in the doorway
Don't block up the hall
For he that gets hurt
Will be he who has stalled
There's a battle outside
And it is ragin'.
It'll soon shake your windows
And rattle your walls
For the times they are a-changin' ".

- Bob Dylan's lyrics, in addition to a profound poetic sense, would introduce another artistic aspect: timelessness.
* The fact that the lyrics listed above are applicable to any generation before or after is a testament to what great art is all about: durability.
2.) Bob Dylan: at the ripe age of 22, was dubbed "Spokesman For A generation" by the media as well as his devoted followers.
- He was now, the poster child of the folk music domain.
* But such elite titles as "Spokesman For A Generation" can always come back to haunt the bearer of those titles – with major consequences…
a.)… including the rejection and alienation of a once devoted following.
- Bob Dylan would experience this consequence first-hand.
b.) By the time of his 1966 tour, he would be booed everywhere he played (but that is another story to be covered later in this chapter).
F.) Bob Dylan: was one of the two major catalysts of rock and roll in the early 60's.
1.) The other, would come from across the ocean about 5000 miles away.

III. THE BEATLES
A.) Personnel:
1.) John Lennon (b. John Winston Lennon,10/09/40, Liverpool, ENG; d. 12/8/80, New York): guitar, vocals, keyboards, harmonica; Paul McCartney (b. James Paul McCartney, 6/18/42, Liverpool): guitar, vocals, bass, keyboards; George Harrison (b. 2/25/43, Liverpool; d. 11/29/01, Los Angeles, CA): guitar, vocals, sitar; Ringo Starr (b. Richard Starkey Jr., 7/7/40, Liverpool): Drums, vocals, percussion.
- In addition: Stuart Sutcliffe (b. Stuart Fergusson Victor Sutcliffe, 6/23/40, Edinburgh, Scotland; d. 4/10/62, Hamburg, GER): bass; Pete Best (b. 1941, ENG): drums.
B.) From The Beginning: Quarry Bank High School (Liverpool).
1.) John Lennon starts The Quarrymen (1956-59).
- Personnel: Eric Griffiths (guitar), Pete Shotten (washboard), Len Garry & Colin Hansen (drums), Ivan Vaughan (tea chest [on occasions]), and John Lennon (banjo).
* Len Garry and John's friend, Ivan Vaughan attended The Liverpool Institute.
C.) Three events: inspired John Lennon to take up music:
1.) Bill Haley's, "Rock Around The Clock" (1954)
- It swept England by storm in 1955 as the song for the hit rebellious film, "Blackboard Jungle".
- It mirrored Lennon's own sense of rebelliousness – his rebel attitude was manifested in fighting and causing trouble.

* It sparked the beginning of John Lennon's recalcitrant nature melded with music (instead of fist-fighting, etc.) that would be with him his entire career.

2.) Lonnie Donegan's, "Rock Island Line" (1/1956)

- With his jazz oriented band and high tenor voice, Lonnie Donegan (b. 4/29/31, Glasgow, Scotland) introduced "Skiffle" to the English masses.

Does Your Chewing Gum Lose Its Flavor
Lonnie Donegan

* Skiffle: a mixture of folk elements (i.e. melodies, simple chord progressions) and jazz elements (mainly perky jazz rhythms). There were three aspects that made this style popular.

a.) Easy to Play: all one needed to know were 1 or 2 chords on the guitar or very simple basic perky rhythms.

- And above all, it was fun.

b.) Instrumentation: acoustic guitar, washboard, tea chest, homemade bass, and drums (optional).

- each "instrument" was easy to acquire.

c.) A Mania: because it was so easy to emulate and it was fun, Skiffle put guitars "in the hands" of every British teenager.

- which spearheaded Skiffle bands in every neighborhood in the UK – it became a craze.

3.) Elvis Presley's, "Heartbreak Hotel" (5/1956)

- Established Elvis as the most inspiring, most influential pop music icon in England.

* He was one of the most important early modals for John Lennon to emulate.

D.) John Lennon's Beginnings: learned to play the guitar from his mother, Julia.

1.) She played the banjo.

- She taught her son chords on the acoustic guitar, but fingered like banjo chords (instead of the conventional acoustic guitar fingerings).

* John learned to play "banjo chords" on the guitar.

2.) June 15, 1956: Ivan Vaughan brought a friend from the Liverpool Institute to a Quarrymen gig at the Woolton Parish Church.

- After the gig, Ivan Vaughan introduced his friend – Paul McCartney – to John Lennon.

* Paul would teach John, the proper way of fingering chords that were indigenous to the acoustic guitar (instead of the banjo).

3.) At this time, John was the only member of The Quarrymen who took the band seriously.

- Other band members would not show up to gigs or to practice sessions except at their convenience.

- When Paul McCartney joined The Quarrymen…

* The group got going in a more serious direction.

4.) George Harrison: another Liverpool Institute student who would be introduced to John (via Paul) and sat in on Quarrymen gigs starting in 1958 but would not become a full-fledged member until 1959.

- George knew many more chords than the rest of the group.

* He taught them to John and Paul.

a.) This new expanded chord language, as well as their drift away from Skiffle towards a more "Elvis" type of beat music…

- inspired their first early original songs.

5.) Their first shot at a professional gig was in Manchester where they played on "Carroll Levis Discoveries TV Show" - a TV talent competition.

- They appeared as "Johnny and The Moondogs".

* They did not win or for that matter, were not even approached by any talent scouts.

a.) John, Paul, and George were disappointed by the outcome.

E.) <u>Their First Official Venue</u>: "The Casbah" in the basement of a house in the West Derby district owned by Johnny Best (a native Liverpudlian) and his wife, Mona (a native of new Delhi, India).

    1.) Summer of 1959, Mona Best converted the basement of her house to create what would become, a private club/coffee house.

        - initially, to create a place for her son Pete and his friends to listen to records.

    2.) They decided to search for a "beat group" to perform there on a regular basis.

        - they The Quarrymen: now John, Paul, George, and Ken brown (guitarist)…

            * …refereed by a girl who knew Ken Brown.

    3.) The club would be entitled, "<u>The Casbah</u>" (inspired by a Heddy Lamar/Charles Boyer film: "Algiers").

        - The Quarrymen debuted there in August of 1959.

            * about 300 people attended.

    4.) After Ken Brown quit the group due to absenteeism and a row dealing with a payment dispute:

        - The Quarry Men began playing in other venues.

    5.) It was through this Casbah connection that Pete Best eventually joined the band as their drummer.

        - In August of 1960.

F.) <u>Their first professional break</u>…

    1.) After their initial stint at The Casbah, they auditioned for talent scout Larry Parnes in Manchester.

        - he was the biggest rock and roll kingpin in England at the time.

    2.) It was during this time that they changed their name to, "<u>The Silver Beatles</u>".

        * naming groups after insects was in fashion at the time.

            a.) John originally wanted to name the band, "The Crickets" but the name was already taken by Buddy Holly's group.

    3.) <u>Stuart Sutcliffe</u>, a friend of John's and fellow art college student had by then, joined the band as bass player (even though he didn't know how to play).

        - Paul and George taught him the basics.

        - Sutcliffe was so self conscious of his inabilities, he usually turned his back to the audience.

            * In order to hide from the audience's view, his rudimentary fingering.

    4.) At the audition, they lacked a drummer (this is before Pete Best had joined).

        - for the audition, a drummer named Johnny Hutch, who belonged to another group, sat in.

    5.) Their audition was successful and, as a result, they were given a back-up band slot for a two-week tour in the remote villages and towns of northern Scotland (1960).

        - The main act they were backing up: <u>Johnny Gentle</u>.

    6.) After that tour, they returned to the Casbah as a regular act (this was when Pete Best joined the group).

G.) <u>Hamburg, Germany</u>: their first extended gig outside of Britain. Their first club, The Indra.

    1.) <u>The Indra</u>: a strip club owned by Bruno Koschmider located in the rough, red-light St. Pauli district of Hamburg. Koschmider wanted to change the club (a sparsely attended strip joint) into a rock 'n' roll club modeled after his other club located nearby called, The Kaiserkeller (it was the success of this club that spearheaded the change for The Indra). All he needed, was an energetic, hard-nosed, rocking British band to turn The Indra around.

        - <u>Beginnings</u>: at first, their performance style was rigid, deadpanned, sedate, and uninspiring. Even their manager, Alan Williams kept encouraging them to "make a show!" but his words failed to connect.

            * Finally, according to author Bob Spitz, it was Koschmider who kept yelling to the band, *"Mach Schau! Mach Schau!"* that finally connected and almost immediately, the performance style of The Beatles became more flamboyant and free of any inhibitions.

a.) The band started joking around and dancing on the stage. Soon after, they worked these new free-spirited moves and flamboyance into their act.

- RESULT: within a few weeks, the word got out about The Beatles and The Indra was packed to the guilds every night – The Beatles were the new main attraction.

- Rearranging Their Repertoire: before their arrival in Hamburg, The Beatles had a sizable repertoire of rock 'n' roll classics by Chuck Berry, Little Richard, Elvis Presley, Jerry Lee Lewis, Ray Charles, et al – but as earlier mentioned, were performed in an uninspiring, deadpan sort of manner.

* Now, The Beatles have rearranged these classic covers to basically rock out the house which further honed in their new, hard-rocking performance style which captivated The Indra crowd and their next venue, The Kaiserkeller.

2.) The "Kaiserkeller": on the same rough side of town (of The Indra) where the "Teddy Boys" (ruffians) hung out.

- The "Teddy Boy" look: white tee shirt, black leather jacket, body-tight black pants that go down only as far as the upper side of the ankles, white socks, black shoes, and a greasy, very high bouffant hairdo (more puffier than Elvis).

* The Beatles by then, had already adopted this "Teddy Boy" look.

- After Bruno Koschmider was forced to close The Indra (due to constant complaints from area residents concerning the late-night noise), The Beatles were booked at The Kaiserkeller: considerably bigger and more hip than The Indra.

* They were hired as the back-up band for "Rory Storm and The Hurricanes" whose drummer was Ringo Starr (Richard Starkey). The gig began on October 4, 1960.

a.) The 2 bands would alternate performing every two hours (i.e. The Beatles, then The Hurricanes, then The Beatles again, etc.) — they lasted nightly into the very late hours.

3.) To Summarize: The experience of The Beatles' tenures at both The Indra and The Kaiserkeller resulted in the following:

- RESULT #1: This experience honed in their solid, rocking, performance style which was a very major development.

* In addition to making them a hit in Hamburg, it would also make them a hit upon their return to England.

- RESULT #2: They rearranged their repertoire of rock 'n' roll classics (mentioned earlier) and presented them in a way that rocked the house. They would also perform extended improvisations of tunes such as "Whole Lotta Shakin' Going On" that would last up to 30 minutes.

* They were also covering Gene Vincent styled rockabilly songs (they would also adopt the Gene Vincent renegade look with black leather outfits).

- RESULT #3: They would begin to nurture a friendly relationship with Ringo Starr.

* They couldn't help but notice that Ringo's drumming style was considerably more advanced than Pete Best's.

- RESULT #4: The famous Beatle haircut (eventually).

* Klaus Voorman and Astrid Kirchherr were college students known as "Exi's" (short for "Existentialists") who were the first native Germans to befriend the Beatles. She was a photography student at a local Art School.

a.) She would be the one who'd take those famous early photographs of the Beatles that included Stuart Sutcliffe and Pete Best.

* In a matter of time, Astrid and Stuart Sutcliffe became romantically involved.

        a.) It was she, who encouraged him to change his hairdo from a "Teddy Boy" look, to the "Exi" style in 1961 (during the Beatle's second Hamburg run).

4.) Because their lack of work permits were discovered by German authorities…

    - The Beatles were deported back to England where for two months, they went their separate ways (after which they would return to the Casbah).

H.) <u>The Litherton Town Hall (Dec. 27, 1960)</u>: Their first important post-Hamburg gig.

    1.) The culmination of their new, accomplished performance style and their new songs (all Kaiserkeller products)…

        …inundated Liverpool on that night.

    2.) In that audience, was Bob Wooller: DJ at <u>The Cavern Club</u>.

    - He was responsible for arranging the Litherton performance.

    - Eventually, he would book the Beatles at the Cavern Club (after they performed on the ballroom circuit).

    - <u>December/1960</u>: was the Beatles' first engagement at the Cavern Club.

        * from 12/60 to 2/62, Bob Wooller would introduce them 292 times.

    3.) <u>In April of 1961</u>, The Beatles made their second Hamburg run this time, at a considerably larger venue called: "<u>The Top Ten</u>".

    - It was during this time that Astrid influenced the famous haircut.

        * She also designed the collarless suits they'd become famous for.

    - It was also during this period, that The Beatles made their first studio recordings.

        * They accompanied a British pop singer named Tony Sheridan (who was performing in Hamburg at the time).

            a.) For these recordings, they named themselves The Beat Brothers.

                - Because the term "Beatles" rhymed with the word "Peedles" a German slang term for male genitalia.

            b.) Most notable of these recordings was a pop/rock version of an old folk tune entitled: "<u>My Bonnie</u>" (with Sheridan as lead singer).

                - It became a hit on the German "Hit Parade" but would flop in England.

        * Before this cut was recorded, Stuart Sutcliffe had left the band.

            a.) And in July of 1961, the four remaining Beatles returned to Britain and left Stuart behind where he married Astrid Kirchherr. (In April of 1962, Stuart Sutcliffe died of an aneurysm).

    4.) They went back to The Cavern Club. Their last gig there was on August 23, 1963

    - In their early Cavern days, they were wild, disorganized, unkept in appearance, and joking with the audience and each other on stage.

        * But all that would change after December 3, 1961…

I.) <u>Brian Epstein</u>: "North End Music Stores (NEMS)".

    1.) He managed two NEMS stores that specialized exclusively in retail record sales.

    - His father, Harry – son of Isaac who emigrated from Poland to escape Nazi Jewish persecution and founded Epstein & Sons, a retail furniture empire – established a new NEMS branch in Liverpool (the first NEMS store in Walton had been part of the family business since 1930) in order to spark his son's interest in the family business.

        * because Brian had no interest in his father's furniture business (for Brian had a history of constantly changing jobs and interests).

a.) Brian became so enthusiastic about managing NEMS, his father decided to open up another branch for him.

b.) He [his father] was hoping that Brian's enthusiasm in both record shops would eventually transfer over to the furniture domain…

- …where his father hoped he would eventually take over.

2.) <u>Brian's retail policy</u>: To have practically every record available in stock (he had a massive index system).

- Pop records he would carry an abundance of.

* With unpopular records, he would try to at least have one copy in stock.

a.) If a customer could not find the record they were looking for, Epstein would order it (whether the customer was interested enough or not).

- <u>RESULT</u>: Epstein's record shops achieved a distinguished reputation of having any record available upon demand.

* No mechanism, however meticulous one may make it, can ever be completely full-proof.

a.) For many, this could be seen as an example of failure, but for Brian, this would unveil a window of opportunity although at the time, he didn't know it yet…

3.) Sometimes, the road to success can begin at a spontaneous, uncalculated moment translated as a blessing in disguise.

My Bonnie
Tony Sheridan &
The Beat Brothers

- <u>Case In Point</u> (October 28, 1961): according to legend, a customer named Raymond Jones came into his [Brian's] shop requesting a record entitled: "<u>My Bonnie</u>" by Tony Sheridan & The Beat Brothers (i.e. The Beatles).

*…and he didn't have it in stock (he was in fact, aware of The Beatles but had never heard the record).

* He began searching for the disk and started inquiring about the group.

a.) He began hearing rumors on how fabulous they were.

b.) He didn't realize the momentum of their popularity.

- He visited The Cavern Club to check them out.

* <u>First visit</u>: a lunch time session on November 9, 1961.

- When he saw them for the first time, he felt they were:

* Untidy, unclean, cigarettes hanging from their mouths, eating on stage, talked and engaged in horseplay with one another on stage, exchanged jokes with audience members of the front rows, and turned their backs on the audience.

a.) Nevertheless, he was fascinated by their magnetism (especially with John Lennon).

- His original reason to see them at the Cavern Club was to find out from them [Beatles] how he could procure a copy of "My Bonnie".

* But he eventually took an interest in managing them.

4.) <u>December 3, 1961</u>: Their first meeting at Brian's NEMS office.

- The following Wednesday, he asks to be their manager.

* The contract was signed the following Sunday at "The Casbah" (their home base).

5.) <u>His first order of business</u>, was to clean up their act.

- <u>No more</u>: smoking, chewing gum, eating, or joking on stage.

* No more talking to the audience.

* Their hair would be neatly coifed.

* Identical clean-cut suits would be worn.

* A clean, well-kept look would be the new norm.

6.) <u>Second order of business</u>, The sacking of Pete Best.

- August 15, 1962: Epstein informs Pete Best that…

* "I've got some bad news for you. The boys want you out, and Ringo in".
    a.) Hence, Ringo Starr became their new drummer.
7.) <u>Third order of business</u>, secure a recording contract.
    - London: Brian Epstein approaches an engineer to record a Beatles demo tape onto an LP (vinyl).
      * The engineer informs Epstein about a producer he knows named George Martin at Parlophone (a subsidiary of EMI).
        a.) As a result of this connection, Brian Epstein and George Martin eventually meet for the first time
    - <u>June 6, 1962</u>: George Martin meets The Beatles for the first time at EMI's No. 3 Studio in the St. John's Wood section of London.
      * Martin found them to be very attractive people possessing a great charisma.
        a.) He would say in an interview that: "They were not great musicians. But the thing they had was charisma. You felt better for being around them".
      * <u>George Martin's Impact</u>: as their producer, he would encourage The Beatles to write their own songs – transforming them from a cover band to a band performing and recording their own original material.
        a.) He would not only encourage them to make the next song better than the last, but also, to never write the same song twice.

Love Me Do
The Beatles

    - Martin's first choice for the Beatles' first release: "<u>Love Me Do</u>" (1962), reached up to #17 on the UK charts (he chose this song because it was the least bad of an array of bad, un-deep songs).

Please, Please Me
The Beatles
From Me To You
The Beatles

      * "<u>Please, Please Me</u>" (1/12/63): reached to #1 on the UK charts (2/16/63).
      * "<u>From Me To You</u>" (4/63): reached #1 on the UK charts.

      * "<u>She Loves You</u>" (8/63): reached #1 on the UK charts.
        a.) Established The Beatles to national prominence in the UK.

She Loves You
The Beatles

    - First American releases: "<u>Please, Please Me</u>" and "<u>From Me To You</u>" (1963) on Vee-Jay Records.
      * "<u>She Loves You</u>" (1963) on Swan Records.
8.) <u>Epstein</u>: arrives in New York City for the first time.
    - Arranges a meeting with Capitol Records (EMI's American affiliate).

I Wanna
Hold Your Hand
The Beatles

      * <u>RESULT #1</u> — "I Wanna Hold Your Hand" (1964): their first US release on a major label (Capitol Records). Brian Epstein had personally contacted Alan Livingston, President of Capitol records (who had rejected The Beatles on three other occasions) and asked if he [Livingston] had heard the record. After he said no, Alan Livingston decided to give the record a listen and as a result, he agreed to release the record in the US which resulted in their first #1 hit on the US pop charts. It appeared on their debut US album, *Meet The Beatles*.

Wake Up
Little Susie
The Everly Brothers

        a.) <u>Influences</u>: They released teenage pop love songs with a style reminiscent of the girl-group sound that was popular in the US at the time.
          - The Everly Brothers: also influenced The Beatles' melodic style as well as their [The Beatles'] approach to vocal harmonization.
    - <u>RESULT #2</u>: Capitol launches an aggressive national ad campaign (at a price of $50,000).
      * Beatles posters/images were everywhere throughout the US.
    - <u>RESULT #3</u>: Epstein negotiates two appearances on The Ed Sullivan Show.
      * Scheduled for February 9th and February 16th of 1964.

- RESULT #4: He successfully booked two Carnegie Hall performances.
- RESULT #5: A cover story on "LIFE" Magazine.
   * America's most popular magazine at the time.
- Other results included:
   * a concert booked for the Coliseum in Washington, DC
     a.) Which would attract 20,000 fans.
   * a concert in Miami.
J.) NOTE: By the time The Beatles would arrive in America…
  - They were already enjoying immense popularity.
    * Feb. 7, 1964: They left London for New York on Pan Am flight 101…
      a.) …and arrived at New York's Idlewild Airport (later renamed JFK International) at 1:35 pm EST…
       - …to 10,000 screaming fans….

IV. THE FIRST SYNTHESIS OF BOB DYLAN AND THE BEATLES

A.) Roger McGuinn (b. James Joseph McGuinn III, 7/13/42, Chicago, IL): a folk artist in LA folk clubs and coffeehouses.
 1.) Added Beatles tunes to his folk sets.
  - He was among the first to recognize the folk influences in their music.
   * He termed it, "electrified folk music" (they did after all, start off with Skiffle).
 2.) He was approached by Gene Clark (b. Harold Eugene Clark, 11/17/41; d. 5/24/91, Sherman Oaks, CA) and later, by another folk artist named David Crosby (b. David Van Cortland, 8/14/41, LA).
  - They established a folk trio called: "The Jet Set".
 3.) Eventually, after a failed attempt as "The Jet Set":
  - Michael Clarke (b. 6/3/44, New York, NY; d. 12/19/93, Treasure Island, FL), a drummer, and Chris Hillman (b. 12/4/42, LA), a mandolin player who played the bass…
   * … joined McGuinn, Clark, and Crosby to form a band.
B.) The new group would work in the studio under the watchful eye of producer, Jim Dixon.
 1.) He forced this group to listen to themselves played back on tape.
  - At first, their sound was crude and unpolished.
   * David Crosby once said, that listening to themselves was at first, "acutely painful".
  - Their sound however, improved dramatically due to more listening as well as a lot of practice.
   * Their sound became more polished and accomplished in a strictly musical sense.
    a.) That notwithstanding, there were two remaining problems.
 2.) Problem #1: they lacked a signature sound, something that would set them apart from the rest.

A Hard Day's Night
The Beatles

  - For that, they decided to see a movie entitled, "A Hard Day's Night" (The Beatles first feature film) in April of 1964.
   * It would be the most inspirational moment of theirs lives thus far.
    a.) David Crosby once said in an interview, that after seeing "A Hard Day's Night", they [the group] knew exactly what they wanted to do.
  - Roger McGuinn: noticed that in the movie, George Harrison was playing an electric "12-string" guitar which had a unique twang to the sound.
   * As a result, McGuinn traded in his acoustic guitar and banjo for a Rickenbacker 12-String electric guitar.
    a.) The solo 12-string timbre in their future themes, would be this group's signature electric guitar sound.
  - The group would also adopt a Beatles style/influence of vocal harmonization.

a.) But, in the act of copying the Beatles sound, it came out as something different and original.
- With folk influences (basically folk influenced chord progressions), a polished sound, the individuality of the 12-string color, and the rich vocal harmonization; this new group would call themselves, <u>The Byrds</u>.
* As a result of all the influences mentioned above (including "A Hard Day's Night") along with countless hours of work in the studio, <u>The Byrds</u> have crafted their own original sound.

C.) <u>Problem #2</u>: They needed a song to cover. For that, they would refer to Bob Dylan.
1.) By this time (1965), Bob Dylan abandoned his "finger-pointing" songs for musical poetics that, in the words of the late poet, Alan Ginsberg, encompassed:
- "Psychological investigations into the nature of consciousness".
* In other words, insights on the nature of identity.
- In addition, the "beat poets" such as Ginsberg and especially Jack Kerouac were inspiring Dylan.
*<u>Beat Poetry</u>: a rejection of academic poetry and a free-form writing style emulating the rhythm of average, everyday speech (of common folk), or the way the poet himself actually spoke.
* Kerouac's prose, as exemplified in his most famous work, "On The Road", is long-winded.
a.) Sentences can last an entire paragraph without any breaks or pauses. This sort of long-winded prose can be found in the Dylan tune that The Byrds would cover.

Mr. Tambourine Man
Bob Dylan

2.) "<u>Mr. Tambourine Man</u>": in addition to the Kerouac prose inspiration, Dylan was also influenced by a night at the Mardi Gras.
- where people were dressed in an array of various costumes (i.e. different identities).
* which sparked his interest in the nature of identity.
- It was these two influences that inspired Bob Dylan to write "<u>Mr. Tambourine Man</u>".
3.) After listening to this record that their producer, Jim Dixon had acquired, The Byrds decided to cover this song.

D.) <u>Strategy and Influence</u>:
1.)

Musical Property	Influence of Musical Property
Vocal harmonization...............	The Beatles
Electric 12-string sound...........	The Beatles
Arpeggiations on the 12-string opening theme...........	Johann Sebastian Bach (1685-1750)
The Beat............................	The Beach Boys', "<u>Don't Worry Baby</u>"
The song/lyrics.......................	Bob Dylan

2.) The combination of these influences melded together, gave The Byrds their own original sound plus:
- They would be the first, to synthesize both the Dylan and Beatles styles together creating a completely new musical paradigm.
* Which would inspire countless others to pursue their own combinations of influences (individual paradigms)...
a.) ...which in turn, would send rock and roll into many different directions at once.
3.) Because of this accomplishment, <u>The Byrds</u> would not only become one of the most important artists in the development of rock and roll
- but also, one of the most underrated.

Mr. Tambourine Man
The Byrds

4.) The Byrds' version of "<u>Mr. Tambourine Man</u>" was released in April of 1965.
- It would set a new trend in motion of artists covering Dylan tunes and achieving success in the interim.
* Which also elevated Bob Dylan to icon status with mainstream audiences.

5.) Dylan at the time, was also undergoing another change that would alienate (as well as outrage) his traditional folk following.

- On the weekend that the Byrd's cover of "Mr. Tambourine Man" reached #1 on the pop charts:

* Bob Dylan was booed by his audience at the Newport Folk Festival.

a.) For performing a new song highlighting his new musical direction.

E.) In his book, "Rock and Roll: An Unruly History", Robert Palmer describes a meeting that took place in August of 1964 at the Delmonico Hotel on Park Avenue in New York City.

1.) This was during The Beatles' second American tour – a 30 city tour of the US and Canada.

- By this time, The Beatles were holed-up in their room, under tight security, and unable to go anywhere at their leisure.

* This was when their disdain for touring to screaming fans began to take hold.

2.) Bob Dylan, his manager, and Al Aronowitz – a rock/pop music journalist, visited the Beatles in their hotel room.

- It was there, that Dylan introduced the Beatles to cannabis for the first time.

* Which thereafter, would become a regular habit for them [The Beatles].

3.) This was one of the most important "summit meetings" in the annals of rock and roll history. What was said exactly amongst themselves was probably lost in history.

- But the results for each of them were monumental.

4.) There were two major turning points as a result of their meeting.

- RESULT #1: Bob Dylan would go electric (thereby rekindling his early pre-New York City blues influences).

- RESULT #2: The Beatles would compose lyrics that were more meaningful, self-effacing, and grittier (as opposed to the teenage, "lovey-dovey" type of lyrics that these mop-tops were presently writing).

F.) "Bringing It All Back Home" (1965): the first of three albums which emanated from the influence of that "summit meeting" and for Dylan, the shape of things to come.

1.) The opening cut on the album: "Subterranean Homesick Blues" – Dylan's first electric piece.

Subterranean Homesick Blues
Bob Dylan

- Drew fire from his fans who still viewed him as their folk/spokesman poster child.

* In fact, going electric would outrage his fan base.

2.) During his 1965 UK tour, Dylan was faced with an identity crisis due to the negative reaction his fans expressed to him regarding his new electric blues direction.

- Upon his return to the US, he seriously considered giving up music altogether.

3.) Instead, he returned to the studio with a new line-up of session players.

G.) "Highway 61 Revisited" (1965): the second of his famous album-esque triumvirate.

1.) Assisting Dylan were artists such as Mike Bloomfield (b. July 28, 1944, Chicago, IL; d. Feb. 15, 1981, San Francisco, CA): electric blues artist par-excellence — also the lead guitarist for the Paul Butterfield Blues Band…

… and Al Kooper (b. Feb. 5, 1944, Brooklyn, NY): organ. He was in his own words, "a mediocre organ player".

2.) Like his previous album, the first cut on "Highway 61 Revisited" would become an important milestone in Dylan's electric blues development.

- "Like A Rolling Stone" produced by Tom Wilson.

Like A Rolling Stone
Bob Dylan

* This song would establish the ingredients of Dylan's electric blues sound:

a.) electric guitar, harmonica, and organ (The Hammond B-3 Organ + Leslie Speaker sound).

* RESULT: Dylan's version of hard-edged, primitive sounding electric blues.

a.) Which would become his first million seller with him as the main recording artist of his own music (as opposed to the traditional cover groups).

- It was a performance of this piece at The Newport Folk Festival that caused him to get booed by his traditionally loyal fans.

H.) By this time, circa 1966, it was becoming "en vogue" for recording artists to cover Dylan's songs.

1.) <u>The Byrds</u>: would do another Dylan cover, "All I Really Want To do".

2.) <u>The Turtles</u>: would cover, "It Ain't Me Babe".

3.) Also, the popularity of Dylan tunes made the recording industry wake up to the potential value of protest music.

- …and began mass-marketing it.

* A legacy of the "Finger-Pointing" songs of Dylan's early career.

4.) But this wasn't the only "venue" where Dylan's influence was penetrating…

V. THE BEATLES AND BOB DYLAN'S INFLUENCE UPON THEM

A.) "<u>HELP!</u>": The Beatles' second full-length motion picture. A very important turning point for the Beatles in the following respects:

1.) By this time, they were smoking cannabis on a regular basis.

- It was said that during the entire filming of "HELP!", they [the Beatles] were constantly "in a haze of marijuana smoke".

2.) <u>George Harrison</u>: began filling in the idle time between takes by experimenting with various instruments that were laying around the set.

- one of these instruments, was a <u>Sitar</u> (from India).

* The twangy, overtone-laden timbre of this eastern instrument would become a part of the Beatles' sound mix in future albums to come.

a.) Which in turn, would help open them up to Eastern influences: both musically and spiritually.

B.) <u>Dylan's Influence</u>: The first consistent manifestation of the Dylan influence could be heard on the album "Help!" (1965) – soundtrack for their second full-length feature film.

1.) "<u>Help!</u>" (the title track): lyrics of insecurity and vulnerability.

- Beginning of a consistent departure from their norm of teenage love songs.

Help!
The Beatles

* <u>Harbinger of Change</u>: an album released in December of 1964, *Beatles For Sale*

a.) Songs like "I'm A Loser" and "Baby's In Black" anticipated their new lyric direction.

* <u>NOTE</u>: The album "Help!" made this new Dylan-influenced formula consistent.

2.) "<u>You've Got To Hide Your Love Away</u>"

You've Got To Hide Your Love Away
The Beatles

- <u>Vocal Delivery</u>: John Lennon: Adopts his own emulation of Dylan-esque vocal twang.

- <u>Instrumentation</u>: A lone acoustic (folk) guitar accompanied by a tambourine

- <u>Lyrics</u>: Expressing vulnerability and self-effacement.

* Containing a new sense of expressive depth.

a.) Again, a departure from their previous teen-oriented-love-song lyric formula.

3.) "<u>Yesterday</u>": Again, lyrics of vulnerability and insecurity with a sense of depth.

Yesterday
The Beatles

- Accompanied by an acoustic (folk) guitar.

* Second Stanza: A string quartet appears in the accompaniment.

a.) <u>String Quartet</u>: 2 violins, 1 viola, and 1 cello.

- A standard classical "chamber" group setup with a sparse string sound (as opposed to the full, thickly textured sound of a string orchestra).

                           b.) <u>RESULT</u>: This arrangement was an example of The Beatles raising the 3-and-a-half-minute single to a highly crafted work of art.

                                  - Giving this arrangement a sense of elegance and sophistication.

4.) <u>Ticket To Ride</u>": perhaps the best example of The Beatles' maturity in a pure compositional sense thus far.

Ticket To Ride — The Beatles

    - In addition to the sophistication of arranging that "Yesterday" brought forth…

        * "<u>Ticket To Ride</u>" brought an elevated level of songwriting craftsmanship from both a theoretical and textural perspective:

                a.) Another sense of sophistication only this time, in the substance of pitch control and harmonic density.

                      - This was "music composition" in the purest sense.

                           * As opposed to conventional song writing.

5.) "<u>Hide Your Love</u>", <u>Yesterday</u>", and "<u>Ticket To Ride</u>" are examples of their version of the three-and-a-half minute single…raised to a highly crafted work of art.

    - The album "Help!" marked a major turning point in the creative development of The Beatles.

        * But their next two albums would advance their creative destinies even further.

                a.) One would be lyrical, the other musical.

C.) "Rubber Soul" (1965): the major lyrical change.

    1.) <u>NOTE</u>: 1965 marks the first year where the "album format" was becoming a highly crafted work of art in it's own right.

        - Before 1965, an artist's musical development was charted more or less by the "single".

            * But now, the album is the new creative benchmark.

    2.) For the first time, an eastern influence is heard.

        - <u>The Sitar</u> (from India) makes its debut in the Beatles' repertoire.

Norwegian Wood (This Bird Has Flown) — The Beatles

            * "<u>Norwegian Wood</u>": a folk-influenced tune featuring the Sitar twang in the opening instrumental theme.

                a.) Lyrically, a stealthy narrative of a possible extra-marital affair (for the first time, risqué subject matter).

            * <u>NOTE</u>: Even though the new direction of lyrics was introduced in the album, "HELP!":

                a.) It is in "Rubber Soul" where the change is made more pervasive and permanent.

    3.) <u>Examples</u>: lyrics of vulnerability in "HELP!" was the starting point. Now there is more of an eclectic expansion of subject matter.

I'm Looking Through You — The Beatles

        - Lyrics of conflict: "<u>I'm Looking Through You</u>" and "<u>Think For Yourself</u>" (musically, "I'm Looking Through You" and "What Goes On" features country music influences).

        - Lyrics of contemplation: "<u>Places</u>".

        - Lyrics dealing with social criticism: "<u>Nowhere Man</u>".

Run For Your Life — The Beatles

        - Lyrics of outright jealousy: "<u>Run For Your Life</u>".

        - Lyrics of love with some French phrases added in: "<u>Michelle</u>".

            * folk plus a French-styled melodic bass line.

    4.) Most important lyrical aspect:

        - Dylan, by this time had given up his mantle as "spokesman for a generation"…

            * …by replacing his "finger-pointing songs" with lyrics dealing with "Psychological investigations into the nature of identity"…

                a.) …spearheaded by the Kerouac/beat poet influence.

        - <u>The Beatles</u> would now take over the mantle and carry the torch as the new spokesmen for a generation.

The Word — The Beatles

            * The song which first signified their new status: "<u>The Word</u>".

a.) In addition, The Beatles – especially John Lennon with his wife, Yoko Ono, would adopt a high profile in protesting the war in Vietnam.

- with their "bed-in's" and "sit-in's" during the late 60's.

5.) One other aspect concerning the "Rubber Soul" era:

- Their look was drastically changing.

* The group was starting to adopt a look of world weariness and disposing with their traditional mop-top/matching uniform look.

a.) John Lennon was wearing round, wire rimmed glasses and a "fu-Manchu" mustache.

b.) George Harrison had long, floppy, unkept-looking hair and a mustache.

- along with rest of the group.

c.) Instead of looking uniform, they all looked different.

- wearing basically street clothes, sometimes, with psychedelic designs (more in-depth information on Psychedelia will be covered in Chapter 6).

- They were no longer, the lovable mop-top cuties that the world grew to love.

* Their personas along with their music, was changing.

a.) To paraphrase the legendary rock critic, Lester Bangs, they [The Beatles] had become four separate individuals as opposed to one unified group.

D.) By the time of their final tour (1966), The Beatles have grown tired of touring and performing live.

1.) They would be holed-up in their hotel rooms – which to them were like prison cells, unable to venture anywhere…

- and living off the take-out food their road assistants picked up for them.

2.) They also hated the fact that they couldn't hear themselves perform due to the multitude of screaming fans.

- Ringo especially, couldn't hear what the rest of the band was doing.

* in spite of his near proximity to the amplifiers.

3.) The Beatles were also frustrated at what they perceived as:

- their failure to reach an adult audience.

* they had had enough of the teen-oriented domain.

a.) They wanted to branch out into new creative territory.

4.) In August of 1966, The Beatles performed their final concert at Candlestick Park in San Francisco.

- The Ronettes were one of the back-up groups.

VI. THE BEATLES' NEW STAGE: THE RECORDING STUDIO

A.) From now on, the recording studio would be their new permanent stage.

1.) It gave them unlimited room to experiment.

- They could do things in the studio that logistically, could not be done live.

2.) In September of 1966, they would release their next album which would mark a new musical milestone.

- in a similar way that "Rubber Soul" marked a lyrical turning point.

B.) "Revolver" (1966): what most aficionados concur, their most creative album (the Beatles took more creative risks on this album than on any other).

1.) "Taxman": Their version of Hard-Edged Blues (Dylan influence).

Taxman
The Beatles

- Featuring a wild, borderline chaotic electric guitar solo (psychedelic influenced).

*NOTE: Another touchstone that sparked their desire for experimentation was LSD.

- The psychedelic experience for them:

* Opened up their minds to many different influences both musically and spiritually (case in point: "Love You To").

Love You To
The Beatles

2.) "Love You To": George Harrison's first full-fledged, Indian/Eastern influenced song.
- Featuring the sitar as the predominant instrument (He was studying under the tutelage of sitar master, Ravi Sankar).
* Accompanied by Indian percussion instruments.
a.) Also, with an underlying drone.
- a part of the Eastern/Indian style.

I'm Only Sleeping
The Beatles

3.) "I'm Only Sleeping": influenced by composer Karlhienz Stockhausen (a very prominent "Art Music' composer during the 60's).
- Stockhausen was known for his experimentation in electronic music with tape manipulations and sound collages (among other things).
* One of his practices – which was common among composers of his ilk – was playing a tape backwards.
a.) This would result in reversing the "envelope" or shape of a recorded sound.
- In this particular song, The Beatles recorded electric guitar breaks (which they imbedded in the verses) and an electric guitar solo…
*…and played the tape in reverse thereby presenting this particular guitar music backwards.
a.) In reversing the envelope of a note on the electric guitar (i.e. the plucked sound followed by a decay), the result was a crescendo of sound (reversed decay)…
- …leading up to the plucked attack.

Eleanor Rigby
The Beatles

4.) "Eleanor Rigby": classically influenced both poetically and musically.
- Lyrically: words written from a classical poet's tradition.
* A story dealing with two people living adjacent to one another, but never making a connection (a subject straight out of classical literature).
* Filled with metaphor: "wearing a face that she keeps in a jar by the door, who is it for?"
a.) Suggesting a deeper meaning below the surface…
- …meant to make the listener think (Dylan influence).
b.) The metaphor, "I look at all the lonely people", refers to their fans (according to the late poet, Alan Ginsberg).
- Musically: a classical string quartet (2 violins, viola, and cello). The arrangement features "spiking" attacks by the bow with each instrument in unison.
* Inspired by the style of film composer, Bernard Hermann (famous for his movie scores in Alfred Hitchcock films).
a.) This string quartet arrangement accompanied Paul's vocal line.

5.) "She Said, She Said": heavy rock sound on the electric guitars that accompanies morbid lyrics.
- "She said, 'I know what it's like to be dead'…"
- In the first person: "She makes me feel like I've never been born".
* A sort of dark twist to the art of metaphor (taking Dylan one better).

Dr. Robert
The Beatles

6.) "Dr. Robert": arguably, The Beatles' first overt drug song.
- About a physician possessing an enthusiastic penchant for writing up amphetamine prescriptions.
* Also possessing a "funky" style of beat (which was something new for them).

7.) "Here, There, and Everywhere" and "Yellow Submarine": both examples of radio-friendly tunes with easily accessible melodic hooks…
- …to cover their "pop" angle.

* in order to "sell" the album.
- "Yellow Submarine": introduces a military-marching-band influenced brass arrangement style that will become a standard feature in their following albums.
8.) "Tomorrow Never Knows": another of the "Stockhausen" influences.

- Also influenced by "The Tibetan book of The Dead" (it's significance will be discussed in Chapter 6, The Psychedelic Era).
* Hence, an Eastern influence as well.
a.) According to George Martin, "John wanted to sound like The Dalai Lama chanting from a mountain top".
b.) Another eastern musical influence - the drone.
- Ringo's sound: instead of blending in with the rest of the group musically...
* ...he plays a loud, highly up-front, aggressive drum beat.
a.) Very unusual for him – but, like the most of the album, a departure from the norm.
- Stockhausen influence: tape loops collaging together.
* Paul was experimenting with various tape loops:
a.) Sped-up music, seagull sounds, broken wine glasses, etc.
* Each fader track in the mixing console contained a specific tape loop.
a.) Which could be faded in and out at will.
* RESULT: a collage of different loops being played from the console making the mixing console itself, a new instrument.
9.) For the traditional mop-top fans, "Revolver" was too much of a radical departure.
- Many of them [traditional fans] felt alienated.
* They also felt the Beatles had reached the end of the creative line and were finished as a pop band.
- Nine months later, they would silence their critics with their next release...
C.) "Sgt. Pepper's Lonely Hearts Club Band" (June, 1967)
1.) More of a "listener friendly" album than "Revolver" and in some ways...
- a more streamlined version [of "Revolver"].
2.) Some comparisons:
- "Within You, Without You": a sitar focused, Indian/Eastern based song in the same style of "Love You To"...
* but with less of an edge.
- "She's Leaving Home": accompanied by a string quartet.
* But instead of the intense, spiky, Bernard Hermann-styled arrangement found in "Eleanor Rigby"...
a.) ...it was a more subdued, more fluid conventional type of string writing.
*The subject matter was also less inventive and intense.
a.) Instead of the classical literature influence...
- ...it was a story about a daughter leaving home and the sadness thereof.
* Like "Within You, Without You", "She's leaving Home" is a more watered-down version of its "Revolver" counterpart.
3.) Brass Arrangements: the "British Marching Band" style of brass arrangements first heard on the opening title track becomes a signature sound.
- which will be featured in subsequent albums such as: "Magical Mystery Tour" (1967) and "The White Album" (1968).
* They originated this type of arrangement with "Yellow Submarine" (again, from "Revolver").
4.) Whatever audience was lost by the extreme experimentation of "Revolver"...
- would be drawn back with the more pop-oriented "Sgt. Pepper's..."
* NOTE: If "Revolver" was their greatest creative achievement...
a.) "Sgt. Pepper's Lonely Hearts Club Band" would be their greatest "pop" oriented album (and, their most celebrated).

VII. DYLAN'S FURTHER QUEST FOR THE ELECTRIC BLUES SOUND

A.) <u>1966</u>: Bob Dylan releases the third album of his electric blues triumvirate.

    1.) "<u>Blonde On Blonde</u>": recorded at Columbia Studios in Nashville, TN.

        - In regard to his session players, the only originals left from his prior two albums, were Al Kooper and Charlie McCoy.

            * One of the newer players was <u>Joe South</u> (who would have a pop solo career in the late 60's with two top ten hits: "Games People Play" and "Walk A Mile In My Shoes").

        - <u>RESULT</u>: Dylan's hardest edged electric blues yet – more so than the previous two albums.

            * - but it would not be his grittiest…

B.) <u>The 1966 World Tour</u>: Dylan embarks on a world concert tour with yet, another personnel change: he deposed of all his session players from "Blonde On Blonde".

    1.) <u>The Hawks</u>: from Canada. A hard-edged electric blues and rockabilly bar band who accompanied rockabilly singer: Ronnie Hawkins.

        - They were a road-hardened band that toured the bar circuit mainly in the US.

            * They performed in dives and bars, that were usually: "on the other side of the tracks".

    2.) Personnel: <u>Robbie Robertson</u>: guitar, <u>Levon Helm</u>: drums, <u>Garth Hudson</u>: organ, <u>Richard Manuel</u>: rhythm piano/vocals, and <u>Rick Danko</u>: bass.

        - They would later be known as: "<u>The Band</u>".

    3.) When Dylan asked them to be his band on the 1966 world tour…

        - He wanted to take his vision of hard-edged electric blues to the limit.

            * And make it harsher, more primitive sounding than anything he had ever attempted.

                a.) The Hawks would be the perfect band to help him accomplish this.

    4.) <u>RESULTING SOUND</u>: loud, raw, hard-edged, borderline crude, and over-the-top.

Just Like Tom Thumb's Blues (Highway 61 Revisited) Bob Dylan

        - A counterpoint of various electric blues lines – on guitars and keyboards – woven together into a full-throttled audio assault.

            * Peppered by Dylan's harmonica and his raw, signature vocal style.

                a.) He brought it all to the extreme.

            * <u>Comparison</u>: "Just Like Tom Thumb's Blues"

                a.) Compare the original version from the album, *Highway 61 Revisited*…

                    - …with Dylan & The Hawks version from *Dylan 1966: The Royal Albert Hall Concert*.

                      * The latter being more grittier, raw, and hard-edged.

    5.) <u>The fans' reaction</u>: outrage.

Just Like Tom Thumb's Blues (Royal Albert Hall) Bob Dylan

        - They were incensed. In fact, Dylan and The Hawks were booed vociferously everywhere they played.

        - "<u>Dylan 1966: The Royal Albert Hall Concert</u>" (actually, it was recorded at the Free Trade Hall in Manchester, England on May 17, 1966).

            * Originally, a bootleg recording that Columbia released on a 2 CD set in 1998.

                a.) The only recording of Dylan and The Hawks on the 1966 tour featuring their hard-edged cracking electric blues sound.

Like A Rolling Stone (Royal Albert Hall) Bob Dylan

                b.) Right before the final track: "<u>Like A Rolling Stone</u>", an audience member went up to the stage and shouted "Judas!"

                  - Dylan replied, "I don't believe you. You're a Liar." (his reaction happened in tandem with the band fading the song in).

                    * Throughout the performance, Dylan kept taunting the protesters as he was singing.

    6.) Extreme hard-edged versions of previously recorded Dylan electric blues songs…

- For example, "<u>Like A Rolling Stone</u>" (Highway 61 Revisited):
> * The original recording was polished with studio production.
>> a.) Where the organ was prominent and mid-ranged, electric guitar breaks occurred between verses.
- <u>The Hawks' version</u>: much more metal.
> * Like draping a metal jacket around the original tune.
>> a.) And Dylan's singing was so over-the-top, he at times was taunting the audience.

7.) For all the negative feedback he received from his fans, Bob Dylan stuck to his guns and never wavered from his extreme, electric sound.
- He took a tremendous risk by alienating his audience which at times, all great artists have to do in order to advance to a higher artistic level.

8.) In the course of the tour, Dylan suffered injuries resulting from a motorcycle accident.
- As a result, the remainder of the tour was cancelled.

C.) <u>Saugerties, NY</u> (near Woodstock): where Dylan and The Hawks (now known as, "The Band") retired in solitude in a big house.

1.) Both Bob Dylan and The Band would do the one thing all artists do when they feel they've reached a limit.
- they went back to their roots, back to basics.
> * <u>The Band:</u> returned to their more traditional folk/blues roots with 2 albums, "<u>The Brown Album</u>" and "<u>Music From The Big Pink</u>".
> * <u>Dylan:</u> returned to his folk roots with the album, "<u>John Wesley Harding</u>".
> * Together, they recorded "<u>The Basement Tapes</u>".
>> - which were originally home recordings not intended for public release. They were of course, bootlegs which were released as an album in the early 70's.

(<u>NOTE</u>: In a similar way, The Beatles returned to their "pop" roots after "Revolver").

VIII. LEGACY

A.) The development of both Bob Dylan and The Beatles would have never happened the way it did...

1.)...without the mutual influences they had upon one another.

B.) They transformed rock and roll into "art music" meant for listening, thinking, and contemplation in a very adult fashion.

C.) For rock and roll musicians, The Beatles and Bob Dylan inspired them in the following ways:

1.) Taking the courage to experiment with your own individual ideas.
- regardless of how esoteric and alienating they may be.

2.) Writing your own songs.

3.) And in turn, producing your own work as well.

<u>TO SUMMARIZE</u>: reigning in and taking full control of all creative endeavors.

D.) <u>RESULT</u>: this inspiration would cause rock and roll to split into infinite directions at once.

1.) Creating a wealth of new and different paradigms.
- because now, it's the individual artist taking full control.

IX. EPILOGUE

A.) <u>The Beatles</u> – and their subsequent British pop bands – were not the only invading force coming out of England, there was one other...

1.) whose musical roots came right out of the American South as well as the heartland.
- that mainstream American had all but forgotten.

2.) But before we go there, a side-step to the roots of the black sanctified church is in order...

CHAPTER III: REVIEW

Who was Bob Dylan's first important folk influence?

    Name this artist's [Dylan's influence] primary musical influence:

        What did this musical influence pioneer and in what context/setting?

What was the first musical example [album] of this influence that Dylan heard?

Name Woody Guthrie's primary lyric influence:

    As a result, what did Guthrie introduce into folk music insofar as literary elements in the following examples?
        1.) In *Oregon Trail*:
        2.) In *Dirty Overhalls*:

    With the birth of modern folk music, what did Guthrie inspire?

        What was his new blueprint for folk music?

What did Bob Dylan find inspiring about Guthrie's writing ability?

    How would Dylan emulate Guthrie's performance style and thereby, acquire an original sound?

Name the other important folk influence for Bob Dylan after arriving in New York (hint: Dylan copied his style "phrase for phrase").

    Dylan once wrote that this influence could…

Which legendary A&R man for CBS Records discovered Bob Dylan?

    Name the two original songs in Bob Dylan's debut album:
        1.)
        2.)

Which folk group successfully covered "Blowin' In The Wind"?

    What was the significance of this single in relation to the Civil Rights Movement?

What was unique about Bob Dylan's lyrics? In other words, what set his words apart from the average lyricist?

> What did Bob Dylan mean by describing his early music as "finger-pointing songs"?

In addition to deep, hidden meanings, Dylan's poetry conveyed a sense of timelessness. Why?

What was the original name of the band that would become The Beatles?

> What was their first musical influence?

> Name the artist who invented that stylistic influence which became a mania in the UK in 1956.

Name three important influences that inspired John Lennon to take up music:
1.)
2.)
3.)

In the summer of 1959, who were the remaining four members of The Quarrymen?

> Where was their first regular performance venue beginning in August of 1959?

What was their first professional break?

> Who became their new regular bass player at that time?

> What was their new name?

Name four important results from their [The Beatles'] tenure at The Indra and The Kaiserkeller in Hamburg, West Germany.
RESULT #1:
RESULT #2:
RESULT #3:
RESULT #4:

Who became the innovator of the Beatle haircut?

What became The Beatles' second regular performance venue begging in late December of 1960?

When and where did The Beatles make their first studio recordings?

Who was the pop singer that they recorded with?

List four important decisions by Brian Epstein that had a major effect on The Beatles:
1.)
2.)
3.)
4.)

Which Beatles single was the first to capture his [Epstein's] interest when a customer named Raymond Jones requested it on October 28, 1961?

Who became The Beatles' producer at Parlophone Records?

What impact did he have upon The Beatles or, in other words, what did he encourage them to do?

Name their first release under the Parlophone label in 1962:

Name their following three releases:
1.)
2.)
3.)

What were the five results of Brian Epstein's visit to the US?
RESULT #1:
RESULT #2:
RESULT #3:
RESULT #4:
RESULT #5:

The Byrds had two problems that needed to be resolved:
Problem #1:

What film was the inspiration that helped resolve Problem #1?

What would be The Byrds' signature solo instrumental sound?

Problem #2:

What was the resolution?

Which single –covered by The Byrds – became the first synthesis of The Beatles and Bob Dylan influences?

Bob Dylan emulated a particular literary figure when he wrote the lyrics for "Mr. Tambourine Man". Who was that figure? (Hint: he was a famous beat poet):

What was Dylan's other influence for "Mr. Tambourine Man"?

List five influences on The Byrd's cover of "Mr. Tambourine Man":
    1.) Vocal Harmonization Influence:
    2.) Electric 12-String Influence:
    3.) Arpeggiation of Opening Theme Influence:
    4.) The Beat Influence:
    5.) The Song/Lyrics Influence:

In August of 1964, The Beatles and Bob Dylan met for the first time at The Delmonico Hotel in New York. What was the result for The Beatles?

What was the result for Bob Dylan?

Name Bob Dylan's first electric single. It was the first cut from the "Bringing It All Back Home" album:

Which single established Bob Dylan's signature electric blues sound?

Name the three instrumental properties of his signature electric sound:
    1.)
    2.)
    3.)

On which album did this single appear?

Name the 1965 Beatles album that became their first consistent manifestation of the Bob Dylan influence:

What was different about their lyrics in this particular album?

Name a folk-oriented example:

How would you describe (in a few words) new quality of their arrangements?

Name a classically oriented example:

Describe (in a few words) the new level of their songwriting craftsmanship.

Name an example:

In the album *Rubber Soul*, what was the significance of the single "Norwegian Wood" insofar as a new foreign influence was concerned?

Name the instrument that manifested this new foreign influence:

Name two other eclectic musical influences in this album:
1.)
2.)

The Word signified The Beatles new status. What was it?

Name the year, month, and venue of The Beatles last public performance?

What was The Beatles' most creative and experimental album in 1966? (Hint: most aficionados consider it their [The Beatles] most creative album):

Name the opening tune that presents their version of hard-edged blues. It featured a wild, psychedelic influenced electric guitar solo.

Which tune was the first, full-fledged Eastern/Indian influenced song featuring the sitar and Indian percussion?

Name the tune from this album that features classical elements of both music and literature:

What type of classical group was used? Name the film composer whose music inspired the style of the arrangement.

Name the German art music, composer who specialized in experimentation with electronic tape manipulations and sound collages.

   Which track on the "Revolver" album did The Beatles play a tape of an electric guitar solo backwards? (It mimicked a sense of laziness).

Which single introduced the use of military-marching-band influenced brass arrangements?

Which track was influenced by both the "Tibetan Book of the Dead" and Karlheinz Stockhausen?

   How was Stockhausen's influence manifested in this single?

   How did Paul McCartney use the mixing console for his tape loops?

What is the comparison between the albums *Sgt. Pepper's Lonely Hearts Club Band* with *Revolver*?

The name of the band Bob Dylan hired to accompany him on his 1966 world tour.

   What was the style of this band?

   What influence did this band have upon Bob Dylan's hard-edged blues style?

How did Bob Dylan and The Beatles inspire rock and roll musicians of their generation and beyond?
   1.)
   2.)
   3.)

What became the legacy of both Bob Dylan and The Beatles?

CHAPTER IV : A TALE OF TWO AND A HALF CITIES
I. BACKGROUND AND IRONY

A.) Nelson George once said in his book: "The Death Of Rhythm And Blues" that:

   1.) whites tend to recycle and Blacks tend to move on…

      - in other words, when a particular genre of black music crosses over to the white, mainstream population:

         * Blacks tend to reinvent their music in order to suit their own constituency (i.e. an African American audience).

   2.) in this case, by the time Fats Domino's or Chuck Berry's styles of black music (i.e. Rhythm and Blues and Black Rockabilly respectively) was being coined as rock and roll:

      - thereby carrying a "white" connotation…

         * Blacks were changing the landscape of the rhythm and blues domain into something new, something clearly distinctive, and something completely derived from their own culture.

            a.) The new musical touchstone would come straight out of the black sanctified church: Gospel.

B.) The irony of gospel-driven ideas imbedded into rhythm and blues would eventually, unveil itself in several ways.

   1.) On one hand, this gospel related music would be packaged and marketed by a black-owned record company:

      - to specifically target a white, mainstream audience.

   2.) On the other, a white owned company would do the same: packaging and marketing black, gospel-derived rhythm and blues:

      - to specifically target an African American audience.

   3.) Also within this gospel driven musical domain, blacks and whites would work harmoniously together toward a common goal:

      - to elevate the artistry and expression that this new type of black music had to offer (at least up until April 4, 1968).

         * as a result, this music would be appreciated the world over.

C.) But before this story of gospel-driven rhythm and blues can be told…

   1.) …it would be helpful to trace the history (in general terms) of what lead up to this gospel tradition.

II. GENESIS

A.) The roots of gospel can be traced all the way back to the West African coastal area circa 400 years ago.

   1.) The area of West Africa is referred to the region such as:

      - Ivory Coast, Ghana, Nigeria, Guinea, Kongo, etc.

         * This is the area where the slave trade abducted thousands of men, women, and children from primarily…

            a.) … the Yoruban and Fon tribes.

            b.) And brought them in slave ships to the new world.

B.) West African traditional music contained the following properties:

Temantei/ Zaouli
IVORY COAST

   1.) Polyrhythmic Grooves: there were three pairs of drums in the Yoruban tradition and hence, three players.

      - Each player would play a different repetitive pattern relating to a specific deity (the specific pattern was called: a "toque").

         * But the various patterns overlapping each other produced cross rhythms resulting in an underlying groove.

   2.) Call and Response: The traditional vocal style inherent in the Yoruban, West African tradition.

Setapa
BOTSWANA

      - One soloist would sing a melody.

         * The group would respond by either:

            a.) Using the same melody and words or…

            b.) With something completely different which serves as an

answering phrase to the soloist.

    3.) <u>Hand Clapping</u>: in syncopation with the "call & response".

        - Usually goes like this: <u>**1**</u>23, <u>**1**</u>23, <u>**1**</u>23, <u>**1**</u>23... (note: the darkened, underlined beat numbers represent the accents within the beat pattern).

          * this pattern is such that, the last beat of the three beat pattern, leads to the following first beat of the next beat pattern (or measure).

    4.) <u>Rhythmic Hierarchy</u>: within the sets of drums, the intensity of rhythmic activity differs from range to range.

Bakisima/
Nankasa
UGANDA

        - On the high-registered pitched drums, the rhythms are the fastest.

        - Consequently, the lowest ranged drums carry the slowest rhythms...

          * ...with the patterns ranging from one to four pitches.

        - The medium range drums contain moderate rhythmic activity (somewhere in between the outer ranged instruments).

    5.) <u>NOTE</u>: All four of the above mentioned properties are inherent elements in rock and roll.

C.) <u>Traditional Purpose</u>: Robert Palmer once wrote that the Yoruban polyrhythmic music: "Mediated social discourse between deity and celebrant".

    1.) It was an integral part of every life and worship .

        - Usually, each tribal member worshipped a particular deity and the drummers were cognizant of each one.

          * When the drummers noticed a particular member getting into the groove, they would play a particular "Toque" of the deity that person was worshipping.

            a.) The celebrant would advance to the middle within a counterclockwise moving circle.

            b.) He or she would then bow to the drummers as a sign of respect.

            c.) Start dancing (as a form of worship) and getting into the groove a.k.a., <u>The Trance</u>.

          * This "trance" concept is similar to when one goes to a dance club or a concert and gets into the groove.

    2.) BATA Drums: traditional Yoruban drums: 3 pairs.

        - <u>6 pitches</u>: each pairs consists of different sized drums.

        - <u>3 pairs</u>: small, medium, and large.

          * Again, according to Palmer, the drums are named after and representative of, the Yoruban family unit.

            a.) <u>Large (Iya)</u>: represents the father.

              - initiates new rhythmic patterns/rhythmic conversations.

            b.) <u>Medium (Ototele)</u>: represents the mother.

              - maintains a steady rhythmic pattern unless cued by the "father" drum to change.

            c.) <u>Small (Okonkolo)</u>: represents the child.

              - maintains a fast, repetitive rhythmic pattern throughout.

          * Sometimes, the "child" drum will rush the tempo and the "father" will pull back in order to prevent the "child's" rushing tempo from going out of control.

            a.) This concept of "push and pull" is an intricate part of both jazz and rock and roll.

D.) <u>Cuba, The First Filtering Unit</u>: where West African polyrhythmic music first became filtered through a new western prism before reaching the Mississippi delta.

    1.) Santiago da Cuba in the Oriente Province:

        - <u>Western styled melodic instruments</u>: were replacing drums.

          * i.e. fiddles, guitars, bamboo fifes, doublebass, brass, etc.

- <u>Stanza Form</u>: each poetic paragraph (stanza) would contain the same musical form.
  - * The concept of an "outer form" in African-derived polyrhythmic music was another innovation of this "filtering" process.
- <u>Call and Response</u>: would occur between a solo, lead voice and the response would be performed by an instrumental section (i.e. brass).
  - * Instead of voices.
- <u>Bass Line</u>: Would be presented as a traditional melodic instrument as opposed to a drum. In this case, a doublebass.
  - * Which would play a two to four note repetitive pattern.

2.) <u>NOTE</u>: These filtering alterations paved the way for the originality of western (New World) polyrhythmic music.
- The first important new genre was called: "Son".
  - * Which contains all of the musical properties mentioned above.

E.) <u>The Mississippi Delta</u>: where the genesis of traditional black American music took place.

Kneebone
Joe Armstrong
Leader, Group A

1.) Because the enslaved were not allowed to use drums (for plantation owners feared they [drums] would be used to send "rhythmically encrypted" messages of insurrection).
- these enslaved had to be creative.
  - * They had to adapt their traditions to a new environment (adaptation, another method of achieving originality).

Read 'Em, John
John Davis
Leader, Group A

  - <u>1st</u>: They gathered in a counterclockwise circle (in accordance to West African tradition).
  - <u>2nd</u>: Call and response vocals.
  - <u>3rd</u>: Hand clapping in syncopation with…

Beaulah Land
John Davis
Leader, Group C

  - <u>4th</u>: …feet stomping: the wooden floor would serve as the drumhead (adaptation).

- <u>RESULT</u>: The Ring Shout: first body of traditional African American music.
  - * This genre would eventually develop into the "Spiritual".

F.) <u>The Spiritual</u>: In the post-civil war era.
1.) Would be the first body of black American music to cross racial lines.
- and become popular with white Americans.
  - * This popularity was spearheaded by spiritual groups such as "The Fisk Jubilee Singers"
    - a.) …who performed throughout America to solicit funds for Fisk University in Nashville.
      - Various black colleges throughout the South were established by charitable contributions generated from touring spiritual groups.
- This scenario of the spiritual group was responsible for spreading awareness of this particular type of music.

2.) <u>The Spiritual</u>: an integral part of black worship.
- <u>Religious Texts</u>: that expressed the power and joy of the Holy Spirit.
- <u>Melodies</u>: Derived from the traditions of West African music.
  - * Improvising ornamentation around a basic melody.
- <u>Structure</u>: Call and Response (again, from the African tradition).
- <u>European Influences</u>: major and minor diatonic scales.
  - * In minor diatonic scales, the development of "Blue Notes" which would become a common fixture in black music genres such as Blues.
  - * These scales would also introduce and solidify:
    - a.) European harmonic structure into black music…
    - b.) and the use of European-styled meter.

3.) <u>Elizabeth F. Barkley</u>: wrote that the Spiritual emerged in rural communities.
- Specifically, in large agricultural plantations of the pre-civil war South.
  - * It became an integral part in the "<u>Invisible Church</u>".
    - a.) They were without any buildings or houses that would equate to a conventional church.

b.) They also had to keep their religious gatherings hidden from whites.

4.) This body of the Spiritual would eventually evolve into <u>Gospel</u>.

G.) <u>Gospel</u>: Evolved in the 20th Century within the black urban communities.

1.) Which grew out of the influence of emancipation.

Oh Lord,
I'm Glad I Got
Good Religion
Starlight Gospel
Singers

2.) In the urban communities, new denominations were sprouting up in place of the more traditional white influenced denominations that were European in style and in substance.

- These new denominations emphasized west African traditions.
  * Which in turn, would lead to the more modern "sanctified" Gospel denominations.
- These churches were where the musical traditions of African-inspired, early black American musical practices — were revitalized.
  * (i.e. hand clapping and foot stomping in crossrhythms, call & response, and melodic improvisations)…
- <u>NOTE</u>: This was where and how Gospel music began.

H.) <u>Modern Gospel</u>: Sung in a homophonic texture.

I Heard
The Lord of
Jesus Say
Bishop Bowen
& Combined
Choirs

1.) <u>Homophony</u>: a musical texture where everyone sings the same rhythms…
- But different pitches which blend together in a satisfying, harmonious manner.
  * Coupled with call and response vocal style.

2.) <u>Texts</u>: Concentrates on themes such as spirituality, salvation, being touched by the Holy Spirit, and conversion.
- These songs contained "quasi-sermons" (i.e. do good deeds, pray, etc.)
  * <u>Spirituals</u>: on the other hand, tended to be about biblical events with an underlying message.

I.) <u>Gospel in the 1950's</u>: Gospel artists were beginning to obtain lucrative recording contracts (on independent labels).

1.) This phenomenon began as a result of a popular event that gained nationwide attention:
- <u>The Negro Gospel & Religious Festival at Carnegie Hall</u>.
  * Gospel singers would become household names in black communities throughout America.

2.) In the midst of 50's Gospel resurgency along with the popularity it was gaining within black America…
- Someone was bound to come along and immerse it into the rhythm and blues domain.
  * and thereby, creating a new musical style.

<u>III. THE GENESIS OF "SOUL"</u>

A.) <u>Ray Charles</u> (b. Ray Charles Robinson, 9/23/30, Albany, GA; d. 6/11/04, Beverly Hills, CA): Originally, a piano playing croon artist who basically copied the sound of Nat King Cole.

1.) As mentioned earlier, one of the ways of achieving originality was that, in the act of emulating someone else – an original sound would result.
- For Ray Charles, the copying of Nat King Cole would instead, have the opposite effect.
  * Artistically, he was going nowhere with it. He was growing tired of trying to be someone that he wasn't.
    a.) This epiphany, caused him to ask a question to himself that would serve as a touchstone to his own road to being an original:
      - instead of trying to sound like Cole, Ray Charles would surmise: "Why can't I be who I am, instead of trying to be like somebody else?"
- <u>With that fateful self-question</u>, in addition to the growing popularity of 50's Gospel:

* Ray Charles returned to his roots and started doing rhythm and blues inspired by music of the sanctified church.

      a.) He reinvented the concept of Gospel by copying it's melodies, rhythms, and expressive quality…

        - while simultaneously secularizing it.

      b.) In other words, rewriting existing gospel tunes and making the lyrics express romantic love…

        - instead of expressing love of God.

I've Got A Woman
Ray Charles

2.) "I've Got A Woman" (1954): was, according to Charles, "Where it all started".

    - The first fruits of this new, secularized gospel approach.

      * It would not only change the direction of black, R&B music…

Hallelujah I Love Her So
Ray Charles

        a.) But would also start a new trend for black music that would last throughout the 60's.

    - Other songs included "Hallelujah, I Love Her So" (which the early Beatles would record a cover of).

Swanee River Rock (Talkin' Bout That River)
Ray Charles

    - "Swanee River": a great example of Ray Charles' gospel inspirations.

      * Call and response, hand-clapping in syncopation, and drum rhythms (inspired by African-based music).

3.) The expressive goal: to capture the rise and fall, give and take intensity of the sanctified gospel service:

    - And condense it into a three-and-a-half-minute singles format.

4.) In addition to revolutionizing a new genre in black music, Ray Charles would also serve as an inspiration for other black artists to follow.

B.) Sam Cooke (b. 1/22/31, Clarksdale, MS; d. 12/11/64, Los Angeles, CA): had a very successful career with a gospel group called, "The Soul Stirrers".

    1.) They were widely appreciated throughout the black community.

    - Cooke however, would leave this group in order to pursue a more lucrative career in pop music.

      * But, like Ray Charles, would use his gospel roots to his advantage.

    2.) He was lean-looking with a flexible and very passionate voice.

    - Cooke skillfully balanced two aspects of his voice:

      * A smooth, creamy, velvety mid-range.

      * And, when warranted, some gospel-styled shouting.

3.) Cooke's major contributions: included his music, his business venues (in the recording industry), and his mass-market, crossover appeal.

You Send Me
Sam Cooke

    - He was a man with a mission — launching his "secular" pop career with his first major release: "You Send Me" (1957).

      * Which sold 2,000,000 copies and reached #1 in the white pop charts.

4.) He molded his gospel-inspired musical sensibilities to appeal to a white mainstream audience.

    - This would define the meaning of the term, "crossover":

      * When black artists write and record music specifically, for white mainstream audience consumption.

5.) Sam Cooke: was among the first to set the standard for black artists/entrepreneurs as:

    - a producer, songwriter, pop icon, and all-around business man….

      *…while injecting in his art, a sense of youth and sexuality.

        a.) These aspects would catapult him to stardom.

6.) Beginnings: He started singing gospel at the age of 10.

    - His father was a Baptist minister in Chicago.

      * After singing for a gospel group while in high school…

        a.) He began his career as the lead singer for the Soul Stirrers (replacing R. H. Harris).

        b.) He brought something to the Soul Stirrers that was never before seen in the gospel domain: Sex Appeal.

    *RESULT: As Nelson George would note, Sam Cooke became gospel's first teen icon.

7.) His smooth, velvety voice would be an inspiration for many other singers of this period including:
- Bobby Womack, Otis Redding, and Johnny Taylor.

8.) Sam Cooke could also compose: starting with gospel and then pop.
- in many ways, Cooke was gradually singing gospel with an increasing R&B feel before he made the break into pop music.
* In doing so, he took an enormous risk.
- Songs such as: "Wonderful World", "Sixteen", and "You Send Me" were pop classics of the late 50's/early 60's.
* Insofar as risk: He alienated the gospel community by going pop.
a.) Which made the risk all the more greater (he would not have the gospel domain to fall back on).

9.) In addition to his performing and writing skills, he along with J. W. Alexander:
- started their own music publishing company: "Kags Music Publishing" (1958).
* And "SAR Records": the first truly black-owned soul label.

10.) Sam Cooke: was one of black America's greatest success stories.
- Both as a great pop performer and songwriter.
* And a great pioneer of black entrepreneurship in the recording industry.
- He would also serve as a major inspiration in the Black American business domain...
* That would resonate long after his untimely death in 1964 from a gunshot wound in a Hollywood motel.
- One of his greatest inspirational legacies was another black entrepreneur who would carry Sam Cooke's crossover formulas to new heights.

IV. MOTOWN

A.) Berry Gordy Jr. (b. 11/28/29, Detroit, MI): grew up in Detroit where early in his life, he became a jazz enthusiast.
1.) He would hang around outside of jazz clubs and listen (because at the time, he was too young to be allowed in).
2.) He spent five years trying to make his way as a professional boxer before joining the Army.
- After his discharge from the Army, he returned to Detroit's East Side and opened up a jazz record store.
*...because of his love for the music.
- As he explained it in an interview featured on the PBS "Rock and Roll" video series:
* "The people in the neighborhood, they had other ideas. They wanted to hear Fats Domino and B.B. King. So I stocked up on those records, but it was too late. It was too late to save my record store...
(His next statement is an example of how originality can be discovered through learning from failure...through an epiphany spearheaded by an unfavorable occurrence that otherwise may not have happened).
* ... But it was not too late for me to realize, the simplicity that people craved that was in me all the time!"
3.) Thus, he took this realization of simplicity and turned it into practice.

B.) Gordy, the Lyricist: collaborated with songwriter: Roquel "Billy" Davis (pseudonym: Tyran Carlo).
1.) Goal: To create gospel-driven music that would have crossover appeal.
2.) "Brunswick" Label: singer Jackie Wilson (managed by Nat Tarnopol).

Lonely Teardrops
Jackie Wilson
- Gordy/Davis songs for Jackie Wilson: "Reet Petite", "To Be Loved", "Lonely Teardrops", "I'll Be Satisfied", "I'm Wanderin", and "That's Why I Love You So".
3.) 1958: "Lonely Teardrops" reached #1 on the R&B charts.

- Also did well on the mainstream pop charts.
  * …Where the Gordy crossover policy took hold.
    a.) <u>For Lyrics</u>: easily memorable and catchy word phrases.
    b.) <u>Musically</u>: danceable, but not "too funky" with easily memorable, catchy tunes.

C.) Gordy started his first label in 1958: "<u>Anna</u>" (later "Tamla") – named after his sister.
  1.) He ran the label with his other sister, Gwen.
    - Distributed by "<u>End</u>" Records (New York) and later on, by <u>Chess</u>.
  2.) First hit: "<u>Money, That's What I Want</u>" - recorded by Barrett Strong.

Money, That's
What I Want
Barrett Strong

    - Written by Berry Gordy and Janie Bradford.
      * Reached #2 in six weeks in 1960.
        a.) This success gave him the financial backing to broaden his new business venture…

D.) "<u>Motown</u>": A recording operation built in an old house on 2648 West Grand Blvd. in Detroit.
  1.) <u>1st Floor</u>: housed the control room and the reception lounge.
    <u>The Garage</u>: became Studio A (the only studio).
  2.) After seeing scant financial returns for leasing out the "Anna" label…
    - Gordy founded his own "Motown" label.
  3.) "<u>Shop Around</u>" (1961): recorded by Smokey Robinson and The Miracles.

Shop Around
Smokey Robinson
& The Miracles

    - Motown's first million seller that reached #2 on the pop charts.
      * written by Berry Gordy and William "Smokey" Robinson.
  4.) "<u>Smokey</u>": was the first of the great Motown staff songwriters.
    - His group was originally called The Matadors.
      * <u>Gordy</u>: was also Smokey Robinson's early songwriting mentor and producer of The Miracles.
  5.) <u>Smokey Robinson</u>: would become Gordy's most prolific songwriter with hits such as:
    - "<u>My Guy</u>" (1964): recorded by Mary Wells.
      * Motown's first #1 hit in the UK.

Mr. Postman
The Marvelettes

    - "<u>The Way You Do The Things You Do</u>"
      * First successful hit written for The Temptations.
    - He wrote additional hits for artists such as: <u>The Marvelettes</u> and <u>Marvin Gaye</u>.
  6.) The success of "<u>Shop Around</u>" and Motown's first #1 in the US: "<u>Mr. Postman</u>" (The Marvelettes)…
    - …inspired Gordy to hone in the Motown "house style" policy.

E.) <u>Policy Of Sound</u>: the key — crossover appeal.
  1.) A black-owned company with black recording artists and black songwriters.
    - Targeting a white, mainstream audience.
      * An Irony.
  2.) <u>The Rules</u>: the Motown "House Style" musically illustrated by *My Guy* written by Smokey Robinson and recorded by Mary Wells.

My Guy
Mary Wells

    - <u>Polish</u>: the music had to have a smooth and polished sound.
      * No raw intensity allowed.
      * A glossy, smooth-strutting essence that was non-threatening to the mainstream audience.
    - <u>Beat Out Front</u>:
      * In conventional rock and roll, the beat resulted from an underlying groove which was buried beneath the surface.
      * With Motown, the beat was emphatically in the foreground.
        a.) To paraphrase Thomas "Beans" Bowles, Saxophonist and Motown's Tour Manager: "They would stomp on 2 by 4's, shake chains, scratch the walls or do just about anything provided it sounded OK" [to make the beat most prominent].
      * The effect added to the danceable quality of their signature sound.
        a.) When you hear it, you can't help but move your hips and sway to the beat.

          - Heard on beats 2 & 4 of a four-beat pattern: the Backbeat.

    - <u>Backbeat</u>:

        * First, a definition of meter is in order.

          a.) <u>Meter</u>: a recurring pattern of strong and weak beats.

            - the actual pattern itself is called a measure.

          b.) Normally, in a four-beat pattern, the first beat (a.k.a. the downbeat), gets emphasis above the rest.

            - it is normally accented.

        * With the backbeat, the accents are on beats 2 and 4 (as opposed to beat 1).

          a.) This became Motown's metric/beat policy.

    - <u>Melodies</u>: Catchy, easily singable, and easily memorable.

        * Designed to be instant.

          a.) Also designed to connect easily with a mainstream audience.

    - <u>Catchy Lyrics</u>: especially in a "hook" fashion.

        * Refrains or musical resolutions especially focus on words that are easily memorable.

          a.) Usually, a phrase of about 2 to 5 words.

        * Words must <u>not</u> deal with controversial subject matter (even though the height of the Civil Rights movement was sweeping America at the time).

3.) <u>RESULT</u>: All of these musical ingredients mixed together would not only insure a consistent sound regardless of the recording artist.

    - But would also insure mass, mainstream appeal that would win over audiences throughout the entire world.

        * But the musical sound itself was not the only crossover policy.

          a.) If you have a non-threatening sound, your artists would also have to be non-threatening.

            - they needed to be groomed…

F.) <u>Artist Development</u>:

    1.) <u>Purpose</u>: To groom the artists for big-time performance venues and to give their appearances, their etiquette, and their routines' crossover appeal.

        - in addition to their music.

    2.) Most of these artists grew up in single parent homes in housing projects and they came from poverty.

        - Their mannerisms were characteristic of a poverty-laden culture. These mannerisms were crude, with no self-awareness.

          a.) They needed to be groomed.

    3.) <u>Artist Development</u>: was a department specifically for this purpose. There were three areas:

        - <u>The Finishing School</u>: headed by Maxine Powell.

          * She taught the artists on the following:

            a.) To walk with a sophisticated gait.

            b.) Proper posture.

            c.) To speak clearly and articulately.

              - For interviews.

            d.) To properly wear make-up

            e.) How to dress elegantly.

              - And choose the proper attire.

            f.) How to engage an audience in a very tasteful manner.

          * <u>REASON</u>: To appear and act elegantly with an air of sophistication for easy acceptance by a white mainstream audience.

        - <u>Choreography</u>: Cholly Atkins.

* He crafted the various dance routines for each performing artist. Again, for crossover appeal.

        a.) He would concentrate on projection, sex appeal (in a very stylish manner), and sophistication.

        b.) His movements tended to be smooth and in total control.

          - Not overtly emphatic and wild.

        c.) His routines always had a touch of class.

* The artists would spend hours and hours every day practicing these dance routines.

* Atkins was trying to groom these dance routines for acceptance in venues where black artists seldom ventured.

        a.) The famous supper clubs such as: The Stork Club, The Copacabana, The Coconut Grove, and other various clubs in Las Vegas.

        b.) And also for TV variety shows such as The Ed Sullivan Show.

* They were trained to perform with polish and class.

        a.) Again, in order to be non-threatening and acceptable to the mainstream.

    - Music Education:

        * They were trained in the basic rudiments of music (i.e. basic theory, harmony, and rhythm).

4.) Artist development: became a quasi music conservatory for these artists.

    - They were given in essence, an education.

G.) Writers/Producers: Motown had a staff of songwriters who also produced as well.

    1.) In sync with the times where the record producer also wrote the music.

    2.) Personnel: William "Smokey" Robinson

                      Ivy Joe Hunter

                      Mickey Stevenson

                      Norman Whitfield

                      Brian and Eddie Holland with Lamont Dozier (H-D-H Team).

    3.) Policy: Gordy's policy regarding these writer/producers was this:

        - A writer/producer would be assigned a performing artist or group that would be exclusively his (or theirs) to produce and write songs for.

        - The PBS Rock and Roll video series gives an excellent example of this policy in action:

The Way You Do The Things You Do
The Temptations

        * Smokey Robinson was assigned to The Temptations where he wrote and produced their first hit: "The Way You Do The Things You Do".

            a.) The success of this record earned Smokey Robinson exclusive rights to The Temptations.

               - For the next two years, they were his exclusive group to compose and produce for.

            b.) Two years later, Robinson wrote and produced a chart failure entitled: "Get Ready"

               - (ironically, in the early 70's, the first white group to ever be signed to Motown – "Rare Earth" – would make this song their debut hit)

Ain't Too Proud To Beg
The Temptations

            c.) As a result of this failure, Gordy gave The Temptations to another writer/producer named Norman Whitfield.

               - Who wrote: "Ain't Too Proud To Beg" which became a massive hit.

    - This quasi "punishment" policy created fierce competition within the walls of Motown rather than from the outside.

        * Gordy had enacted a formula that would guarantee success: a company competing against itself.

           - A sure way to elevate their quality.

4.) <u>RESULT</u>: This "self competition" of Motown would insure a string of top ten hits throughout the 60's.

- Hits with The Supremes, Martha Reeves and The Vandellas, Mary Wells, The Four Tops, Marvin Gaye, The Temptations, etc.

* Top flight talent on a consistent level was not exclusive to just the performing artists.

a.) That polished, classy, background sound performed by the session band was also important to the Motown equation.

H.) <u>The Funk Brothers</u>: Formerly Joe Hunter's Combo, came out of the vibrant jazz scene in Detroit. Gordy, who knew them from his jazz appreciation days, personally recruited them to be his session band.

1.) Personnel: <u>Ivy Joe Hunter</u>: keyboards
<u>Earl Van Dyke</u>: keyboards (eventually took over for Ivy Hunter)
<u>Robert White</u>: guitar
<u>Eddie Willis</u>: guitar
<u>Benny Benjamin</u>: drums
<u>James Jamerson</u>: bass
<u>Joe Messina</u>: rhythm guitarist

2.) The two most important: <u>Benny Benjamin</u> and <u>James Jamerson</u>.

- <u>Benny Benjamin</u> (1925-1969): had that signature smooth, swinging snare drum slap.

* Smooth rolls on the Tom-Toms as well.

Come See About Me
The Supremes

a.) His overall suave, easy sound blended perfectly with the crossover polish.

- a great musician in every sense.

- <u>James Jamerson</u> (1936-1983): probably their most innovative musician.

* He wrote his own bass lines around a given chord chart.

a.) And his bass lines can always be heard.

* He could play in a smooth, strutting swing style as in: "<u>Come See About Me</u>".

*You Keep Me
Hangin' On*
The Supremes

a.) Or, in an aggressive, rhythmically vibrant manner as in: "<u>You Keep Me Hangin' On</u>".

- Both songs written for The Supremes (by Holland-Dozier-Holland).

- His sources for inspiration that led to his originality:

* African, Cuban, and Indian (India) scales/modes.

a.) He once said: "My feel was always an Eastern feel, a spiritual thing".

* His inspiration to create original bass lines came from two other sources:

a.) By listening to the way people spoke…

- through their voice intonations.

b.) By watching the way they walked…

- Getting a certain beat from watching their gait.

- <u>SOURCE</u>: originality being forged out of sources completely outside of music in which his imagination could then relate to specific musical ideas…

* Thereby conveying a unique musical perspective.

3.) <u>James Jamerson</u>: was the first, great virtuoso bass player in rock and roll.

- Elevating the bass to a new level of artistry never before seen.

I.) <u>Motown</u>: from a standpoint of success, marked a new milestone for black entrepreneurship.

1.) Berry Gordy had proven that, with a unique vision, hard work, and tireless energy as well as a level playing field:

- Black businesses could compete with white enterprises and become highly successful.

2.) But not all of black America was enthusiastic of Motown's success.

- For them, Motown was a sell-out.

     * Selling out their black identity in order to appeal to white audiences.
- They also felt that Motown's music – as polished and as beautiful as it was:
     * ...was not truly authentic, gospel-driven black music.

V. STAX/VOLT RECORDS (MEMPHIS): THE SECOND OF THE TWO-AND-A-HALF CITIES
  A.) Proponents of "Southern Soul" felt that their brand of gospel-driven rhythm and blues was the real thing.
    1.) Raw Intensity: no polish, no elegance, no desire for crossover appeal.

     - They let it all hang out.
      * If a performer wanted to scream, sing out of tune, or jump all over the stage working themselves into a sweat: that's OK.
       a.) The key: authenticity.
        - Example: Compare the Sam & Dave southern soul single "Hold On! I'm Comin' " with Marvin Gaye's Motown hit "Ain't That Peculiar"
    2.) The description stated above, was the policy of Stax/Volt records in Memphis.
     - Irony: A white owned record company...
      *...that targeted an African American audience.
  B.) Stax/Volt: founded in 1958 by Jim Stewart and his sister Estelle Axton. (Hence, the acronym: Stax – ST for Stewart and AX for Axton).
    1.) They started out recording local R&B talent such as radio DJ, Rufus Thomas.
     - He recorded a single with his daughter, Carla entitled: "Cause I Love You".
      * Which caught the attention of a producer for Atlantic Records in New York named Jerry Wexler.
  C.) Jerry Wexler (b. 1/10/17, Bronx, NY): former writer for Billboard Magazine (he first coined the term, Rhythm and Blues).
    1.) He was now a producer for Atlantic Records:
     - An independent label specializing in black music.
    2.) Wexler entered into a distribution agreement with Stax.
     - Which supplied Stax with an extensive, African American distribution base (he leased "Cause I Love You" for $1000, which initially started the Wexler/Stax collaboration).
    3.) He was also responsible for bringing in recording artists that define the Southern Soul sound.
     - Sam and Dave: "Hold On, I'm Comin" and "Soul Man"
     - Wilson Pickett: "Midnight Hour"
  D.) Booker T. & The MG's: Stax's session group. (initials MG's denote: Memphis Guitars).
    1.) The only true rivals of The Funk Brothers.
     - Whereas the Funk Brothers were jazz schooled.
      *The members of Booker T. & The MG's grew up appreciating and playing rhythm and blues.
       a.) Their original name: The Mar-Keys
    2.) Personnel: Booker T. Jones (b. 11/12/44, Memphis, TN): keyboards
        Al Jackson Jr. (b. 11/27/35, Memphis; d. 10/1/75, Memphis): drums
        Donald "Duck" Dunn (b. 11/24/41, Memphis): bass
        Steve Cropper (b. 10/21/41, Willow Springs, MO): guitar
    3.) They were an early prototype for the racially mixed band.
     - Jones and Jackson were black.
     - Cropper and Dunn were white.

    4.) "Green Onions" (1962): their first hit (and one of the first instrumental hits in rock and roll to climb the charts).
     - An after hours jam tune turned into a single.
    5.) They were the superb rhythm section backing up main artists during Stax recording sessions.

- Stax also had a separate, great horn section that played alongside them during recordings.
    E.) <u>Isaac Hayes and David Porter</u>:
        1.) Stax's in-house songwriter/producer team.
    F.) <u>Wilson Pickett</u> (b. 3/18/41, Prattville, AL): first of Wexler's new York artists to arrive in Memphis.
        1.) Pickett's first hit under the Memphis umbrella, which would mark a new beat policy for Stax:
            - Was written in collaboration with Steve Cropper on Pickett's first night in Memphis at the <u>Lorraine Motel</u> (an important/infamous landmark of the Civil Rights movement – more on that later).
        2.) The song was: "<u>In The Midnight Hour</u>" (1965).

In The Midnight Hour
Wilson Pickett

            - Would have a lasting impact on the Stax "house style" because of an idea that Jerry Wexler had for the beat.
                * He wanted the beat to sound a certain way.
                    a.) He demonstrated during the recording session (a day after the song was written) a dance called <u>The Jerk</u>.
                        - <u>In a four-beat pattern</u>: one raises both arms up above the head – on beat 1 — and swings them down to waist level – on beat 2. The sequence is repeated on beats 3 & 4.
                        - Also, while raising the arms, the pelvis moves forward, when lowering the arms, the pelvis moves backward.
                    b.) Usually, in dancing "The Jerk", the arms are raised slightly higher on the second beat than on the fourth.
                        - This causes a <u>slight delay</u> on the second beat for the dancer.
                * In demonstrating this dance, Wexler wanted exactly that: a backbeat with a <u>slight delay</u> on the second beat.
                    a.) And along with the slight delay, a slightly more accented emphasis.
                * <u>RESULT</u>: This "Delayed Backbeat" (a.k.a. "Delayed Two") on "Midnight Hour" would become Stax's new signature, backbeat policy.
        3.) This single not only became a big hit, it also put the Southern Soul sound squarely on the map.
            - Along with Sam & Dave, Wilson Pickett opened the door for another gospel, church-sounding artist to follow:
                * Who would become Stax's greatest success story.
    G.) <u>Otis Redding</u> (b. 9/9/41, Dawson, GA; d. 12/10/67, Madison, WI):
        1.) His first stint as a vocalist in the recording industry:
            - A Little Richard screaming sound-alike.
                * Although it never lead to anything important, this early Little Richard influence of raw intensity would pay its dividends later.
        2.) The job that would first connect him to Stax:
            - He worked as a backup singer and chauffeur for Stax recording artists: "Johnny Jenkins and The Pine Toppers"
                * After the group finished a recording session earlier than planned (there was forty minutes of studio time left),

These Arms Of Mine
Otis Redding

                    a.) They allowed Otis Redding to record two ballads:
                      - one of them, "<u>These Arms Of Mine</u>" (1964) caught the attention of Booker T. Jones.
        3.) <u>John R. Richberry</u>: of WLAC radio in Nashville, was a huge promoter of Stax recordings.
            - It was his relentless promotion of "<u>These Arms Of Mine</u>" on WLAC:
                * that gave Otis Redding his first big break.

a.) It also helped that John R. Richberry had partial publishing rights to this song as an added incentive.

4.) Otis Redding's natural singing style was much "churchier" than the other Stax artists.
- That sanctified church influence (along with the early Little Richard emulation), had a major impact on his style.
* For slow ballads, his voice had a pleading, prayer-like vulnerability.
* For fast music, he could scream in the mike and sing with the all-out intensity of a Pentecostal linkage with the Holy Spirit.

5.) He wrote much of his own music, as well as arrangements.
- He was especially particular about the brass arrangements.
- RESULT: A raw, gritty, and intense brand of deep Southern Soul.
* With brassy arrangements and deep emotion.

6.) One of the greatest recordings that demonstrates (in the span of one single), the extent of Otis Redding's complete expressive arsenal: "Try A Little Tenderness".

Try A Little
Tenderness
Otis Redding

- Begins slowly where he sings with that vulnerability.
- The song suddenly changes to a moderate tempo highlighted by Al Jackson's constant, clock-like rim shots.
* Within this new context, Redding begins a vocal lyricism with a churchy, chant-like subtlety, but possessing an element of subdued power waiting to be unleashed.
- The next section begins with the MG's playing in contrapuntal syncopation.
* While Redding's intensity is picking up momentum.
- Finally, the apex of a massive, polyrhythmic groove at full-throttle which marks the densest and loudest part of the song.
* Which he sings with all-out, screaming intensity.
a.) This section is the culmination of a direction which began as soft and subtle and ended fast and furious.

7.) It was the performance of this song,
- at the Monterey Pop Festival in June of 1967…
* That made Otis Redding a crossover success for the first time.

8.) "Sittin On The Dock Of The Bay": his last recording, which became a crossover hit in 1968…
- …after his untimely death in a plane crash in Madison, WI on Dec. 10, 1967.

9.) Otis Redding: His originality stemmed from a sanctified church musical background.
- In collaboration with the rhythmically vibrant rhythm and blues style of Booker T. & The MG's.
* Along with the brass influence of the Stax horn section.

H.) Jerry Wexler however, was embroiled in a major conflict with Stax executives: Al Bell and Jim Stewart.

1.) Atlantic Records (Wexler's label): had gained control of Stax's master-tape inventory.
- This was part of the original distribution agreement that was buried technically in the contract.
- Wexler tried using this element of the contract as a negotiating tactic.
* Bell and Stewart reacted by selling Stax to the "Paramount Pictures Music Division"…
a.) …which was part of the "Gulf Western" conglomerate.

2.) This move, ushered Stax into the quilt of corporate America…
- …and sending Jerry Wexler in search of a new studio.

VI. MUSCLE SHOALS, ALABAMA: THE "HALF" CITY.

A.) Rick Hall (b. 1/31/32, Franklin County, AL): songwriter, country fiddler, and whiskey bootlegger built a studio reminiscent of "cinderblock adobe shacks" (he knew from Nashville) next to a cotton field in the small town of Muscle Shoals, AL.

1.) He called it Fame Studios (Florence Alabama Music Enterprises).
- A name he inherited from Tom Stafford who originally set up "Fame" in nearby Florence, AL.

2.) A rural, bible belt, KKK infested area.
- Irony #1: In this rural and racist area, some of the greatest recordings of black, Soul music would be made.

B.) Fame Studios: caught the attention of Jerry Wexler when he heard a Muscle Shoals recording by Percy Sledge: "When A Man Loves A Woman".
1.) Wexler was impressed enough, that he solicited Rick Hall into a possible distribution arrangement.

C.) Rick Hall: founded Fame Studios in 1962.

When A Man Loves A Woman
Percy Sledge

1.) His first success story was a singer named Arthur Alexander (b. Arthur Bernard Alexander Jr. 5/10/40, Florence, AL; d. 6/9/93, Nashville, TN)...
- ...who became the first true star of "Country Soul".
* Southern black gospel-driven music written in a country-styled structure and flavor.
1.) Which in turn, was played and appreciated by white musicians.

You Better Move On
Arthur Alexander

- "You Better Move On"(1962): reaching #24 on the pop charts, was the first hit recorded at Fame Studios.
* The success of "You Better Move On" not only put Fame Studios on the map, it also gave Fame much needed financial backing.
- From the outset, Arthur Alexander was highly revered and covered by his contemporaries:
"Anna" - The Beatles
"Soldier Of Love" - The Beatles, Marshall Crenshaw
"Burning Love" - Elvis Presley
"Rescue Me" - Percy Sledge, Fontella Bass
- Arthur Alexander's originality of soul mixed with country made him a harbinger of Southern Soul and its artists to come.

D.) Wilson Pickett: was the first of Jerry Wexler's artists to be sent to Muscle Shoals after he [Wexler] reached a distribution agreement with Rick Hall.
1.) When Wilson Pickett touched down in Muscle Shoals, Rick Hall was waiting.
- Pickett: who said in an interview how nervous and dumbfounded he was when he arrived, felt that way for several reasons:
* He didn't expect a tall, white person like Rick Hall to know anything about producing a raw-sounding, gospel-driven singer like him [Pickett].
* As they drove on a dirt road through a cotton field, he couldn't believe he was seeing people (black people) picking cotton.
* When he arrived in the studio for his first recording session there, he noticed that the entire studio band was comprised of white southerners.
2.) Irony #2: This session group – known as The Peckerwoods – would play authentic, gospel-driven rhythm and blues even though their racial and cultural backgrounds were far removed from the black experience.

E.) Personnel:
1.) Jimmy Johnson: rhythm guitar extraordinaire
David Hood: bass (later replaced by Junior Lowe)
Spooner Oldham: electric keyboards
Roger Hawkins: drums

Land Of A Thousand Dances
Wilson Pickett

- They constituted the core session group.
* Their sound was soulfully, very authentic.
2.) After breaking in to: "Land Of A Thousand Dances",
- Wilson Pickett needed no more convincing.
* He became totally sold on the session group's authenticity as well as Rick Hall's abilities as a full-fledged producer of black, gospel-driven music.

Mustang Sally
Wilson Pickett

- They would go on to record other Wilson Pickett classics such as "Funky Broadway", "634-5789 (Soulsville, USA)", and "Mustang Sally".

3.) But Wilson Pickett would not be the final chapter on the rise of Southern Soul out of Muscle Shoals.

F.) <u>Aretha Franklin</u> (b. 3/25/42, Memphis, TN): daughter of the Reverend C. L. Franklin out of Detroit, MI (who had a syndicated radio broadcast on WLAC).

    1.) She began recording gospel music when she was 14.
- Motown even expressed an early interest in her.

    2.) Aretha was signed instead by <u>John Hammond</u>.
- The legendary A&R man for CBS Records (he had also signed Bob Dylan).

    3.) She sang occasional R&B tunes with Columbia (CBS) but mostly, she sang easy, "cool" jazz.
- As a result, she was not completely utilizing her gospel talents.
        * She sounded contained and not full.
- She was virtually unknown in the recording business (she did have one top 40 single: "Rock-A-Bye Your Baby With A Dixie Melody").

    4.) CBS Records basically didn't know what to do with her.
- But Jerry Wexler did.
        * He bought out her contract from Columbia and brought her immediately to Muscle Shoals.
            a.) Wexler: wanted to bring out the full gospel spirit and energy that was so much an integral part of her background and upbringing.
            b.) He brought out Aretha's uniqueness by basically, bringing her back to herself.

    5.) "<u>I Never Loved A Man (The Way I Love You)</u>": was her first and only recording at Fame Studios.

I Never Loved A Man The Way I Love You
Aretha Franklin

- Backed up by The Peckerwoods and a slew of other musicians hired directly for this occasion.
- <u>Teddy White</u>: her husband at the time, got involved in a drunken brawl with one of the brass players.
        * That, in addition to being uncomfortable in backwards/redneck environment.
            a.) Prompted Aretha and Teddy to immediately leave Muscle Shoals and return to Detroit.

    6.) <u>Wexler</u>: had aggressively promoted "<u>I Never Loved A Man</u>…" to radio DJ's throughout the country by sending them recorded examples of the song.
- It resulted in such a massive and positive response, these DJ's were requesting the actual record to be sent.
        * <u>The Problem</u>: no record, because there was no Side B.

Do Right Woman, Do Right Man
Aretha Franklin

- He did have the instrumental tracks to the Side B song: "<u>Do-Right Woman, Do Right Man</u>" in his possession.
        * All he needed, was for Aretha to come to New York and record the vocal track.
            a.) She, along with her sisters: Carolyn and Erma completed the vocal tracks themselves thereby, completing the song.
- She also finished recording the remainder of the album accompanied by The Peckerwoods (Wexler had brought them to New York).

    7.) "<u>I Never Loved A Man</u>…" (Side A) along with "<u>Do-Right Woman</u>…" (Side B) was released by Atlantic Records in the spring of 1967 to a phenomenal, worldwide response.
- Not only did it immediately hit the top of the charts.
        * It also became a crossover sensation (without intending to be).
- <u>Otis Redding</u>: opened the "crossover" door for Southern Soul at Monterey.
        * But Aretha solidified Southern Soul's place in the mainstream (right along side Motown).

    8.) Her additional Atlantic recordings: "<u>Chain Of Fools</u>", "<u>Respect</u>" (written by Otis Redding), "<u>Baby, I Love You</u>", etc.
- Would also become massive hits.

9.) Aretha not only became a star, she also became a symbol.
- A symbol, of what Black Americans could achieve in an era where the Civil Rights movement was moving at full speed.

G.) <u>Momentum</u>: the great momentum of gospel-driven black music was being appreciated the world over.
1.) Mirroring the momentum of the Civil Rights advances.
2.) The popularity of this music seemed like an unstoppable juggernaut.
- But usually, when one thinks the juggernaut train will run invincibly:
* it usually gets blind-sided and derailed.
3.) The event that changed the landscape of gospel-driven music as well as the momentum of the Civil Rights movement (Soul's musical mirror), took place on April 4, 1968.
- The assassination of Dr. Martin Luther King at the Lorraine Motel in Memphis.

H.) <u>Aftermath</u>: as a result, black artists slowly stopped coming to Muscle Shoals to work with Fame Studios.
1.) The goodwill and camaraderie between black and white artists/producers working together (so important to the development of gospel-driven music throughout the South)…
- Began to dissipate.
2.) Eventually, white pop artists would replace them at Fame Studios.
- Artists such as: Rod Stewart, Paul Simon, Cat Stevens, The Osmond Brothers, and the Rolling Stones.
* The Stones would record cuts from their "Sticky Fingers" album (released in 1971) during their "Gimme Shelter" American tour in 1969.
3.) There was also, a new trend on the horizon in black music.
- Music with a greater focus on rhythm than on gospel based ideas.
* This new music also produced a more aggressive sound.
* And it spoke about black pride and black identity.
- as opposed to love and romance.
* There was in addition, an overt sexual aura surrounding the music.
* The catalyst for this revolution in rhythm with lyrical emphasis on an identity statement:
- was <u>James Brown</u> (he will be covered in depth in the chapter on "Funk").

Say It Loud
(I'm Black And I'm Proud) Pt. 1
James Brown

a.) His song <u>*Say It Loud (I'm Black and I'm Proud)*</u> (released in the Fall of 1968), became a symbol of this new direction in black music.
4.) Even though Funk would now become the new rubric in black music…
- it did not mean that the flame of the "Soul" torch had been completely extinguished.

VII. AL GREEN (b. 4/13/46, Forrest City, AR):
A.) The first great soul singer of the 70's.
1.) And also, the last of the great Southern Soul artists.
2.) Produced by songwriter <u>Willie Mitchell</u>, Al Green would launch a string of hits throughout the 70's…
- With songs that he either wrote or co-wrote with Willie Mitchell.
* Mitchell's influence upon Al Green was profound.
B.) <u>Willie Mitchell</u> (b. 1/3/28, Ashland. MS): started out as a trumpeter and bandleader.
1.) In 1959, he signed with "<u>HI</u>" Records in Memphis where he basically created the "HI" signature sound:
- Organ fill-ins, a smooth steady beat, and horn section punctuations.

          * This would be one of the signature sound policies associated with Al Green recordings.

    2.) The other, would be the marriage of Southern Soul to the "Philadelphia ("Philly") International" sound:

You Ought To Be With Me

Al Green

          - the latter's signature sound consisted of lush, up-front, orchestral strings.

          * Taking that lush string influence and putting them more to the background would lend perfect support for Al Green's falsetto sound.

C.) The Al Green/Willie Mitchell collaboration also put the emphasis on beat one (as opposed to backbeats).

    1.) This "On the One" concept was a product of James Brown's funk style which was prominent at the time.

    2.) RESULT: Al Green's sexy, suave, laid-back falsetto voice.

Here I Am (Come And Take Me)

Al Green

          - Singing easily catchy melodies.

          - And supported by the "HI"/"Philly" smooth arrangements.

          * Songs such as: "Here I Am (Come And Take Me)", "You Ought To Be With Me", and "Call Me" all became top ten singles.

D.) 1976: He became an ordained minister for the "All Gospel Tabernacle" in Memphis where he bought a church.

    1.) Even though he became a pastor, he still pursued R&B until 1979:

        - The year he gave up secular music altogether.

    2.) There would be other scant R&B projects in the future but for all practical purposes:

        - His departure from the secular music arena was in 1979.

          * As a result of his departure, 1979 marked two major things:

             a.) The last great music to come out of Memphis.

             b.) And the final end of the Soul Era.

CHAPTER IV: REVIEW

Define the four properties of traditional West African music.
    1.) Polyrhythmic Groove:
    2.) Call & Response:
    3.) Hand Clapping (describe the beat pattern):
    4.) Rhythmic Distribution (Hierarchy):

What was the role of Yoruban polyrhythmic music?

What were the BATA Drums?

    List the different pairs of drum sizes and what each pair represented:
        1.)
        2.)
        3.)

Which island became the first filtering unit of West African polyrhythmic music?

    What did this filtering unit change in regard to instrumentation?

    How did the concept of "outer form" enter into African-derived polyrhythmic music?

    Instead of voices in the response section [of call & response], what did this filtering unit incorporate?

    What type of repetitive bass pattern was used and what instrument replaced the drums?

    What was the first important new genre of western polyrhythmic music?

What was the significance of the Ring Shout?

    Name its four properties:
        1.)
        2.)
        3.)
        4.)

What was the first body of African American music to be appreciated by post-Civil War white America?

    List its four properties:
        1.)
        2.)
        3.)
        4.)

From where did the Spiritual emerge?

How did Gospel evolve?

List two elements of Modern Gospel:
    1.)
    2.)

What was the significance of The Negro Gospel and Religious Festival at Carnegie Hall?

The significance of Ray Charles and the name of the musical movement he started:

    What did he do to gospel music?

    Name his first important single in 1954 which in his words "was where it all started"?

The significance of Sam Cooke (both musically and business-wise):

    Name his label and publishing company:

    The significance of his single, "You Send Me" (1957):

Name the gospel group with which he launched his professional career:

    What did he bring to gospel that was never before seen?

His smooth, velvety, mid-range voice would be an inspiration for other singers such as:

Why was Sam Cooke considered one of black America's greatest success stories?

Name the founder of Motown:

    His policy as a lyricist:

    Name the songwriter he collaborated with on singles released by the Brunswick label:
        What was his songwriting policy?

    List several of these singles and the artist who recorded them.

What was Berry Gordy's first hit under his TAMLA Label that he co-wrote with Janie Bradford?

    What did the revenue generated from [the success of] this record afford Berry Gordy to establish?

Motown's first big hit (i.e. their first million seller):

    Name the Gordy protégé who wrote it:

List the five elements of Motown's "House Style " regarding music policy:
    1.)
    2.)
    3.)
    4.)
    5.)

Name the three departments of "Artist Development":
    1.)
    2.)
    3.)

    What was the goal of Artist Development?

What was Motown's policy regarding songwriters? How did they get a lock on a particular artist?

    Name the Motown staff of songwriters:

1.)
2.)
3.)
4.)
5.)

Name the session band for Motown:

    List the personnel of this session band:
        1.)
        2.)
        3.)
        4.)
        5.)
        6.)

    What was the significance of this group's bass player? (What was he a first of in rock and roll?)

        What type of scales/modes did he use to give his music "an Eastern Feel"?

        What were his two inspirations for creating original bass-lines?
            1.)
            2.)

What was the difference between the sound of Motown and Southern Soul?

Name the Memphis-based label of Southern Soul:

    Name this label's first important single recorded by Rufus and Carla Thomas.

    Which Atlantic record producer took an interest in this song, which led to his interest in this label?

Name Stax's session group.

    List their personnel:
        1.)
        2.)
        3.)
        4.)

Also, who comprised Stax's songwriting/producer team?

Name the first Atlantic Records artist to record at Stax Studios:

Name his first hit recorded there in 1965:

Who were the other Atlantic Records artists [a vocal duo] who recorded at STAX?

Explain Stax's metric policy of the "delayed backbeat":

Who was Stax's most successful recording artist? He was also Southern Soul's first crossover success.

What single became his first big break?

Who was the WLAC DJ who promoted it?

List two aspects of Otis Redding's sanctified church-influenced singing style?
1.)
2.)

What was the significance of his performance at the Monterey Pop Festival in June of 1967?

What was his last recording?

Where was Fame Studios located and who founded it?

Name the single (1962) and artist that became this studio's first success:

Which single, recorded at this studio, caught the attention of producer Jerry Wexler (name the artist of this single as well)?

Name the session band of FAME Studios.

Name the personnel:

1.)
2.)
3.)
4.)

Name the first Atlantic Records artist that Jerry Wexler sent to Fame Studios and the first single he recorded there:

Name at least three additional singles that he recorded there:
1.)
2.)
3.)

Name the most successful artist to record at Fame Studios (hint: this artist made only one recording there):

Which legendary A&R man at CBS Records discovered her?

Why did Jerry Wexler buy out her contract from CBS?

Name the two (both A and B sides) singles that were released in the spring of 1967:

What was the significance of this two-sided smash hit in regard to Southern Soul crossover? (Hint: the important word here is, "solidify"):

List the two turning points in that changed the momentum of gospel-based Soul music (hint: one had to do with a tragic event at the Lorraine Hotel in Memphis, the other had to do with a new black genre in rock and roll):
1.)
2.)

Name the last great artist of the Soul Era:

Who was his producer/co-songwriter?

List the three elements that make up the "Hi! Records" sound:
1.)
2.)
3.)

In what year did Al Green leave secular music in order to preach the Gospel on a full-time basis (thereby marking the end of the Soul Era)?

CHAPTER V: BRITISH BLUES REVISIONISM

I. SEEDS TO THAT "SECOND INVASION"

    A.) The First British Invasion (1964): the first wave of English pop bands were invading America.

        1.) Spearheaded by The Beatles, their music grew out of a more pop tradition.

        2.) But not all artists in Britain were happy with it.

        3.) Students attending art colleges throughout suburban England were interested in an entirely different inspiration:

            - they discovered American Blues.

    B.) Why American Blues? What was it about this art form they found attractive?

        1.) They were entranced with the raw intensity derived from gospel-driven emotion and sense of passion.

            - transformed to the strings of the electric guitar.

        2.) The Grit: The sound had a certain grit or "dirt" to it that gave it an air of authenticity as opposed to what they saw, was the fakeness of Liverpool-styled pop.

            - American blues to them [art school students], had the substance.

        3.) Sexuality: The music was very sexual in energy.

        4.) Foundation: For these artists, the blues marked a starting point.

            - By covering blues tunes, they would achieve the following:

                * Technique: it helped them acquire the "chops" or technical ability that would eventually enable them to play lines of immense complexity.

                    - They would start by emulating various artists by memorizing their [blues artists'] guitar riffs verbatim.

                * Artistic Expression: The better their chops became, the more they could focus on expressing emotion through their playing.

                    - For example, by copying such expressive techniques as "pitch-bending" or vibrato on an important note that realizes the direction of a melodic line.

                        a.) By copying, they would make it their own.

                * Truth: to them, blues was the truth.

                    - As Van Morrison once said: "You can't glamorize it. It is what it is".

                        a.) To British artists, the lyrics of American blues spoke of real life's struggles and hardships.

                            - that they themselves could relate to first hand.

                    - Lyric examples: "I woke up this morning, and my baby was gone", "I've been working in a coal mine all day and my body is aching", "I'll drink a bottle of whiskey, to wash my troubles away", etc.

                * The Mystique: In England, blues records were extremely difficult to find.

                    - Which added to the mystery and legend of the sound.

                * A "Classical" Style of Music: each cover gave them an artistic goal to accomplish.

                    - They were to copy American blues in an authentic manner as possible.

                        a.) But it would come out as something completely different.

                * NOTE: The following, was the key to their originality.

                    - They were not African American and thereby, never experienced the racial culture that their American counterparts did.

                        a.) Nor did they experience the depressing results spawned by racism.

- They were far removed from the hardships of day to day living.
> a.) the impoverishment as sharecroppers or inner-city ghetto life.
- As opposed to a single front-man format (for all American blues artists were presented as individuals like Muddy Waters, Howlin' Wolf, etc.).
> a.) British blues artists presented their interpretation of American blues in a "group" format.

5.) <u>RESULT</u>: Their music was bound to be different.

C.) British artists would make it their business to emulate and learn about these American blues artists.

1.) And, in the process, become virtuosos in their own right.
- transforming the electric guitarist, from a background person in rock and roll:
  * To an accomplished artist standing front and center.

2.) Chuck Berry was rock and roll's first "guitar hero" by not only bringing the electric guitar twang up front:
- but also, by inspiring generations to pick up the electric guitar.
  * These British artists would solidify the primacy of the guitar front-man as a permanent fixture in the rock and roll domain.
> a.) Artists like <u>Eric Clapton</u>, <u>Jeff Beck</u>, and <u>Jimmy Page</u>.

3.) They would emulate an American musical genre that mainstream America had basically forgotten.
- They [British artists] would adapt it as their own.
  * And import it back to American soil making mainstream America aware of blues' existence for the first time.

4.) <u>RESULT</u>: A new wave of British blues-based bands will make their way to America.
- In the wake of The Beatles styled "first wave" pop bands.

D.) In order to understand these artists and what they accomplished:

1.) it would be useful to understand the make-up of the American blues genre.

II. THE BLUES

A.) <u>The Structure</u>: lyrical (a,a,b)

1.) <u>a</u>: same words
<u>a</u>: same words   = <u>1 stanza</u>
<u>b</u>: different words
- This structure of lyrics holds true for each stanza in a blues song.
  * The words in the first verse are always repeated in the second.
  * The third verse contains wording different from the prior two verses.

Empty Bed Blues

Elizabeth Johnson

- <u>Example</u>: from the 1st stanza of a blues tune, "<u>Empty Bed Blues</u>" recorded by Elizabeth Johnson.
  * <u>a</u>: "I woke up this morning with a awful aching head"
  <u>a</u>: "I woke up this morning with a awful aching head"
  <u>b</u>: "My new had left me just a room and an empty bed".

B.) <u>The Structure</u>: musical - the I,IV,V chord progression.

1.) To understand what a chord progression consists of, one must first become familiar with the structure of the diatonic scale.
- <u>Diatonic Scale</u>: consists of seven pitches in an octave segment. A number is assigned to each sequential pitch starting with the home (or "tonic") pitch.
  * <u>Example</u>: with C as the home pitch: C=1, D=2, E=3, F=4, G=5, A=6, B=7, C=1 (at the octave: where a pitch –in this case C – duplicates itself on the next highest level).
> a.) The numbers assigned to the pitches are called: <u>scale degrees</u>.
- <u>Chords</u>: a Roman numeral is assigned to each chord in accordance to the scale degree.

* Example: a "I" chord is a triad (consisting of three pitches) whose "root" of foundation tone rests on the first scale degree: 1.

    a.) Again, with C as the home pitch:

Root: C   D   E   F   G   A   B   C
Chord: I   II   III   IV   V   VI   VII   I

2.) The standard chord progression in the blues tradition is: I, IV, V.

- Structure: <u>Lyrics</u>   <u>Chord</u>
           a   I
           a   IV
           b   V

- Again, using a previous example:

    * <u>a</u>: "I'm a real good woman but my man don't treat me right" - <u>I</u>
    <u>a</u>: "I'm a real good woman but my man don't treat me right" - <u>IV</u>
    <u>b</u>: "He takes all my money and stays out all night".   - <u>V</u>

C.) <u>Country Blues</u>: first body of black American music to lay down these basic blues structures.

    1.) Started with musicians working as sharecroppers and living on Southern plantations.

    - Country blues is a genre consisting of a lone person singing and playing the acoustic guitar.

    2.) Among the most inspirational to the British art school students:

Jersey Bull Blues
Charlie Patton

    - <u>Charlie Patton</u> (b. April,1891, Bolton, MS; d. 4/28/34, Indianola, MS)

    - <u>Son House</u> (b. Eddie House, 3/21/02, Riverton, MS; d. 10/19/88, Detroit, MI)

My Black Mama Pt. 1
Son House

    - <u>Robert Johnson</u> (b. 5/8/11, Hazelhurst, MS; d. 8/16/38, Greenwood, MS)

    * They served as early romantic symbols of the lone blues guitarists from the South who had no other choice other than to sing and play.

    - <u>Robert Johnson</u>: the artist who best embodied this romantic myth.

Cross Road Blues
Robert Johnson

    * Legend has it, that he sold his soul to the devil at the crossroads in exchange for an incredible musical ability.

        a.) One example of his great ability: he could play the guitar behind his neck.

    * What added to the legend, was the circumstances surrounding his death.

        a.) During a gig at a roadhouse, a jealous girlfriend slipped poison into his drink.

        b.) <u>RESULT</u>: he writhed in pain onstage, his eyeballs rolled up to the back of his head (showing only the whites of his eyes), and foam was seeping from the corners of his mouth.

    - It was this type of legendary embodiment that added to the allure of the lone blues artist.

    * which further attracted the British art school student.

D.) <u>Urban Blues</u>: The addition of different timbres to the traditional blues mix.

    1.) Trumpets, Clarinets, Doublebasses, Piano, Banjo, and Drums.

    2.) <u>Breaks</u>: the first structural, post "country blues" addition to the musical tradition.

Empty Bed Blues
Elizabeth Johnson

    - <u>Definition</u>: Instrumental solos – usually, improvised around a basic melody that occurs at the opening of the song and in between sung verses.

    -<u>Example</u>: Using the first stanza from "<u>Empty Bed Blues</u>".

    * <u>Trumpet solo</u>: beginning of the song (accompanied by piano).
    <u>a</u>: "I woke up this morning with a awful aching head"   - <u>I</u>
    <u>Trumpet Break</u>
    <u>a</u>: "I woke up this morning with a awful aching head"   - <u>IV</u>
    <u>Trumpet Break</u>
    <u>b:</u> "My new had left me, just a room and an empty bed" - <u>V</u>
    <u>Trumpet Break</u>: the link between first and second stanzas.

    3.) With these two new elements: different instrumental colors and instrumental breaks, the needed ingredients were now in place for the next developmental step.

E.) <u>Electric Blues</u>: the biggest blues influence in Britain.

1.) Began due to a need of amplification.
- Where, in urban blues joints, acoustic instruments could not be heard above the crowd noise.
* Chicago, would become the Mecca for this new style hence the term: "Chicago Blues".
- Out of this blues style, a new instrumental timbre would be added to the blues tradition:
* the electric guitar.
2.) Mass Migration: Millions of black Americans migrated to various industrial cities in the North in order to find better paying factory jobs and a better life.
- And escape their futile, depressing lives in southern plantations as sharecroppers.
- In moving to the North, they brought their culture with them, including music.
* Many of the artists who set the standard for Chicago blues were part of this mass migration.

3.) The first to capture the Chicago Blues sound in the studio were the Chess brothers: Phil and Leonard.

*I Can't Be
Satisfied*
Muddy Waters

*I Feel Like
Goin' Home*
Muddy Waters

- Aristocrat Records (1947 - 1950): started recording electric blues.
* Muddy Waters (b. McKinley Morganfield, 4/4/15, Rolling Fork, MS; d. 4/30/83, Chicago, IL).
a.) His recording of "I Can't Be Satisfied" was the first recording engineered by Leonard Chess (Phil ran the business end)…
- …to feature an electric guitar solo.
* Muddy Water's next electric tune: "I Feel Like Goin' Home"…
a.) would begin with a long extended electric guitar solo.
4.) 1950: The Aristocrat label was renamed: Chess Records.
- This new label that would be synonymous with classic Chicago blues.
5.) The list of artists grew:
- John Lee Hooker (b. 8/22/17, Vance, MS; d. 6/21/01, Los Altos, CA):
* Foot-stomping, gospel styled chanting in a blues format.
- Howlin' Wolf (b. Chester Arthur Burnett, 6/10/10, West Point, MS; d.1/10/76, Hines, IL).

Keep It To Yourself
Sonny Boy Williamson

*So Many Roads,
So Many Trains*
Otis Rush

* Originally recorded with Sun Records in Memphis.
- Sonny Boy Williamson (b. Willie "Rice" Miller, 12/5/1897, Glendora, MS; d. 5/25/65, Helena, AR):
* Specialized in the harmonica -- another traditional blues instrument.
a.) One of the pioneers in standardizing this instrument into the electric blues domain.

*First Time
I Met The Blues*
Buddy Guy

- Otis Rush (b. 1935, Philadelphia, MS):
* Combined the raw emotion of gospel singing with the classic bending of strings (downward) for expressive and dramatic flair.
- Buddy Guy (b. George Guy, 7/30/36, Lettsworth, LA): among the many who took the urban blues structure…

The Sun Is Shining
Elmore James

Tool Bag Boogie
Elmore James

*…and transformed it (breaks and all) into the electric guitar/electric blues format.
- Elmore James (b. Elmore Brooks, 1/27/18, Richland, MS; d. 5/24/63, Chicago, IL):
* Added the "slide; sound on the electric blues guitar.

29 Ways
Willie Dixon

- Willie Dixon (b. 7/1/15, Vicksburg, MS; d. 1/29/92, Burbank, CA):
* One of Chess' most prolific songwriters, talent scouts and producers.
a.) With the latter, his musical suggestions were crucial to artists like Bo Diddley.
- NOTE: These artists were among the ones most responsible for making the electric guitar, the primary instrument in blues.

6.) <u>Vee-Jay Records (1952)</u>: Chess' cross-town rival which, unlike Chess, was black owned.

Bright Lights
Big City
Jimmy Reed

- by James and Vivian Bracken along with Calvin Carter.
* They leaned towards a more streamlined version of electric blues.
a.) Their primary artist, was the legendary <u>Jimmy Reed</u> (b. 9/6/25, Dunleith, MS; d. 8/29/76, Oakland, CA).

F.) <u>Key To British Blues Originality</u>: In the act of emulating the original black American blues artists...

1.) The British blues revisionists would sound different and therefore, original in their own distinct way.

- Various British groups had their own interpretations of American blues classics.

Boom Boom
John Lee Hooker

* <u>Case in Point</u>: "Boom Boom" by John Lee Hooker.
a.) <u>The Animals</u>: did their own interpretation of this blues tune.

Boom Boom
The Animals

- <u>The Yardbirds</u>: did their own interpretation that resulted in a radically different rendition than that of The Animals.

Boom Boom
The Yardbirds

* <u>NOTE</u>: Although they both had tried to achieve as authentic an interpretation as possible, they wound up sounding different for two reasons that were mentioned earlier:
a.) They were white, middle-class suburbanites.
- They were far removed from the poverty and racism that black American artists were facing.
b.) They presented their brand of blues in a group format (i.e. The Yardbirds, The Animals, etc.).
- As opposed to the solo/lead artist context of the original American artists (i.e. Muddy Waters, Elmore James, etc.).

G.) In the beginning of the blues movement in England, recordings on Chess and Vee-Jay were difficult to find.

1.) That changed when Chess Records agreed to a distribution contract with an English label called: "<u>P.Y.E. International</u>".

Smokestack
Lightnin'
Howlin' Wolf

- <u>RESULT</u>: Chess recordings became readily available.
* Among the first Chess recordings to benefit from this new arrangement, was: "<u>Smokestack Lightnin</u>" by Howlin' Wolf.
a.) It became a big hit on the white, pop charts.

2.) Starting in the late fifties, artists like Muddy Waters and Big Bill Broonzy started performing in England.
- Primarily in folk and jazz clubs on off-nights.
* When no prior folk or jazz bookings were scheduled.
* They would sometimes perform in town halls as well.

3.) One of the earliest English blues artists, was about to be inspired when he heard the screaming electric guitar sounds of Muddy Waters emanating from the Newcastle Town Hall...

III. <u>THE EARLY BRITISH BLUES BANDS</u>

A.) <u>Eric Burdon</u> (b. 5/11/41, Newcastle upon Tyne, ENG): a singer/blues enthusiast from Newcastle heard those sounds coming out of the Town Hall in his city.

1.) He started a group called: "<u>The Animals</u>" ...
- which included keyboardist/songwriter, Alan Price, Bryan "Chas" Chandler (bassist), John Steel (drums), and guitarist, Hilton Valentine.

2.) <u>The Idea</u>: to perform authentic American blues.
- they would rise to the top of the Newcastle club scene.

135

3.) Although they did not know it at the time when they were starting out, their passion for the blues was being shared by other enthusiasts throughout the UK.

B.) <u>Problem</u>: throughout the UK, folk/jazz clubs were now booking English blues acts on "off nights" but...

    1.) These clubs were starting to express their ire over the loud, electric sounds invading their clubs.

    2.) <u>Needed</u>: a central club completely devoted to electric blues.

        - Which could also serve as a magnet for UK blues musicians to interact and perform.

    3.) <u>Solution:</u> a new London venue entitled: <u>The Ealing Club</u> would become the nexus for the British blues movement.

        - <u>Alexis Korner</u> (b. Alexis Koerner 4/19/28, Paris, FRA d. 1/1/84, London): an electric blues guitarist for his band, "<u>Blues Incorporated</u>" was the founder of the club.

            * In fact, the British blues movement would have never developed the way it did without the initiative and vision of Alexis Korner.

                a.) For this reason, he stands among the most important of rock and roll influences who were not rockers by trade.

    4.) It was at The Ealing Club, where a new blues-based band would form.

        - <u>Brian Jones</u>, a former guitarist with Blues Incorporated, met up with Michael Jagger and Keith Richards and formed: <u>The Rolling Stones</u>.

C.) <u>The Rolling Stones</u>: started as a group whose initial policy was to perform authentic Chicago blues.

    1.) Emulating Muddy Waters, Howlin' Wolf, Jimmy Reed, Willie Dixon, etc.

        - They began be covering these artists

    2.) Their one major limitation: they lacked a fluid, virtuoso lead guitarist.

        - An irony of sorts for the key element of electric blues after all, was a fluid lead melodic solo line on the electric guitar.

    3.) Sometimes, the key to originality rests on turning disadvantage into advantage.

        - For the Rolling Stones, their disadvantage was complemented by their tight rhythm section:

            * <u>Brian Jones</u> and <u>Keith Richards</u>: two top-flight rhythm guitar aces.

            * <u>Charley Watts</u> and <u>Bill Wyman</u>: a great underlying rhythm support force.

        - These four equated to a first rate rhythm machine which supported Mick Jagger's vocals.

            * They focused mainly on Bo Diddley/Chuck Berry/Jimmy Reed types of rhythmically based blues/R&B covers.

                a.) This rhythmic emphasis would eventually lead the Stones in a direction different from their early blues counterparts.

D.) <u>The Animals</u> (from Newcastle) and <u>Them</u> (from Belfast, Northern Ireland): both had great ensemble styles themselves.

    1.) Backing up blues tested singers: <u>Eric Burdon</u> from The Animals and <u>Van (George Ivan) Morrison</u> of Them.

E.) <u>The Yardbirds</u>: unlike The Rolling Stones, The Animals, and Them:

    1.) The Yardbirds' musical approach was <u>improvisation</u>.

        - The first of their three great lead guitarists was <u>Eric Clapton</u>.

            * Because of Clapton's virtuosity, The Yardbirds would be the first band to transform the electric guitarist:

                a.) from sideman to front-and-center star.

    2.) Original Personnel (1963): <u>Keith Relf</u> (vocals, harmonica), <u>Chris Dreja</u> (rhythm guitar), <u>Paul Samwell-Smith</u> (bass), <u>Jim McCarty</u> (drums), and <u>Anthony "Top" Topham</u> (lead guitar).

        - Anthony Topham's tenure with The Yardbirds was very brief because at the age of 16, his parents pressured him to leave the group.

            * <u>Eric Clapton</u> (b. Eric Clapp, 3/30/45, Ripley, ENG): a friend of Keith

Relf at art college, replaced Topham.

3.) At the time, Clapton was emulating electric blues legend <u>Freddy King</u>.

- This act of emulating King would inadvertently result in an original sound for Clapton.

* One of his earliest great examples was a song called: "<u>Got To Hurry</u>" featuring an extended King-influenced electric blues guitar solo in the song's beginning.

a.) but, with Clapton's original essence within a group context.

4.) <u>Paul Samwell-Smith</u> (bass): would guide the group along with improvised tempo changes.

- Gradually accelerating the musical speed up to a temponic climax called "<u>Rave Up</u>"…

* Then, gradually relaxing the tempo.

5.) Underlying the improvisations of gradual tempo shifts and extended lead guitar solos…

- The band generally followed two basic blues structures:

* <u>Lyrical</u>: a, a, b form for each stanza.

* <u>Musical</u>: I, IV, V chord progression.

- On the one hand, they were practicing structural tradition.

* On the other, they were venturing "outside of the box".

a.) Stretching the musical language above a traditional I, IV, V blues format.

- The support that this traditional blues structure gave, allowed them to experiment with the material hovering above it.

* thereby sending blues-derived revisionism in a new direction.

6.) Clapton's tenure with The Yardbirds was brief due to the group's desire to record a light weight "pop" tune in order to attract some much needed notoriety.

- which in turn, could lead to better bookings.

* "<u>For Your Love</u>": a pop tune featuring a harpsichord in the accompaniment.

a.) Clapton was so infuriated by what he felt was a "sell-out" that he quit the group.

b.) He wanted to delve deeper into the blues and the rest of the band wanted to lighten up in a pop direction.

7.) There would however, another single that, rather than "sell-out"…

- would instead, unleash the grit of the British blues revisionism while simultaneously topping the pop charts.

* Both in Britain and in America.

F.) <u>The Animals</u>: their first big break was a slot on the Chuck Berry tour (1964) and, as Eric Burdon once said that "everyone's going to try to out-rock Chuck Berry"…

1.) They would instead, play a slower song in a minor key with a catchy tune that would be different from all of the rest of the songs.

- which they hoped would "stick in peoples' memories".

* It worked.

2.) "<u>The Rising Sun Blues</u>": an old country blues song written by John A. & Alan Lomax and recorded by Woody Guthrie.

- The Animals recorded their own arrangement and called it: "<u>House Of The Rising Sun</u>" (1964). Modeled on Bob Dylan's version from his debut album.

* It became the first British blues hit in America.

a.) This song opened the door for other British blues songs to follow and gain wide US acceptance.

3.) Initially, it was The Beatles' invasion of the US that was crucial to opening up the doors for English blues acts to follow.

G.) <u>The Rolling Stones</u>: took advantage of that opening. Their musical style was undergoing a change.

1.) Which was due in part, to their focus on rhythm.

- A byproduct of their early performance style.

2.) Within this context, The Rolling Stones established the following:
- Jones/Richards: were not the first rhythm section with a tight ensemble style.
* But their dovetailing of different guitar grooves into an effective, riff-laden counterpoint, gave visibility on a wide scale...
a.) ...to the artistic value and accessibility of great riff-craft.
* Backed up by the tight rhythmic mechanism of Bill Wyman (bass) and Charley Watts on the drums. (This example would become influential to scores of other bands across the US).

3.) Mick Jagger: Even though there were other lead singing front men in other bands at the time including Eric Burdon of The Animals...
- As well as the formulaic "British invasion" pop bands like Herman's Hermits, Manfred Mann, The Zombies, etc.
* Mick Jagger gave the lead singer/front man scenario, the highest and most prolonged exposure.
* He presented himself as a raw, more sexier, rough-shod, "bad boy" alternative to the mop-top, clean-cut image of The Beatles (for Jagger, it was part of his blues influences to be raw in nature).
- RESULT: Mick Jagger would provide the long term modal for the rock and roll lead singer/front man which would lead to many imitators.

4.) Since establishing themselves as icons throughout the civilized world, their longevity would present them as the most visible band in rock and roll history.
- Long after The Beatles, Jimi Hendrix, and Led Zeppelin have disappeared from the scene.

H.) The Rolling Stones: a brief background.
1.) Brian Jones and Charlie Watts: played for Alexis Korner's "Blues Incorporated" at the Ealing Club in London.
- Mick Jagger eventually became their lead singer.

2.) The original Rolling Stones:
- Mick Jagger (b. Michael Phillip Jagger, 7/26/43, Dartford, ENG): vocals.
- Keith Richards (b. 12/18/43, Dartford): guitar, vocals.
- Brian Jones (b. Lewis Brian Hopkins-Jones, 2/28/42, Cheltenham, d. 7/3/69, London): guitar.
- Mick Avory (b. 2/15/44, London): drums.
- Dick Taylor: bass, Ian Stewart: keyboards.
- "The Rolling Stones": named after a title of a Muddy Waters tune: "Rollin Stone".
* Their debut performance: July 12, 1962 at the Marquee Club in London.
a.) Shortly thereafter, Bill Wyman (b. William Perks, 10/24/36, London):
- would replace Dick Taylor on the bass.
b.) Charlie Watts (b. 6/2/41, Islington):
- would replace Mick Avory on the drums (who left the band to join "The Kinks").

3.) The Crawdaddy Club: where they built their first original fan base.
- After which Andrew Loog Oldham would become their manager.
* A talented promoter who came up with the idea of marketing the Rolling Stones as the "Anti-Beatles" "Bad Boy" alternative.
a.) He also insisted on firing Ian Stewart for being too heavy set which would not fit into the modal that he [Oldham] had envisioned.
- Stewart would remain with the Stones as a roadie and keyboardist on Rolling Stones' recordings until his death in (1985).
* Oldham also got them signed to Decca Records.

a.) under the Abkco subsidiary.

4.) The Rolling Stones' initial singles were mostly blues covers.

- Chuck Berry's: "Come On" (1963) - reached #21 on the pop charts.
- The Beatles': "I Wanna Be Your Man" (1963) - #15.

Not Fade Away
The Rolling Stones

- Buddy Holly's: "Not Fade Away" (1964) - #3.
   * From their 1964 debut album: "The Rolling Stones (England's Newest Hitmakers).

a.) Their first US hit climbing to #48.

5.) In 1964, The Rolling Stones were beginning to gain notoriety for their bad-boy/Beatles rivalry persona.

It's All Over Now
The Rolling Stones

- Their second album: "12 x 5 "(1964), included their first #1 hit in the UK: "It's All Over Now".
- Summer of 1964: during their first US tour, they recorded their first EP at Chess Studios entitled: "5 x 5".
   * Definition of EP (Extended Play) : A 10 inch, 45 rpm vinyl record containing 4 to 6 songs:

a.) Artists release an EP when they do not have enough new songs to fill an album but more than a side A/side B single.

6.) By the time their first US tour ended in 1965, their third album: "Rolling Stones Now" was released.

- Resulting in their second, #1 hit in England.
   * Howlin' Wolf's "Little Red Rooster".

7.) Andrew Loog Oldham's publishing company was making little profit from the Rolling Stones consistently doing covers. In order to turn a greater profit, he encouraged them to start composing their own music.

- "Tell Me (You're Coming Back)" (1964): their first original single and also their first US top 40 hit….
   … featured on their debut album, "The Rolling Stones (England's Newest Hitmakers)".
- "Time Is On My Side" (1964): written by Irma Thomas
   * Their first US top 10 hit from the "12 x 5" album.

The Last Time
The Rolling Stones

- "The Last Time" (1965): #1 in the UK, Top 10 US,
   * Began a string of hits -- where their new, original riff-craft style became honed in.
   * Ingredients of the new riff-craft style:

a.) A repetitive, catchy guitar riff that gave the song instant accessibility.
   - Brain Jones would usually play the repeated riff and Keith Richards strummed the chords giving the repetitive riff solid harmonic support.
b.) Mick Jagger's catchy pop tunesmithism.
   - Adding another instantly memorable tune atop of the already catchy, repeated guitar riff.
c.) Catchy, easily memorable choruses/refrains.
   - Usually, the chorus/refrain carries the title of the song (giving it more focus) and, it is normally performed by vocal harmonization.

(I Can't Get No)
Satisfaction
The Rolling Stones

   * "Satisfaction" (1965): first #1 hit in the US (4 weeks).
a.) The hit that made them superstars.
b.) Featured a repetitive fuzz guitar riff to mimic a horn section - which became the hook. (both "Time Is On My Side" and "Satisfaction" are on the "Out of Our Heads (US)" album of 1965).

8.) "(I Can't Get No) Satisfaction": solidified the new Rolling Stones songwriting, signature formula:

- a repeated blues influenced riff split between the two rhythm guitars backing up Mick Jagger's easily memorable vocal lines.

I.) <u>Next Two Years</u>: a list of top ten singles.

    1.) <u>Song</u>   <u>Album</u>

"Get Off Of My Cloud"

"As Tears Go By"   <u>December's Children (And Everybody's)</u> (1965)

"19th Nervous Breakdown"   <u>Big Hits: High Tide & Green Grass</u> (1966)

" Have You Seen Your Mother Lately Baby Standing In The Shadows" (recorded in 1965)   <u>Flowers</u> (1967)

IV. 1966: AN IMPORTANT YEAR FOR ALBUMS

(<u>Note</u>: Even though the album format rose to a level of artistic importance in 1965, 1966 produced some of the most important, seminal albums in rock and roll.)

    A.) "<u>Aftermath</u>": The Rolling Stones' first album to be completely composed of original songs.

        1.) A major turning point.

            - was also a response to the ingenuity The Beatles' "<u>Revolver</u>" (not the last time they would respond to a Beatles album).

                * "<u>Their Satanic Majesty's Request</u>" (11/67): their response to The Beatles' "Sgt. Pepper's Lonely Hearts Club Band" album.

        2.) This album also marks the blossoming of Brian Jones' eclecticism.

Paint It Black
The Rolling Stones

            - He would use various instrumental colors most of which were not indigenous to rock and roll.

                * "<u>Paint It Black</u>" (Sitar), "<u>Under My Thumb</u>" (Marimba), "<u>Lady Jane</u>" (Dulcimer).

Under
My Thumb
The Rolling Stones

        3.) "<u>Aftermath</u>" would also solidify one branch of the direction of British blues revisionism -- pop riff-craft:

            - that would eventually lead to a more blues traditionalist sound for the Stones in the late 60's/ early 70's.

    B.) "<u>Roger, The Engineer</u>": through this album, The Yardbirds would solidify the other branch of blues revisionism to a completely new direction of blues "distortionism" (as opposed to traditionalism).

        1.) The Key: their new guitarist: <u>Jeff Beck</u> (b. 6/24/44, Surrey, ENG).

            - He was not the blues purist that Eric Clapton was (although he too, had developed his style by covering American blues legends).

                * As a result, he was open to experimentation which would prove crucial to the evolution of the "distortion' line of blues revisionism.

        2.) His experimental properties:

            - Dive-bomber runs, harmonic sustain, fuzz-tone, feedback, and explosions.

                * Expressive techniques that superseded musical notation. Because he didn't read music, Jeff Beck used an expressive arsenal that could not be expressed in that [notated] manner.

                    a.) He would instead, use these noise-laden sounds to express emotional intensity in his own way.

Lost Woman
The Yardbirds

        3.) Perhaps most noticeable in this particular album: the use of amplitude-laden chords (or power chords) as a main thematic element.

            - As opposed to one line riffs.

              * "<u>The Nazz Are Blue</u>" is an example.

The Nazz
Are Blue
The Yardbirds

                    a.) Opens with loud, repeated guitar chords as the hook.

                        - alternating with single lines breaks/solos.

                    b.) Guitar solo in the middle of the song: features a long, one-note harmonic sustain that is panned from one speaker to the other.

                      - Then returns to the thematic power chords. Then alternates into an extended, blues derived guitar solo.

- This style of power chord-laden thematic material is the first harbinger of what would later become known as "Heavy Metal".
4.) For the reasons previously mentioned, this album marked a pivotal point where a new paradigm was beginning.
- That power chord, amplitude-laden guitars will gradually distort the original blues influences into a music totally different and unprecedented.
C.) "John Mayall's Bluesbreakers Featuring Eric Clapton" (1966)
1.) Clapton's first major blues project following The Yardbirds.
2.) A continuation of his blues "purism"…
- Example: "Have You Ever Loved A Woman?"
* A Freddie King influenced extended guitar solo in the opening of the song.

Have You Ever Loved A Woman (Live)
John Mayall's
Bluesbreakers

a.) Again, in the act of emulation, he managed to convey an original sound.
3.) Clapton's association with The Bluesbreakers (like The Yardbirds) was very brief.
- He would go on to start a new band that would inadvertently continue the distorted blues paradigm started by Jeff Beck.

IV. THE ADVENT OF HIGH ENERGY, SUPER-CHARGED BLUES REVISIONISM
A.) Eric Clapton: decided to start a new band devoted to emulating traditional American blues.
1.) He finds two other players:
- Jack Bruce (b. 5/14/43, Glasgow, Scotland): bass.
* Former Alexis Korner player with jazz leanings.
a.) Very adept at improvisation.
- Ginger Baker (b. Peter Baker, 8/19/39, Lewisham, ENG): drums, vocals.
* Another of the Alexis Korner players who also had jazz improvisation influences.
a.) And with it, great improvisational skills and an aggressive style.
2.) A new element added to the new mix: amplitude.
- Featuring a wall of Marshall amplifiers.
* Resulting in an amplitude-laden, loud sound.
3.) A New Influence On Eric Clapton: Albert King – the great blues guitarist from St. Louis, MO.

Answer To The Laudromat Blues
Albert King

- His stylistic focus: a unique and highly focused electric guitar sound that carried a sense of presence. In other words, he made the guitar "sing".
* This focus on the unique sound with slower rhythms made up for the absence of highly rhythmic, virtuostic ornamentation.
a.) Eric Clapton would emulate the Albert King focus on sound during his tenure with The Cream.

Strange Brew
The Cream

* Case in Point: compare the opening of Albert King's guitar solo in "Laundromat Blues" with the guitar solo in The Cream's "Strange Brew".
a.) Clapton's emulation of Albert King is evident.
- In the act of emulating Albert King, Eric Clapton, in he context of The Cream's " heavy blues", sounded original.
B.) RESULT: The Cream (formed in 1966): rock and roll's first "Power Trio".
1.) Strategy: all players would usually be in sync with one another (playing a pre-conceived arrangement) during the verse portions of a song.
- However, during the extended guitar solo/improvisation section:
* All three players would simultaneously improvise in a rhythmically aggressive manner.
a.) And all with a very loud, heavy and somewhat distorted sound.
2.) RESULT: a new style called: "Heavy Blues".

Cross Road Blues
 Robert Johnson

Crossroads
 The Cream

    - <u>Example</u>: The Cream would do a revisionist version of a Robert Johnson classic.

        * "<u>Crossroads Blues</u>" (recorded in 1928): a country blues tune for voice and acoustic guitar.

        * "<u>Crossroads</u>" – The Cream (1967): a wildly electric, amplitude-laden distorted version of the original song.

C.) In the fall of 1966, Eric Clapton invited a guest artist to play a set with The Cream at a gig at the London Polytechnic Institute.

    1.) When he saw this artist perform, he immediately realized he had met his match.

<u>V. JIMI HENDRIX</u> (b. 11/27/42, Seattle, WA; d. 9/18/70, London): The guitarist who appeared on stage with The Cream in that Fall '66 concert.

    A.) He started out as a sideman for The Isley Brothers, Little Richard, and King Curtis.

    B.) <u>Background</u>: The Animals were breaking up in the summer of 1966.

        1.) However, they decided that in the interest of fulfilling their contractual obligations in the US that fall:

          - They would remain together until their obligations were complete.

            * Which meant one last US tour.

        2.) <u>Bryan "Chas" Chandler</u> (bass): decided he was going to delve into artist management.

          - He arrived in America (New York City) several weeks ahead of the band to see a woman he was dating at the time.

          - They went to a nightclub in Greenwich Village called, "<u>The Café Wha</u>?" to see a guitarist who arranged pick-up bands that day.

            * The first song Jimi Hendrix played was his arrangement of "<u>Hey Joe</u>".

              a.) A song Chandler's girlfriend introduced to him earlier that was recorded by a folk artist (he had planned to arrange a cover of this song made upon his return to England).

        3.) After being blown away by Hendrix's performance, Chandler offered to become his [Hendrix's] manager.

          - And take Hendrix back to England with him (he accepted on the condition that he [Chandler] would introduce him to Jeff Beck).

    C.) <u>Hendrix's Influences</u>:

        1.) <u>Earl King</u> (b. Earl Silas Johnson, New Orleans, LA, 2/7/34, d. 4/17/03): an early pioneer in exploring the sonic resources of the electric guitar's upper register.

          - Jimi Hendrix emulated King's upper-register explorations.

            * Hendix recorded an Earl King classic: "Come On".

        2.) <u>Johnny Jenkins</u> (b. 7/8/24, d. 4/17/05): known for his flamboyant, onstage guitar acrobatics.

          - He could play the electric guitar behind his head, pick the guitar with his teeth, etc.

            * Hendrix first saw him perform during a concert in Johnson's hometown of Macon, GA.

              a.) Hendrix emulated Johnson's performance style acrobatics in his own unique way (which became part of his [Hendrix's] legend.)

        3.) <u>Jeff Beck</u>: As mentioned earlier, Jeff Beck introduced his expressive arsenal of electric guitar noises to British blues revisionism such as feedback, harmonic sustain, etc.

          - Hendrix would emulate these as well.

            * He also borrowed various riffs from Jeff Beck's music.

        4.) RESULT: The upper guitar-register influence of Earl King, the flamboyant performance style inspired by Johnny Johnson, and the noise elements inspired by Jeff Beck, became the bedrock of Jimi Hendrix's style.

          - He blended these influences together and created his own unique stylistic signature that set him apart from his peers.

            * And is still unique today.

D.) Britain would mark the beginning of the Hendrix phenomena.

> 1.) Chandler would solicit a rhythm guitar player, <u>Noel Redding</u> to play the bass in Hendrix's first jam session in England.
>> - Chandler would also solicit <u>Mitch Mitchell</u> for the drums.
>>> * Mitchell: had a very aggressive, highly polyrhythmic style that was mainly influenced by drummer <u>Elvin Jones</u>, John Coltrane's drummer (Ginger Baker was also influenced by him).
>
> 2.) RESULT: <u>The Jimi Hendrix Experience</u> – rock and roll's other great power trio of the late 60's.

E.) <u>Hendrix's Playing Style</u>: a unique way of playing both lead and rhythm guitar at the same time.

> 1.) Normally, on a bar chord (a type of chord used by rhythm guitarists), the index finger on the guitar neck hand stops all of the strings at once.
>> - This type of hand position can only facilitate the playing of that chord only.
>
> 2.) Hendrix however, would stop the strings normally reserved for a bar chord with his thumb.
>> - Because of his big hands, he could easily position his thumb over the top side of the guitar neck (thumb pointing downward) to stop the strings.
>>> * Thereby leaving his remaining fingers in a perfect position to play lead riffs on the bottom three strings (which are the higher register melodic strings).
>
> 3.) <u>RESULT</u>: Jimi Hendrix could play lead and rhythm guitar and sing simultaneously on stage in a very overt manner.
>> - making him the consummate front-man.
>>> * By giving the front-man/guitarist persona, the most visibility (the same that Mick Jagger did for the front-man/lead singer).

F.) His debut album: "<u>Are You Experienced</u>" (1967).

> 1.) It featured three top ten hits in the UK.
>> - "<u>Hey Joe</u>", <u>Purple Haze</u>", and "<u>The Wind Cries Mary</u>".
>
> 2.) He made his name first in Britain before returning to the US.

Manic Depression
The Jimi Hendrix
Experience

>> - He became an overnight sensation in America due to his performance at the Monterey Pop Festival in June of 1967.
>>> * He received a lot of press coverage not for his music, but for smashing and burning his guitar on stage using lighter fluid.

G.) In the two years that The Jimi Hendrix Experience was together, they released only three albums.

Fire
The Jimi Hendrix
Experience

> 1.) "<u>Are You Experienced</u>"(1967), "<u>Axis, Bold As Love</u>"(1967), and "<u>Electric Ladyland</u>"(1968)
>
> 2.) It's worth noting that Hendrix's unique musical style:
>> - Was fueled in great part by the rhythm section of Noel Redding and Mitch Mitchell. They provided a highly energized support that Hendrix fed brilliantly off of.
>>> * But he would never be able to recapture that super-charged style when he performed with "<u>Band Of Gypsies</u>" starting in 1969.
>>>> a.) With Buddy Miles (drums) and Billy Cox (bass).
>>>> b.) They released one live album: "<u>Band Of Gypsies</u>" (1970).
>
> 3.) <u>The Experience</u> reformed briefly in early 1970.
>> - After which Hendrix formed his last group with Mitch Mitchell and Billy Cox.
>>> * He had not recorded another studio album since "<u>Electric Ladyland</u>" in 1968.
>>>> a.) He was in the process of recording a new studio project when he died of a drug overdose in London on September 18th of 1970.

VI. THE ROLLING STONES' NEW DIRECTION

   A.) At approximately the same time that Hendrix was at his musical peak.

      1.) The Rolling Stones were debuting a stand-in for Brian Jones.

         - Jones' behavior was becoming increasingly erratic due to his heavy abuse of alcohol and drugs.

            * The new person was <u>Mick Taylor</u> (b. 1/17/48, Hertfordshire, ENG):

               a.) The first true lead guitarist for the Rolling Stones.

                 - He got his start, playing for John Mayall's Bluesbreakers.

      2.) Mick Taylor's contribution to The Stones' traditional roots/blues paradigm would result in arguably, two of the best Stones albums ever: "<u>Sticky Fingers</u>" (1971) and "<u>Exile On Main Street</u>" (1972).

         - But this new direction of a more traditional blues influence had begun before the start of Taylor's involvement with the group.

   B.) "<u>Beggar's Banquet</u>" (1968): would mark in earnest, the beginning of the Stones' new direction.

      1.) Songs such as "<u>Salt Of The Earth</u>" and "<u>No Expectations</u>" marked a turn to the Mississippi Delta blues influence.

No Expectations
The Rolling Stones

         - "<u>Street Fighting Man</u>": on the other hand, was a straight forward rock and roll tune that was radio friendly (to help sell the album).

Street Fighting Man
The Rolling Stones

         - "<u>Sympathy For The Devil</u>": the first cut on the album with the shape of things to come.

            * Traditional African rhythm influences with a blues-inspired occultist obsession.

               a.) And a biting guitar solo in the middle.

      2.) This album also marked the beginning of the end for Brian Jones.

         - Because of his problems stemming from drug and alcohol abuse, he was absent for some of this album's recording sessions.

            * It is assumed that he did play the slide guitar in "<u>No Expectations</u>".

   C.) "<u>Let It Bleed</u>" (1969): Brian Jones' last album with The Rolling Stones.

      1.) He was only on two cuts: "<u>Midnight Rambler</u>" (percussion) and "<u>You Got The Silver</u>" (autoharp).

         - On July 4th, 1969 Brian Jones was found dead floating face-down in his swimming pool (coroner's report: "Death by misadventure").

      2.) This album also marked the debut of his eventual replacement: <u>Mick Taylor</u> (he would become a full-fledged member following the death of Brian Jones).

Country Honk
The Rolling Stones

         - "<u>Country Honk</u>" (slide guitar): Mick Taylor's rendition adds to the traditional country blues influence.

            * This song would later be released in it's revised version as "<u>Honky Tonk Woman</u>" (1970) without Taylor in the line-up.

Live With Me
The Rolling Stones

         - "<u>Live With Me</u>": Both Taylor and Keith Richards play rhythm guitar.

            * They play in rhythmic counterpoint with one another – especially during the verses.

         - Like Brian Jones, Mick Taylor only appears on two cuts.

      3.) For the entire album, there was a collaborative effort with mostly American artists who espoused blues/roots traditions in rock and roll. Their influences greatly added to this album's eclecticism.

         <u>Mary Clayton</u>: singer ("Gimme Shelter")

         <u>Ian Stewart</u>: piano ("Let It Bleed")

         <u>Bobby Keys</u>: tenor Saxophone ("Live With Me")

         <u>Jimmy Miller</u>: percussion ("Gimme Shelter")

         <u>Ry Cooder</u>: mandolin

         <u>Byron Berline</u>: country fiddle

         <u>Leon Russell</u>: piano (wrote the horn arrangement in "Live With Me")

         <u>Nicky Hopkins</u>: piano/organ

         <u>Al Kooper</u>: organ and French Horn ("You Can't Always Get What You Want")

         <u>The London Bach Choir</u> ("You Can't Always Get What You Want")

D.) "<u>Sticky Fingers</u>" (1971): Mick Taylor's second album as a full-fledged member (his first was "Get Yer Ya-Ya's Out" (1970) but it was a live album).

      1.) For Taylor, this was the first Stones album where his guitar solos/leads are heard throughout the entire format of original songs created for this album.

Sway
The Rolling Stones

        - The traditional electric blues influences are becoming more pronounced due to Mick Taylor's blues-derived solos.

Can't You Hear Me Knocking
The Rolling Stones

        * "<u>Sway</u>" (2:40 into the song which lasts to the end), <u>Can't You Hear Me Knocking</u>" (4:40 into the song), "<u>Bitch</u>", "<u>Dead Flowers</u>", and "<u>Moonlight Mile</u>"

        a.) solos and breaks in the electric blues tradition.

E.) "<u>Exile On Main Street</u>" (1972): arguably, The Rolling Stones' greatest artistic achievement (a 2 album set).

      1.) Mick Taylor's electric slide sound, reminiscent of country influences, is added to his eclectic blues vocabulary.

Torn And Frayed
The Rolling Stones

        - "<u>Torn And Frayed</u>" (at 1:43 into the song) and "<u>Stop Breaking Down</u>" (at 1:19) are examples.

      2.) Their last album to delve deeply into the American blues/country/roots influences.

Stop Breaking Down
The Rolling Stones

        - starting with their next album: "<u>Goats Head Soup</u>" (1973), the Rolling Stones would move in a more pop-oriented direction.

      3.) Nevertheless, while British blues revisionists were busy distorting their blues influences on a gradually greater scale.

        - The Rolling Stones – from "Beggar's Banquet" to "Exile On Main Street"…

          * were busy re-injecting traditional roots/blues sounds back into their brand of revisionism.

F.) Mick Taylor's last album with the Stones was: "<u>Oh No! It's Only Rock and Roll</u>" (1974).

      1.) He wanted to pursue a solo career.

      2.) He was eventually replaced by <u>Ron Wood</u> formerly, of Rod Stewart's band: "<u>Faces</u>".

        - The Ron Wood era would usher in more metal to the Stones' pop structure.

      3.) According to most aficionados, their last great album was "<u>Some Girls</u>" (1978).

        - Their remaining albums, "<u>Tattoo You</u>" included rejected cuts from prior album sessions.

          * Their albums later on, would become surface-y, over-produced affairs.

            a.) They would never again create with the artistry and bluesy flare that they did up to 1972 (with the exception of "Some Girls").

G.) Insofar as the "<u>Distortionist</u>" line (the other line) of blues revisionism, the legacy for this was already well in place by the time The Stones released "Exile".

      1.) But to track what lead to this legacy, there is one more group to discuss that would usher it in.

VII. LED ZEPPELIN: THE CONTINUATION OF THE DISTORTIONIST PARADIGM

A.) Originally, to be named "<u>The New Yardbirds</u>".

      1.) <u>Jimmy Page</u> (b. James Patrick Page, 1/9/44, Heston, ENG): became the third lead guitarist of the Yardbirds replacing Jeff Beck.

      2.) <u>Summer of 1968</u>: Keith Relf (vocals) and Jim McCarty (drums) left the band.

        - Leaving Jimmy Page and Chris Dreja, the rights to the "Yardbirds" name.

      3.) Jimmy Page solicited singer, <u>Terry Reid</u> to replace Keith Relf and drummer <u>P.J. Wilson</u> (of "Procal Harum") to replace McCarty.

        - Both were unable to do so.

          * Reid consequently suggested <u>Robert Plant</u> (b. 9/20/48, Bromwich, ENG) who, at the time was in a band called, "Hobbsteedle"

a.) He [Plant] would suggest <u>John "Bonzo" Bonham</u> (b. John Henry Bonham, 5/31/48, Redditch, ENG, d. 9/25/80, Windsor):

- ...to join the group as their new drummer.

- In August of 1968: Chris Dreja left the group to pursue another project.

* He was replaced by <u>John Paul Jones</u> (b. John Baldwin, 1/3/46, Sidcup, ENG).

4.) <u>The New Yardbirds</u>: fulfilled previously booked engagements in September of 1968.

5.) In October, they went into the studio to record their first album together.

- under their new name: "<u>Led Zeppelin</u>".

B.) <u>Led Zeppelin's Style</u>: Their contribution to the development of British Blues Revisionism.

1.) More Distortion: In the distortionist line initially laid out by The Yardbirds (with Jeff Beck), and The Cream...

- ...Led Zeppelin distorted their original blues influences even further.

2.) Stylistic Elements:

- <u>Texture</u>: A more thickly textured, chordal sound as opposed to superimposing different solo melodic lines over one another (i.e. single bassline, single guitar line, etc.).

* With amplitude-laden harmonic chords carrying the main thematic instrumental tunes.

- <u>Rapid-Fire Guitar Solos</u>: Many of Jimmy Page's electric guitar solos are performed in rapid tempos with his fingers move from one note to the other at blinding speed.

* This fast-moving virtuosity was something the original blues guitarists never encompassed.

- <u>Eclecticism</u>: The addition of outside elements into the distorted blues revisionist mix.

* Indian and Arabic scales/modes.

* Celtic influences.

* Folk influences.

- In some of their singles, both folk and metal elements are featured (in the same single).

a.) "Stairway To Heaven" was one such example..

- <u>All-Riff</u>: Where all band members are simultaneously performing the same melodic line (i.e. riff) -- sometimes in different octaves -- or the same melodic rhythm [of a line].

* Most effective in a thickly textured, chordal context.

C.) "<u>Led Zeppelin I</u>" (1969): featured a "heavy blues" sound in the tradition of The Cream although with some differences.

1.) A more heavy, amplitude-laden chord sound or a chord riff.

2.) More rhythmically vibrant guitar solos and breaks.

- A distorted version of traditional electric blues.

* With a harsher electric sound.

3.) <u>Robert Plant</u>: he emulated the country blues twang of Robert Johnson in his own [Plant's] revisionist manner.

D.) "<u>Led Zeppelin II</u>" (1969): begins with a harshly distorted version of Willie Dixon's Chess recording of "<u>You Need Love</u>".

Whole Lotta
Love
Led Zeppelin

1.) Renamed, "<u>Whole Lotta Love</u>".

- Presented in a thickly textured, amplitude-ladened chordal context.

2.) Within this album, Jimmy Page added some additional elements to his revisionist mix.

- Putting both folk and heavy blues – 2 contrasting elements -- in the same song.

* which added a stark sense of variety in a singles format.

a.) An example: "<u>What Is And What Should Never Be</u>".

3.) Also, this album solidified their signature style: a heavy, amplitude-laden chordal riff (instead of a single line) as the main musical element of the song.

4.) <u>Rapid-Fire Guitar Solo</u>: At the 2-minute mark in the track, "Heartbreaker", Jimmy Page delivers an electric guitar solo with rapid, rhythmic speed.

Heartbreaker
Led Zeppelin

- Virtuosity on an unparalleled scale.
* A distorted rendition of the original blue artists' guitar solos (which were all rhythmically slow by comparison).

E.) "<u>Led Zeppelin IV</u>" (1971): shows more examples of heavy power chord elements as main riff ideas (a good example is the song: "<u>Rock And Roll</u>").

1.) At this time, Jimmy Page was adding Indian, Arabic, and Celtic scales/modes to his mix.

Battle Of Evermore
Led Zeppelin

- "<u>Battle Of Evermore</u>": has traditional Irish/Celtic folk influences in the guitar accompaniment.
* Backing up Robert Plant's vocal line.

When The Levee Breaks
Led Zeppelin

2.) "<u>When The Levee Breaks</u>": a Chicago blues influenced harmonica style accompanied by a heavy blues-laden texture.
- and a heavy, John Bonham-styled beat.

3.) "<u>Stairway To Heaven</u>": an artistic composition as opposed to a song.
- Contains both folk and heavy blues styles (highly contrasting).
- Also features a gradual increase in tempo.
* Starts off slowly and gradually increases in speed and intensity until the very end when, a sudden contrast of Plant's solo line: "And she's buying the stairway to Heaven", is presented.
a.) A very effective technique: stark contrast.

4.) This album presents the heaviest blues yet of this distorted revisionist tradition.

F.) "<u>Houses Of The Holy</u>" (1973): continuation of the heavy blues sound with all of the other aforesaid elements.

1.) The heavy blues idiom taken to the limit.
- Featuring their signature "all-riff" style.

The Ocean
Led Zeppelin

* "<u>All-Riff</u>": where every band member is simultaneously playing the same exact riff.
a.) Resulting in a simultaneous, thick musical texture.
- Example: "<u>The Ocean</u>"

VIII. LEGACY: WHERE DO WE GO FROM HERE?

A.) British blues revisionism from a distorted development paradigm.
1.) Produced some great virtuoso who put the lead guitarist in the spotlight.
- At a time where rock and roll audiences were obtaining sophisticated musical tastes nurtured by the artistry of these players.
* They [the players] turned blues inspired rock and roll into a serious form of art.

B.) <u>Problem</u>: it was difficult for the next generation of guitarists to emulate on a wide scale.
1.) They were not the dedicated blues aficionados that their predecessors were. In fact, they [the next generation] knew very little of the blues.
- As a result, they lacked the chops needed to play these technically demanding, blues-derived leads.
*they had no material – with a long and rich tradition like the blues -- to cover, that would elevate their playing skills to a virtuoso level.

C.) <u>Solution</u>: Lack of playing ability can force one to be resourceful.
1.) In other words, limitations or lack of ability can, by absolute necessity, lead to originality.
- The plan to originality: take something that was originally difficult:
* And streamline (or simplify) it.

D.) <u>Case-In-Point</u>: "Black Sabbath"
1.) They would the first to greatly simplify the heavy blues style into a musical form that would be easy for other artists following them, to emulate.
2.) <u>The Key</u>: "All-Riff", where every band member is simultaneously playing the same exact riff.

- Some players, like the bass, will play the melodic part of the riff an octave below the others.
- The drummer plays the exact same rhythm as the others.
- Even the singer performs the same riff in concert with the rest of the band.
    * The heavy blues, chord-laden texture of Led Zeppelin was the genus of this technique.
- Add fuzz-tone and feedback.

3.) <u>RESULT</u>: A style that would become known, as "<u>Heavy Metal</u>".

4.) <u>Tony Iommi</u>: the lead guitar player for Black Sabbath. Robert Palmer once wrote that Iommi was the most widely imitated rock and roll guitarist of all time.
- Because his and Black Sabbath's style in general, was easy for practically any band or guitarist to copy.
    * When something is easy to emulate, it spreads like wildfire.

5.) Mostly all of the formulaic bands in the wake of Black Sabbath came onto the heavy Metal scene in the early 70's.
- "<u>Deep Purple</u>", "<u>Foghat</u>", "<u>Aerosmith</u>", "<u>Grand Funk Railroad</u>", "<u>Kiss</u>", etc.

6.) 80's legacy:
- "<u>Def Leppard</u>", "<u>Van Halen</u>", "<u>Loverboy</u>", "<u>AC/DC</u>", etc.
    * And the so-called "Hair Bands" of the 80's & 90's: "<u>Poison</u>", "<u>Slayer</u>", "<u>Ratt</u>", etc. (a.k.a. "Cock Rock" bands).

E.) As extensive as British blues revisionism was with it's style and heavy metal legacy:
1.) It wasn't the only blues revisionism in town (so to speak).
- There was one other with a completely different "prism" from which the blues influence would filter through.
    * Resulting in a completely different, unsuspecting legacy of it's own...

CHAPTER V: REVIEW

Name the six reasons why white, middle class, British art school students found black American blues so attractive:
    1.)
    2.)
    3.)
    4.)
    5.)
    6.)

What type of artist (instrumentalist) did British blues revisionism transform from a sideman to a front and center virtuoso icon?

> What were the keys to the originality of the British artists? In other words, why would they sound different from their American counterparts?
>   1.)
>   2.)
>   3.)

What transformation would the background, sideman electric guitarist experience as a result of this movement known as British Blues Revisionism?

> What American musical style would they emulate thereby achieving originality?

What was the traditional blues structure for lyrics (in stanza form)?

> What was the traditional blues chord progression?

> What do you call an improvised melody line inserted between sung verses?

What was Country Blues?

> Name three country blues artists that were most celebrated by British blues artists:
>   1.)
>   2.)
>   3.)

> Of these artists, who was the one that best embodied the so-called romantic myth of the lone blues guitarists?

What was the difference between country and urban blues?

What type of electric blues was most influential to British Blues artists? (Hint: it's named after a city)

> Name at least seven of those blues artists:
> 1.)
> 2.)
> 3.)
> 4.)
> 5.)
> 6.)
> 7.)

Who were the first to capture the sound of Chicago Blues in the recording studio?

> What was their label's name from 1946-50?

> The new name in 1950 was:

Which English label distributed Chess Recordings throughout the UK thereby making these records easy to obtain?

> Which Chess recording was among the first to benefit from this distribution arrangement? It became a hit on the white charts.

Who was Vie Jay Records' primary blues artist?

Name the club that Alexis Korner's founded?

> What was the significance of this venue?

> Name his band:

Name the three most important early British blues bands:
1.)
2.)
3.)

Who was the lead singer of The Animals?

What was The Rolling Stones' one main limitation? In other words, what did they lack?

How did they turn this disadvantage into an advantage?

Name their two rhythm guitarists: Name their underlying rhythm support force:
1.)   1.)
2.)   2.)

In their early years, which rhythm-based Chicago Blues artist did they cover that would contribute to their rhythmic emphasis?

How was The Yardbirds' performance style different from the other early bands just mentioned? What did they do that the others did not?

Name The Yardbirds' three important electric guitarists:
1.)
2.)
3.)

Which black American blues guitarist did Eric Clapton try to emulate when he was with The Yardbirds?

Which Yardbird member guided the group with improvised tempo changes?

Define the term "Rave Up".

Name the first British blues hit and the band that recorded it.

What was the original version of this song, who wrote it, and who was among the first to record it?

How would you describe The Rolling Stones model as opposed to The Beatles? In other words, what alternative model did they [The Rolling Stones] standardize in rock and roll?

What type of alternative [image wise] was Mick Jagger in comparison to The Beatles?

Name the six original members of The Rolling Stones:
     1.)
     2.)
     3.)
     4.)
     5.)
     6.)

     Which of these original members left the group and who were their replacements?

At which venue did the Rolling Stones build their initial fan base?

Who became their manager?

     What were the three things that this manager accomplished or changed?
          1.)
          2.)
          3.)

\
Name The Rolling Stones' debut album (include the year).

     Name their debut single.

What did Andrew Loog Oldham encourage The Rolling Stones to do on a regular basis in order for his publishing company to generate a profit?

     Name their [The Stones'] first original single.

In which single did they hone their new, original riff-craft style?

     Briefly describe this style:

Name the Rolling Stones' first #1 hit in the US that transformed them into icon status?

Name the first Rolling Stones album that was completely comprised of original singles:

    List three singles that shows Brian Jones' eclecticism (include name and instrumental color):
        1.)
        2.)
        3.)

Name the Yardbirds' pivotal album of 1966.

    Who was their lead guitarist for that album?

    What was the main difference between this guitarist and Eric Clapton?

    List his experimental properties:

What was the greatest impact that The Yardbirds' second lead guitarist had on the development of British blues revisionism?

    What would the eventual legacy be? In other words, what was he the first harbinger of (what process did he set in motion)?

With the first power trio, The Cream (Eric Clapton, Jack Bruce, & Ginger Baker), did they all improvise simultaneously?

    What other sonic aspect made their sound completely different from conventional blues thereby creating a genre called "Heavy Blues"?

    Which black American blues guitarist was Eric Clapton's main influence when he [Clapton] performed with The Cream?

List three of Jimi Hendrix's most important influences and the reasons they were influential:
        1.)
        2.)
        3.)

List the members of The Jimi Hendrix Experience:
        1.)
        2.)
        3.)

    Name the title and year of their debut album:

Jimi Hendrix had a unique approach to the guitar, which was a combination of two specific playing techniques. What were those two techniques? (Hint: he played a particular way on the upper three strings and a particular way on the lower three strings)

At which performance venue did Jimi Hendrix become an overnight sensation in the US?

What aspect of that performance received the most publicity?

What were two elements of Jimi Hendrix's sound that made his style unique?
1.)
2.)

What new direction did the album, *Beggar's Banquet* mark for The Rolling Stones?

Who became The Rolling Stones' first true lead guitarist following the demise of Brian Jones?

What was the first Rolling Stones album that this guitarist appeared on?

Which Rolling Stones album in 1971 featured his guitar solos/leads throughout the entire format of original songs?

Which album was arguably, The Rolling Stones' greatest artistic achievement?

Name the third great lead guitarist of The Yardbirds:

What were the following important elements that made Led Zeppelin sound original?

a.) Type of texture:

b.) Approach to lead guitar solos. What did Jimmy Page do that the original American blues guitarists did not?

c.) What eclectic elements did they introduce into the blues revisionist domain?

d.) Describe the concept of "all-riff":

The blues "distortionist" process began with Jeff Beck's power chords. Did Led Zeppelin bring this process to the logical artistic limit?

What was the legacy of the British blues revisionist movement?

Which group was the catalyst for this new legacy?

Which Led Zeppelin musical property did they streamline and use extensively? (Hint: it has to do with the word " riff")

CHAPTER VI: PSYCHEDELIA – THE OTHER BLUES REVISIONISM

I. LSD: THE NEW "PRISM"

    A.) <u>British Blues Revisionism</u>: distorted and reinvented the traditional American blues into a new original sound.

        1.) But there would be another type of blues revisionism.

           - Only this time, through the filtering prism of LSD.

    B.) <u>LSD</u> (Lysergic Acid Diethylamide): was invented in 1938. A small amount could trigger haphazard, somewhat non-sensible visual hallucinations.

    C.) <u>The CIA</u>: in the early 60's was conducting tests on this drug at Stanford University in Palo Alto, CA.

        1.) <u>Purpose</u>: to see whether this mind-altering drug could be useful in covert operations.

        2.) <u>Every Tuesday</u>: about 100 subjects (who served as the "guinea pigs") were paid $20 each to ingest either.

           - LSD, LSD 6, LSD 25, mescaline, or a placebo.

              * Among the testees were two men who become the personification of the counter-culture movement:

                  a.) <u>Ken Kesey</u> (author): most notable work was "One Flew Over The Cuckoo's Nest".

                  b.) <u>Alan Ginsberg</u> (poet): one of the most notable of the beat generation poets during the 1950's

        3.) Eventually, the CIA concluded that the effects of LSD were too spontaneous to control.

           - Covert operations have to be carefully planned and must be prepared for any contingency and also, that the outcomes can be predictable to an acceptable degree.

              * LSD's effects were too unpredictable to meet those standards.

              a.) <u>RESULT</u>: the trial tests at Stanford were terminated.

        4.) To the chagrin of <u>Kesey</u>, <u>Ginsberg</u>, and others: Kesey decided to secure his own LSD supply (for it was legal at the time) and conduct his own acid tests.

           - In order to venture into what he called "uncharted territory".

    D.) He procured an old school bus and painted it with a myriad of different colors and liquid shapes which blended together.

        1.) These different colors and shapes blended together in a somewhat blurry fashion creating a "melting pot" of various images.

           - The concept of a "melting pot" of various, sometimes disparate properties that "bleed" in together is an inherent part of psychedelic art.

        2.) He also equipped the bus with speakers and strobe lights.

        3.) He traveled along with several friends. Among them: <u>Neal Cassaday</u> who Jack Kerouac refers to as Dean Moriarty in his classic: "<u>On The Road</u>".

           - Cassaday usually drove the bus.

           - Kesey's and his cohorts who drove around conducting acid tests called themselves: <u>The Merry Pranksters</u>.

              * These acid tests would be known as "<u>Happenings</u>".

                  a.) Each person paid one dollar at the door to enter.

                  b.) Then, at 11:00 pm the acid (legal and in liquid form) was passed around.

                  c.) Within an hour, an entire myriad of different hallucinogenic experiences in one area would occur.

           - Insofar as live music, there was a band. But the people attending these "happenings" were not interested in the music that was being played. The only thing that mattered was the that the LSD "tripping" experience was positive...

              * ...and that the live music was danceable.

    E.) The genus band in question was originally named: "<u>Mother McCree's Uptown Jug Champions</u>".

        1.) In 1965, they changed their name to "<u>The Warlocks</u>".

2.) Then, through randomly choosing two words from the "Oxford English Dictionary"
- They juxtaposed them to be "The Grateful Dead".

3.) They performed at their first Happening on December 4, 1965 at a house in San Jose, CA.

4.) Personnel:
- Jerry Garcia (b. Jerome John Garcia, 8/1/42, San Francisco; d. 8/9/95, Forest Knolls, CA): guitar, vocals.
- Bob Weir (b. Robert Hall, 10/16/47, San Francisco): guitar, vocals.
- Phil Lesh (b. Philip Chapman, 3/15/40, Berkeley, CA): bass, vocals.
- Ron "Pigpen" McKernan (b. 9/8/45, San Bruno, CA; d. 3/8/73, San Francisco): vocals, harmonica, keyboards.
- Bill Kreutzman (a.k.a. Bill Sommers, b. 4/7/46, Palo Alto, CA): drums.
* Later on: Mickey Hart (b. 1950, Long Island, NY), secondary (additional) drummer.

5.) The group consisted of musicians from various musical disciplines and backgrounds.
- Garcia and Weir: bluegrass, folk, and jug-band styles.
* Self-taught musicians.
- Phil Lesh: Educated. Experienced at composing electronic compositions.
* Never played the electric bass before joining the band.
a.) He supposedly played acoustic bass in swing jazz.
- McKernan and Kreutzman: Hard-edged blues backgrounds.

6.) NOTE: This combination of various musicians from different aesthetic backgrounds in one group would fit the "melting pot" scenario of what would constitute Psychedelia.
- in addition to the mixture of self-taught and schooled musicians.
* This scenario would become the norm rather than the exception.

F.) Their music started out as straight-forward rock, blues, and rhythm & blues.

1.) Which later became a combination of styles in the context of long, extended improvisations.

2.) According to Jerry Garcia, they played: "R & B plus, an awful lot of weirdness to it".
- They would start out playing a rhythm and blues tune which would then, turn inadvertently into a 30 minute extended improvisation piece.
* "There was no way we could not, not do it", he would say in an interview.

3.) Because they were playing to a crowd of dancers tripping on LSD (as opposed to a watching, waiting audience)…
- They were afforded the opportunity to develop their crafts as musicians.
* Because the audience was not there to see them.
a.) They [the dancing, tripping audience] were patient and forgiving of wrong notes, improvised passages with no direction, sloppy playing, jagged ensemble-work, etc.
- As long as the music was danceable.

4.) In this context, The Grateful Dead was given the opportunity to learn from their mistakes without suffering any fallout as a consequence.
- And thereby, honing in their musicianship talents.

5.) Recording Debut: They began recording demo tapes under the name: The Emergency Crew, at Golden Gate Studios for a local label, Autumn Records.

Can't Come Down
The Grateful Dead

- "Can't Come Down" (11/65): was one of those Autumn Records early singles.
* Written by Jerry Garcia in a hard-edged blues style (a la Bob Dylan).
- Garcia's Songwriting Turnabout: The beginning of his long collaboration with lyricist Robert Hunter.
* Who, beginning in 1967, brought songwriting craftsmanship of the Grateful Dead to a new elevated level.

Dark Star
The Grateful Dead

a.) Among His Early Collaborations: "Dark Star" and "China Cat Sunflower".

II. WHAT CONSTITUTES PSYCHEDELIC MUSIC?

A.) To understand the concept of the Psychedelic experience, one must understand that among other things...

    1.) ...it involves (as mentioned earlier) the mixing or bleeding of disparate elements.
- Psychedelic visual art for example, constitutes the blending together of many different colors and shapes into an amalgamation of a wild, quasi-chaotic work of art.

        * Psychedelic music follows a similar concept.

B.) The various elements that make up Psychedelic music are as follows:

1.) <u>Garage Band</u>: for the first time thus far, another important touchstone for rock and roll is introduced.
- <u>Definition</u>: music that is rudimentary, crude, unpolished, at times out of tune (especially with the vocals), and usually drenched in reverberation.

Shape Of Things
To Come

Max Frost & The Troopers

    * It is said that The Beatles inspired kids in practically every suburban neighborhood in America to start their own bands.

        a.) They would literally play and practice in their parents' garages (hence the term).
- The mid to late 60's saw a proliferation of so-called "<u>garage bands</u>" whose enthusiasm far outweighed their playing abilities.

    * Garage Bands will also be discussed as inspirations when we get to the chapters dealing with the Proto-Punk, Punk, and Post-Punk movements.

2.) <u>Blues or Rhythm & Blues</u>: as mentioned in the beginning of this chapter, psychedelic music is referred to as: "The Other Blues Revisionism".
- <u>Definition</u>: Blues or R&B filtered through the prism of the LSD experience in conjunction with the Garage Band ethos.

    * Often times, Psychedelic bands will cover traditional blues songs. However, instead of attempting to sound authentic like the British Revisionists did (which resulted in something different)...

        a.) Their interpretation would have a more crude, reverb-laden sound.

The Hunter

Blue Cheer

        b.) An example: "<u>The Hunter</u>" (written by Booker T. Jones) and recorded by <u>Blue Cheer</u> from their "Inside, Outside" album of 1967.

           - Incidentally the name "Blue Cheer" is a name of a particular "brand" of LSD.

3.) <u>Eastern Influences</u> (mainly Indian and Arabic): The psychedelic movement was responsible for opening up young Americans to Eastern music, culture, and spirituality.
- Among the most important musical signatures:

Within You
Without You

The Beatles

    * <u>The Sitar</u> (India): a highly rhythmic, string plucking instrument reminiscent of an oversized mandolin with a neck so long that one has to sit down cross-legged in order to play it.

        a.) it's most notable essence is the nasally twangy, overtone-laden sound.

    * <u>The Drone</u>: in Eastern music, the drone is the foundation similar to the foundation of an underlying sustained chord in western music.

        a.) A pitch that is sustained indefinitely underneath the lead instruments.

        b.) Is ripe with overtones.

    * <u>Eastern Melodies</u>: in eastern melodies, there is a mantra-like vocal chant style that rock and rollers adopted into their own psychedelic mixes along with the eastern twang.

        a.) Within this context, Eastern modes (or scales) were also being experimented with.

           - As well as Eastern-styled melodic ornamentation.

4.) <u>Noise</u> (mainly electronic): the genus for this, started with the "Futurist Movement" of

the 1920's.
- They started developing new instruments whose purpose was to generate new timbres dealing with noise.

Glissandi
György Ligeti

* <u>The Idea</u>: to reinvent both pitch and musical structure in completely non-traditional ways.
a.) No great enduring works resulted from this era although it did inspire a new musical genre.
- The Futurist Movement will be discussed in greater detail in Chapter XIV which focuses on industrial dance music.
- <u>Electronic Music</u>: the first legacy of substance to result from the Futurist movement.
* <u>2 types</u>:
a.) <u>Music Concrete</u>: recording sounds of life and nature on to magnetic, reel-to-reel and then:
- electronically or manually manipulating the tape (i.e. playing it backwards or suddenly speeding it up with the hand) in order to produce a new sound.

Artikulation
György Ligeti

b.) <u>Analog</u>: where oscillators generate electronic wave shapes (i.e. sine waves, square waves, etc.) and noises (i.e. white noise)…
- and create a non-traditional musical composition from these timbres onto 4-channel tape.
* <u>Karlhienz Stockhausen</u>: prominent art-music composer of the 60's and 70's who not only specialized in electronic composition:
a.) But also inspired rockers to experiment with electronic/noise ideas of their own.
5.) <u>Experimentation</u>: as mentioned several times earlier, one of the essences of Psychedelic art is the bleeding together of disparate elements.
- Another essence, is <u>experimentation</u>: the very backbone of Psychedelia for after all, it is the reason that artists "turned-on" to the LSD experience in the first place.

At The Mountains
Of Madness
HP Lovecraft

* LSD opened up new doors of consciousness to new areas of awareness.
a.) And also, the search for that "one-step-beyond" premise.
- Even corporate record labels were uncharacteristically tolerant of the various experimental paths these artists have taken…
*…in the quest to find something different.
C.) <u>Early Psychedelic Music</u>: consisted of the blending of "<u>Garage band</u>" plus <u>blues (or R&B)</u> and drenched in <u>reverberation</u>.
1.) Later on, <u>eastern influences</u>, <u>noise</u>, and <u>more experimentation</u> were added into this "melting pot" of Psychedelia.
- Coalescing into the very foundation of it's music. which leads us to the next section…

III. WHY LSD?

A.) Artists have utilized drugs of one type or another to inspire artistic creativity ever since art has become a part of humanity.
1.) Various Examples:
- <u>Opium</u>: in the late 18th and early 19th centuries, opium was a common drug of choice in the artistic inner circles.
- <u>Absinthe</u>: a green, alcoholic beverage widely used in the 19th century in which the intoxication causes one to hallucinate.
* This beverage can be seen as background decor in many paintings of that era. Just look for the bottle or glass with green liquid in it.

a.) Today, the only country where it is still available (legally) is in Spain.
- <u>Cocaine</u>: along with <u>Heroin</u>, were for many artists in the 20th century, the drug of choice.
* especially, in rock and roll.
- <u>Cannabis</u>: had also been around for decades in the 20th century up to the present time (along with Heroin and Cocaine) and for centuries before.
* again, in the rock and roll community.

B.) According to Robert Palmer, many artists from Louis Armstrong smoking cannabis his entire adult life to Charlie Parker's addiction to heroin:
1.) Drugs were never the "label" attached to the music. In other words, the drug culture was separate from the musical genre.
- They were not publicly associated with one another.
2.) But LSD was different.
- For the first time, a new artistic movement will manifest itself around this drug.
* There will be no mistaking it's association.

C.) <u>So. Why LSD?</u>
1.) When one becomes intoxicated on alcohol or high on cannabis:
- The experience is nevertheless, "head intoxication" and even though equilibrium or thought processes are skewed, it is in many ways:
* A routine brand of intoxication limited to the head effecting one's perception.
2.) With LSD, the entire body from head to toe is "intoxicated" not unlike the "head-rush" feeling from cannabis only this time:
- the whole body is experiencing this.
* At times, one can feel their heart beating in their chest.
3.) Because of the sheer intensity of this bodily intoxication, one can feel a very "near death" experience with the sense that this experience will eventually subside and the body will return to normal.
- For many others, the effects of this near death/shaking feeling was highly destabilizing and resulted for some, in terrifying experiences (i.e. bad trips).
4.) <u>The effect</u>: can drive one to think of issues foreign from those dealing with everyday, "normal life" or, as Dr. Timothy Leary would call it, "Game Reality".
- <u>Instead</u>: one thinks of spirituality in a do-it-yourself sense.
* writing poetry that sometimes makes sense only to the writer.
* Staring at a light bulb watching the halo around it for a period of time (part of the hallucinogenic state of the drug).
* Playing one pitch slowly and repeatedly on the piano and intently listening to the ringing overtones.
* <u>NOTE</u>: in other words, activities where the perception of passing time ceases to exist for the one experiencing the LSD trip.
5.) Along with the extreme bodily intoxication comes the hallucinations where one's perception can become completely altered.
- Viewing colors, shapes, halos, trails of light (when one turns away from the light) that do not exist in "game reality"…
* …which must be done in a peaceful, non-violent setting.
- <u>RESULT</u>: The experience develops a different "reality" quite separate from the real world on one hand.
* On the other, (according to LSD proponents) it can open the mind to completely new experiences and open doors that, in Paul Kantner's words: "may never be closed again".
6.) It is due to this powerful, often destabilizing effect on the mind and body that LSD would have a unique place in rock and roll history…
- and would spearhead a new movement.

* Psychedelia would not only become a musical movement but also, a psychological one.

D.) The main psychedelic philosophy, would develop into one of "peace and love".

    1.) Resulting in part, from the so-called "do-it-yourself" spirituality associated with the acid trip.

    2.) It would also become the touchstone for a new insurgency.

        - Which would become manifested in the anti-Vietnam war protests of the late 1960's.

        *A war where 58,000 Americans were killed in action.

    3.) As a result, a massive anti-establishment movement in the US took place on such a large scale.

        - That would eventually change the way the US government conducts war.

IV. "QUEST FOR PURE SANITY" AND OTHER PSYCHEDELIC PHILOSOPHIES

A.) The first rock and roll band to extol a psychedelic philosophy was: "The 13th Floor Elevators" from Austin, Texas.

    1.) Which made them the first psychedelic band on record.

B.) "The Psychedelic Sounds Of The 13th Floor Elevators" (1966): their debut album.

    1.) The liner notes for this album contain the "us against them", "do-it-yourself spirituality" manifesto entitled: "Quest For Pure Sanity".

    2.) "Quest For Pure Sanity" (as quoted from the liner notes):

"Album Liner Notes," by the 13th Floor Elevators, reprinted from The Psychedelic Sounds of the 13th Floor Elevators. Collectables Records COL CD-0550: 1993, by permission of Charly Licensing.

"Since Aristotle, man has organized his knowledge vertically in separate and unrelated groups – science, religion. Sex. Relaxation, work, etc. The main emphasis in his language, his system of storing knowledge has been on the identification of objects rather than on the relationship between objects. He is now forced to use his tools of reasoning separately and for one situation at a time..."

"...Recently, it has become possible for man to chemically alter his mental state and thus alter his point of view (that is, his own basic relation with the outside world which determines how he stores his information). He can then restructure his thinking..."

"...so that his thoughts bear more relation to his life and his problems, therefore approaching them more sanely..."

"...It is this Quest for Pure Sanity that forms the basis of the songs in this album."

    3.) These liner notes (yes, liner notes!) are basically saying that there is a battle between the "new" and "old' reasoning.

        - "old": materialism, "new": a do-it-yourself spiritual connection with the cosmos.

        * Those who take in the "new" are both spiritually and philosophically in-the-know while those who don't, are lost in, and blinded by, their materialism.

    4.) Each song, dealing with the conflict behind the "Quest" contains their own liner notes.

        "Tried To Hide: was written about those people who for the sake of appearances take on the superficial aspects of the quest..."

You're Gonna Miss Me
The 13th Floor Elevators

        "...The dismissal of such a person is expressed in You're Gonna Miss Me".

    5.) Their musical style is a combination of the following:

        - Rhythm & blues elements mixed with garage band (and it's associated reverb drench).

        * RESULT: early establishment of the psychedelic musical style of R&B revisionism through the psychedelic prism.

C.) The first Psychedelic hit: inspired by John Coltrane who himself embarked on his own pure sanity "Quest".

    1.) John Coltrane: an artist with an excellent jazz background made his own change doing the following:

        - extended improvisation over either a drone or one chord held indefinitely.

    2.) This simplicity of accompaniment allowed him the freedom to be experimental on both a rhythmic and modal approach.

        - He could literally be as rhythmically complexed or as energized as he wanted to be:

            * without clashing with the rest of the group.

        - It also allowed him the freedom to experiment with Indian/Eastern and Arabic scales and modes.

            * Opening up his brand of jazz to a world music influences.

    3.) His example would be a touchstone for rockers to adopt their own brand of extended improvisation over an extended chord or a drone.

        - Much easier to emulate as opposed to improvising over complexed chord progressions.

            * In addition to the openness inspired by LSD, Coltrane's example would inspire rockers to investigate world influences (i.e. Eastern modes, etc.) as creative sources.

    4.) "India": a Coltrane work that would inspire the first psychedelic hit.

        - Coltrane's B-flat soprano saxophone performing rhythmically free, highly energized improvisations.

India

John Coltrane

            * Fast, complexed rhythms with a melodic arch.

            * Over one extended chord.

            * Utilizing Indian scales/modes.

        - Focus Of The Work: a 4-note theme heard intermittently throughout the piece.

            * More of a reference point bracketing sections of rhythmically vibrant improvisations.

            * This theme would also, in it's slightly varied form:

                a.) … become the main thematic element for Psychedelia's first hit.

D.) "Eight Miles High" (1966): The Byrds. The first psychedelic hit.

(Note: once again, we focus on one of rock and roll's most underrated bands. As you may recall, they were the first to synthesize both The Beatles and Dylan sounds together sending rock and roll in many different directions/paradigms.)

    1.) "India" (John Coltrane) was a direct influence on "Eight Miles High" in the following ways:

        - The 4-note theme of "India" (as mentioned earlier) is the main thematic element or reference point of the song giving "Eight Miles High" a sense of thematic cohesion.

            * The difference in The Byrd's rendition is that the theme is transposed to a new key (or pitch center).

                a.) And is played on Roger McGuinn's "Rickenbacker" 12 - string electric guitar (the signature timbre of the group).

        - Roger McGuinn: wanted to emulate the sound of John Coltrane's soprano saxophone on his electric 12 string.

            * Right down to emulating the sustained quality of the wind instrument (by giving the guitar sound, a sustaining ring to it).

                a.) as well as the sounds of the valves (on the soprano saxophone) opening and closing.

        - Improvisation: McGuinn took the highly rhythmic, spontaneous, and energized quality of Coltrane's improvisation on "India" and again:

            * Emulated it on the 12 string.

            * Only this time, a sort of blending/bleeding together of a collage of rhythmic sounds results in a blurry, chaotic effect.

a.) In accordance with the collaging ethos of psychedelic art.

- RESULT: the first psychedelic hit is born.

2.) "Eight Miles High": however, would fall victim to a brand of de facto censorship called, the "Gavin Report".

- A tip sheet sent to radio stations all over the US.

* It displayed songs that they felt were either acceptable or unacceptable for broadcast.

a.) They would object to the "unacceptable" and request that those songs stop being played on the air.

- The Gavin Report accused "Eight Miles High" of being a drug song and they suggested that radio stations refrain from playing it and radio stations all over the country complied.

* Actually, the title of this song refers to an airliner's cruising altitude (of their first trip to Europe).

- It stopped "Eight Miles High" (then climbing up the charts) dead in it's tracks and before long, it was off the charts.

E.) "Tomorrow Never Knows"- The other landmark psychedelic single: inspired by "The Tibetan Book of The Dead".

1.) Dr. Timothy Leary: an adjunct professor in psychology at Harvard University created a treatise on the psychedelic experience aptly titled: *The Psychedelic Experience*.

- An instructional manual on properly taking an LSD trip using the Tibetan Book Of The Dead as a model.

2.) He begins his treatise by saying: "A psychedelic experience is a journey is a journey to new realms of consciousness…"

"…it's characteristic features are the transcendence of verbal concepts, of space-time dimensions, and of the ego or identity".

3.) He goes on to say: "Most recently, they have become available to anyone through the ingestion of psychedelic drugs such as LSD, psilocybin, mescaline, DMT, etc. …"

"…Of course, the drug dose does not produce the transcendent experience. It merely acts as a chemical key – it opens up the mind, frees the nervous system of it's ordinary patterns and structures".

4.) He is saying in so many words that, according to his viewpoint, the psychedelic experience already exists in the area of the mind unattainable because of what Leary called "game reality" or, everyday life.

- So, the drug is just a vehicle to open that, which was lying dormant in the mind all along.

5.) He states his purpose: "…to enable the person to understand the new realities of the expanded consciousness, to serve as road maps for new interior territories which modern science has made accessible…"

"…The Tibetan modal, on which this manual is based, is designed to teach the person to direct and control awareness…"

"…to reach a level of understanding variously called liberation, illumination, or enlightenment…"

6.) He explains the Tibetan meaning: "The Tibetan Book of The Dead was called in it's own language the BARDO THODOL, which means 'Liberation by Hearing On The After-Death Plane' …"

"…that the free consciousness has only to hear and remember the teachings in order to be liberated…"

7.) The Tibetan Book Of The Dead: is a "how-to" manual for the soul (Buddhism believes in reincarnation) to leave one body after it [the body] is deceased and move into a new one.

- There are three stages:

* Chikhai Bardo (1st Period): complete transcendence. When the soul leaves the body.

a.) For The Manual: it's the onset of the LSD gradually taking effect and transforming the person from "game reality".

Eight Miles High
The Byrds

Tomorrow Never Knows
The Beatles

     * <u>Chonyid Bardo</u> (2nd Period): where the soul (now out of the body) experiences "karmic apparitions".
       a.) <u>For The Manual</u>: the hallucinogenic state or "tripping".
     * <u>Sidpa Bardo</u> (Final Period): where the soul enters a new body.
       a.) <u>For The Manual</u>: the gradual return to "game reality".
  8.) <u>Timothy Leary</u>: was dubbed, "The High Priest of LSD" for synthesizing the eastern with the psychedelic experience.
    - It was within this context that the Tibetan Book inspired the creation of "<u>Tomorrow Never Knows</u>" (the song and the logistics behind it, were discussed in Chapter 3).
 F.) "<u>Eight Miles High</u>" and "<u>Tomorrow Never Knows</u>": were two lasting examples of psychedelia embraced in a three-and-a-half-minute singles format.
  1.) Carrying a considerable level of artistic skill, thematic coherence, and outright innovation.
    - From a singles viewpoint, a high-water mark in the psychedelic domain was solidified.
     * But the singles format, is only part of the psychedelic equation…

V. <u>THE SAN FRANCISCO SCENE</u>: Where extended improvisation was the rule rather than the exception.
 A.) <u>The Culture</u>: the legendary "Haight-Ashbury" district featuring:
  1.) A psychedelic shop.
  2.) <u>Psychedelic comics</u>: entitled "<u>Zap Comics</u>" depicting the adventures of a character named "Mr. Natural".
    - Written and illustrated by art legend <u>Robert Crumb</u>.
     * These comics sometimes bordered on the pornographic.
  3.) <u>Psychedelic "B" Movies</u>: focusing on plots depicting acid trips (of which Jack Nicholson was a producer).
  4.) <u>A Psychedelic Newspaper</u>: the "San Francisco Oracle" espousing mainly two things:
    - Ending the Vietnam War.
    - Promote the psychedelic way of life (i.e. a new modal of living).
 B.) <u>Venues</u>: "Happenings" by the end of 1966 have become bigger, more popular events.
  1.) Therefore, they moved from private homes to ballrooms, theaters, and parks.
    - Three most important venues: <u>The Avalon Ballroom</u>, <u>The Fillmore</u>, and <u>Golden Gate Park</u>.
 C.) Three most important bands: <u>The Grateful Dead</u>, <u>The Jefferson Airplane</u>, and <u>Big Brother & The Holding Company</u>.
  1.) The so-called lower tiered bands included:
    - <u>Moby Grape</u>, <u>The Charlatans</u>, <u>Santana</u>, <u>Quicksilver Messenger Service</u>, and <u>Country Joe & The Fish</u>.
  2.) For the most part, these bands were accustomed to performing extended improvisations to dancers tripping on LSD.
    - as opposed to the singles format.
     * Eventually, a "happening" that would achieve national attention peaked the interest of major record labels.
 D.) "<u>The Human Be-In</u>" (1/67): at Golden Gate Park (also refered to as "The Gathering Of The Tribe").
  1.) A prototype of the great outdoor concerts that would identify itself with the era.
    - Featuring live music that was sometimes, more like an accompaniment to the party going on in the audience (about 20,000 people).
  2.) <u>The idea</u>: that 20,000 people can gather in love and peace without any violence ensuing.
  3.) Also, a major drug event. It was said that a massive cloud of pot smoke perpetually floated over the audience.
  4.) This so-called "<u>Gathering of The Tribe</u>" brought the psychedelic culture of San Francisco…
    - national attention for the first time.

* and introduced mainstream America to the Hippies.
     5.) <u>Part of the result</u>: major record labels sent their A&R people to the Haight-Ashbury district.

E.) <u>Adjustments to recording for these labels</u>: these groups, who were so accustomed to performing in an extended improvisational format to an audience of dancers high on LSD (who were not paying much attention to them [the performers])...
     1.) Were now being called upon to switch to a singles format and...
       - Using the recording studio as a new stage.
     2.) Results of an extended improvisational format:
       - Improvisations that led nowhere.
       - Solos that were highly adolescent.
         * In other words, these solos had no artistic depth
           a.) <u>Result</u>: they could not stand up to the scrutiny of repeated listenings and therefore, not maintain any long term, musical interest).
       - Sloppy ensemble playing where the players were out of sync with one another.
       - Little consideration of playing within a succinct, tightly structured outer form (i.e. a singles format).
       - Necessity of drawing on-the-spot, creative energy from the audience.
     3.) These "results" had to be corrected once these bands entered the studio.
       - They had to learn the art of the three-and-a-half minute singles format.
       - They had to learn to create ideas that would stand the test of time.
         * In other words, they had to learn how to <u>compose</u>.
       - They had to polish up, and tighten their ensemble work.
       - Most of all, they had to accomplish this adjustment within the isolated walls of a recording studio.
         * As opposed to drawing their creative energies off the audience.

F.) <u>The Jefferson Airplane</u> (formed 1965): the first of these bands to sign with a major record label (RCA).
     1.) Personnel:
       - <u>Grace Slick</u>: (b. Grace Barnett Wing, 10/30/39, Chicago, IL): vocals, keyboards.
       - <u>Paul Kantner</u> (b. 3/17/41, San Francisco): guitar, vocals.
       - <u>Marty Balin</u> (b. Martyn Jerel Buchwald, 1/30/42, Cincinnati, OH): vocals.
       - <u>Jorma Kaukonen</u> (b. 12/23/40, Washington, DC): guitar, vocals.
       - <u>Spencer Dryden</u> (b. 4/7/43, New York, NY): drums.
       - <u>Jack Casady</u> (b. 4/13/44, Washington, DC): bass.
     2.) They would also be the first of the San Francisco bands to achieve national notoriety.
       - Thereby, becoming the first personification or "face" of the Haight-Ashbury scene (on a worldwide scale).
     3.) They would also boast the first female "rock star": <u>Grace Slick</u> (FYI: Ronnie Bennett was rock and roll's first female sex symbol).
     4.) The group consisted mainly of ex-folkies who have had the most experience with the singles format.
       - Which in turn, expedited their adjustment to the recording studio.
     5.) <u>Their sound</u>: a polished, reverb-laden sound with garage band influences plus:
       - Electric guitar solos exhibiting a quasi Eastern-styled twang.
         * A great match for Grace Slick's loud, and at times, mantra-like vocal style.
     6.) "<u>White Rabbit</u>" (<u>their anthem</u>): a musical embodiment of not only the San Francisco sound but also, the drug-laden psychedelic culture as well.
       - Grace Slick: takes images from the Lewis B. Carrol's stories of "<u>Alice In Wonderland</u>" and "<u>Alice Through The Looking Glass</u>".
         * And uses them as metaphors for drug use.

Somebody
To Love
The Jefferson Airplane

White Rabbit
by Jefferson Airplane,
reprinted from *The Best of*
Jefferson Airplane, BMG/
RCA 66197-2; 1993, Irving
Music.

- Example:
>
> "One pill makes you larger
> And one pill makes you small,
> And the ones that mother gives you
> Don't do anything at all.
> Go ask Alice
> When she's ten feet tall."

> a.) A reference to the story where Alice drinks out of a bottle that displays the words, "Drink Me" and she becomes larger in size. She drinks out of it again, and becomes smaller.

> " Tell 'em a hookah smoking caterpillar
> Has given you the call.
> Call Alice
> When she was just small."

> a.) In the Carrol story, Alice approaches a caterpillar sitting atop a mushroom (psilocybin?) and smoking a hookah (cannabis?).
> b.) Alice eats a piece of the mushroom (in the real story) and her neck extends so "high", her head is far above the ground.

> "When the men on the chessboard
> Get up and tell you where to go"

> a.) A reference from "Alice Through The Looking Glass" where she sees the chess pieces come to life before her eyes.
> - For the song, a reference to an LSD, hallucinogenic experience.

- Both in sound and metaphor-laden subject matter relating to drug use, "White Rabbit" captured the art and attitude of an era.
> * This single in conjunction with several others, would launch The Jefferson Airplane as the first major success to come out of the psychedelic scene in San Francisco.
>> * Thereby, becoming this scene's first well known embodiment.

G.) <u>Big Brother and The Holding Company</u> (formed 1965, San Francisco): a ragged, scruffy garage band that made it's initial reputation by playing straight-ahead, hard edged blues.
- 1.) Personnel:
  - <u>Peter Albin</u> (b. 6/6/44, San Francisco): guitar, bass, vocals.
  - <u>Sam Andrew</u> (b. 12/18/41, Taft, CA): guitar, saxophone, piano, vocals.
  - <u>James Gurley</u> (b.12/22/39, Detroit, MI): guitar.
  - <u>David Getz</u> (b. 1/24/40, Brooklyn, NY): drums, vocals, piano.
  - <u>Janis Joplin</u> (b. 1/19/47, Port Arthur, TX; d. 10/4/70, Hollywood, CA):
- 2.) Because of their garage band "chops", their playing abilities were highly limited.
  - They played in a somewhat sloppy, sometimes out of tune manner.
    * They would however, be remembered as the band that gave <u>Janis Joplin</u> her beginning in the music business of San Francisco.
- 3.) <u>Janis Joplin</u>: grew up in Port Arthur, Texas distressed by her inability to fit in with her peers.
  - As a blues enthusiast, one of her biggest influences was the late blues singer, <u>Bessie Smith</u>.
    * By the time she moved to San Francisco in 1966, she had already developed her own blues revisionist style of singing.
      a.) That would turn out an all-out assaultive style of blues performance (as opposed to the self-effacing vulnerability in the traditional sense).

- She joined <u>Big Brother and The Holding Company</u> in 1966.
> * Their first album together on the "<u>Mainstream</u>" label consisted of rough, sloppy psychedelic blues.
>> a.) With Janis singing lead on some cuts but not on others.
> * Their breakthrough came in June of 1967 at the Monterey Pop Festival.
>> a.) Where her revisionist rendition of the blues classic, "<u>Ball And Chain</u>" was captured on film and made her into a star.

Ball And Chain (Live)
Janis Joplin
(with Big Brother & The Holding Co.)

4.) Big Brother and The Holding Company signed a management deal with Albert Grossman and signed up with Columbia Records for their second album: "<u>Cheap Thrills</u>" (1968).
- The album cover featured the "Zap" comics illustrations of Robert Crumb.
- It was their first album to top the charts.

H.) <u>Janis Joplin</u>: would become the first female artist in rock and roll to invent her own sense of beauty, out of what most would see as ugliness.
> 1.) She had acne, sloppy unkept hair, no make up, and cheesy looking psychedelic outfits.
>> - She had a very aggressive performance style that turned this "ugliness" into something attractive.
> 2.) Janis would leave "Big Brother and The Holding Company" in pursuit of a higher, star quality profile.

Try (Just A Little Bit Harder)
Janis Joplin
(with The Kozmic Blues Band)

>> - <u>The Kozmic Blues Band</u>: a group with a more polished sound featuring a horn section.
>>> * "<u>I've Got Those Kozmic Blues Agin</u>" (1968): her only album with this band.
>> - <u>Full-Tilt Boogie</u>: her last band and probably, the most bluesiest she had ever worked with.

Cry Baby
Janis Joplin
(with Full-Tilt Boogie)

>>> * "<u>Pearl</u>" (1970): her last album which featured some of her most notable hits: "<u>Cry Baby</u>", "<u>Me And Bobby McGee</u>", and "<u>Move Over</u>".
>>>> a.) Produced by Paul Rothschild (who also produced The Doors).
> 3.) Her untimely death occurred in July of 1970 of a drug overdose in Hollywood, CA.

I.) By this time, The Grateful Dead had not only secured their contract with the Warner Brothers label, but they had also honed in their hybrid of traditional American music styles to an elevated level.
> 1.) <u>General Influences</u>: Mountain ballads, bluegrass, blues, country, R&B, and rock n' roll.
>> - The Howlin' Wolf growl, the Bakersfield country twang, the stomping sound of jug band music, 60's folk music, Mariachi influences, jazz, and disco.
>>> * <u>NOTE</u>: The main difference between country and bluegrass is that bluegrass tends to focus more on instrumental virtuosity.
>>>> a.) Country tends to focus on vocal expression.
> 2.) <u>Key</u>: It were not just about their various influences but rather, it was all about how they *synthesized* these influences.
>> - In the process, they added some strange, weird twists to their traditional influences.

On The Road Again
The Grateful Dead

>>> * <u>American Musical Traditions</u>: Was their foundation that they could bend and shape to their improvisatory whims.
>>>> a.) Extended Improvisation was their main vehicle synthesizing these influences.
> 3.) <u>Individual Influences</u>:
>> - For "<u>Pigpen</u>" McKernan: Texas blues artist, "Lightnin' Hopkins.
>>> * Hopkins could improvise his blue lines out of thin air.
>>>> a.) McKernan referred to this as "air music".
>> - <u>For Garcia</u>: Scotty Stoneman, bluegrass fiddler for a group

called, The Kentucky Colonels.

        * Garcia once referred to him as "The Charlie Parker of bluegrass".

            a.) Garcia was enamored by his [Stoneman's] technical virtuosity and his ability to stretch a small musical phrase into a long, extended improvisation.

                - While simultaneously expressing a wide range of musical emotions.

        * The great jazz saxophonist <u>John Coltrane</u> also influenced Garcia.

            a.) Like Stoneman, Garcia was inspired by Coltrane's ability to turn a riff or melodic fragment into an extended improvisation that expressed great virtuosity and emotional flair.

                - <u>NOTE</u>: According to Eric Pooley, "John Coltrane [and Scotty Stoneman] inspired Garcia to elongate his musical phrases, soloing in paragraphs rather than in licks and riffs".

    - <u>For Phil Lesh</u>: jazz, classical, electronic composition, and new music.

        * His wondering bass lines would serve as a counterpoint for Jerry Garcia's extended guitar solos.

4.) <u>Their Approach to Collective Improvisation</u>: To Jerry Garcia, improvisation (i.e. making up the music as you go along), was what true musical expression was all about.

    - A sort of instrumental conversation where conceptually, the various instruments are "talking" to one another.

        * One instrument would begin where the other left off.

            a.) Applying jazz improvisational concepts to American traditional influences such as bluegrass.

                - Bluegrass was about precision while the jazz influences allowed for a looser approach enabling spontaneity for the music to shift in new directions.

    - <u>Their Improvisational Formula</u>:

        * <u>Jerry Garcia</u>: Improvisational skills that focused on a melodic, noodling style of extended solos.

            a.) A sort of jazz meets bluegrass approach.

        * <u>Phil Lesh</u>: Compliments Garcia's extended lead guitar with long, meandering, flowing basslines (a counterpoint to Garcia).

        * <u>Bob Weir</u>: Rhythm guitar playing improvising creative chord progressions…

            a.) …was the glue that held the Garcia/Lesh counterpoint together.

        * <u>Bill Kreutzman</u>: a deceptive, simple beat that provided a rhythmic foundation which drove the collective improvisation forward.

5.) "<u>Anthem Of The Sun</u>" (1968): their first album under the Warner Brothers label (their second album overall).

    - Each side was mixed extensively and continuously in Garcia's words, "like an electronic composition".

        * Both he and Phil Lesh did the mixing.

            a.) A result no doubt, of their extended improvisational influence.

    - <u>NOTE</u>: As the 60's came to a close, The Grateful Dead would concentrate on writing more concise songs in a three-and-a-half minute singles format.

6.) The successful honing in of songwriting in the traditional singles format would begin to reach fruition in 1970 with two albums: "<u>Workingman's Dead</u>" and "<u>American Beauty</u>".

    - For the time being, they would develop their new skills with free, unlimited studio time.

        * Which they negotiated into their contract with Warner Brothers.

*Eyes Of The World
(Live)*
The Grateful Dead

VI. OTHER PSYCHEDELIC SCENES

    A.) Los Angeles: bands such as: "Kaleidoscope", "Love", and "The Beach Boys".

    B.) "Pet Sounds" (1967) by The Beach Boys: Brian Wilson's LSD drenched contribution to Psychedelic music.

        1.) Initially inspired as a reaction to The Beatles' British invasion.

Wouldn't It   - Which forced Wilson to become resourceful.

Be Nice   2.) The album begins with a "Love" anthem entitled: "Wouldn't It Be Nice".

The Beach Boys   - It is said that art is a reflection of the times.

             * In this case, the rise of cohabitation in the late 60's forced society to gradually accept this as a norm.

                a.) "Wouldn't It Be Nice" spoke to that brilliantly.

        3.) "God Only Knows": a more heartfelt, serious view of love through the psychedelic prism.

             - Done in a laid back, classy manner with a catchy sequence that anyone could sing to.

God Only Knows   * And remember on the spot.

The Beach Boys   4.) Most of the cuts on this album, including "Sloop John B", fit in with the reverb-laden flavor of psychedelic music.

Sloop John B.   - Along with some unique electric keyboard timbres.

The Beach Boys   * The music in general, does not sound so much like surf music as their previous releases did.

I Just Wasn't Made   a.) It sounds instead, more introspective as illustrated in a song

For These Times   called, *I Just Wasn't Made For These Times*.

The Beach Boys

        5.) This album would go on to inspire Paul McCartney in his creation of the "Sergeant Pepper's Lonely hearts Club Band" album.

    C.) West Berlin: "Can", "Faust", and "Neu".

Why Don't You 1.) Musical Emphasis: Noise experimentation

Eat Carrots   - The focus of the German/European psychedelic experience.

  Faust   * Example: "Why Don't You Eat Carrots" by Faust

           a.) Opens with a free-formed sequence of electronic noise.

VII. THE LONDON PSYCHEDELIC UNDERGROUND

    A.) Pink Floyd (formed 1965, London, ENG): England's first important psychedelic band.

      1.) Original Lineup:

        - Syd Barrett (b. Roger Keith Barrett, 1/6/46, Cambridge, ENG – d. 7/7/06, Cambridge, ENG), vocals, guitar.

        - Roger Waters (b. 9/6/44, Surrey, ENG), vocals, bass.

        - Richard Wright (b. 7/28/45, London, ENG), vocals, keyboards.

        - Nick Mason (b. 1/27/45, Birmingham, ENG), drums.

          * In 1968, David Gilmour (b. 4/6/44, Cambridge, ENG), vocals, guitar: would eventually replace Syd Barrett.

    B.) Beginnings: the band's name – taken from two obscure blues artists in Syd Barrett's record collection:

      1.) Pink Anderson: a blues artist from Georgia and Floyd "Dripper Boy" Council.

        - Barrett dubbed the band, The Pink Floyd Sound.

      2.) Early Music: Covering the songs of conventional blues-derived artists such as The Rolling Stones and garage band classics.

        - But in an unconventional manner.

          * Within instrumental breaks or solos: distortion, feedback, and Stockhausen-influenced experimentations on the keyboard.

            a.) Wild, avante garde performance practices initiated by Syd Barrett.

- Barrett was their initial songwriter, guitarist, frontman, and visionary.
- Their debut gig in late 1965: The Countdown Club.
3.) Their First Attempt at Using Mixed Media: another eventual signature element.
- Early 1966: Essex University.
* A film made by a paraplegic who filmed London from the vantage
point of his moving wheelchair was shown on a movie screen behind
the band during a performance.
a.) This became the initial spark that led to their common
practice of showing images on the wall behind them during
performances.
4.) Pete Jenner and Andrew King were The Floyd's early managers.
- Jenner encouraged Syd Barrett to use techniques that were inspired by an
experimental jazz band called AMM.
* AMM: They wore lab coats and used various theatrical lighting
effects.
a.) Style: Free improvisation that bore no resemblance to any
standard musical genre.
- They made some of their own instruments to further
their esoteric, experimental sound.
* One of Jenner's suggestions to Barrett (inspired by AMM):
a.) Slide metal ball bearings up & down the electric guitar
strings.
- NOTE: It was during this period that they started
calling themselves "The Pink Floyd" (thereby
dropping the word "Sound" at the end).
5.) Their First Regular Performance Venue: The London Free School's weekly Friday
night benefit at the All Saints Church in the Notting Hill district.
- In the beginning, these concerts were known as "The Sound and Light
Workshop".
* One night, strange-looking images were displayed from a slide
projector onto the wall in back of The Pink Floyd during a
performance.
a.) These images were timed to the music.
- This was the inspiration for Pete Jenner to come up
with what he believed was a bona fide "psychedelic"
lighting show that would eventually be integrated
into Pink Floyd's live performances.
* He [Jenner] believed he was duplicating
what he *imagined* was the psychedelic scene
in America.
C.) Syd Barrett's Influences: what he termed as "music in colors".
1.) Children's stories, JRR Tolkien sagas (i.e. *The Lord of The Rings*, etc.), English folk
tunes, electric blues, and electronics experimentation.
- In addition, The Rolling Stones, The Beatles, and Donovan Leitch (a.k.a.
Donovan).
* These influences were what initially inspired his artistic leadership of
the group.
2.) Barrett's Performance Practice:
- Extended improvisations: with feedback and other various noises.
* Noise: the key to British/European approach to the psychedelic
experience.
a.) In America, the psychedelic approach was achieved by
more conventional means (i.e. blues-influenced extended
melodic guitar solos).

- For Pink Floyd (and Europeans in general), the psychedelic experience stemmed on the creation of actual new sounds (mostly from noise).

Astronomy Domine
Pink Floyd

* Free Form: extended improvisations (with experimental noises included) of some of their early works.
    a.) "Interstellar Overdrive": an extended instrumental piece and "Astronomy Domine".
      - Extended improvisations could make one song last for up to 45 minutes.

Interstellar Overdrive
Pink Floyd

* Light Shows: Barrett would create shadows on the wall in back of him.
    a.) Waving his arms in the colored lights and projecting shadows on the screen.

- NOTE: Through these unique performances, Syd Barrett became a charismatic figure in the London Psychedelic underground.

D.) Their First Major Show: A benefit concert launching a first psychedelic newspaper called *IT* (meaning, *International Times*).

    1.) Venue: The Roundhouse "All Night Rave" on October 16, 1966.
      - A gathering of all of the disparate underground psychedelic London tribes (sort of their version of the "Be-In").
        * It was a major event – promoting "peace & love" — that was covered from as far away as San Francisco.
          a.) Another early English psychedelic band, The Soft Machine, was also on the bill.

    2.) The UFO (pronounced "U-FO"): Britain's first psychedelic club managed by Joe Boyd (this venue was originally known as The Blarney Club).
      - December 23, 1966: opening night.
        * Modeled after what they believed, was a typical San Francisco psychedelic nightclub.
          a.) It was also an "all-night" club (alcohol-free).
        * The Pink Floyd were the UFO's featured band on Friday nights.
          a.) In fact, they were UFO's de facto house band.
            - It was here that Pink Floyd honed in their signature light shows, which would forever be associated with their performances.

      - Extended Improvisational Style At This Time:
        * According to one witness: "atonal, non-melodic, walls of sound, and lots of feedback".
          a.) Syd Barrett: led the way while the rest of the band accompanied him.

      - Songwriting: Barrett was writing psychedelic songs that combined the following:

Lucifer Sam
Pink Floyd

        * Psychedelic arrangements of dark guitar sounds and space-like organ licks.
          a.) With catchy, easily memorable pop melodies and humorous, child-like pop poetics.
            - In some case, awash with reverberation (another psychedelic trait).
        * 1967: They were signed by the EMI label.

E.) Recording: An emphasis would be placed on the album format as opposed to the conventional single (a radical idea in this time period).

    1.) They did however, begin by releasing their first single, *Arnold Layne*.

Arnold Layne
Pink Floyd

      - A listener/radio-friendly pop tune brandishing a heavy English accent.
        * A comic story of a kleptomaniac transvestite.
          a.) Made the top 20 on the British pop charts.

See Emily Play
Pink Floyd

- Their following single, "See Emily Play" made the top ten.

2.) "The Piper At The Gates Of Dawn" (1967): Their debut album.
- Recorded at Abbey Road Studios in London.
* Initial Influence: The title of Kenneth Grahame's seventh chapter from his children's novel: *The Wind In The Willows*.
- Released the same year as Britain's other great psychedelic album: "Sergeant Pepper's…" (in the eyes of most critics, "The Piper.." as a great British psychedelic album ranks second to Sgt. Pepper's).
* Many of these songs, written mostly by Syd Barrett, contain a sense of childish, humorous whit and whimsy.

Scarecrow
Pink Floyd

a.) But filtered through the prism of LSD.
- Musical properties:
* Catchy melodies balanced with psychedelic experimentation:

Pow R. Toc H.
Pink Floyd

a.) Dissonance and chromaticism on the organ.
- by keyboardist, Richard Wright.
b.) Strange vocal noises.
c.) Weird sound effects.
- All of this fits the mind "mind expansion" ethos of the European, LSD/Psychedelic experience.
* Along with the dichotomy of mental disorder and derangement.

3.) Whit, Weirdness, Derangement: this combination made "The Piper At The Gates Of Dawn" one of the greatest psychedelic albums.
- And Pink Floyd's only album to involve Syd Barrett.
* He began taking too much LSD and began to lose his senses to the point where he would become catatonic and could no longer perform.
a.) Suddenly, Pink Floyd found themselves without a chief songwriter, lead singer, and visionary.
- He would be replaced by guitarist, David Gilmore (b. 4/6/44, Cambridge, ENG).
* Roger Waters (bass): would emerge as their new dominant writer.

4.) "A Saucer Full Of Secrets" (1968): their next album.
- Would start them on a new direction of a more formal, classically oriented, progressive direction.
* Featuring long instrumental sections.
a.) With darker, more somber colors in a "concept" album format.
- But mixed with the psychedelic influences that they started out with in the beginning.

5.) "Dark Side Of The Moon" (1972): the culmination of this direction.
- Where the new direction engineered by Roger Waters becomes totally solidified.
* And became the benchmark sound for Pink Floyd's musical identity in which the world would henceforth, identify them with.
a.) The album itself, operatic in scale, would serve as the blueprint for their subsequent albums such as; "Wish You Were Here" (1975), "Animals" (1977), "The Wall" (1979)..

VII. THE LATE PSYCHEDELIC ERA
A.) 1968: In America, the album format was achieving dominance over the "single".
1.) This was when albums began outselling singles for the first time.
2.) Albums were also becoming the new benchmark for overall artistic expression and achievement.
B.) "Anthem Of The Sun" (1968): by the Grateful Dead was an example of this format becoming

the preferred vehicle of expression.

      1.) They spent six months recording this album: a combination of both studio songs and live recording.

        - They mixed and edited each album side as a whole.

          * And did it continuously without stopping between songs.

            a.) Conceptually, this continuous editing and mixing was sort of a one-sided composition in and of itself.

              - that held the songs together in a continuum.

C.) In 1968, albums were starting to become conceptual rather than an amalgamation of separate songs.

      1.) But the album was not the only example (during the psychedelic era) of taking something composed of separate entities and eventually presenting it on a more complete, substantive, and higher in scale.

        - The concept of the "Human Be-In" (1/67) would also be brought to new heights.

VIII. A TALE OF TWO GATHERINGS

    A.) The first was <u>Woodstock</u> (8/69). The "Human Be-In" scenario brought to the ultimate extreme.

      1.) The largest concert the world had ever seen up to then.

        - On the schedule: <u>Paul Butterfield Blues Band</u>, <u>Janis Joplin</u>, <u>Sly & The Family Stone</u>, <u>The Who</u>, <u>Crosby, Stills, and Nash</u>, <u>Richie Havens</u>, <u>Ravi Shankar</u>, <u>Country Joe & The Fish</u> (famous for the "Fish Cheer" (i.e. "Give me an F! Give me a U!"), and <u>Jimi Hendrix</u> among many others.

I'm Going Home
Ten Years After

          * Featuring a vast array of psychedelic blues revisionism.

            a.) Example: "<u>I'm Going Home</u>" by Ten Years After.

              - Featuring lead guitarist, Alvin Lee.

      2.) According to <u>Mike Lang</u>, promoter of the Woodstock Festival (and that "other" gathering to be mentioned later):

        - 500,000 people were on sight.

        - They closed the New York Thruway.

        - The Canadian border was also closed.

        - It was estimated that at least 2,500,000 people attempted to get there.

      3.) This concert was not only the "Be-In" concept of the "Gathering of the Tribe" brought to the logical extreme:

        - But also, the publicity this concert generated promoted the peace/love ethic to the mainstream and made it an indelible stamp on pop culture in the late 60's.

          * After all, 500,000 people gathered in one place without any violent

*I-Feel-Like-I'm-
Fixin'-To-Die Rag*
Country Joe & The Fish

          breakout was a shining example.

            a.) In addition, protests against the Vietnam war were expressed by some of the artists the most well known being the: "<u>I-Feel-Like-I'm-Fixin'-To-Die Rag</u>" by Country Joe & The Fish (pre-empted by the infamous "Fish Cheer").

      4.) In addition to turning the "Be-In" into a full blown movement:

        - <u>Woodstock</u> would usher in a new era in rock concerts.

          * For the big names, outdoor festivals and stadiums would be the new norm.

            a.) As opposed to ballrooms and theatres.

        - Woodstock also anticipated the major outdoor concerts of the 70's such as:

          * <u>Watkins Glenn</u>, <u>The California Jam</u>, etc.

            a.) And no doubt served as a modal for the <u>Lollapalooza</u> tours of the 90's and today.

      5.) The other major gathering of the psychedelic era would become the total antithesis of Woodstock.

    B.) <u>Altamont</u> (12/6/69):

1.) The Rolling Stones were creating a documentary film of their "Gimme Shelter" tour of 1969 on the heels of their new album: "Let It Bleed" featuring their new guitarist, Mick Taylor.

- The original plan was for The Stones to make a surprise appearance in a concert at Golden Gate Park in San Francisco on December 6th.

* No one but the concert "insiders" were supposed to know of it.

a.) They would play for about 30 to 40 minutes in the midst of this concert headlined by, among others, The Grateful Dead.

- When The Rolling Stones arrived in New York City, they kicked off the promotion of their tour with a press conference.

* In which Mick Jagger announced that they would play a free concert at Golden Gate Park on December 6th.

a.) Within minutes of the news, the San Francisco Parks Department called the concert organizers and revoked the permit given for this event.

- As a result, a new venue had to be found quickly because people from all over the US were already heading to San Francisco for this free concert.

2.) At the last minute (48 hours before the concert):

- They found a rundown speedway (auto racing track) on the outskirts of San Francisco.

3.) Altamonte Speedway: the new venue of what would be called: "The Woodstock of the West"

- Supervised by the same promoter of Woodstock: Mike Lang.

* Scheduled performers: The Flying Burrito Brothers (featuring Gram Parsons and Chris Hillman), The Jefferson Airplane, The Grateful Dead, and The Rolling Stones.

a.) Security for the concert would be provided by members of The Hell's Angels motorcycle gang.

4.) RESULT: A fiasco in which peace and love were in very short supply.

- The Hell's Angels used brute violence brandishing baseball bats and using them to beat on audience members who tried to get close to the stage.

* A singer for the Jefferson Airplane, Marty Balin, was beaten while on stage during a performance.

a.) The violent situation involving the Hell's Angels members was spiraling out of control.

- For their part, The Grateful Dead, in protest of the violent behavior instigated by this "security detail"…

* Refused to perform on stage.

5.) After sundown, The Rolling Stones appeared on stage and the violence began to re-escalate.

- An individual brandishing a hand gun and pointing it toward the stage was tackled and stabbed to death by Hell's Angels members.

* Immediately in front of the stage.

6.) Altamont: for all practical purposes…

- Was the event that marked the end of the Psychedelic Era.

IX. LEGACY

A.) The legacy of the Psychedelic Era was spearheaded by Gram Parsons (b. Ingram Cecil Conner on 11/5/46, Winter Haven, FL; d. 9/18/73, Joshua Tree, CA).

1.) The father of "Country Rock".

- He originated the concept of country music being performed by a rock band.

2.) He grew up in Waycross, FL where in 1956, he saw Elvis Presley perform for the first time.

- The event became the touchstone that changed his life in the following ways:

* He started listening to radio and buying lots of records

a.) <u>Radio</u>: a mixture of rockabilly and country western.
* He was especially enamored with country artists, The Louvin Brothers.
- He also loved R&B and Rock n' Roll.
b.) He wrote his first tune at the age of 11.
* He began studying piano and learning the art of boogie-woogie.
a.) He later started learning to play the guitar, which would become his main instrument.
- By the age of 15, he was playing in bands.
* He eventually played in a band called The Shilos which featured a banjo and doublebass with a musical influence reminiscent of The Kingston Trio.
3.) He enrolled at Harvard University shortly after the death of his mother (from alcohol poisoning). He majored in Theology.
- He formed a band called <u>The Like</u>.
* In addition to Parsons, the members included John Neuese, guitar; Ian Dunlop, bass; and Mickey Gauvin, drums.
a.) These band members reintroduced Gram Parsons to his country roots.
- Country influences such as George Jones, Ray Price, and Merle Haggard.
b.) As a result, Parsons began playing straight-ahead country music for the first time.
- He also played covers of Southern Soul (especially of STAX artists).
* They became <u>The International Submarine Band</u>.
a.) After which in 1966, the band moved to New York City.
4.) During their New York residency, they developed a heavily country influenced sound mixed with rock.
- After two failed singles on the Columbia label:
* They moved to Los Angeles and recorded their only album: "<u>Safe At Home</u>" (1968) on the "LH1" label (owned by Lee Hazelwood).
a.) The first "country rock" album on record.
- Which Gram Parsons original songs such as "<u>Luxury Liner</u>"

Luxury Liner
The International
Submarine Band

b.) By the time of it's release, the group disbanded.
- Which meant that there was no band to go on tour to promote the album.
B.) After the band's dissolution, Parsons met Byrds bassist, Chris Hillman.
1.) Through Hillman's connection, Gram Parsons joined <u>The Byrds</u> in 1968.
- Hillman became enamored with Parsons' insight into country and R&B which Hillman dubbed as "working man's music".
2.) The subsequent influence of Gram Parsons pushed The Byrds firmly into the country rock sphere.
- RESULT: "<u>Sweetheart Of The Rodeo</u>" (1968) Because he was still under contract with LH1 Records, Parson's voice could only be heard on two singles.
* "<u>Hickory Wind</u>" (written by Parsons) was one of those singles.

Hickory Wind
The Byrds

- NOTE: Although "Safe At Home" became the first country rock album, "<u>Sweetheart Of The Rodeo</u>" became the first *important* country rock album because it introduced the concept of country rock on a much wider scale.
* As a result, it became the touchstone that anticipated the country rock trend of the 1970's.
a.) Artists like <u>The Eagles</u>, <u>Jackson Browne</u>, <u>Crosby, Stills, Nash, & Young</u>, etc.

* Once again, The Byrds would chart a new course in rock and roll that would result in a solid legacy.

C.) <u>Gram Parsons</u>: Eventually left The Byrds out of protest against a scheduled tour of South Africa (in protest against the South African policy of "apartheid).

1.) He would form his next group, <u>The Flying Burrito Brothers</u> along with Chris Hillman (who had left The Byrds after the South African tour).

Christine's Tune (Devil In Disguise)
The Flying
Burrito Brothers

- Hence, the period of the Parsons/Hillman collaboration to country-influenced rock (example: "Christine's Tune").

*The band was devoted to, among other things, the synthesis of R&B and country.

Do Right Woman
The Flying
Burrito Brothers

a.) Example: "<u>Do Right Woman</u>", originally recorded by Aretha Franklin.

- Presented in a country-styled format complete with a pedal-steel guitar sound.

- Their debut album: "<u>The Gilded Palace Of Sin</u>" (1969).

* Sold only 40,000 copies due to no airplay on FM radio.

a.) Radio stations thought their [Burrito's] sound to be too "country".

- And country radio detested the idea of The Burritos putting country influences into their rock n' roll musical mix.

* In an attempt to streamline their musical approach, they released their second (and last) album called, "<u>Burrito Deluxe</u>".

a.) This release marked the end of the Parsons/Hillman collaboration.

2.) Parsons eventually launched into a solo career in the early 70's.

Streets Of Baltimore
Gram Parsons

- And subsequently recorded two critically acclaimed solo albums: "<u>G.P.</u>" (1972) and "<u>Grievous Angel</u>" (1973).

* Which introduced eventual country music legend: <u>Emmylou Harris</u>.

3.) Gram Parsons died in Joshua Tree, CA of an overdose of morphine and tequila on September 18, 1973.

D.) <u>Epilogue</u>: Former psychedelic bands would venture back and rediscover their country/ bluegrass roots (i.e. going back to their basics).

1.) <u>The Grateful Dead</u>: would come out with two country rock/folk albums in 1970:

Uncle John's Band
The Grateful Dead

- "<u>Workingman's Dead</u>" and "<u>American Beauty</u>"

a.) Modeling their vocal harmonizations after the Crosby, Stills, and Nash style.

- And featuring introspective lyrics (another country rock property that Gram Parsons helped spearhead).

CHAPTER VI: REVIEW

LSD (Lysergic Acid Diethylamide): when was it invented?

What could a small amount of this drug do?

Where were the CIA trials held in the early 1960's?

Why did the CIA terminate the LSD trials?

Name two early counter-culture gurus who took part in the LSD trials.
1.)
2.)

They would become known for conducting their own "acid tests". With the addition of other people such as Neal Cassaday, what did they call themselves?

What were "Happenings"?

Name the band that played regularly at these events:

List the original lineup of The Grateful Dead:
1.)
2.)
3.)
4.)
5.)

What was the musical backgrounds for each of these players?
1.) Garcia and Weir:
2.) Phil Lesh:
3.) McKernan and Kreutzman:

In what type of performance context did The Grateful Dead present their combination of styles?

When and where was their recording debut?

What marked Jerry Garcia's songwriting turnabout?

What effect did this collaboration have on Garcia's songwriting craftsmanship?

List the five basic elements that make up the Psychedelic "melting pot" sound:
    1.)
    2.)
    3.)
    4.)
    5.)

Why did artists partake in the sheer intensity of LSD?

    What was the effect of LSD on these artists?

What was the impact of The Thirteenth Floor Elevators?

    What was the name of their treatise (i.e. the liner notes on their debut album)?

List four musical properties of John Coltrane's "India" that would be influential to Psychedelic artists:
    1.)
    2.)
    3.)
    4.)

Name the first Psychedelic hit and the band that recorded it:

    List three influences of this hit derived from Coltrane's "India":
        1.)
        2.)
        3.)

What was the impact of the Gavin Report upon this first Psychedelic hit?

What literary/spiritual source did Dr. Timothy Leary use as a model for his "How-To" manual?

List four items of the San Francisco Psychedelic scene in the Haight-Ashbury district:

1.)
2.)
3.)
4.)

Name the three most important performance venues in the San Francisco psychedelic scene:
      1.)
      2.)
      3.)

Name the three most important bands of the San Francisco Psychedelic scene:
      1.)
      2.)
      3.)

What was the first big event (January 1967) that gave major exposure of the San Francisco psychedelic scene to the American mainstream?

What did they have to learn once they went into the recording studio?

What were the four "results" that San Francisco bands had to correct once they had entered the studio?
      1.)
      2.)
      3.)
      4.)

Name the first San Francisco psychedelic band to sign with a major record and thereby, become the first to gain national notoriety:

    They recorded a single that became the "singles-format embodiment" of what the San Francisco psychedelic scene was all about (events from a famous children's story was used as metaphor). What was that single?

Who was the most authentic blues revisionist of the San Francisco psychedelic scene?

    Who was her main influence?

        Which blues band was she first associated with?

Which breakthrough performance launched her to national notoriety?

Which blues tune did she perform at that event?

Name two other bands that she would later be associated with:

Name her last, and most commercially successful album of 1970:

List five of The Grateful Dead's general influences:
1.)
2.)
3.)
4.)
5.)

How did they synthesize these American Musical Tradition influences?

List the significance of the following individual (improvisational) influences:
1.) Lightnin' Hopkins (for "Pigpen" McKernan):

2.) Scotty Stoneman and John Coltrane (for Jerry Garcia):

3.) What were Phil Lesh's influences?

By the mid to late 60's, The Grateful Dead had honed in a specific approach to their extended improvisational style. There were three major elements to that style assigned to three different players. Which element were the following players responsible for?

Jerry Garcia:
Phil Lesh:
Bob Weir:
Bill Kreutzman:

Name two albums from 1970 where The Grateful Dead honed in their songwriting in a traditional singles format:
1.)
2.)

Which album was Brian Wilson's most notable contribution to Psychedelic music?

If you could use one word to characterize the music in this album, what would it be? (Hint: it's not the word, "psychedelic")

What Beatles album would this [Brian Wilson's] album have a major impact upon? (At least insofar as this [Beatles'] album's conception)

What was the most important difference between the extended improvisations of European Psychedelic bands and those bands in America?

Name the three most important West Berlin Psychedelic bands:
    1.)
    2.)
    3.)

What was their musical emphasis?

Name the first important psychedelic band in England:

List four members of their original lineup:
    1.)
    2.)
    3.)
    4.)

Which member was this group's original visionary, songwriter, and front man?

List two obscure blues artists that became the source of this band's name:

During their early years, what was Pink Floyd's approach to covering songs of blues-derived artists – what did they do during instrumental breaks or solos?

When and where was their first attempt at using mixed media?

Pete Jenner (their manager) encouraged Syd Barrett to use techniques inspired by an experimental band – name that band:

What was their [the experimental band's] style?

What was one of the techniques that Pete Jenner suggested to Syd Barrett?

Where was Pink Floyd's first regular performance venue and what were these concerts known as?

What were Syd Barrett's literary influences?

What were his primary and additional musical influences?

What was Syd Barrett's performance practice in regard to his extended improvisation?

Where was their first major show?

Name the first psychedelic club in London.

Name this band's debut album, which, incidentally, is the only album Syd Barrett was involved in.

1968 marked first milestone for albums in comparison to singles. What was this milestone? (Hint: it had to do with sales)

The impact of Woodstock ushered in a new era in rock concerts involving major acts. What was that impact?

Which concert marked the end of the Psychedelic era?

Who was credited as the father of country rock?

Who were his country roots influences that he was reintroduced to?

Name the first "country rock" album on record.

The Byrds released the first important country rock album in 1968. Name that album. (Hint: the father of country rock was involved in this album)

What was the legacy of the Psychedelic movement?

CHAPTER VIIa: ANTAGONIZATIONS: PROTO PUNKS

I.THE INTRODUCTION OF NEW CONCEPTS IN ROCK 'N ROLL
    A.) The Birth of a Postmodernist Movement [in Rock 'n' Roll]:
        1.) Definition of the term "postmodernism: where the boundary between so-called high art (i.e. avant-garde) and pop art is blurred (in this case, pop art refers to "garage band").
            - Bands that were involved in this movement had synthesized their own individual styles with elements derived from avant-garde influences – musical, literary, or theatric.

Dirty Water
The Standells
                * In other words, these artists reached up and borrowed from these high art influences and manifested them within a garage band format. An example of garage band is illustrated in The Standells', *Dirty Water*.
            - In addition to borrowing high art influences some of these artists had direct connections to visual art or theatrical art inner circles.
                * These inner art circles played a major role in influencing outside avant-garde elements, which garage band artists would adopt into their own unique, musical mix.
        2.) Additional New Concepts: Besides the birth of postmodernism, there were two other important concepts:
            - The challenge against conventional success.
            - Extreme expression out front in the absence of traditional musical skill.
    B.) Conventional Success Is Challenged: Sometimes, not all of Rock and Roll stories are measured by chart successes in the commercial sense.
        1.) Some of the most important innovators in Rock and Roll have been complete commercial failures.
            - Barely selling any records during their most creative periods.
        2.) Reasons:
            - Inaccessibility: Their body of work was too esoteric to connect with a mainstream audience.
            - Too Precursory: Their work may have been so far ahead of its time, that it would take mainstream audiences decades to mature to the innovator's level and thus, appreciate the work.
            - Subject Matter: It was either too morbid, negative, or "anti". Subjects that mainstream audiences were definitely not accustomed to. These artists would delve into areas of taboo such as:
                * Heroin addiction (in the first person).
                * Sado-masochism.
                * Tough NYC street life.
            - Androgyny: Another realm of taboo [that they delved into] which horrified mainstream America.
                * Due to their [mainstream American society's] mostly Puritan heritage and homophobia (in England, it was always treated as camp or satirical).
            - The Grit: The sound would be crude, unpolished, and in many cases, aggressive.
                * Complete with annoying noises/sounds such as feedback (among other things).
        3.) All of these elements – together or separately – insured that this music, back in the mid to late 60's, would experience commercial failure (with one notable exception to be discussed later).

                * Thereby, becoming a touchstone for a new movement that would have one of the most important legacies in rock and roll.
            - There is also certain romanticism in failure that leads to an indelible legacy.

* The supreme sacrifice for the sake of art (i.e. be destitute now, become a major legend later).

C.) <u>Extreme Expression Out Front</u> In the absence of highly skilled musicianship, these artists will concentrate primarily on extreme expression "out front" (making up for diminished skill level),

    1.) In other words, what one *says* is more important than the skill level on which they say it. Musicianship skill – or lack thereof – is irrelevant. The door will now become open for rudimentary-skilled artists to make a significant musical contribution.

        - Rock n' roll will adopt a more proletariat nature.

    2.) <u>NOTE</u>: It is worth noting that the focus of the first six chapters of this course dealt mainly with the concept of elevated levels of artistic expression through great musicianship (i.e. Motown, Blues Revisionism, The Beatles, Little Richard, etc.).

        - Beginning with this chapter and throughout the remainder of the course, the focus will deal various expression-out-front alternatives such as punk, alternative, hip hop, etc.). <u>The only exception</u>: Chapter XI covering the development of Funk.

II. <u>THE IRONY</u>:

    A.) In many ways, this is a tale of some of rock and roll's greatest success stories.

    1.) And one in which America and the rest of the civilized world needs to hear because it runs contrary to the standard successes (i.e. money, power, popularity, etc.) that those in the mainstream are socialized to believe.

        - In other words, the greatest achievements can be measured by artistic innovations and the legacy that they leave, rather than by monetary wealth -- especially in the face of commercial failure.

    B.) <u>Genus: Audience Antagonization</u>:

    1.) At that time, the psychedelic peace/love movement was in full gear.

        - But these new innovators would challenge this positive ideal by confronting the audience to the point of becoming outright offensive and disturbing -- sometimes, in a highly aggressive manner.

        - They would also act out certain fantasies and inhibitions on stage along with their insecurities.

    2.) As a result, they considered the mass rejection from the Woodstock generation a badge of honor.

        - They reveled at being the outcasts because they felt that they spoke for a small segment of the New York under-society who shared their [outcasts'] views.

        * They also anticipated that in the long run, their movement would develop in a wider scale.

C.) These outsiders were frowned upon by the record industry and dismissed as incompetent, crude, grotesque, negative, and above all, scum.

    1.) It is now time to focus on the outsiders/commercial failures that will have one of the greatest impacts on the development of rock and roll for decades up to the present day.

    2.) The story begins in New York City with an artist who wanted to "shake things up".

        - The artist in question was <u>Andy Warhol</u> and the group he sponsored was <u>The Velvet Underground</u>.

        *Who along with <u>The Stooges</u> and <u>MC5</u> would constitute a new movement known as the "<u>Proto-Punks</u>".

III. <u>THE VELVET UNDERGROUND</u>

    A.) First postmodernist artists [in rock and roll] that synthesized high art and low art namely, avant-garde influences with the garage band ethos. Named after a book of sado-masochism by author Michael Leigh (Found in a gutter in the Bowery section of lower Manhattan by M. Conrad).

    1.) Original line-up:

        - <u>Lou Reed</u> (b. Louis Furbank, 3/2/42, Brooklyn, NY): vocals, guitar.

        - <u>John Cale</u> (b. 12/5/40, Garnant, Wales): viola, guitar, bass, keyboards.

        - <u>Sterling Morrison</u> (b. Holmes Sterling Morrison Jr., 8/29/42, Westbury, NY; d. 8/30/95, Poughkeepsie, NY): guitar, bass.

- Angus MacLise (b. 3/14/38, Bridgeport, CT; d. 6/21/79, Katmandu, Nepal): drums, percussion.
    * Later replaced by Moe Tucker (b. Maureen Tucker, 8/26/44, Levittown, NY)
B.) Lou Reed: as a child, he was trained in classical piano (according to the liner notes in "The Velvet Underground" box set).
    1.) As a teenager, he joined a group called "The Shades" and in 1958, recorded his first single with them entitled, "So Blue". His early influences were:
        - 50's R&B vocal groups: The Paragons and The Diablos.
        - Rockabilly: Warren Smith and Carl Perkins (both were Sun Records artists).
            * These influences would remain a part of Reed's influential foundation throughout his adult career.

Rock 'n' Roll Ruby
Warren Smith

    2.) Syracuse University: where he was an English major and enrolled in the film and drama schools.
        - Was also a DJ at the campus radio station.
        - It was at Syracuse where he met and jammed with Sterling Morrison (a non-matriculating student there).
C.) His avant-garde poetic/literary influences:
    1.) Delmore Schwartz (poet in residence and Lou Reed's mentor at Syracuse): taught Reed the art of the English language and the art of *being* a poet. In addition, he also inspired Reed to fall in love with the language's creative possibilities.
        - To Schwartz, the writing of language was more than just a career. As he alludes to in his work, "In Dreams Begin Responsibilities" that, in a fearful age of anxiety that encompasses civilization:
            * "...the poet must be prepared to be alienated and indestructible".
        - In other Words: The poet, in order to maintain the sacred trust, must forgo any aspiration of commercial success in order to protect the integrity of the art and to truly interpret his contemporaneous life and times (and not be blinded by materialism).
            * This attitude of eschewing commercial gain would prove crucial to the artistic development of The Velvet underground later on.
    2.) Reed's Other Literary Influences:
        - *Last Exit to Brooklyn* by Hubert Selby
        - *Naked Lunch* and *Junky* by William Burroughs
            * The latter influential to the song, "Heroin", which Reed wrote while at Syracuse).
        - Raymond Chandler: perhaps his greatest influence. Lou Reed loved Chandler's ability to create "profound images in a very simple language" (which would become Reed's signature approach to lyric writing).
            * Chandler became famous for his crime novels featuring the detective Phillip Marlowe that included *The Big Sleep* (1939) and *Farewell My Lovely* (1940).
            * In addition to simplicity, Chandler's literary style was famous for two other things:
                a.) Dialectics depicting a union of opposites.
                b.) The catchy one-liner. For example: "The big foreign car drove itself, but I held the wheel for the sake of appearances" from *Farewell My Lovely*.
    3.) Reed's first professional gig was as an artist for Pickwick Records.
        - Where he developed his own personal melodic/tunesmith art form and chorus (refrain) style -- critical to his eventual work with the Velvet Underground.
            * It was also at Pickwick where he met John Cale.
D.) John Cale: grew up saturated in traditional music. Especially Welsh choral music.
    1.) Was also influenced by a relative who wrote hymns and another who played the fiddle.

- <u>His initial rock and roll influence</u>: Alan Freed's weekly shows in the late 50's broadcast on Radio Luxembourg.
2.) <u>Formal education</u>: Goldsmith College of Art in London.
   - Where he composed his first symphony.
   - He also was a recipient of the "Leonard Bernstein Scholarship" at the <u>Tanglewood Music Center</u> (Lenox, MA - summer home of the Boston Symphony Orchestra).
        * Following that experience, John Cale moved to Manhattan for the following reasons:
            a.) The New York avant-garde Movement.
            b.) The "Fluxus" Movement (da-daism).
   - New York is also where he joined Lamont Young's "<u>Dream Syndicate</u>".
        * Performing drone-laden pieces with repetitive minimalist rhythmic motives.
        * He also started playing the viola, which he would tune to the hum of the amplifier.
3.) <u>Cale's Avant-Garde Influences</u>:
   - <u>Lamont Young</u>: The Drone.
        * <u>Lamont Young's theories</u>: involving basic chords was this:
            a.) If you could find 3 basic chords that share the same pair of identical pitches, you could hold those identical pitches indefinitely throughout the entire piece (like a drone), thereby creating a dreamlike quality.
            b.) <u>NOTE</u>: These "Dream Syndicate" influences became the primary musical foundation for John Cale's compositional approach with the Velvet underground.
   - <u>Terry Riley</u>: Minimalism.

In C
Terry Riley

        * <u>Minimalism</u>: A rhythmic technique derived from Eastern influences which involves perpetual repetition of a rhythmic fragment or idea.
            a.) <u>Terry Riley</u>: a former Lamont Young collaborator, helped introduce the art of minimalism into the New York art music scene.
   - <u>Small Faces</u> (and to a lesser degree, The Who): Electric Guitar Noises.
        * Inspired during a trip that Cale took to the UK. Small Faces were one of the early Mod groups in England.

*Watcha Gonna
Do About It*
Small Faces

            a.) Their use of noise was the key especially: the use of feedback and other crackling electric guitar noises.
               - "<u>Watcha Gonna Do About It</u>": the noise-ridden Small Faces single that inspired John Cale.
            b.) This constituted a major influence in The Velvet's use of noise to convey the following:
               - Extreme expression "out front".
               - Annoyance and antagonization of audiences.
4.) Sterling Morrison's guitar influences:
   - <u>Bo Diddley</u>: his 1955 hit single, "Bo Diddley" was Morrison's first major influence.
   - <u>Additional early influences</u>: Mickey Baker, T-Bone Walker, and Jimmy Reed.
   - <u>Later influences</u>: Lonnie Mack, Steve Cropper, and D'Jange Reinhardt.
        * <u>NOTE</u>: Even though Lou Reed and Sterling Morrison loved the blues, they were not devotees attempting to emulate the blues style.
E.) The Formation of The Velvet Underground.
   1.) <u>Early 1965</u>: after hearing songs written by Lou Reed that included "Heroin" among other things: Cale and Reed decided to form a band.
   - Cale invited guitarist <u>Sterling Morrison</u> to join the group.
   - <u>Angus Maclise</u>: who was also associated with Lamont Young's "Dream Syndicate" became the drummer.

2.) They were originally called, "The Warlocks". They later named themselves, "The Falling Spikes" until they finally settled on The Velvet Underground.

- By that time, "Venus In Furs" – a song dealing with sado-masochism -- was already written (inspired by Sacher-Masach's volume of the same name).

* For Reed and The Velvets, writing about S &M was not about sexual deviance but rather, a literary exercise.

3.) Debut Performance: Spring of 1965 – *Film-Maker's Cinematheque*, New York City.

- The show entitled, "The Launching of the Dream Weapon" was arranged by Piero Heliczer. It was a show for mixed media.

* The Velvet Underground performed behind the film screen.

* NOTE: This was an early example of the high art/rock and roll synthesis in live performance (to be suggestive of postmodernism).

a.) In addition, it began the New York tradition of rock 'n' roll artists having direct connections to visual art scenes and inner circles that would remain in place throughout the punk and post punk eras.

4.) Al Aronowitz: arranged the Velvet Underground's first paid gig at Summit High School in New Jersey for $75. Angus MacLise considered this paid gig, a "sell-out" of artistic principal and subsequently left the band.

- Drummer, Moe Tucker, replaced him

5.) Café Bizarre (New York City): their first bar gig (6 sets for $5 apiece).

- They were fired for performing "The Black Angel's Death Song" one too many times. But as fate would have it, on that same night, Andy Warhol happened to be in the audience and liked what he saw.

The Black Angel's Death Song
The Velvet Underground

* The Black Angel's death Song: Poetry that makes no literal sense. Instead, the poetry is focused on the rhythmic flow of the syllables.

a.) To quote Lou Reed: "The idea here was to string words together for the sheer fun of their sound…" (another example of a poetic idea from a high art perspective).

F.) Andy Warhol (b. Andrew Warhola, 1928, Pittsburgh, PA; d. 2/22/87, New York): pop artist who sponsored The Velvet Underground.

1.) Background: After an early career as a successful commercial artist for major magazines such as *Vogue, The New Yorker*, and *Harper's Bizarre*; he launched his first individual art show in 1952 entitled: "Fifteen Drawings Based on the Writings of Truman Capote".

- But it was during the 1960's that he made his initial impact upon the art world.

* He took mass-culture images that were well known among the populace and presented them as art. Some images included the Campbell's soup can and various celebrities such as Marilyn Monroe.

2.) Postmodern Concept: By highlighting mass-culture images, Warhol's work blurred the line between high art and advertising – it was shown in high art museums such as the Guggenheim, but maintained the essence of popular art.

- He also kept his 16mm video camera rolling (sort of foreshadowing YouTube), perpetually in his studio chronicling activity of his entourage like a fly on the wall.

* He also released films such as *Chelsea Girls*.

3.) The Factory: Warhol's home and studio located on 33rd Street and Madison Avenue in New York – a non-stop activity center of his inner circle/entourage and whoever else happened to drop in. It was also his perpetual film set.

- The Velvet Underground became a regular part of The Factory culture.

* Lou Reed was always taking notes of the activity surrounding him [at The Factory] and would use them as subject matter for his songs.

a.) The song, *All Tomorrow's Parties* was one example.

4.) Warhol's Mission for The V.U: To disturb and antagonize audiences as a viable art form.

- In Lou Reed's words: "To shake things up a bit".

* In addition, Warhol wanted to jolt the audience out of their apathy and to revolt against what he felt, was the gimmickry of the "peace/love" ethos.

      a.) His goal was to spark uneasy/disturbed reactions from the audience as they were leaving the theatre or club.

5.) He wanted The Velvet Underground to accompany a dance duo called "The Exploding Plastic Inevitable" --- Gerard Melanga and Mary Woronov.

- They basically performed sado-masochistic fantasies under a strobe light.

      * They would sometimes, aggressively bring the show to the audience.

- NOTE: For all practical purposes, The Velvet Underground/Exploding Plastic Inevitable collaborations introduced a sense of theater in rock and roll for the first time in live performance – this concept (theatre art synthesized with rock and roll) would grow on a considerably larger scale in the mid 70's.

G.) Their Debut Album: In 1965, they recorded their first demo tape at John Cale's Ludlow Street apartment in New York. It was a crude, roughshod affair where traffic could be heard in the background.

1.) They later recorded a more professional demo tape at Scepter Studios.

- As a result, producer Tom Wilson (who produced Bob Dylan's hit, "Like A Rolling Stone"), signed The Velvet Underground to Verve Records (a subsidiary of MGM).

2.) The Velvet Underground and Nico (1967): their debut album. A compilation of songs worked up thus far.

- They re-recorded "I'm Waiting For The Man", "Venus In Furs", and "Heroin" (which were previously on their Scepter Studio demo tape) under producer Tom Wilson at T.T.G. Studios in Los Angeles.

      * The remaining songs of the album were directly from the Scepter demo tape except one.

- "Sunday Morning": the only new song for the album (not previously recorded) that was composed following the Los Angeles recording session at T.T.G .

Sunday Morning
The Velvet Underground

      * John Cale noticed a Celeste sitting in the studio: a small, compact keyboard instrument that sounds like little bells or chimes being played.

          a.) Lou Reed wrote "Sunday Morning" as a result of this Celeste discovery and the group recorded it in New York (it became the opening track on the album).

- Warhol: brought to the band, a female singer or, as he would refer to as, a "Chanteuse" named Nico (b. Christa Päffgen, 10/16/38, Cologne, GER; d. 7/18/88, Ibiza, SP).

      * He tried to convince the band to accept her as a part of the group, which they never completely did.

      * She had a small, walk-on role in Frederico Fellinni's film, "La Dolce Vita" and also became a famous modal.

All Tomorrow's Parties
The Velvet Underground

      * She would record three songs with her voice as the lead:

          a.) Femme Fatale", "All Tomorrow's Parties", and "I'll Be Your Mirror".

3.) Style of The Velvet Underground and Nico: Basic, sometimes crude garage band essence elevated by various avant-garde influences – both musical and poetic.

- Avant-Garde influences: The Drone (Lamont Young Influence), Minimalism (Terry Riley Influence), and Electric Guitar Noises (where the Mod group, Small Faces and The Who were influential).

      * In addition, Lou Reed's literary influences from, among others: William Burroughs, Hubert Selby, and Raymond Chandler.

- NOTE: By synthesizing these musical and literary avant-garde influences into a garage band format, The Velvet Underground raised the artistic level of their sound while keeping the garage band ethos intact.

      * Thus the concept of postmodernism – the blurring of the line between high art and low art -- was introduced into rock and roll.

4.) Examples:

- "I'm Waiting For The Man": a first person account of a heroin addict experiencing the initial onset of withdrawal symptoms while waiting for his drug dealer. The story takes place in a black neighborhood in upper Manhattan (in Harlem).

* Contains a simple, steady, and highly repetitive eight-note pulse that every member of the band is performing – a minimalist feature.

   a.) With everyone doing it, this driving, minimalistic pulse remains the song's prominent feature.

   b.) Like their drummer Mo Tucker said in an interview: "It's like a train. It starts and then takes off".

- "Venus In Furs": a poetic account of sado-masochism.

   * Drone: Contains a drone on an open fifth interval (D - A) that is expressed rhythmically (in the percussion) and multi-tracked on the viola.

   * Minimalist Essence: Repeated string-slides on the viola (portamento) throughout the song.

   * Only two harmonic regions: D and E .

   * Poetics: Words that are simple yet full of depth (from a poet's perspective):

   a.) Example: " Comes in bells, your servant don't forsake him. Strike dear Mistress and cure his heart"…

- "Heroin": quasi Shakespearian in nature.

   * Lyrically: a soliloquy for a heroin addict reflecting upon a life with no direction.

   a.) The effect of the heroin's intoxication gives him a temporary (albeit false) sense of exuberance that is detached from the realism of his actual situation.

      - Hence, the Raymond Chandler dialectic of opposites: reality vs. unreality (his self-destructive real life vs. the intoxicated fantasy of his imaginary escape). Then back to reality again.

   * Musical High Art (Avant-Garde) influences:

   a.) The Drone: Screechy drone on the viola (an interval of a fifth) heard on adjacent open strings.

   b.) Minimalism: Alternation between the D and G chords that persists throughout the entire song.

   c.) Feedback Noise: during the fourth stanza, after the tempo acceleration, a wall of feedback begins to appear. This happens at the point where he describes the intoxicating effects of the heroin reaching to the center his head (the feedback representing the "head rush") -- a stark example of extreme expression "out front".

      - This feedback wall eventually becomes massive. Then, at the end of the song, it dissipates.

   * Tempo: acceleration and de-acceleration. Tempo accelerates along with the gradual increase of words.

   a.) Expresses the feeling of heroin being injected into the vein (in the first person).

   b.) The tempo acceleration also mimics the sensation, both physically and emotionally of the "rush" involving the incoming heroin.

      - This tempo acceleration is featured in the middle point of every stanza.

   c.) After the stanza is complete, it slows down to the original slow tempo.

H.) <u>Spring of 1966</u>: Andy Warhol took the Velvet Underground and The Exploding Plastic Inevitable to the epicenter of the hippie peace/love movement: <u>San Francisco</u>.

    1.) The concert series was scheduled at the Fillmore Auditorium from May 27th through the 29th.

        - The audience according to Moe Tucker, liked them. But in her words the critics, club owners, and music people didn't like them at all.

    2.) Among the audience members, was a young, UCLA film student who made the long trip from LA to see them.

        - He would return to LA inspired to begin writing his own material.

    3.) In addition, the Velvet Underground performances either in New York or in the many other venues throughout the US, would inspire other artists and bands to make there start.

        - <u>Brian Eno</u> (Roxy Music), <u>Rick Ocasek</u> (The Cars), <u>Chrissie Hynde</u> (The Pretenders), <u>Iggy Pop</u> (The Stooges), and <u>David Bowie</u>.

            * <u>Joy Division</u> (Manchester, England), <u>Can</u>, and <u>Faust</u> (both psychedelic bands from Berlin, Germany).

                a.) The inspiration of The Velvet Underground created quite a line-up.

        - Their performances at places in Cleveland like La Cave and The Masonic Auditorium also become a touchstone for an early to mid 70's Punk movement in that city.

    4.) Their first major influence however, rested upon that film student from Los Angeles...

IV. JIM MORRISON (b. 12/8/43, Melbourne, FL; d. 7/3/71, Paris, France)

    A.) <u>Background</u>: as a son of a Rear Admiral in the US Navy, his family had consistently moved to many different locations.

    1.) His father was also a strict disciplinarian.

        - Which may explain Morrison's rebelliousness once he broke away from his home environment.

    2.) He attended St. Petersburg Junior College and Florida State University for one year each.

        - and then enrolled at UCLA majoring in film and theater.

    3.) His first literary influence: the quirky humor of *MAD Magazine*.

        - His first serious literary influence: *On The Road* by Jack Kerouac.

        - His other literary influences were author <u>William Blake</u>, theatre artist <u>Antonin Artaud</u>, and the late 19th century German philosopher: <u>Frederick Nietzche</u>.

    4.) His studies began to taper off when he began to seriously pursue his interest in poetry.

        - and taking LSD.

    5.) For him, an LSD trip didn't unlock the doors to a hallucinogenic world rich with beauty and spirituality.

        - Instead, his acid trip perceptions dealt with morbidity, dark theatrics, and twistings of psycho-sexuality -- another key to his poetic creativity.

    B.) <u>Musical Beginnings</u>: after his experience with the Velvet Underground concert, Morrison started writing lyrics for songs. Among his early musical influences was the LA band: *Love*.

    1.) He showed them to a fellow cinematography student at the UCLA film school: <u>Ray Manzarek</u> (b. 2/12/35, Chicago, IL).

A House Is Not A Motel

Love

        - He became so impressed with Morrison's talent for lyricism (from a poet's perspective). They decided to form a band.

            * <u>Manzarek</u>: was also a writer himself. He studied classical piano early in his life and was currently in a blues band called Rick & The Ravens.

                 a.) He was also making quality films as a student at UCLA.

    2.) <u>Robbie Krieger</u> (b.1/8/46, Los Angeles, CA) and <u>John Densmore</u> (b. 12/1/44, LA): who both played for a band called: "The Psychedelic Rangers" reunited to join Morrison's/Manzarek's band.

        - <u>Robbie Krieger</u>: among his talents, he was an experienced flamenco guitarist.

* He could also play the guitar in a slide fashion using a bottleneck. His additional influences were rock, folk, and blues.

> a.) Of all the band members, his musical background was the most eclectic -- he could also compose.

- John Densmore: originally, a jazz drummer with a flare for theatricality.

3.) Ray Manzarek knew Densmore and Krieger from a meditation/yoga class that they were all attending. It was there that Manzarek eventually recruited them to form a band.

- RESULT: The Doors -- a group with diverse musical backgrounds. The only problem was that they had no bass player. Ray Manzarek had the solution.

> * His acquired a Fender bass keyboard. He played the bassline with his left hand and with his right hand, played melodies, riffs, and chords on the Vox organ/keyboard.

> > a.) Sometimes though not always, a bass player would be hired to play in [some of] their studio recordings.

- Stylistic Ingredients of The Doors:

> * Jim Morrison's poetry, angst, theatrics, and dramatic delivery.
> * Krieger's eclectic mix of blues, rock, and flamenco styles.
> * Densmore's jazzy influences.
> * Manzarek's Vox organ as the most significant signature instrumental sound introducing the main thematic elements.

4.) Jim Morrison's High-Art Literary & Theatric Influences: The common element within each of these influences was that they challenged the conventional norms of their time.

- Friedrich Nietzche (1844-1900): A philosopher who challenged the norms that were firmly in place in the latter 19th Century namely: Christianity and conventional morality.

> * He also believed in what he called "Life Affirmation":

> > a.) Instead of focusing on eternal salvation of the afterlife, he believed in focusing on good health, the creative spirit, and the daily life of the world in which we live and deal with.

> * Another Focus: The quest for power as the motivation of people's actions. Some of those aspects include:

> > a.) An emphasis of the power of the will, uprightness, and self assertion: especially in music.
> > b.) A megalomaniacal sense of power of one over the masses.
> > c.) The concept of violence as an acceptable tool (to include in one's metaphysics).

> * Nietzche's most influential work (upon Morrison): The Birth of Tragedy from the Spirit of Music.

> > a.) Investigates the dialectic duality between the art of the free spirit (being music) and the art of the intellectual (being sculpture).

- Antonin Artaud (1895-1948): Pioneered the concept of audience confrontation by creating more direct contact between actors on stage and the audience.

> * Concept: To bring out the inner darkness and cruelty of the characters to the surface and in the process, disturb the audience emotionally.

> > a.) He attempted to shake the audience out of their voyeuristic complacency in order to make them feel the inner depths of humankind (portrayed in an extreme manner by the actors).
> > b.) In addition, by forcing an emotional reaction from the audience, Artaud turned that audience into participants (as opposed to detached spectators).

> * His Mental Instability (actually an illness): was interpreted by the public as a rebellious streak against conventional morality, rationale, and institutionalized conventions.

> > a.) Influential quote by Artaud: "We must recognize that the theatre, like the plague, is a delirium and is communicative.."

- <u>William Blake</u> (1757-1827): poet, mystic, and illustrator who championed imagination over rationality by creating poetry and illustrations that were apocalyptic and mythical
  * No doubt initially due in part, to his visions of seeing God and angels in a tree when he was a child. This partly inspired his creation of fantasy creatures that captured one's imagination.
    a.) His characters rebelled against the authority of organized religion and the law (especially that of the monarchy).
  * He wrote both short poems and long narrative poems (at times, in one long extended stanza as opposed to sections).
    a.) One such poem (dealing with latter): *Auguries of Innocence* -- a poem that was influential to Jim Morrison in his own attempts to write long extended poems ("The Lizard" being one of his examples).
  * "When the doors of perception are cleansed, man will see things as they truly are infinite" -- from Blake's *The Marriage of Heaven and Hell.*
    a.) <u>Aldus Huxley</u>: inspired by this William Blake quote, titled his book on psychedelic experiences with LSD and mescaline: *The Doors Of Perception.* It was from this title that Jim Morrison got the inspiration for the name of his Group: "<u>The Doors</u>"..

- <u>Arthur Rimbaud</u> (1854-1891): As someone who was pugnacious and irreverent, Rimbaud spent his early adulthood testing real-life and moral boundaries to the extreme. This led to excessive bouts of debauchery, intoxication, and scandalous behavior. He was also one to engage in shocking behavior (like urinating in public on the work of a poet that he detested).
  * He gave up any semblance of caution when it came to experiencing the chaos of his primal senses.
    a.) For Jim Morrison, Rimbaud was a role modal of life (he once said that he was the reincarnation of Rimbaud).
  * Rimbaud was iconoclastic against the conventional French literary circles.
    a.) Unlike conventional poetry, Rimbaud's was considerably <u>angst</u> ridden. A noteworthy example was his last masterpiece, *A Season In Hell* that he wrote when he was 19 years of age (he started writing seriously when he was 16).
  * Of language, Rimbaud wrote: "Gives rhythm to the words, speaks directly to, and unites souls. The alphabet of the soul! Pristine, Indestructible".

- <u>Norman O. Brown</u> (1913-2003): Freudian-influenced philosopher whose best known work, *Life Against Death* (1959), was highly influential to Jim Morrison.
  * A shocking piece of Freudian interpretation for its time. He stated that humankind was subconsciously geared toward self-destruction due in big part, to its collective sexual repression which he viewed as, "the universal neurosis of mankind".
    a.) In his view, the path to resurrection from mass repression was for society to partake in a reconnection with the natural world – to transcend class or personal boundaries and become one with nature.
    b.) <u>The Key To This Unity with Nature</u>: Liberation by means of total expressive freedom and the embracing of childlike playful abandon.
  * Through Brown's influence, Morrison saw through audience confrontation (and control), a way to affect such crowd liberation from what he felt, was their repression-induced apathy.

5.) <u>Morrison's Lyrics</u>: Could be overt expressions of insanity, darkness, sexuality, and deathly, angst-ridden visions.
- He chose the words first and then, put a simple tune to them by singing [the tune].
6.) The Doors' first club gig: The London Fog (in Los Angeles) – nobody showed up.
- <u>The Whiskey a Go Go</u>: The club where The Doors built their initial fan base. In time, Jim Morrison, due to his melodramatic, eccentric, and sometimes crazy antics on stage, was starting to develop his notoriety.
* And in the process, actually *became* the art.

C.) <u>The Education of Jim Morrison, the Performer</u>:
1.) At first, Jim Morrison was a neophyte on stage.
- Very shy. At times, he would turn his back to the audience.
- The more accustomed he grew to performing, the more bold his gestures became. <u>Example</u>: he started using the mike as a phallic symbol.
2.) He began to adopt a new persona: the threatening "<u>Lizard King</u>" – another example of theatre synthesized with rock 'n' roll.
- Due in part to the influence of The Velvet Underground/Exploding Plastic Inevitable theatrics he witnessed in San Francisco as well as his literary, and theatrical influences.
* In this case, Morrison created a character that he played like an actor.
3.) He also realized that he had a certain power to move audiences into a frenzy.
- <u>Audience confrontation</u>: Purpose - to rouse the audience – in his personal view -- out of their apathy.
* The <u>Antonin Artaud</u> and the <u>Norman O. Brown</u> (among others) influences were the touchstones for this.
* The other, was <u>Julian Beck's Living Theatre</u>.
a.) Their main emphasis was both extreme audience confrontation and acting out extreme scenarios of pain and torture. -- right down to the actors venturing out into the audience and screaming in their [audience members'] faces.
b.) <u>GOAL</u>: to make the audience FEEL. To bring out an emotional reaction.
c.) Morrison himself attended six performances of the "Living Theatre" and took Julian Beck's lessons to heart which manifested in his own audience confrontations.
4.) <u>RESULT</u>: In addition to his approach on audience confrontation, the melodramatic interpretations of his lyrics, and his Shaman-like dancing, Jim Morrison developed a highly dramatic persona on stage. He not only added drama into rock 'n' roll but also…
- Due to the synthesis of his high-art theatric, philosophical, and literary influences presented in a pop music format, Jim Morrison introduced the concept of a pop/rock postmodernist movement* to the mainstream public.

* The postmodernist movement as that initiated by The Velvet Underground. Where, within this context -- as opposed to experimentation (inherent in the Psychedelic Movement) -- these [postmodernist] artists incorporated high-art influences within their basic, blueprint structures of musical, lyrical, and performance practice. In other words, their high-art/low-art synthesis was part of their modus operandi.

D.) <u>Their Debut Album</u>: After being dropped from the CBS label, they were signed with an independent label, Elektra Records – founded by Jac Holzman.
1.) They were be produced by Paul Rothschild who once said that The Doors, "Added *drama* into rock 'n' roll" (the ever-growing audiences at The Whiskey a Go Go noticed that drama, too). The result, their debut album: "<u>The Doors</u>" released in January of 1967.
- "<u>Break On Through</u>" (1967): their debut single from this album.

* The Doors utilized their film expertise to create an artsy promotional video of this single.
* This single and accompanied video began the process of The Doors' eventual climb to widespread notoriety and commercial success.

- "Light My Fire": Their second released single and their first to reach #1 on the pop charts on July 25th of 1967. The notoriety generated from this record transformed Jim Morrison and The Doors into pop/rock, mainstream icons.

* This song was written mostly by Robby Krieger with some assistance by Morrison.

- "The End": 11 minutes and 41 seconds of epic drama in an extended singles format. Lyrics depicting separation and departure complete with a controversial Oedipal narrative passage inspired by Nietzche's *The Birth of Tragedy from The Spirit of Music*.

* Musical Character: Begins softly and slowly then builds in volume and dramatic intensity – especially in lengthy instrumental passages between sung verses. Once the passage recedes and subsides, the diminuendo leads to the beginning of a quietly new, sung verse.

> a.) The new verse ushers in a new "scene" and the climactic instrumental passages in between are the lead-ins to other new verses (reminiscent of a film sequence).

* The Climactic Dramatic Moment: Jim Morrison delivers a dramatic spoken narrative reminiscent of an actor in a Shakespearian-like play. With music quietly subsiding, the spoken narrative begins: "The killer awoke before dawn and put his boots on." It ends with the notorious Oedipal passage.

> a.) The Oedipus Legend: A man who murders his father, marries his mother, and answers the ancient riddle of the Sphinx.
>
> b.) Morrison's Oedipal Passage: "Father? Yes Son? I want to kill you". "Mother…I want to...FUCK YOU!!!"

* A whirling, fast tempo'd instrumental passage ensues that gradually accelerates to a temporal, instrumentally dramatic climax (a musical narrative following the spoken one).

> a.) When it's at its loudest and chaotic (an extended cadential ending), the words "Kill, Kill…Kill" are heard. Then, a gradual return to a soft and slow passage that fizzles out and ends the song.

E.) Commercial Success: Wild, negative subject matter notwithstanding, The Doors (unlike The Velvet Underground) would achieve immense commercial success.

1.) This success, was due in part with Morrison's ability to write catchy, easily memorable tunes supporting those dark, droning lyrics.

- Lyrics depicting dark, noire subject matter complete with theatrics and twisted psycho-sexual soliloquies (i.e. "Lament For My Cock"). Some of his lyrics dealt with negativity.

2.) Like Lou Reed, Morrison wrote lyrics from a poet's perspective thereby elevating the artistic quality of his music.

3.) A Notorious Touring Group: As mentioned previously, The Doors success meant massive draws on their concert tours which were becoming the subject of controversy and consternation from various municipal authorities.

- Because of his confrontational reputation, Jim Morrison and The Doors were banned from performing in various cities.

* The police hated and harassed him (sometimes backstage) in practically every concert he performed. It all culminated at the legendary Miami concert in 1969.

- Miami Concert: Jim Morrison was arrested on stage for indecent exposure and allegedly inciting a riot.

* Plus "Lewd and lascivious behavior".

* The ensuing two-month trial resulted in a guilty verdict which drained the group both emotionally and financially.

* This episode basically ended The Doors' career as a touring band.

    a.) Although they would perform in subsequent, individual concerts from time to time.

F.) They returned to the studio and made it their center stage.

    1.) Musically, they re-ignited themselves with two hard rocking albums:

      - "Morrison Hotel" (1970) and "LA Woman" (1971).

    2.) After more police harassment in their subsequent concerts…

      - Jim and his wife Pamela Courson, moved to Paris in order [for him] to seriously pursue his poetry.

        * His first publicly published collection of poems: "The Lords & The New Creatures" (Simon & Shuster,1970).

G.) In Paris, the one thing he was missing, was his band.

    1.) Densmore, Kreiger, and Manzarek deliberately took "second stage" (so to speak) and allowed Morrison the exposure and the glory of being the front man or "face" of the group.

      - In turn, they would keep him in line and become his anchor protecting him from self-destruction (their need of each other was quite mutual).

        * Without the band looking after him, Morrison started to believe his "Lizard King" persona and started acting out his fantasy (at times, dangerously).

    2.) He was found dead in his bathtub, apparently from a heart attack on July 3, 1971 at the age of 27.

      - He was buried in the "Poets' Corner" of Pere Lachaise Cemetery in Paris.

        * In the same vicinity as Balzac, Moliere, and Oscar Wilde.

H.) Someone else would carry on the audience confrontational tradition that Morrison had spearheaded only this time…

    1.) …the concept would be brought a few steps further.

V. THE STOOGES, MC5 AND THE HARD-EDGED, DETROIT ELECTRIC GUITAR SOUND

A.) Iggy Pop (b. James Newell Osterberg, April 21, 1947, Muskegon, MI): A man with two personas: Jim Osterberg – quiet, average-Joe, golfer, and well read individual. The other: Iggy Pop – a rough-hewn, in your face, Wildman type of performance artist.

    1.) The former: his real self, the latter: his on stage persona.

B.) Early Years: Growing up in mobile homes in Ypsilanti – one of which stood within a cornfield (where he once said he hung out in and invented little games).

    1.) He began playing drums when he was in the fourth grade. At that time, he also began his fascination with various noises such as:

      - His father's electric razor.

      - The hum of electric space heaters within his mobile home.

      - The heavy industrial sounds booming out of gigantic auto plants in the Ypsilanti area.

        * This began his interest in sounds from beyond the conventional scope of rock 'n' roll.

    2.) At 15, he became a drummer for a group called, The Iguanas (this was where he was first called Iggy). His favorite influences at this time: The Kinks, The Rolling Stones, and Them.

      - The rest of the band members were enamored with The Beatles and The Ventures.

        * The Iguanas were basically a frat house/local resort band.

    3.) The Prime Movers: Iggy's next band located in the adjacent city of Ann Arbor, Michigan. An uppity blues band who were influenced mostly by The Paul Butterfield Blues Band (featuring guitarist Mike Bloomfield – who also collaborated with Bob Dylan).

- They brandished sophisticated musical tastes that included some avant-garde experimentation.

* They were also influenced by various Chicago Blues artists (who recorded for Chess Records) as well as Mississippi Delta blues.

- He played drums for them for about a year and a half during which time he met the Ashetons (more on that later).

4.) Iggy's Blues/R&B Stints: He was also, a drummer for hire accompanying Motown artists such as The Four Tops, The Marvelettes, and The Contours.

- He noticed through these experiences, various aspects behind the art of performance presentation while sitting [at the drum set] behind these artists

- Chicago: His first trip to Chicago was with his group where he met Chess artists Muddy Waters and Chuck Berry. It was there that he met his blues-drumming mentor, Sam Lay (formerly of The Paul Butterfield Blues Band).

* Iggy also took his training by drumming for blues artists such as Big Walter Horton. It was at this point where Iggy started to seriously practice his singing.

- NOTE: Through his Chicago blues experiences, he learned that the *building blocks* of the creative process were more important than the *actual* finished product. And those *building blocks* [of the creative process] were the manifestation of a unique environment from which that process developed.

* RESULT: Although Iggy realized that he would never be able to capture the blues in an authentic manner, he could adapt the blues influence in an alternative way: by applying it to songs depicting the boredom and delinquency of Midwest, low-rent life (hence the *unique environment*).

a.) It was then, that he decided to be a lead singer in a band. When he returned to Ann Arbor, he contacted the Ashetons.

C.) Ron Asheton: Started off playing the accordion when he was a kid. His brother Scott was interested in playing the drums.

1.) They were both from the "wrong side of the tracks" which would become influential to Iggy's outlandish free-spirited performance style later on. Their juvenile delinquent mentality would become The Stooges' main characteristic.

2.) Ron Asheton: Took up guitar, his brother started playing the drums, and they were joined by bassist Dave Alexander and formed a group called The Dirty Shames.

- A garage band of beginners who exhibited rank amateurism and instrumental ineptitude. They also made a lot of noise.

* The only thing missing was a front man.

D.) The Psychedelic Stooges: Iggy Pop, vocals; Ron Asheton, guitar; Scott Asheton, drums, and Dave Alexander, bass.

1.) In addition to singing, Iggy was also playing on "homemade" Instruments such as a vacuum cleaner, a kitchen blender, and a 50 gallon oil drum with a microphone suspended in it (he beat the oil drum with a metal mallet).

- He also danced rhythmically on a washboard with spiked golf shoes. Dave Alexander engaged in lots of feedback noise.

* In the words of Iggy himself, he described it as "Clang-bang and very annoying -- the more annoying, the better". His use of noises from his homemade instruments were in part, due to the influence of composer Harry Partch.

- Harry Partch: was an art music composer who specialized in microtones and noises. He built his own instruments in order to realize his creative goals.

* It was through the Ann Arbor avant-garde scene that iggy became exposed to some of the high art influences.

2.) Anne Wehrer's House: was the nexus for avant-garde artists (such as Warhol) who came to town and the locals who interacted with them.

- <u>1966</u>: It was there that Iggy first met John Cale (who would later produce The Stooges' debut album), composer Robert Ashley, and Nico among others. (he also saw The Velvet Underground perform in Ann Arbor for the first time).

 * Mixing and interacting with these avant-garde artists were one of his influences.

- <u>Additional influences</u>:

 * <u>Jim Morrison</u>: his low-registered baritone croonsmanship and dramatic way of vocalizing by shouting into the microphone. In addition, his irreverence for the status quo – he played by his own unique performance rules. He inspired Iggy to become a lead singer.

 * <u>Bo Diddley</u>: the repeated rhythmic riff pattern that supported a call & response pattern that was easy to improvise words over.

 * <u>Chuck Berry</u>: subject matter that focused on white teen concerns that effectively focused on catchy phrases like "Sweet Little Sixteen", "School Days", etc. – a cultural focus.

 * <u>Lou Reed</u>: his style of vocalizing over a visceral groove.

3.) <u>Their First Public Performance</u>: a Halloween party at a local teacher's house.

- An avant-garde show complete with his requisite homemade instruments (vacuum cleaner, blender, etc.) and other bizarre instruments like the Theremin. He was also banging noises on an amplified steel guitar.

- <u>Their First Real Gig</u>: as the opening act for Blood, Sweat, & Tears at Russ Gibbs' Grande Ballroom in Detroit (the first of many gigs that they would do there and where they would hone in their unique performance style).

 * The venue itself held about 2000 people.

- NOTE: In time, the various noise/homemade instruments went by the wayside and in their place, was a conventional, minimalist guitar-driven rock 'n' roll band format.

 * But heir wild, kamikaze sense of extreme theater – that eventually led to audience confrontation in order to get a reaction – remained intact.

4.) <u>Their minimalist approach</u>: Music that was stripped down and very basic right down to the bare essentials -- unsophisticated, crude, and simplistic. And because of they were unskilled beginners, a blatant amateurism to their sound resulted. But instead of shunning this amateurism, they embraced it and in the process, became the first true blueprint for what would later become, the conventional punk band.

- Their songs would normally based on a particularly simple repetitive riff and then jam on top of it or improvise in various free-form directions.

 * The crazier Iggy's performance practice became, the crazier the music got (along with guitar noises added in for good measure).

  a.) In essence, The Stooges engaged in extreme expression out front which made up for their amateurish ineptitude. This became another part of their punk band [harbinger] blueprint.

E.) <u>Recording Contract</u>: The group now known as The Stooges (after dropping the "Psychedelic" moniker), were signed to a former folk label, Elektra Records after being discovered by Danny Fields – their [Elektra's] representative sent to Detroit.

1.) He was initially sent to check out the MC5 (Elektra was looking for more rebellious natured artists on the heels of their earlier signing: The Doors). The Stooges however, had caught his attention even more [than the MC5].

- <u>Reason</u>: Iggy Pop's free spirited, rambunctious, in your face performance style. To Danny Fields, Iggy Pop was in a class by himself. Especially when it came to Iggy's approach to audience confrontation – where, if he felt he wasn't getting the reaction he wanted, he would jump out into the audience and "take the show them".

 * As far as Iggy Pop was concerned, his performances were more like meetings (or minglings) with the audience (as opposed to traditional watching and waiting audiences type of shows). In other words, he

made the audience become part of the show (another approach to theater in rock 'n' roll).

2.) <u>Their Debut Album</u>: *The Stooges* (1969). The first record that John Cale produced for Elektra Records. His goal: to capture the essence of their live show and transform it into the studio.

- <u>Technique</u>: To record the instrumental tracks first, then add the vocal track later.

* <u>Songs' subject matter</u>: dealing with boredom, directionless ness, alimentation, and delinquency of Midwest/Michigan life. Examples are "<u>1969</u>" and "<u>No Fun</u>". There was also the element of the bizarre: "<u>I Wanna Be Your Dog</u>".

- Birth of a blueprint of a new guitar sound that would become punk: the repeated, aggressive riff with lots of noise and energy added in.

* That, in addition to shocking audiences with his confrontational, assaultive antics was what made The Stooges so blatantly unique.

3.) *Fun House* (1970): their second album. Produced by Don Gallucci (former keyboardist of one of *the* classic garage bands, The Kingsmen). It was also at this point, that a jazz influenced saxophone player joined them, Steve Mackey.

- Like John Cale, Don Gallucci also wanted to capture the full power of The Stooges' live performance style (and energy) in the studio.

* <u>Solution</u>: To record the entire band in the studio as if they were performing live (instead of instrumental and vocal tracks separately).

a.) They also livened up the studio by stripping the walls of all the baffles that normally muffle and absorb the sound. In other words, the studio was turned into a "live" theatre.

- As a result, this caught a truer essence of their live style.

*<u>Reason</u>: unlike their debut album where John Cale recorded the instrumental track and added the voice later, Gallucci had the group record together as if mimicking a live performance and recorded it into a mono mix.

a.) This approach was a better fit for The Stooges whose playing abilities were very basic/unskilled.

- Yet, whose highly raw, energetic style was best manifested in a live performance format.

- Singles of interest on the "Funhouse" album:

* "<u>Down On The Street</u>": machine riveted drumbeat essence with a powerful electric guitar wall of sound accompanying Iggy Pop's screaming vocals.

* "<u>TV Eye</u>": an "in-your-face" musical assault reminiscent of The Velvet Underground's second album: "White Light, White Heat" (1968).

a.) Where most cuts are noise/distortion ridden with all-out aggression and some dissonance (result of distortion).

- Producing the in-your-face sound.

b.) Compare The Stooges' "<u>TV Eye</u>" with the Velvet Underground's' "<u>I Heard Her Call My Name</u>" (from their *White Light, White Heat* album of 1968)

- For the "in-your-face" comparisons.

* "<u>l.a. Blues</u>": 4 minutes & 55 seconds of no-holds-barred sonic aggression with a cacophony of noise.

a.) A free-form version of the "Wall Of Sound" - Iggy style.

- "<u>Freak-Out</u>": Sounding like noise improvisation. Noisy on the one hand while deliberately annoying on the other. Basically, a collectively improvised amalgamation of their previous sets in one noisy, free-formed piece.

          * This was how they usually ended their live performances.

    4.) The idea of being annoying and offensive to an audience was a combination of both The Velvet underground and The Doors influences.

C.) <u>To summarize Iggy Pop's Music/Performance Style</u>: taking Morrison's concept of audience confrontation even further.

    1.) <u>Musically</u>: would pioneer the concept of musical expression over technique. In other words, the importance of accomplished playing ability was irrelevant.

      - The focus instead, was on pure emotional expression -- even if the band members' performance skills were rudimentary (i.e. at a beginner's level).

        * A framework that would be a musical template for Punk.

    2.) He would in his words, "take the show to the audience".

      - He would jump out into the audience and "mix it up" with them.

        * In order to unleash the rowdy elements, to work them up into a frenzy.

      - At times, an arrest by the police would result on some of his audience confrontations.

        * Especially when he lost his clothes during the confrontational process.

    3.) The development of The Stooges would be stymied because of their increasing problem with drug abuse.

    4.) In addition to The Stooges, there would be another Detroit band.

      - Also signed by Danny Fields, they would unleash their own version of the hard-edged Detroit guitar sound.

D.) <u>MC5</u> (Motor City 5): from Lincoln Park, Michigan - formed in 1964 by…

    1.) <u>Rob Tyner</u>: vocalist, <u>Fred "Sonic" Smith</u>: guitar, <u>Wayne Kramer</u>: guitar, <u>Pat Burrows</u>: bass (would be replaced by Michael Davis), and Bob Gaspar: drums (would be replaced by Dennis Thompson).

      - Another of the bands (like The Stooges) who would adopt the concept of musical expression [taking precedence] over accomplished technique.

        * They started out during their high school years performing at local parties and dances.

    2.) After high school, Smith and Kramer began experimenting with guitar noise (i.e. feedback, distortion, etc.).

      - Because the original bass and drummer didn't relate to this experimentation, they left and were replaced by Davis and Thompson.

Ramblin' Rose
The MC5

    3.) They began performing regularly at <u>Russ Gibb's "Grande Ballroom"</u> in Detroit (where their legendary live album, "Kick Out The Jams" was recorded).

      - They would develop a loyal, local following.

        * And their would be anarchic and frenzied affairs.

    4.) <u>Their Signature Sound</u>: an assaultive, loud, noise-laden, aggressive electric guitar wall of sound.

Borderline
The MC5

      - Flavored with intermittent feedback noise, dissonance, and distortion.

        * <u>Example</u>: "Borderline" from their "Kick Out The Jams" album.

          a.) A perfect example of the above description.

    5.) <u>John Sinclair</u>: a former high school teacher and later, a jazz critic for "Downbeat" magazine.

      - He was at the time of MC5, a Detroit counter-culture guru.

      - He founded his own organization called, "<u>Trans Love Energies</u>".

        * Which had within it's organization, various underground enterprises one of which was, "<u>The White Panther Party</u>".

          a.) It's [The W.P.P.'s] treatise: "A total assault on the culture by any means necessary, including rock & roll, revolution, dope, and fucking on the streets".

- He became MC5's manager in 1967 and made them, the official band of the White Panther Party.

    * <u>RESULT</u>: they became the official "Mouthpiece" for John Sinclair's revolutionary rhetoric.

        a.) Which among other things, would spawn conflicts with the police.

6.) <u>Their most famous performance</u>: August of 1968 at Grant Park in Chicago during the 1968 Democratic National Convention.

    - "<u>The Chicago Seven</u>": Abbie Hoffman, Jerry Rubin, Tom Hayden, etc. organized "<u>The Yippies' Festival of Life</u>" to protest the convention.

        * A major clash between the anti-convention crowd and the Chicago police ensued.

            a.) On the foreground, one could see the police (at the behest of mayor, Richard Daley Sr.) violently beating the daylights out of the protesters with billy-clubs.

                - In the background, one could hear the raw, noisy s sounds of MC5 emanating from nearby Grant Park.

E.) <u>NOTE</u>: Both MC5 and The Stooges developed the style of the Hard-Edged Detroit Electric Guitar Sound.

    1.) But because of it's assaultive, highly aggressive sound...

    - it would not become appreciated by a wide, mainstream audience.

    2.) Another Detroit artist would come along and do something different to this sound:

    - One of the keys to originality is to take a sound too esoteric for mainstream audiences to appreciate...

        * and streamlining it, making it more palatable for mainstream radio and audience.

F.) <u>Alice Cooper</u> (b. Vincent Furnier: 2/4/48 in Detroit. MI).

    1.) The first Glam rocker to achieve commercial success on the American mainstream market.

    - GLAM: referring to cross dressing/androgyny.

        * Which grew out of his love for stage theatrics and for shock value.

    2.) <u>Musical Influences</u>: garage band and the Detroit hard-edged sound.

    - He added simple, catchy melodies above a streamlined, more palatable metallic sound.

        * These catchy tunes had a role in taming the harsh Detroit sound.

Under My Wheels
Alice Cooper

    - Another "taming' factor was the concentration and focus on the stage show.

    - <u>RESULT</u>: these elements enabled Alice Cooper to make inroads to mainstream success.

    3.) "<u>Love It To Death</u>" (1970): his first successful album featuring his breakthrough single, "<u>Eighteen</u>" (reached to #21 on the Pop charts).

    - And featured the entire band as cross dressers.

        * With Alice Cooper wearing old women's outfits and loud facial eye makeup.

            a.) His Glam success notwithstanding, Alice Cooper decided to give up the cross dressing personae.

                - And adopt horror personae instead.

    4.) His new horror image, would bring the concept of theater in rock and roll to an entirely new level.

    - Complete with gallows, boa constrictors, guillotines, fake blood, and electric chairs.

    5.) Both the streamlined, palatable Detroit sound and his horror-laden stage show theatrics became widely popular.

    - <u>IRONY</u>: He became more popular for adopting a horror persona than that of a cross dresser.

* As <u>Jane County</u> (b. Wayne Rogers, 7/13/47, Dallas, GA), cross-dressing actor for <u>Andy Warhol's Factory</u> theatre troupe production of "Pork" in New York City once said:

> a.) "People in America can understand horror and dead babies but could not understand male/female sexuality or bisexuality".

6.) Alice Cooper's next three albums: "<u>Killer</u>" (1971),"<u>School's Out</u>" (1972), and "<u>Billion Dollar Babies</u>" (1973)… all reached gold.

G.) As far reaching as Alice Cooper's persona had become, there was another artist who would bring the androgynous personae even further to arguably, the logical limit.

1.) And, like Lou Reed and Iggy Pop, adopt an approach to rock and roll from an "underside" perspective.

- Unlike Reed and Iggy, he would hail from Britain and spearhead a movement that would mix the "avante garde" of New York…

* with the Glam rock style out of England.

CHAPTER VIIb: ANTAGONIZATIONS: GLAM

<u>I. THE GLAM MOVEMENT</u>

A.) Prominent during the first half of the 70's.

B.) <u>Style</u>: Simple, metal-laden guitar sound presented in the context of outrageous theatrics.

1.) Featuring catchy tunes.

- Derived and influenced by both "bubble gum" pop and dance beats of early rock and roll.

2.) But what set Glam Rock aside was not so much the music…

- as much as the delivery.

* Which was campy, full of glitter, outlandish showmanship, and of course, sexuality.

C.) <u>Glam</u>: had a difficult time cracking the mainstream American market for the following reasons.

1.) American mainstream's Puritan/conservative background.

- Which was religious in nature.

2.) Homophobia

3.) Distaste of gender-benders doing outlandish things on stage.

- In wearing women's outfits and make-up.

D.) <u>Two Schools of Glam</u>:

1.) Where the substance and surface are one.

- Where fashion was more important than musical artistry.

* Trashy, easily disposable, but fun.

- "<u>T-Rex</u>": featuring <u>Marc Bolan</u> (b. Mark Feld, 9/30/48, London, ENG; d. 9/16/77, London).

Baby Boomerang

T-Rex

* First international star of Glam.

a.) Even though Pink Floyd's <u>Syd Barrett</u> pioneered the concept of androgyny in the rock and roll domain.

* <u>Marc Bolan</u>: became the first high-profile "face' of the Glam movement.

- Other artists of this genre would follow such as:

* <u>Slade</u>, <u>Sweet</u>, and <u>Gary Glitter</u>.

a.) They perpetuated a movement of camp, glamour, and whit which was fun and sexy.

2.) The other school was that of the Art Music side.

- These artists had more creative ambition from both a musical and lyrical perspective.

* Their main goal both musically and visually was to make a serious artistic statement.

> a.) In part, by exploring the dark underside that lurked beneath the glam/glittery surface.
- Like the avante artists in America, they acted out their fantasies and inhibitions on stage.
> * Only they [Glam artists] did it with more of a sense of style added to their artistry.
- There were two artistic entities that would become the personification of this school:
> * <u>Roxy Music</u> and <u>David Bowie</u> (both were from England).
>> a.) It is these two artists of the "second school' that this discussion will focus upon.

3.) <u>Performance Concept</u>:
- Emphasis on the acting out of fantasies and inhibitions on stage in front of a live audience.
> * This emphasis also includes the persona of the artists.
>> a.) If the proto punks established extreme musical expression "out front", GLAM established extreme expression of the persona (as well as fantasies and inhibitions) out front as well.
>>> - Sometimes, in an in-your-face sort of manner.

II. ROXY MUSIC

A.) Basically, a story of two strong personalities: <u>Bryan Ferry</u> and <u>Brian Eno</u>.
1.) <u>Bryan Ferry</u> (b.9/26/45, Washington, ENG): vocals, keyboards.
- Was a devoted fan of American gospel-driven soul and the Beatles/Liverpool rock pop sound.
2.) <u>Brian Eno</u> (b. Brian Peter George St. John le Baptiste de la Salle Eno, 5/15/48, Woodbridge, ENG): synthesizer, electronics.
- Inspired by The Velvet Underground's style of avante garde rock as well as electronic experimentalism.
3.) Remaining Members:
- <u>Andy MacKay</u> (b. 7/23/46, ENG): saxophone, oboe.
- <u>Phil Manzanera</u> (b. Philip Targett-Adams, 1/31/51, London): guitar.
- <u>Paul Thompson</u> (b. 5/13/51, Jarrow, ENG): drums.
- <u>Graham Simpson</u>: bass.

B.) <u>RESULT</u>: A creative tension between them that would lead the band in separate directions at once.
1.) Mixture of a glamorous, guitar-ridden pop sound (Ferry)…
- With primitivism and avante garde (Eno).
2.) Add to that, Ferry's vampiric/goth-like crooning…
3.) <u>RESULT</u>: a sound that is experimental, glamorous, and accessible.
- But yet, somewhat crude amid the shimmer.
> * Their accessibility at least was initially, to a British audience.

C.) They also dressed in chic, stylish outfits that had a bizarre twist.
1.) Their hairstyles ranged from the androgynous (Eno), to quasi-spiked/stand up (pre-punk) hair of Bryan Ferry, to conventional long. Floppy hair.

D.) To summarize, the glam look along with the guitar pop/avante experimental sound…
1.) Marked the initial personality/direction of Roxy Music.

E.) Roxy Music's first two albums sold well in England but not in America.
1.) Due primarily to their bizarre, androgynous appearances.
2.) "<u>Roxy Music</u>" (1972): Their debut album.

Remake/Remodel
Roxy Music

- "<u>Remake/Remodel</u>":
> * Angular vocal segments in the melody.
>> a.) With a non-emotional, vampiric timbre.
> * <u>Instrumental Section</u>: counterpoint between guitar and saxophone.
>> a.) Each performing independent, free formed, jagged angular lines.
>>> - Held together by an underlying, aggressive groove.

        * <u>Note of Interest</u>: Saxophone sounds like it is mimicking the electric guitar sound.

            a.) Resulting in a perfect match between the electric guitar and saxophone.

      - "<u>Virginia Plain</u>":

        * Their first hit on the UK charts.

            a.) Straightforward rock and roll accompanied by Eno's synthesized electronic flavor (in the background).

              - A sleek yet simultaneously primitive sound.

            b.) Accessible.

      - "<u>Ladytron</u>":

        * First minute features layers of synthesized sound.

        * Once the vocals and bass guitar appear:

            a.) A synthesized sound hovers in the background.

              - Anticipating the "Post-Punk" sound of the late 70's/early 80's.

     - <u>NOTE</u>: This album stylistically is a mixture of electronic avante garde, primitivism (garage band), the glam metal sound, and pre-gothic styled vocals.

   3.) "<u>For Your Pleasure</u>" (1973): Their second album.

     - "<u>Do The Strand</u>":

        * More metallic with raw power.

        * A thicker texture.

            a.) Like a wall of sound accompanied by a walking bass figure.

     - "<u>Editions of You</u>":

Editions Of You
Roxy Music

        * Raw energy with a simple pop melody.

            a.) With Bryan Ferry's quirky and angular vocals.

        * A full-throttled saxophone solo.

        * Most striking moment:

            a.) A wild, angular electronica-styled synthesizer solo where Brian Eno slides emphatically from one note to the other.

              - Sounding highly spontaneous in character with a unique sense of originality.

                * Melds brilliantly into Phil Manzanera's following guitar solo.

     - "<u>The Bogus Man</u>":

        * A musical tug-of-war between Eno and Ferry.

            a.) Avante experimentation [Eno] vs. traditional pop [Ferry].

              - Melded together by a bass-laden underlying groove.

        * <u>NOTE</u>: This song greatly illustrates that practically anything will work – no matter how bizarre sounding – as long as a bass-heavy, drum-laden groove is prominent underneath.

            a.) This also holds true in the case of atonality.

In Every Dream Home
A Heartache
Roxy Music

        * This song sums up the Roxy Music (conceptually) in this album.

     - "<u>In Every Dream Home A Heartache</u>":

        * Eerie, gothic sounding vocals.

        * Accompanied by some atonality.

            a.) And shimmering synthesizer textures.

  F.) The tension between <u>Eno</u> and <u>Ferry</u> in wrestling for artistic prominence led Eno to quit the band after their second album.

    1.) "<u>Country Life</u>" (1974): first album of the "Post-Eno" era.

     - "<u>The Thrill Of It All</u>": continues the thick metal textures that became an integral part of their previous album: "For Your Pleasure".

The Thrill
Of It All
Roxy Music

        * An even thicker wall of sound contrasted by softer sections/textures.

            a.) Which made the heavy metal sections more prominent.

              - This opening track sets the tone for the entire

album.
2.) <u>NOTE</u>: The absence of the Eno-synthesized "avante" textures is made up by a more full-throttled metallic sound.
- Hard driving.
* As personified by other songs such as;
a.) "<u>All I Want Is You</u>" and "<u>Prairie Rose</u>".
G.) <u>Roxy Music</u>: in the early 70's…
1.) Greatly anticipated the dark, electronically textured sound of post-punk and new wave.
- As well as the Goth sound of the late 70's/early 80's.
2.) And were a direct influence on post-punk pioneers such as "<u>Joy Division</u>" and "<u>The Cure</u>".
- Who in turn, had a significant influence on the development of the "alternative" sound.
3.) But as far as expressing Glam's artier side by pushing the envelope on creativity…
- They were only half of the equation…

<u>III. DAVID BOWIE</u> (b. David Robert Jones, January 8, 1947, ENG):

<u>Pre-Teen Years</u>: In his childhood, his earliest musical memory was the song, *Inchworm*, performed by Danny Kaye in a Hans Christian Anderson film. The melodic style of would be influential to his [Bowie's] melodic style later on. From a cultural standpoint, he first became enamored with fantasies of outer space/science fiction from an early 1950's television show, *The Quatermass Experiment* (his interest in imagining space travel as a song motif would be realized in the 1969 song, *Space Oddity*).

<u>Rock 'n' Roll's First Golden Age</u>: from a musical and cultural approach, the rebellious essence of rock 'n' roll's first golden age swept the UK by storm and David Bowie rode along with it. He loved the sound and androgyny of Little Richard, the rebelliousness the film, The Blackboard Jungle, and the rebellious icons such as Elvis Presley (music) and James Dean (film) – inspirations that millions of British kids could relate to. His father used to buy him 7 inch, 45 RPM pop records of various artists such as Buddy Holly, Jerry Lee Lewis, Eddie Cochran, Chuck Berry, Gene Vincent, and Fats Domino.

<u>Teen Years</u>: Bowie had discovered jazz via his half-brother, Terry Burns. As a result, he began studying jazz saxophone under virtuoso, Ronnie Ross for several months. Bowie was also at the time, a big fan of jazz saxophone great, Jerry Mulligan. After his interest in jazz saxophone had faded, he turned to learning the guitar while a student at Bromley Technical High School (along with fellow classmate, Peter Frampton).

<u>Mod</u>: in his mid-teens, he got into the Mod fashion trend that was sweeping the UK at the time. Mod was the antithesis of the Teddy Boy look that had been in fashion up to this point. It was basically an androgynous look that was strictly English in influence (whereas the Teddy Boy look, with the greasy quiff of hair, was more macho and more American influenced). The clothing consisted of suits that were sleek, stylish, and tight with sharp creases that looked like angular lines. The three-button, suit jackets were an identifying trademark. It was all about the "new" – it would set the initial tone for Bowie's life-long obsession with style seeking.

<u>Musically</u>: Mod was influenced by African American music namely, gospel-driven soul. Mod bands performed covers of soul within the context of heavy amplitude, speed tempos, and rank amateurism (i.e. garage band ethos).

<u>Bands</u>: during this period, Bowie was involved in a number of blues bands such as

What Kind Of
Fool Am I?
Anthony Newley

The London
Boys
David Bowie

The Hooker Brothers (named after John Lee Hooker) for a brief time before moving on to the King Bees (another blues revisionist outfit). He also had brief tenures with Mod bands such as The Manish Boys and The Lower Third. After he lost interest in playing the blues, David Bowie discovered a new influence that would bear artistic fruits later on: singer <u>Anthony Newley</u> – an artist with a more theatrical approach to singing with a dance hall type of flair (a sort of English version of Tin Pan Alley). At this point, Bowie had ended his pursuit of blues revisionism.

<u>Game Changers</u>: after signing with his first agent, Kenneth Pitt, David Bowie would undergo a number of life-changing experiences that, all told, influenced his future uniqueness.

The Velvet Underground & Nico: Kenneth Pitt obtained an acetate of this album following a meeting with artist, Andy Warhol in New York and gave it to Bowie upon his return to England. This album initiated two things for him [Bowie]: first, the beginning of his long-lived enthusiasm for New York City. And secondly, the advent of rock 'n' roll as serious art -- which opened up an entirely new musical awareness for Bowie. It was an album where the artists felt indifferent to the listener's reaction, while also charting the possibilities of where rock 'n' roll could go. It opened up a whole new world for him -- especially when it came to Lou Reed's poetry dealing with the underside of tough, New York City street culture.

<u>Syd Barrett</u>: the frontman/guitarist/songwiter of The Pink Floyd (as they were known at that time) became the model for Bowie on how to be the ultimate, English rock singer and frontman -- this was due to Barrett's originality and theatrics. Instead of using an innocuous accent like most British singers, Barrett was very British in his vocal inflections and pronunciations (which Bowie would also adopt). Other models that David Bowie would emulate: Barrett's cryptic lyrics and intense stage presence that was (in Bowie's view) truly charismatic. Part of that charisma came from his noise improvisations where he made the nastiest, wildest guitar sounds that no one in the London scene had ever heard.

<u>Lindsay Kemp</u>: a collaborator who helped David Bowie to eventually connect to his physical vision -- in other words, to loosen him up (for Bowie as pretty rigid on stage). Kemp was a controversial dancer, movement instructor, and choreographer. He studied the art of mime under the world-renowned miming artists, Marcel Marceau. Through mime, Lindsay Kemp could be whatever he wanted to be while adding some wittiness and camp to his approach.

When I Live
My Dream
David Bowie

<u>NEMS</u>: (an artist management company founded by Brian Epstein) managed Lindsay Kemp's career as an opening act for various rock 'n' roll shows throughout Britain. He discovered Bowie through his NEMS connection and soon after, heard Bowie's debut album and loved it – especially the song, *When I Live My Dream* (recording of which he played during his theatre troupe's performances). Their first collaboration, *Pierrot in Turquoise*, which was influenced by Bowie's love for Eastern art forms including Kabuki Theatre.

<u>Kemp's Impact</u>: he taught Bowie to be audacious and loosen him up, getting him to break out of his timid shell. Up to this point, Bowie had been tight and inhibited on stage. In addition, Kemp had taught him the technique of holding a somewhat hypnotic force over the audience and then, get them to adore you.

<u>Tony Visconti</u>: an American-born producer and musician (from Brooklyn, NY) would help David Bowie find his original musical voice. He first met Bowie through a meeting set up at the Essex Publishing Office by producer Denny Cordell – he wanted Visconti to

figure out what to do with David Bowie's talent. The first time he had previously heard Bowie, was from his debut album.

They both shared an interest in Eastern spirituality and philosophy as well as art films which quickly developed a new friendship. Due to his love of The Beatles from a vocal perspective, Visconti transferred that influence onto Bowie. As a result, Visconti molded Bowie's voice into a more powerful, polished, finished sound that he [Bowie] never had up to that point. They began their collaboration in September of 1967.

Mick Ronson: the artist who would add electric guitar metal to the Bowie mix. His early influences: rockabilly and blues heard on the radio. In 1965, he became a devoted fan of Jeff Beck. One of his earliest bands was The Rats – a Hull (home town) band that Ronson had joined. They specialized in loud, blues-based rock. The Rats included drummer John Cambridge. He eventually left the band to record with Bowie and his producer, Tony Visconti for the *Space Oddity* sessions. During the Spring of 1970, he returned to Hull and recruited Mick Ronson to relocate to London and join David Bowie's band.

Production and Arranging: he learned the art of producing from Visconti which began during *The Man Who Sold The World* sessions in 1970. It was during this session, that Ronson added a heavy blues guitar style (influenced by The Cream), which initiated metal to the Bowie sound. As an arranger, he would write arrangements for string orchestra in songs such as *Life On Mars?* (from the *Hunky Dory* album of 1971) and Lou Reed's *Perfect Day* (from his *Transformer* album of 1972).

Early Recording Career: *David Bowie* (1967), his debut album released on the Deram label. Musically, none of the influences of various "game changers' mentioned previously are present. Instead, the main influence was mostly derived from Anthony Newley -- stylistically, a Broadway-esque, music-hall-show type of sound. Some of the more notable tracks were *Love You Till Tuesday*, *Uncle Arthur*, and *Sell Me A Coat* (as well as *When I Live My Dream*).

Love You Till Tuesday
David Bowie

Man of Words Man Of Music (1969): the album with a hippie-like, folk strumming essence that contained his first local hit, *Space Oddity* (released shortly after the first lunar landing). But soon after, Bowie would move beyond folk once he met Mick Ronson who, as mentioned earlier, initiated metal into the Bowie mix. Together with Tony Visconti on bass, and John Cambridge on drums, they formed a band called The Hype.

Space Oddity
(Original Version)
David Bowie

Space Oddity
(Revised Version, 1972)
David Bowie

The Hype: inspired by attending an Alice Cooper concert. Bowie and Ronson had noticed Cooper's shock treatment for his audience by performing violent motifs like hanging himself on the gallows and his Frankenstein-like horror persona – it was considerably more accessible than Lindsay Kemp's Mime Troupe. Bowie had an idea: he wanted to transcend Alice Cooper's macabre approach and replace it with overt sexuality, theatre, and advanced songwriting craftsmanship. The eventual result: The Hype – David Bowie's first dive into the GLAM arena.

They dressed up as super heroes with costumes made by Bowie's wife, Angie (b. Mary Angela Barnett). Bowie was "Rainbow Man", Ronson was "Gangster Man", Visconti was "Hype Man", and Cambridge was "Cowboy Man"

In addition to Alice Cooper's influence, Bowie's flair for the flamboyance was first inspired by Lindsay Kemp who, in Bowie's words (regarding Kemp's mime troupe), "were a highly flamboyant bunch who'd been opening my eyes since the late 60's". Kemp's inspiration drew Bowie's initial theatrical road map.

This band would follow-up with an album that would mark the beginning of Bowie's new artistic direction…

The Man Who sold The World (1970): the start of a new process that ushered in Bowie's classic period. This was his second time working with producer Tony Visconti (the first was the _Space Oddity_ sessions). It was also the beginning of the Bowie/Ronson collaboration where [electric] guitar metal would become a regular fixture on Bowie's recordings. On the album's cover, he poses in a woman's outfit -- It was the shape of things to come. (NOTE: the woman's dress album cover was for the UK version only. For the American version, a cartoon figure was presented).

January 1970: David Bowie's first trip to America – a nationwide visit. Everywhere he went, he noticed a plethora of different radio stations plying hit after hit. The key that he discovered in regard to these hits: the catchy, instant thematic hook. As a result of this constant exposure [to American radio], he understood what the art of writing the hit song was all about -- especially, when it came to writing the catchy, easily memorable chorus sections (which became his trademark). Up to this point, his music consisted of a number of various separate elements: music dance hall (Newley influence), folk (hippie-folk influence), and metal (Ronson). The next step was to synthesize these disparate influences together.

Changes
David Bowie

Hunky Dory (1971): the turning point, the breakthrough album where all of his prior influences were synthesized for the first time. In addition, his American influence on the art of writing hits became realized – especially when it came to writing choruses that were catchy, instant, and durable. Some of the more notable examples included _Life On Mars?_ And _Changes_. This album had also set the tone for the remainder of his albums throughout the 1970's in terms of highly skilled songwriting craftsmanship and synthesis of influences.

Life On Mars?
David Bowie

Oh! You Pretty Things
David Bowie

Coming Out: In the song, _Oh! You Pretty Things_, Bowie was setting another precedent – his eventual "coming out" and admitting his bisexual/gay identity. It happened in an interview with _Melody Maker_ magazine in January, 1972 when he said, "I'm gay and always have been, even when I was David Jones". This admission received a lot of attention and he would play up his gay/effeminate stereotype in an overtly GLAM format. The process that led to GLAM began with a visiting theatre troupe headed by Andy Warhol.

Pork: debuted in the summer of 1971 in the East Village section of New York City. The source of the main subject, were hours of taped conversations between Warhol and Brigid Berlin (his best friend). The main character was Amanda Polk with her downtown escapades of syringe-driven, urban street life that featured full-frontal nudity, masturbation, and perverted acts of gallantry. Polk was played by Warhol star, Cherry Vanilla.

The London debut was on August 2, 1971 at The Roundhouse. Bowie, an already devoted Warhol fan (in part, due to his association with The Velvet Underground), was instantly enamored with cross-dressing, Glam-oriented cast – he and his wife Angie hung out with them and attended multiple performances. These cast members, with their wild, off-stage antics, were always "in character" as they carried an outrageous, expressive freedom that was foreign to the proper British context.

They became key to influencing Bowie to go the Glam route and to create his own outrageous persona. They (along with Angie) decided to help him go in that direction. He would change his image completely and that change would help grab more attention. He would transform from a hippie-looking guy with long, floppy hair to one of the most unique Glam personas of all time. Not only would he be a cross-dresser, but a cross-dresser from outer space…

Ziggy Stardust: David Bowie's first important persona. A number of influences were synthesized into this androgynous, extraterrestrial rock star character: the "outer space" ethos of Stanley Kubrick's film *2001, A Space Odyssey*, the androgyny of the menacing Alex character in *A Clockwork Orange* (another Kubrick film) – Ziggy portrayed a twisted, non-violent version [of the character] Alex as gang leader of his group The Spiders From Mars (in homage to *Clockwork Orange*, the band opened with a synthesizer version of "Ode To Joy" from the film's soundtrack). Additional influences [to the Ziggy persona] included Kabuki Theatre, mime and living theatre (the Lindsay Kemp influence), plus the decadence inspired by The Velvet Underground. The red rooster-styled haircut along with heavy make-up (which hid the eye brows) gave Bowie this outrageous, otherworldly, androgynous type of look (*Pork* cast influences). In America, his character was seen as outrageous and in many cases anathema (due to the American mainstream's homophobic attitudes).

Ziggy Stardust
David Bowie

Rise and Fall of Ziggy Stardust (1972): his first release in the RCA label – the contract was negotiated by his second manager, Tony Defries. Although it only reached up #75 on the pop charts, the album's sound was full of shimmering metal juxtaposed with folk-styled influences and a flair of theatrics. *Ziggy Stardust*: a song directly about the Ziggy character and his "Spiders" further brought this character into a life of its own. His vocals stress an effeminized, gay-stereotyped-inflection in a highly overt "in your face" manner (further playing up the gay identity).

Suffragette City
David Bowie

In addition to his up front persona, his metal sound would be hard rocking in an upfront manner as well, which accompanied the boldness of his character as illustrated in a song called *Suffragette City*.

Vicious
Lou Reed

Bowie As Producer: that same year (1972), David Bowie, along with Mick Ronson, produced Lou Reed's second solo album, *Transformer*. This album featured Lou Reed classics such as *Vicious, Perfect Day, Satellite Of Love*, and another influenced by Warhol's drag queen entourage at The Factory, *Walk On The Wild Side* – an anthem for this entire "underside of American culture" movement. It was Lou Reed's

Walk On The Wild Side
Lou Reed

most notable, successful, and artistically viable solo project ever. He to, through the Andy Warhol influence, had also adopted an androgynous look at this time.

His Gradual Expansion to Further Eclectic Influences: for the remainder of the 1970's, David Bowie progressively added a number of various eclectic influences into his original mix.

Time
David Bowie

Aladdin Sane (1973): the resurfacing of a new influence from his teen years: jazz. In the track entitled *Time*, the song opens with an introductory stride jazz piano solo (played by Mike Garson) followed by an old dance hall type flavor which at times – during loud passages – is grandiose and quasi-operatic in sound.

Watch That Man
David Bowie

Watch That Man: lyrical influence of Jack Kerouac chronicling someone else's partying and debaucherous episodes while musically inspired by the nostalgic, doo-wop chorus/back-up singing in a song called *Time Warp* from The Rocky Horror Picture Show. His metal/Glam influence still abounds in a song called *The Gene Genie*.

The Gene Genie
David Bowie

In 1973 at the last concert of the Aladdin Sane tour of the UK, at the Hammersmith Odeon in London, David Bowie retired the Ziggy Stardust persona. For his next album and tour, a new persona would be unleashed.

Diamond Dogs (1974): his first success in America. Inspired by the George Orwell novel, *1984*. He wanted create a musical adaptation & theatre production [of the novel] but when MainMan Entertainment – the Tony Defries-owned company managing Bowie's career – applied for the rights, Orwell's widow, Sonia Blair, rejected it. In response, Bowie eventually created the concept album, *Diamond Dogs*: a loose adaptation of the *1984* novel (his first concept album). He would use classical elements -- both literary and musical.

1984
David Bowie

> Setting: rough teenage punks living in urban, dark, apocalyptic squalor with characters relative to the Orwellian novel. Instead of the *1984* hero Winston Smith, Bowie's hero was Halloween Jack. Instead of Orwellian London, it was Hunger City. Songs included in the album had titles relative to the novel such as *Big Brother* and *1984* with other dark songs like *We Are The Dead*. *Rebel, Rebel* was Bowie's last metal-driven Glam single.

Rebel, Rebel
David Bowie

The Diamond Dogs Tour: in lieu of his original theatric idea, he decided to take the "theatre production" on tour with a Broadway set designed by set designers Jules Fisher and Mark Ravitz.

> The Stage Set: a reflection of German expressionism inspired by the 1927 film by Fritz Lang, *Metropolis* depicting the degradation of modernist, urban decay. The set featured two silk-screened skyscrapers connected by a bridge lined with streetlights – it slid up and down powered by a hydraulic lift. At the show's end, Bowie tore them down (i.e. urban decay). The band played in a makeshift pit just like a normal Broadway show (as opposed to on stage). The band members (with the exception of Mike Garson) were all new.

>> Impact: the Diamond Dogs tour marked the first time that an actual stage set was used in rock 'n' roll. The concept of theatre in rock 'n' roll – with its genesis from The Velvet Underground/Exploding Plastic Inevitable performances has now become full-blown. From now on, all major rock 'n' roll acts had to have huge theatrical stage shows in order to compete. One of the acts that adopted this extravagant concept, was Alice Cooper's *Welcome To My Nightmare* tour (1975).

>> The pinnacle of the extravagant stage show was the Kiss *Destroyer Tour* of 1976 (set designed by Fisher & Ravitz) featuring a wealth of wild pyrotechnics.

> New Influence: during the Diamond Dogs Tour, Bowie was in the process of a new fascination with an old musical love from his Mod days: an American, gospel-driven style known as "Philly Soul".

Young Americans (1975): post-Ziggy Bowie had fallen in love with the "Philly Soul" sound and began emulating it for himself. Philly Soul (a.k.a. The Philadelphia International Records or P.I.R. sound) was the brainchild of the writer/producer team of Kenny Gamble and Leon Huff. Their style featured a glossy, symphonic approach that added a touch of elegance to soul-driven funk. In addition to catchy pop tunesmithism, gospel-styled vocal ornamentations, and a funky dance groove, Gamble & Huff also used orchestral string arrangements (which would become a model for mainstream disco). Their recording sessions took place at Sigma Sound Studios (owned by engineer Joe Tarsia) in Philadelphia.

Bowie recorded the *Young Americans* album at Sigma studios and was joined by a new guitarist & songwriting collaborator: Carlos Alomar. Bowie's new emulation of the Philly sound would be called "Plastic Soul" with songs such as *Young Americans* title track (with artistic input from a then unknown singer, named Luther Vandross). Included in the album was a song he co-wrote with Carlos Alomar and John Lennon entitled *Fame* – his first #1 hit single on the mainstream American charts.

<u>Station To Station</u> (1976): the artistic juncture between his previous soul influences and his new and his new avant-garde electronic influences which became an early harbinger of synth-driven post punk and New Wave of the early 80's. In addition to his continuing love of soul, he became influenced by the robotic, futuristic electronic sounds of the German group, Kraftwerk. *Station To Station* became the bridge to an even more electronic approach of the Brian Eno influence/collaborations to come. One example of this electronic bridge is the song, *TVC 15*.

<u>Golden Years</u>: a dark, soul-driven approach with a quasi-disco flavor was his most notable single [from the album] and his second major hit in the US.

<u>New Persona</u>: The Thin White Duke. It was during this time in Los Angeles that David Bowie had developed a massive cocaine habit and, as a result, became increasingly paranoid (some of which could be heard in the album). He was also going broke – his manager Tony Defries (who ran MainMan Entertainment) was bankrupting the company that supported Bowie. Bowie decided that a change was in order. He moved to West Berlin, Germany to start over (i.e. go back to basics) along with Iggy Pop (who was also managed by Defries).

<u>The Brian Eno Period</u>: an era where the two twin towers of Glam as serious art (i.e. Bowie & Roxy Music) joined their creative forces. They recorded three albums together: *Low*, *Heroes*, and *Lodger*. *Heroes* was recorded at Hansa Studios in Berlin, *Lodger* was recorded at Mountain Studios in Montreaux France, and *Low* was recorded at both Hansa & Mountain [Studios]. The creative impetus was from a purely post-modernist approach – the synthesis of high-art and pop. At the time, Bowie was developing a fascination with electronic, textural music which was Brian Eno's specialty – a byproduct of his [Eno's] avant-garde influences inspired in big part, by The Velvet Underground.

<u>Low</u> (1977): a product of their first collaboration. As always, Alomar and Visconti were also heavily involved in the creative process. Examples of various tracks include *Always Cashing In The Same Car* – straightforward rock 'n' roll with fluttering, experimental synthesizer colors in the background. Other examples include:

<u>Subterraneans</u>: an electronic-styled soundscape. A composition in a full fledged sense that is both textural and picturesque. (image-evoking).

<u>Weeping Wall</u>: avant-garde marimba-like melody emulating a minimalist (high art) style supporting electronic, synth-driven melody lines.

<u>Warszawa</u>: a dark, haunting, electronic work that would become directly influential to the first British post-punk band, Joy Division (they previously had named themselves Warsaw in commemoration of *Warszawa*). Joy Division would adopt their own stripped-down, direct version of the Bowie/Eno influence and synthesize it with punk influences, which spearheaded the post punk movement in Britain.

<u>Heroes</u> (1977): another Bowie/Eno collaboration focusing on a stripped-down, sparse electric sound in both the electric guitar and synthesizers. A harbinger of the New Wave movement to come (starting in the early 1980's).

The Title Track (*Heroes*): co-written with Brian Eno is about two lovers – one from East Berlin (communist country) and the other from West Berlin (free country) – who were separated by the Berlin wall. The track includes a prominent guitar riff by Robert Fripp (from the band, King Crimson).

Like the *Low* album, side B was primarily instrumental from an avant-garde influenced perspective.

Lodger (1979): included the same artists as in the previous two albums: Eno, Alomar, & Visconti (the three albums combined were known as the "Berlin Trilogy").

Lodger adopted a "world beat" type of funk that would become influential to artists like The Talking Heads' *Remain In Light* album (produced by Brian Eno) and Paul Simon's *Graceland* – employing world music styles.

NOTE: this album concludes an era of arguably, Bowie's most creative period, which was due in big part, by his collaboration with Brian Eno, Carlos Alomar, and Tony Visconti.

IV. SUMMARY

A.) Roxy Music's and David Bowie's joint legacies: Post-Punk, 80's Synth-Pop, and New Wave.
B.) Post-Punk: Would become one of the influences in shaping the "Alternative" sound beginning in the early 1980's with artists such as "Sonic Youth".
    1.) Which would eventually lead to the alternative explosion in the early 90's by "Nirvana", et al.
        - Which in turn lead to the alternative bands of the late 90's/early 2000's such as "Incubus", "Limp Bizkit", "Linkin Park", "Nickleback", etc.
            * Alternative eventually became mainstream.
C.) But Post-Punk was not the only influence that molded the alternative sound.
    1.) The Velvet Underground was also an important influence.
        - In fact, the genesis of this entire story can be traced directly back to them with their influences on the following:
            * Rock and roll as theatre.
            * The introduction of avante garde elements into rock and roll.
            * The underside of American culture as legitimate subject matter.
                a.) As well as being influential on The Doors, The Stooges, and David Bowie.
            - The Velvet Underground would also inspired the genesis of an additional movement that would form the other half of the alternative equation: Punk.

Chapter VII: Review

List three examples of early protopunk subject matter:

      What were some of the music characteristics of the early protopunks?

What was the genus (the intention) of this movement?

      How did the mainstream record industry view these artists?

What became the new concept in regard to lacking musicianship skills?

List the three most important early protopunk bands (the ones who were commercial failures):
      1.)
      2.)
      3.)

Who were Lou Reed's four early musical influences? (Hint: two were R&B and two were rockabilly):
      1.) R&B Influences:
      2.) Rockabilly Influences:

Who was Lou Reed's poetic mentor at Syracuse University?

      Which important ideal did he instill into Lou Reed in regard to *being* a poet?

Who was Lou Reed's most important poetic influence? (He loved this one above all else):

      What was his influence upon Lou Reed?

Name the three most important musical influences on John Cale:
      1.) _____
                 - Name the main musical property of this artist that influenced John Cale:

      2.) _____
                  - Name the main musical property of this artist that influenced John Cale:

3.) _____

              - Name the main musical property of this group that influenced
              John Cale:

Name at least three of Sterling Morrison's guitar influences:

     1.)

     2.)

     3.)

List the original lineup of The Velvet Underground

     1.)

     2.)

     3.)

     4.)

Where was their first New City Bar gig? (It became their first regular performance venue)

On the night they were fired, which prominent pop artist was in the audience who would change their lives/careers?

What was the name of this artist's theatre troupe?

Name the two members of the Exploding Plastic Inevitable?

What did they act out on stage when they performed alongside the Velvet Underground?

This collaboration introduced a new concept into rock and roll. What was it? (Hint: one word)

Name the Velvet Underground's debut album:

What was the key stylistic element of this album?

What was the subject matter in the poetry of "Venus In Furs"?

What was the subject matter in the song "Heroin"? What was it a soliloquy for?

What John Cale musical property appeared in the fourth stanza of this song?

List at least four artists who became influenced by The Velvet Underground:
1.)
2.)
3.)
4.)

Why were Jim Morrison's LSD experiences not Psychedelic?

In addition to Jim Morrison, name the other members of The Doors:

Name Jim Morrison's three most important literary influences:
1.)
2.)
3.)

What type of performance art did these influences inspire in him?

What was his rock and roll persona?

What was the goal of Morrison's approach to audience confrontation?

Name the LA theatre troupe that further inspired Jim Morrison in his confrontational approach:

What was this theatre troupe's ultimate goal?

Name The Door's debut single:

What did they achieve that the other protopunk bands did not?

List two types of noises that intrigued Iggy Pop when he was a child:
1.)
2.)

Name at least four of Iggy Pop's eclectic influences:
1.)
2.)
3.)

4.)

What influence did Jim Morrison have upon him?

What was the basic sound of his band, The Stooges?

What would they set the blueprint (template) for as a band and why? What was it about The Stooges that was different from conventional bands discussed in prior chapters?

What did they emphasize to replace their lack of musical skill?

What musical genre would they inspire later on as a result of this blueprint?

How was Iggy Pop's audience confrontational style different from Jim Morrison's?

What were some of the musical properties of MC5's signature style?

Who was MC5's manager and impresario?

Which organizational subgroup did MC5 become a "mouthpiece" for?

How did Alice Cooper's style make the Detroit hard-edged guitar sound palatable for a mainstream audience?

Chapter VIIb: Antagonizations – The Rise of the Underside of American Culture Part II: "The Underside Gains Exposure"

What was the essence of GLAM?

Describe the two schools of GLAM:
1.)
2.)

Who were the two artists representing the second school?

What were Bryan Ferry's two main musical influences?
1.)

2.)

What were Brian Eno's two main musical influences?
1.)
2.)

What were the three resulting sound ingredients of this creative union?
1.)
2.)
3.)

Which later musical movements did the style of Roxy Music anticipate?

After signing with his first agent, Kenneth Pitt, David Bowie would undergo a number of life-changing experiences that, all told, influenced his future uniqueness. Name 5 of these "game changes".

1.)
2.)
3.)
4.)
5.)

Which artist (singer) was most influential to David Bowie's debut album with his Braodway-esque, music hall type of sound?

What was David Bowie's first local hit in 1969? What event took place shortly before its release?

Which 1970 album ushered in David Bowie's classic period?

With which guitarist did he begin collaborating with?

As a result, what type of sound would become a new regular fixture?

Which 1971 album became David Bowie's turning point where all of his prior influences became synthesized?

What American influence on the art of writing hits had become realized in Bowie's songwriting?

Who became key to influencing David Bowie to go the Glam route and create his own, outrageous persona?

What play/production were they associated with?

What was David Bowie's first important persona?

Name 2 Stanley Kubrick films that were influential to this androgynous, extraterrestrial, rock star character.
1.)
2.)

Which 1972 album became his first release on RCA?

What was Lou Reed's most notable, successful, and artistically viable solo project?

Who produced this album?

Name the anthem for the entire "underside of American culture" movement featured on this album.

Which new musical influence appeared on David Bowie's *Aladdin Sane* album? (a resurfacing of an influence from his teen years)

Which film inspired the nostalgic, doo-wop chorus/back-up singing in *Watch That Man*? What was this song's lyrical influence?

What album marked David Bowie's first success in America?

Which classic novel inspired this concept album?

What was his last, metal-driven Glam single?

For the *Diamond Dogs* tour, Bowie decided to take the "theatre production" on the road with something designed by Jules Fisher and Mark Ravitz. What was it?

The stage set was a reflection of German expressionism. What was the 1927 film that inspired this stage set and what did the film depict?

What was the impact of the *Diamond Dogs* tour?

What became the pinnacle of the extravagant stage show?

Which musical influence appeared on David Bowie's 1975 album, *Young Americans*?

Who became his new guitarist and songwriting collaborator?

What was Bowie's first #1 hit single (from this album) on the mainstream US charts?

The 1976 album, *Station To Station*, became an artistic juncture between 2 influences. What were they?
    1.)
    2.)

What did these influences become an early harbinger of?

Which German group was influential [to this album] by their robotic, futuristic electronic sounds?

Name 3 albums of the David Bowie/Brian Eno collaboration. (They were known as "The Berlin Trilogy")
    1.)
    2.)
    3.)

What was Brian Eno's high-art specialty that influenced David Bowie's new, postmodern approach?

Which of these albums was the first product of their collaboration?

        Name 3 examples from this album of the high-art, electronic synthesis.
            1.)
            2.)
            3.)

What was the musical focus of the 1977 album, *Heroes*?

What musical movement did this album become a harbinger of?

What type of "beat" was adopted in David Bowie's 1979 album, *Lodger*?

Name two albums that were influenced by this type of world music approach.
1.)
2.)

What period in David Bowie's career did this album mark the conclusion of?

Who were his 3 collaborative colleagues that made this period as creative as it was?
1.)
2.)
3.)

What was the Roxy Music/David Bowie joint legacy?

What was the most important musical legacy of the entire protopunk movement initially spearheaded by The Velvet Underground? (You can answer it in one word)

CHAPTER VIII: PUNK PROPER
I. THE STATE OF ROCK AND ROLL IN THE EARLY 70'S
    A.) There were several major entities in early 70's rock and roll.
        1.) Progressive Rock:
            - Definition: Rock and roll mixed with the complexity of classical stylistic elements.
                * The songs themselves became bona fide "works".
                    a.) Lasting anywhere from 15 to 30 minutes.
                    b.) In some cases, could be in multiple movements.
                        - Like a classical composition.
                    c.) Concept albums were the norm.
                        - Concept album: where every song is connected either by variants of the same thematic material or same thread of thought.
            - The idea of classical complexity in rock and roll was started by the group: "King Crimson" (founded on January 13, 1969).
                * Personnel: Robert Fripp, Greg Lake, Ian McDonald, and Michael Giles (Peter Sinfeld wrote their lyrics).
                    a.) "Court Of The Crimson King" (7/1969): Progressive rock's first major album (reached to #5 in the UK).
                        - An album that took enormous artistic risks.
                        - Dominant instruments: Ian McDonald's mellowtron, Robert Fripp's guitarwork, and McDonald's saxophone.
                        - Lyrics of dark, ominous visions.
                        - Fripp's guitar style: elegant, explosive (Hendrix-like) and jazzy (virtuostic).
                * This was the only King Crimson album featuring the original line-up.
                    a.) Fripp would eventually be the only one left to carry on the King Crimson name.
                    b.) Greg Lake: Would go on to another group that would take progressive rock from obscurity…
                        -…and put it on to the world stage.
            - Emerson, Lake, and Palmer (founded in 1970):
                * Keith Emerson: keyboards.
                    a.) Formerly with an early progressive band called: "The Nice".
                * Greg Lake: guitar and bass.
                    a.) Formerly with "King Crimson".
                * Carl Palmer: drums/percussion.
                    a.) Formerly of the band: The Crazy World of Arthur Brown.
                    b.) He was chosen by Emerson and Lake.
                        - After auditioning several drummers including Mitch Mitchell (formerly of The Jimi Hendrix Experience).
                * They transformed progressive rock from a small following to a worldwide phenomenon.
                    a.) Thereby making progressive rock one of the dominant forces in early 70's rock and roll.
                * Emerson: Also brought the Moog synthesizer sound to the rock mainstream (starting with their first hit single: "Lucky Man").
                    a.) Which eventually, would become a fixture in 70's rock and roll.
                * They recorded and performed progressive rock arrangements of classical pieces such as:

Epitaph
King Crimson

a.) "Hoedown": by composer Aaron Copeland and "Piano Concerto No. 1", 3rd Movement: by Alberto Ginastera.

- The Ginastera arrangement was renamed, "Toccata".

* They also recorded their own multi-movement extended suites.

a.) "Karn Evil 9" from the "Brain Salad Surgery" album (1973).

- 1st, 2nd, and 3rd Impressions (movements).
- with lyrics assisted by Peter Sinfeld (King Crimson).

b.) "The Endless Enigma" and "Trilogy" (from their second album: "Trilogy").

- Both multi-movement in a continuous sense.

* They made artistic "intellectualism" a normal fixture in the early 70's rock and roll landscape.

a.) In tandem, the average rock and roll listener was developing sophisticated musical tastes.

- Along with large, sophisticated stereo systems (complete with huge cabinet speakers, reel-to-reel tape players, fancy receivers, etc.).

b.) Progressive rock had become "adult" medium and was transforming rock and roll into a very serious art form.

- NOTE: The success of Emerson, Lake and Palmer opened the door for other progressive rock bands to step onto the world stage such as:

* "Yes", "Triumverat" (from Germany), and "Kansas".

- PROBLEM: As innovative as this music was, it was extremely difficult to emulate.

* For the average rock musician, the technical facility required to play progressive rock was far beyond their means.

a.) They did not possess that type of virtuosic playing ability.

2.) The Rise of FM Radio:

- In the late 60's, FM radio was primarily "underground" emanating form college campuses.

* The DJ's sounded as if they were perpetually "stoned" and sometimes, with slurry speech.

a.) At night, these stations had a certain "mystique" to them.

b.) They would play music not normally programmed on the predominant, pop-oriented AM radio.

- In the early 70's (circa 1972), FM radio exploded into a mass marketing commercial enterprise – they were becoming corporate.

* And by 1975, became the new standard in rock and roll broadcasting complete with various gimmicks.

a.) For example: WORJ (Orlando, FL) started broadcasting in full "Matrix Quad" instead of stereo.

- A testament to the sophisticated stereo systems en vogue at the time.

- Their programming consisted primarily of "listener friendly" music such as:

* The California (Country Rock) sound including "The Eagles", Jackson Browne, Linda Ronstadt, "Pure Prairie League", etc.

* Southern Rock (Country Rock with a metal edge draped under the Confederate flag) with artists like:

- "Lynard Skynard", "Wet Willie Band, "Marshall Tucker Band", "ZZ Top", etc.

- PROBLEM: FM radio, due to their listener friendly policy and their corporate status, would usually program only "safe' music.
       * They shied away from music that would take creative risks or sounded definitely out of the mainstream.
             a.) Especially if the music was experimental.

3.) <u>Post Woodstock</u>:
- As mentioned earlier in Chapter 6, The Woodstock Music and Art Festival marked the end of the theatre/ballroom venue circuits for major rock and roll acts.
       * During the theatre/ballroom era, experimental (garage) bands had a performance outlet that gave them exposure.
             a.) They sometimes were the back-up bands for the main acts.
                 - Because these venues were small, audience size was not a major issue.
- But with the post-Woodstock era transforming rock concerts to large arenas and outdoor stadiums (i.e. considerably larger venues):
       * Bigger venues meant that more notoriety was needed even for the back-up bands in order to sell more tickets.
- PROBLEM: Experimental "garage bands" were now relegated back to the nightclubs, bars, and occasionally in small theatres.
       * Which gave them little exposure.

4.) <u>Corporate Rock</u>: The primary rock and roll of the early 70's.
- A sort of pre-fabbed, generic sound that was easy to listen to, predictable, and non-threatening (examples of various artists listed earlier).
       a.) With little sense of youth and energy.
             - Rock and roll had become a grown-up medium indulging in leisure (and corporate rock became the personification of this).
- PROBLEM: Little sense of youth, energy, and above all, fun.

B.) <u>Take these four elements</u>: Progressive Rock, FM Radio, Post-Woodstock venue norms, and Corporate Rock…
    1.) And you have a musical medium in danger of fizzling out into something bland, unemotional, and far removed.

C.) NEEDED: A revitalization of youth, energy, simplicity (the latter translating into something that's fun to do).

II. HARBINGERS OF A NEW MOVEMENT

A.) <u>Jonathan Richman</u> (b. 1951, Boston, MA): and his group, "The Modern Lovers".
    1.) Directly influenced by <u>The Velvet Underground</u> and <u>The Stooges</u>.
       - Once again, the Velvet Underground influence looms large.
    2.) <u>Richman</u>: Was the first to lay down the structure in the early 70's of what would later become Punk.
       - <u>Musically</u>: Songs that were stripped-down and direct.
          * <u>Simplicity</u>: Music that is easy to play.

Roadrunner
The Modern Lovers

             a.) With only a few chords.
             b.) In some cases, a "drone" effect (a V.U./John Cale influence).
             c.) Music that was "straight ahead", nothing fancy.
       - <u>Lyrics</u>: Again, simple.
         * But, with an air of irreverence.
             a.) Expressed in lyrics like: "Pablo Picasso was never called an asshole" (from the song, "Pablo Picasso").

Pablo Picasso
The Modern Lovers

       - <u>Attitude</u>: Jonathan Richman also had an "I-don't-care-what-you-think" type of demeanor to accompany the irreverence of his lyrics.
         * Again, a precursor to the Punk attitude that would eventually border on the anti-social.

3.) "The Modern Lovers" (1973): Their only album. Produced by John Cale.
- Featuring the stripped-downed (sometimes droning), simple, direct songs that made this album so seminal.
* Even though it sold poorly due to its eccentric nature.
a.) It would however, become highly influential to the New York City underground scene.
b.) Richman's stripped-down, direct nature of his songs struck a nerve with a certain segment of the New York underground that would eventually flourish into a full-fledged movement.

B.) New York City: where the first true punk movement began.
1.) New York Dolls: The first to develop an underground movement that would eventually become Punk.
- Some musicians who attended their performances would become inspired to form their own, Punk harbinger bands.
* The New York Dolls had a noisy, guitar-ridden sound influenced in part by Glam Rock elements from Britain.

Personality Crisis
New York Dolls

a.) Along with a kamikaze, crash & burn essence to their sound.
b.) Their basic style consisted of repeating the same noisy guitar riff.
- They kept it simple and at times, vulgar.

Trash
New York Dolls

c.) Vocally: Their shrill screaming became a trademark along with the sometimes out-of-tune vocalisms of David Johansen (who would later reinvent himself as Buster Poindexter).
d.) Their Glam influences included "Slade", "T-Rex".
- They were also influenced by The Rolling Stones' "trashy" style of rock.
- The New York Dolls formed in 1971.
* Original line-up: Johnny Thunders (b. John Genzale, 7/15/54; d. 4/23/91, New Orleans, LA), Billy Murcia (b. 1951, New York; d. 11/6/72, London, ENG): drums, and David Johansen (b. 1/9/50, Staten Island, NY): vocals, Rick Rivets: guitar, Arthur Kane: bass.
a.) They not only adopted musical influences from the British Glam sound:
- They also adopted the Glam look: cross-dressing.
- The Mercer Arts Center: The theatre in lower Manhattan where the New York Dolls first developed their following.
* It would take a few months to accomplish this.
a.) Even though at the time, they were not signed by any record label (who were afraid to sign them due to their gender-bending and outright raunchy sound).
- And even though this "raunchy sound" bucked the dominant treads in rock and roll at that time.
- 1972: Their first tour of Britain where, at Wembley Stadium, they backed up Rod Stewart's band, "Faces" (a metal/Glam sound).
* in the midst of this tour, drummer Billy Murcia died of a drug/alcohol overdose.
a.) He was replaced by Jerry Nolan.
- 1973: After the tour they finally secured a recording contract with Mercury Records.
* Todd Rundgren: A well-known pop artist ("Hello It's Me') would be their producer.
a.) An irony that someone as pop-oriented as Rundgren would produce a raunchy-styled by the New York Dolls.

b.) "New York Dolls" (1973): Their debut album received great reviews but nonetheless, sold poorly (reaching #116 on the pop charts).

* George "Shadow" Morton: A producer of girl-group fame (with" The Shangri-La's"), produced the Doll's second album.

a.) "Too Much Too Soon" (1974): Although more accessible than their first album, it still sold poorly (#167 on the charts).

- After being dropped by Mercury (due to poor sales), The New York Dolls hired producer Malcolm McClaren.

* McClaren – the King of Outlandishism – tried to use his outrageous, attention-getting tactics in order to get The Dolls to shock their audiences.

a.) He had The Dolls clad completely in red leather outfits performing in front of the Soviet (Communist) flag.

- Due to strong sentiments concerning the on-going Cold War, this tactic completely turned off the audience and resulted in a complete failure

b.) Following this failure, the band itself began to dissipate.

- Its influence however was, by this time (1975), already etched in stone.

* Their commercial failures notwithstanding, The New York Dolls did leave an important legacy.

a.) Their success in gathering an audience in the midst of rebelling against the dominant trends, spearheaded a new underground movement in New York City.

- That would grow into a new music genre as well as a new rock and roll movement.

- The music would be based on metal along with very basic, rudimentary, unskilled playing chops.

* Back during the Mercer Theatre days, a young guitarist a basic, garage-band facility, was so inspired by the performances of The New York Dolls and the following they gained…

a.) He decided that he wanted to gather an underground following of his own…

2.) Television: Original Lineup: Tom Verlaine (b. Thomas Miller, Dec. 13, 1949, Wilmington, DE): guitar, vocals. Richard Hell (b. Richard Meyers, Oct. 2, 1949, Lexington, KY): bass. Richard Lloyd, guitar, vocals. Billy Ficca, drums. Their total effort into their music ran opposite of their outside career concerns.

- Thomas Miller: Turned his back on classical music to embrace jazz. His initial high art jazz influences: John Coltrane, Eric Dolphy, and Albert Ayler – these artists became his inspiration to pursue improvisation and to play the saxophone.

* His High Art Poetic Influences: Baudelaire, Lautreamont, Arthur Rimbaud, Huysmous, and Celine: basically known as the French decadents who delved into the twisted aesthetics of darkness and the derangement of the senses.

* He moved to New York City with his old friend Richard Hell and began writing poetry together using an old typewriter. He reinvented himself as Tom Verlaine taking the surname of the classic French poet Paul Verlaine (1844-1896).

a.) Later on, Verlaine and Hell would move in completely opposite directions: for Verlaine, it was toward serious art and for Hell, it was toward pop. This would lead to an indelible friction between the two.

- Beginnings: After seeing the New York Dolls at the Mercer Arts Center, it was Richard Hell's idea to form a band (Verlaine would teach Hell the basics of playing the bass). Billy Ficca on the drums and Richard Lloyd on the guitar would join them. The result: they called themselves <u>The Neon Boys</u> (it was Richard Hell who eventually came up with the name, <u>Television</u>).

* From a rock 'n' roll perspective; they were inspired by garage bands (featured in Lenny Kaye's legendary compilation, *Nuggets*) such as The Standells, The Seeds, The Chocolate Watchband, and The Shadows of Night.

- <u>Improvisation</u>: Tom Verlaine wanted to extend beyond the conventional three-and-a-half minute format to delve into improvisation especially, with noises and other sonic explorations on the electric guitar -- this, despite their sloppy, unskilled, and rudimentary garage band limitations. One of their main improvisational influences was jazz saxophonist, <u>Albert Ayler</u>.

* Robert Palmer (*Rock & Roll: An Unruly History*) once quoted Albert Ayler: "Sounds, not notes. Feeling, not phrases".

a.) He wrote that Albert Ayler's style was to play noises on his tenor saxophone (honks, squawks, groans, etc.) for the sake of expression that one could not achieve through conventional means: this was his approach to extreme expression out front. Television, would take a similar approach.

- For them, the act of synthesizing high art influences of Ayler (among others) with their limited garage band chops [low art] resulted in a unique approach to their noise-laden extended improvisations.

b.) NOTE: The concept of extreme expression over skill and technique became the very foundation of what would eventually become Punk.

- <u>1974</u>: Tom Verlaine and Richard Hell approached Hilly Kristol, owner of a runned-down, bluegrass/country bar in the Bowery section of Manhattan called CBGB (Country, Bluegrass, & Blues).

* <u>Television's CBGB debut</u>: Sunday, March 31st. It became the venue where they developed their initial following.

a.) Thereby, transforming CBGB into the new ray of light for the New York City underground replacing the Mercer Arts Center (which became dilapidated and uninhabitable).

- <u>1977</u>: By this time, the conflict between Verlaine's serious art focus and Hell's pop sensibilities became too much for either one to handle and as a result, Hell left the band and moved on (first, to The Heartbreakers and then The Voidoids). He was replaced by Fred Smith (not to be confused with Fred "Sonic" Smith of the MC5).

* <u>Elektra Records</u>: Through Danny Field's involvement – by alerting Elektra's publicity director Karen Berg – Television was signed to a recording contract.

a.) *Marquee Moon* (1977): Their debut album produced by Andy Johns (of Led Zeppelin and Rolling Stones fame). It took only three days to record and produce the album comprised of songs that they have been performing for quite awhile (only in the recording, the songs were in tune).

- Although critically acclaimed, this album (like those of the New York Dolls) sold poorly.

- In addition to his band's short recording career (including another album, *Adventure* released in 1978), Tom Verlaine collaborated on a book of poems with another poet who shared the same passion for the French decadents.

3.) <u>Patti Smith</u> (b. Dec. 30,1946, Chicago, IL): A poet who entered the world of rock 'n' roll by combining her serious [high art] poetry to music. Moved to New York City in 1967.

- <u>1971</u>: She first began reciting her poetry at St. Mark's Place with the back-up of pianist Richard Sohl and guitarist, writer, & rock critic <u>Lenny Kaye</u>.

* <u>Her Poetic Flavor</u>: confrontational, raw, and pointed. She transformed her poetry into performance art.

    a.) <u>Her Poetic influences Included</u>: Arthur Rimbaud's total derangement of the senses as exemplified in his epic work, *A Season In Hell*, Baudelaire's *Les Fleur du Mal* (Flowers of Evil), Lautreamont's *Moldoror*, etc. (influences that were similar to Tom Verlaine's). She also collaborated on a rock influenced play with Sam Shepard called *Cowboy Mouth*.

* She began performing regularly at the Mercer Arts Center in 1972.

- <u>CBGB</u>: By the time she started at CBGB in 1974, her act with Lenny Kaye not only continued, but would expand with addition of two new players: <u>Ivan Kral</u> on the guitar and <u>Jay Dee Daugherty</u> on the drums. They would be known as The Patti Smith Group. Their initial mission was to perform garage band classic repertoire. This was a manifestation of Lenny Kaye's revolt against the complexities of progressive rock.

    * <u>Lenny Kaye</u>: He once said in an interview that, "Progressive rock had made rock 'n' roll very complicated where artistry and instrumental prowess were the key -- it had also made rock 'n' roll into a very adult medium. The idea of someone learning 2 or 3 chords on the guitar and getting on stage two weeks later, was being lost".

        a.) He not only played garage band classics, he also reissued them on a compilation album entitled, *Nuggets*. An example from this album was *Pushin' Too Hard* by The Seeds.

            - In his view, "Garage band music was the reason why people wanted to rock 'n' roll in the first place", because it was simple, fun, and easy to play. *Little Girl* by The Syndicate Of Sound was an example of the fun and simplicity that garage band music [in Kaye's view] had to offer.

- <u>Patti Smith</u>: Would also become obsessed with music that focused on emotion and feel as opposed to skill and technique.

    * But this music would serve as a supporting [musical] platform for her poetry to flourish (which she injected into the music). This was her way of "pushing music over the edge". As a result, the [postmodern] synthesis of high art poetics and garage band became her trademark.

- <u>1975</u>: The Patti Smith Group and Television shared a regular house billing together at CBGB where her incantations now took on a viable rock 'n' roll form.

    * In the process, it was her notoriety that brought exposure to the underground CBGB scene by expanding the audience to artists from other artistic scenes [outside of music] in New York and synthesized them into the garage rock crowd.

        a.) She became one of the main embodiments of the CBGB scene.

        b.) NOTE: Around this time, other artists would begin their tenures at CBGB including <u>The Talking Heads</u>, <u>Blondie</u>, <u>Johnny Thunders Heartbreakers</u>, and many others.

- <u>Her Debut Album</u>: She was signed to Arista Records by the company's chief executive Clive Davis. RESULT: *Horses* (1975), produced by John Cale.

    * A mixture of Smith's poetry and music with classic garage band motifs used as raw material. Some motifs include, *Gloria* (by Van Morrison) and *Land of 1000 Dances* (Cannibal & The Headhunters).

        a.) She fluctuated between garage band motifs and original free verse. Again, injecting her poetry into rock 'n' roll by using these classic motifs as structural [musical] support.

- <u>NOTE</u>: Patti Smith began performing at CBGB in 1974 but around that time, another group would pave the way sending the garage band influenced genre in a completely new direction.

    * Or, to put it another way, to completely codify this genre that would result in a stylistic policy/consistency that many other artists could emulate and make their own.

        a.) There would also be a new name attached to this genre because of what this next group would accomplish. But before we get to that, a slight detour out of New York is needed…

C.) <u>Cleveland</u>: Had an active, early garage band influenced scene. Initially inspired by The Velvet Underground's regular performances at a Cleveland nightclub called "La Cave". A number of garage-based bands sprouted up such as Rocket from The Tombs, The Electric Eels, The Mirrors -- they only recorded singles. Eventually, former members of Rocket from The Tombs would form a new band that would become the epitome of Cleveland's underground scene with their own postmodernist approach…

<u>PERE UBU</u>: from the ashes of Cleveland's underground garage band, punk scene.

Personnel: <u>David Thomas</u> (vocals); <u>Peter Laughner</u> (guitar), <u>Tom Herman</u> (guitar), <u>Tony Maimone</u> (bass), <u>Scott Krauss</u> (drums), and <u>Allen Ravenstein</u> ("EML 200" synthesizer). Of the five members, Thomas and Laughner were the original founders.

<u>Origin of Name</u>: *Ubu Roi* (1896), a play by Alfred Jarry (1873-1907) – one of the first harbingers of what would become the "Theatre of The Absurd" (in the 1930's/40's). *Ubu Roi* is basically, an absurdist re-writing of Shakespeare's *MacBeth*. The main character, Pere Ubu (Papa Ubu), is a highly grotesque, childish, vulgar, obese, demonic despot that was Jarry's metaphoric representation of modern man. <u>Brief Synopsis of the Play</u>: Pere Ubu kills the Polish king Venceslas, assumes the throne, and gets defeated by Venceslas' son, Bongrelus (who recaptures the throne of his father).

<u>Beginnings</u>: Thomas and Laughner were in a previous band, Rocket From The Tombs – a more straightforward, aggressive approach to the Detroit hard-edged guitar sound of The Stooges and The MC5. His [Thomas'] other influences were artists who were more personally and progressively unique namely, the tape collaging of Frank Zappa and the avant-garde approach of Captain Beefheart (especially from his *Trout Mask Replica* album). The Velvet Underground's raw, primitive, postmodern approach and their "live-for-the-art-first" attitude plus Lenny Kaye's *Nuggets* compilation, were also key ingredients to the influential mix.

<u>Early Cleveland Scene</u>: as early Cleveland garage bands were inspired by the rebelliousness of the proto punks, groups like The Electric Eels had worn what would be known, as punk regalia (i.e. safety pin piercings, swastikas, etc.) -- two years ahead of the punk culture in the UK. They referred to their approach as "artistic terrorism". On the heels of this scene, Pere Ubu had formed and, in the character of *Ubu Roi*, Dave Thomas (lead singer/frontman) and the band adopted a dark, grotesque persona.

<u>Synth Effect</u>: an anomaly in early American punk (anticipating the synth-driven British post punk movement of the late 70's). Allen Ravenstein experimented with the EML 200 synthesizer for several years. Instead of learning in a traditional keyboard-oriented way, Ravenstein explored the usage of what would resemble "found sound" (but in a synth-driven manner). "Found Sound" is defined as recording the sounds of everyday life, electronically processing them, and taking them out of their original context. <u>Result</u>: an original, abstract, dissonant jumble of controlled chaotic sounds – a postmodern, high art synthesis that they had dubbed, "avant-garage".

<u>Further Abstractions</u>: like Ravenstein, Dave Thomas had an obsession with the abstract in a postmodern tradition. One of his tenants was to avoid all

semblances of black music influence. This energized the "abstract" obsession by initiating his dark, grotesque, and throaty vocal approach.

Resulting Style: dark, apocalyptic – abstract on one hand (controlled, chaotic synthesis), combined with straightforward rock accompaniment on the other (i.e. guitar, bass, & drums) – an avant + garage band synthesis.

Debut Recording: *30 Seconds Over Tokyo*, attempting to [musically] encapsulate a sonic environment within a WWII bomber plane equipped with powerful incendiaries that would leave the Japanese capital in flames and destruction. Released on their label *Hearthan* in 1975 (they were the first punk band in America to initiate their own independent label).

Their Following Singles: *Final Solution* and *Street Waves* were influential in the UK to the emerging post punk bands of the late 70's like Joy Division. In America, these singles became influential to alternative bands such as Hüsker Dü, R.E.M., and The Pixies.

30 Seconds Over Tokyo
Pere Ubu

With regard to *Final Solution*, the single contains many of the bands characteristics – from a high art perspective, the use of dissonance and scattered rhythms from the synthesizer (in between sung verses). And from the vocal line, a dark melodic and apocalyptic essence (in Dave Thomas' throaty voice). From a garage/punk band approach, the use of guitar, bass, and drums with the anomalous synthesizer added in. The result: an example of their postmodern (high art + garage band) approach conveying a grotesque characteristic reminiscent of the Alfred Jerry play.

Final Solution
Pere Ubu

Street Waves: was reminiscent of the area of Cleveland that they rehearsed in – an area known as The Flats. The Flats: a locale along the heavily polluted Cuyahoga River that was home to massive factories, industrial plants, and warehouses that was dark and bleak. *Street Waves* attempted to capture that bleak "industrial" essence.

Street Waves
Pere Ubu

New Label: Cliff Bernstein, A&R man for Mercury Records signed Pere Ubu to a subsidiary label called Blank. Their next release, *The Modern Dance*: their debut album released in March of 1978 followed by their second album, *Dub Housing* in 1979. Both albums received underground, critical acclaim and influence in the UK. These albums contained dissonant abstractions and "found Sound" collages that in some ways were representative of the "Absurdist Theatre" in a post punk, roll 'n' roll sense.

Dub Housing
Pere Ubu

An "absurdist theatre" example is shown in the title track of the album, *Dub Housing,* which was conceived on a tour trip though Baltimore as they were driving stoned-out in their tour van. The term "dub housing" was their initial reference to a set of row houses that they were passing – a sort of one row unit echoing the other (the use of echo effects was a prime component of the Jamaican dubbing tradition used by King Tubby among others). Dave Thomas' histrionic, dramatically exaggerated vocal delivery was reminiscent of an absurdist, "dada-art" expression – while a repeated vocal chorus in the background suggested the repetitiveness of the uniformed, row houses.

In some ways, similar to what New York garage bands were doing, Pere Ubu, through their dissonant found-sound collages (on the synthesizer) and their absurdist theatre influences were contributing their own postmodernist efforts via their "avant garage" approach.

D.) The state of garage-based music: Jonathan Richman laid down the structure for the stripped-down, direct approach. Others who had followed such as Television, Patti Smith, Pere Ubu, etc., created their own distinct musical voices within this structural approach.

- <u>PROBLEM</u>: There was no unifying set of elements that would create a "official" genre that would be identifiable.
- <u>NEEDED</u>: A codification (i.e. a set of rules) that would create a foundation for a new style that others could easily emulate on the one hand.
  - And on the other, create a unifying "school" of a particular style.

III. PUNK BECOMES A NEW GENRE

A.) <u>The Ramones</u> (1974): were the first of the CBGB artists to acquire a distinct musical signature that set them apart from the other CBGB bands.

1.) <u>Style</u>: Simple, rapid tempo'd, aggressive, and extremely energetic, with a furious wall of electric [guitar] chordal texture. In addition, their lyrics were purposefully deadpan and adolescent (ex: "Beat The Brat With A Baseball Bat", "I Wanna Sniff Some Glue", "Go Mental" etc.). -- presented within simplistic, twisted bubblegum melodies.
- <u>Presentation</u>: A minimalist format (i.e. the basic guitar, bass, drums, lead singer model) and a very basic, bare-bones musical approach. The key: simplicity.
  * In the process, they established the new rules for New York-based Punk that would be easy for others to emulate on the one hand while maintaining an individual voice on the other.

2.) Personnel: They would all change their onstage, professional surnames to Ramone.
- <u>Joey Ramone</u>: (b. Jeffery Hyman, 5/19/51; d. 4/15/01, New York, NY): vocals.
- <u>Johnny Ramone</u>: (b. John Cummings, 10/8/51, Long Island, NY; d. 2004): guitar.
- <u>Dee Dee Ramone</u>: (b. Douglas Colvin, 9/18/52, VA; d. 2002): bass.
- <u>Tommy Ramone</u>: (b. Tom Erdelyi, 1/29/52, Budapest, HUN): drums.

3.) <u>Early Years</u>: A need for rebellion against the boredom of their upbringing in Forest Hills, NY. In addition, to 60's garage bands, they liked blues revisionists, The Yardbirds and Them. They also liked the late 60's pop group, The Young Rascals.
- <u>Their First Major Inspiration</u> The New York Dolls. To Tommy Ramone, they demonstrated that, if you had the true rock 'n' roll essence, it didn't matter what your skill levels was.
  * This inspiration gave them the go-ahead to form a band in March of 1974 and it was then, that they dubbed themselves <u>The Ramones</u> (a satirical goof on Paul McCartney's "Paul Ramon" pseudonym that he adopted during his Silver Beatles days in 1960).

4.) <u>Their CBGB Debut</u>: August, 1974. During their residency, they established their own distinct black leather jacket look and their own sound: ultimate form of minimalism that was musically stripped down to the absolute, back to basics essentials.
- In the process they became the first to establish the initial rules that would transform American Punk into a unifying aesthetic – one that anyone could easily emulate (thereby becoming a part of that aesthetic identification), while simultaneously, maintaining a sense of unique individualism.
  * <u>The Rules</u>:

I'm Against It
The Ramones

I Wanna Be Sedated
The Ramones

  a.) No more than 3 chords in a song (4 is pushing it).
  b.) Catchy, simple, twisted "bubblegum" tunes.
  c.) Sing only about what you know (if you've never owned a car, then don't sing about cars).
  d.) Rapid, quick tempos (or, as Johnny Ramone once said, "Slow songs played quickly")
  e.) Song duration: about two and a half minutes – tops.
  f.) All-out, assaultive, aggressive energy.
  * <u>Simplicity</u>: The simplicity of these rules, were the result of The Ramones working strictly within their limited skill levels (i.e. no solos, no fancy tunes, no slow tempos, no elaborate chord progressions, etc.).

With relentless efficiency, these rules helped them make the most of their limitations while establishing an unmistakable artistic signature and (countless other punk bands, also with limited skills, would follow suit).

> a.) This became serious art in its own right, which laid down the blueprint for New York Punk.
>
> b.) In addition, they re-injected the basic elements of energy, and youth (as well as simplicity) back into rock 'n' roll via their high-octaned, punk-oriented approach:
>
> -.

5.) <u>Their Debut Album</u>: *The Ramones*, released by the Sire Label on April 23, 1976.

Go Mental
The Ramones

- Contained 14 tracks that, in the aggregate, clocked in at just less than 30 minutes at a production cost of $6200 – another example of The Ramones getting the most out of the least.

> * This mimicked their performance sets where they'd synchronize their watches to exactly twenty minutes.

Bad Brain
The Ramones

6.) <u>Longevity</u>: Whereas most punk bands crash and burn within a short time period…

- The Ramones managed to stay and tour relentlessly for 20 years.

> * Finally disbanding in 1996.

7.) <u>Legacy</u>: Because The Ramones were the first to establish the rules mentioned above:

- They would be forever known as the first "Punk" band on record. (where the term "Punk" carried a strictly musical connotation).

> * Thereby sending the punk movement into full gear.
>
> > a.) Especially with their first British tour, which started on July 4, 1976…
> >
> > > -… where they influenced many British artists.

C.) <u>Malcolm McClaren</u> (b. 1/22/46)

1.) <u>The French Situationist Movement</u>: supposedly, his first major influence.

- Advocated both the absurd and provocative (controversial) actions in the following ways:

> * Making a political statement or…
> * In the presentation of a performance art context.
>
> > a.) This movement began in the 1950's but peaked during the Paris riots of 1968.

- He would begin the application of these "situationist" influenced ideas into the pop domain.

2.) Also, he began an interest in clothes designing while attending the <u>Goldsmith College of Art</u> (the same Art College that The Velvet Underground's John Cale attended).

- He [McClaren] attended there from 1969 - 1971.

> * After dropping out, he opened his first fashion boutique in 1972 with business partner, <u>Vivienne Westwood</u>.

3.) <u>1975</u>: After his public relations fiasco as manager of The New York Dolls…

- McClaren took an interest in Richard Hell's look.

> * Clothes held together by safety pins.
> * Spiked up hairdo.
> * A vacant mien like that of a heroin addict.

- He wanted to take Richard Hell back to England, but he [R. Hell] declined the invitation.

> * McClaren subsequently returned to the UK armed with the New York underground influence, look, and attitude.

- Later that year [1975], he opened a boutique in London with his business partner, Vivienne Westwood and named the venue, "SEX", which in his words, "Sold primarily leather and fetish artifacts". In addition, they sold tee shirts displaying swastikas among other things.

* It would be at this shop where two rockers who had jammed on old rock covers together and a bass player who worked at the shop, would form a band.

        a.) The two rockers were guitarist <u>Steve Jones</u> (b. Sep. 3, 1955, London) and drummer <u>Paul Cook</u> (b. July 20, 1956, London).

        b.) The employee/bass player was <u>Glenn Matlock</u>.

* They started rehearsing in the back room of McClaren's shop.

4.) <u>Steve Jones</u>: His musical influences were the following:

- <u>Glam Bands</u>: T-Rex, New York Dolls.

- <u>Mod Band</u>: Small Faces

- <u>Proto-Punk</u>: The Stooges.

    * These bands represented a rich and aggressive metal sound.

- A word about <u>MOD</u> (which influenced "Small Faces"). <u>MOD</u>: was more about lifestyle and fashion as opposed to music.

    * First adopted by UK teenagers.

        a.) They dressed in stylish, neo-Italian fashions while listening to American R&B genres such as Motown and Southern Soul.

    * <u>Mod Bands</u>: who dressed in this style, eventually developed into outlandishness. They originally covered R&B songs.

        a.) But presented it [R&B] in a more rapid, more hard-rocking interpretation (sort of like an amphetamine edge to it).

        b.) Their original songs would become a hard rocking version of their R&B soul influences.

Whatcha Gonna Do About It
Small Faces

        c.) <u>Small Faces</u> and <u>The Who</u> would become the first two Mod bands to crack the American market (they were widely popular in the UK).

    * With the rise of the Psychedelic movement in the late 60's, Mod began to fizzle out of fashion.

        a.) <u>It's Legacy</u>: the cross-dressing and metal-laden genre of GLAM (metal sound derived from the hard rock, soul sounds of Mod).

- <u>Steve Jones</u>: was so broke (and a kleptomaniac by nature), he stole his musical equipment. Legend has it, that he stole his equipment from <u>The Spiders From Mars</u>' final performance at the Hammersmith Odeon in 1973.

    * He befriended <u>Paul Cook</u> who began playing drums as a teenager. Cook's style was a thunderous, hard-hitting, Charley Watts style of drumming.

        a.) His drumming style became the underlying backbone of The Sex Pistols' sound.

    * <u>Cook and Jones</u>: developed a friendship by jamming in rock and roll covers together. They began hanging out at Malcolm's shop and jamming with Glenn Matlock.

        a.) The only thing missing was a front man….

D.) <u>John Lydon</u> (b. John Joseph Lydon, Jan. 31, 1956, London): The real brains behind the new group: <u>The Sex Pistols</u>. Introduction of noisy rage and anger that rebelled against the class-oriented British establishment. In his own words, he once said that, "Chaos was my philosophy".

1.) A shy kid who grew up in a rough, Irish, low-income working class slum.

- He felt that the working class always turned against those who were one rung below on the socio-economic pecking order.

    * <u>To Lydon</u>: It should be the other way around – rebel against the upper classes that were smothering you down to begin with.

2.) At age 7, he contracted spinal meningitis and was brought to Wittington Hospital in Highgate where he was in and out of a coma for six months. He began to recover after approximately one year.

- <u>The Fallout To His Health</u>: The Lydon Stare – the illness brought him bad eyesight, which forced him to intensely stare at an object in order to focus on it.

* It took him quite awhile to catch up after the illness with his schoolwork – he had to restart the same grade level over again. At this point, he began to feel that he'd never fit in.

3.) Mid Teens: He began becoming overtly rebellious in school by openly confronting and questioning his teachers' assertions [in class]. He did so in an antagonistic manner that included the no-blinking, eye-boring stare. He would be thrown out of schools for disruptive behavior.

- He began to seriously buy and listen to records. His favorites were: The Stooges' album, *Fun House* and the group, Hawkwind featuring Lemmy (of later Mötörhead fame). Other musical favorites were the album *Tago Mago* by Can, Miles Davis' *Bitches Brew*, Captain Beefheart, Alice Cooper, T-Rex, and some of David Bowie. He also loved Reggae.

* When he was 16, he saw Iggy & The Stooges perform at a club in Kings Cross. He witnessed Iggy physically abusing himself on stage while the guitarist (James Williamson) was constantly noisy and out of tune – Lydon loved it.

- His literary favorites were: Oscar Wilde, Ted Hughes, and some Shakespeare.

4.) At 17, he began ripping and slashing his clothes apart with a razor blade, then hold them together with safety pins. As he hung out and lived in squalor with his long time friend, Sid Vicious (b. John Simon Ritchie), Lydon cropped his [Sid's] hair by cutting out chunks which made his hair look spiky.

- According to Lydon's autobiography, this was where the so-called punk look originated (long before anyone else had caught on).

E.) Beginnings of The Sex Pistols: As previously mentioned, Steve Jones (guitar), Glenn Matlock (bass), and Paul Cook (drums) began practicing in the back room of Malcolm McClaren's "SEX" boutique. They were basically doing covers of Mod groups such as Small Faces. They had no direction at that time because they were missing something namely, a front man/lead vocalist.

1.) Bernie Rhodes (future manager of The Clash): discovered John Lydon wearing an "I Hate Pink Floyd" Tee Shirt (the words "I Hate" were written in) and as a result, Rhodes arranged a meeting with McClaren. The meeting took place at the Roebuck Pub where he also met Steve Jones and Paul Cook (neither of them were impressed).

- The Audition: Immediately following this meeting, they went to Malcolm's shop and had Lydon mime to a song off of the jukebox – he [Lydon] chose "Eighteen" by Alice Cooper -- he used a showerhead as a fake microphone. The "audition" was successful.

* NOTE: Lydon had no musical experience, a terrible voice, but he definitely looked the part and had the right rebellious attitude.

- Lydon: Became the new front man and wrote the lyrics that were full of rage and rebellion projecting lower-class anger from the bottom rungs upward.

* In the words of rock critic Caroline Coon who first attached the "punk' moniker to Then Sex Pistols, "The Pistols was dramatized rage".

2.) Their Debut Performance: November 1975 at St. Martins College. They played twenty minutes of absolute chaos and the audience didn't know what to make of it. Lydon wrote that they had, "energy and sheer, brazen honesty".

- The 100 Club: their first regular performance residency where they built their initial audience base. Other clubs that they regularly performed in were The Nashville Rooms, The Marquee, and Screen on the Green – it was at these clubs where the initial punk underground developed.

* The Audience: former fans of Roxy Music, David Bowie, and Glam Rock. Many of them started wearing plastic garbage bags, torn-up clothes (held together with safety pins), swastikas, and cropped, spiky hairdos. Goal: to rebel against the establishment – to antagonize the status quo.

a.) Some of the other punk bands who were formed around this time and played in these venues were <u>Siouxsie & The Banshees</u>, <u>The Adverts</u>, <u>The Damned</u>, and <u>The Clash</u>.

3.) <u>The Punk Essence</u>: Before the term "punk" made its way to London, it was used in America as a strictly *musical* description – first, to denote the nostalgia of 60's garage band music and then, to denote the music coming out of the CBGB bands -- especially that of The Ramones (where the common thread was an anti-corporate sentiment).

- In London, ushered in by rock critic Caroline Coon, the term "punk" was introduced [into the lexicon] as a more *cultural* description that captured the essence of The Sex Pistols.

* The Pistols had an aura that generated activism against the caste-minded British establishment with sometimes, violent results (although The Pistols were not violent themselves).

a.) What was once a term denoting music, "punk" was now a moniker for rebellion, anti-establishment, and radicalism completely devoid of any nostalgia or connection with the past.

F.) <u>The Impact of The Sex Pistols</u>: They would spend only two years together but in that period, they would redefine the character and the place of Punk within rock 'n' roll. In addition, they would also introduce and export the rebellious, snarly punk essence/attitude to the mainstream world. And in the process, become the first recognizable, international "face" of punk (that the world would become familiar with).

1.) The Impact that The Sex Pistols had upon standardizing the anti-establishment brand of punk were the following:

Pretty Vacant
The Sex Pistols

- <u>Musically</u>: Injecting a sense of sheer abrasiveness into the music (that went along with blatant amateurism).
- <u>Subject Matter</u>: Lyrics dealing with rage, anger, violence, apathy, abortion, and anarchy (i.e. personal, class-oriented commentary)
- <u>Attitude</u>: Confrontational accompanied by an "in your face" snarl.
- <u>The Look</u>: Creating an image that captured the essence of Punk, which would stick into the awareness of the mainstream – and inadvertently, turn it into fashion.

2.) NOTE: These new elements that the Sex Pistols had standardized would forever become an indelible part of the punk idiom.

G.) <u>Their First Signing</u>: EMI records. Their first release: *Anarchy In The UK* (1976) – sold 55,000 copies.

1.) EMI was embarrassed by the appearance of The Sex Pistols on *Today* -- a live morning television talk show on the ITV network hosted by Bill Grundy. As a result, the label would drop The Sex Pistols from their roster.

Anarchy in The UK
The Sex Pistols

- <u>Instant Fame</u>: While they were rehearsing for their upcoming "Anarchy Tour" (the tour would include Johnny Thunder's Heartbreakers, The Damned, and The Clash), a limo appeared on front of their venue. It was sent by ITV to transport The Pistols and their entourage to the studio – the interview was arranged by EMI. It took place on January of 1976.

* Their entourage was dressed in full punk regalia, which included Nazi swastika armbands, spiky hair, and safety pins through their noses.

a.) The British mainstream en mass, had never seen anything like this before.

* The live broadcast (with no seven second delay) eventually turned into a cussword free-for-all, which was initially nudged on by Bill Grundy himself. This live TV swear-fest sparked outrage and controversy throughout the UK and overnight, The Sex Pistols achieved instant notoriety.

a.) Their irreverent, rebellious, punk-driven attitude had now been exposed to the mainstream. As a result, the British tabloids viewed them [The Pistols] as a social pariah resulting in unanimously negative [mainstream] press.

- And due to this negative publicity, their antics would give them more fame than their music.

2.) <u>Case in point</u>: *God Save The Queen* (1977) – Released as a protest song against what they felt, was the self congratulatory patriotism surrounding the celebration of Queen Elizabeth's 25th year Silver Jubilee.

- On the night of the festivities, The Sex Pistols chartered a tourist boat – complete with a plethora of friends, artists, and in Lydon's words, "Plenty of Tarts" to accompany them.

God Save The Queen

by the Sex Pistols, reprinted from *Never Mind the Bollocks: Here's the Sex Pistols*, Warner Bros. 3147-2: 1977, by permission of Alfred Publishing Co., Inc.

* While the boat cruised up the Thames River, The Sex Pistols played the song quite loudly. Because of a rash of complaints, the police responded en mass [on their own boats] to put an end to the affair of which some were arrested.

- *God Save The Queen* would have the distinction of becoming the first punk single to reach #1 on the UK pop charts or, for that matter, on any important pop chart.

* Even though radio stations refused to play it on the air and that both the song and the name of the group were blackened out on the official printed pop chart list.

a.) The lyrics said it all:
"God Save The Queen,
The fascist regime,
They made you a moron,
Potential H-Bomb…
…there's no future for you".

3.) "<u>Never Mind The Bullocks, Here's The Sex Pistols</u>" (1977): Released on the Warner Bros. label. Their first album and, until their reunion in 1996 to celebrate their 20th anniversary – <u>their only album</u>: one of the highest rated in all of rock and roll.

- <u>Glenn Matlock</u>: Who became increasingly distressed by the recalcitrant, offensive direction that The Sex Pistols had headed in, decided to call it quits.

* He did possess however, the best musical facility in the group especially from a melodic standpoint.

* After leaving the group before the start of this album's recording sessions, he was rehired to record most of the baselines in the album primarily, because his eventual replacement, Sid Vicious, couldn't cop a lick due to his neophyte status as a musician.

- <u>Sid Vicious</u> (b. John Simon Ritchie 5/10/57, London; d. 2/2/79, New York, NY). In the absence of any musicianship, he instead became the embodiment of what the Punk ethos was all about.

* <u>His Legend</u>: the one-man embodiment of anarchy, violence, nihilism, dying young, apathy, and all-out recalcitrance.

a.) A revolt against the blandness and boredom of the status quo paralleled by an inevitable path to self-destruction.

b.) A romantic tragedy that was pre-ordained in conjunction with chic and glamour of the junkie cult.

* <u>His Reality</u>: lack of intelligence and common sense.

a.) A soulful, gentle person in real life who was easily given to self destructive behavior if he hung out with the wrong crowd/person.

- Such a person, <u>Nancy Spungen</u> – a heroin addict/groupie – would be one who would lead Sid Vicious down that road to personal destruction.

- He was the only member of the Sex Pistols who could not play his instrument.

* Although he made a valiant/early attempt to learn the bass, his interest in learning and practicing began to diminish due to his rising fame and heroin addiction.

    a.) He would become a complete non-entity in regard to the creating and recording of the music.

- <u>Beginnings</u>: Him and John Lydon grew up together and eventually, Sid became a devoted Sex Pistols follower.

    * <u>Influences</u>: T-Rex, David Bowie, and Roxy Music (Glam sounds).

    * He was originally a drummer for <u>Souxsie and The Banshees</u>.

    * <u>4/4/77</u>: His first onstage appearance with The Sex Pistols.

4.) <u>Their Only American Tour</u>: Their *Never Mind The Bollocks* album would support their impending tour of the US, which would last only 14 days starting in January of 1978.

- They would perform in a string of small roadhouses (country western joints mostly) throughout the deep south.

    * Causing a total ruckus everywhere they played.

- Their tour ended at the Winterland Ballroom in San Francisco in late January.

    * By this time, they were not speaking to one another. This was where John Lydon delivered the famous quote: "Ever get the feeling you've been cheated?"

    a.) Which was aimed towards the band for wasting their opportunity.

5.) The Sex Pistols broke up after that San Francisco performance but it didn't mean that their legacy broke up with them.

- On the contrary, in addition to being the UK's first Punk band, their legacy would be monumental.

    * Because of their influence, Punk would eventually split in three different directions:

    a.) One in which Punk would carry a <u>Reggae</u> influence.

    b.) Birth of the <u>Post Punk</u> movement.

    c.) And the spawning of Punk's extreme: <u>Hardcore</u>.

IV. THE EVOLUTION OF REGGAE'S INFLUENCE INTO PUNK

A.) <u>The Clash</u>: the consummate UK Punk band.

1.) Introduced political statement/commentary into Punk.

- From a left-wing, working class perspective.

2.) Introduced a sense of eclecticism into Punk as well.

- Opening it up to many different influential styles which included:

    * <u>Rockabilly</u>, <u>Pop</u>, <u>Jazzy Elements</u>, <u>Rhythm & Blues</u>, and above all, <u>Reggae</u> (more on that later).

3.) In the context of making political statements in Punk…

- They developed their own type of recalcitrance but, unlike The Sex Pistols:

    * They did not take on an anti-social/nihilistic stance but rather…

    a.) …an outlandish sort of rebellious attitude from a left-wing, blue-collar perspective.

4.) Beginnings:

- <u>Joe Strummer</u> (b. John Graham Mellor: 8/21/52, Ankara, TUR; d. 2003)

    * Grew up in an upper-class environment with a boarding school education.

    a.) Began playing in pub bands in his early 20's.

    - His most noted band: <u>The 101'ers</u>.

- <u>Mick Jones</u> (b. Michael Jones, 6/26/55, London): unlike Joe Strummer, he [Jones] grew up in a working class environment in Brixton, UK.

    * Started playing in rock bands as a teenager.

    a.) <u>Influences</u>: "Mott The Hoople" and "Faces".

- Both hard-rocking bands (Steve Jones of The Sex Pistols [no relation], was also influenced by "Faces").
  b.) Mick Jones' most notable group: "The London SS"
   * NOTE: Both Joe Strummer and Mick Jones would eventually become very important songwriters for The Clash.
- Paul Simonen (b. 12/15/55, London): joined up with his childhood friend Mick Jones after attending a performance of The Sex Pistols.
  * He played bass guitar for "The London SS".
- Joe Strummer was also influenced after hearing The Sex Pistols.
  * He broke up with The 101'ers and ventured into a more hard-edged direction.
   a.) RESULT: He joined a revamped version of "The London SS" which would rename itself, The Clash.
5.) The Clash (UK) (released on 4/8/76): their debut album.
- Included their first single: "White Riot" (British CBS label).

White Riot
The Clash

  * Was not released in the US because the music wasn't "radio friendly".
   a.) It would not be until July of 1979 (with different songs than in the original) that this album would make it's US debut.
- Eclecticism: examples from the UK album:
  * "Cheat": rockabilly influences.
  * "White Riot": raging Punk guitars with political influences.
  * "Police and Thieves": written by Junior Mervin and Lee Perry (a.k.a. the Phil Spector of Reggae).
   a.) Their first track in the Reggae influenced domain.

White Man In Hammsmith Palais
The Clash

    - "White Man In Hammersmith Palais" is another reggae influenced example.
     * Reggae meets punk.
- US Release: for "The Clash (US)", the following songs were scratched from the album and replaced by original "B-sides".
  * "Cheat", "Protex Blues", "Deny" and "48 Hours".
   a.) Replaced by: "Complete Control" (produced by Lee Perry), "White Man In Hammersmith Palais", "Clash City Rockers", "I Fought The Law", and "Jail Guitar Doors".
   b.) "Police and Thieves" and "White Man In Hammersmith"
    - marked the beginning of The Clash's experimentation with Reggae which would later become a major influence to other Punk artists.
B.) The Attraction of Punk Artists to Reggae: the reasons…
 1.) Spirituality: because of its Rastafarian roots, Reggae imbued a sense of spirituality that was missing in Punk.
  - That some in the Punk domain wanted to embrace.
 2.) Accessibility: Reggae was more easily acceptable to the masses…
  - As opposed to Punk's loud, aggressive and sometimes anti-social sound.
 3.) Rebelliousness: accessibility and spirituality notwithstanding, Reggae had a rebellious essence to it.
  - Which could fulfill the confrontational nature these Punk artists had.
   * Without alienating the mainstream.
   * And enjoying a more popular appeal and commercial success.
    a.) While simultaneously avoiding the impression of "selling out".
C.) Reggae: to understand the essence and meaning of Reggae, some background into the development of Jamaican music is in order.
 1.) Mento (1940's):
  - Played on homemade drums, bamboo fifes, fiddles, etc.
   * Drums were the main instrument.

- Basically, they were songs made for dancing.
  * Sung or "Toasted" (quasi Rap) over an African influenced polyrhythmic groove.
    a.) With a heavily syncopated beat.
- Artists: Slim & Sam, Lord Flea, Sugarbelly, and Count Lasher.

2.) Bluebeat (1950's):
  - Influenced by American "Swing" (big Band) music.
    * With simple, repetitive, catchy tunes.
    * And that heavily syncopated beat.
  - Very "brassy".
  - Don Drummond: one of perennial Bluebeat artists.
    * He helped popularize the style in Jamaica.

Feeling Fine
Don Drummond

3.) SKA (1960's):
  - In 1962, Jamaica achieved independence.
    * RESULT: They would encourage their artists to create works that were purely "Jamaican" in character.
  - SKA: an invention of a Jamaican group called The Skatalites: Ernest Ranglin, guitar; Cluett "Clue-J" Johnson, bass; Theophilus Beckford, vocals; and Roland Alphonso, saxophone
    * Mixed indigenous Jamaican folk music with American R&B influences.
      a.) With some jazz influences as well.
  - Laurel Aitken: was one of the premiere SKA artists.
    * With songs such as "Little Sheila" and "Rudy Wedding"

Little Sheila
Laurel Aitken

Rudi Wedding
Laurel Aitken

4.) Rudie: transition from SKA to Rock Steady.
  - A sort of pre-ordained "Gangsta Rap" (long before it was ever conceived).
    * A youthful criminality from the ghetto.
      a.) And a rejection of normal, traditional values.
      b.) Romanticization of living dangerously and dying young.

5.) Rock Steady: experimented with rock and roll instrumentation.
  - Especially electric guitar, electric keyboard, and electric bass.
    * Most prominent of melodic instruments: guitar and keyboard.
    * The electric bass sound becomes most prominent and "out front".
      a.) Along with the bass, an emphasis on drums.
        - In keeping the rhythm section prominent.
  - Another characteristic feature: a slow, bluesy beat.
    * Rock Steady's signature tempo.
      a.) with the signature Jamaican syncopated beat.
  - Most prominent artists: Clement Dodd and Jackie Mittoo.
  - Lyrics: dealt mostly with social commentary.

Hot Milk
Jackie Mittoo

6.) Reggae: basically, a combination of all previous Jamaican music forms.
  - African Influence: polyrhythmic layerings resulting in an underlying groove.
    * A Mento derivative.
  - Catchy Tunes: easily singable and memorable
    * Embedded in Jamaican tradition by Bluebeat.
  - Melodic Instrumental Emphasis: on electric guitars and keyboards.
    * Rock influences: electric guitar solos and organ fill-ins.
    * Bass out front: bass timbre most prominent adding a lot of "bottom" to the music.
      a.) Both elements above derived from the Rock Steady influence.
  - Tighter, Faster Tempo:
    * In fact, it was Lee Perry who took Rock Steady and sped up the tempo.
      a.) This was the original concept behind the creation of Reggae.

- <u>Meaningful Lyrics</u>:
* Black awareness.
* Speaking for the world's oppressed people.
* Social Commentary.
* A longing for redemption in a Rastafarian sense.
- <u>RESULT</u>: A musical genre that had something in it for everyone to appreciate thereby, crossing all of the lines.
* <u>For Rock Enthusiasts</u>: rock guitar riffs and solos.
* <u>For Funk Enthusiasts</u>: polyrhythmic grooves with a heavy bass.
* <u>For Pop Enthusiasts</u>: Catchy, easily singable and memorable tunes.
* <u>For Political Activists</u>: Lyrics of social commentary and activism.
- Because these elements made Reggae all-inclusive...
* It became appreciated by mainstream audiences the world over.

V. <u>Bob Marley</u> (b. Nesta Robert Marley, Feb. 6, 1945, Nine Miles/St. Ann's Parish, Jamaica; d. May 11, 1981, Miami, FL) -- the artist who exported Reggae to the mainstream world.

A.) Grew up in a one-room stone hut in the remote, back country of Jamaica. As a child, he worked the fields along with his grandfather.

1.) <u>Early Musical Experiences</u>: choir music on Sundays, his one day off. To young Bob Marley, singing was a spiritual uplift. Especially the vocal harmonizations.
- <u>Radio</u>: Marley loved listening to dance music of Fats Domino and Ricky Nelson on the radio (whenever they could get radio reception in their remote village).
* <u>NOTE</u>: His early love of dance music and vocal harmonization would be a significant inspiration as a songwriter later on.

2.) He first began singing when he was four years of age.
- At Stepney School located at St. Ann's Parish, he met his first permanent singing partner: <u>Bunny Livingston</u> (b. Neville O'Reilly Livingston). He [Livingston] used to play songs on his homemade guitar by artists such as Louis Jordan or anyone else he had heard on the radio. This was the inspiration that led Bob Marley to begin playing the guitar.

3.) Soon after Bunny's father and Bob's mother became intimately involved, they decided to move to the capital city of Kingston. Bob Marley and Bunny Livingston moved to the city with them.

B.) <u>Trench Town</u>: the area where Bob and Bunny lived (in the same household). Trench Town, as it was called, was one of the main ghetto areas of Kingston. There was plenty of racial conflict and Bob Marley was constantly harassed for being of mixed-race origin (his father, Norval Marley, was Caucasian, his mother, Cedella was Afro/Jamaican).

1.) <u>Music In The Air</u>: Throughout Trench Town, there was music was piping out of churches – tiny churches that were reminiscent of small storefronts (the music was playing throughout the entire week). Music was also piping out of dance halls, bars, and being played by street musicians.
- These "in-the-air" musical inspirations along with the struggle of living in poverty would have a profound effect on Marley's future musical expressive arsenal.
* He turned to writing poetry but eventually (again, due to Bunny Livingston's inspiration), Marley would take a vested interest in songwriting and devote his full time to becoming a singer.

2.) <u>His First Studio Recordings</u>: February, 1962 as a solo artist. "Judge Not", "One Cup Of Coffee", and "Terror" were recorded at the Federal Studios in Kingston. They were recorded with the help of artist/producer Jimmy Cliff.
- These singles – recorded on the Beverley's label – were unsuccessful in the Jamaican hit market.

C.) <u>His First Group</u>: He wanted to start a vocal group in the tradition of vocal groups such as The Platters, The Drifters, and Frankie Lyman & The Teenagers.

1.) They started off naming themselves The Teenagers (after Lymon's group), then, they renamed themselves The Wailing Rudeboys then finally, <u>The Wailers</u>.

- The group consisted primarily of <u>Bob Marley</u>, <u>Bunny Livingston</u>, and <u>Peter Tosh</u> (b. Winston Hubert McIntosh, October 19, 1944).
  * <u>Tosh's influences at the time</u>: James Brown, Al Green, Curtis Mayfield, and Otis Redding.
- Other members included Franklin Delano Alexander Braithwaite (a.k.a. "Junior"), Beverly Kelso, and Cherry Green.

2.) <u>Joe Higgs</u> (b. June 3, 1940): Marley's first important influential mentor. Higg's influences included Louis Armstrong, Mambo, and Billy Eckstine.
- He taught vocal harmonization to The Wailers as well as execution of that harmonization with absolute precision.
  * In addition, he taught Bob Marley various musical styles (especially jazz) and also taught him how to sing with an uncontrived, emotional authenticity. In other words, he taught Bob how to keep it real.
- He trained and prepared The Wailers for their first studio recordings (as a group) at Clement "Sir Coxson" Dodd's "Studio One" (founded in 1962).
  * Among the most prominent, was their first Jamaican Hit, "Simmer Down" released in December, 1963.

3.) <u>The Skatalites</u>: Dodd's studio session band. They were on the cutting edge of Ska's innovation.
- <u>Personnel</u>: Ernest Ranglin, guitar; Cluett "Clue-J" Johnson, bass; Theophilus Beckford, vocals; and Roland Alphonso, saxophone.
  * <u>First Ska single</u>: "Easy Snappin' " – arranged by guitarist Ernest Ranglin whose influences included European jazz acoustic guitarist Django Reinhardt and the first great jazz electric guitarist Charlie Christian.
    a.) <u>Feature</u>: Downbeat accent on the second beat of a four-beat pattern (second beat was the strongest of the four). Tempo was normally fast and free-spirited.

4.) <u>Rude Boy</u>: a tough, impoverished, rebellious ghetto boy who was considered a social outcast, an outsider. Ska was the music that the Rude Boy community had identified with and they saw The Wailers as their de facto spokesmen.
- Songs such as "Simmer Down", "Hooligan", and "Trench Town Guerillas" became their [Rude Boys] theme songs.
  * This established Bob Marley's love of rebellious lyrics that would bear fruit on a considerably wider scale later on. By this time, The Wailers were a trio (Bob, Bunny, & Peter) modeling their sound after an American R&B group, The Impressions which featured Curtis Mayfield.

D.) <u>Lee "Scratch" Perry</u> (b. Hugh Rainford Perry, March 26, 1936, Hanover, Jamaaica): As a prize-winning dancer, he became inspired by dance music.
  1.) He recorded his first single at Coxson Dodd's Studio One entitled, "Chicken Scratch" (hence the name "Scratch" Perry).
- Perry would become a gifted producer in his own right. He was quick to recognize the artistic potential of The Wailers. He not only thought they were rebels but also, that they had star potential.
  2.) <u>Musical Shift</u>: 1966-68, Rock Steady, the slow, blusy beat Jamaican aesthetic was en vogue throughout the island. Legend has it, that due to the unseasonably hot summer of '66, the fast tempos of Ska was not conducive to dancing in dance halls – none of which had any air conditioning. Hence, the slower tempos made dancing more tolerable.
- <u>1968</u>: Perry came up with a new take on Rock Steady. Instead of the conventional slow tempos, he started speeding things up to a more moderate tempo.
  * <u>RESULT</u>: "People Funny Boy" moderately tighter, faster tempo than Rock Steady with rhythmically focused guitar lines and heavy bass sound out front. Slower than Ska yet slightly faster than Rock Steady. This marked the beginning of what would be known as Reggae.

a.) Another landmark single around this time was, "Do The Reggay" by Toots & The Maytals.

- Perry's new band for his new sound were The Upsetters. They also be his studio session band.

* Personnel: Glenroy Adams, keyboard; Alva "Reggie" Lewis, guitar; Carlton "Carly" Barrett, drums; and Aston "Family Man" Barrett, bass.

3.) Marley's Second Mentor: under the guidance of Lee Perry as their producer, Bob Marley elevated his music to a more indigenous Jamaican style (not an American emulate) and a more spiritual level of emotion. Like Marley, he too, was a Rastafarian (but without the dreadlocks).

Small Axe
The Wailers

- It was under Perry's direction, that The Wailers became a bona fide reggae group with singles such as "My Cup", "Small Axe", and "Duppy Conqueror".

* They recorded two albums under Lee Perry in 1970-71: "Soul Rebel" and "Soul Revolution". They [The Wailers] also started their own label known as "Tuff Gong". Their first release was "Trench Town Rock".

Trench Town Rock (Live)
The Wailers

- Soon after a few additional releases on the Tuff Gong label, Perry and The Wailers had a dispute regarding royalty payments and as a result they parted ways.

* Although Perry brought The Wailers into the reggae domain and although The Wailers had almost 200 recordings to their credit, they were still broke and unknown outside of Jamaica. But all of that was about to change.

E.) Chris Blackwell: founded his own record label called Island Records in 1959 – first in Jamaica and then moved to an old church in London. He discovered The Wailers through a publicist named Brent Clarke (publicist for pop artist Johnny Nash).

1.) When he first met them, they had the rebellious charisma of true and tested renegades. He gave them £4000 to record an album upon their return to Jamaica thereby giving them total creative freedom. He would later visit them on the island to monitor their progress.

2.) "Catch A Fire" (1973): was initially recorded in three different studios in Kingston: Dynamic, Harry J's, and Randy's Studios (they commenced work in October of 1972).

Concrete Jungle
The Wailers

- This would be reggae's first concept album and the one that would finally give The Wailers widespread notoriety outside of Jamaica. It would also introduce reggae to the mainstream world.

* Singles: "Slave Driver", "No More Trouble", "Stop That Train", "400 Years", "Rock it Baby" etc. (including previously recorded but now revised, "Concrete Jungle" and "Stir It Up").

Rock it Baby
The Wailers

- The recording sessions in Jamaica were basically primary sessions. The secondary, finishing touches sessions would take place at Island Record studios in London.

Slave Driver
The Wailers

* Chris Blackwell took charge and wanted to evolve this reggae album into a reggae rock album. Blackwell felt that instilling a rock essence would enhance its popularity potential. Rock elements that were added were guitar and keyboard solos.

a.) Example: "Concrete Jungle" – an electric, rock-oriented guitar solo recorded in an impromptu session by Wayne Perkins (of the group Smith Perkins Smith). It took three takes to get it right.

Stir It Up
The Wailers

- Perkins: also played the guitar solo in "Stir It Up" and played a country-oriented slide guitar in "Baby We've Got A Date (Rock It Baby)" giving a sort of back-woods/country feel.

- Another ingredient that would add to their cache (according to Blackwell) was to present them in a black group context. Again, a format familiar to a rock-oriented, mainstream audience.

* The photograph on the back cover shows the core group of The Wailers (Bob, Bunny, and Peter) along with drummer Carlton "Carly" Barrett and bass player Aston "Family Man" Barrett (the latter two, former members of The Upsetters, were not officially part of The Wailers).

- Mainstream Rock Audiences: always possessed a rebellious spirit to begin with. Because of the rebellious essence and presentation in a rock band format, Bob Marley would be launched on the threshold of international stardom. It was the notoriety of "Catch A Fire" that made it possible.

* The three main ingredients that made this album successful were: Reggae, Rock Elements, and Expressive Authenticity (the latter proving that mainstream audiences were yearning for something real, authentic).

a.) "Catch A Fire": released on April 13, 1973 on the Island Records label exported Reggae to the mainstream world and in addition, made Bob Marley into the first international face of Jamaica which in essence, introduced that country to the world.

3.) Follow-Up Albums:

The Wailers

- "Burnin" (1973): a album-length study on revolution and social commentary.
* Most notable singles: "Get Up, Stand Up", "I Shot The Sheriff", "Burnin & Lootin", and "Rastaman Chant".
- "Natty Dread" (1974): the album that solidified Bob Marley as an international icon.
* "Lively Up Yourself", "Revolution", and "No Woman, No Cry" among the more notable tracks.
- "Rastaman's Vibration" (1976): Bob Marley's first Top 10 album in the US.
* Solidified Marley and Reggae music in the American pop mainstream.

F.) Reggae's Influence On The Post-Clash Punk Bands:
1.) P.I.L. (Public Image Ltd.):
- Personnel: John Lydon, formerly of The Sex Pistols, (vocals); Keith Levine, formerly of The Clash, (guitar); Jah Wobble (John Wordle, bass); Jim Walker (drums).
* Style: droning, noisy, bottom-laden, and slow.
- "Metal Box" (1979): presented in a film canister with 3, twelve-inch 45 rpm vinyl disks inside (UK only).
* It's US release: "Second Edition" (1980).

The Suit
P.I.L.

a.) Influenced by a Lee Perry style called: "Dub".
- Where the instruments accompanying the voice are an ultra-heavy bass guitar sound and drums (very "bottom heavy").

2.) Elvis Costello (b. Declan McManus, 1955): another artist to incorporate elements of Reggae into his sort of Punish influenced sound.
- "My Aim Is True" (1977): his debut album.
* Borrowed elements not only from Reggae, but also…
a.) Elements of Country and Tin Pan Alley influences.
* RESULT: Eclecticism within a Punk influenced format (in addition to The Clash's initial eclectic direction).
- Elvis Costello's punk connection was more emotional than stylistic.
* Because he was not a Punk purist, he was open to more outside influences.
a.) Which resulted in the eclecticism.
3.) The Police: were another band of influenced Punk artists that did not have the Punk

Get Up Stand Up

purist sound (but were Punk in spirit).

- One Reason: they were accomplished musicians with solid, technical skills (unlike the average Punk artists whose skills were at best, rudimentary).

* RESULT: they were bound to be more eclectic and different because their advanced musicianship enabled them to branch out to various other influences.

a.) Most important influence: Reggae.

- Personnel: Andy Summers (guitar), Stuart Copeland (drums), and Gordon Matthew Sumner – a.k.a. Sting (bass/vocals).

* Sting : previously performed in both jazz and rock bands.

- 1978: they signed with A&M Records.

* "Outlandos d'Amour" (1978): their debut album.

a.) "Roxanne": their first white reggae single to become a hit in America in1979 (after an initial release in 1978). Formalistically, the reggae style accompanies the verses and the choruses are accompanied by straight-forward rock pop beat (a formula they would use consistently for the next several albums).

- With it's 1979 release, it reached the UK top ten and the US top 30.
- RESULT: the concept of Reggae influenced pop music (i.e. white reggae) was introduced and appreciated for the first time by the American mainstream.

- Songs in each of the following albums would feature Reggae influenced pop music as a focal point thereby making it the norm.

* "Regatta de Blanc" (1979): literally meaning "White Reggae"
* "Zenyatta Mondatta" (1980): blurring the line between both Reggae and conventional pop influences.
* "Ghost In The Machine" (1981): their last Reggae influenced album.

a.) Example: "Spirits In The Material World"
- Reggae influenced beat/music.
- Reggae influenced lyrics (i.e. social commentary)

b.) In addition, the consistency of a more hard-driving pop approached focus (without the reggae) carrying the well-played, punk spirit as illustrated in tracks such as *Hungry For You* and *Too Much Information*.

b.) This album also had a dark element to it.
- Again, highlighted by the "Spirit of Punk" and Reggae influences.

c.) This was arguably, their last great album.

* "Synchronicity" (1983): became completely pop oriented.

a.) No longer, with the Reggae-focused/risk taking elements of earlier albums. Also gone: the punk spirit.

- RESULT: the Reggae-influenced sound would fizzle out into pop.

4.) The Reggae influenced sound was one of the legacies Punk.

- There would however, be several other punk legacies….

Chapter VIII: Review

Define Progressive Rock:

Who was the first progressive rock group?

    Which group transformed progressive rock from a small following to a worldwide phenomenon?

What was the problem of Progressive rock in the early 70's?

What was the problem with corporate FM radio in the early 70's?

What was the problem with the bigger venue requirement of the post-Woodstock concert era?

What was the problem with corporate rock of the early 70's?

What three elements needed to be revitalized in rock 'n roll?
    1.)
    2.)
    3.)

What was the significance of Jonathan Richman?

    How would you describe his songs?

    What were they an eventual musical blueprint for?

    What were two of his important influences?

    Ho produced The Moderns Lovers album?

What were the New York Dolls develop the first to develop that would eventually become Punk?

List at least three stylistic elements of the New York Dolls:

1.)
2.)
3.)

Name several of their musical influences:
1.)
2.)
3.)

Name the performance venue where they first developed their following?

What was the New York Doll's legacy? What did they accomplish?

In which venue did the group, Television, build their initial audience?

Briefly describe their performance style:

Which jazz saxophonist, who once said, "Sounds not notes, feelings, not phrases", became their greatest musical influence?

What was unique about this saxophonist's performance style?

How did Television emulate this stylistic influence?

Where did Television develop their underground audience??

Name the club's proprietor.

What was Patti Smith's original artistic vocation before she teamed up with guitarist Lenny Kaye performing garage band classics?

Against which musical genre did Lenny Kaye launch a one-man revolution by reissuing and performing garage band classics?

What was Patti Smith's "first accomplishment" in relation to the rest of the CBGB artists in 1975?

Name her critically acclaimed album.

Name three of the early garage bands form Cleveland:

    1.)

    2.)

    3.)

What was the origin of the name, Pere Ubu and how did it relate to the "Theatre of the Absurd"?

Who were 4 of Dave Thomas' influences that were more personally and progressively unique?

    1.) Tape collaging of _____.

    2.) Avant-garde approach of _____.

    3.) Primitive, postmodern approach of _____.

    4.) Lenny Kaye's _____.

Which of the early Cleveland bands was wearing punk regalia (safety pin piercings, swastikas, etc.) 2 years ahead of the UK punk culture? They referred to their approach as "artistic terrorism".

What type of instrument did Alan Ravenstein experiment with that anticipated the British post punk sound to come?

    What was the name of his synthesizer?

    Describe the term "found sound".

    What was the result – the properties – of the postmodern, high art synthesis that they had dubbed "avant garage"?

What 3 elements made up Dave Thomas' abstract vocal approach?

    1.)

    2.)

    3)

How would describe Pere Ubu's resulting musical style?

Name their independent label.

Name Pere Ubu's first 3 original singles.
    1.)
    2.)
    3.)

    Which two of these singles were influential to emerging post punk bands of the late 70's like Joy Division?

Name Pere Ubu's debut album of 1978.

In their second album released in 1979, which single was an example of Dave Thomas' absurdist theatre approach with a Dada-art expression?

What was the problem with the state of garage-based music?

    What was the needed solution?

Who was the first true punk band?

    List six of their rules that would codify the punk genre:
        1.)
        2.)
        3.)
        4.)
        5.)
        6.)

    What the three ingredients that they injected back into rock and roll?
        1.)
        2.)
        3.)

What was Malcolm McClaren's initial artistic influence?

    What did this influence inspire him to do artistically in regard to audiences?

Name the original members of The Sex Pistols:
    1.)
    2.)
    3.)

4.)

Who was the musical brain of the group?

What were his musical influences?
1.) Glam Bands:
2.) Mod Band:
3.) Proto-Punk:

Which member was the brain behind the group's anti-social attitude that henceforth, would forever be associated with punk?

Which event gave them instant fame?

What was the difference between Sid Vicious' legend and his reality? (list several aspects of each):
His Legend:

His reality:

List three elements that the Sex Pistols introduced and, as a result, standardized into punk:
1.)
2.)
3.)

Name their debut single:

Name their single written and recorded to protest Queen Elizabeth's 25th Jubilee:

What was the significance of this single in regard to pop-chart success?

Name The Sex Pistols' 1977 debut album:

The Clash: what type of statement did they introduce into punk?

What eclectic influences did they introduce musically into punk?

Of all the musically eclectic influences, which one was the most important (that would carry a legacy)?

Name their debut track of this influence:

List three reasons as to why punk artists adopted reggae?
1.)
2.)
3.)

Describe the following Jamaican musical styles:
Mento:
- It's main musical influence:
Bluebeat:
- It's main musical influence:
Ska:
- It's main musical influence:
Rock Steady:
- It's main musical influence:

List at least five elements that make up the eclecticism of reggae:
1.)
2.)
3.)
4.)
5.)

Who exported Reggae to the mainstream world?

List two elements of Bob Marley's approach to artistic expression:
1.)
2.)

Name the original members of his group (in addition to Marley):
1.)
2.)
3.)
4.)

Name their first Jamaican hit:

Which of the original members would be part of the re-formed Wailers in October of 1966?

       1.)

       2.)

       3.)

IN 1969, who became the producer of The Wailers?

How did he set the basic foundation for reggae?

Name his first important album (1973) that released reggae outside of Jamaica:

Name his first album-length study (1973) on revolution and social commentary:

Name the album (1974) that made him into an international icon:

Describe the "Dub" technique:

Name the band that utilized this technique in addition to reggae influences:

The Police did not have a punk purist sound but rather, a sound that captured the punk spirit. Why?

What was the first white reggae single to become a top 30 hit on the US pop charts?

What was the result of this single's popularity?

What was The Police's last great album featuring white reggae?

What was the result /legacy of the white reggae style?

CHAPTER IX: BRITISH POST PUNK

I. THE BRITISH POST PUNK SCENE

A.) <u>Beginnings</u>: a local Manchester punk band, <u>The Buzzcocks</u>, arranged a concert for the Manchester debut of The Sex Pistols at Lesser Free Trade Hall in the June 4, 1976 (only 42 people attended).

        1.) <u>The Buzzcocks' style</u>: perky melodic treatment coupled with aggressive, driving guitars and stripped-down rhythmic treatment.
- Pop, quasi-bubblegum oriented vocal lines.
    * With repeated note support in the bass.
- Aggressive, super-charged energy inspired by The Sex Pistols.
    * Instead of the Sex Pistols' anti-social message…
        a.) A more humorous, crisply pop-bubblegum essence.
        - Superimposed over the energetic guitars (stripped-down, direct).
- <u>Pete Shelley</u> (b. Peter McNeish, 4/17/55), guitarist/vocalist met through participation in an electronic music clique, vocalist <u>Howard Devoto</u> (b. Howard Trafford).
    * They were both heavily influenced by <u>The Velvet Underground</u>, <u>The Stooges</u>, and <u>Brian Eno</u>.
    * After seeing two performances of The Sex Pistols in London, they formed the band: <u>Rock Follies</u>.
        a.) Which they later changed to <u>The Buzzcocks</u> (eventually, bassist Steve Diggle and drummer John Mayer joined the group).
        b.) After Devoto eventually left, the group revamped itself leading to their first single…
- "<u>Orgasm Addict</u>" (1979): their debut single.
    * Debuted on the first "do-it-yourself" (DIY) independent label of the UK Punk scene: "<u>New Hormones</u>".
- The Buzzcocks's style of Punk already ushered in a new, independent sound in Manchester.
    * But there was more to come from other Manchester artists that would turn an even more independent sound into a movement.
- The Buzzcock's legacy:
    * A pop-oriented Punk that would be highly influential.
    * Also, the Sex Pistols concert that they arranged at the Lesser Free Trade Hall would inspire several bands that would eventually send the Punk influence in a new direction thereby, sparking a whole new movement.
        a.) With extreme implications of it's own., a new group would form as a result of attending this concert…
        -…and would chart the initial way.

What Do I Get
The Buzzcocks

B.) <u>Joy Division</u> (formed in 1976, Manchester, ENG): the first British post punk band and the innovators of the British post punk movement.

Personnel: <u>Ian Curtis</u> (b. July 15, 1956, Macclesfield, ENG; d. May 18, 1980), vocals; <u>Bernard Albrecht</u> (b. Bernard Dicken, Jan. 4, 1856), guitar; <u>Peter Hook</u> (b. Feb. 13, 1956, Salford, ENG), bass; <u>Stephen Morris</u> (b. Oct. 28, 1957, Macclesfield, ENG), drums.

Background: Sumner and Hook initially formed a band after seeing The Sex Pistols debut performance at the Lesser Free Trade Hall in Manchester on June 4, 1976. They originally called themselves, The Stiff Kittens. When Ian Curtis -- who also attended that concert – had joined the band (after answering an add posted in a Virgin records store), they changed their name to "Warsaw". They did this for two reasons: one, was their initial inspiration stemming from David Bowie's single, *Warszawa* (from the *Low* album of 1977) and the other, the Polish capital of Warsaw (both pre and post WWII). In their view, Warsaw was the embodiment of urban decay and desolation. Once they became aware of another band called Warsaw Pakt, they changed their name to Joy Division.

Warszawa
David Bowie

The source of this [Joy Division] name originated from a novel written by a holocaust survivor whose alias was Ka-Tzetnik 彡5633 (his tattooed prisoner number) entitled, *House Of Dolls*. The "Joy Division" was a section of the Auschwitz concentration camp that housed inmates who were forced into sexual slavery. In the band's [Joy Division's] view, that name was meant to identify with the victims and not with the oppressors.

For Ian Curtis, the German allure was partly inspired by the caché of the Berlin legend as decadence, where his idols: Iggy Pop, Lou Reed, and David Bowie had once lived. Incidentally, the urban decay motif was a key component of David Bowie's *Diamond Dogs* album (Bowie was an important influence on Ian Curtis).

Debut Recordings: as Joy Division's debut single, *Digital* sounded more like metal-driven, conventional punk. It was only after slowing the tempo that they disposed of punk conventions and in its place: a mood-driven aura of sparse electric guitars (as opposed to aggressive), dark synthesizer colors, and distinct melodic focus. This became the initial framework of a new punk-derived aesthetic known, as British Post Punk.

Curtis' Influences: in addition to Lou Reed, Iggy Pop, and especially David Bowie, the dark, baritone vocalizing of Jim Morrison. Curtis was also enamored with artists expressing the darker, abrasive, and insane side of life. Like Morrison, Ian Curtis' literary influences would originate from high-art levels of dark literature such as Franz Kafka. The Morrison vocal influence can be heard in the excerpt of *Atmosphere*.

The Dark Side of Life – Curtis' Modus Operandi: whatever he was reading or whenever pondering, it was all about human suffering and hardship (according to his wife Deborah). In the end, in addition to a dark, moody, melodic focus and sparse guitars, there was this eeriness of deep, expressive character.

Martin Hannett: producer for Tony Wilson's *Factory* label. He recorded one instrument at a time (a departure from the standard punk practice of recording the entire band at once – like a live performance). He then processed each instrument through an AMS digital delay device, which gave the instrument a slight echo. All instrumental tracks were superimposed into an overall sound/mix that, though sparse on one hand, filled up musical space on the other.

Disorder
Joy Division

Transmission
Joy Division

I Remember
Nothing
Joy Division

The End Result:
* Sparse, stripped-down electric guitar sound (as opposed to the abrasiveness of conventional punk).

* The bass, at times, carrying the melodic theme (as opposed to exclusively carrying harmonic support).

* Dark, moody, synth-driven sound (as opposed to the rage & anger of conventional punk)

* Use of slow tempos as a standard feature in a punk-derived aesthetic (unlike the consistency of moderate to rapid tempos in standard punk).

* A distinct melodic focus (as opposed to a focus on aggression).

Unknown Pleasures (1979): their debut album recorded and released on *Factory* – the label that would dominate the Manchester post punk scene with its owner Tony Wilson as local impresario. The Cover Art: graph of a Fourier analysis of 100 light spasms released in succession by a Pulsar

CP 1919. The album itself, received critical acclaim along with an increasingly broader following. On the heels of several UK hits such as *She's Lost Control, Transmission,* and *Love Will Tear Us Apart,* Joy Division embarked on their 1980 tour of England and Europe, which furthered their critical acclaim. In March of 1980, with the health of Ian Curtis rapidly deteriorating, they recorded their final album [as Joy Division] called, *Closer.*

Ian Curtis: in December of 1978, he suffered his first epileptic seizure. As a result, he was prescribed with heavy dosages of tranquilizers, which eventually rendered him dysfunctional. As his condition worsened, Curtis sank deeper into depression and his ability to effectively fulfill his role [with the band] became increasingly difficult. Much of this deeper, depressive state was expressed in a darker, more somber manner in his last album with Joy Division entitled: *Closer.* At the age of 23, on the eve of Joy Division's first American tour, with Iggy Pop's album, *The Idiot* playing on the turntable, Ian Curtis committed suicide by hanging in his apartment on May 18, 1980.

C.) The Fall (formed in 1977, Manchester, ENG): another component of the Manchester-based, British Post Punk movement.

Original Lineup: Mark E. Smith (b. Mar. 5, 1957, Broughton, Selford, ENG) vocals, Keyboards, harmonica; Martin Bramah (b. March, 1957) guitar; Una Baines (b. 1957, Manchester, ENG) keyboard; Tony Friel (b. May 4, 1958, Birkenhead, Merseyside, ENG) bass; Karl Burns (b. 1958, Manchester, ENG) drums.

Postindustrial Manchester: setting from where The Fall originated. What was once a prosperous behemoth of the industrial revolution, was now -- starting in the 1970's -- a city with abandoned factories, unemployment, and bleak, dark neighborhoods. The once proud, affluent working class was now given to downing pints, bingo halls, or drug abuse (legal or illegal) in order to ease their collective, depressing pain.

Mark E. Smith, through his straightforward, simple approach, would transform this scenario into art by expressing the dreariness and darkness of Northern post-industrial life in a biting, caustic, grotesque sort of manner. It was his way of expressing authenticity.

Background: in the apartment occupied by Una Baines, they'd read their own poetic writings to one another. Their poetic influences were of high-art origins such as Raymond Chandler, William Burroughs, Yeats, and Albert Camus. Usually, they would be under some drug intoxication to aid in their literary escapades. Drugs of choice ranged from hallucinogenics such as LSD or psilocybin mushrooms to amphetamines (the latter being most influential to their musical approach).

Smith's Literary influences: short stories of cosmic horror by 19th century occultists such as M.R. James, Arthur Machen, Algernon Blackwood, and H.P. Lovecraft. Phillip K. Dick, an author who wrote sci-fi novels on amphetamines (who influenced the concept of "psychic time travel") furthered Mark E. Smith's obsession with the supernatural.

Musical Influences: groups that were experimental, postmodern, and primitive (the latter in an unskilled, amateurish manner): Can, The Velvet Underground, The Seeds (a 60's garage band whose best known single, *Pushin' Too Hard* was featured on Lenny Kaye's *Nuggets* compilation). They were also influenced by skiffle and rockabilly.

Musical Ingredients: "Raw music with really weird vocals on top" – Mark E. Smith. Sources of this "rawness": quasi-cacophonous, atonal, thin/jangly electric guitar lines coupled with repetitive, garage-band-type organ licks. On top of that -- the sneering, sarcastic, sing-speech, English-working-class vocalizing of Mark E. Smith. Resulting sound: primitive, simple, crude -- combined with a dissonant, twangy, "garage band" essence.

Lyrics: dealing with the societal effects of over-prescribed drugs and illegal drug use as an escape from the monotony of dreary, post-industrial life. In addition, they deal

Bingo Master
The Fall
with the depressive state of the low paid, enslaved workers and the depressive dreariness of the unemployed. On example, *Bingo Master* – a bingo number caller decides that after a life of no direction, commits suicide through a drug overdose to escape his dark, dreary, and meaningless life

Live At The Witch Trials (1979): their debut album that was recorded in one day. Injected with lyrics of crime and horror; dark, dreary essences of the post-industrial north; and the primitive musical influences of The Velvet Underground.

Industrial Estate
The Fall
Mark E. Smith delves in a highly caustic commentary of drug-ridden, post-industrial British life in songs like *Industrial Estate, Underground Medicin,* and *No Xmas for John Quays.*

Underground Medicin
The Fall
Smith's Lyric Development: Smith's lyrics would gradually increase in abstraction. That, and his occultist fascination culminated in the album *Hex Induction Hour* (1982). This was The Fall at their most primal and forbidding -- what most aficionados believe was their last great album (the album cover features "found text" clips furthering Smith's reputation for the abstract).

D.) The Smiths (formed 1982, Manchester, ENG): one of the definitive British bands of the 1980's. They transferred post punk from a sparse, synth-driven sound, to an exclusively guitar-based sound that would dominate English rock into the 1990's -- they also expanded the audience of British post punk to the American mainstream. As a result, they turned British post punk into pop.

Original Lineup: Morrissey (b. Stephen Patrick Morrissey, May 22, 1959, Manchester) vocals; Johnny Marr (b. John Maher, Oct. 31, 1963, Manchester) guitar; Andy Rourke (b. 1963, Manchester) bass; Mike Joyce (b June 1, 1963, Manchester) drums.

Pop Roots: They were initially indebted to the pop-melodic focus and 3-minute song structures of the 60's "British Invasion" bands. In addition, Morrissey and Johnny Marr were inspired by the D.I.Y. (Do-It-Yourself) ethos of punk but they were also fond of rockabilly and the early 60's American girl-groups.

An Opposite Dichotomy: Johnny Marr was into rock tradition while Morrissey broke with tradition by employing a dark, sometimes keening, crooning vocal quality that was self-absorbed in nature. In reference to Morrissey's voice, The Smiths made up for the lack of dark, moody synth-driven sounds (of the initial UK postpunk model ushered in by Joy Division) by his dark, crooning vocal sound. In addition, he was the first truly accomplished, polished singer in the punk-influenced tradition. As a result, the sound of Morrissey's voice added a more conventional [pop] melodic focus that became more accessible to a broader audience.

Guitar Approach: in the absence of a synthesizer, Johnny Marr multi-tracked his electric guitar lines in the studio thereby giving his guitar-focused sound more density. The repeated tunesmithism in his guitar lines added another vehicle of accessibility that would connect with a rock guitar-literate, mainstream audience.

Morrissey's Background: he grew up with a passion for both music and film. In his teens, he regularly wrote to Melody Maker magazine and at times, his letters would get published. His first book, *James Dean Isn't Dead*, was a bio/tribute to the late, famous actor -- it was published in the late 1970's by Babylon Books. He also wrote another book about the New York Dolls and was president of their UK fan club. Although he became a member of a band called The Nosebleeds, his vocation was still first and foremost, a writer. It all changed when he met Johnny Marr in 1982. Marr was searching for a lyricist and the eventual result was The Smiths.

Oscar Wilde (1854-1900): Morrissey's high art literary influence. Wilde had a devotion to "art for art's sake" – he carried around sunflowers and peacock feathers. His writings were delicate, highly emotional, and full of aphorisms (one-liners as commentary) that demonstrated his sharp whit. He was a celebrity and legend in his own time. Although he was married with children, he was secretly engaged in an intimate relationship with another man, Alfred Douglas for years. When this relationship went public, Wilde was tried and convicted of sodomy and gross indecency – he was sentenced to 2 years of hard labor. After his release, he drifted throughout Europe but never again recaptured his creative edge and was a victim of financial ruin.

Morrissey: was an Oscar Wilde devoteé and the embodiment of his [Wilde's] ethos in an indie rock format (right down to wearing a bouquet of gladiolas out of his back pocket). He made obvious references to Oscar Wilde in a 1986 single, *Cemetery Gates* (from *The Queen Is Dead* album) where he claimed, that "Wilde is on my side". Like the author, Morrissey engaged in wordplay that on the surface, seemed innocuous but underneath, carried a serious undertone that included biting metaphors. Similar to his literary influence, Morrissey's sexuality (along with his self-avowed celibacy) was a source of controversy. Reason: he never comes out to admit it but rather, engages in undertones of intricate wordplay regarding veiled references to being gay -- especially with his early singles *Hand In Glove*, *This Charming Man*, and *How Soon Is Now*.

Hand In Glove
The Smiths

In each example, Morrissey makes cryptic references to a secretive gay life full of stigma, shame, and isolation (again, in reference to Oscar Wilde's life experiences). Much of their debut album of 1984 *The Smiths* deals with this subject in addition to others. On an activist scale, Morrissey added to his controversial persona by his biting, outspoken criticism of then British Prime Minister Margaret Thatcher and his passion of promoting animal rights.

Musically: Guitar-based: jangly, multi-track electric guitar layerings of Johnny Marr that were raw in nature but not overproduced like many of their contemporaries. Like Morrissey's vocal lines, Marr's guitar tracks had a repetitive, pop melodic focus that added more depth to their accessibility. The Smiths utilized a no-frills, minimalistic approach (i.e. lead singer, guitar, bass, & drums).

How Soon Is Now
The Smiths

Meat Is Murder (1985): Morrissey engages in a dichotomy between croon-smithism and tortured soul; lyrical and soulful, self-deprecating and self-aggrandizing (or self-loathing and self-parody). Included in the album is the first, British post punk-influenced hit in America: *How Soon Is Now* – one of the main reasons for its popularity: the video that was heavily promoted on MTV.

E.) Summarization: of the Manchester-based, British Post Punk sound.

Joy Division: provided the initial template for British post punk with a dark, moody, synth-driven sound and an emphasis on melodic focus in the guitar, voice, or bass.

The Fall: gave it a raw, edgy sound with Mark E. Smith's sarcastic sing/speech and the crude dissonance in the instrumentation – a reflection of the dark, depressing state of post-industrial Manchester. In other words, British post punk as social commentary.

The Smiths: transformed British post punk into pop with a post modern flair in the lyrics inspired by Oscar Wilde: high-art lyrical influences injected in a guitar-driven, post punk sound with the dark, croonsmithism of Morrissey.

The next significant contribution to the development of British post punk will come from outside of Manchester. The catalyst would be the artist who inspired the genesis of the Manchester post punk scene at that landmark concert in June of 1976: John Lydon with his band/outfit known as Public Image Limited.

F.) <u>Public Image, Ltd</u> (P.i.L): founded by John Lydon from the ashes of The Sex Pistols which, according to him, was nothing more than rock convention with searing, incendiary lyrics dealing with anarchy, nihilism, and class warfare. In contrast, Public image Ltd. would veer away from punk convention and become an important part of the synth-driven, British post punk scene. They accomplished this by injecting outside, eclectic influences into British post punk such as reggae-dub basslines, disco, and primitive, tribal-like percussion.

Original Lineup: <u>John Lydon</u> (b. Jan. 31, 1956, London, ENG) vocals; <u>Keith Levene</u>, guitar, synthesizer/electronics; <u>Jah Wobble</u> (b. John Wardle) bass; <u>Jim Walker</u>, drums.

<u>Influences</u>: Lydon had an eclectic array of various musical tastes [beyond punk] from the kraut-rock of Can to the mutant blues art of Captain Beefheart. One of his greatest musical passions however, was reggae – especially when it came to the studio production of Jamaican dub.

<u>Dub</u>: where the bass and drums are produced to resonate in musical space left vacant by cancelled-out melodic instruments (such as the guitar and keyboards). This resonance is so pervasive, that it completely fills up that vacant musical space. It was the dub model along with Jamaican reggae/riddim that made up the foundation for John Lydon's post-Sex Pistols career beginning with Public Image, Ltd. (PiL). He decided on the idea during an all-expense-paid trip to Jamaica compliments of Virgin records owner, Richard Branson. It was there, that Lydon met some of his favorite Jamaican artists such as Prince Far I, U-Roy, and Big Youth.

<u>Background</u>: Lydon recruited an old friend named <u>John Wardle</u> (a.k.a. Jah Wobble) as bass player – he already had a fanatical passion for playing Jamaican dub (before joining the band). For guitar, he recruited <u>Keith Levene</u>, former member of The Clash who also had an extensive passion for reggae (he was another of the "dub fanatics"). At this point, Lydon had disposed of his snarly "Johnny Rotten" image and used his real name and identity thereby, making a new fresh start for the next leg in his career.

Public Image: First Issue (1978): their debut album. Although Lydon wanted to adopt

Public Image
Public Image Ltd.

a more "anti-music" approach, this album did have its conventional rock elements such as the hard-rocking, aggressive guitar sound (as opposed to abrasive), synthesizer lines, and prominent dub-influenced bassline in the title track, *Public Image*. In addition, Lydon continues with his biting lyrics of rage only this time, against religion (*Religion I, Religion II*) and his vocal screeds of lamenting the fallout of his "Johnny Rotten" fame and persona (basically, anger against the unrealistic expectations of his Sex Pistols fans).

Fodderstampf
Public Image Ltd.

In the album's final track, *Fodderstampf*, a funky bassline, ethereal synthesizer lines, studio-processed vocals and heavily produced drum sounds point the way to the shape of things to come -- their next album in 1979 that arguably, became their greatest artistic achievement and one of *the* standard bearers of the British post punk aesthetic: *Metal Box* (which would be re-released as *Second Edition* in 1980).

Metal Box (1979): featuring another musical influence on John Lydon: disco. In homage to disco's 12-inch, 45-RPM format, *Metal Box* was originally released in a film canister with three, 12-inch vinyl disks (50,000 original limited copies were released). For the American version, it was released as a standard, vinyl LP under the name *Second Edition* in 1980.

<u>Stylistic Focus</u>: a musical, post punk style that is basically a combination of disco grooves, some reggae dubbing, heavy bass, and metallic dissonance on both the guitar and the synthesizer.

Swan Lake (formerly *Death Disco*): featured Wobbles hard funk basslines,

Swan Lake
Public Image Ltd.

John Lydon's torturing, banshee-like wailing, and Keith Levene's edgy, and at times, an atonal, searing electric guitar accompaniment.

Memories: another disco/dance-oriented single displaying Lydon's love of disco. Levene doubles between the synthesizer and jangled, edgy guitar work with percussive shards and metallic scrapes like abstract brush strokes – giving Lydon's vocal line, dissonant accompaniment while juxtaposing with Wobble's tonal-oriented bass (the latter giving Lydon's vocal line harmonic support).

Careering: another example of atonality mixed with a postpunk aesthetic with Levene's ominous, dissonant soundscaping from his Prophet 5 synthesizer.

Overall Production Quality: very dark and bass-heavy (a la Dub) with John Lydon's vocal screeds, but lighter in the middle (a CAN influence).

The Flowers Of Romance (1981): on the heels of bass player Jah Wobble being fired for his unauthorized use of P.i.L.'s pre-recorded tracks for his solo project, The Flowers of Romance (1981) had no dub-heavy basslines (or for that matter, no bass at all). In addition, Keith Levene's dissonant shards that were featured in the previous album were also no longer there (except for one track, *Go Back*) – in its place, his growing obsession with the synthesizer.

What was left, was an album heavy on percussion and primitivism that was almost anti-rock in nature. They were after a tribal/percussive feel where exotic percussion instruments were used (as in *Hymie's Him*) and other second-hand instruments such as the ukulele, banjo, violin (the latter in *Flowers of Romance*), etc. – all to be processed via the studio mixing board and that was what the album was all about: using the recording studio as the "primary" instrument. In the end, according to Keith Levene, it was an anti-music "get-away-with-anything" attitude along with Lydon's lyric negativity.

II. THE EXTENSION OF BRITISH POST PUNK: NEW POP, GOTH, SYNTH POP & THE NEW ROMANTICS

A.) New Pop: a movement where postpunk groups turned to the world of mainstream pop to attain stardom yet maintain serious (postpunk influenced) artistic expression. According to author/critic Simon Reynolds, the term "New Pop" was first coined by Paul Morley, columnist for the *New Music Express* in the December 1980 issue.

The idea: to clean up the darkness and self-indulgence of British postpunk and add a sense of brightness, romantic illumination, and overall healthiness. In addition, by taking on the consumer market, they too would focus on pop tunesmithism and skilled writing as an means of serious artistic expression – especially when it came to adding reggae, funk, and disco influences. There were three bands [among others] who adopted this mode in their own distinct ways (that will be covered): Scritti Politii, ABC, and Orange Juice.

1.) Scritti Politti (formed in 1977, Leeds, Yorkshire, ENG): initially, a Marxist-inspired postpunk outfit who traded in an esoteric sound for a more mainstream-driven pop sound (dubbed New Pop) in the early 1980's. As a result, they did see some significant chart success. Personnel: Green Gartside (b. Paul Julian Strohmeyer, June 22, 1955, Cardiff, WALES), vocals, guitar; Nail Jinks, Bass; Tom Morley, drums; and Mathew Kay, manager and [sometimes] keyboardist.

Initial Inspirations: Green Gartside's attendance of the the Sex Pistols Anarchy Tour concert on December, 6, 1976 at the Leeds Polytechnic – this event inspired him to form a band that would become Scritti Politti. Another initial inspiration was a group called Desperate Bicycles.

Desperate Bicycles: their viewpoint had a direct connection to Green's Marxist/Communist roots (he was once a member of the Young Communist League). After dropping out of art college in Leeds, he (along with Nial Jinks) embraced the

Desperate Bicycles influence. Their [Desperate Bicycles') main influence – <u>Situationist</u> <u>International</u> (SI): a revolutionary organization established in 1957 whose influence peaked with the general strike and Paris riots in France, in May, 1968.

> <u>The Idea of SI</u>: as champions of Marxism and 20th century modernist artistic styles, they promoted life structures that served as alternatives to those encouraged by the modern capitalist system (which they dubbed, "The Spectacle"). According to Guy Debord's work *Society of Spectacle*, the "Spectacle" is a fake reality that serves a distraction to society's underlying degradation and decay spawned by modern capitalism. The remedy: overthrow the system (as illustrated by the 1968 Paris revolts asking workers to take over factories run them – a D.I.Y. ethos attached to social revolution).

>> This D.I.Y. ethos (inspired by SI) was adopted by Desperate Bicycles in the following way: the music industry represented "The Spectacle" and needed it be overthrown. The solution: make your own art/entertainment, your own label, and connect it to fellow (like-minded) travelers.

>> *The Medium Was Tedium*, their 2nd release – a manifesto of how "cheap and easy" it is to make your own records. Their maxim: "Go and do it!"

> <u>Antonio Gramsci</u> (1891-1937): whose works revolted against what he called, "cultural hegemony over the working class" was another of Green's Marxist-oriented influences.

<u>*Skank Bloc Bologna*</u> (1978): Scritti Politti's debut single which initially sold 2500 copies and following its release through Rough Trade, an additional 15,000. According to journalist Andrew Harrison, "The song alluded to political upheaval in Italy and specifically, Gramsci's theory of the historical bloc of the underclass". It was also about Green's love of cryptic, brainiac wordplay.

Skank Bloc
Bologna
Scritti Politti

> <u>Musically</u>: Jangly, edgy, dissonant chords on the electric guitar repeated throughout most of the song superimposed over a reggae/skank bassline. Green's vocals were influenced by British soul singer, Robert Wyatt.

> <u>Early Singles</u>: their early musical style was for the most part, dissonant guitar-driven edgy chords that bordered on the cacophonous mixed with reggae-influenced basslines. Some examples include *Messthetics*, *Bibly-O-Tek,* and *Is And Ought The Western World*. In both sound and brainy, Gramsci-influenced wordplay, Green Gartside was a devoted challenger to rock 'n' roll's conventions at every turn.

Messthetics
Scritti Politti

>> Especially when it came to live performance where he and his band would make up songs on the spot – a sort of deconstruction of typical rock 'n' roll songwriting convention.

<u>Turning Point</u>: after suffering what appeared to be a heart attack at the age of 23 (some sources say it too much drug use), Green Gartside convalesced in his parents' summer home off the coast of Wales. Over the course of this time, he would completely rethink the musical direction of Scritti Politti into a more pop-driven direction.

After becoming disillusioned with the influences of Marxism and Situationist International, as well as the taxing, overall exhaustion from questioning everything that the status quo represented -- Green decided that the best course of action, was to *within* the [music capitalist] system rather than *against* it. His new vehicle of expression became pop.

Musical Influences: American black soul and dance music in the form of Michael Jackson and Aretha Franklin among others. Lyrically, he was also taking a keen interest in the "deconstructionist" theories of Jacques Derrida (they would eventually become friends). The result: the continuity of abstract language experimentation but within the veneer of pop (soul, funk, & reggae) – through this new context, Green would finally embrace convention.

The Sweetest Girl (1981): Gartside's first manifestation of a new pop direction. His vocals had a soulful, Robert Wyatt-influenced sound and a skank/reggae type of groove (a.k.a. "Lover's Rock") but this time, without the edgy, dissonant guitar chords [of earlier singles]. The key: a pop-driven melodic focus that was listener-friendly.

Lyrics: cryptic social commentary imbedded beneath the surface of what appears to be a love song – Green's Derrida-influenced example of deconstruction (in this case, deconstructing a love song).

Songs To Remember (1982): their debut album and first chart success (#12 on the UK). This success notwithstanding, Scritti Politti was still seen by many as a niche/cult type of group. One reason was the lyrics: they were too brainy/philosophical to qualify as teen anthems and the other, the recordings were under-produced – not slick enough to capture the mainstream market. He eventually fired his group and once again, began rethinking the direction of the Scritti project. What he needed, were new collaborators.

New Lifeline: two New York-based artists – David Gamson (keyboards/computer music programmer) and Fred Maher (drummer). With his new collaborators, Green Gartside would pursue a new inspiration: New York-styled, synth-driven funk and electro-pop. His goal: dance pop that would be executed within machine-like precision (one of his technological tools, was the Linn Drum Machine – one of the first available [digital] drum machines).

First Hit of this New Direction: *Wood Beez (Pray Like Aretha Franklin)*. Released in 1984, it reached #10 in the UK. But his first US hit was *Perfect Way* (#11, US), which became influential to a new wave of black dance-pop records (listen to *Control* by Janet Jackson and notice the similarity of grooves).

Cupid & Psyche 85 (1985): the album presenting his new dance pop direction [and pop hits] including his biggest US hit, *The Word Girl* (#6). With the album's success, Green's big talk of future pop success and stardom was finally realized – long after his New Pop contemporaries (ABC, etc.) had come and gone. Part of his success, lied within his gender-bending falsetto voice sound (adding a Glam-ish flavor) that was inspired by Michael Jackson.

2.) ABC (formed in 1980, Sheffield, ENG): although Green Gartside was among the first post punk artists to espouse a pop-driven artistic goal, he was one of the last to realize it. ABC on the other hand, had no such problem. In the early 1980's, they would have a number of hits on both sides of the Atlantic several years ahead of Scritti Politti. Like Scritti however, they would accomplish their notoriety through the dance-pop, disco-driven medium.

Beginnings: while writing for his own music fanzine called *Modern Drugs*, Martin Fry was interviewing members of a group called Vice Versa: a band that formed in 1977 with Stephen Singleton, Mark White, and David Synenham. They had established their own label, Neutron Records releasing an EP, *Music 4* – basically, postpunk electronics somewhat similar to early Human League.

After Martin Fry had interviewed the band, he was invited to join them as synthesizer player (which he accepted). Shortly thereafter, the band became known as ABC and Martin Fry took over as lead singer/frontman and artistic visionary.

Influences: the synth-driven, R&B influenced pop of David Bowie and Roxy Music. In fact, Martin Fry's vocals would be reminiscent of David Bowie's (a.k.a. Thin White Duke era) and Bryan Ferry (of Roxy Music).

It was Fry who steered ABC into a more pop-driven direction but it would be a producer named Trevor Horn (formerly of The Buggles' *Video Killed The Radio Star*), that would guide the group toward a more sumptuous, glamorous, lush, string-oriented disco sound supporting Martin Fry's lyrics of intellect and wordplay.

Tears Are Not Enough
ABC

Debut Single: *Tears Are Not Enough* released in October of 1981 on their Neutron label. It became their first British pop hit. For the next several months, more synth-driven dance hits would follow and usher in their pop successes in the US.

Poison Arrow, Look of Love, and *All Of My Heart* – all from the Trevor Horn-produced album *Lexicon of Love*.

Poison Arrow
ABC

Poison Arrow (2nd single): lyrics with an underlying sentiment of a betrayed lover revealing his true feelings to someone whose feelings were not mutual and in the end, he gets burned. On the surface, the lyrics convey a sense of poetry with an underlying meaning (but presented in a disco-driven, synth-sweeping format).

Postpunk Influence: the lyrics (as in *Tears Are Not Enough* and *Poison Arrow*) carry a postpunk-driven wariness and pessimism [of love & romance] within the gloss and elegance of disco (whereas Green Gartside dealt with postpunk wariness from the standpoint of social commentary and deconstruction).

The Look of Love
ABC

The Look of Love (3rd single): complete with lush, disco-oriented string orchestra arrangements with all of the disco elegance and glamour added in.

Debut Album: *The Lexicon of Love* (1982): featuring Martin Fry's continuity of wordplay of the postpunk weary take on the subject of romance – postpunk pessimism masked beneath the lush, disco glitter-ball façade, pop melodic focus, and sweeping synth lines. The album also contains the three previously mentioned singles (listed above). It would be ABC's first big success in the US.

All Of My Heart
ABC

All Of My Heart: lyrics of ambivalence of one in love who dares not reveal his true feelings but hopes that somehow, his longings may be realized. However (with the postpunk wariness intact), he is also fearful that if the line is crossed, and his longings become reality, she may be disappointed [with him] and the friendship will end.

This is again, the postpunk tradition of pessimism and ambivalence masked beneath the Hollywood-styled glamour (Fry basically masquerading himself).

<u>New Direction</u>: following the conclusion of a world tour in 1982, they returned to their hometown of Sheffield only to find it decimated with abandoned factories, massive unemployment, and the scourge of drug-use among the disenfranchised (a depressive state due to rapid de-industrialization). As a result, Martin Fry decided to close the gap between the luxuriousness and glamour of his New Pop aura and the depressive state of his hometown's harsh realities. In other words, he is going to change his tune.

Beauty Stab (1983): Martin Fry's protest album that launched his new direction in terms of both sound and lyrical expression.

<u>Sound-wise</u>: a complete turnaround from *Lexicon of Love*. Gone are Martin Fry's clever romantic wordplay, the elegance of his glamour-driven synths & orchestration, and catchy, melodic tunesmithism that added sparkle with glitzy sophistication.

In its place, electric guitars – the new vehicle (as opposed to the glossy synth & drum machine sound) supporting songs like *King Money, The Power of Persuasion,* and the title track, *Beauty Stab*. It was a return to his postpunk roots in terms of both sound and more direct wariness regarding subject matter.

<u>Lyrics</u>: postpunk influenced in a more direct manner and without the romance. In this case, a more direct protest against what he saw, as the plight of the unemployed working class and the repression that they face at the whims of the ruling elite. Its class warfare but not in the sense of conventional punk's rage & anger but rather, through simple poetics that are not as elegant & sophisticated as in *Lexicon*. But yet, it has the same dark, revealing sensibilities as in the postpunk tradition.

That Was Then But This Is Now: the album's only significant hit. The song – as well as the album – became a hit in the UK (due primarily to the commentary of urban decay that a UK audience can relate to). It was not however, a hit in the US. In fact, it wouldn't be until 1987 that the next significant hit in the US for Martin Fry would occur–*When Smoky Sings* –a song where he returns to his more pop-oriented sound.

That Was Then But This Is Now
ABC

3.) <u>Orange Juice</u>: (formed in 1979, Bearsden, Glasgow, Scotland): a postpunk band who revolted against the angst and macho aggression of Scottish punk and in the process, became the epitome of a New Pop insurgency that championed the nostalgia of romance & innocence (while rejecting postpunk's darkness and depressive states). Personnel: <u>Edwyn Collins</u> (guitar, vocals), <u>Steven Daly</u> (drums), and <u>David McClymont</u> (bass). Debut performance: the Victor's Café in Glasgow on April 20, 1979.

<u>Inspirations</u>: initially, The Buzzcocks (performing in Glasgow as part of The Clash's White Riot Tour in 1979). They [The Buzzcocks] were not a typical British punk band. The difference: although their playing was energetic, they did possess a bubblegum-like melodic focus with lyrics of twisted whit and humor. In other words, they were campy and they went against the [conventional punk] grain.

<u>Another Inspiration</u>: The Subway Sect, one of the original British punk bands who were contemporaries of The Clash and The Sex Pistols back in the early days at The 100 Club. They were led by <u>Vic Godard</u>, whose lyrics were unconventional by London punk standards. Instead of rage & anger, his words were poetic with deep, personal, and hidden meanings.

Collins would inject a similar sensibility into his own lyrics. His poetics would deal with feelings of romantic inferiority, shyness, and insecurity. He used his subjects of wimpiness and insecurity as a means of rebelling against the Scottish punk status quo -- in other words, his lyrics were a symbol of non-conformity.

<u>Early Musical Influences</u>: Edwyn Collins and his Bearsden band-mates (who came of age together), took a special interest in New York namely, the CBGB scene. Bands such as Television, Patti Smith and The Talking Heads – in Collins' view -- were more interesting than their Scottish punk counterparts (Collins' group would later promote themselves as: "A New York band forming in the Bearsden area").

<u>Retro Guitar Sound</u>: his New York obsession was furthered by The Velvet Underground's *Live 1969* album from a nostalgic point of view. Lou Reed played a Gretsch electric guitar. In Collins' view, playing a Gretsch (as opposed to the more contemporary Fender and Gibson) was all about a return to a 1960's type of sound. Their retro approach would also be influenced by the jangly guitars of 60's folk-rock bands such as The Byrds.

An additional influence was the disco-driven guitar sound of Chic, featuring Niles Rodgers and Bernard Edwards. Their signature guitar sound (heard in songs such as *Good Times*) features strumming rhythms at twice the speed as the kick-bass drum.

<u>Original Sound</u>: the ingredients [of their original style] were a combination of several elements -- 60's guitar-driven [jangly] nostalgia; touches of contemporary, late-70's disco (a la Chic); and pop-styled vocalizing that matched the sentimentality of their lyrics.

<u>Debut Single</u>: *Falling and Laughing* (1982) released on the independent label, Postcard – founded jointly by Edwyn Collins, and Alan Horne and distributed by Rough Trade. *Falling and Laughing* cost £100 to make and established Orange Juice as the label's signature band (Horne would later add groups like Aztec Camera and Josef K to Postcard's catalog).

Falling
And Laughing
Orange Juice

Falling... received critical acclaim from the British pop press on the heels of Ian Curtis' untimely death by suicide – in their view, Orange Juice had progressed from the dark side of British postpunk into something more fun and romantically illuminating. Their subsequent releases included *Blueboy* (sold ca. 20,000 copies), *Consolation Prize*, and *Poor Old Soul*.

<u>Debut Album</u>: because Postcard lacked the finances to produce a full-fledged album, Orange Juice signed with Polydor and the result was their debut album, *You Can't Hide Your Love Forever* (1982). Included in this album were their previously released singles.

<u>Changes</u>: later in 1982, Collins purged several of his band members, which resulted in the acquisition of Zimbabwe-born drummer, <u>Zeke Manyika</u>. He gave Collins a new outlook of possibilities the most important being: the exploration of a more complex synthesis of pop and blue-eyed soul.

Rip It Up
Orange Juice

The result, their second album *Rip It Up* (1982): a more artistically ambitious project than their previous debut album. Included, was a tribute to their soulful Motown roots, *I Can't Help Myself* and the title track, *Rip It Up*, which became their first (and only) top ten hit in the UK.

B.) <u>The Goth Movement</u>: a tradition born out of reaction to both punk and New Pop with an attraction to all things macabre, mystical, and eternal. Although they tended to differentiate themselves, Goths did have several things in common with New Pop with regard to Glam influences. One was the impact of David Bowie and Roxy Music and the other, a return to glamorous adornment and the individuality of stardom.

Their individualized thirst for stardom was spawned by the art of expressive uniqueness resulting from Goth's wide-ranged potential for adaptability. In other words, there was little constraint with regard to both sound and theatrics. One could become statuesque and macabre while shrieking out a banshee wail, expressing lyrics of death & despair. There was also a collective identity within this subculture that was vigorous and tribal-like (dressed in complete black-leather clad). Their reaction against New Pop (as well as the New Romantics) was a dislike for New Pop's conventionalism and blatant, pop-commercial ambition.

Musical Foundation: foreboding, darkly sorrowful, and at times, epically grandiose. Specific traits include edgy, rapid-cutting, repeated guitar riffs; melodic basslines that lie in the upper register (a Joy Division trait); and grooves that are funereal or primitive in nature. Vocals could either be low and depressingly droning (a la Ian Curtis) or carrying an operatic, shrieking quality.

Lyrics: romanticism with old, timely things such as morbidity, mysticism, the supernatural, and religious metaphor/symbolism. And eternal longings such as death, despair, and doom & gloom.

Intent: The expression of timeless, eternal feelings -- an escape from the "rage & anger" mendacity of present-life punk. Another escape: from the depressing drudgery of everyday British life to one of ritual, magic, and mystique. Lyrics would also be personal, intelligent, and reflective.

Personal Attraction: for Goths, an attraction to all things taboo: a fixation on debauchery, sexual fetishism, and vampyric-styled fashion. The Goth look was a menacing combination of deathly sallowness, jet-black hair that stood up straight (teased), and black-leather, fetish outfits (sometimes, with Nazi regalia). Jewelry consisted of religious, magical artifacts and faces & ears were pierced. Overall, it was a macabre/dark sense of personal glamour.

As a result of its focus on personal adornment, Goth would connect especially to women.

The Batcave: London's first Goth club that opened in July of 1982. It was originally not intended to be a "Goth" club but rather, an alternative to the funk-driven New Romantics, New Pop, and dance music played at other London nightclubs. Its original goal was to reconceive Glam (Bowie/Roxy-styled), into a darker, fetish-clad, horror-movie type of scene. They started out playing records of glam and electro-synth with DJ Hamish McDonald. Soon after, a number of Goth bands were in residence fitting well within the club's darker, macabre setting -- among the earliest of these resident Goth bands, was Bauhaus.

1.) Bauhaus (formed 1978, Northampton, ENG): one of the founding fathers of the Goth-rock movement. They created a shadowy, horror-film-like essence of darkness within the context of lyrics expressing psych-sexual theatrics, idolatry, and blasphemy. Musically, their sound consisted of scratchy, jagged, & knife-edgy guitars; high registered bass lines; and throaty, dark, vampyric vocals that were either low and austere, or high up and intense (like an Ian Curtis voice on Steroids). At times, the character of the music was cold and distant.

Original Lineup: Peter Murphy (b. July 11, 1957, Northampton, ENG) vocals; Daniel Ash (b. July 31, 1957, Northampton) guitar, vocals, saxophone, keyboards; David J (Jay) (b. David Jay Haskins, April 24, 1957, Northampton) bass, vocals, keyboard, guitar; Kevin Haskins (b. July 19, 1960, Northampton) drums. Daniel Ash and the two Haskins brothers originally formed a group called The Craze. Once vocalist Peter Murphy joined, the name was changed to "Bauhaus 1919" (commemorating the German architecture movement with the maxim that "less is more").

Debut Single: Bela Lugosi's Dead, released on the independent label, Small Wonder, in August of 1979. Although it failed to gain any pop-chart traction, it did become Goth's first, bona fide anthem (which did achieve long-term success on the UK indie charts). This single contained many signature elements attributed to Goth mainly, a vampyric vocal sound (made to sound distant via studio-produced echo-effects); edgy, atmospheric guitars; high registered bass lines (which at times carried the instrumental melodic hook); and a cold, darkly distant aura. The lyrics carry a horror-film/ritualistic essence as in the following excerpt:

> *The virginal brides file past his tomb*
> *Strewn with time's dead flowers*
> *Bereft in deathly bloom*
> *Alone in a darkened room*
> *The count*
> *Bela Lugosi's dead*

"Bela Lugosi's Dead" by Bauhaus, reprinted from Bauhaus Crackle, BEGL 2018 CD: 1998, Beggars Music.

*A Kick
In The Eye
(Alternate Version)*
Bauhaus

On the printed record label, the "1919" was dropped from their name. Three months following the release, Bauhaus signed with 4AD (founded in 1979 by Ivor Watts-Russell), a subsidiary of Beggar's Banquet Records. They followed with singles such as *Dark Entries* and *Terror Couple Kill Colonel*.

Debut Album: *In The Flat Field* (released in October of 1980). With success on the independent charts, it also broke into the pop charts at #72. As a result, Bauhaus would have two "crossover" hits charting into the UK top 60 – *A Kick In The Eye* and *The Passion of Lovers*. Both singles were theatrical from a distant, tales-from-the-crypt-like essence with an austere, vampyric flavor.

*The Passion
Of Lovers*
Bauhaus

This marked the earliest example of Goth-driven singles crossing over from the cryptic underground to the British mainstream. This British mainstream success was furthered by their second album, *Mask,* in 1981.

Bauhaus: was among the earliest transitions from British postpunk to Goth within the context of a burgeoning subculture centering around a dark, horror film-oriented club. They represented a culture that reacted against the more pop-driven New Pops and New Romantics -- they shunned funk and used black leather, macabre motifs and various sounds reflective of those dark-driven theatrics (with a vampire-like aura).

There would be other groups emanating other locales that would build their own transitions to Goth and in the process, create their own unique reactions against what they saw, as the mediocrity of pop. These groups include Siouxsie & The Banshees, The Birthday Party, and Killing Joke.

2.) Siouxsie & The Banshees: hailing for the original London punk underground – they were among the most successful and longest-lived groups to emerge from that scene. Bandleader and visionary Siouxsie Sioux captured the artistic attitude that became the hallmark of the Goth spirit – outright rebellion against the mediocrity of conventional rock. Not only would they maintain that spirit, but they would become the "last bastion of punk purity". They were a combination of several things: art makers, intellectuals, and poseurs posting a voodoo vibe. They were the uncompromising embodiment of all things punk in terms of radical rhetoric.

Original Lineup: Siouxsie Sioux (b. Susan Dallion, May 27, 1957, London, ENG) vocals; Steve Severin (b. Steven Bailey, Sept. 25, 1959, London) bass; Sid Vicious (b. John Simon Ritchie, May 10, 1957; d. Feb. 2, 1979) drums; and Marco Pironni (b. April 27, 1959, London) guitar.

Beginnings: her initial inspiration happened while recuperating in the hospital from a blood transfusion and difficult operation. She was watching on TV, David Bowie's performance of *Starman* on the popular show, Top of The Pops. She loved what she had referred to as, "the skinniness, the alienation, and otherworldliness" – the androgyne of the future: a platform to accentuate your own sense of individuality. Due to this epiphany, she transformed herself from being shy, to openly flaunting her "freak" status.

: a motley crew of rabid Sex Pistols fans from which Souxsie Sioux and members of the Banshees would emerge. They flaunted their rebellious spirit and non-conformity. They were also devoted fans of Glam attracted to its sense of theatre and drama (Severin & Sioux first met at a Roxy Music concert in 1974). They also hung out at Malcolm McClaren's shop, "Let It Rock" (later to be named "SEX").

Debut Performance: September 20, 1976 at the legendary Punk Festival, arranged by Malcolm McClaren, at The 100 Club in London. Insofar as her band's name, she had gotten the idea several days earlier from a Hammer Horror film on TV called "Cry of The Banshee". The performance was an extended rendition *The Lord's Prayer* – they posed on stage looking incredible but couldn't cop an instrumental lick otherwise. They knew that they couldn't play but in the typical punk tradition, they decided to "give it a go". At this point, they were first and foremost, Poseurs.

Gigging: they would progress from being poseurs to actual musicians. Steve Severin's musical influences were similar to his postpunk contemporaries: The Velvet Underground, Can, Captain Beefheart, and Roxy Music. As for Siouxsie Sioux, she wanted the electric guitar to sound like a slashing dagger reminiscent of the shower scene in the film, *Psycho*.

This knife-edged guitar sound was produced by a device known as a Flange. It merged two identical signals together with one of those signals slightly delayed producing a microscopically echoed copy of itself. The result was a grating, glassy, shining guitar sound that was different from their more abrasive contemporaries.

Siouxsie Sioux's vocals were different, too – icy, distant, staccato-like incantations that could shriek at dramatic moments. Her vocal essence was somewhat similar [in a female version] to Bauhaus' Peter Murphy – dark, dramatic, and articulate in a purely Gothic/Horror-film manner.

Her early attire included Nazi/fascist imagery that evolved into fetish/vampy outfits laced with fishnet hosiery, dark eye shadow, and jet-black, teased-up hair (a more witchy characteristic that women of Gothic culture would emulate).

Resulting Sound: iconoclastic. They all shared a vision of their band as an outright rebellious work of art posting a voodoo type of vibe and a glam-driven drum sound – a cymbal-free drum sound reminiscent of the Velvet Underground's Moe Tucker. In addition, Siouxsie Sioux's voice was superimposed over the flanged/stabbing guitar sound carrying an ominous, fearful presence.

Recording Contract: on June 9, 1978, they signed with Polydor Records. Debut single: *Hong Kong Garden,* which charted as well as their debut album, *The Scream.* The lyrics (from *The Scream*) deal with the morbid, macabre side of human nature that at times, verges on dark humor.

Example: *Carcass*, a mutilation love story. In order to seal the ultimate act of love, the narrator hacks off a part of herself to be one with the refrigerated meat – the object of her undying affection.

Suburban Relapse: stabbing-like, panning guitars open up the song: about a suburban wife who has had enough of a life of blandness and no direction. She asks herself, "…what for?" -- an expression of rebellion against blandness reminiscent of the punk-influenced tradition.

Hong Kong Garden
Siouxsie &
The Banshees

Suburban Relapse
Siouxsie &
The Banshees

Their Second Dramatic Chapter: in support of their second album, *Join Hands* (1979), they were two days into their tour in Scotland when John McKay (guitarist) and Kenny Morris (drummer) abruptly left the group. They were replaced by Budgie (b. Peter Clark, Aug. 27, 1957, St. Helen's, ENG) on drums and guitarist John McGeoch (b. May 28, 1955, Strathclyde, Scotland). Following the release of their third album, Kaleidoscope (1980), they released their most poignant Gothic statement, *JuJu* (1981).

With songs like *Spellbound, Halloween, Sin In My Heart*, and *Voodoo Dolly* (the latter exhilarating a black, macabre approach to drama), *JuJu* explored themes that would forever be synonymous with Goth – sin, magic, and the dark side of the supernatural – common fare for many Goth artists to come.

NOTE: in their 1982 album, *A Kiss In The Dreamhouse*, The Banshees took on a more eclectic, melodic-driven approach, which gave them pop success throughout the UK mainstream. Their style had synth elements and characteristics more reminiscent of Joy Division than their previous Goth-driven sound. Because of their pop success, the band transcended beyond being cult idols. Since they were no longer seen as Gothic figures (having transcended their niche audience), the torch would be passed to another group who was arguably, more extreme, more noisy, and more brutal than anyone who had ever preceded them...

3.) The Birthday Party (formed in 1976 as The Boys Next Door): whereas Bauhaus came out of The Batcave, and Siouxsie & The Banshees hailed from a London punk background, The Birthday Party's loud, angst-driven, cacophonous racket was crafted out of a uniquely American influence: Delta Blues. With the addition of the dark, morose vocalizing of Nick Cave, the Birthday Party was an extremely Gothic, death-of-rock version of blues revisionism (English Goth meets the voodoo essence of blues).

Original Lineup: Nick Cave (b. Nicholas Edward Cave, Sept. 22, 1957, Warracknabeal, Australia) vocals, guitar; Mick Harvey (b. Sept. 29, 1957, Rochester, Australia) guitar, keyboards, drums, bass; Tracy Pew (b. 1958; d. Nov. 7 1986) bass; Phil Calvert, drums.

Background: originally from Australia, they began as The Boys Next Door after Nick Cave (a petty thief and misfit) met Mick Harvey at boarding school. Following the release of their debut album *Door Door* and the *Hee Haw* EP, they moved to London, England (after finding the Aussie scene as too constrained). Following their arrival, they gradually changed their name to The Birthday Party where their enthusiasm [for London] was soon dampened -- they thought that there would be an explosion of innovative groups only to find that things had cooled down considerably.

Nick Cave: he and his band were renegade outsiders. He engaged in rough-hewed, swaggering blues that was at odds with the New Pop/New Romantics of the early 80's. He was also among the first of the London scene to go against the anti-religious grain of British postpunk by using Old Testament themes of damnation, sin, and retribution (among others) – a source that would match well with his Delta blues, voodoo influences. He had a fascination with the language of violence and bold, stylistic experimentation.

Musical Style: brutal, assaultive, extreme, and raw to the core. Nick Cave's vocals were drooling and guttural on the one hand, yet screechy and angst-driven on the other – animalistic and grotesque with in-your-face macabre dramatics. With the electric guitar -- a brutally dissonant, edgy, aggressive onslaught.

Recording Contract: because of their notoriously assaultive, musically aggressive live performances, on John Peel's BBC-1 radio program, they eventually got noticed by the UK indie label, 4 AD (the same label as Bauhaus) and were signed.

Prayers On Fire (1981): the title gives a taste of Nick Cave's focus on the gloomy, cataclysmic side of religion delivered in a raucous, assaultive, Dionysian inferno. This was his group's first, international album.

Zoo Music Girl
The Birthday Party

Example: *Zoo-Music Girl* – to quote Greg Maurer: "It's the religion of depraved sexuality, bestial urges, and sadomasochism". Nick Cave howling out his grotesque, guttural incantations upon Zoo-Music Girl's pagan altar. To accentuate his idol worship, tribal-like drumming (on the floor toms), cheesy garage-band organ licks, and funky background trumpet, add a voodoo-rite/Gothic-like Caribbean essence.

Junkyard (1982): the apex of their extreme, Gothic approach in an album-length format. Its rock 'n' roll meeting the incendiary, fiery depths of a Kamikaze inferno. It was Nick Cave's further exploration of extreme Gothetics from an Americanized, voodoo-based, blues influence. The sound itself, matched the drooling grotesqueness of the album cover's cartoon monster illustrated by Ed Roth.

The Album's Sound: brutal, extreme, and raw to the core. Songs like *Dead Joe*, are teemed with noisy, edgy, dissonant guitars and guttural, shouting vocals that match the violent, dramatic essence.

Big Jesus Trash-Can
The Birthday Party

Big-Jesus-Trash-Can: screaming, howling vocals (like the cry of a Werewolf). The guitars were cacophonous, dissonant, and abrasive superimposed over a back-alley, blues-driven groove – reminiscent of clanging trashcans. The lyrics were a cryptic, extreme exposé of an evangelist who was rotten to the core (a very American theme).

Release The Bats
The Birthday Party

Release The Bats: their most influential single from Goth-driven perspective. Yelling, vampire-like vocals that were characteristic of absurdist theatre/horror movie dramatics -- an expression of what sex would be like in a bloodthirsty, vampire world. This single topped the UK indie charts

NOTE: The Birthday Party followed up *Junkyard* with two EP's that were a continuation of their extreme Gothic expressive nature: *The Bad Seed* and *Mutiny* (the latter being their final release).

Aftermath: with former members of The Birthday Party plus Blixa Bargeld, (front man for a German industrial band called Einstürzende Neubauten), Nick Cave formed his new group – The Bad Seeds (a.k.a. Nick Cave & The Bad Seeds). They would take a more refined, controlled approach while maintaining their earlier, gloomy, dark-driven intensity. He would also delve more heavily into the mystical, voodoo-like swampy influence, of Delta Blues.

4.) Killing Joke (formed in 1978, London, ENG): whereas Nick Cave derived his inspiration from Delta Blues, Killing Joke would embrace a more funk-derived aesthetic: disco (but, with a twist). They stripped away disco's shining, burnished, pop surface and replaced it with harsh, aggressive, and dissonant noise on the electric guitar. Insofar as the disco groove, they maintained a hammering, heavy dance beat supported by a Giorgio Moroder [Euro-disco] four-on-the-floor kick-drum style. They became the crossroad, by which Gothic rock and Industrial dance music would intersect -- but they were also a bridge [to Goth] *from* British postpunk.

Their greatest [postpunk] influence was P.i.L. Jaz Coleman's vocals were reminiscent of John Lydon going dark, and hardcore – shouting, yelling, and barking with outright ferocity In addition, the guitar treatment of Geordie was like Keith Levene going off the savage deep-end (Martin Atkins [of P.i.L.], would later join Killing Joke as drummer).

Original Members: <u>Jaz Coleman</u> (b. Feb. 26, 1960, Cheltenham, ENG) vocals, synthesizer keyboards; <u>Geordie</u> (b. Kevin Walker, Dec. 18, 1958, Newcastle-upon-Tyne, ENG) guitar; <u>Youth</u> (b. Martin Glover, Dec. 29, 1960, Africa) bass; <u>Paul Ferguson</u> (b. March 31, 1858, High Wycombe, ENG) drums.

<u>Background</u>: Paul Ferguson was the drummer of The Matt Stagger Band when he met Jaz Coleman in the late 1970's – he soon became part of the band. Both he and Ferguson soon left to form their own band and after the recruitment of Geordie and Youth, they formed Killing Joke.

<u>*Wardance*</u> (1980): their debut single – hammering rhythms with a mechanized feel supporting Jaz Coleman's harsh vocals spewing anger-driven ferocity. John Peel, legendary DJ for his BBC-1 radio program, gave the single an intense amount of airplay. He thought they were someone famous operating under a pseudonym (an assumed name).

This single was included in their debut album of 1980, <u>*Killing Joke*</u>. Although it was dark, bleak, and full of rage, it would have widespread influence inspiring many future imitators. It would also become the first to anticipate the "aggro" industrial sound of Ministry and Big Black in the late 1980's.

<u>Controversy</u>: they gained a notorious reputation for their offensive, inflammatory posters and 7" record sleeves. The imagery included Pope Pius XII receiving Nazi hand salutes from marching German storm troopers and one of Fred Astaire dancing over corpses piled within a World War I trench.

<u>*What's THIS For...!*</u> (1981): the last great album of the original lineup and the first of where of their P.i.L. influences would gradually slip away. They emerged with more hammering, tribal-like wallops matching Geordie's edgy, punishing dissonant guitar riff-craft while Coleman's synth treatments remained intact (but not P.i.L.-like) and the vocals featured chorus-like shout outs.

One of the primary examples from this album, was *Follow The Leaders* – hammering tribal drum-machine beats with synth-driven, looping echo effects and hardcore, scything guitar rhythms.

<u>Disintegration</u>: because of Jaz Coleman's growing obsession with the occult – beginning during the recording of their third album, *Revelations* (1982) -- the band was in the process of breaking up. Following the break up (after the album's release), Coleman, thinking that the end of the world was near, moved to Iceland. He remained there until he decided that world was going to stick around after all…

<u>NOTE</u>: the previously covered Goth artists – Bauhaus, Siouxie & The Banshees, The Birthday Party, and Killing Joke -- each had their own underground, cult-oriented following. But a mainstream, commercial-type success – due to their cult status – seemed out of reach (<u>exception</u>: it was only after transcending their cult audience that The Banshees achieved some pop-based success in the UK). But not all Goths would share the same fate [of perpetual underworld cult existence]. Unlike the previously mentioned bands, The Cure would achieve pop success in the UK while maintaining their dark, gloom & doom-driven "mope-rock" sound.

5.) <u>The Cure</u> (formed in 1976, Crawley, West Sussex, ENG): the band that formed the bridge from Goth rock into pop. Although they experienced many different lineups, the one constant mainstay was singer/guitarist Robert Smith. His notably gruesome appearance – complete with funereal-white makeup, red lipstick, and teased jet-black hair – became the first "face" of Goth that reached mainstream awareness in the UK and US. They did not begin that way however, but rather, as a postpunk group playing stripped-down, sparse electric guitar with melodically driven pop sensibilities. In 1980, they began a new process toward minor-keyed, dark synthesizer colors with thick, gloomy, textural layers.

Original Lineup: <u>Robert Smith</u> (b. April 21, 1959, Blackpool, ENG) vocals, guitar; <u>Michael Dempsey</u> (b. Nov. 29, 1958) bass, vocals; Laurence "Lol" Tolhurst (b. Feb. 3, 1959) drums.

Background: Robert Smith hailed from Crawley, a working-class suburb of London. Having an emotionally difficult childhood (with both his parents and the police), he formed a band called The Obelisk – he was 17 at the time. It was his first artistic outlet by which he'd vent his rebellious energy. With the emergence of punk rock in the UK, he became swept up in its influences and in turn, formed <u>The Easy Cure</u>.

*Killing
An Arab*
The Cure

Early Sound: sparse electric guitar with pop melodic focus supporting lyrics that were literature-inspired. The latter was evidenced in their debut single, *Killing An Arab* (1979) – inspired by a two-part novel called, *The Stranger* by Albert Camus. Released in December of 1978, at the behest of Chris Parry, A&R man for Polydor -- he released it on the Small Wonder label (same label as Bauhaus). It was at this point, that they condensed their name to The Cure. (Parry re-released the single on the Fiction label in 1979).

Three Imaginary Boys (1979): their debut album that received positive, UK press reviews. While they toured throughout the UK in support of the album, they were the opening act for Siouxsie & The Banshees. When The Banshees' guitarist abruptly quit the band, Smith filled in beginning a dynamic collaborative association [with The Banshees].

*Boys Don't
Cry*
The Cure

Turn of Events: following the release of pop-styled singles, *Boys Don't Cry* and *Jumping On Someone Else's Train*, the band would turn to a more darker, minor-keyed, synth-driven sound due in part, to their new fourth member (and synth player). Mathieu Hartley. (they were also joined by Michael Dempsey's replacement on bass, Simon Gallup). The result: *Seventeen Seconds* (1980), the album that introduced their new direction. – a progression to a darker, Goth-essenced type of sound complete with obsessed lyrics and thick synthesizer textures. Unlike their Gothic predecessors or contemporaries, The Cure's sound would be devoid of brutality, edgy dissonance, and grotesque vocalizing (which was why they became pop-friendly).

A Forest
The Cure

A Forest: their first hit in the UK pop charts rising to #31. A minor-keyed synth-driven sound that was Gothic on the one hand, pop accessible on the other – what Simon Reynolds called "Goth-lite".

Lyrics: about one who is lost in a forest. The idea of being lost with no direction and feelings of alienation are both an inherent part of Gothic subject matter.

*Charlotte
Sometimes*
The Cure

Faith (1981): their darkest album to date – melancholy, funereal with a sense of despondence. Atmospheric in a Gothic sense, pop on the other with gloominess of Robert Smith's vocals. Perhaps their darkest, thickly textured, Gothic statement was a 1981 single release *Charlotte Sometimes* (eventually included in the 1986 compilation, *Staring At The Sea: The Singles*). Complete with processed vocals that give a faraway, detached essence superimposed over a dense murky wall of synthesizer sounds.

Close To Me
The Cure

Continuing the gloom and neurosis with the albums *Pornography* (1982) and *The Top* (1984), The Cure would eventually transcend beyond Goth and adopt a more mainstream pop approach with the 1985 album, *The Head to the Door*. This would become their first pop success in America with listener friendly songs like *Close To Me,* and *In Between Days*.

> NOTE: By the time of The Cure's thickly textured, dark synth-driven Gothic statements and their eventual transition to a more pop-related direction, a new trend in synthesizer music had a already been well underway. It happened first in the UK and then eventually, it caught on in the US. By the time we get to 1985, (the year of The Cure's pop statement *The Head To The Door*), the synth pop phenomenon was filling the mainstream charts and video airtime on MTV. Among its earliest successes on both sides of the Atlantic, was a man who became known as the father of synth pop – a former punk artist named Gary Numan.

C.) <u>Synth Pop</u>: an aesthetic that centered around synthesizers as the predominant, lead instrument. Although its developmental process started in the late 1970's, its prominence began in the early 1980's and remained so, for the rest of the decade. In addition, devices such as drum machines and computerized sequencers became the norm – in some cases, replacing traditional instruments (guitars, drums, etc.). Since most of the early synth pop artists hailed from postpunk (where technical skill was mostly irrelevant); their transition to this pop melodic, keyboard-driven genre was relatively easy. Another transition was in the attitude – punk was about authenticity, postpunk was about demystification, while synth pop was mostly about artificiality. In the process, glam influences of gender bending and painted faces with a disco-oriented flair (especially in the grooves) became commonplace. Among the first to embody this new concept was a group called Tubeway Army featuring synth pop's first international icon…

> 1.) Original Lineup: <u>Gary Numan</u> (b. Gary Anthony Jones Webb, March 8, 1958, London, ENG) guitar, vocals; <u>Paul Gardiner</u>, bass; <u>Jess Lidyard</u>, drums.
>
> <u>Gary Numan</u>: one of the main progenitors of the synth pop era ushering in its initial popularity and early mystique. His synth-dominated style was the result of several influences – <u>Ultravox</u>, <u>Kraftwerk</u>, and <u>David Bowie</u>. In turn, he became influential to the Gothic-driven dance genre known as "Darkwave". He had the persona of an extraterrestrial, character with a clinical sense of detachment, gloom, and alienation. His sound matched his robotic, space-alien persona with austere, dark, and heavy synthesizers supporting a Ziggy Stardust, creature-like style of vocalizing.
>
> > <u>Background</u>: while being swept up in the British punk movement, Numan joined a [punk] group called The Lasers as a guitarist in 1976. He was already a prolific sing writer with an eye for pop/commercial success. The Lasers had originally released punk songs following their signing with the Beggars Banquet label in 1978. Shortly thereafter, Numan and Gardiner left The Lasers and along with his uncle Jess Lidyard on drums, they formed the Tubeway Army.
>
> > <u>Game Changer</u>: during a recording session at Spaceward Studios in the summer of 1978, he discovered a minimoog synthesizer that was used by a previous band but the rental company had not yet picked it up. The synth setting was left on its heaviest mode, which produced a sound unlike anything he had ever heard – powerful, space-like, and futuristic. He immediately began experimenting with it and included it in his new songs.
>
> > *My Shadow In Vain* Tubeway Army
>
> > <u>Debut Album</u>: *Tubeway Army* (1979), an album that began with a guitars-only concept that evolved with the addition of synth sounds. It consisted mostly of sparse, postpunk-driven electric guitars with David Bowie, Ziggy Stardust-styled vocalizing (in songs like, *My Shadow In Vain* and *Life Machine*). The synthesizer could be heard in a clinical, robotic sense (reminiscent of the Kraftwerk influence) in songs such as *Zero Bars (Mr. Smith)*. Although this album marked the beginning of Numan's transition into the synth realm, it still consisted mostly of postpunk-based, electric guitar riffing. The next album however, would complete this new transition and solidify a radically new sound and austere alienated focus.
>
> <u>*Replicas*</u> (1979): his breakthrough – Numan's first bona fide, synth-pop focused, New Wave album. Gone are the sparse electric guitars and in, are the predominant, futuristic

synth-heavy textures. In addition to the futurism, it had a solid dance beat anticipating the pop-driven New Wave movement to come.

Lyrics: science fiction-oriented inspired by writer Phillip K. Dick (Numan was known to have attempted writing a science fiction novel of his own).

Are Friends Electric? His first #1 hit the UK charts and the one that opened the door to a proliferation of synth pop hits by other various artists such as Ultravox, Visage, and Human League. The popularity of this single launched *Replicas* to #1 on the UK charts as well.

Characteristic: thick, ominous, doomy synth sounds presented in a robotic manner. His vocals were detached, clinical and David Bowie-like – especially, when articulating a heavy British accent with an androgynous sound. As synth-driven as this single was, the rhythm section was not programmed but rather, played by actual musicians (bass, drums, etc.).

With *Replicas*, Numan was continuing his extraterrestrial mystique with a song called *Praying To The Aliens*. He was also seen by critics, as bridging the gap between synth pop and Goth – one example was *Down In The Park*.

The Pleasure Principle (1979): their next album and the first to be released under Gary Numan's name (instead of Tubeway Army). Although he still used a conventional rhythm section, his heavy synthesizer sound was *the* dominant force; it had a grandiose, almost symphonic level of presence.

This album contained his first international hit, *Cars*. It reached the US top 10 (his first big success in America) and #1 in the UK. For his tour (in support of the album), he put together a hugely elaborate, futuristic science-fiction-type stage show that subsequently lost money. He also began indulging in his new hobby as an airplane pilot with his newfound wealth.

Note on His Lyrics: within the context of his space alien, science fiction subject matter, there was something else lying beneath the surface: feelings of seclusion, uneasiness, suggestions of sexual ambivalence, and a distant, emotional disconnect – perhaps the very essence of what being an isolated space alien is all about.

Telekon (1980): his third consecutive chart success in the UK. He scored a couple of top ten hits in the UK with *We Are Glass* and *I Die You Die* plus a top 20, *The Wreckage*. For all of his newfound notoriety, *Telekon* would be Numan's last significant success but his legacy and influence (by this time) had already been set in stone.

Within two years, there would be a proliferation of synth pop artists releasing chart topping hits on a monumental scale. In fact, the charts would overflow with synth pop classics expanding Gary Numan's innovations. His long-term influence would last for decades into the 1990's. But his immediate legacy revolved around a collective known, as the New Romantics.

2.) The First of The Synth Pop Harbingers: Before Gary Numan, there was Ultravox -- the first to embrace the lush, romantic sounds of the synthesizer while turning against the raging, abrasive guitars of their punk-era contemporaries. As a result, they became one of *the* early important influences of British synth pop that emerged in the early 1980's.

Ultravox's Original Members: John Foxx (b. Dennis Leigh, Chortley, ENG) vocals, synthesizer; Steve Shears vocals, keyboards; Billy Currie (b. William Lee Curtis, April 1, 1952) violin, synthesizer, keyboards; <u>Chris Cross</u> (b. Christopher Allen, July 14, 1952) bass; <u>Warren Cann</u> (b. May 20, 1952, Victoria, CAN) drums.

<u>Background</u>: they formed in London in 1974 and were led by vocalist, <u>John Foxx</u>. He had taken an interest in music while dabbling in tapes and synthesizers at school. After moving to London in 1974, he began writing songs and later, formed Ultravox. Their influences were the Glam sounds of <u>David Bowie</u> and <u>Roxy Music</u> (which brought the no respect from a punk-biased audience). In 1977, they signed with Island records and released their eponymous (self-titled) debut album produced by Brian Eno.

<u>Imagery</u>: the approach, both for him and his band, was to reject American rock influences and instead, look eastward – mainly to Germany and Eastern Europe. In fact, this deliberate avoidance was conscientious to the point where keyboardist, Billy Currie, refused to play anything relating to a blues scale.

<u>Germany</u>: they followed in the footsteps of David Bowie's German residency by having a German residency of their own – in Köln. They worked with Kraftwerk producer Conrad Plank and the result was *Systems of Romance*, their 3rd album released in 1978. Even before this release (which failed commercially like their prior two albums), John Foxx was anticipating the early 80's synth pop phenomenon – both in terms of music and of imagery: the latter with a European, Glam influenced aura with lyrical themes of urban decadence, disillusionment, and human depravation (which caught the attention of a young Gary Numan).

I Want To Be A Machine
Ultravox

<u>Examples</u>: Songs such as *I Want To Be A Machine* and *My Sex* (their first minor hit in the UK), created an atmosphere of alienation and detachment (again, anticipating Numan).

<u>NOTE</u>: with the failure of their first three albums, Island Records dropped Ultravox from their contract in 1978. At this point, John Foxx went solo – he would never achieve the chart-topping success of his young acolyte, Gary Numan.

New Frontman: <u>Midge Ure</u> became Ultravox's new frontman. He was formerly of a Scottish group called SLIK and also of ex-Sex Pistols', Glenn Matlock's band Rich Kids. Unlike John Foxx, Midge Ure was a more dynamic performer and less foreboding in character.

Vienna
Ultravox

Vienna (1981): the album that became their first UK success which included hit singles, *Sleepwalk* (#2, UK) and the title track, *Vienna* which remained at #2 in the UK for several consecutive weeks. The title track, *Vienna*, was completely synth-driven with a title reminiscent of their European [Eastern] obsession. Although Ultravox achieved great success in the UK, they would never achieve that status in the US. In fact, Ultravox, and several other bands known as The New Romantics, would find success exclusively in the UK with both a look and sound all their own. It began with a venue known, as The Blitz Club.

3.) <u>The Blitz Club</u>: following the demise of Ultravox'x first incarnation marked by John Foxx'x departure and Island Records dropping their contract, Billy Currie (former Ultravox member), began hanging out at a club called Billy's – a club in London's SoHo region where a DJ named Rusty Egan spun records (he was a former member of Glenn Matlock's band, Rich Kids).

<u>Egan's Record Selections</u>: sounds that looked toward Europe, namely Germany, with selections from David Bowie's "Berlin Trilogy" albums, Iggy Pop's Berlin period, Kraftwerk, and the Eurodisco-based sounds of Giorgio Moroder. Glam artists from the UK such as Roxy Music were also included. Eventually, the scene moved to a larger venue called <u>The Blitz Club</u> located on Great Queen Street. The clientele who frequented there – highly ultra-chic for their period -- were known as <u>The New Romantics</u>.

Steve Strange: was the man who spearheaded this scene and it was his mission, to preserve and maintain the club's "in crowd", fashionable elitism. It was he (as doorman) who was very selective in deciding whether someone entered the club or not.

Cultural Purpose: a reaction against the current punk scene. Whereas British punk was all about confrontation -- against the systemized, caste-based, dreariness of everyday life -- the New Romantics were all about escapism. Instead of expressing rage and anger, they favored fantasy and oblivion. Instead of dressing to offend [like swastika armbands], they chose the Glam route – dressing to be someone else.

> Style of Dress: a Bowie-esque flair for fashion, which was basically, a mixture of retro and futurism. From the retro side, a blend of various classic hats (pillbox, bolero, etc.), Cossack-looking waistline cummerbunds, and 19th century, European-styled military tunics with knee high boots. The futuristic side was twofold, first, were the hairdos: angular with precise geometric shapes and secondly, the makeup. Again, with the Bowie influence, face painting that was otherworldly which included abstract designs and a Ziggy-like personification.

> Result: a fashion statement containing a mixture of androgyny, the extraterrestrial, and faux nobility – their expression of fantasy and escape from the drudgeries of everyday life.

First Recording: Both Steve Strange (former member of punk band, The Moors Murderers) and Rusty Egan shared the idea of making their own recordings to fit into the club's regular playlist. Midge Ure (another Rich Kids alum) offered studio time and along with Egan and Strange, recorded a single in 1978 – an aptly futuristic cover of the Zager & Evans late 60's pop tune, *In The Year 2525*. This was the debut of the group that would forever be known as Visage.

Original Lineup: Steve Strange (b. Steven John Harrington, May 28, 1959) vocals; Rusty Egan (b. Sept. 19, 1957) drums; Midge Ure (b. James Ure, Oct. 10, 1953) guitar, vocals, keyboard; Billy Currie (b. William Lee Curtis, April 1, 1952) keyboard, violin; plus three former members of the group, Magazine – John McGeoch (b. John Alexander McGeoch, Aug. 25, 1955 – d. March 4, 2004) guitar; Dave Formula (b. David Tomlison, Aug. 11, 1946) keyboard; and Barry Adamson (b. June 11, 1958) bass.

> Musical Style: electro-disco grooves with synth-driven pop focus – a style reminiscent of a David-Bowie-meets-Teutonic-Kraftwerk, but with a fun, pop effervescence.

> Debut Album: *Visage* (1980), their self-titled debut album which included their earlier recorded, first original single, *Tar*.

> > *Fade To Grey*: a French woman's evocative spoken voice over a dark, minor-keyed, repetitive synth-riff and pulsating electronic groove. Its character sounded Cabaret-like -- reminiscent of a New Romantic's desire to escape from life's utter exhaustion. It was their first major single that heralded synth pop's commercial breakthrough – it was followed by another hit (from the same album) *Mind Of A Toy*.

NOTE: By the time of their follow-up album, of 1982, *The Anvil*, the fashion-flaired obsessive, club-conscious, New Romantic movement was on the decline. Steve Strange's lyrics were delving more into melancholy than ever before with songs such as *The Damned Don't Cry* superimposed over driving electro-disco beats.

Fade To Grey
Visage

But influences spearheaded by The New Romantics and Blitz Club connections were already rearing their collective heads onto the international, pop arena. One such Blitz Club connection was <u>Martin Rushent</u>. He owned an independent label called Genetic, that recorded the "<u>Big 3</u>" of The New Romantics: <u>Ultravox</u>, <u>Visage</u>, and <u>Spandau Ballet</u>. Following the eventual failure of this label, Martin Rushent would finally strike gold as the producer of a band that would become synth pop's first international mega-stars [in a band format...

4.) <u>The Human League</u> (formed 1977, Sheffield, ENG): Synth pop's first international icons and undisputed leaders of the British synth pop movement. In 1982, they topped the charts in both the US and UK – they were among the most innovative artists to ride the pop wave of synthesizers and electro-dance beats. Their synthesis of sumptuous melodies with the latest, state-of-the art technology, became highly influential to many who followed in their wake.

Original Lineup: <u>Phil Oakey</u> (b. Oct. 2, 1955, Sheffield, ENG) vocals, synthesizer; <u>Martyn Ware</u> (b. May 19, 1956, Sheffield) synthesizer; <u>Ian Craig Marsh</u> (b. Nov. 11, 1956, Sheffield) synthesizer; and <u>Phillip Adam Wright</u> (b. June 30, 1956, Sheffield) stage/multi-media visuals.

Later: <u>Suzanne Sulley</u> (b. March 22, 1963, Sheffield) vocals; <u>Joanne Catherall</u> (B. Sept. 18, 1962, Sheffield) vocals; <u>Ian Burden</u> (b. Dec. 24, 1957) bass, synthesizer. (the three of them joined after the departure of Martyn Ware and Ian Marsh).

Background: Martyn Ware and Ian Marsh (formerly of the duo, Dead Daughters), had briefly formed Future in 1977 as duo synthesizer players. When singer Phil Oakey came on board, they rechristened themselves as The Human League. Soon after, they enlisted Phillip Adam Wright as "Director of Visuals" -- he would put on multi media slide shows using synchronization units (a new technology) that synched the slide selections with the music during live performances. They also relied on pre-recorded tape accompaniment [during their live shows].

Early Recordings: in 1979, they signed with Virgin Records and released their first two albums -- *Reproduction* (1979): grim, rigid, and austere emulating Kraftwerk's robotic style & mystique. The other was *Travelogue* (1980): more polished, upbeat, and lively [than *Reproduction*]. Modest sales [for both albums] notwithstanding, they failed to score a hit pop single (which was what they aspired to more than anything).

Internal Tensions: because of Phil Oakey's trepidation of relying on pre-recorded tapes for live shows (which he deemed "dishonest"), Martyn Ware and Ian Marsh left the group (they would go on to form a production outfit known as B.E.F. -- British Electric Foundation). They were replaced by Ian Burden (bass) and "The Girls" – vocalists <u>Joanne Catherall</u> and <u>Suzanne Sulley</u>. As important as these editions were, there was one more element that they needed in order to cement their new direction – a new producer...

Martin Rushent (b. July 11, 1948 – d. June 4, 2011): a former regular of The Blitz Club. Following the demise of his own label called Genetic, he invested over £200,000 to build his own private recording studio. Included in this new enterprise, was state-of-the-art equipment with the purpose of making electronic music (which included a Linn Drum Computer – among the first of timbral, programmable drum machines). In early 1981, he came to the rescue of the newly revamped Human League, whose morale was at an all-time low due to their failure to create a hit.

The Sound Of The Crowd (1981): a single that marked the first result of the Phil Oakey/Ian Burdon songwriting collaboration. It also marked the debut of their new backup singers, "The Girls" – their romantic charm would transform Human League's essence from a robotic, geeky coldness, into a more humanizing, connective, populist persona.

In addition, Oakey's lyrics would shift to an everyday, mainstream-connecting formula of romance thereby "humanizing" the aura of electro-pop -- that is, an electro-pop being more about humanity than machinery.

New Hit Making Formula: with Phil Oakey writing the songs, The Girls singing backup, Martin Rushent programming the rhythms and working with Ian Burden on the bass lines; The Human League now had a solid hit-making formula in place. It also helped that Rushent crafted their synth sounds to fit perfectly within a pop-oriented, accessible context -- non-dark, non-robotic, non-distant.

Dare! (1981): their first blockbuster album. It served as an example of manipulating new technologies by means of a time-honored tradition – using traditional orchestration to create textures for modern synthesizers. Martin Rushent was the man who made this happen. He had learned the art of arranging and voicing of instruments while working under orchestra-leader, Johnny Harris. He took this experience and applied it to cutting-edge technology in the following way: to arrange each individual line [on the synth] to be simple, melodic, and rhythmically articulate. Then, by superimposing these [individual] lines, a new sound emerges where the overall texture is clear, rhythmically vibrant, and sumptuous. In other words, instead of arranging for orchestra, he arranged for machines.

The Roland MC-4 Microcomposer: released in 1981, it was a music sequencer run by microprocessors containing enough connections to control four separate synthesizers. In other words, it was like a central brain. The programmer could control tempo, assign specific pitch intervals, and can also cut and paste. In addition, it allowed the user to program complex note and rhythmic patterns.

Result: the ultimate precision on one hand, and emotional passion on the other – it did not sound robotic and detached like Kraftwerk but rather, [it sounded] lush, tuneful, and romantic.

Don't You Want Me: the classic mega-hit from DARE! – a conventional single using cutting-edge technology (old meets new). It was also the song that gave "The Girls" the most prominence by putting them in the spotlight during the second verse (answering to the Svengali-like character portrayed by Phil Oakey).

Pop Success: at long last, Phil Oakey's dream of a pop-driven, international success had now become a reality, By Christmas of 1981, DARE! had sold over 5,000,000 copies (mostly due to the chart success of Don't You Want Me). It was also their first major success in the US market (while still maintaining their strictly European influences).

1983: following a US tour, and a remix recording of Love and Dancing, The Human League finally released their follow-up: an EP entitled, Fascination! On this EP, were two hits – Mirror Man and (Keep Feeling) Fascination.

They would not release their next full-length album until 1984 – the long anticipated Hysteria, which heralded a more forceful sound [than their earlier releases]. But they would never again, match the massive success of DARE!

Chapter IX: Review

What groundbreaking concert was arranged by The Buzzcocks?

Name the first British post punk band:

    Which David Bowie single (from his *Low* album of 1977) became an inspiration to change their name to Warsaw? In addition, what did the city of Warsaw, Poland symbolize for them?

Who was the literary source (and its author) of their new name, Joy Division?

Name four of Ian Curtis' musical influences;
    1.)
    2.)
    3.)
    4.)

Who was the producer for Tony Wilson's *Factory* label?

    What was his production technique?

What were the 5 main elements of Joy Division's sound?
    1.)
    2.)
    3.)
    4.)
    5.)

    How was the British post-punk sound compare to conventional punk in regard to these elements?

Name their debut album of 1979.

    Describe the cover art of this album.

    Name their final album that they recorded together (as Joy Division).

Briefly describe the state of post-industrial Manchester in the early to mid 1970's.

How did Mark E. Smith transform this scenario into art?

Who were some of The Fall's initial poetic influences when they read poems at Una Baines' apartment?

Name 5 of Mark E. Smith's specific literary influences.

    1.)
    2.)
    3.)
    4.)
    5.)

    List his musical influences.

What were the musical ingredients of The Fall that were sources of their "rawness"?

    What became their resulting sound?

Briefly list the various issues of post-industrial life expressed in their [The Fall's] lyrics.

Name The Falls' debut album of 1979.

    Name the 1982 album that was their most primal and forbidding with abstract "found texts" on the album cover. It's an album that most aficionados consider as The Fall's last great album.

The Smiths transformed post punk from a sparse, synth-driven sound to something else. What was it?

    They expanded British post punk to an American audience. As a result, they turned British post punk into _____.

How did The Smiths make up for the lack of dark, moody, synth-driven sounds?

    Who was the first truly accomplished singer in the punk-influenced tradition?

In the absence of synthesizers, what was Johnny Marr's guitar approach?

    Why would this approach connect with a rock guitar-literate mainstream audience?

Who was Morrissey's high-art literary influence?

       Like the author, what type of wordplay was Morrissey engaged in?

       Why were Morrissey's lyrics controversial?

       Name s singles that were examples of his controversial lyrics.
           1.)
           2.)
           3.)

Which Smiths single became the first British Post-Punk hit in America? (It was from the *Meat Is Murder* album of 1985)

       What was the reason for this song's popularity/exposure?

Which British post punk band injected outside, eclectic influences into post punk?

       Name 3 of those outside, eclectic influences:
           1.)
           2.)
           3.)

Who was the frontman/visionary of Public Image Ltd. (P.i.L.)?

       What were his various musical tastes that were beyond punk?

       Describe Dub.

What was P.i.L.'s debut album of 1978?

       What were 3 conventioinal rock elements featured in this album?
           1.)
           2.)
           3.)

       What did John Lydon's lyrics express?

       Which track – with funky basslines, synthesizer, processed vocals, and heavily produced drums sounds – pointed the way for the shape of things to come?

Metal Box (1979) featured another musical influence on John Lydon. What was it?

What was the name of this album for the American, vinyl LP version of 1980?

The musical, post punk style of this album is a combination of 4 elements. What were they?
    1.)
    2.)
    3.)
    4.)

In the album, *The Flowers Of Romance* (1981), what instrumental sound was no longer a part of the band?

In addition (with the exception of one track), Keith Levene's dissonant guitar shards were no longer a feature in the P.i.L. sound. What did he replace it with?

What became the main musical focus of this album? (In other words, what was left in the absence of bass and guitar?)

What was the "primary" instrument in this album? (In other words, what was this album all about?)

What was "New Pop"?

What was the "idea' behind it?

What 3 influences were added to New Pop in addition to brightness, romantic illumination, and overall healthiness?
    1.)
    2.)
    3.)

Name the three most important New Pop groups.
    1.)
    2.)
    3.)

Who was Scritti Politti's artistic visionary?

Besides attending a Sex Pistols Anarchy Tour concert, who was the other group that inspired Green Gartside to form a band?

What was the idea behind Situationist International (SI)?

What was the "spectacle"?

What was the significance of Antonio Gramsci in terms of this – what did his works revolt against?

Name Scritti Politti's debut single.

What type of bassline was used?

Which British singer inspired Green Gartside's vocals?

During Green Gartside's "turning point", he would completely rethink his band's musical direction. What was that direction?

What was his specific influence for this musical direction?

Who was his lyric influence? (hint: he specialized in "deconstructionist" theories)

What song was Green Gartside's first manifestation of a new pop direction?

What was Scritti Politti's debut album and first UK chart success in 1982?

Name the two New York City-based artists that became Green Gartside's new lifeline.

With these two collaborators, what new musical inspiration would Green Gartside pursue?

What was his artistic goal (of this new inspiration)?

Name the first hit of this new direction.

What was his first US hit?

Name Scritti Politti's 1985 album that accompanied a new dance pop direction.

What was Green Gartside's biggest US hit from this album?

Like Scritti Politti, what other band would accomplish their notoriety through the dance pop, disco-driven medium?

Who was this band's lead singer/frontman and artistic visionary?

Describe Martin Fry's musical influences.

Although Martin Fry steered ABC, into a more pop-driven direction, who was the producer that would guide the group?

What type of sound would he guide the group toward?

Name ABC's debut single of 1981. It became their first British pop hit.

With ABC's lyrics, what was the postpunk influence in the lyrics of songs like *Tears Are Not Enough* and *Poison Arrow*?

What was ABC's debut album of 1982? It was also their first big success in the US.

What type of album was *Beauty Stab* (1983) that launched Martin Fry's new direction?

As opposed to the glossy synth and drum machine sound, what instrument was ABC's new vehicle?

What was the album's first significant hit?

Which Scottish postpunk band revolted against the angst and macho aggression of Scottish Punk?

With their New Pop insurgency, what did they champion?

Who was Orange Juice's original inspiration?

This inspiration was not a typical punk band – what was the difference (between them and a typical punk band)?

Which Subway Sect artist was influential to Edwyn Collins in terms of lyrics?

Instead of rage and anger, what were this artist's words expressing?

Who and what album, influenced Edwyn Collins' retro guitar sound?

What type of guitar did Collins use as a revolt and what type of sound was he after?

How was the disco band Chic influential?

What were the ingredients of Orange Juice's original sound?

Name Orange Juice's 1982 debut single and name the independent label that released it.

Zimbabwe-born Zeke Manyika gave Edwyn Collins a new outlook of possibilities with an exploration of a more complex synthesis. What 2 elements were synthesized?
1.)
2.)

Name their 1982 album that was more artistically ambitious than their previous debut.

The Goth movement was a tradition born out of reaction to both punk and New Pop. What were they attracted to?

What was Goth's musical foundation?

What type of subject matter did Goth lyrics romantically address?

What was the intent behind their lyrics?

What were trying to escape from (through these lyrics)?

Name London's first Goth club that opened in July of 1982.

What was this club a reaction against?

Which band became one of the founding fathers of the Goth-rock movement?

What sort of essence did they create?

What did their lyrics express?

Which single became Goth's first bona fide anthem in 1979?

List 4 signature elements attributed to Goth that are featured in this single.
1.)
2.)
3.)
4.)

Name Bauhaus' debut album of 1980.

What were two singles from this album that became "crossover" hits in the UK?

What artistic attitude did Siouxsie Sioux capture that became the hallmark of the Goth spirit?

While recuperating in a hospital, Siouxsie Sioux discovered her initial inspiration and this inspiration became a platform to accentuate her own individuality. Who was that inspiration?

Following their debut performance, what were Steve Severin's musical influences (they were similar to his postpunk contemporaries). List all 4.
1.)
2.)
3.)
4.)

What did Siouxsie Sioux want the electric guitar to sound like?

What did her vocals sound like?

What was her early attire and what did it evolve into?

Name Siouxsie & The Banshees' debut single released on the Polydor label.

Name their debut album.

Within this album, what did the lyrics deal with?

What 1981 album by Siouxsie & The Banshees was recognized as their most poignant Gothic statement?

This album explored several themes that would be forever associated with Goth. List three.
1.)

2.)

3.)

The Birthday Party's loud, angst-driven, cacophonous racket was crafted out of a uniquely American influence. What was that influence?

Who was the main artistic visionary/frontman of The Birthday Party?

    Which Old Testament themes did he use, to go against the anti-religious grain of British postpunk?

What was the musical style of The Birthday Party?

    Describe Nick Cave's vocal style.

    What were the electric guitar's stylistic elements?

Name The Birthday Party's debut album of 1981.

    In the song *Zoo Music Girl*, what were several musical elements that accentuated Nick Cave's idol worship (adding a voodoo rite/Gothic-like Caribbean essence)?

Name the 1982 album that marked The Birthday Party's apex of their extreme Gothic approach.

    Describe the album's sound.

    In *Big Jesus Trashcan*, the lyrics were a cryptic exposé of a very American theme. What was it?

Which funk-derived aesthetic would the band Killing Joke embrace?

    After stripped way disco's shiny, burnished pop surface, what did they replace it with?

Who was Killing Joke's greatest postpunk influence?

Name Killing Joke's debut single from 1980.

    This single would become the first to anticipate a late 80's sound of Ministry and Big Black. What was that sound?

323

What was Killing Joke's last great album of 1981 with their original lineup?

In the wake of their P.i.L. influences slipping away, what emerged as their new sound in regard to the following:

Type of drumbeat:
Geordie's guitar sound:
Coleman's synth treatments:
Vocals:

Which band formed the bridge from Goth rock into Pop?

Who was their frontman/artistic visionary?

What was the basic sound of The Cure's early postpunk style? In other words, describe their early sound.

Name their debut single inspired by Albert Camus' *The Stranger*.

What became the turning point for The Cure in the album, *Seventeen Seconds*?

How did this turning pint change the character of their music?

Unlike their Gothic predecessors or contemporaries, what would The Cure's sound be devoid of?

What was The Cure's first hit on the UK charts?

Following the release of their darkest album to date, Faith (1981), which single became their darkest, most thickly textured Goth statement?

What new direction did their 1985 album *The Head To The Door* unveil?

Which aesthetic centered around synthesizers as the predominant lead instrument?

Who was one of synth pop's first main progenitors?

Who were his three main influences?
1.)

2.)
3.)

Name his band.

What was his game changer that he discovered during a recording session at Spaceward Studios in 1978?

Name Gay Numan's breakthrough album of 1979. It was his first, bona fide synth pop focused album.

Who inspired the science fiction-oriented lyrics?

Name Gary Numan's first #1 hit in the UK.

List several characteristics of this single.

Which 1979 album was the first to be released under Gary Numan's name (instead of Tubeway Army)?

This album possessed his first international hit. What was it?

Lyrics: within the context of his space alien, science fiction subject matter, list several elements that were lying underneath the surface.

Before Gary Numan, which band was the first of the synth pop harbingers?

Name their lead singer/visionary.

By rejecting American influences, to which direction did Ultravox look to?

Following the departure of John Foxx, who became Ultravox's new frontman?

Who were the clientele that frequented The Blitz Club known as?

What was the cultural purpose of The Blitz Club?

Instead of expressing rage and anger, what were the New Romantics all about?

Describe the New Romantics' style of dress.

Name the group that included The Blitz Club's Steve Strange, Midge Ure, and Rusty Egan.

What was their musical style?

Name their debut album of 1980.

Who was synth pop's first international icons and undisputed leaders of the British synth pop movement? They formed in 1977.

Name the producer who came to the rescue of the newly revamped Human League in 1981.

Name the first result of their songwriting collaboration.

What effect did their new backup singers "The Girls" have on their new sound?

What role did Martin Rushent have on Human League's hitmaking formula?

Name their first blockbuster album of 1981.

Name the classic mega-hit from this album.

CHAPTER X: POST PUNK IN AMERICA & THE ALTERNATIVE SOUND

I. POSTPUNK IN THE US: A TALE OF TWO DIRECTIONS. THE FIRST: HARDCORE PUNK
    A.) The Dead Boys (1976: Cleveland, OH): the first harbinger of the hardcore punk sound.
        1.) Personnel: Cheetah Chrome (b. Gene O'Connor) guitar, Johnny Blitz (John Madansky) drums.
            - Their influences: The Stooges, Alice Cooper, and The New York Dolls.
                * Additional personnel: Stiv Bators (b. Steve Bator, 10/22/49, Cleveland; d. 6/4/90, Paris, FRA): vocals, Jimmy Zero (b. William Wilden) guitar, and Jeff Magnum (Jeff Halmagy) bass.
        2.) Chrome and Blitz: when they were with "Rocket From The Tombs", their other band mates were David Thomas and Peter Laughner (the latter two would be in "Pere Ubu").
            - Thomas and Laughner were becoming too artsy for Chrome's and Blitz's aggressive Punk tastes.
                *RESULT: Chrome and Blitz started a new band called: "Frankenstein" (along with Bators, Zero, and Magnum).
                    a.) They moved to New York City and, with the help of Joey Ramone…
                        - Auditioned for Hilly Kristol (proprietor of CBGB).
                    b.) They were hired and as a result, performed there on a regular basis.
        3.) "Young, Loud, & Snotty" (1977): their debut album.
            - Style: raging, aggressive electric guitar onslaught.
                * The first to inject a sense of nihilism into the Punk domain.
                    a.) With shouting-styled vocalizing over an extremely violent metal Punk sound.
                      - This sound was the first to anticipate the coming hardcore sound of the early 80's.

Sonic Reducer
Dead Boys

            - "Sonic Reducer": the opening track that spawned a new direction.
                * The consummate hardcore-harbinger Punk anthem.
    B.) Hardcore Punk: a definition.
        1.) Ingredients: loud, thrashing, and extremely aggressive.
            - A sonic, distortion-laden onslaught.
            - Highly rapid tempos.
            - Shouting, sometimes screaming vocals.
            - Punk at it's most basic, bare bones, extreme, and simple.
                * So simple, that the music itself sounded as if anyone could go on stage and perform it.
            - The recordings sounded with a crude "basement sound" essence.
        2.) The bands themselves had very basic, rudimentary skills.
            - When their skills did eventually develop, their sound would become somewhat more palatable.
                * Without compromising their hardcore ideals.
        3.) A number of important hardcore scenes would develop in the US.
            - The three most important were in Washington DC, Los Angeles, and San Francisco.

II. WASHINGTON DC, DISCHORD, AND THE SCENE THAT CHANGED THE INDEPENDENT RECORDING INDUSTRY
    A.) 1979: the beginning of the DC hard-edged sound.
        1.) Bad Brains: The initial inspiration that spearheaded the DC underground hardcore movement.
            - Personnel: HR (b. Paul D. Hudson, 2/11/56, London, ENG), vocals; Dr. Know (b. Gary Wayne Miller, 9/15/58, Washington, DC), guitar; Darryl Aaron Jenifer (b. 10/22/60, Washington, DC), bass; Earl Hudson (b. 12/17/57), drums.
                * An African American band that started off playing jazz-fusion rock in the mid 70's.

        a.) <u>Jazz-Fusion Rock</u>: A complexed style mixing the rhythmic virtuosity of jazz improvisation with the musical conventions of rock n' roll.

           - Requiring a considerable amount of technical skill.

        b.) Popularized in the mid 70's with artists such as Chick Corea, Stanley Clarke from a group called: *Return To Forever* and Al DiMeola, virtuoso guitarist.

- <u>New Direction</u>: playing reggae and punk.

    * 1977: Dr. Know had grown tired of the "Fusion" complexity.

        a.) Their artistic change-of-heart was inspired by the music of Bob Marley and The Sex Pistols.

           - In their view, Punk and Reggae complimented one another and could appear side by side in performance sets (as was the case in the UK).

    * <u>RESULT</u>: the Reggae/Punk inspiration, along with their highly skilled playing technique ushered in a new sound consisting of:

        a.) High-speed, revved-up, tempos.

        b.) Absolute rhythmic precision within those faster tempos.

        c.) Extreme energy and exhilarating, "in-your-face" emotional passion.

           - These three elements formed the musical blueprint for the DC Hardcore Punk sound.

        d.) <u>Lyrics</u>: A message of righteous political views and Rastafarian spirituality.

Pay To Cum
Bad Brains

    * "<u>Pay To Cum</u>": their first hardcore punk classic.

        a.) Pure hardcore punk fury and energy.

- <u>Inspiring A New Movement</u>: Their message of Rastafarian Spirituality and political message struck a chord with a host of fledgling, DC underground punks.

    * Inspiring these punks to do the same both lyrically and musically.

        a.) One of those who became inspired was <u>Ian MacKaye</u>.

           - <u>MacKaye</u>: felt that the highly energized style of Bad Brains was within his reach (an anyone-can-do-it sound).

                * Especially, for beginning, rudimentary musicians such as himself and his colleagues.

           - This was what inspired him to form his first band called: <u>The Slinkees</u>

                * Other DC area bands such as <u>The Penetrators</u>, <u>The Enzymes</u>, and <u>State Of Alert</u> would follow suit.

2.) <u>The Slinkees</u>: Ian Mackaye, Jeff Nelson, Geordie Grindle, and Mark Sullivan.

    - The rubric of a new band that would chart a new direction.

        * Began by doing rapid speed, punk versions of covers.

B.) <u>The Teen Idles</u> (1980): from the ashes of The Slinkees.

    1.) Same personnel with the exception of Nathan Strejeck (who replaced Mark Sullivan).

        - they would be the catalyst for the development of the DC underground punk scene from a recording perspective.

    2.) <u>Skip Goff</u>: a local record storeowner who gave The Teen Idles advice on how to both record and press records.

Get Up and Go
The Teen Idles

        - He produced The Teen Idles' first two singles.

           * <u>Style</u>: an all-out sonic, amplitude-laden assault with rapid, speedy tempos.

                a.) …from a band with no prior studio experience.

        - <u>RESULT</u>: This experience would lead them to a new studio that would change everything.

    3.) <u>Inner Ear Studios</u>: a basement studio owned by <u>Don Zientara</u>.

           - "Minor Disturbance": a 7-inch EP containing 8 songs.
               * The Teen Idles' first release.
                        a.) Even though the band broke up soon after this release…
                             - the new paradigm was already set in motion.
        - RESULT: The "Dischord" label.
               * The independent label that would serve as a sonic chronicle of the DC underground movement.
                        - Resulting in one of the first, and most important scenes of the development of the early hardcore punk style.
   C.) 1981: The development of the new label.
       1.) Minor Threat: Ian Mackaye's new band. Debuted on December 17, 1980 as the opening band for Bad Brains.
           - At this time, Don Zientara became Ian MacKaye's recording arts mentor.
               * MacKaye: would go on to become Dischord's premiere producer.
                        a.) He produce a slew of local DC punk bands whose common trait was to explore the hardcore punk style in their own way.
                             - They were mostly kids attending either Woodrow Wilson High School of the Georgetown Day School.
                        b.) Thereby making Dischord, the nexus and "face" of the underground DC hardcore punk scene.
      - Minor Threat's style: typical of hardcore Punk.
               * Rapid tempos, aggressive/loud/abrasive sound, screaming and shouting into the microphone.
                        a.) Very simple: 1 to 3-chord structure (on average).
                        b.) Simple, very basic melody lines.
                        c.) An electric guitar wall of distortion.
                           - An aggressive sonic onslaught.
                        c.) With a "recorded in the basement" essence to it's sound.

Straight Edge
Minor Threat

     Philosophy: a lifestyle of no drugs or alcohol consumption (among other things).
               * Exhibited in the lyrics to the song entitled: "Straight Edge".
                   I'm a person just like you
                   But I've got better things to do
                   Then sit around and fuck my head
                   Hang out with the living dead
                   Snort white shit up my nose
                   Pass out at the shows
                   I don't even think about speed
                   That's something I just don't need.

                   I've got the straight edge.

               * RESULT: this philosophy expressed above would spawn the "Straight Edge" movement.
                        a.) Which would spread out to other various underground hardcore punk scenes throughout the US.
      - Other lyrics deal with criticism in a very direct, one on one, confrontational manner (Ian Mackaye addressing society as a "person").

Filler
Minor Threat

               * "Filler": a confrontational view against religion.
                        a.) Between MacKaye and the "representative".
               * "I Don't Want To Hear It":
                        a.) Against dishonesty.
               * "Bottled Violence":
                        a.) Against violence resulting from alcohol abuse.
      - Other songs such as "Stand Up" and "Guilty Of Being White"
               * Fit the same confrontational, I'm-against-it, critical mode.
   D.) Dischord House (1981: Arlington, VA): an old green house where the members of the group, Minor Threat, lived.

1.) And where the Dischord office (in the kitchen) was located.
- Business/artistic philosophy in Henry Rollins' words:
* "Music over marketing, content over profit, and ethics over strategy".
- RESULT: a label without hyperbolic adds, devoted to low prices (always marked on the back label).
* Vision: "To attract listeners, instead of consumers".
2.) Dischord's Importance: a small, independent label with a major impact in getting the hardcore punk sound on the map of rock and roll.
E.) Various other DC bands recorded and produced by the Dischord label.
1.) State OF Alert (SOA): featuring Henry Garfield (a.k.a. Henry Rollins).
- Began association with the DC underground as a roadie for The Teen Idles.
* Would later achieve notoriety as the vocalist/frontman for the LA group, Black Flag.

Public Defender S.O.A.

2.) Other bands included: Void, Scream (with Dave Grohl, future drummer of Nirvana), Government Issue, Red C, Faith, The Rites of Spring, Iron Cross, etc.
- Iron Cross: the first American punk group to adopt the "oi" essence.
* "oi": a mostly dress style from the UK which was basically, the "skinhead" look.
a.) They were the first to mix that look with the hardcore punk sound.
- In the case of most DC bands, they interchanged band members with one another on a regular basis.
F.) Activism: the beginning of Dischord brought, in addition to musical activism, a philosophical and social activism as well as an anti-commercial sentiment.
1.) But it was not exclusive to the DC scene.
- There would be others….

III. OTHER NOTABLE UNDERGROUND PUNK SCENES
A.) Black Flag (Hermosa Beach, CA, 1977): Most notable of the bands from the LA area underground punk scene (others included X, Fear, Germ, and later on, The Circle Jerks).
1.) Original Line-up:
- Gregg Ginn (a.k.a. Dale Nixon), guitar; Chuck Dukowski (b. Gary McDaniel), bass; Keith Morris (a.k.a. Johnny "Bill" Goldstein), vocals: Brian Migdol, drums.
* Chavo Pederast (b. Ron Reyes), vocals, would eventually replace Keith Morris.
a.) Morris moved on to start a new band called: The Circle Jerks in 1980.
* Robo (b. Roberto Valverdi), drums, would eventually replace Brian Migdol.
* Dez Cadena: guitar, vocals, eventually replaced Pederast.
* Henry Rollins: vocals.
* Emil Johnson: drums, replaced Robo.
2.) Black Flag: the first to nationalize hardcore punk and its underground.
- They were the initial trailblazers.
* Hardcore scenes before Black Flag, were disparate, underground localities/ societies spread throughout the US, with virtually no connections between them.
a.) Because Black Flag was the first hardcore punk group to tour nationally; they started providing connections between these disparate [hardcore] scenes throughout the US.
- And in the process, paved the way for other hardcore bands to follow in their wake.
* The key: Networking.
- They were also the first hardcore group to develop an underground, national following that would inspire many others to start their own bands.

- In addition, they also set an example for other punk scenes by being among the first to seriously adopt the Do-It-Yourself (D.I.Y.) ethos.

    * The Idea: if you did not like the system already in place, create a new one of your own. Especially, your own label.

        a.) RESULT: SST Records. Founded by Black Flag guitarist, Greg Ginn.

            - SST: would become one of *the* most important indie labels of the 1980's ushering in many of the most important artists to develop the indie/alternative sound.

                * Some of the artists included: Sonic Youth, The Descendents, Minutemen, and Hüsker Dü.

3.) Influences: for founding member Greg Ginn, punk rock was a rebellious statement against conformity.

    - Because there was a lack of punk recordings, Ginn became initially influenced by the aggressive, abrasive types like the MC5, The Stooges, and Black Sabbath.

        * The rapid tempos of The Ramones were also an important musical influence.

            a.) The combination of aggressive, abrasive influences [mentioned above] mixed with the rapid speeds inspired by The Ramones…

                - …ushered in the creation of the west coast, hardcore sound.

            b.) Inspired by the first Ramones concert he had attended, Ginn started his first band: "Panic"

                - Richard Pettibone: (Ginn's younger brother), suggested that they'd change their name to Black Flag.

                    * After discovering another band by the same [Panic] name.

Nervous Breakdown
Black Flag

    - First Release: *Nervous Breakdown EP* (January, 1979), catalogued as SST #001.

        * It set the initial Black Flag musical blueprint.

            a.) Rapid, quick tempos with loud, abrasive, aggressive electric guitar sound and wailing, angst-driven vocals.

Jealous Again
Black Flag

                - Ginn: abrasive, rhythmically strident guitar work with scratchy, tangled leads and fill-ins.

                - Dukowski: pounding, percussive, rapid machine-like bass playing.

4.) Early Local Concerts: violence-ridden affairs where police and audience members clashed on a regular basis.

    - Because of their notorious reputation for violent concerts, local clubs would not allow Black Flag to perform in their venues.

        * The solution? Road Trip.

            a.) They began touring in the summer of 1979.

                - At first, throughout the west coast then eventually, nationwide.

        * Road Trip: the opening of a new underground performance network that other hardcore punk bands would follow.

            a.) By becoming the first to tour nationally, Black Flag opened the door for other hardcore bands to do the same.

                - Especially by discovering various, small performance venues that allowed such bands to play.

                    a.) And also, to tour as financially cheap as possible.

                        - Including the use of an old, beat-up, rickety van.

5.) <u>Henry Rollins</u>: when Dez Cadena wanted to concentrate strictly on guitar, Henry Rollins was recruited to join Black Flag in mid-tour.

Louie Louie
Black Flag

- He was already a devoted fan of Black Flag and knew their repertoire.
* <u>Spring of 1980</u>: During a Black Flag concert in New York City, Rollins was allowed to jump on stage and sing a tune called "Clocked In".

Clocked In
Black Flag

a.) The rage and anger behind his singing style, impressed the band to the point of giving him the call to join them on tour.
- <u>Damaged</u> (1/1982): Black Flag's debut album and the first recording to include Rollins.

Damaged I
Black Flag

* Featuring slower but no less abrasive sounds.
a.) Beginning the process of Greg Ginn returning to his earlier, initial rock influences of the MC5, The Stooges, and Black Sabbath.
- <u>Reason</u>: a need for expressing rage and aggression without constantly resorting to rapid speeds.
* In other words, rage, anger, and aggression at considerably slower tempos. A new twist on an old expression. It also opened the door for them to do covers of classic garage band tunes (again, in a moderately tempo'd, hardcore manner) as illustrated in *Louie Louie*.

B.) <u>Dead Kennedys</u> (1978, San Francisco, CA): combined hardcore punk with biting political commentary.
1.) <u>Influences</u>: British Punk especially the anti-social recalcitrant nature of <u>The Sex Pistols</u>.
- The British Punk art of the brazen repeated electric guitar riff, which gave the music an element of familiar melodic focus without becoming pop.
* The "in-your-face' rebelliousness was lead by vocalist, <u>Jello Biafra</u> (b. Eric Boucher, 6/17/58, Boulder, CO).
a.) His vampiric sounding voice and his overtly nasty lyrics earned him the ire of the conservative right-wing.
- Who felt that he (i.e. his lyrics/attitude) was dangerous.
- <u>Psychedelic Rock Influences</u>: Especially pertaining to abstract guitar intros in singles such as "Holiday In Cambodia".
* Melodic focus was also a key ingredient.
2.) Personnel: in addition to <u>Biafra</u>, the other original members were <u>Klaus Flouride</u> (b. Geoffrey Lyall): bass, <u>East Bay Ray</u> (b. Raymond John Pepperell): guitar, and <u>Ted</u> (b. Bruce Slesinger) drums.
- Ted would eventually be replaced by <u>Darren H. Pelligro</u> (b. Derron Henley): drums.
3.) "<u>California Uber Alles</u>" (1978): their debut single.
- Definite British Punk influences (especially The Sex Pistols) in this single.

California Über Alles
Dead Kennedys

* In both sound and rebelliousness.
a.) Raging punk guitars supporting a repeated riff conveying a sense of familiarity.
- Rather than the conventional hardcore barrage of distortion.
b.) <u>Jello Biafra</u>: his vampiric vocal sound was also a departure from what would be the conventional hardcore shouting.
- with nasty, rebellious, and offensive lyrics.
* In this case, against then California governor Edmund Brown.

c.) <u>Contrasting sections</u>: sections of minimal, relatively quiet accompaniment vs. sections with the raging, roaring electric guitar support.

    4.) "<u>Holiday In Cambodia</u>" (1978): their second single.
       - Quasi-Psychedelic influenced opening with garage band/reverberated sound and experimental improvisation with sliding guitar overlays.

          * Bass gets matched with guitar in an "all-riff" style of accompaniment.
            a.) Turns into an electric guitar-laden onslaught.
            b.) Like "California Über Alles":
               - a refrain on the title words reminiscent of quasi pop structure.
            c.) Main riff gets developed as song and verses progress.
               - Develops into a musical journey of twists and turns leading to a variety of musical peaks and valleys.
                  * Unlike the bare bones approach of hardcore punk.

    5.) "<u>Fresh Fruit For Rotting Vegetables</u>" (1980): their debut album.
       - It was at this point where Darren H. Pelligro (drummer) joined the group.
          * Following their debut album (which included their first 2 singles mentioned earlier)…
            a.) They formed their own independent label in 1981 entitled: "<u>Alternative Tentacles</u>".

    6.) "<u>Too Drunk To Fuck</u>" (1980): the first hardcore punk hit cracking the UK top 40 at reaching #36.
       - Or for that matter, the first hardcore punk single to crack any top 40 chart.
          *Initially released as a single only, it became part of a later album: "<u>Give Me Convenience Or Give Me Death</u>" (1987).
            a.) It ["Too Drunk…"] was successful as a single even though it was banned from the radio airwaves.

    7.) "<u>Plastic Surgery Disasters</u>" (1982): their second album.
       - It was during this period that the "Alternative Tentacles" label was achieving notoriety among underground audiences and artists.

    8.) "<u>Frankenchrist</u>" (1985): the album that transformed Dead Kennedy's notoriety to outside of the underground.
       - <u>REASON</u>: they were prosecuted under California's anti-obscenity law.
          * Because of a poster that was included with the album in which prosecutors found to be pornographic.
            a.) The poster was a creation of serial artist, <u>HR Giger</u> (Switzerland) entitled: "Penis Landscape #XX"
            b.) Prosecutors claimed that the Dead Kennedys, through this poster, was distributing pornography to minors.
               - The trial, which lasted two years, was eventually dismissed because the jury could not reach a unanimous decision.
                  * Dead Kennedys broke up soon after the dismissal (they would later reunite).

    9.) <u>Dead Kennedys</u>: were the first highly visible hardcore Punk band of the 80's exposing the [hardcore] Punk style to many outside the underground.
       - They aggressively pushed the envelope of decency and in addition…
          *Pushed the envelope of artistry within a style that was not given to much musical depth. In other words, they added compositional depth to the hardcore Punk genre.

C.) <u>Hardcore Punk's Legacy</u>: Emocore (a.k.a. Emo).
    1.) <u>Definition</u>:
       - <u>Lyrically</u>: Emotionally charged lyrics.
          * Introspective , confessional, and personal.

　　　　　　　　　　a.) Subject Matter: includes heartbreak, confusion, searching for a meaning [in life], catharsis, and hope.
　　　　　　　　　　　　- Less macho then hardcore lyrics.
　　　　　- Musically: melodic focus with injection of rock conventions.
　　　　　　　　* Somewhat tuneful, crooning vocalizing (as opposed to barking, yelling, or ranting).
　　　　　　　　　　a.) Slow to moderate tempos.
　　　　　　　　　　b.) Guitar solos.
　　　　　　　　　　c.) Cleaner less distorted chords on the electric guitar.
　　　　　　　　　　　　- Clearer harmonies.
　　　- Attitude: anti-commercialism.
　　2.) Rites of Spring: the first emo band. Founded in the spring of 1984.
　　　　　- Personnel: Guy Picciotto, vocals, guitar; Brendan Canty, drums; Mike Fellows, bass; Eddie Janney, guitar.
　　　　　　　　* Part of the DC underground hardcore scene.
　　　　　　　　　　a.) Goal: to concentrate on a more heartfelt/emotional thing as opposed to aggression.
　　　　　　　　* "Drink Deep": one of their earliest recordings on the Dischord label.
　　　　　　　　　　a.) All of the earmarks of emocore mentioned above are in place.
　　　　　　　　　　　　- Picciotto's approach to croonsmanship: an intense, pleading, melodramatic quality.
　　　　　　　　* Ian MacKaye was one of their most loyal supporters.
　　　　　　　　　　a.) Recording their album on Dischord in 1985 and later, after the group had broken up, an EP of previously unreleased recordings.
　　　　　　　　　　　　- In fact, for a group that held such importance in the pioneering of a new punk-derived genre, they only did 14 performances.
　　　- RESULT: Rites of Spring created the initial music and lyric templates for the Emo sound.
　3.) Fugazi (1987): standardization and continuity of the Emo template that scores of other bands would emulate.
　　　　　- Personnel: Ian MacKaye, guitar; Joe Lally, bass; Guy Picciotto, vocals, guitar; Brendan Canty, drums (the later two were former members of the Rites of Spring).
　　　　　　　　* "Fugazi" acronym: **F**ucked **U**p, **G**ot **A**mbushed, **Z**ipped **I**n.
　　　　　　　　　　a.) A slang term used by American soldiers during the Vietnam War (according Nam, a book by Mark Baker).
　　　　　- MacKaye: was also looking for a new direction away from the aggression of hardcore.
　　　　　　　　* He felt that it had spawned an unintended culture of violence that he was powerless to stop. He wanted a change.
　　　　　　　　　　a.) The inspiration of the Rites of Spring led the way.
　　　- Attitude: a no-frills approach to performances/touring.
　　　　　　　　* No magazine interviews.
　　　　　　　　* Would play exclusively for all-ages shows only.
　　　　　　　　　　- Their set cover-charge: $5 (affordability for everyone).
　　　　　　　　* No Middle Man: Mackaye was manager, booking agent, and advertiser.
　　　　　　　　* NOTE: this D.I.Y. (Do-It-Yourself) ethos was MacKaye's only continuity from his hardcore, "Minor Threat" days.
　　　　　　　　　　- Everything had changed.
　　　- Musically:
　　　　　　　　* New Influences in addition to Rites of Spring: Reggae and Funk.
　　　　　　　　* Slow to moderate tempos.
　　　　　　　　　　a.) Replacing the rapid-fire, high-speed tempos of hardcore.
　　　　　　　　* Sudden Dynamic Contrasts:

Drink Deep
Rites Of Spring

Turnover
Fugazi

a.) From soft to suddenly loud.

b.) From solo instrument to suddenly, the entire ensemble.

c.) Sudden stops to sudden starts.

* Clearer, cleaner guitar chords and conventional melodic lines.

a.) Sung in a crooning, sometimes dramatic approach.

* Lyrics of angst and vulnerability.

a.) With some ecological and political protest added in.

- But not confrontational like hardcore.

Blueprint
Fugazi

* Example: "Blueprint" from Fugazi's debut album *Repeater* (3/90).

a.) Slower tempo, more harmonic focus (i.e. less distortion and dissonance), and more palatable melodies (w/ some harmonic vocalizing).

- Hardcore gives way to less abrasive sound.

* NOTE: these musical aspects became standardized in the Emo genre that would facilitate emulation by countless other artists.

- To Summarize:

* Rite of Spring provided the initial Emocore structure.

* Fugazi standardized that structure and in the process, opened it up to outside (eclectic) influences such as reggae and funk.

a.) While also standardizing sudden dynamic contrasts.

* The next step? Mainstream accessibility.

4.) Sunny Day Real Estate (1992: Seattle, WA): first to define the mainstream Emo style.

- Personnel: Dan Hoerner, guitar, vocals; Nate Mendel, bass; William Goldsmith, drums; Jeremy Enigk, lead vocals.

* Elements that made their brand of Emo mainstream:

a.) Jeremy Enigk's high-registered, soaring melodic vocal quality.

- Adding a more catchy focus to the melody.

* With crooning, underlying sensitivity in his lower-registered melodic lines.

b.) Quiet, instrumental arpeggiations accompanying Enigk's voice in soft passages.

c.) Sudden dynamic contrasts (i.e. soft to loud).

d.) Grunge influences in the loud guitar passages.

e.) Straight-forward rock sounds.

* RESULT: a palatable sound that mainstream audiences could embrace.

- "Diary" (1994, Sub-Pop): their debut album.

* Single-handedly defined the mainstream Emo sound for the 90's.

In Circles
Sunny Day
Real Estate

a.) "In Circles": a single from this album that brilliantly illustrates the standard mainstream elements of Emo.

- A sound that became widely imitated by scores of other "alternative" bands.

IV. THE ROAD TO THE ALTERNATIVE SOUND: 80's (INDIE) STYLE

A.) NO WAVE (1978-80): the ultimate rock rebellion -- an anti-music movement whose mission was to eradicate rock history and re-begin from square one or, in the words of their proponents, "year zero". They wanted to create a clean slate from which all previous, accepted conventions in rock 'n' roll, have been expelled. Although they presented their sound in a punk band format, they synthesized it [that format] with brash, dissonant, noise experimentation -- an extreme experimentation that bore no resemblance to tradition or convention. They hailed from New York City's lower east side.

Attitude: their disdain for punk traditionalism was pointed toward the New York punk bands playing at CBGB and Max's Kansas City. These bands such as Television, Patti Smith, Johnny Thunders Heartbreakers, The Ramones, etc (a.k.a. the first wave) were the object of their [No Wavers'] artistic ire. In the eyes of "first wave", punk was about a "return to something lost" in the face of progressive rock's massive popularity and complexity. (i.e. a return to "garage band" values where rock was simple, fun, and easy to play). In addition, first wave bands represented a rebellion against a mainstream rock culture that focused on commercialism (and show business) as opposed to art.

Response: in contrast, No Wave artists (a.k.a. the second wave) defined radicalism not as a "return" to one's artistic roots but rather, the "obliteration" of those roots. Their shared determination, their unifying principle, was to sever all connections with the past. Although there were other artists who tried a similar disconnect such as The Velvet Underground (a post-modern, garage band approach) or Captain Beefheart (with his mutant blues abstractions) – they both reached back to their [musical] ancestries. No Wave artists on the other hand, acted as if they had no ancestry.

The Irony: although they focused on a clean break from tradition, No Wavers performed through the use of conventional rock instrumentation (guitar, bass, & drums). In other words, they used a traditional platform in order to deliver their anti-art radicalism.

Artistic Background: No Wave artists, like their first wave counterparts, were mostly beginning-level, rank amateur players. And, like some of their punk counterparts, they hailed from artistic disciplines outside of music. Whereas punk artists used conventional harmonic language and song structure, No Wavers invented their own rules. They created their own rules, because they didn't know what the [normal] rules were to begin with -- for none of them, with the exception of James Chance, had ever played an instrument before. As a result [of their beginning-level status], experimentation with the most unorthodox of concepts, was simple and easy to attain.

Experimentation: the easiest starting point was the guitar. They had a fascination with sonic possibilities that the electric guitar had to offer by experimenting with new timbres and noises. One of them was alternate tunings: tuning the guitar strings at their own whim in non-traditional ways – they also made up their own chords that were fingered in contorted, non-traditional ways. The result was an atonal dissonance where guitar chords had an out-of-tune-like of sound. They also played slide guitar by sliding a beer bottle or a knife up and down the strings making dissonant, eerie-sounding noise-chords. The result in all cases was a highly amplified, noise-driven assault.

No Wave Shows: along with their highly amplified noise-ridden onslaught, No Wave performances also involved forms of audience confrontation including physical aggression. The source: Iggy Pop's influence [of audience confrontation] that blurred the line between stage and audience transforming the performance into a "situation" or a "mingling". James Chance, saxophonist and frontman for The Contortions (and Iggy Pop devotee) was notorious in creating melees with the audience where he would get beat up by audience members. In addition to the Contortions, the other important No Wave bands engaging in these confrontational, sonic assaults were Teenage Jesus & The Jerks, Mars, and DNA.

Backgrounds of No Wave Artists: New York City during the late 70's, was a worldwide epicenter of aesthetic border crossings and conceptual "total art". Avant-garde ideas dating back to the 60's from the Fluxus Movement to the Vienna Aktionists had trickled down to art-literate kids in the early 1970's who were interested in expanding their horizons. The idea: to push creative boundaries as far as possible.

Pat Place (The Contortions): was a visual artist who studied painting and sculpture but instead joined the current trend of NYC performance art (a breeding ground for No Wave artists). Other artists who joined the fray were Arto Lindsay and Robin Crutchfield (DNA), and Mark Cunningham (Mars) -- all of whom came from experimental theatre and performance art backgrounds and Lydia Lunch (Teenage Jesus & The Jerks) whose main vocation was poetry.

For the most part, these artists had no prior experience in the playing and performing of rock 'n' roll. But because they arrived from other artistic disciplines, they possessed a more distant/detached approach, which enabled them to use their instruments as tools or foreign objects to be misused, abused, or reinvented.

The Lower East Side: home to the Bohemian No Wave scene, which at the time was cheaper and more crime-ridden than the rival art world of SoHo. In fact, the traditional, upscale, elitist SoHo galleries were their enemy. And since tradition was the enemy to fight against, art became their weapon to exact change. As a result, the concept of No Wave lived between art and anti-art (or rather, between avant-garde art and anti-traditional-art).

The Catalyst: in May of 1978, Artists Space, a gallery in the TriBeCa region of New York City hosted a multi-day festival of underground art bands. The highlights of the festival: Friday and Saturday nights. On Friday: DNA and The Contortions and on Saturday: Mars and Teenage Jesus & The Jerks. This weekend's events – which included an altercation between James Chance (The Contortions) and members of the audience – was attended by Brian Eno. He became inspired enough to produce a No Wave compilation entitled, *No New York* – it only included the "Big 4" (DNA, Mars, The Contortions, & Teenage Jesus) from the lower east side.

Excluded from this compilation were art bands that hailed from the SoHo district [who also had performed at this event]: Theoretical Girls featuring Glenn Branca and The Gynecologists featuring Rhys Chatham -- they would eventually be known, as the "Downtown" artists. Branca's use of No Wave influences, in a more high-art, skillful manner, would be the link between No Wave and it's musical legacy (to be discussed later in this chapter).

Mars: the first of the No Wave bands to form. Personnel: Sumner Crane (guitar, vocals); China (Connie) Burg (guitar, vocals); Mark Cunningham (bass, vocals); and Nancy Arlen (drums).

Tunnel
Mars

They began by using rock conventions but gradually, disposed of these conventions. The first to be expunged was unified tempo, then soon after they disposed of tonality. The catalyst for the latter, alternate tunings on the guitar: either by detuning it, retuning it within songs, or constantly shifting tunings (either within the song or from one song to another).

Helen Forsdale
Mars

Example: in the song *Helen Forsdale*, both Connie Burg's guitar and Mark Cunningham's bass are detuned. And, in an attempt to make their guitars "buzz", the resulting sounds were insect-like sound-swarms (reminiscent of record scratches being revved up). Vocally, Connie Burg's and Sumner Crane's were disturbingly angst-ridden, tortured sing/yell/speech vocalisms that furthered their atonal approach.

NOTE: their dissonant, insane-sounding, non-conventional approach had definitely polarized their audiences. But they went on to inspire another of the No Wave artists who would contribute significantly to the genre…

Teenage Jesus & The Jerks: led by poet, Lydia Lunch (b. Lydia Koch, 1959, Rochester, NY), guitar, vocals. Additional personnel: Gordon Stevenson (bass) and Bradley Field (drums). James Chance was an original member but left to form another band called, The Contortions.

Background: Lydia Lunch, who had never played music before, adopted it because it was the most immediate vehicle for artistic (or, in her case, anti-traditional) expression. Her goal: to completely destroy convention by being, in her words, "coarse, harsh, and bitter". She and her band were able to achieve this [goal] because none of them had played any instrument before so, as a result, they invented their own anti-music style and techniques.

Lunch's Vocal Approach: her one-note shrieking, spastic wail that reeked of angst and outright pain. Her songs were short/minimalistic but primal and brashly dissonant. A standard performance lasted about 10 minutes with hammering beats performed in a tight, well-rehearsed ensemble. Her performance approach was rigid and alienating. She made no eye contact with the audience and insured that other members did the same.

James Chance & The Contortions: the innovators of funk/punk. Personnel: James Chance (saxophone, vocals), Pat Place (slide guitar), Jody Harris (guitar), George Scott III (bass), Adele Bartei (acatone organ), and Don Christensen (drums).

James Chance's Influences: Iggy Pop, James Brown, and Albert Ayler. Unlike the other No wave artists, James Chance was an accomplished, jazz-influenced musician.

The James Brown Influence: *Super Bad Parts 1 &2*, the saxophone solos had an altissimo (extremely high range), shrieking sound of an Albert Ayler type expressive quality (noises from the saxophone for extreme expression) that inspired Chance to delve into the musical world of James Brown.

The Iggy Pop Influence: audience confrontation that transformed both stage and audience into one entity (rather than separate).

Resulting Sound: fast, atonal, angular melodies emanating from James Chance's saxophone. His solos sound spastic over repeated bass and guitar riff repetitions.

The groove's tonal center [in guitar, keyboard, & bass] accompanies his atonal, dissonant, and angular melodic lines. These lines are performed either by shouting, screaming vocals or spastic, jagged (angular) saxophone solos. Characteristic: James-Brown-meets-dissonant-rackety-jagged-sound.

In the James Brown tradition, James Chance took total control by instructing his players on how to play their instruments (which none had ever played before – he felt that novices had "fresh ideas").

RESULT: because of the funk/punk synthesis plus a semblance of tonal center in the accompaniment, The Contortions became the most accessible of the No Wave bands. According to Chance, he created songs by interlocking parts played by each instrument, which was exactly what James Brown had done.

DNA: according to their frontman Arto Lindsay, their musical character was, "Skeletal, stop/start, lots of silences". Personnel: Robin Crutchfield (organ, vocals), Ikue Mori (drums), and Arto Lindsay (guitar, vocals).

Musically: highly abstract and deconstructive with an improvised type of essence. They sounded chaotic but in reality, it was all well rehearsed -- right down to the tiniest detail. Vocally: animalistic bark/growls and tribal-like howling incantations. As students in experimental theatre, they engaged in vocal experimentations & exercises that utilized the voice in many different, unorthodox ways.

Musical Ideas: basic, formalistic, sonic onslaughts as opposed to melodic focus -- with massive use of noisy, and dissonant repetitions. It also carried an "in-your-face" aggressive quality. Instead of sounding like a conventional group, DNA sounded more like one big unified instrument going from one global noise repetition to another. Characteristically, it was a noise-driven, repetitive hypnosis with shouting, aggressive vocalizing – an example of the deconstruction of rock convention.

The Decline of No Wave: although the funk/punk/No Wave hybrid of The Contortions had some crossover/mainstream potential, it still failed to catch on to a wider market. A commercial success for the avant-garde/punk/funk fusion was never realized. No Wave's sound – no matter if it had mainstream potential or not – would never go beyond a small underground inner circle. In some ways, the extremism of No Wave was a cultural/artistic spasm that could only exhaust itself. There were changes in the air: Max's Kansas City had closed, CBGB was becoming more of a rock club, and the Mudd Club (located in TriBeCa) was now the new underground hot spot. The vibe in the New York music scene (now centered at the Mudd Club), was shifting toward music that was fun and danceable.

In 1982, the last remaining No Wave band was DNA and by then, they were only gigging once every 4 months. Thus in 1982, once DNA stopped performing, the movement known as No Wave officially came to an end. By then, No Wave's legacy had already begun the process of a new movement in rock 'n' roll known as "alternative". But first, some background that led to this new process…

"Downtown" (a.k.a. the 3rd Wave): the bridge to No Wave's indelible legacy. Out of the ashes of No Wave's demise in the early 1980's came the so-called "Downtown" artists from SoHo (enemy territory of the No Wavers). These artists such as Glenn Branca and Rhys Chatham became the new symbols of the Downtown school starting in the 1980's (replacing those of the 70's such as Phillip Glass and Robert Ashley). Unlike the No Wavers from the lower east side, Downtown artists were trained and experienced musicians – they would create their own No Wave approach.

Whereas the original No Wavers synthesized a punk band format with extreme noise experimentation and aggressive audience confrontation, Downtown artists took on a more cerebral approach -- the mixing of highly amplified rock instrumentation with specific avant-garde influences such as minimalism (a high art byproduct of the 70's Downtown artists). In addition, they used the No Wave practice of alternate tunings to create a loud, multi-guitar-driven sustained resonance that highlighted shimmering, ringing overtones that clashed dissonantly together. The ringing overtones were presented in a minimalist format completely devoid of melody and punk influences -- they never engaged in audience confrontation.

Glenn Branca (b. Oct. 6, 1948, Harrisburg, PA): began studying theatre at Emerson College in Boston and had an early career in playwriting before entering into the world of music.

Although rooted in experimental theatre, Branca had started out in the punk rock scene before entering into the world of high-art, music experimentation. Following his move to New York City, Branca met composer Jeff Lohn. After working to combine their respective theatre operations – Branca's "Bastard Theatre" and "No Theatre" of Lohn's they decided to form a band called Theoretical Girls. Their first show was at the Experimental Intermedia Foundation – they were soon labeled as a No Wave band (following their performance at Artists Space, they were considered to be the "5th band" in the *No New York*, Brian Eno compilation). After Lohn left the group to (in order to pursue a solo career), Branca formed a new group called The Static. It was at this point, that he began experimenting with a highly amplified, multiple-guitar format.

Multi Guitars: the first of Glenn Branca's works for "guitar orchestra" was *Instrumental for Six Guitars* premiered at Max's Kansas City in the spring of 1979. He eventually began recording his multi-guitar works with a group dubbed "The Ascension Band" which included guitarist Lee Ranaldo and eventually, Thurston Moore (both of whom would form the band, Sonic Youth). For this group, the guitar orchestra was divided like a choir: soprano, alto, tenor, baritone, and bass – each guitar was tuned differently in a non-conventional manner namely: octave and unison tunings (among others).

The Idea: utilize alternate tunings that produced a wide variety of dissonant harmonies resulting from sustained resonances of the vibrating strings (producing an array of ringing overtones). The sustained, ringing resonances of overtones were possible due to the heavy, aggressive downstroking and multi-strumming [on the strings]. This extremely loud, imposing sound was presented within a minimalist, avant-garde influenced format displaying no melodies – and no punk influences. The Result: a high-art aesthetic synthesized over a rock-influenced, guitar foundation.

Legacy: by 1980, with his former band members Lee Ranaldo and Thurston Moore, Glenn Branca's and No Wave's legacy would become sealed in a band would become known, as Sonic Youth – the band who helped launch the alternative movement into motion.

B.) Sonic Youth (1980, New York): the group that nationalized the transformation of American Post Punk into the foundation of a new musical genre called "Alternative".
    1.) Original Lineup:
        - Thurston Moore (b. 7/25/58, Coral Gables, FL): vocals, guitar, bass.
        - Kim Gordon (b. 4/28/53, Rochester, NY): bass, vocals.
        - Lee Ranaldo (b. 2/3/56, Glen Cove, NY): guitar.
        - Ann DeMarinis: keyboards. Vocals.
        - Richard Edson, drums.
            * Their first live performance:
                a.) "The Noise Festival" (Summer 1981, New York): after which DeMarinis left the group.
    2.) Influences: Glenn Branca, Rhys Chatham, The Velvet Underground, MC5, and The Stooges (i.e. avante garde and noise experimentation).
        - Minor Threat: their initial hardcore punk influence (1982).
            * Minor Threat's musical aggression and D.I.Y. organization (Sonic Youth adopted the spirit of hardcore rather than the actual style itself).
                a.) Like Minor Threat, Sonic Youth shunned mainstream commercialism and chose instead to advance via their underground, networking connections.
    3.) Basic Early Style: a combination of No Wave influenced dissonance, alternate tunings, and noise experimentation otherwise known as "Noise Music".
        - Placing an emphasis on instrumental tone colors and varying degrees of dissonant harmonic textures.
            * An arty approach to noise music influenced in part by the New York art culture (like the Velvet Underground, Sonic Youth had a direct connection with the New York art scene).
                a.) Sonic Youth became a rock byproduct of that culture.
        - Alternate Tunings: Furnished by an array of about a dozen guitars on stands behind the group.
            * Configured with different tunings.
                a.) Each song called for a prescribed, specific tuning (instead of having to re-tune between each song, the pre-tuned array of guitars made it easy to go from one song to the next).
        - Timbre Changes: Either drumsticks or screwdrivers wedged beneath the strings.
            * Giving the electric guitar a bell-like, percussive tone.
        - RESULT: a total redefinition of what the electric guitar in rock and roll could do by expanding its sonic vocabulary…
            * …while introducing a new musical landscape into rock and roll.
                a.) This was the seed that marked the beginning of the art-pop sound.
                    - Setting in motion, the development of the "alternative" sound.
            * In the mid 80's: Sonic Youth would take a more conventional approach with solid melodic focus added in (No Wave + "Tunesmithism").

4.) Early Artistic Development:
- "Confusion Is Sex" (1983): their debut album on Glenn Branca's *Neutral* label.
* "(She's In A) Bad Mood": dissonant-laden thick chordal texture inspired directly from No Wave.
a.) With vocal lines/melodic verses inserted between the dissonant chordal riffs and instrumental sections.
* "Inhuman": opens with heavy dissonant, noisy textures.
a.) Then sequeways into a faster tempo with shouted vocal lines (Lydia Lunch influenced) accompanied by thick dissonance.
* RESULT: the introduction of melodic focus mixed with No Wave dissonance/textures presented in an experimental approach.
- "Kill Yer Idols" an EP released on the Zensor label (Germany).
* "Brother James": a continuing process of melodic focus in the guitars with a dissonant sonic landscape.
a.) With shouted vocals from guest artist Lydia Lunch.
b.) More experimentation with electric guitar noise and dissonance.
- "Bad Moon Rising" (1985): where they first combine their No Wave influences with pop-oriented song structures.
* "Death Valley 69": Opens with more melodic focus on the guitars with a groove in the bass line.
a.) Not as experimental-sounding as in previous recordings.
b.) Song Structure more conventional.
c.) Music more repetitive.
* It was at this point where Steve Shelley (b. 6/23/62, Midland, MI) became their permanent drummer.
- NOTE: Although Sonic Youth had delved in some melodic focus and song structure, their music/reputation up to this point was that of an arty "Noise Band" with a very small, limited audience.
* This perception would begin to change beginning with the next set of albums.

5.) Their 3 most seminal albums: "Evol", "Sister", and "Daydream Nation".
- Both "Evol" (1986) and "Sister" (1987) were recorded and released by Greg Ginn's SST label.
* "Daydream Nation" was released on the Blast First-Enigma label.
a.) These 3 albums set the tone for the remainder of Sonic Youth's musical output.
- A turning point in their musical development.
* Solidifying a more conventional, accessible rock approach than in any of their previous albums..
a.) Using pop melodic focus and conventional song structure that will make their music more palatable to a wider, college radio-listening audience (but not mainstream).
- With each album (i.e. *Evol, Sister, Daydream Nation*), their sound becomes more palatable and conventional.
* While maintaining the spirit of no wave.
- "Evol" (1986): where the evolution of No Wave, pop song structures, melodic focus, palatability develop in a more solid direction.
* More Conventional: A result of opening themselves up to more mainstream influences such as Bruce Springsteen, Prince, and Madonna.
a.) At this time, Sonic Youth would begin achieving national exposure due to the following:
- Signing with SST Records: the most powerful label in the indie movement.

Inhuman
Sonic Youth

Death Valley 69
Sonic Youth

- <u>College Radio</u>: the new conduit for the spreading of the indie/alternative style.

    * NOTE: college radio was not mainstream but rather, a more expansive underground audience on a national level.

* Schemata: "<u>Tom Violence</u>"

a.) Sung verses are of conventional song structure.

b.) Instrumental Section:

- Improvisational sounding dissonance, noise elements, and amplitude-laden expressive momentum in the electric guitars.

    * <u>Key</u>: expression was the main focus.

c.) Then a return to the sung verse structure (which they were doing before in "Death Valley 69").

* "<u>Shadow Of A Doubt</u>": a soft, slow tempo with a minimalist repeated melodic fragment on a "prepared" guitar (i.e. wedged with a screwdriver or drumstick under the strings) sounding like a marimba with a tonal essence plus quiet whispered lyrics.

a.) In the middle of the song: dissonant, loud, and thickly textured with shouted vocals of <u>Kim Gordon</u>.

- Again, the Lydia Lunch influence.

b.) Then back to an abbreviated version of the first section.

c.) <u>RESULT</u>: very effective stark contrasts between both the tonal and dissonant sections.

- "<u>Sister</u>" (1987): where conventional tonal-influenced melodies and harmonies become a more (somewhat) regular fixture (in addition to conventional song structures adopted earlier) – while maintaining the Post-Punk/No Wave spirit. In addition, more consistently faster, rocking tempos than their previous norm.

* "<u>(I Got A) Catholic Block</u>": opens with a short rendition of electronic noises reminiscent of a short circuiting fuse-box.

a.) Then proceeds gradually (through guitar noise) into a somewhat conventional sounding repeated guitar riff.

- Familiar riff transforms into the vocal line.

b.) This technique of a dissonant/noise/experimental opening leading into conventional song craft…

- is used in several of the album's songs.

c.) This is also one of several tracks in the album to use religious imagery.

- "White Cross" and "Cotton Crown" are the others.

* "<u>Tuff Gnarl</u>": very tuneful in a pop-styled fashion with traditional pop structure.

a.) But as in all of the songs:

- a semblance of No Wave influence and ideal.

* "<u>Beauty Lies In The Eye</u>": strummed harmonies on the guitars that are tonal but non-tonal (i.e. tonally ambivalent)

a.) Consonant, but not completely.

- Supporting Kim Gordon's speech-singing.

* "<u>Pacific Coast Highway</u>" and "<u>Hot Wire My Heart</u>"

a.) The standard dissonance (ala. No Wave) meets convention.

- but very aggressive and noise laden.

* <u>NOTE</u>: All songs contain dissonant, distortion-laden instrumental sections in contrast with sung/verse sections that are more traditional in nature.

* <u>RESULT</u>: An album making stylistic crossroads between their standard dissonance and more traditional tonal influenced qualities.

Tom Violence
Sonic Youth

Shadow Of A Doubt
Sonic Youth

(I Got A) Catholic Block
Sonic Youth

Tuff Gnarl
Sonic Youth

- "Daydream Nation" (1988): the culmination of Sonic Youth's development into a consistency of palatable songs.

    * "Teen Age Riot": catchy, melodic tunesmith-ism with clear, consonant accompaniment while maintaining their Post Punk spirit and a fast-rockin' tempo.

        a.) Their first hit on the national college radio circuit.

            - Which solidified the new alternative sound as the standard style of rock and roll promoted in college radio.

                * Gradually throughout the 80's, college radio became the outlet for the new emerging alternative sound.

    * RESULT: Sonic Youth was the group that invented the first true "alternative" sound as an influential genre on a national level (when it was really alternative) by laying down alternative's sonic foundation.

        a.) Taking the American Post-Punk sound (i.e. No Wave) and adding melodic focus and palatability to it that would slowly build an audience.

            - Albeit on a limited basis.

- NOTE: there would be two other important examples of groups who would bring additional musical elements into the alternative mix.

    * One would include hardcore Punk influences.

    * The other: sharp contrasts and stop/start dynamics.

        a.) Both would imbue a palatable flair by utilizing pop melodic focus and conventional song structures.

            - And present them within the context of esoteric, punk-derived genres.

    * But before going there, one more Sonic Youth postscript is in order...

6.) DGC (David Geffen Company): would later be known as Geffen Records.

- Sonic Youth signed with DGC (a major record label) in 1990.

    * And in doing so, still managed to maintain their creative independence.

        a.) Thereby establishing the new "norm" for other indie bands to follow (insofar as contracts with major record labels).

    * "Goo" (1990): their first album under DGC.

        a.) A more streamlined sound albeit maintaining the No Wave influenced alternative/indie spirit.

        b.) In support of this album, they became the backup group for the "Ragged Glory" tour of Neil Young.

            - Sonic Youth's first mainstream exposure.

    * "Dirty" (1991): produced by Butch Vig.

        a.) Who also produced Nirvana's breakthrough album: "Nevermind".

    * NOTE: it was Sonic Youth who brought Nirvana to the DGC label and to producer Butch Vig.

        a.) But before focusing on the Nirvana phenomenon,

            - a few more important examples of 80's indie bands that were crucial to the development of the new alternative mix.

A NOTE ON COLLEGE RADIO: by the time of Sonic Youth's *Teen Age Riot*, college radio had already spread its wings throughout the US via low-powered [radio] stations. In fact, it became a vital conduit for indie bands to attract larger audiences, enhance their careers, and solidify their reputations. It was all due to a vacuum – commercial [corporate] radio stations were not sanguine when it came to programing artists who -- by virtue of risk taking -- were more innovative than their mainstream, chart-friendly, pop counterparts. As a result, college radio stepped into the gap by becoming the only place where this new, innovative sound could be heard.

Beginning in the early 1980's, college radio provided a soundtrack for the development the indie sound that would progress and culminate into the alternative explosion of 1991 – the year, the underground went mainstream. Among the first of the bands that made their name (and reputation) via the college radio circuit (starting in the early 1980's) was a band from Minneapolis called Hüsker Dü…

C.) Hüsker Dü (formed in 1979, Minneapolis, MN): the band that was monumental in defining the very nature of "college rock" – a vibrant blend of an extreme, punk-derived aesthetic (in this case, hardcore) with catchy, melodic focus sung in a mostly conventional manner (connecting with a rock-literate audience). Their massive walls of speed and noise, with injected elements of other rock traditions, were key to transporting hardcore [punk] into wider accessibility, while placing themselves as the pied pipers of underground indie rock.

They had also transformed college radio into a new conduit for promoting like-minded bands from independent labels thereby, expanding their audiences.

In 1986, they sparked controversy by becoming the first of the underground bands to jump to a major record label (paving the way for others to follow suit). In addition, they transformed indie labels into quasi prep schools for mainstream, major-label appeal. And, were highly influential in setting a new tone that others like Charles Thompson (of later Pixies fame) would follow namely – the legitimacy of hardcore punk/pop melodic synthesis (that Thompson would eventually inspire on Kurt Cobain).

Personnel: Bob Mould (b. Robert Arthur Mould, Oct. 16, 1960, Malone, NY) guitar, vocals; Greg Norton (b. Gregory James Norton, March 13, 1959, Rock Island, IL) bass, vocals; Grant Hart (b. Grantzberg Vernon Hart, March 18, 1961, St. Paul, MN) drums, vocals.

> Background: Bob Mould was a Beatles fan who also delved into 60's rock – his father bought him used 45 rpm singles for a penny apiece. After transcending metal-based music from his early teen's, he discovered [in his late teens] the big game changer: The Ramones. Their rapid-speed, simple approach inspired Bob Mould to pick up the guitar.

> > 1978: he attended Macalester College in St. Paul, MN and soon after, became disillusioned with the demise of their tradition of 60's era social activism (and politics of the College Republicans). He began hanging out with punk rock fans and attending concerts. He transformed himself into one-man welcoming committee for big name punk artists stopping over during tours.

> > > During his freshman year, he met Grant Hart who, like Mould, had a passion for 60's pop hits. They'd sit together in Mould's dormitory room listening to records for hours on end (Hart noticed how adept his friend was at playing the guitar along with the records).

> > March 1979: Charlie Pine, a keyboardist, had secured a gig at a local, twin cities-area bar but did not yet have a band. He asked Grant Hart to help form a band so Grant recruited his friends, Greg Norton (bass) and Bob Mould. His [Mould's] style was evident from their first rehearsal in that he whipped up a lot of distortion-ladened noise with his Ramones-inspired Flying V guitar.

> > > They started out doing covers of Eddie Cochran, The Buzzcocks, and The Ramones (among others). But once they ditched Charlie Pine, the road to their new artistic progression had begun. With the trio of Mould, Hart, and Norton, the band that would be forever known, as Hüsker Dü was born.

> Early Style: in the summer of 1979, they were playing loud, rapid-tempo'd punk and audiences absolutely hated it – so, in response, they just kept playing faster. Although they had a hardcore punk style, they despised the hardcore punk culture because in their [The Hüsker's] view, these

punks were spoiled white kids pretending to be revolutionaries – it was fake, and the band wanted no part of them.

Reflex Records: their own independent label where some of their earliest singles were released (the name "Reflex" was a reaction against the then dominant, twin cites area record label: Twin/Tone).

Debut Single: *Statues* (1981) – a slow-tempo'd, P.i.L. type of dirgy single that was robotic and distant (it did sell 2,000 copies).

Debut Album: *Land Speed Record*, recorded for only $350. It had 17 songs within a time span of 26 minutes. At this time, they were vying for rapid tempo'd supremacy with an explosive sense of passion.

Pop Sensibilities: Johnny Ramone once said in an interview that The Ramones, "played slow songs quickly" -- although there is a hint of sarcasm in that statement, the concept was not beyond the realm of possibility. Author Michael Azzerad alluded to something similar with The Hüskers by suggesting that – although they were recognized as hardcore -- what they were really playing was folk rock at lightning fast speeds with a wall of electric guitar distortion. Add to that, reckless drumming and ear-splitting amplitude and the picture is complete.

Result: with their folk rock influences, Hüsker Dü injected outside, eclectic elements that would change the face of hardcore punk into something more accessible beyond [hardcore] inner circles and thereby, connecting to a national, college radio-driven, alternative audience. As a result, they began selling more records than their underground counterparts starting with an EP called, *Everything Falls Apart* – released on the Reflex label in January 1983. It was their first release to sell throughout the entire US.

Reason: they were bucking against the conventional hardcore punk doctrine by experimenting with pop tunesmithism. They had grown tired of the entire punk scene and wanted to transcend beyond what they saw, were hardcore's finite, musical restrictions.

Metal Circus (1983): in 1983 Hüsker Dü signed with Greg Ginn's SST label (the first non-Californians to do so) and the immediate result, was a seven-song EP called *Metal Circus*.

Real World
Hüsker Dü

It's Not Funny
Any More
Hüsker Dü

Musically: although they maintained their loud and furiously fast trademarks, their sound was more melodically focused than in any of their previous releases. Oftentimes, Greg Norton's bass carried the main instrumental melody while Bob Mould's guitar blazed the wall of distortion (with some hint of harmonic clarity). It was at this point, that they were further transcending conventional hardcore punk and thereby setting a new standard.

College Radio: with the release of *Metal Circus* in October of 1983, college radio nationwide began playing its tracks and relentlessly pushing the EP. Because of their tunefulness, The Hüsker's sound was connecting to a college radio-based, national audience establishing a new [alternative] formula on college radio (even though they were still hardcore).

When they embarked on their first east coast tour, they were surprised to see so many packed venues. It was at that point when they realized that college radio was the reason – they were already playing the heck out of The Hüskers and would continue to do so for the next several years. In fact, it was this band that established college radio as the new conduit for artists who were not mainstream but were yet appreciated on a national albeit underground level.

Next Phrase: The Great Triumvirate – *Zen Arcade*, *New Day Rising*, and *Flip Your Wig* – their three most important albums. With each album release, their sound became gradually more accessible. By the time of *Flip Your Wig*, (the last of the three) Hüsker Dü was at their most palatable to date.

Transcendence: as previously mentioned, Hüsker Dü had grown tired of hardcore's limitations in terms of both rhythm and harmony and wanted to transcend them – to go beyond the norm. For their next album, they would record songs that they had already been working on during their last concert tour – which made them ready to zip quickly through the recording process (which a lot of saved time and money). It would all begin with a 40-hour session…

Zen Arcade (1984): a double-LP, concept album recorded in one, amphetamine-laced, 40-hour studio session for the price of $3200. This was their true transcendence beyond the hardcore punk dogma with harmonic language expansion and pop melodies that went beyond the conventional [hardcore] norm.

*Turn On
The News*
Hüsker Dü

Story: an adolescent runaway becomes a big city vagabond trying to figure out his role in life. He meets a girl (and hooks up with her), he OD's, lives in a perpetual nightmare, and in the end – it was all a dream (an entire album concept working its way up to a letdown). It's a story of alienation, loneliness, betrayal, and outright emotional pain – a story that many adolescents could realistically relate to.

*Pink Turns
To Blue*
Hüsker Dü

This was also the album that transformed Hüsker Dü into nationally known status while expanding hardcore's exposure and audience well beyond the underground. It also expanded the tentacles of college radio to the point that major labels were starting to take notice. By setting a new standard for the hardcore-derived sound, The Hüskers made pre-Zen Arcade, conventional hardcore punk into something passé, gimmicky, and archaic. In other words, traditional Pre-*Zen* hardcore, was now dated.

*Celebrated
Summer*
Hüsker Dü

New Day Rising (1985): an album where the focuses on melody and rapid-tempo'd, distorted guitars were becoming more coherent – both in terms of tunesmithism and harmonic clarity. They were also vocalizing in a more conventional manner.

*The Girl Who Lived
On Heaven Hill*
Hüsker Dü

Compared to *Zen Arcade*, the songs in *New Day Rising* were more concise with conventional song structures (verse, chorus, verse, etc.), more melodic focus, and more maturely written arrangements (due to their growing musicianship skills). In addition, because of its prominence on college radio, *New Day Rising* sold 30,000 copies *before* Hüsker Dü even went on tour. In essence, this became the first true college radio-based "commercial" album and in the process, Hüsker Dü became SST's top selling band.

Flip Your Wig (1985): the most palatable and accessible of the 3-album triumvirate. Unlike their previous SST albums produced by Spot (b. Glen Lockett, 1951), the Hüskers produced this album entirely on their own – the process took several months to complete (instead of their previously rapid, speed-driven sessions).

*Makes No
Sense At All*
Hüsker Du

As previously mentioned, *Flip Your Wig* became their most accessible, well-recorded,
and consistent album to date – completing the palatability process initiated by *Zen Arcade* and furthered by *New Day Rising*. Released in September 1985, it gave The Hüskers more college radio play than ever – it also became the first album released by an indie label, to reach #1 on the *CMJ* (College Music Journal) charts. They would remain there for nearly six months.

Some tracks on this album, especially *Makes No Sense At All*, saw some crossover into limited airplay on mainstream radio.

Jump To A Major Label: following the success of *Flip Your Wig*, there was an ominous sign – JEM, the most prominent distributor of indie labels, filed for bankruptcy protection. This was a major catalyst for the band to do something that no other college radio/underground indie success had ever done – sign with a major label. That label was Warner Bros. and once Hüsker Dü signed on the dotted line, a shock wave resonated throughout the indie cult community there by marking the end of an era. It had also marked the beginning of the end for the band...

Although Warner Bros. had promised the band complete artistic freedom, the label did not live up to it – especially in regard to managing their affairs. The band had wanted to recruit their own management team but the label wanted instead, to exert their own control [on this matter].

Their debut album on Warner Bros. was *Candy Apple Grey* (1986) -- a mere four months after they recorded *Flip Your Wig*. But unlike the previous triumvirate, *Candy Apple Grey* was a considerably weaker album in terms of artistic expression.

Hardly Getting Over It
Hüsker Dü

Although they still sounded like The Hüskers, it was cleaner, more pop-oriented which included two acoustic guitar songs one being, was *Hardly Getting Over It*. Overall, they had lost that explosive sense of passion that was a vibrant part of their previous classic releases.

In addition, Grant Hart had become a heroin addict and the animosity between the band members had grown considerably. By the time they went on tour in December of 1987 in support of their last album (from this era) *Warehouse: Songs and Stories*, the band had had enough and later on that month, The Hüskers broke up and went their separate ways.

And although this was a sad ending to a great story, their legacy by this time, was already set in stone. Back in the east coast in the city of Boston, in a cold studio situated in an abandoned warehouse, there was another band directly influenced by Hüsker Dü, who would carry on the torch of college radio/indie success and make their success not only in the US, but in the UK as well – they would also become a direct link to punk's eventual crossover to the mainstream American public...

D.) Pixies (formed in 1986, Boston, MA): the band that would make their own unique contribution to the development of the indie/alternative sound. They did it by mixing roaring, (hardcore punk influenced) blistering guitars with conventionally sung vocal lines (with some shrieking added in) and vocal harmonization -- this gave the melody a clear, pop-oriented focus that enabled a potentially esoteric sound (due to abrasive guitars) to become considerably more palatable. In addition, they standardized the use of stop/start sudden dynamic change, which became an indelible part of the indie developmental framework. With some mysterious Latin lyrics/flavors added in, they became one of the most revered and influential acts in the independent music scene.

Original Lineup: Black Francis (b. Charles Michael Kitteridge Thompson IV, Apr. 6, 1965, Long Beach, CA) guitar, vocals; Joey Santiago (b. Joseph Alberto Santiago, June 10, 1965, The Philippines) guitar; Kim Deal (a.k.a. Mrs. John Murphy) (b. Kimberly Ann Deal, June 10, 1961, Dayton, OH) bass, vocals; David Lovering (b. December 6, 1961, Burlington, MA) drums.

Background: Charles Thompson's father owned a bar in the LA region and he listened to a lot of 60's singles from his father's jukebox. He also sought records from used record stores, or by checking them out of the library. Since his mother was a hippie, he heard many folk tunes that would echo with him for years to come. When he was 13, he discovered one of his first important influences – a Christian rocker named Larry Norman who, in the words of Thompson, "Did his own thing" (Thompson would somewhat emulate him as well).

His Teen Years: during his teen years, he hung out with the misfits – he once said that he was part of the, "Listen to odd-music crowd". The oddball music he referred to: 60's records and religious music. He had heard of punk but never listened to it. By the time he began writing for the Pixies, he had already discovered non-punk entities that became highly influential – Iggy Pop (whose inspiration led Thompson to rename himself, Black

Francis), Captain Beefheart, The Talking Heads, Violent Femmes, and Hüsker Dü (in his view, Hüsker Dü was postpunk – more related to hardcore [than conventional punk]).

College Years: as a student at UMass/Amherst, he shared a suite with guitarist Joey Santiago. Before meeting Thompson, he listened to classic rock then went on to David Bowie and Iggy Pop. Once he heard The Velvet Underground's second album, *White Light/White Heat*, he felt that this abrasive, aggressive style was simple and attainable. He also introduced Black Francis to the sound of David Bowie and 70's punk.

Francis' College Tenure: in his own words, during college, he had this, "oddball collection of records" of artists like XTC (*English Settlement*), Violent Femmes (*Violent Femmes*), and Iggy Pop, (*The Idiot*, and *Lust for Life*). He also loved The Cars. In his view, they possessed a gunning vibe that was highly influential [to him] namely -- a rhythmic, clicky type of new wave essence (an example of one of his [Pixies'] Cars-influenced songs – *Is She Weird* from the *Bossanova* album of 1990).

1984: following a student exchange residency in San Juan, Puerto Rico, he returned to Boston to start a band. During this time, he was listening to albums such as *Spotlight Kid* by Captain Beefheart and *Zen Arcade* by Hüsker Dü – he was also continuing his steady diet of Iggy Pop records. At this time, he was writing songs using an acoustic guitar and writing lyrics (at times, while travelling by subway).

Starting The Band: while Thompson and Santiago were working up original songs together, they wanted to recruit a new member (preferably, a bass player). Thompson placed an add in the *Boston Phoenix* saying that he was looking for a harmony – a cross between Peter, Paul & Mary and Hüsker Dü and "please, no chops" (implying that they were not interested in heavy metal players). The only person who answered the call was Kim Deal (it turned out, that Thompson also wanted a female voice). At first, it was not his intention to have a loud band but once drummer David Lovering began beating the daylights out of his drums – they became loud. They started playing gigs throughout the Boston area – especially in a Kenmore Square club called The Rat (short for The Rathskeller). Rich Gilbert, local Boston musician (and alumni of bands such as, The Zulus and Human Sexual Response) once referred to The Rat, as "the CBGB's of Boston".

Fort Apache Studios: founded by Joe Harvard (b. Joseph Incagnoli), Sean Slade, Paul Kolderie, and Jim Fitting. They wanted to capture the sound of a burgeoning, underground Boston scene that centered around The Rat club in the mid/late 1980's. It was during this period that the Pixies would enter the studio together for the first time (at this point, they were influenced by a local group called The Zulus with their weird, unorthodox vocal arrangements).

Locale: Fort Apache Studios was located in an abandoned upper-floor warehouse in the high-crime-ridden, Roxbury district of Boston. They opened in October of 1985 and would cater mainly to Boston-area bands of which the Pixies would be one.

The "Purple Tape" of 1987: a demo tape recorded at Fort Apache Studios in March of 1987 that contained 18 songs and took three days to complete.

Gary Smith: studio manager at Fort Apache, offered free studio time for the Pixies (who were broke at the time) to record a demo tape. The reason: because he saw a big time potential in them -- he told the management team [at Fort Apache] that they would not regret it. The only caveat, was that one of the in-house [sound] engineers had to donate their time -- in response, Paul Kolderie said yes.

<u>4 AD Records</u>: an independent British record company that was owned and operated by Ivor Watts-Russell. He was the first to say yes to the Pixies' demo tape. Gary Smith had been circulating the tape to many different record labels and was rejected by each one until Watts-Russell heard it and agreed to sign them – in his view, they sounded a bit like Violent Femmes. Up to this point, the label recorded mostly Gothic bands like Bauhaus and The Birthday Party.

<u>Come On Pilgrim</u> (1987): Ivor Watts-Russell was the one who decided which songs from the demo tape would be released – he chose eight of them. The result, an album called *Come On Pilgrim*, words that Thompson had ripped off from one of his biggest influences, <u>Larry Norman</u> (who once wrote, "Come on pilgrim, you know he loves you"). Thompson felt that although Larry Norman was a Christian rocker, he was also rebellious in a rock-driven manner (at the age of 14, Thompson had emulated Norman's look and sound).

Released in October of 1987, *Come On Pilgrim* made an immediate impact on the indie record scene garnering critical acclaim from various indie record publications. Stylistically: a more rock version of Violent Femmes plus the hardcore guitar aggression of Hüsker Dü.

The key to the album's initial success: punk-oriented guitars supporting a pop, melodic focus made accessible due to conventionalized singing (with at times, a woman's voice) and harmonization that a wider, rock/pop literate audience could relate to.

Isla de Encanta
Pixies

This is also the introduction of their trademark stop/start sudden dynamic contrast. As illustrated in the selection *Isla de Encanta*, a wall of rapid-tempo'd, hardcore-influenced guitars that suddenly stops and Kim Deal's solo voice appears, then suddenly, the wall of guitars resurface (this sequence is repeated throughout the song).

<u>Surfer Rosa</u> (1988): one of the most influential college rock/indie albums of the 1980's. Six months following the release of *Come On Pilgrim*, they were back in the studio. This time, they would work under the watchful eye of engineer <u>Steve Albini</u> – formerly of the Chicago-based bands Big Black and Rapeman. It was Watts-Russell's idea to recruit Albini in order to help the Pixies with their first proper album (not derived from demo tapes).

<u>Q Division</u>: a Boston-based studio where the album would be recorded. Steve Albini possessed a unique recording vision – to use the natural acoustics of the studio by strategically positioning the microphones, especially for the drums (as opposed to fancy, slick production effects that were artificial) – in other words, natural ambience was what mattered most. He saw himself as an engineer rather than a producer.

Gigantic
Pixies

In addition to "live miking" he had the guitarists use metal picks (instead of plastic), to give their sound an added edge. For songs like the classic, *Gigantic*, he put the amps in a cemented-walled bathroom in order to get a "real", natural echo instead of an artificial – tech based -- studio effect.

Something Against You
Pixies

<u>Result</u>: a raw, potent, muscular sound that was more powerful and aggressive than their previous album. It also marked a new standard in their approach to original songwriting, which featured abrasive, intensive dynamics. *Surfer Rosa* would top the UK indie charts and was highly rated by both *Melody Maker* and *Sounds* magazines as album of the year.

Broken Face
Pixies

Examples: regarding elements of stop/start sudden dynamic change in a song called *Broken Face*, the onslaught of aggressive, roaring guitars suddenly stop and all you hear are solo vocals (ending a phrase). Then the next phrase begins with an abrupt reappearance of the same aggressive wall of guitars (a Pixies trademark).

Where Is My Mind?
Pixies

Slower Tempos: with the song, *Where Is My Mind?* The guitars take on a more melodic-focused, thematic role (as opposed to the roaring, rapid abrasion). An ethereal melody of wooing vocals hovers above the guitars evoking a mystique – it was more of a light, poppy type of song (the polar opposite of their rapid-tempo'd, aggressive/abrasive tracks).

Tony's Theme
Pixies

Anticipation: in a playful, whimsical song called *Tony's Theme*, the Pixies were already anticipating the character of their next album called *Doolittle* (1989). That album would take a tighter, more pop-driven direction with considerably less abrasiveness than *Surfer Rosa.*

E.) <u>Summarize</u>: Pop, melodic focus and conventional song structure were fused with the following esoteric, punk-derived styles by the following bands:
  1.) <u>No Wave</u>:
    - Sonic Youth
  2.) <u>Hardcore Punk</u>:
    - Hüsker Dü
  3.) <u>Stop/Start sudden dynamic change</u>:
    - The Pixies
  4.) In each of these circumstances, no artists had followed these bands to make their respective styles more palatable to a mainstream audience.
    - In other words, no one followed Sonic Youth, Pixies, or Hüsker Dü to close the mainstream deal.
      * In the case of Grunge – another punk-derived esoteric style –
      the results would be totally different.
        a.) Someone would indeed accomplish the mainstream follow-through.

VI. THE ALTERNATIVE EXPLOSION OF THE EARLY 90'S : THE SEATTLE SOUND (a.k.a. GRUNGE)

A.) <u>Green River</u> (1984): the first harbinger of the "Seattle Sound" by introducing the sonic rubric that would later become known as <u>Grunge</u>.
  1.) Personnel: <u>Mark Arm</u> (b. Mark McLaughlin 2/21/62), guitar, vocals; <u>Steve Turner</u> (b. 3/28/65, Houston, TX), guitar; <u>Jeff Ament</u> (b. 3/10/63, Big Sandy, MT), bass; <u>Alex Vincent</u> (b. Alex Shumway), drums.
    - and later on, <u>Stone Gossard</u> (b. 7/20/66, Seattle, WA), guitar.
  2.) Influences: <u>American (Hardcore) Punk</u>, <u>Heavy Metal</u> (a la Black Sabbath), and <u>Blues-Derived Hard Rock</u>.
    - Specific Influences: <u>The Stooges</u> and <u>Aerosmith</u>.
  3.) <u>Style</u>: hard rock/heavy metal riff-laden grooves (sometimes "all-riff") and punk-styled tempos.
    - With shouting, punk-styled vocalizing (and some hard-rock styled legit vocalizing as well).
      * Heavy Metal meets Hardcore Punk.
  4.) "<u>Dry As A Bone</u>" (1987): their second EP (the first was "Come On Down").
    - Produced by Jack Endino and released on the legendary Seattle indie label: <u>Sub Pop</u> (Green River's first release on that label).
      * Stylistically in line with their early style.
      * At this point, Steve Turner was replaced by <u>Bruce Fairweather</u> on guitar.
  5.) "<u>Rehab Doll</u>" (1988): in the opening track, a new sound emerged that would be the shape of things to come.

Forever Means
Green River

- "Forever Means": features a metal-laden, thickly textured chordal sound.
  * This particular sound would be the rubric for Grunge.
- Shortly following this release, Green River broke up but two members would go on to form a new band called Mudhoney…
  * Which would go on to further the development of Grunge (more on Mudhoney later).

The Melvins: the founding fathers of a style that would become known as Grunge. Their debut album, *Gluey Porch Treatments* (1987), was the first grunge album. It marked a synthesis of punk rock, heavy metal, and hard rock influences (the latter including bands such as Kiss and Aerosmith), which formed into grunge.

Echo/Don't
Piece Me
The Melvins

Background: they started out playing covers of The Who and The Jimi Hendrix experience – what is referred to, as their "pre-punk" phase. Once they began their "punk phase", they played rapid-tempo'd hardcore punk. But after everyone else began playing hardcore punk, The Melvins purposefully, played slow tempos in order to make everyone angry. Soon after, they completed the transition to their originality by injecting heavy metal and hard rock influences into the mix.

NOTE: By 1985, bands such as Soundgarden, Green River, Skin Yard, etc. had all adopted this grunge synthesis of punk, hard rock, and heavy metal.

RESULT: The Melvins would add a more heavy-laden chordal sound to the Seattle rubric which would culminate into the Grunge sound that would become familiar to the mainstream.
- This culmination would be further refined in another group which would combine Matt Lukin with two former members of Green River.

C.) Mudhoney (1988, Seattle, WA): featured Mark Arm and Steve Turner from Green River and Matt Lukin from The Melvins (incidentally Ament, Gossard, and Fairweather – the other Green River members – went on to form "Mother Love Bone" and later, Ament and Gossard along with singer Eddie Vedder formed "Pearl Jam").
  1.) Sub Pop's first success story.

Touch Me
I'm Sick
Mudhoney

  - Influences: the hard-rocking sounds of Green River and the Black Sabbath textural influences of The Melvins mixed together…
    * …but with a pop melodic focus and conventional song structure that gained them a wider audience through college radio airplay.
      a.) But not a mainstream audience (in other words, they did not close the mainstream deal).
  2.) Style: highly energized, metal-laden thick textural guitar chords, melodic hooks, and at time, screamed vocals.

Let It Slide
Mudhoney

    - A heavy-metal influence mixed with the energized emotion of American (hardcore) punk.
  3.) Other Influences: basically, The Stooges, Black Sabbath, American Hardcore Punk, and 60's style garage band music.
    - Bands such as Sonic Youth were big fans of Mudhoney.

Good Enough
Mudhoney

  4.) In spite of their groundbreaking sound and their success in the European underground (along with fellow Sub-Pop artists "Soundgarden")…
    - Their would be another band of three people who were devoted followers of The Melvins…
      * That would streamline the Mudhoney sound into something more palatable for mainstream consumption.
        a.) For Mudhoney's uncompromising style was perhaps too esoteric to reach a wider, mainstream audience.

D.) Nirvana (1987, Aberdeen, WA): the band that transformed the grunge style into a mainstream phenomenon – unlike other genres such as no wave (Sonic Youth), hardcore punk (Hüsker Dü), and stop/start sudden dynamic change (The Pixies), Nirvana followed Mudhoney to close the mainstream deal.

Original Lineup: <u>Kurt Donald Cobain</u> (b. Feb. 2, 1967, Hoquiam, WA; d. Apr. 5, 1967, Seattle, WA), vocals, guitar; <u>Krist Anthony Novoselic</u> (b. May 10, 1965, Compton, CA), bass; <u>Aaron Burckhard</u>, drums (he would eventually be replaced by Chad Channing (b. Jan. 31, 1967, Santa Rosa, CA) and then, <u>Dave Grohl</u> (b. Jan. 14, 1969, Warren, OH).

<u>Kurt Cobain</u>: in 1982, Buzz Osborne (The Melvins' guitarist, vocalist, and lead visionary), introduced Kurt Cobain to the world of punk rock. He made a cassette tape compilation that included songs by hardcore punk bands, <u>Flipper</u> (from San Francisco) and <u>Black Flag</u> (from Los Angeles). He also introduced Cobain to other punk influenced bands such as <u>MDC</u> and <u>Butthole Surfers</u>.

Along with fellow Melvins bandmate Matt Luken, Osborne furthered Cobain's [punk] interest The Sex Pistols (an interest that Cobain had up to that point) by introducing him to other punk artists and proto-punks like The Velvet Underground, New York Dolls, Patti Smith, and Richard Hell -- these influences would transform Kurt Cobain into a devoted punk artist (especially after hearing the nasty, abrasive sounds of Black Flag's *Damaged II*).

Fecal Matter: Kurt Cobain's first punk band that he formed along with Dale Crover on bass (member of The Melvins), and Greg Hokanson, drums. He recorded his first demo tape [with this group] featuring stylistic elements that would reappear in his sound with Nirvana namely: heavy riffing, melodic hooks, thrash-oriented tempos, and a rugged, somewhat twisted sense of song structure. Fecal Matter was Cobain's first artistic outlet where the seeds of his originality first appeared.

<u>Cobain's First Live Performance</u>: was in 1986 with a band called Brown Towel, which included Melvins members Buzz Osborne and Dale Crover at the GESCO Hall in Olympia, WA.

<u>Krist Novoselic</u>: after he befriended Matt Luken and Buzz Osborne (of The Melvins), they introduced him to punk rock namely, The Sex Pistols, Circle Jerks, and Black Flag. Although he would continue to like Aerosmith and Led Zeppelin – as a result of his punk discovery – Novoselic turned his back on all of his previous likes of metal (which included bands like Iron Maiden and Judas Priest). The punk album that completely sold him to punk was *Generic Flipper* by the San Francisco punk band, Flipper.

When he and Kurt Cobain first crossed paths, they discovered a mutual liking for the same bands. Eventually, they made their first collaboration in a Melvins-oriented collective called Stiff Woodies (they also hung out at the Melvins' practice space).

Following a brief stint as a Credence Clearwater Revival cover band called The Sellouts -- Cobain (drums), Novoselic (guitar), and Steve Newman (drums) – Cobain and Novoselic formed a new band with drummer Aaron Burckhard in 1987. They originally had called themselves Skid Row but also appeared under other names such as Ted Ed Fred, Throat Oyster, Bliss, and Windowpane -- they later settled on Nirvana.

Human Cannonball
Butthole Surfers

Kurt Cobain's Influences: during his early days with Nirvana, his influences were a mixture of post punk bands such as Butthole Surfers, Scratch Acid, and Gang of Four (i.e. art-driven on the one hand, but dissonant sounding on the other). His guitar proficiency had improved considerably since his early hardcore punk days. He was now writing and improvising – the latter of which, helped him to discover new melodies.

His Strength: the eclecticism, which came with an extensive repertoire of covers. This gave Cobain a sense of flexibility in his improvisations when it came to stumbling upon new tunes and melodic hooks.

Bleach (1989): their debut album and first college radio success -- recorded at Reciprocal Studios in Seattle and released June 15, 1989 on the Sub Pop label. In addition to Cobain and Novoselic, Chad Channing was now their new drummer (also credited was guitarist Jason Everman). The album was produced by Jack Endino – architect of the Sub Pop house style and a highly important influence on the establishment of the Seattle-based sound. His goal: to successfully record a band exactly as they sound in live performance (in other words, no slick production techniques that other producers were using).

Floyd
The Barber
Nirvana

The earliest recordings were made during a session in January of 1988. The stylistic approach was a combination of two influences: American Indie Punk and melodically focused hard rock. Of the songs recorded during that session, three of them made it onto the _Bleach_ album – _Floyd The Barber_, _Paper Cuts_, and _Downer_ (the drummer for this particular session was Dale Crover formally of The Melvins).

Love Buzz
Nirvana

Along with the live aura of the record, Kurt Cobain's lyrics dealt primarily with personal angst and written in a minimalist manner: one verse, repeated multiple times. His guitar style carried a punk-meets-hardrock-meets-metal essence (NOTE: "hard rock" is defined as a metal-driven guitar sound with a _pop melodic focus_ whereas "metal" is defined by a focus on the _repeated, amplified guitar riff_. Hard rock is more pop/radio-friendly whereas metal is more about the artistry).

Sub Pop: a record label founded in 1986 by Jonathan Poneman and Bruce Pavitt – two former radio Deejays who shared a passion for the indie-punk sounds. Due to the inexpensive recording sessions of producer Jack Endino, they became _the_ outlet by which the Seattle-based bands would record thereby, adding a pointed, focused cohesion to the Seattle movement.

House Style: hardcore punk-edged guitars synthesized with the tunesmithism of [melodically focused] hard rock. They also had an eye for promotional flair by hiring photographer Charles Peterson for their album covers. Peterson specialized in the action-packed, grainy style of black & white photography that immediately captured the eye of punk/metal fans.

They [Poneman & Pavitt] carefully studied the success formulae of other independent labels from _Sun_, _Stax_, and _Motown_, to more contemporary indie labels such as _SST_ and _Touch & Go_. Their research notwithstanding, by 1991, Sub Pop was on the verge of bankruptcy but the sales of _Bleach_ and Nirvana's next album (on the Geffen label) would not only earn Sub Pop the necessary revenue to survive but also, the financial backing produce other bands.

Exodus: in the wake of Sub Pop's financial problems and rumors that were circulating with regard to their negotiations with major labels such as Columbia for a distribution deal, Cobain felt it necessary for the band to sign with a major label. These labels were aware of a tape that Nirvana had recorded at Smart Studios just outside of Madison, WI (in April of 1990). It was within this tape, that Cobain's vision of punk/metal-meets-pop-melodic focus was first realized.

Sonic Youth: Gold Mountain Entertainment – the same firm that managed Nirvana, managed them. At a time where other major labels were courting Nirvana, Kim Gordon (bass player for Sonic Youth), was encouraging Nirvana to sign with Geffen (DGC) Records. They signed with DCG on April 30, 1991. Their next release would become their first major success…

Nevermind (1991): Nirvana's breakthrough album released by DGC (David Geffen Corporation) on September 24, 1991. In order for Nirvana to sign with Geffen, DGC had to buy out Nirvana's contract from Sub Pop. Geffen Records paid $75,000 for the contract buyout and gave Sub Pop 3 percent of the listed price sales of *Nevermind* (approx. $2.50 for each copy sold).

Impact: this album that marked punk's first crossover to the American mainstream thereby blurring the line between pop and punk in America (for the first time). It was produced by Butch Vig (who also produced the Smart Studios session tape) and engineered by Andy Wallace. It was also the first album featuring their new drummer, Dave Grohl (formerly of the DC hardcore punk band, Scream).

Recorded: May through June of 1991 at Sound City Studios in Van Nuys, CA. Some of the songs were re-recordings from the Smart Studio sessions a year earlier. In these re-recordings, Dave Grohl had emulated Chad Channing's original drum parts.

Background: *Bleach* was not the "heavy sounding" type of album that Cobain had originally intended. The music itself was contained, at times the guitar slightly understated with more emphasis on the vocals and most of all, lacking in catchy melodic focus.

Dichotomy: Kurt Cobain loved the heavier side of guitar-based metal like Black Sabbath but also identified himself with his punk credentials. He became further ambivalent because he also possessed a pop, melodic side that he could not ignore. All he needed was "permission" to explore that pop side without the guilt. He would find that permission from a legendary indie-based album...

Surfer Rosa: the landmark 1988 album by The Pixies that spoke directly to Cobain's ambivalent pop sensibilities. The Pixies' style: roaring, extreme, aggressive guitars supporting pop-melodic, conventionally sung melodies. Before he heard this album, Cobain felt too intimidated to follow his pop-oriented muse. After hearing it, *Surfer Rosa* gave him the confidence – and permission -- to act upon his pop-muse. A muse that he would combine with his punk and metal influences...

Smells Like Teen Spirit: Kurt Cobain's pop/punk/metal realization and the main catalyst for the success of *Nevermind*. The first significant anthem of the post baby boom generation, which -- along with the video -- touched a nerve with the mainstream twenty-somethings. (the idea for the title came from Kathleen Hanna, leading member of the "riot grrl" group, Bikini Kill. She spray-painted the words: "Kurt smells like Teen Spirit" on his apartment wall following a drinking/graffiti-spraying binge).

Smells Like Teen Spirit
Nirvana

Musical Character: piercing, screeching, invigorating, and well written in a conventional singles format with sharp dynamic contrasts and a very catchy chorus (climactic in nature). Verse sections have softer, quieter dynamics with a growing transition that leads to the loud climactic chorus: dissonant, roaring punk-influenced guitars supporting vocalized tunesmithism (synthesis of punk & pop influences) – these soft to loud dynamic changes were a definite Pixies influence.

Lyrics: the obscurity of the lyrics notwithstanding, *Teen Spirit* not only became immensely successful but also, ignited debate as to what, if anything, these vague, muddied lyrics had meant. Some believe that the implied negativity spoke to a disgruntled, mainstream audience of the early 1990's (relative to the way punk had spoken to a disgruntled British audience in the mid 1970's thereby touching a collective nerve).

Landmark Video: directed by Sam Bayer but in concert with the overall, controlling veto power of Kurt Cobain. Many of Cobain's ideas appeared in the video such as the mosh pit, overweight cheerleaders, dim lighting, etc. evoking a sense of darkness and anarchy. This sense of rebelliousness has always been a part of rock 'n' rolls tradition. The difference was that rebellious elements [in this video] were revised with images that connected with the new post-baby-boom generation (such as the band wearing torn-up jeans and flannel shirts).

MTV: with the increase of sales of *Nevermind* and the eventual, constant radio airplay of *Teen Spirit*, MTV was showing this video on a highly consistent basis – from 6 to 7 times in the afternoon, to at least 11 to 12 times a day. It got to a point that one couldn't switch to MTV *without* seeing this video.

RESULT: by late October (1991), *Teen Spirit* reached gold (500,000 copies sold); by late November, the top 40, and during the Christmas holiday season, 70,000 copies sold per day.

NOTE: on the heels of *Teen Spirit's* popularity along with the raw nerve that it touched in the post-baby-boom generation, *Nevermind* unleashed almost overnight, the advent of what became known, as the alternative explosion of late 1991/early 1992. And as earlier mentioned, it marked point where punk crossed over into the American mainstream for the first time.

In Bloom
Nirvana

In the process, Cobain transcended from his initial punk audience into that of the mainstream thereby becoming punk's first American celebrity – the difficulties that he experienced due to this new status of fame would haunt him for the remainder of his life. But it did not mean that he wouldn't take advantage of this newfound notoriety. On the contrary, he saw it as a license or a vehicle, to more independent artistic freedom. He believed that because he made Geffen Records millions of dollars in profits, they would be somewhat tolerant when it came to his vision for a riskier, follow-up project.

NOTE: In the song, *In Bloom*, Cobain addresses his new, mainstream fan by saying that he [the new fan] loves the "pretty songs" and he "likes to sing along, but he knows not what it means". In Cobain's view, the new mainstream fans had no understanding of what Nirvana was truly all about (which was one of Cobain's frustrations about mainstream notoriety).

In Utero (1993): Nirvana's final studio album. In February 1993, Pachyderm Studios, located 50 miles south of the Minneapolis/St. Paul area, would be Nirvana's next recording locale. They traveled there to work with Steve Albini (producer of The Pixies *Surfer Rosa* album, and other artists such as The Breeders, PJ Harvey, and Helmet). Cobain was particularly enamored to the drum sounds of albums that he [Albini] had produced – sounds resulting from skillful microphone placement as opposed to slick production techniques.

The Albini Sound: in Cobain's view, it's the sound that he's had in his head for years. That sound? "No Fi": a natural sound containing no studio effects and no radio-friendly compressed mixes. It was all about using the right microphones in the right places in order to capture the studio's natural acoustics. The key: natural resonance. Even Kurt Cobain's vocals were recorded naturally – without special effects giving the illusion of resonance.

Scentless
Apprentice
Nirvana

RESULT: a back-to-basics approach: something that the band had wanted to do for years. In some ways, Cobain saw *Nevermind* as a sellout. In Steve Albini's words, *Nevermind* was, " a very controlled, compressed radio mix". So for Albini, he wanted to make a record *the way the band wanted it to be* rather than at the producer's whim (in this way, Albini did not see himself as a producer but rather, as a sound engineer).

The resulting sound of *In Utero* was that of a band recorded in a low-tech, No-Fi, authentic "live band" format, as opposed to slick, high-tech studio gloss. This approach was fast-becoming a new trend in the indie rock scene.

Lyrically: synthesizing the nihilism/pessimism of punk lyrics in a more hidden, cryptic format (as opposed to being blatantly direct) with pop melodic focus and punk influenced guitars and vocalizing (shouting). Examples include track such as *Scentless Apprentice, Heart Shaped Box, Serve The Servants,* and *Frances Farmer Will Have Her Revenge On Seattle.*

Final Curtain: The final album of Nirvana was released posthumously in November of 1994 following the untimely suicide death of Kurt Cobain. It was entitled *MTV Unplugged In New York.*

Chapter X: Review

What was the style of their debut album of 1977, *Young, Loud, & Snotty*?

    Name the opening track that became the consummate hardcore-harbinger anthem:

Name the former jazz-fusion rock band that was the initial inspiration for the DC hardcore punk sound.

List two influences that spearheaded their new direction in 1977:
    1.)
    2.)

Name four elements of their new sound:
    1.)
    2.)
    3.)
    4.)

Which important new artist would become inspired enough [by The Bad Brains] to start his own band?

    Name the group that thus artist founded (from the ashes of The Slinkees).

    What was their style?

In which studio did they make their first recording?

    Name their debut EP:

How was Don Zientara influential to Ian MacKaye?

    Name the legendary label founded by Ian MacKaye that served as the sonic chronicle of the underground DC punk scene:

Name Ian MacKaye's next important band (following the Teen Idles):

    What was their basic style that was typical of Hardcore Punk?

    Name four additional specific elements of their style:

1.)
2.)
3.)
4.)

Which lifestyle philosophy did Ian MacKaye champion? (It was the subject of one of his songs):

In regard to other lyrics, how would you briefly characterize MacKaye's approach?

In the words of Henry Rollins, what was Dischord's business/artistic philosophy?

What was their vision?

What was the importance of Dischord?

Which group was the first to tour nationally and thereby, nationalize the hardcore punk sound and opening the networking door for other such bands to follow?

Name the indie label founded by Black Flag members Greg Ginn:

List four of Greg Ginn's musical influences:
1.)
2.)
3.)
4.)

What was Black Flag's first release?

What was Black Flag's initial musical blueprint that was set by this record?

When did Henry Rollins join the group?

Name their debut album which was the first recording to include him:

With Black Flag's debut album, what was the difference in Greg Ginn's writing approach in regard to musical speed?

Who was the first punk band to achieve mainstream visibility/notoriety?

What were their main musical influences?

Name their indie label.

What was the significance of "Too Drunk To #%*@&"?

What type of statement did Dead Kennedys introduce [in an offensive and extreme manner] into hardcore punk?

List at least four elements of Emo (Emocore):
　　Lyrically:

　　Musically:
　　　　1.)
　　　　2.)
　　　　3.)

　　Name the first Emo band:

Which Ian MacKaye group standardized the Emo sound?

　　List their three approaches to sudden dynamic contrasts:
　　　　1.)
　　　　2.)
　　　　3.)

Which band streamlined the Emo sound thereby making it palatable for a mainstream audience?

　　List their five elements:
　　　　1.)
　　　　2.)
　　　　3.)
　　　　4.)
　　　　5.)

What was the mission of the anti-music movement known as No Wave?

　　Although they performed in a punk band format, what type of sounds did they synthesize this format with?

What was the difference of attitudes between the "first wave" and "second wave" artists?

<u>Experimentation</u>: what was the starting point for No Wave artists? (In other words, what was the first instrument they experimented with?)

They had a fascination with sonic possibilities that the electric guitar had to offer. What were 2 of them? (Hint: one was about tunings, the other about chords)
1.)
2.)

Which area of New York City was home to the Bohemian, No Wave scene?

Art became their weapon to exact change. What were they fighting against? (In other words, what was their enemy?)

In May of 1978, what landmark event (located in TriBeCa) became the catalyst that inspired Brian Eno to create a compilation of No Wave artists?

Name that compilation.

Name the four bands that were featured in this compilation.
1.)
2.)
3.)
4.)

List four elements involved in the no Wave approach of Glenn Branca:
1.)
2.)
3.)
4.)

Would you define Branca's No Wave approach as refined?

Who was the first of the No Wave bands?

After disposing of rock conventions, what was the first of these conventions to be expunged?

How did they dispose of tonality (Hint: it had to do with the guitar)

What was Lydia Lunch's artistic goal?

Because neither she nor her bandmates had ever played an instrument before, what artistic goal were they able to achieve? (What sort of rules were they able to make?)

Who were the innovators of funk/punk?

Who were 3 of James Chances influences?
1.)
2.)
3.)

What was the resulting sound emanating from James Chance's saxophone?

Musically, what was the main characteristic of DNA?

What were their vocal characteristics?

Which 2 artists were the symbols of the "Downtown" movement starting in the 1980's?
1.)
2.)

In terms of musicianship (i.e. skill level), what was the main difference between these artists and their no Wave counterparts?

Downtown artists took a cerebral approach (as opposed to their No Wave counterparts) by blending highly amplified rock instrumentation with a specific avant-garde influence. What was that influence?

Name the first of Glenn Branca's works for "guitar orchestra".

What was "the idea" behind his use of alternate tunings? (in one sentence)

With former Ascension Band members Lee Ranaldo and Thurston Moore, their new band would become No Wave's and Glenn Branca's legacy. Name that band.

What movement did they help launch into motion?

What were their avante garde/noise experimentation influences?
1.)
2.)
3.)
4.)

Their hard core punk influence?

What two musical properties did they eventually add in the mid 80's to their No Wave influences that ushered in the initial development of the "alternative" sound?
    1.)
    2.)

List Sonic Youth's three most important albums:
    1.)
    2.)
    3.)

Of the three albums, which one was the most palatable?

Name their first college radio hit:

Name the Minneapolis band that was monumental in defining the very nature of "college rock".

What was college rock a vibrant blend of?

How did Hüsker Dü transform college radio?

In 1986, they had sparked a controversy. What was it?

Who was Bob Mould's big game changer and what did this game changer inspired him to do?

In the summer of 1979, what was their early style?

Name Hüsker Dü's own indie label.

Name their debut album.

With their folk rock influences, what elements did Hüsker Dü inject [into their sound] that would change the face of hardcore punk?

They bucked against the conventional hardcore punk doctrine by experimenting with a particular musical element. What was it?

Name Hüsker Dü's 1983 EP. Although it maintained their loud, furiously fast trademarks, what separated this EP from their previous releases?

Name Hüsker Dü's three most important albums that made up their great triumvirate.
     1.)
     2.)
     3.)

Name Hüsker Dü's first concept album.

     Although this was a concept album about an adolescent runway, what underlying emotions did this album address (that many adolescents could relate to)?

Name their next album from 1985, where their focuses on two musical elements were becoming more coherent. What were those two musical elements?

What was Hüsker Dü's most palatable and accessible album of their 3-album triumvirate?

What ominous sign was the catalyst for Hüsker Dü to jump to a major record label?

     Name that label.

Which Boston-based artist would carry on Hüsker Dü's legacy?

How did The Pixies make their own unique contribution to the development of the indie/alternative sound?

     In addition, what type of dynamic change did they standardize that became an indelible part of the indie developmental framework?

At the age of 13, Charles Thompson discovered his first important influence. Who was this influence?

By the time Charles Thompson began writing for The Pixies, he had discovered non-punk entities that became highly influential. Name 5 of them (the last of which was more related to hardcore [as opposed to conventional punk]}.

    1.)

    2.)

    3.)

    4.)

    5.)

During Black Francis' college tenure, there was another influence that he loved. In his view, this band/influence possessed a gunning vibe that was highly influential [to him]. Name that band/influence.

Name the club that Boston musician Rich Gilbert referred to as "the CBGB of Boston".

    Name the studio that wanted to capture the sound of a burgeoning underground Boston scene centered around this club.

What was the "Purple Tape" of 1987?

What 1987 Pixies album resulted from this tape?

    Stylistically, this album was a more rock version of _____ plus the hardcore guitar aggression of _____.

    What was the key to this album's initial success?

    This album also marked the introduction of their trademark element. What was it? (hint: it was illustrated in the song *Isla de Encanta*)

What was The Pixies' first proper album? It was one of the most influential college/indie rock albums of the 1980's.

    Who was the sound engineer that The Pixies worked with on this album?

    What was the result in terms of sound?

In a playful, whimsical song called *Tony's Theme*, The pixies were already anticipating the character of their next album called *Doolittle* (1989). What was that new direction?

What did grunge have in relation to the mainstream that Sonic Youth, Husker Dü, and The Pixies did not?

American hardcore punk combined with blues-derived heavy metal (a la Black Sabbath) was known as grunge. Name the first harbinger (anticipator) of this style.

Who were the founding fathers of a style that would become known as grunge?

    Name the first grunge album.

    There 3 elements that were synthesized to create grunge. What were those elements?
        1.)
        2.)
        3.)

Which band transformed grunge into a mainstream phenomenon?

    Who were some of the punk bands that Kurt Cobain first became aware of ? (because of Buzz Osborne)

    In addition to The Sex Pistols, what other punk and proto-punk influences would transform Kurt Cobain into a devoted punk artist?

    Name Kurt Cobain's first punk band.

During his early days with Nirvana, who were 3 of Kurt Cobain's post punk influences?
    1.)
    2.)
    3.)

    Why was his eclecticism his strength?

Name Nirvana's debut album of 1989 and the label it was released on.

    What was the essence of Kurt Cobain's guitar style? In other words, what did it carry? (Hint: in the book, the descriptive words are all hyphenated)

Who founded the independent label, Sub Pop?

    Who was Sub Pop's producer and what was the label's "house style"?

Name Nirvana's breakthrough album of 1991 and the label that released it.

What was the impact of this album in regard to crossover?

Which landmark 1988 album by The Pixies gave Kurt Cobain the confidence and permission to act upon his pop muse? (A muse that he would combine with punk and metal influences)

Which single (and it's landmark video) became the main catalyst for the success of *Nevermind's* crossover success?

What new phenomenon did *Nevermind* unleash (on the heels of *Teen Spirit's* popularity) in late 1991/early1992?

What was Nirvana's final studio album?

Who produced this album?

Describe the "No-Fi" sound.

What was the resulting sound of this album?

CHAPTER XI: POST SOUL AND FUNK'S DEVELOPMENT

I. James Brown (b. May 3, 1933, Barwell, SC; d. Dec. 25, 2006, Atlanta, GA): Born in abject poverty in South Carolina but raised in Augusta, GA.

> A.) Childhood: Stealing items out of cars. After he and several of his friends were caught stealing clothes out of cars parked on Broad Street [in Augusta], he was convicted of theft and sentenced to a series of juvenile institutions including the Georgia Juvenile Training Institute (GJTI) and lastly, the Boys Industrial Institute in Toccoa, GA.
>
>> 1.) It was during his incarceration at the Boys Institute that he started a gospel voice quartet and gained a reputation for his musical ability – his nickname was Music Box.
>>
>>> - One day, he spoke across the prison fence to an outsider named Bobby Byrd with whom, he [Brown] would eventually have a life long collaborative partnership.
>>
>> 2.) He was eventually allowed parole, but on two conditions: that he had a hold a steady job and that he could no longer return to Richmond County (where Augusta, GA was located).
>>
>>> - Brown worked for an Oldsmobile dealership called Lawson Motors. Also, as part of the parole deal, he had a sponsor, Bobby Byrd.
>>>
>>>> * He lived with the Byrd family for a brief period before moving into a more long-term stable life with Dora & David Nathaniel.
>
> B.) Mt. Zion Baptist Church: he formed his own gospel vocal group: The Ever Ready Gospel Singers. They performed throughout the Toccoa area.
>
>> 1.) The Avons: Bobby Byrd's vocal group. They began as a gospel group, but switched to secular R&B.
>>
>>> - Their Initial Influences: The Dells and The Moonglows.
>>>
>>>> * James Brown later joined the group, which would eventually be known as The Flames.
>>>
>>> - The Avons (1953): James Brown, Bobby Byrd, Sylvester Keels, Doyle Oglesby, Fred Pulliam, Nash Knox, Baby Boy Scott, and later on, Nafloyd Scott (on the electric guitar).
>>>
>>>> * Influences: The Dominoes (featuring Clyde McPhatter), The Five Royales, The Orioles, The Clovers, and The Five Keys.
>>>>
>>>>> a.) Debut Performance: Bill's Rendezvous Club in Toccoa, GA.
>>>
>>> - Instrumentation: at first, only a piano (Bobby Byrd), then eventually, a crude version of a drum set plus a guitar and small amplifier.
>>>
>>>> * Eventually, James Brown became the lead singer – that's when they named themselves The Flames.
>>
>> 2.) James Brown's Influences: In addition to the previously mentioned groups such as The Clovers and The Moonglows other influential models were Big Joe Turner and especially, Hank Ballard & The Midnighters (they [Ballard & The Midnighters] were the first professional artists that James Brown saw in live performance).
>>
>>> - The Flames: would play in many clubs, dives, and juke joints throughout the South.

Let's Go, Let's Go, Let's Go
Hank Ballard

>>> * They signed on with a manager named Clint Brantly (Little Richard's manager at that time) and the group moved to Macon, GA.
>>>
>>>> a.) Soon after, they became The Famous Flames.
>>>
>>> * Once Little Richard went big time and left Georgia for California, The Famous Flames took over the remainder of his scheduled gigs (at the request of Clint Brantly).
>>>
>>>> a.) James Brown performed covers of "Tutti Fruitti", Hank Ballard & The Midnighters, and Roy Brown. He also started performing his first original tune: "Please, Please, Please".
>
> C.) Recording Contract: After recording a demo tape at the radio station studio of WIBB, Clint Brantly tried circulating it but was constantly turned down.
>
>> 1.) After a lot of radio airplay by DJ Hamp Swain of WBML, Brown took the demo tape to Gwen Kessler of Southend Record Distributing Company in Atlanta.

- She was a former employee of King Records but still had a significant business connection with that label. That business connection was Ralph Bass, a talent scout for King Records.

      * After Kessler played the tape for Ralph Bass, he signed The Famous Flames to a recording contract with King Records (during one of their gigs at Sawyer's Lake in January of 1956).

2.) <u>King Records</u>: Founded in 1945 by Syd Nathan. By the time The Famous Flames had arrived, King was recording R&B artists such as Hank Ballard & The Midnighters, The Five Royales, Bullmoose Jackson, and Wynonie Harris.

Your Only Love
The Five Royales

- <u>Feb. 4, 1956</u>: The Famous Flames' first recording session at King – they recorded "<u>Please, Please, Please</u>" (using sevenths as passing chords) – initially inspired by a song called "Baby Please Don't Go" by The Orioles. Syd Nathan hated the record but decided to release it anyway.

      * <u>March 3, 1956</u>: "Please, Please, Please" was released on the King Records subsidiary, *Federal*.

Please, Please, Please
James Brown
& The Famous Flames

           a.) It eventually sold 1,000,000 copies and reached to #5 on the R&B charts.

That Dood It
James Brown &
The Famous Flames

- "<u>Try Me</u>": After nine subsequent failures including songs such as "That Dood It", "You're Mine, You're Mine", "I Walked Alone", and "Begging, Begging", Brown's 1958 single "<u>Try Me</u>", became his first #1 record on the R&B charts.

      * Before this recording, Syd Nathan no longer had any interest in releasing another James Brown record. In response, James Brown offered to pay (and paid for) for the recording session for "Try Me".

Try Me
James Brown
& The Famous Flames

           a.) James Brown distributed acetates to various radio DJ's and the response was quite favorable. As a result, King Records received 20,000 orders before the actual record was made.

      * At the request of Brown, the song was re-recorded in a more professional manner (the initial recording lacked great session musicians and production). The finished record was released on September 18, 1958.

           a.) It reached to #1 on the R&B charts and #48 on the pop charts. Still, Syd Nathan showed little respect.

- "<u>(Do The) Mashed Potatoes</u>": James Brown had wanted to record an instrumental single to help popularize a dance he was doing called the Mashed Potatoes. Syd Nathan vetoed Brown's request to make the record. (Nathan thought it would be a flop).

      * Brown decided to record on the Dade label under the name of Nat Kendrick & The Swans (Kendrick was Brown's drummer).

(Do The)
Mashed Potatoes
Nat Kendrick
& The Swans

           a.) <u>King Colman</u>: a radio DJ dubbed his voice over Brown's so as to not violate his [Brown's] contract with King Records.

           - Released in February of 1960, "Do The Mashed Potatoes" reached the R&B top ten. Once again, James Brown's foresight out-did Syd Nathan's.

3.) <u>Touring</u>: Throughout the remainder of the 1950's and throughout the early 60's, James Brown & The Famous Flames were touring about 350 days out of the year – most of them as one-nighters.

- <u>1959</u>: He made his successful debut at the legendary Apollo Theatre in New York in a revue headlined by Little Willie John.

      * Eventually, James Brown would become a regular headliner there.

- "<u>Live At The Apollo</u>" (1963): James Brown had wanted to record a live album recorded at the Apollo Theatre but Syd Nathan emphatically rejected the idea.

      * Because Syd Nathan refused the project, Brown paid $5700 of his own money to make the album.

a.) It was recorded on October 24, 1962 but released in January of 1963 and eventually reached #2 on the mainstream pop charts.

- The success of this album proved that there was still a significant part of young white America that still craved a frenzied, free spirited performer that had been missing since Little Richard.

D.) <u>Beginning Of A New Direction</u>: In early 1960, a synthesis of Gospel and Jazz – what he called "rhythm hold" — became his new musical foundation in the song: "<u>Think</u>" (originally released in 1957 by The Five Royales – one of James Brown's early R&B influences).

1.) By 1961, James Brown's approach to rhythm was also influenced by his dancing abilities.

Night Train
James Brown

- "<u>Night Train</u>" (released in March of 1962): an experimentation with shuffle dance rhythms.

* He also experimented with Latin rhythms in a song called: "<u>Good Good Lovin'</u> ".

2.) "<u>Papa's Got A Brand New Bag</u>" (1965): James Brown's breakthrough single – another new musical beginning. Fashioned out of onstage improvisations involving a "give and take" between singer and audience (later recorded at Arthur Smith's Studio in Charlotte, NC).

- <u>A new rhythmic direction</u>: superimposing different repetitive rhythmic layers simultaneously — in other words, a polyrhythmic groove.

Papa's Got A Brand New Bag Pt. 1
James Brown

* <u>Structural Schemata</u>: Different repetitive layers on the guitar, horns, bass, drums, and James Brown's voice.

a.) Instruments normally used for melody (horns, guitar, even voice) are now purely rhythmic instruments.

* <u>New Guitar Sound</u>: "Chank" – A metallic, percussive-like, one-chord rhythm guitar break played by guitarist <u>Jimmy Nolan</u>.

a.) He'd squeeze the strings tightly and rapidly against the fret board creating a non-sustained, ringing type of sound.

* <u>More Bottom</u>: The Bass guitar (played by Bernard Odum) taking on a more prominent role.

a.) The sound itself is more accentuated, more audible, and the driving force behind the pulse of the song (something totally new).

* <u>Traditional Song Structure Replaced By The Vamp</u>:

a.) <u>The Vamp</u>: An originally improvised introductory riff (initial horn blast followed by a repetitive pattern in the accompaniment) was repeated throughout the entire song. In Robert Palmer's words, the Vamp became the song itself.

- Conventional song structure (i.e. Verse, chorus or refrain) was no longer applicable.

- <u>RESULT</u>: The combination of these musical properties marked the initial foundation of a new genre called: <u>Funk</u>.

3.) <u>The JB's</u>: James Brown's band led by bandleader/arranger <u>Pee Wee Ellis</u> who came directly out the Louis Jordan tradition of "Jump Blues". He greatly aided Brown in the initial creation of Funk.

- The JB's incorporated two drummers:

* <u>Primary Drummer</u>: to keep the steady beat.

* <u>Secondary Drummer</u>: to mimic James Brown's dance movements.

a.) Every dance move of James Brown was highlighted by a particular sound on the drums (be it a rim shot, a bass drum kick, or a flam on the snare drum).

- He took this concept of live performance with the secondary drummer into the recording studio.

- <u>Pee Wee Ellis</u>: kept revising old arrangements evolving the James Brown funk sound/structure over the course of multiple performances as well as the test of time.

     * In addition to guitarist Jimmy Nolan and bassist Bernard Odum, other great musicians of The JB's included:

         a.) <u>Fred Wesley</u>: trombone, <u>Maceo Parker</u>: saxophone, <u>Clyde Stubblefield</u> and <u>Jabo Starks</u>: drums.

     * <u>RESULT</u>: The JB's had the tightest band in the business and James Brown insured that it stayed that way.

         a.) By fining his players whenever they missed a note or a rhythm.

4.) "<u>Cold Sweat</u>" (1967): James brown's next landmark single.

Cold Sweat Pt. 1
James Brown

- By this time, one more basic ingredient was added to the funk structure.

     * "<u>On The One</u>": metric accentuation on the downbeat of the measure or on beat one.

         a.) As opposed to the traditional backbeat where the metric emphasis rested on beats two and four.

- <u>The musical focus of "Cold Sweat"</u>: tight polyrhythmic groove. Solidifying the James Brown funk style by standardizing its properties.

5.) <u>RESULT</u>: James Brown provided the musical structure for funk.

- But he also created the new norm of "being" a funk singer.

     * For him, being a singer alone was not enough — he had to be a spokesman for a cause. Another legacy to be adopted by other funk artists to follow (more on that later).

         a.) He was also pro-active from a business sense.

E.) "<u>The Hardest Working Man In Show Business</u>": James Brown became in Nelson George's words, "a living symbol of black self determination".

1.) He became the embodiment of what black America could achieve by pursuing his own vision (both artistic and business) even in the face of barriers — both social and personal.

- He single-handedly demonstrated the pay-off of persistence.

     * He also used his personal reputation and prestige to promote his musical creativity and the marketing of that music.

2.) He co-managed his enterprises with manager: <u>Jack Bart</u> and later, with his son, <u>Ben</u>.

- Brown was privy to all decisions made in his business and artistic ventures.

3.) <u>As a self promoter</u>: he cut out the middleman.

- He and his staff contacted the performance venues themselves to arrange dates.

     * Brown and his road managers Alan Leeds and Bob Patton planned the tours themselves using a Rand McNally road map while the staff booked the performances.

- In exchange for promotional consideration, Brown offered black retailers and radio DJ's a piece of the pie (i.e. payola, which was legal).

     * In exchange, local DJ's would coordinate radio time purchases and Brown's main office would buy ad spaces in the local black press.

         a.) All within two weeks prior to his appearances.

- To ascertain whether more promotional efforts were needed by way of free tickets or more radio ads, Brown's office consistently monitored ticket sales.

4.) His usual tour during the mid 60's to the early 70's:

- Five to six one-nighters a week for about nine to eleven months out of the year.

     * It was James Brown's choice to embark on such a taxing schedule.

- The entire "<u>JB Revue</u>" consisted of about 40 to 50 people.

     * As well as all of the equipment (i.e. a few spotlights, amplifiers, etc.)

         a.) The personnel fit into one bus and the equipment into one truck — compact and easy to move.

- As gritty as his style was, James Brown put on a show that was clean enough for the entire family — no swearing/cussing and no overt sexuality onstage.

E.) "<u>Number One Soul Brother</u>": this entails James Brown's new norm establishing the concept in funk that being a singer alone was not enough.

    1.) He celebrated his black identity.

      - He never polished his image or his message to appeal to white audiences.

        * His musical message was straight-forward: "I don't need nobody to give me nothin', just open up the door, I'll get it myself".

    2.) He backed up his words with action in part, by donating millions of his own money into black, inner-city enterprises.

    3.) In the wake of Martin Luther King's assassination, James Brown would become the new de facto spokesperson for black America.

      - In Nelson George's words: "James Brown spoke for every brother on the corner".

        * Hence the title: "Number one soul brother".

    4.) "<u>Say It Loud, I'm Black and Proud</u>" (1968):

      - Brown's most classic example of a message celebrating black identity and awareness — wrapped in an aggressively funk rhythmic format.

    5.) <u>James Brown</u>: as a social activist, would set the tone for subsequent funk singers/artists to do the same.

G.) <u>Musical Legacy</u>: James Brown completely reinvented the concept of rhythm in black music thereby creating a new genre.

    1.) Others inspired by the innovations of James brown would try their own hand at reinventing rhythmic concepts.

II. SLY & THE FAMILY STONE

    A.) <u>Sylvester Stewart</u> (b. 3/15/44, Dallas, TX)

      1.) His family moved to the San Francisco during the 50's.

        - At age 4, he began singing gospel.

          * Beginning his basic musical foundation, which in addition to gospel, would eventually include Soul.

      2.) <u>Vallejo Junior College</u>: where he studied trumpet plus theory & composition.

        - His theory/composition experience may have aided in his eclectic musical writing approach later on (more on that later).

          * During this time, he was musically active in the Bay Area music club scene.

            a.) He would form several short-lived groups with his brother, Fred.

      3.) <u>A Radio DJ</u>: at a San Francisco soul station: KSOL.

        - He was also a producer for <u>Autumn Records</u>.

          * He produced bands such as:

            a.) <u>The Beau Brummels</u>: they had two hits that Sly produced.

              - "Laugh, Laugh" and "Just A Little" both in 1965.

            b.) <u>The Great Society</u>: Grace Slick's first band.

            c.) He also produced artists such as <u>Bobby Freeman</u> and <u>The Mojo Men</u>.

        - He later worked as a DJ for KDIA.

      4.) <u>1966</u>: he started a band called <u>The Stoners</u>.

        - Which included a trumpeter named <u>Cynthia Robinson</u> (b.1/12/46, Sacramento, CA).

          * Again, it was another of his short-lived bands.

            a.) But they would go on to form a new band that would have considerably more durability.

      5.) <u>NOTE</u>: Up to now, two things were developing for Sly Stone (a.k.a. Sylvester Stewart).

        - He was developing artistically in a world far removed from traditional black culture and…

- He wanted to harness the Psychedelic rock elements that were flourishing in the Bay Area at that time.

 * …and mix it up with the gospel and soul feel that he already knew and performed starting in his youth.

B.) <u>Sly & The Family Stone</u>: formed with Cynthia Robinson in 1967.

 1.) Also included: <u>Freddie Stone</u> (b. Fred Stewart, 6/5/46, Dallas): guitar, vocals; <u>Larry Graham Jr.</u> (b. 8/14/46, Beaumont, TX): bass, vocals; <u>Greg Errico</u> (b. 9/1/46, San Francisco, CA): drums; and <u>Jerry Martini</u> (b. 10/1/49, Colorado): saxophone.

 - They would be joined later on by <u>Rosie Stone</u> (b. 3/21/45, Vallejo, CA): keyboards, vocals.

 * Unlike Sly's previous bands, this one made an immediate impact in the Bay Area.

 2.) "<u>I Ain't Got Nobody</u>" (1967): their debut single on the "Loadstone" label.

 - "<u>A Whole New Thing</u>" (1967): their debut album.

 3.) "<u>Dance To The Music</u>" (1968): their second album and the first which would give them notoriety.

 - The title cut would be their first hit reaching #8 on the pop charts and #9 on the R&B.

 * It also solidified their signature combination of musical elements that set them apart and created an original sound.

Dance To The Music
Sly & The Family Stone

 a.) Catchy, easily singable and easily memorable pop melodies.

 - Including catchy, memorable refrains.

 b.) Constant shifting of voicings and instrumentation within a three-and-a-half minute singles format.

 - <u>EX</u>: voices solo and harmonized, with or without instrumental accompaniment.

 c.) A massive funk groove with the bass guitar sound out front in the foreground.

 - A product of bass player <u>Larry Graham</u>: the father of the funk bass who became enormously influential to other funk artists to follow.

 * He was the first to develop this concept (i.e. the bass "out front").

 - He could also play percussively and melodically at the same time.

 * By plucking the bottom strings giving a snapping sound while simultaneously playing the upper strings with his thumb (thereby creating a more conventional melodic sound).

 a.) "Thank You (Falettinme Be Mice Elf Agin)" is one example.

 d.) Rock guitar and Hammond B3 organ solos.

 - <u>Rock guitar solos</u>: derived from Psychedelic music prominent in the Bay Area.

 - <u>Organ solos</u>: no doubt a combination of the psychedelic rock sound and gospel/church influences.

 e.) Horn blasts and horn punctuations.

 - A conventional part of the black music tradition especially that of James Brown.

 f.) The polyrhythmic groove structure laid down by James Brown.

 g.) <u>His message of optimism</u>: "Everyday People", "Dance To The Music", and "Thank You (Falettinme Be Mice Elf Agin)" are examples of his optimism.

Thank You
(Falettinme Be Mice Elf Agin)
Sly & The Family Stone

- His message was also enhanced by the make-up of his band: multi-raced (black and white people) and multi-gendered.
* A reflection of American society.
- RESULT: with the massive funk bass, constant variety within a singles format, elements of rock (especially Psychedelic), horn blasts/punctuations, the James Brown influenced polyrhythmic groove, catchy easily memorable pop melodies, and lyrics conveying a message of optimism…
* Sly Stone created a musical style that anyone could appreciate.
a.) Funk Bass: for black audiences.
b.) Rock Guitar Solos and Pop Tunes: for mainstream audiences.
c.) Polyrhythmic Groove: for dance lovers.
d.) Message of Optimism: for those with a more activist bent.
* RESULT: his music crossed all of the lines and became enormously successful with both black and mainstream audiences. In the process, Sly Stone's success made him funk music's first crossover sensation.
- "Dance To The Music": established all of these parameters that enabled Sly Stone to open up the James Brown structure to an array of outside influences.
4.) "Stand!" (1968): became Sly & The Family Stone's first hit album (the preceding third album, "Life" released earlier that year, was a commercial flop).
- "Stand!" included the song "Everyday People" which was first released as a single…
*…which hit pop chart success reaching #3.
a.) And remaining on the pop charts for over 100 weeks.
- Other hits on this album included:
* "Sing A Simple Song", "Stand!", "I Want To Take You Higher", and "Don't Call Me Nigger, Whitey".
a.) The latter marked the beginning of political commentary in Sly Stone's music.
5.) The success of "Dance To The Music" to the hits from the album "Stand!" solidified Sly Stone's international notoriety.
- By becoming the first great black artist in rock and roll to achieve success under a corporate label: CBS.
* He was signed by Clive Davis who wanted to expand black music operations under CBS after he became president of that label.
- Stone's notoriety was heightened with the release of Sly & The Family Stones "Greatest Hits" album of 1970.
* With hits like "Hot Fun In The Summertime", "Everybody Is A Star", "Thank You (Falletinme Be Mice Elf Agin)".
a.) The album reached #2 on the pop charts.
6.) As mentioned earlier, James Brown provided the funk structure and Sly Stone opened that structure up to outside influences…
- Norman Whitfield: would combine the elements of both artists together.

III. FUNK'S FURTHER DEVELOPMENT: THE MOTOWN INFLUENCE

A.) Norman Whitfield (b. 1944, New York, NY): started off as a pool shark before going into music.
1.) Beginnings: after being stranded in Detroit, due to the breakdown of his father's car (on a return trip from a relative's funeral in California):
- Whitfield remained in Detroit.
* At first, in the pool hall culture.
2.) At age 18: he became a writer and producer for a Detroit label called: Thelma Records.
- Among the artists he wrote and produced for was Richard Street: a member of a group called The Distants.

* Who would later become <u>The Temptations</u>.

     a.) This was where his vision for the group's [Temptations] potential would begin and bear fruit later on.

3.) <u>Motown</u>: he started hanging out at Motown strictly as an observer (much at times, to the chagrin of Berry Gordy), soaking in the recording and production techniques that would produce a quality record.

    - His first Motown gig was in quality control.

      * Rating the records then presenting his feelings about these records to Berry Gordy.

        a.) He [Whitfield] listened to them "cold" (not knowing beforehand who the artists or the writers of a particular song were).

    - <u>1962</u>: He became a songwriter at Motown.

      * He also became a talented arranger and producer.

        a.) Among his early hits:

          - "<u>I Couldn't Cry If I Wanted To</u>" for The Temptations

          - "<u>Too Many Fish In The Sea</u>" for The Marvelettes

          - "<u>Needle In A Haystack</u>" for The Velvettes.

    - <u>1966</u>: Beginning with the hit song, "<u>Ain't Too Proud To Beg</u>", Gordy gave Whitfield exclusive rights to write for and produce The Temptations.

      * Other big singles he wrote and produced for The Temptations were "<u>Beauty Is Only Skin Deep</u>" and "<u>I Know I'm Losing You</u>".

        a.) These hits were crucial for Motown in the late 60's.

      * In the early 70's, the black musical landscape was undergoing a profound change: Funk was now the rubric.

        a.) It was Whitfield who became the catalyst for steering Motown into that funk direction through his work with The Temptations.

          - He would combine two of funk's greatest influences: <u>James Brown</u> and <u>Sly Stone</u>.

4.) <u>Strategy</u>: of the James Brown/Sly Stone combination.

    - <u>Brown's Influence</u>:

      * The use of polyrhythmic Funk groove structure.

      * Lyrics depicting the black American experience or activism (more on the lyrics shortly).

    - <u>Stone's Influence</u>:

      * The constant use of variety within a singles format (i.e. constant shifting of rhythms, voicings, and instrumentation.)

        a.) <u>NOTE</u>: Whitfield would go one better by using the variety of the different vocal ranges of The Temptations, one after the other to add more contrast within a verse.

      * The Larry Graham technique of the bass guitar sound out front.

        a.) In that case, Whitfield would arrange the bass sound to be even heavier than what Graham had been doing, thereby adding more "bottom" to the massive funk groove.

      * In the words of Robert Palmer, Norman Whitfield's goal was to "Out sly Sly"

    - This Brown/Stone combination would be the musical foundation for Whitfield's efforts in taking Motown into the contemporaneous funk domain.

5.) <u>The Lyrics</u>: pertaining to the current state of the decay of the black inner-city neighborhoods at that time.

    - In the wake of the race riot s that were in practically every major city in America throughout the late 60's:

*Ball Of Confusion
(That's What The World
Is Today)*
The Temptations

Papa Was A Rollin' Stone
The Temptations

* Black inner-city neighborhoods were destroyed by burning and looting but there was also another major catalyst: <u>Heroin</u>.

    a.) For the first time in history, the black inner city areas in every major city affected by the race riots were inundated with heroin.

        - It was heroin saturation at a cosmic scale (i.e. mass marketing).

- <u>RESULT</u>: the destruction of a once prosperous urban black culture.

    * Left in it's wake:

        a.) Poverty, unemployment, the rise of single-parent homes, massive drug addiction, and the rise of violent street crime.

            - And yet, mainstream America seemed far removed from these day-to-day inner city realities.

* <u>Norman Whitfield</u>: and other Motown artists such as <u>Stevie Wonder</u> and <u>Marvin Gaye</u> felt that it was their artistic and humanistic responsibility to make mainstream America aware of the black, inner city plight through their music.

    a.) Whitfield's productions with The Temptations would tackle these issues within the Brown/Stone influenced musical context.

        - Songs like: "<u>Cloud Nine</u>", "<u>Runaway Child Runnin' Wild</u>", "<u>Papa Was A Rollin' Stone</u>", and "<u>Ball Of Confusion</u>"

            - All spoke directly – one way or another — to these issues.

6.) With the constant variety within a singles format taken to a greater extreme than Sly Stone (including the variety of different vocal ranges like falsetto, deep bass voice, etc.)

- And the bass guitar sound being considerably heavier and more "out front".

    * In addition, being built upon the polyrhythmic structure inspired by James brown along with the activist message…

        a.) The Temptations under the production and creativity of Norman Whitfield had achieved an original voice within the new funk domain.

            - Thereby bringing Motown up to date on this new "sea-change" in black music.

- But The Temptations under Norman Whitfield were not the only Motown funk artists that Berry Gordy reluctantly handed total artistic control over to.

    * In the next case, it will be the individual lone artist giving out the message, which in some ways, would resonate more than the deliverance of the same message coming from a group context.

        a.) But before we go there, a little change of direction is warranted before we return to the subject of Motown.

B.) <u>Donny Hathaway</u> (b. 10/1/45, Chicago; d. 1/13/79, New York City): would further introduce new elements into black R&B that would resonate throughout the 70's and beyond.

1.) Raised in St. Louis by his grandmother, Martha Pitts, he started singing in her gospel church at age 3.

- Also began learning piano at a young age as well.

    * His prodigious talent eventually earned him a full scholarship to Howard University as a music major in 1964 (following high school).

        a.) This would be crucial to his professional artistic development.

2.) <u>Howard University</u>: not offering jazz studies in it's curriculum, the theory composition studies that it did offer were from a traditional European perspective.

- Hathaway studied music theory and composition in this context by day.

    * While at night, he played jazz in a group called: <u>The Ric Powell Trio</u> (he was also hanging out with Roberta Flack).

a.) His musical development was happening simultaneously both inside and outside of academia.

- In his early professional years, he signed with <u>ATCO,</u> a subsidiary of Atlantic Records.

3.) "<u>The Ghetto</u>" (1969): his debut ATCO single and the record that would serve as the first harbinger of a new black R&B sound.

- Basically, a combination of Hathaway's prior influences:

The Ghetto
Donny Hathaway

* <u>Gospel</u>: gospel-type singing and chanting (especially in and around the repeated words: "The Ghetto").

a.) In addition, gospel-driven vocal ornamentation.

* <u>Subject Matter</u>: a lament of the black inner city plight that slightly predated the Norman Whitfield productions of similar subject matter with The Temptations.

* <u>Latin Influences</u>: a Latin styled beat with a smooth bottom-laden groove.

a.) Played on congas and other Latin or African derived percussion instruments.

- There was no conventional drum set in this song.

* <u>Jazz</u>: use of jazz influences harmonic language thereby expanding the harmonic scope of black R&B music.

a.) In addition, jazz influenced improvisations and melodic treatment on the electric keyboard.

- Adding a dark essence to the music.

- <u>RESULT</u>: this mixture of gospel, jazz, and social commentary that was introduced into black R&B in a funk context...

* ...became the first harbinger of 70's black R&B (and beyond) that is characterized by the musical elements that Donny Hathaway ushered in.

a.) The artists who would standardize these elements into 70's black music were <u>Isaac Hayes</u>, <u>Stevie Wonder</u>, <u>Curtis Mayfield</u>, and...

C.) <u>Marvin Gaye</u> (b. Marvin Pentz Gay: 4/2/39, Wash. DC; d. 4/1/84, Los Angeles): son of a minister from a denomination called, "The House Of God": a combination of Pentecostal Christian and Orthodox Jewish practices – very strict codes of conduct.

1.) Began singing in the church choir at age 3 and eventually became a vocal soloist.

- He later learned to play piano and drums.

2.) <u>By the early 70's</u>: he was about to embark on the second half of his Motown career.

- The first half was marked with pop chart successes in the early to mid 60's such as:

* "<u>Stubborn Kind Of Fellow</u>", "<u>Hitchhike</u>", "<u>Can I Get A Witness</u>", "<u>How Sweet It Is (To Be Loved By You)</u>", and "<u>Ain't That Peculiar</u>".

- <u>In the late 60's</u>: under the direction of Motown songwriting/producing team of Nikolas Ashford and Valarie Simpson:

* "<u>Ain't No Mountain High Enough</u>" (1967) and "<u>Ain't Nothing But the Real Thing</u>" (1968).

a.) He recorded and performed these singles in collaboration with singer, <u>Tammi Terrel</u>.

* His last great hit of the late 60's: "<u>I Heard It Through The Grapevine</u>" (1969).

a.) Although highly successful, Gaye was shaken by the current death of his performing partner Tammi Terrel of a brain tumor.

- <u>NOTE</u>: success notwithstanding, Marvin Gaye was continuously frustrated by the lack of artistic control over his own work.

* Because Berry Gordy was interested only in churning out hits and therefore, would not allow his artists to take creative risks.

a.) But Marvin Gaye wanted to and asked Gordy for that opportunity in which he [Gordy] reluctantly granted.

- The result would culminate in the last great Motown music to come out of Detroit (by this time, Motown had moved it's operations to Hollywood).

2.) "What's Going On" (1971): the album that marks the beginning of Marvin Gaye's second half of his Motown career, and would also become his creative masterpiece.

- Standardization: although "What's Going On" was not the first album in black music to utilize Latin rhythms/timbres, gospel feel, and jazz elements in a funk idiom (all anticipated by Donny Hathaway)...

* It was the first important album to completely standardize these elements thereby making them a permanent fixture in black music of the 70's and beyond.

- Another Standardization: soundtracks of blaxploitation films such as "Shaft" (Isaac Hayes) and "Superfly" (Curtis Mayfield) featured along with the new elements previously mentioned — orchestral string arrangements.

* "What's Going On": would pioneer the use of orchestral string arrangements inspired by blaxploitation soundtracks...

a.) And use it as background accompaniment making it an integral part of the black, funk music landscape.

- Thereby making strings a regular musical fixture.

- Another Soundtrack Inspiration: continuity and unity of a dramatic narrative throughout an entire album.

* Translation: The Concept Album where every track in an album is either connected by the same thread of thought or...

a.) By variants of the same thematic (musical) material.

- Similar to a Song Cycle.

- "What's Going On": became black music's first concept album in the following ways:

* Subject Matter: the consistent theme regarding subject matter dealt with everything bad going on in America at the time.

a.) Police brutality, poverty, and unemployment in the black inner city.

b.) The Vietnam War, destruction of the environment ("the ecology", as was known at the time), and racism.

* Music Matter: at about 1:38 into the opening title track, subordinate theme appears that is used in varied forms in some of the other tracks in the album thereby creating a musical thread.

a.) It begins the second track entitled "What's Happening Brother".

b.) A varied form is background music for "Save The Children".

c.) In "Mercy Mercy Me (The Ecology)", the varied theme appears about 2:14 into the song thereby appearing at the end of the track.

* Music Specifics: jazz oriented chordal language and jazz inspired saxophone solos.

a.) Latin Rhythms with Latin styled percussion instruments.

b.) Gospel Feel: the re-standardization of gospel elements into black music under the funk umbrella.

- Which had been missing in the wake of James Brown's total rhythmic focus.

- With the creation of a concept album as a vehicle of protest and black awareness...

*...along with standardizing the previously mentioned musical elements...

What' Going On
Marvin Gaye

What's Happening Brother
Marvin Gaye

Mercy Mercy Me (The Ecology)
Marvin Gaye

391

a.) "What's Goin On" became one of the most important and influential albums in black music or, for that matter, in rock and roll.

IV. JAMES BROWN REVISITED AND THE RISE OF THE NEW FUNK ATTITUDE

A.) Meeting (late 1969): James Brown's reputation as a stern taskmaster (among other reasons) contributed to a mutiny within his band.

1.) They gave Brown an ultimatum (according to his former road manager Alan Leeds): "They [the band] said that 'If you don't agree to A, B, or C, we won't go onstage tomorrow night' ".

- Among the recalcitrants were Fred Wesley (trombonist) and Maceo Parker (saxophonist).

* Brown, ever the ego-driven alpha male who would not allow anyone to hold him hostage, already had a replacement band ready to step in: The Pacemakers.

2.) The Pacemakers: from Cincinnati, Ohio featuring a young bass player named William "Bootsy" Collins and his brother, guitarist Phelps "Catfish" Collins.

- Bootsy (b. William Collins, 10/22/51, Cincinnati, OH): started his career as a session musician for King Records.

* At age 18, he and The Pacemakers would be recruited by James Brown.

a.) He would add considerably more bottom and aggressive bass rhythms to the James Brown funk mix.

B.) The New Sound: completely focused on rhythm in an aggressive manner with a complete repetitive polyrhythmic groove – even more so than before.

1.) The Reason: a youth-oriented injection of energy – there was more "youth" to his sound.

- For his band was much younger.

2.) The JB's: featuring Bootsy's rhythmically aggressive bass sound out front.

- Adding a sonic bottom resonance never before heard in James Brown's music.

* While other instruments carried a busy, repetitive melodic sense.

a.) Giving great counterpoint with the various simultaneous rhythmic schemes.

- RESULT: the most aggressive rhythmic onslaught that James Brown would have up to then.

Get Up (I Feel Like Being A) Sex Machine
James Brown

* Songs like: "Get Up (I Feel Like Being A) Sex Machine" and "Give It Up Or Turnit A Loose"…

a.) Became staples of this new, aggressive James Brown sound.

- As brilliant as this collaboration was, it lasted for only one year.

* James Brown, ever the control-freak, would not allow Bootsy to expand or explore his [Bootsy's] funk vision while association with The JB's.

3.) "The Houseguests": the band of former JB members including Bootsy.

- Took on the flamboyant MOD look with outrageous costumes and oversized sunglasses.

* They thought they were totally original in the arena of outlandishness, but they weren't.

a.) Everywhere they went, people kept asking them if they had ever seen Funkadelic…

C.) Funkadelic: the vision of writer/producer George Clinton.

1.) George Clinton (b. 7/22/40, Kannapolis, NC): grew up in Plainfield, NJ.

- In his teens, he worked for a local barbershop straightening hair.

* It was in this same venue where he started a vocal group called: The Parliaments – a direct emulation of The Temptations in both sound and presentation.

- <u>Mid 60's</u>: he moved to Detroit and worked for Motown as a staff writer.
   * While there, The Parliaments signed a deal with <u>Revilot Records</u>.
      a.) They achieved their first hit in 1967: "<u>I Wanna Testify</u>" (#3 on the R&B charts, #20 pop).
- He was also hanging out with Detroit's hippie/psychedelic culture.
   * This is where he took an interest in the music of <u>The Stooges</u> and <u>MC5</u>.
      a.) These specific influences would be crucial to Clinton's unique musical development.

2.) <u>Funkadelic</u>: made up of the Parliament vocal group members plus their back-up band.
- Due to an impending lawsuit with Revilot Records, George Clinton was forbidden from using "The Parliaments" name. Hence, the new name.
   * <u>Stylistically</u>: an amalgamation of the Detroit hippie/psychedelic influence combined with the Motown essence.
      a.) <u>Musically</u>: it was Motown meets MC5/Stooges style.
- Once the lawsuit with Revilot was resolved:
   * Clinton was allowed to use the Parliament tag again only it had to be a singular format (without the "s" at the end).
- <u>Inspiration</u>: through watching both MC5 and The Stooges in action, Clinton noticed the wall of Marshall amps as a consistent fixture.
   * This led him to ask a question to himself that would lead to his originality: "Why isn't there any walls of Marshall amps in black music?"
- <u>Resulting Style</u>: acid rock guitars, horny horns, comic book sense of humor, and lots & lots of amplitude.
   * Mixed with Motown inspired vocal melodies and harmonizations.
      a.) Under the Funkadelic umbrella: experimental.
      b.) Under the Parliament umbrella: more pop.
         - Eventually, the two sides would blend together into <u>Parliament/Funkadelic</u>.
   * A very "open" approach to musical development.
      a.) Performance-wise, very open as well.
         - Originally, appearing on stage wearing diapers and later, outlandish costumes (which contributed in part to the comic book humor for each band member would have a comic book name).
            * Mimicking overt sexual acts onstage and smoking cannabis while performing.
         - These outrageous performance tactics were a regular feature of the Funkadelic legend.
   * <u>Musically</u>: although very unique, there was a missing element that Bootsy Collins would contribute to the George Clinton funk mix (once they crossed paths).

3.) <u>Hard Funk</u>: Bootsy brought the James Brown essence into Clinton's Funkadelic mix.
- <u>The JB Staples</u>: polyrhythmic groove, prominent bass sound, and metric emphasis "On The One".
   * <u>Polyrhythmic Groove</u>: superimposed repetitive schemes modeled on the James Brown funk structure.
   * <u>Motown Influence</u>: Motown-influenced, gospel-driven melodic focus.
   * <u>Bass</u>: the sonic booming bass sound of Bootsy Collins. If Larry Graham was the father of the funk bass, <u>Bootsy</u>: took the art of the funk bass to the logical, artistic limit — the funkiest, "out front" bass sound of this era.
   * "<u>On The One</u>": George Clinton would make sure that everyone in the band gravitated to the "one".

Give Up The Funk
Parliament/Funkadelic

a.) <u>RESULT</u>: a massive, pulsating "down beat" that drove into your subconscious. In Clinton's words: "It's better when everybody's on the one".

* <u>Amplitude</u>: a wall of Marshall Amps in the background (another Detroit hard-edged rock influence).

- <u>Another Result</u>: The James Brown vibe mixed with acid rock (Detroit style) influences resulted in a massive funk sound called "<u>Hard Funk</u>".

* By which Parliament/Funkadelic would set a new standard in black music.

- <u>In Addition</u>: with the outlandish costumes, comic book humor, and overt sexuality mixed in…

* George Clinton took funk and turned it into a movement of humor, extravagance, and above all, <u>attitude</u>.

a.) Which in turn, made Parliament/Funkadelic, the funk standard bearer for the remainder of the 70's.

D.) <u>NOTE</u>: During this period, African Americans were the primary audience of funk music.

1.) White, mainstream audiences were not listening to or buying albums of artists such as P/Funk or Marvin Gaye (although few of their singles did see pop chart success).

- It did not mean however, that black artists would not attempt a more listener-friendly sound.

Getaway
Earth, Wind, & Fire

* <u>Case In Point</u>: The group, <u>Earth, Wind, & Fire</u> adopted a pop melodic focused, FM radio-friendly sound that reached a wider audience. — a more streamlined/pop approach to funk.

- But not completely crossover (again, they along with other funk artists, were more popular in the African American community).

V. THE ROAD TO FUNK'S CROSSOVER

A.) <u>Kenny Gamble and Leon Huff</u>: harbingers of a new sound to come.

1.) <u>Kenny Gamble</u> (b. 8/11/43, Philadelphia, PA): singer, lyricist.

<u>Leon Huff</u> (b. 4/8/42, Camden, NJ): pianist, arranger.

- They met as members of a 1950's vocal group called: <u>The Romeos</u>.

* Their first writing/producing collaboration: "<u>The 81</u>" (1964) for a little known group called "Candy & The Kisses".

a.) Another early collaboration included "<u>I Can't Stop Dancing</u>" for Archie Bell & The Drells.

- <u>Gamble and Huff</u>: would further develop through the talents of an arranger named <u>Thom Bell</u> (b. 1941, Philadelphia, PA).

* And their core session group: <u>Ronnie Baker</u> (bass), <u>Early Young</u> (drums), and <u>Norman Harris</u> (guitar).

- "<u>Only The Strong Survive</u>" (1969): written and produced for Jerry Butler.

* Their first major success reaching #4 on the pop charts and #1 on the R&B.

a.) Featuring Butler's smooth singing style.

- <u>Wilson Pickett</u>: for whom Gamble & Huff wrote and produced several songs.

* To present Pickett's raw style in a Gamble & Huff format namely:

a.) Funky bass groove, Latin styled beat/percussion, and horn punctuations.

- "<u>Don't Let The Green Grass Fool You</u>" (1971: #2 R&B, #17 Pop)
- "<u>Engine No. 9</u>" (1970: # R&B, #14 Pop)

- <u>NOTE</u>: The Gamble & Huff style of funky bass grooves, horn punctuations, Latin-styled percussion use, and catchy pop tunes and the success that accompanied this formula…

* Elevated their status as writers and producers in the recording industry.

2.) <u>Kenny Gamble</u>: wanted to use his status in an attempt to emulate Motown by starting his own label.
- Resulting in <u>Gamble Records</u> and also, the <u>Neptune Records</u> label.
* Due to a lack of a reliable and powerful distribution wing, these labels failed.
a.) <u>Needed</u>: a strong, stable business arm that could serve as a highly effective and influential distributor.
- <u>Clive Davis</u>: president of CBS Records stepped in and together with Gamble & Huff, formed the legendary <u>Philadelphia International Records</u> label.
* <u>CBS</u>: would be the distributor and business backbone that allowed Gamble & Huff the freedom they needed to both create and produce.
a.) Working out of Sigma Studios in Philadelphia with recording engineer <u>Joe Tarsia</u>, Gamble & Huff created an array of hits for mainly three different groups (among others):
- <u>The O'Jays</u>, <u>The Stylistics</u>, and <u>Harold Melvin & The Blue Notes</u>.
3.) <u>The "Philly International" Style</u>:
- <u>Lyrics</u>: lyrics dealing with commentary of some kind with a basic message (i.e. lyrics that make one think).

Back Stabbers
The O'Jays

Love Train
The O'Jays

* For the O'Jays: social commentary.
a.) "<u>Back Stabbers</u>", "<u>For The Love Of Money</u>", "<u>Ship A-Hoy</u>"
b.) Also, a message of enlightenment: "<u>Love Train</u>" and "<u>I Love Music</u>".
* For Harold Melvin & The Blue Notes:
a.) "<u>The Love I Lost</u>" (heartbreak), "<u>If You Don't Know Me By Now</u>" (asking for trust), "<u>Bad Luck</u>" (corruption), and "<u>Wake Up Everybody</u>" (spiritual).
* For The Stylistics (under the production control of Thom Bell):
a.) "<u>You Are Everything</u>", "<u>You Made Me Feel Brand New</u>" (love and gratitude).
* <u>RESULT</u>: communicating a message through a classy, sophisticated sound.
- <u>Musical Style</u>: the elements of this classy, sophisticated sound that became the "Philly International" trademark.
* Catchy, easily singable, and easily memorable pop melodies.
* Funky, bass drum focused dance beat.
a.) Featuring Latin-styled percussion sounds and instruments.
* Orchestral sting arrangements: their most notable trademark.
a.) <u>String sound up front</u>: conveying the main instrumental theme.

If You Don't Know Me By Now
Harold Melvin & The Blue Notes

- Also used to musically reinforce the background accompaniment.
- The "up front" nature of the thematic strings help give the Gamble & Huff style, an air of sophistication and a glossy, symphonic sound.
* Catchy, easily memorable, simple lyrics (especially in the refrains) that one could memorize instantly.
- <u>RESULT</u>: a style that would catapult their music to pop crossover success.

The Love I Lost
Harold Melvin & The Blue Notes

* Which caught on in dance clubs all over the America.
a.) Dubbed the "Philly International" style.
* This particular style – illustrated by "The Love I Lost" by Harold Melvin & The Blue Notes — would become the template for a new dance genre that would sweep the nation by storm: <u>Disco</u>.
B.) <u>The Rise Of The Disco Craze</u>: perhaps in no other era in rock and roll has such a dance/cultural mania occurred with such magnitude.

1.) The Music Harbingers: <u>Kool & The Gang</u> ("Jungle Boogie"), <u>Eddie Kendricks</u> ("Keep On Truckin", "Boogie Down Baby"), <u>Carl Douglas</u> ("Kung Fu Fighting"), <u>George McCrae</u> ("Rock Your Baby"), and <u>KC & The Sunshine Band</u> ("Get Down Tonight", "That's The Way I Like It").

Kung Fu Fighting
Carl Douglas

- <u>Common Musical Denominator</u>:
* Catchy pop tunes.
* Repetitive, monolithic funky dance groove or melodic riff (in the accompaniment).

Jungle Boogie
Kool & The Gang

* Moderate tempos.
* The main dance style: <u>The Bump</u> (harbinger to disco) – a popular dance usually done to more moderately tempo'd dance tunes like those of KC & The Sunshine Band. It eventually lost it's appeal around the same time that disco mania began.

2.) <u>The Philly International Sound</u>: the signature Gamble & Huff sound stripped of it's meaningful lyrics, would gradually inject it's way into disco eventually becoming the template for the disco style of the late 70's.

T.S.O.P.
MFSB

- <u>Beginnings</u>: "MFSB" - the Philly International studio orchestra with a song (mostly instrumental) written by Gamble & Huff called <u>T.S.O.P.</u> (The Sound Of Philadelphia) in 1974.
* It ushered in the "Philly" sound into funk dance music by becoming both a #1 hit and becoming the theme song for a popular black dance show: "<u>Soul Train</u>".
    a.) A sound complete with massive horn section melodies, orchestral strings up front on the main theme, and the ever-present funky dance groove.
    - Becoming a new model in black music that would resonate eventually on a much wider scale.
* When MFSB became the <u>Salsoul Orchestra</u> (for the Salsoul label)…
    a.) It pumped the "Philly" sound template into an almost cliché status accompanying various artists.
    - Hence, the disco sound was born.

- <u>Offshoots</u>: Eurodisco - developed in Germany and in France.
* A derivative of the Euro-Pop style made famous by ABBA.
    a.) <u>Eurdisco</u>: cold, machine-like, emotionally detached, and metronomic. Very repetitive.
    - Simple and catchy.
    - Frothy, simple, repetitive lyrics that involved only a few words in an entire cut.
        * Requiring very little need of translation (i.e. designed so that language isn't a factor).
    - Beat was the most emphasized musical property.
    - Dark, distant vocalizing.
    - Emphasis on the single rather than the album format.
    - Signature "Philly International" styled orchestral string arrangements.

Fly Robin Fly
Silver Convention

* "<u>Fly Robin Fly</u>" (1975): by a German group called <u>Silver Convention</u>.
    a.) First Eurodisco hit in the US and the first of many Eurodisco one-hit wonders.

- <u>NOTE</u>: Both black dance music (i.e. the harbingers, MFSB, etc.) and Eurodisco constituted the disco landscape of the early to mid 70's.
* <u>Common factor</u>: emphasis resting primarily on the dance beat.
    a.) <u>Next logical step</u>: a new star would be needed to elevate disco into pop.

3.) <u>Donna Summer</u> (b. Adrian Donna Gaines, 12/31/48, Boston, MA): Disco's first true superstar.

    - While working and performing in Europe, she was produced by <u>Georgio Moroder</u> and <u>Peter Bellotte</u> of Oasis Records.

        * Donna Summer recorded a number of European hits on the Oasis label.

            a.) <u>1975</u>: Moroder signed an agreement with <u>Casablanca Records</u> to contract Donna Summer in America.

                - "<u>Love To Love You Baby</u>" (1975): became her first of many hits in the US.

    - <u>Neil Bogert</u>: president of Casablanca Records heavily promoted Donna Summer.

I Feel Love
Donna Summer

        * <u>RESULT</u>: "I Remember Yesterday" (1977), the album that furthered her disco credentials.

            a.) "<u>I Feel Love</u>": a Eurodisco styled single complete with synthesizer textures.

                - And "<u>Once Upon A Time</u>" for which she wrote the lyrics.

    - "<u>Last Dance</u>" (1978): from the "Thank God It's Friday" movie soundtrack (an imitation of another influential Disco film released a year earlier – more on that later).

        * This single launched Donna Summer into disco-icon/superstar status.

            a.) Was written by <u>Paul Jabara</u> earning him an Academy Award.

        * <u>NOTE</u>: By this time, another iconic disco act was already sweeping the nation ushering in the apex of the disco era mania.

            a.) They would put a white face on the funky disco sound thereby exporting it to the far reaches of white suburbia.

C.) <u>The Bee Gee's</u>: the first important "blue-eyed soul" group since the Righteous Brothers.

    1.) Personnel:

        - <u>Barry Gibb</u> (b. 9/1/47, Manchester, ENG): vocals, guitar.

        - <u>Robin Gibb</u> (b. 12/22/49, Isle of Mann, UK): vocals.

        - <u>Maurice Gibb</u> (b. 12/22/49, Isle of Mann, UK; d. 1/12/03, Miami, FL): vocals, bass, keyboards.

            * They formed in 1958, Brisbane, Australia (their family moved there in 1955).

                a.) They eventually rose through the ranks in Australia but failed to make any impact outside [of Australia].

    2.) <u>1966</u>: they relocated to Britain, then the center of rock and roll in the wake of The Beatles' popularity.

        - They signed with manager <u>Robert Stigwood</u> who at the time, was an associate of Brian Epstein working at NEMS.

New York
Mining Disaster 1941
The Bee Gee's

        * They started releasing singles in 1967, the first:

            a.) "<u>New York Mining Disaster 1941</u>" (1967): became a hit.

                - A Beatle-esque type of sound.

        * Their following releases — primarily slow ballads — were hits in both the UK and the US.

            a.) "<u>To Love Somebody</u>", "<u>Holiday</u>", "<u>Massachusetts</u>", "<u>Words</u>", "<u>I Started A Joke</u>".

                - Melodic in a classic, tuneful sense with a touch of elegance and sentimentality (they were not rockers).

                    * Featuring their signature, tight 3-part vocal harmony style that became their trademark.

    3.) <u>Early 70's</u>: more of their trademark ballads.

        - "<u>Lonely Days</u>" (1970) and "<u>How Do You Mend A Broken Heart</u>" (1971)

* Featuring catchy pop melodies and orchestral string arrangements.
>> a.) Both were, again, big hits on both sides of the Atlantic.
- From late 1971 to early 1975: they launched a string of failed releases and seemed to be finished.
>> * Robert Stigwood: who by now owned RSO Records (a subsidiary of Atlantic Records) made an extremely bold move that would eventually re-ignite the careers of The Bee Gee's.
>>> a.) He called upon an Atlantic Records colleague for some much needed help.

4.) Arif Mardin: a staff producer of Turkish descent at Atlantic Records who specialized in producing black R&B music.
> - He coached the Bee Gee's in everything he knew about the current black R&B style (ca 1975), thereby transforming the Bee Gee's from sentimental balladeers to falsetto singing blue-eyed soulsters.
>> * Ingredients:
>>> a.) Vocalizing:, falsetto singing (a mid 70's black music staple at the time) .
>>> b.) Groove: a funky bass dance groove.
>>> c.) Tempo: moderate to faster speeds.
>> *RESULT: A profound redirection in their music.
>>> a.) Robin Gibb: falsetto and Barry Gibb: lower tenor range.

> - "Main Course" (1975): the album that both re-ignited their careers and unveiled their new musical direction.
>> * "Jive Talkin' " (#1 on the pop charts), "Nights On Broadway" (#3, Pop), and "Fanny (Be Tender With My Love)"…

>>> a.) …marked the Bee Gee's entrance into the blue-eyed soul/funk domain.
>> * "Main Course": became their first platinum album.
>>> a.) At a time when the popularity of disco was on the rise.

5.) RSO: became an independent label breaking away from its parent company, Atlantic Records.
> - Because Arif Mardin was under contract with Atlantic, the Bee Gee's (now under an independent RSO), could no longer use his services.
>> * Nevertheless, the group still maintained his influence.
>>> a.) Their new production team would be Albhy Galaten (arranger) and Karl Richardson (engineer).
>> * RESULT: four more hit singles:

>>> a.) "You Should Be Dancing" (1976): reached to #1, Pop.
>>>> - Their first bona fide disco single.
>>> b.) "Love So Right" (1976): reached up to #3.
>>>> - A resurgence of their ballad sensibilities as well as:
>>> c.) "Boogie Child" and "You Stepped Into My Life".

6.) Robert Stigwood: in addition to being a gifted manager/producer, he also had experience in producing two rock-oriented hit films:
> - "Jesus Christ, Superstar" and "Tommy"
>> * Through Stigwood's connection in the film industry, he found out about a new movie project dealing with a white, working-class disco hero to be played by John Travolta called: "Saturday Night Fever".
>>> a.) He solicited the Bee Gee's to write and record about 5 songs to be included in the upcoming soundtrack.

7.) "Saturday Night Fever": a recipe for guaranteed blockbuster success.
> - A white, sexy working-class hero and funky dance blue-eyed soul equaled a mainstream, nationwide phenomenon.
>> * The Album: a compilation of disco classics by various artists that would find it's way into every white home in suburbia.

a.) Sold 30,000,000 copies and remained on the charts for two years.
- <u>Musical Style</u>: In addition to the Arif Mardin influence on the Bee Gee's (i.e. falsetto harmonies and funky dance grooves)…
* The string orchestra sound (i.e. the Philly International influence) made it's way into these disco tunes.
a.) These elements together, provided the rubric for the signature disco sound of the late 70's.
- Example: "<u>More Than A Woman</u>" – The Bee Gee's
- <u>NOTE</u>: Both the movie and the music of Saturday Night Fever launched the mainstream disco mania. Before this mania, clubbing was more underground, especially in gay clubs. Now, with the concept of clubbing gone mainstream, everybody it seems, was clubbing (it was the new hot thing).
* <u>Culturally</u>: this was the height of the sexual revolution and the beginning of the mass-marketing of cocaine into the American mainstream.
a.) The disco era became the "era of excess" and everyone, it seemed, jumped on the disco bandwagon.
* Practically everyone had a disco hit:
a.) <u>Ethel Merman</u> ("Disco Duck"), <u>Dolly Parton</u> ("9 to 5"), <u>Barry Manilow</u> ("The Copacabana"), <u>The Rolling Stones</u> ("Miss You"), <u>Barbara Streisand</u> ("Enough Is Enough" in collaboration with Donna Summer).
b.) One could set the "Battle Hymn Of The Republic" to a disco beat in the Saturday Night Fever style and it would become a hit – that's how crazy the disco mania was at the time.
- Example: "<u>A Fifth Of Beethoven</u>" by Walter Murphy (from the "Saturday Night Fever" album) uses actual music from Beethoven's 5th Symphony to a disco beat.
* <u>This "era of excess"</u>: was not just limited to the culture, but the music as well.

8.) <u>Disco' Extended Influence</u>: In addition to others jumping on the Disco train previously mentioned, other artists such as The Grateful Dead incorporated the disco influence into their massive, eclectic array of influences.
- Example: "<u>Shakedown Street</u>" (1978).

9.) <u>Disco's Musical Fallout</u>: it was no longer, true Funk. It had severely watered down the Funk ingredients that it [Disco] had become a legacy of.
- In some ways, similar to white big-band "Swing" music of the early 1940's.
* With repetitive pop themes that reached the lowest common denominator and a formulaic dance beat.
a.) White big bands (Benny Goodman notwithstanding) had drained the true jazz traditions out of their music in order to become totally pop.
- The saviors of the true jazz tradition were the black big bands of <u>Count Basie</u> and <u>Duke Ellington</u> among others.
* They not only kept the jazz tradition alive but also maintained it as a serious art form.
a.) They were the keepers of the true art form [jazz tradition] that allowed it to develop into the next level namely: <u>Bebop</u>.
- In a similar parallel, <u>George Clinton</u> was the one who kept the true Funk tradition alive as a highly crafted, serious art form during the height of disco's popularity.

More Than A Woman
The Bee Gee's

Miss You
The Rolling Stones

A Fifth Of Beethoven
Walter Murphy

Shakedown Street
The Grateful Dead

D.) <u>The Keeper of the Funk Flame</u>: In spite of the many black artists jumping on the disco bandwagon such as <u>Gloria Gaynor</u>, <u>Thelma Huston</u>, or <u>Donna Summer</u>…

    1.) <u>George Clinton</u>: stuck to his guns and his experimental grooves in order to keep the true funk tradition alive in black music.

      - Disco had become bland with lyrics that had no true substantive meaning.

        * With overly repetitive, light-weight vamps and over-usage of one formulaic groove…

          a.) The substance of disco's original influences were completely drowned out.

            - It no longer could be considered true funk or soul.

    2.) <u>George Clinton</u>: kept the true funk tradition alive in the following ways.

      - <u>Experimentation</u>: with various funk grooves.

        * Never settling on just one type allowing for much needed variety within the funk groove lexicon.

          a.) Variety being a hallmark of creative imagination.

      - <u>Personality</u>: personas of "Dr. Funkenstein", "Star Child", and "Mr. Wiggles" (of George Clinton)…

        * That experimented with non-logical, non-linear rantings of a lunatic persona.

          a.) And in the process, maintaining the humor, slang, and parody that transformed Funk into a movement of humor and above all: <u>attitude</u>.

      - <u>Other Musical Ingredients</u>:

        * Synthesizer colors, booming Funk bass, and Clinton's unique vocal techniques that reflected his personas.

      - <u>The Maintaining of Great Musicianship</u>: another aspect sorely lacking in disco.

        * <u>Junie Morrison</u> and <u>Bernie Worrell</u>: keyboards, synthesizers.

        * <u>Gary Shider</u> and <u>Mike Hampton</u>: guitar.

        * <u>Gary (Mudbone) Cooper</u>: vocals (with a gospel-driven essence).

        * <u>William "Bootsy" Collins</u>: funk bass extrordinaire.

        * <u>Maceo Parker</u>: saxophone, arranger.

        * <u>Fred Wesley</u>: trombone, arranger.

          a.) Parliament/Funkadelic offshoots that benefited from the success of George Clinton were:

            - <u>Bootsy's Rubber Band</u>, <u>Horny Horns</u>, <u>Zapp</u>, <u>The Brides Of Funkenstein</u>, and <u>Phillipe Wynne</u>.

              * This loose collective emanating from P/Funk was a testament to the openness of George Clinton's approach to both the music and it's production.

      - <u>NOTE</u>: It was the combination of these ingredients that fueled George Clinton's "anti-disco" insurgency and maintained Funk as a serious form of art.

    3.) <u>RESULT</u>: George Clinton's P/Funk collective became the sole standard-bearer for the Funk tradition creating an array of hits on the black R&B charts.

      - Among P/Funk's greatest successes on the R&B:

        * "<u>The Mothership Connection</u>" (1976): the album that introduced <u>Bootsy Collins</u>, <u>Fred Wesley</u>, and <u>Maceo Parker</u> (all former James Brown players) into the collective.

          a.) "<u>Give Up The Funk (Tear The Roof Off The Sucker)</u>": P/Funk's first single to reach gold.

          b.) Other notable singles included:

            - "<u>Mothership Connection (Star Child)</u>" and "<u>P/Funk (Wants To Get You Funked Up)</u>".

        * "<u>Funkentelechy vs. The Placebo Syndrome</u>" (1977) their first album to achieve platinum status.

a.) "Placebo Syndrome": George Clinton's description of the blandness and emptiness of conventional disco music.

b.) "Flashlight" (#1 on the R&B charts; #14, Pop):

- The first single to feature the synthesizer carrying the bass line.

* Touchstone: Larry Graham's influence on P/Funk's Bernie Worrell on the synthesizer. (This "invention" would be highly influential on the synth-driven "New Wave" movement of the early 80's).

c.) "Aqua Boogie" (#1 on the R&B charts):

- Also employed a synthesized bass line.

d.) "Bop Gun": another Funk classic off the album.

- In addition to turning Funk into a movement of whit, attitude, and in keeping the Funk genre as a serious art form, there was one other aspect that George Clinton injected into the Funk domain…

4.) Extravagance: Not only in terms of a big sound but also, in his stage show entitled: "The Earth Tour".

- Featuring a spaceship that lands on stage and an army of performers   as many as 40 — performing on stage together.

* This fit the 70's tradition of the elaborate stage show set in motion by David Bowie's "Diamond Dogs Tour" in 1974.

a.) NOTE: In terms of both musical substance and absolute extravagance, George Clinton brought the concept of Funk to the logical artistic limit.

- Again, turning it into a movement of extravagance, humor, and above all, attitude.

- Problem: this extravagance and the musical substance of funky "high art" was out of reach to the poverty-stricken neighborhoods in black, inner city America such as the South Bronx.

* It was too costly, too complicated, and too extravagant for the average inner city youth to emulate. In other words. logistically out of their reach.

a.) Needed: a return to simplicity both musically and logistically.

- In this case, all one needed were two turntables, an ability of making clever rhymes, no need to even sing (a stylistic speech form was good enough), and…

*…a pulsating, heavily slamming beat…

CHAPTER XI: REVIEW

Name the undisputed innovator of funk:

Who were his two early R&B influences that inspired him to go secular?
    1.)
    2.)

His group, The Famous Flames, signed a recording contract with King Records (Cincinnati, OH). Name their debut single (1956) that rose to #5 on the R&B charts:

Name The Famous Flames' first #1 hit on the R&B charts in 1958:

On the heels of the single, "(Do The) Mashed Potatoes", what would become James Brown's new source for musical ideas? (Hint: it was based on a particular ability)

Name James Brown's breakthrough single of 1965:

Name at least four elements from this single that would make up the funk structure:
    1.)
    2.)
    3.)
    4.)

What was the result of the combination of these musical properties?

What was the role of James Brown's secondary drummer?

What was the role of Pee Wee Ellis?

With the single, "Cold Sweat" (1967), what new metric policy did James Brown introduce that would also become part of the funk structure?

In addition to providing the musical structure for funk, James Brown also provided the model of what in meant to be a funk singer. What was that model?

List four elements that earned James Brown the title of "Number One Soul Brother".
  1.)
  2.)
  3.)

  Name a musical example of a message celebrating black identity.

What became James Brown's legacy?

What were Sly Stone's two most important influences?
  1.)
  2.)

  Name his first hit with Sly and The Family Stone:

Name seven elements of his music:
  1.)
  2.)
  3.)
  4.)
  5.)
  6.)
  7.)

  What became the result of this combination in regard to mainstream appeal?

Name the father of the funk bass:

  Name two playing techniques that he could do on the bass simultaneously.

What did Sly Stone contribute to the James Brown funk structure?

Which writer/producer ushered Motown into the funk domain beginning in 1970?

  He combined the influences of James Brown and Sly Stone. Name two influences
  from each:
    James Brown:
      1.)
      2.)

Sly Stone:
        1.)
        2.)

What was the subject matter of Whitfield's lyrics when he wrote/produced The Temptations (starting in 1970)?

    Name at least one of those singles:

Name the first harbinger of 70's funk:

There were four elements that he introduced into funk that would become standard later on. Name those four elements:
    1.)
    2.)
    3.)
    4.)

    Name his single that introduced these elements into funk.

Name the artist and the album that standardized the harbinger elements (just previously mentioned) into 70's funk:

    Name at least four important elements of this album that greatly impacted black music:
        1.)
        2.)
        3.)
        4.)

What's Goin On became black music's first concept album in the following ways:
    1.)
    2.)
    3.)

What was the reason for James Brown's new sound in the early 70's?

    Who was his new bass player?

Name George Clinton's original vocal group:

Who did they emulate? (Hint: a Motown vocal group)

What were George Clinton's two main influences for his group The Funkadelics?
1.)
2.)

What did Bootsy Collins add to the Funkadelic musical mix?

List three JB staples that became part of the Parliament/Funkadelic sound:
1.)
2.)
3.)

What was the new sound called, which would set a standard for funk?

What additional ingredients did George Clinton use to give this P/Funk extravagance a sense of attitude?

Which funk group adopted a more pop melodic focused, FM radio-friendly sound?

Name the writer/producer duo that created the "Philly International" sound.

Complete the following elements that make up the "Philly International" sound:
1.) Type of melody:
2.) Type of beat:
3.) Type of lyrics (i.e. subject matter):

List three vocal groups that Gamble & Huff wrote for and produced:
1.)
2.)
3.)

What became unique about their string arrangements? In other words, what purpose did these arrangements serve insofar as thematic material?

For what musical genre did the Gamble & Huff structure become a template?

What were the two common musical denominators for the disco harbingers?
    1.)
    2.)

    Name five of these artists:
        1.)
        2.)
        3.)
        4.)
        5.)

Name the record and recording artist group that first introduced the Philly International sound in 1974.

Name at least several aspects of Euro disco:

    What became the first Eurodisco hit in the US?

Name the first disco star:

    What was her first US hit?

    Who was her writer/producer? (Hint: look for the Italian first name):

Name the manager of The Bee Gee's:

Name three elements of The Bee Gee's early balladic style:
    1.)
    2.)
    3.)

    List two of early 70's trademark ballads:
        1.)
        2.)

What impact did Arif Mardin have upon the musical development of The Bee Gee's?

List the two black/R&B ingredients that he influenced that would mark a profound redirection in their [The Bee Gee's] music:
1.)
2.)

What 1975 breakthrough album became the result [of Mardin's influence] that reinvigorated The Bee Gee's career?

Name their first bona fide disco single of 1976:

What became the impact of the soundtrack [and movie], "Saturday Night Fever"?

What was disco's musical fallout?

Name the artist who kept the funk tradition alive during the era of what he called, "The Placebo Syndrome" (i.e. disco):

Name the elements that George Clinton the true funk tradition as a serious art form alive:
1.)
2.)
3.)
4.)

Name the first single where the synthesizer – under the artistry of Larry Graham devotee, Bernie Worrell — was used to carry the main bass line:

What became the fallout of funk's massive extravagance?

CHAPTER XII: HIP HOP

<u>I. RISE OF A NEW STYLE</u>

A.) <u>Jamaican Influences</u>: the art of Rap in the US can be traced back to it's roots in Jamaican tradition namely, <u>Toasting</u> and <u>The Dub</u>.

1.) <u>Toasting</u>: speaking over the microphone accompanied by a record.

- <u>Beginnings</u> (late 50's): toasting first developed at dances in Jamaica known as "Blues Dances" in large dance halls or yards within the ghetto communities.

* Black American R&B records were played.

a.) <u>Fats Domino</u>, <u>Louis Jordan</u>, <u>Amos Milburn</u>, and <u>Roy Brown</u> among others.

b.) <u>Reason for these records being played</u>: the absence of Jamaican bands musically proficient enough to perform R&B well (in other words, necessity being the mother of invention).

* <u>Sound Systems</u>: began to develop in order to play these records in large halls or yards.

a.) They began to get elaborate due to the big sound that was required for large venues and in the process, spawned the first wave of modern Jamaican producers.

- These producers further elaborated their sound systems that eventually developed into a booming bass sound so prominent, that one felt the booming bass resonance before hearing it.

* Early producers in the late 50's/early 60's: <u>Prince Buster</u>, <u>Duke Reid</u>, and <u>Clement "Sir Coxone" Dodd</u>.

a.) <u>Sir Coxone Dodd</u>: most prominent of the early producers at the "Studio One" label.

- Developed the first sound system he called, "<u>The Downbeat</u>", that truly accentuated the booming bass resonance previously mentioned.

- <u>The Birth Of The Modern Jamaican Toasting DJ</u>:

* In the beginning, DJ announced records and played them. And then, a new artist stepped up to the mic and changed the rules in 1956.

a.) <u>Winston "Count" Machuki</u>: the original Jamaican DJ. The first to speak in rhyming phrases over the mike using Sir Coxsone's "Downbeat " sound system.

More Scorcha
Count Machuki

- Originally inspired by the rhyming and jive language of American radio DJ's.

* This rhyming became known as "toasting" and it was Machuki who first put it on the map.

- Other legendary Toasters to follow were: <u>Denis Alcapone</u>, <u>Dillinger</u>, and <u>Prince Far I</u>.

2.) <u>The Dub</u>: (ca 1969): taking a pre-recorded popular Jamaican song and wiping out the melody and mid-range instrumental lines...

- ...while keeping the drums and the bass line intact.

* This accomplishes two things:

a.) It accentuates the dark, droning sound of the bass and drums giving the arrangement a heavy bottom.

- Especially with the signature Jamaican syncopated beat.

b.) It allows more focus on the Toaster.

- Without the original song melody or mid-range instrumental lines to compete against for sonic supremacy...

* The Toaster can be heard over the drums and bass in a very clear, concise manner.

415

- <u>Beginnings</u>: Reggae producers such as Lee "Scratch" Perry began issuing singles with instrumental "B-Sides" that focused on the "<u>Riddim</u>" (i.e. the base line and rhythmic pattern of the drumbeat extracted form the "A-Side" with some remnants of the melody remaining).
- It became a regular practice among Jamaican producers.
 * <u>1971</u>: the first true Dub recordings.
  a.) "<u>Voo Doo</u>" by the Hippie Boys: <u>the first original Dub</u>.
   - A dubbed version of "<u>Hard Fighter</u>" by Little Roy and mixed by <u>Andy Capp</u> (a.k.a. Lynford Anderson).
 * <u>King Tubby</u> (b. Osbourne Ruddock): further developed and popularized the Dub sound.
  a.) A sound engineer and sound systems operator who developed from his small home studio with a 4-track mixing board at 18 Drumilly Avenue, Kingston 11.
   - He tirelessly experimented with the possibilities that the art of Dub had to offer.

Ghetto Dub
King Tubby

3.) Both of these Jamaican elements [Toasting and the Dub], in conjunction with an American invention known as the <u>Mixer</u>, would form the initial building blocks for a new musical domain in America.
- <u>The Mixer</u>: a device which started coming into use during the early 70's, allowing the club DJ to synchronize two turntables together.
 * <u>Concept</u>: to smoothly switch from one turntable to the other in a seamless, non-breakable pattern.
  a.) Thereby creating a continuum of endless sound.
4.) <u>NOTE</u>: With three DJing properties in place that no Toaster could do without, it was just a matter of time that this tradition, like it's Reggae counterpart before it, would become another Jamaican export.
B.) <u>The South Bronx and the Birth of Hip Hop</u>.
 1.) <u>DJ Kool Herc</u> (b. Clive Campbell, 1955, Jamaica): the one who introduced the art of Jamaican styled DJing to the South Bronx and inventor of the "B-Boy" persona.
- <u>Beginnings</u>: his family moved form Jamaica to New York City in 1967 (he was 13).
 * He started out as a break-dancer.
  a.) During this time, he was constantly frustrated by Coxsone-styled DJ's not playing a record out to a considerably longer length.
   - Break dancers by nature, prefer longer cuts.
  b.) This experience inspired him to become DJ taking his musical approach from dancer's perspective.
 * He debuted his DJing at a party his sister arranged at his housing block's recreation room at 1520 Sedgewick Tower in the South Bronx.
  a.) She rented the room for $25 and charged a small admission fee.
- <u>His Unique DJing Angle</u>: to establish a niche, his idea was to find records that no one else had owned.
 * He was among the first to play breaks from James Brown's "<u>Get Up (I Feel Like Being A) Sex Machine</u>" which at the time practically no one owned – he borrowed it from his father.
  a.) He made it his business to research local jukeboxes in order to test a song's notoriety.
 * He shopped at record stores specializing in obscure records namely: "<u>Downstairs Records</u>" (on 42nd St.) and "<u>The Rhythm Den</u>".

a.) <u>His credo</u>: "This is where your recognition, your rep comes from. You have a record nobody else got, or you're the first one to have it. You've got to be the first, can't be the second".

* He was the first to standardize the "Break Spinning" and the use of climactic instrumental sections of a record. He normally used Dub versions of Jamaican records.

a.) "<u>Break Spinning</u>": continuous clipping of various instrumental breaks or bridges from different records.

- He would buy two copies of the same record to mix the same 15 - 20 second instrumental break back and forth from one turntable to the other thereby extending the break (no doubt inspired by his break dancing experiences in wanting longer clip lengths).

b.) Also, by expanding these breaks (i.e. from one turntable to the other) he created something significant out of something originally subservient.

- Resulting into a new work.

* "<u>Merry-Go-Round</u>"(a.k.a. The Breakdown): another of Kool Herc's techniques.

a.) Mixing instrumental breaks of James Brown's "…<u>Sex Machine</u>" into "<u>Bongo Rock</u>" by Michael Viner and back into Babe Ruth's "<u>The Mexican</u>"

- Made for dancers waiting for a particular favorite instrumental break to come along. Kool Herc's solution?

* Clip all the great breaks together.

- <u>RESULT</u>: DJ Kool Herc made the mixer – two synchronized turntables – into a new instrument.

* Thereby, reinventing the music from disparate clips into something totally original.

- He started out as his own MC (Master of Ceremonies) with small little rhymes such as:

* "Yo, this is Kool Herc in the joint-ski saying my mellow-ski Marky D's in the house".

a.) As a result these "Party Shouts" would evolve into something more elaborate using schoolyard rhymes and "dozens".

* He turned over his MC responsibilities first to <u>Coke LaRock</u> to be joined shortly after by <u>Clark Kent</u> and dubbed them: <u>The Herculords</u>.

a.) Kool Herc wanted to devote his full attention to the growing sophistication of his DJing.

- MC Coke LaRock, by incorporating more elaboration in his shouts, laid down the new model of what would become known as Rap.

* As a result, he became Hip Hop's first true American rapper.

- <u>SUMMARY</u>: For all practical purposes, DJ Kool Herc laid down the initial structure for the art of Hip Hop DJing and planted the rhyming seed (with his "Party Shouts") that a host of other artists, would develop on a considerably larger scale beginning with Coke LaRock.

C.) <u>Hip Hop Culture</u>: conceptually, the art of collaging.

1.) <u>Music</u>: the collaging of various musical clips in a continuous string of events from one turntable to the other.

- Thereby completely reinventing the clips of sampled material into something totally original.

417

* The samples themselves were in a sense, like notes (or pitches) in a scale -- all done over a driving beat.

* Collaging through the art of DJing, also reinvented the idea of musicianship.

      a.) One did not have to play an instrument or sing on key to make original music. In other words, the rules concerning traditional musicianship were no longer applicable.

- The Art of Rapping: getting up to the mike to engage in the art of rhythmic rhyming.

      * Or, to put it another way, a collaging of rhyming verses that speak directly of the Rappers' experiences that others in the neighborhood could relate to.

            a.) Speaking in a highly stylized manner similar in concept, to an actor reciting verses.

                - And very accessible for inner city youths to emulate.

      * Egocentric: for a Rapper, letting the world know of his (or her) existence with the art itself [rhythmic rhyming] serving as vehicle of affirmation.

            a.) And a thirst for respect and attention within the inner city peer group.

2.) Graffiti Art: in the 70's, it became an art form rather than a nuisance (an eyesore).

- De Witt Clinton High School (South Bronx): near a parking yard for subway cars not in use.

      * Armed with spray cans et al., they created collages of various liquid shaped letters with collages of different colors splashed together and scribbled designs.

            a.) These mural-like creations Nelson George coined as "guerrilla art".

                - To denote it's insurgent nature.

      * They painted as serious art, their "Tags" (or pseudonyms) in order to hide their real identities from the authorities.

            a.) "Phase Two" (a.k.a. Lonnie Wood): was the most well known whose tag could be seen on the sides of many subway cars.

                - In a sense, these subway cars were like canvasses.

- Graffiti Art: was attached with an egocentric tendency identical to Hip Hop music.

      * The artists' thirst for attention.

            a.) To let the world know or for that matter anyone viewing, that the creator of that particular art exists.

                - In other words: "Hey, I'm alive!"

3.) Break Dancing: conceptually, a collage of various spinning moves in continuity that could lead one into injury status but yet, exhibit a spirit of competition.

- Unlike other segments within the Hip Hop world, the break dancing style as we know it, developed in the Puerto Rican community in New York.

      * Upon its introduction into the black community, it was viewed early on as a fad that gave way to DJing and Rapping.

            a.) The Puerto Rican community was the first to make break dancing competitive.

                - Especially between rival gangs as an alternative to violence.

- Spinning moves in a highly stylized manner that required an enormous amount of skill.

      * Like other Hip Hop forms such as Djing, Rapping, and Graffiti Art.

- The Music: early classics requested at break dancing parties and other Hip Hop events:

    * "Apache" (The Incredible Bongo Band), "It's Only Just Begun" (Jimmy Caster), and "Dance To The Drummer's Beat" (Herman Kelly).

        a.) DJ's played these records often at the request of break-dancers and subsequently, made them into hits.

            - Break dancers influenced the music that DJ's played very early on in Hip Hop thereby shaping it's initial musical direction.

                * As mentioned previously Kool Herc started out as a break dancer and the experience led him to becoming THE groundbreaking DJ of early Hip Hop.

4.) Hip Hop Fashion: a collage of different clothing labels worn simultaneously by one person.

    - For example: Addidas shoes, Nike Shorts, New York Knicks basketball shirt, and a New York Yankees baseball cap all worn in the same outfit.

        * Expressing the individual's taste that was both Hip Hop and personally unique.

            a.) Hip Hop Fashion: was (and still is) one of the segments that enabled the Hip Hop domain to bend, sway, and morph with the development of time.

                - In other words, Hip Hop's immense flexibility allowed it to change with the times and survive on a resilient level.

                * Music was just a part of it...

D.) Rap's Initial Introduction To The Masses: mainstream America in the late 70's had no idea that Hip Hop was currently in existence. But that was about to change...

    1.) Sylvia Robinson: had her first hit as part of a pop duo – "Mickey and Sylvia" – in 1957 called "Love Is Strange".

    - As a soloist, her one big hit was "Pillow Talk" (1973).

        * Along with her husband, Joe, they owned several independent R&B labels -- Vibration, Turbo, and All Platinum – starting in 1968. Because of the difficulty they had in receiving distribution payments [for these labels], they decided to streamline everything under the All Platinum name.

            a.) The change notwithstanding, they still had trouble making money even though they scored a crossover hit in the early 70's called, "Love On A Two-Way Street" by The Moments.

        * In order to make for the continuing loss of revenue, Sylvia Robinson started selling records in black neighborhoods throughout the NYC area. It was through her business interactions in these neighborhoods, and through her son, that she first learned of rap music and the hip=hop scene.

    - Touchstone: She attended a birthday party at the Harlem World Disco in 1978.

        * There was no band or a conventional disco record spinner.

            a.) Instead, the entertainment featured Rap artists performing to a highly enthusiastic crowd.

        * A light bulb went off in Sylvia Robison's head. Her prior experience with "All Platinum" taught her how to seize on an idea.

            a.) The idea in this case: to establish a new independent label completely devoted to the new art of Rap.

                - RESULT: the legendary "Sugar Hill Records" label (named after a section in Harlem that produced a lot of musical talent). It was to be housed in the old "All Platinum" location in Englewood, NJ.

* "Sugar Hill Records" (1979): the first important Rap music label that would not only spawn the most influential early Rap recordings but also…

    a.) …would be THE most powerful record business force in early Rap music.

- "Rapper's Delight" (1979): Sugar Hill Records' first important single.

    * The "Sugar Hill Gang": backed up by a crack recording session band.

        a.) Dub: they rapped over a dub of a highly popular disco tune in mainstream America entitled: "Good Times" by Chic. Written by two of its members, Nile Rodgers and Bernard Edwards. The last great dance hit of the disco mania era.

Good Times
Chic

           - The popularity of this single opened the door for "Rapper's Delight" to become immediately successful.

        b.) Stripped of it's original melody, all there was left was the familiar bass line, the drum groove, and the occasional signature rhythm guitar breaks (that reminded listeners of the original song's familiarity).

Rapper's Delight
The Sugar Hill Gang

           - Hence, the Dub quality consistent with the Jamaican influence prevalent in the earl Hip Hop community.

               * In this case, the dub was recorded by a studio band and not DJ'd.

    * The Sugar Hill Gang members rapped over the "Good Times" dub

        a.) It was subsequently played in mainstream discos all over America and in Europe (this was the height of the disco era after all).

           - It reached to #36 in the US pop charts and even higher on the European charts.

- Sugar Hill Records: would go on to record some of the most important early Rap singles and Rap album formats from 1979 to 1983.

2.) Rap Reaches Gold: Kurtis Blow (b. Curtis Walker, 8/9/59, New York).

- Beginnings: started out as a disco DJ in Harlem (1976).

    * His first rapping influence was DJ Hollywood (Anthony Holloway).

        a.) He copied Hollywood's style word for word.

           - But it came out as something different, something original.

    * He was also mentored in the art of track DJing and editing by DJ Grandmaster Flash (Joseph Sadler).

- Recording Contract: on the heels of the Sugar Hill Gang's success which proved that there was a market for disco-driven Rap:

    * Kurtis Blow was signed to Mercury Records in 1979. This marks the first time that a Rap artist is signed with a major label. They first took interest in him upon hearing his previously recorded single, *Christmas Rappin'*.

Christmas Rappin'
Kurtis Blow

        a.) The original recording was spearheaded at the behest of his manager, Russell Simmons. He convinced Robert "Rocky" Ford (a writer for Billboard Magazine) and J.B. Moore (a prominent NYC musician) to record this single with Kurtis Blow. It was basically "The Night Before Christmas" rewritten and delivered in a bona fide hip-hop, B-Boy manner.

           - Because it initially sold 600,000 copies, Kurtis Blow caught the attention of Mercury Records.

    * Mercury's re-release of Christmas Rappin' marked the first foray of a major label entering the world of hip-hop.

        a.) Released on a 12" vynal format, it reached #4 on the R&B charts and #87 on the mainstream pop charts.

- "The Breaks" (1980): first Rap single to reach gold.
    * Also released in a "12-inch" record format.
        a.) The "12-Inch": literally a 45 rpm record that is 12 inches across to accommodate long dance tracks that the standard 7 inch format could not.
        b.) "The Breaks": the second 12-inch to reach gold.
            - The first: "Enough Is Enough" by Barbara Streisand and Donna Summer.
    - "The Breaks' and "Rapper's Delight": they were made for discos and were basically, Rap in a disco tune-driven format (i.e. dance music).
        * Made to be a hit with mainstream audiences.
    - In addition, the first prominent white artist to attempt rapping in an authentic manner: Blondie.
        * "Rapture" (1980): About 2 minutes into the single, Blondie (Debra Harry) goes into a rap mode.
            a.) A rhythmic speech-rhyming where the words made little sense (insofar as their meaning).
                - After a brief return to song mode, she alternates once again to rapping.

3.) The State Of Rap In The Early 80's: basically, a dance-oriented idiom with lyrics that deal with partying or other frothy subject matter.
    - At a time when disco-oriented dance music was going out of style and giving way to a different style of dance music (more on that in the next chapter), Rap and it's association with disco needed a change.
        * Needed: a new template that Rap artists could emulate, develop, and build upon -- especially those [Rap artists] from the inner city.
            a.) And also, a new Rap focus on expression "up front" that would say something meaningful.
                - As opposed to the previously mentioned status quo.

II. RAP MUSIC'S NEW STRUCTURE FOR THE 80'S (AND BEYOND)
    A.) DJ Grandmaster Flash (b. Joseph Sadler, 1/1/58, Barbados): the man who completely reinvented the concept of Hip Hop DJing.
        1.) As a disciple of DJ Kool Herc, Grandmaster Flash got his start by spinning records in the South Bronx.
            - He was also attending technical school studying electronics.
                * NOTE: When Kool Herc spun records, he did not go from one turntable to the other on the beat – there were brief pauses between records.
                    a.) Grandmaster Flash on the other hand, would alternate from one turntable to the other exactly on the beat with no pause in between.
                        - He referred to this as "quick mixing".
        2.) He became not only the first virtuoso DJ in Hip Hop but also, he set the artistic standard for DJing in the 80's (al a the "Old School") in the following ways:
            - "Cutting": between tracks on two turntables exactly on the beat.
            - "Back Spinning": turning a record backward by hand in order to make the needle repeat the same brief chunks of a groove.
            - "Phasing": changing turntables speeds in order to create sound collages.
            - "Punch Phrasing": playing a short clip from one record while it continues on the other record (of the other turntable).
            - The "Clock Theory": his ability to "read" a record by using the label's logo to find the right break.
            - The Beat Box: a converted drum machine that sampled additional percussion sounds to his mixing.

The Breaks
Kurtis Blow

Rapture
Blondie

421

* No doubt a product of electronic training expertise.

a.) Also a harbinger to the eventual use of drum machines as the norm in Rap recordings.

3.) <u>Grandmaster Flash</u>: also standardized into the Hip Hop lexicon, the "scratch" sound.

- But it was <u>Grand Wizard Theodore</u> (who worked briefly with Flash) who originated the sound.

* Grandmaster Flash however, made it standard.

4.) <u>Virtuosity</u>: Flash utilized all of the previously mentioned elements in an acrobatic and entertaining manner.

- And in doing so, created the template of the "Hip Hop DJ-as-serious-artist" that would inspire subsequent great DJ's throughout the 80's and beyond.

* "<u>Adventures Of Grandmaster Flash On The Wheels Of Steel</u>" (1981): The first "quick mix" studio recording completely made up of turntables (in this case, three) and vinyl records.

Adventures Of Grandmaster Flash On The Wheels Of Steel
Grandmaster Flash

a.) In other words, the first studio recording of Hip Hop DJ'ing.

- He used mainly hit records that were familiar to a DJ wider audience.

5.) He first collaborated with Kurtis Blow in 1977 and then, with "<u>The Furious Five</u>": Flash's crew of MC's.

- The Furious Five: "<u>Cowboy</u>" (b. Keith Wiggins, 9/20/69; d. 9/8/89); "<u>Mellie Mel</u>" (b. Melvin Glover); "<u>Kid Creole</u>" (b. Nathaniel Glover); "<u>Mr. Ness</u>" (b. Eddie Morris); and "<u>Reheim</u>" (b. Guy Williams).

* <u>Cowboy</u>: came up with some original phrases that became Hip Hop staples.

* <u>Creole and Mel</u>: the earliest of the great rhyme-masters…

a.) …alternating sentences back and forth between one another.

6.) "<u>The Message</u>" (1982): by Grandmaster Flash & The Furious Five recorded on the Sugar Hill Records label.

- The single that set the new structure in Rap music for the 80's.

* <u>Impact</u>: the first example of Rap music being used as a vehicle of protest.

a.) Forever changing the subject matter.

- <u>The Structure</u>:

* Heavy Funk-influenced groove/beat.

a.) With heavy percussive drums samples emanating from the beat box (i.e. drum machine sound).

- An essence of the R&B tradition.

* <u>Synthesizer</u>: samples of instrumental thematics acting as the initial hook.

The Message
Grandmaster Flash
& The Furious Five
(featuring Mellie Mel)

* <u>The Lyrics</u> (by Mellie Mel and Duke Bootee):

a.) The hardships and dangers that are a regular part of New York City street life.

- A harbinger of the Social Commentary and Gangsta Rap lyrics to come.

* <u>Gritty, Direct Rapping Style With An Attitude</u>:

a.) <u>Mellie Mel</u>: Acting as a narrator in the first person (as opposed to being a party MC).

b.) An "in-your-face", "street sense", direct style of delivery.

- In a highly stylized, forceful manner complete with an attitude.

c.) An inspiration to MC's throughout the remainder of the 80's by setting the Rapping style standard that is still prevalent today.

- "The Message": first Rap tune to achieve critical acclaim.
  * Primarily due to the social commentary nature of the lyrics.
    a.) This single earned Rap music respect for the first time outside of the Hip Hop world.
7.) With singles like "The Message", Sugar Hill Records set in motion Rap music's first developmental period starting in 1981 and lasting through other labels until 1985.
- Sugar Hill Records opened the door with some of THE most important early Rap records.
  * But to the corporate record labels at this time, Rap music was absolutely anathema.
    a.) But there would be other independent labels devoted to Rap music that would fill in the vacuum left by the avoidance of the major labels.
- (NOTE: In addition to DJ Kool Herc and DJ Grandmaster Flash, the other important pillar of the early Hip-Hop period -- DJ Afrika Bambaataa (b. Kevin Donovan) -- will be discussed in the following chapter on electronic dance music).
  * His groundbreaking single that ushered in the birth of electro-funk was: "Planet Rock" (1982).
    a.) This single became an important inspiration for the birth of electronic dance music (again, to be discussed in detail in Chapter XIII).

Planet Rock (Original Vocal Version) DJ Afrika Bambaataa & The Soulsonic Force

B.) "Def Jam Records": founded by Rick Rubin (a producer) who went into partnership with Russell Simmons.
  1.) Rubin: was the first to originate the idea of supporting Rap tracks with rock elements as opposed to traditional R&B.
  - Rubin himself was a Punk rocker who loved Rap music.
    * He took the rock-influenced metal guitar sound/sampling and superimposed it over a driving beat.
      a.) Thereby producing an original sound.
  - The Rubin/Simmons partnership not only believed in and marketed rap music as rock...
    *... but also harnessed the rebellious attitude in their artists that was also indigenous with rock.
      a.) The first of their artists to display elements of both musical and rebellious elements of rock was Run DMC.
  2.) Run DMC (formed 1981 in Hollis, Queens, NY): Run (b. Joseph Simmons, 11/14/64); DMC (b. Darryl McDaniels, 5/31/64); Jam Master Jay (b. Jason Mizell, 1/21/65; d. 1/30/04, Jamaica, Queens)
  - Hardcore Rap: raw, shout-like, in-your-face, Rapping style.
    * Would introduce Rap in "The Message" tradition (as opposed to the "Rapper's Delight" disco-rap tradition) to a white teenage, mainstream American audience.
      a.) Along with gold chains and laceless Addidas sneakers.
  - Beginnings: they grew up together in the middle class district of Hollis, Queens.
    * When Joseph Simmons was in his mid-teens, his older brother Russell Simmons was emerging as an important figure in the rise of Hip Hop.
      a.) At the encouragement of his older brother Russell, Joseph Simmons started rapping with Darryl McDaniels.
        - 1982: they recruited a friend Jason Mizell (a.k.a. Jam Master Jay) to be their DJ.
      b.) "It's Like That" (1983): their debut single.
  - Their original style: a booming Rap sound with a raw in-your-face intensity.

* They also finished each other's rap lines like a "tag-team" (as opposed to trading off complete verses as was the norm).

   a.) As mentioned earlier, they were more rock than R&B.

      - They started out rapping over rock grooves and [rock] clips in the park – which, with their loud, in-your-face rapping style, matched perfectly.

King Of Rock
Run DMC

   b.) In addition to rapping over rock guitars samples…

      - They also rapped over the 808 Drum Machine. The first mass-produced computerized drum machine that would be the norm throughout the 80's.

   c.) Also, no melodies (except when rock guitars were added in), and no bass lines.

      - Usually, just the 808 Drum Machine, their hardcore rapping style, and at times, rock guitars.

- "Run DMC" (1984): their debut album and the first Rap album to reach gold.

Rock Box
Run DMC

* "Rock Box": the first of the hit Rap videos to be shown on MTV (at a time when it was MTV's policy not to show black Rap videos).

   a.) The MTV exposure catapulted the success of the single (#22 on the Pop charts) and the album sales.

      - Also among the first albums to spearhead the importance of the album format in Rap which up to now, centered mostly around the single.

         * In addition, this success marked the beginning of Run DMC paving the way for Rap music's journey into mainstream acceptance.

- "Raising Hell" (1986): the album that solidified their success in white mainstream America.

* On the heels of their second album "King Of Rock" (1985)

   a.) Which introduced Rick Rubin's heavy metal production techniques (into Rap music) to a wider audience.

      - And solidified Run DMC's tradition of Rap as rock music.

- "Walk This Way": the "Raising Hell" album's most prominent single that made Run DMC into superstars.

Walk This Way
Aerosmith

* Rick Rubin: wanted to include a rock cover tune into the album and came up with the idea of using an old Aerosmith tune – "Walk This Way" – from their [Aerosmith's] "Toys In The Attic" album of 1975.

   a.) The Aerosmith original had rock/metal guitar thematic hooks and a beat that would lend itself well to Rap.

      - Including Steven Tyler's rap-like vocalizing on the original – a natural for a rap cover.

* Because of Steve Tyler's and Joe Perry's (original Aerosmith members') appearance on the video along with the fact that the cover (with rock influences) lent itself well to mainstream accessibility…

Walk This Way
Run DMC

   a.) "Walk This Way" became the first black rap video to be aggressively promoted by MTV.

      - Thereby further solidifying black rap music into the white mainstream.

   b.) NOTE: once again, the idea of rap artists reinventing old material into something totally original is being continued by Run DMC under the watchful production of Rick Rubin.

- "My Addidas" also from the "Raising Hell" album that reached up to #5 on the pop charts.

My Addidas
Run DMC

* Reason: Russell Simmons (of Def Jam) wanted to make certain that Hip Hop could not only sell records but also: fashion.

a.) <u>1986</u>: Run DMC performs to a sellout crowd at Madison Square Garden.

- A few executives from the Addidas company flew over from Germany and stood backstage.
- Before breaking into the tune "My Addidas", Run DMC asked the audience to show off their Addidas by waving the sneaker over their heads.

* The executives themselves saw a sea of white Addidas "Three Stripes" waving throughout the vast arena.

- <u>RESULT</u>: Run DMC became the first Hip Hop act to sign a big fashion deal – worth $1,500,000 – with an athletic wear outfit (instead of the usual athletic star).

b.) Hip Hop was now becoming about fashion merchandising as well as the music.

- <u>Run DMC</u>: by taking Rick Rubin's production vision of turning Rap into rock, Run DMC introduced black Rap music (from "The Message" paradigm) into the white mainstream population.

* And greatly opened the door to black Rap music's commercial success thereby making it an integral part of American pop culture.

3.) <u>The Beastie Boys</u> (formed in 1981): the first prominent white Rap group that would carry the "Rap as Rock" mantle and transport this "pop fixture" once and for all -- into every white home in suburbia.

- Personnel: <u>MCA</u> (b. Adam Yauch, 8/5/65, New York) vocals, bass; <u>Mike D</u> (b. Michael Diamond, 11/20/66, New York) vocals, drums; <u>King Ad Rock</u> (b. Adam Horovitz, 10/31/67, New York) vocals, guitar.

* Originally started out as a Punk band in the New York underground scene that included <u>Kate Schellenbach</u> and <u>John Berry</u> (guitar).

- <u>1983</u>: they began pursuing Rap but didn't make any headway until they crossed paths with Rick Rubin.

* Coming from similar punk rock backgrounds and sharing a passion for Rap music, both The Beasties and Rubin began their artistic collaboration.

a.) With the blessing of Russell Simmons, The Beastie Boys were signed with Def Jam Records in 1985.

- <u>Their first break</u>: as back-up band for Madonna's "Virgin Tour" in support of their debut album released by Def Jam entitled "<u>Rock Hard</u>" (1985).

* This was where they started working up their obnoxious image by yelling obscenities at audiences – and getting booed off stage in the process.

a.) They were also the back-up band for Run DMC's "Raising Hell" tour…

-…which was rowdy in it's own right.

- "<u>Licensed To Ill</u>" (1987): their breakthrough album that sold 4,000,000 copies making it the biggest selling Rap album up to date.

* Including their first hit single on both the charts and on MTV: "<u>Fight For Your Right</u>".

a.) like Run DMC, this single solidified their rock (in this case punk rock) style of Rap produced by Rick Rubin.

- As well as their bratty, obnoxious image fueled by their hormone-driven essences.

b.) Also like Run DMC, The Beastie Boys would also rap in a boisterous, in-your-face, yelling [Def Jam] style.

- As illustrated in "No Sleep Till Brooklyn".

Fight For Your Right
The Beastie Boys

No Sleep Till Brooklyn
The Beastie Boys

* <u>RESULT</u>: The Beastie Boys were stirring up controversy for their offensive lyrics and their antics both on and off the stage thereby elevating themselves as "public enemy number one".

  a.) Their notorious reputation led in part (along with the nasty, misogynous lyrics of Luther Campbell's "2-Live Crew") to the creation of the <u>PMRC</u> (Parents Music Resource Center).

   - Led by <u>Tipper Gore</u> (wife of then Tennessee senator Al Gore) and <u>Susan Baker</u> (wife of Treasury Secretary, Howard baker) who, along with other members, testified before the Senate Commerce Committee chaired by Tipper's husband, Senator Al Gore. They complained of what they felt, were highly offensive lyrics in rap music (and heavy metal) and requested that something should be done to alert parents (in order to, in their view, protect the children).

    * Resulting in the "<u>Parent Advisory</u>" label seen on CD's.

C.) By 1987, rock-oriented Rap music -- first by <u>Run DMC</u> and later by <u>The Beastie Boys</u> under the "Def Jam" label – has gone completely mainstream.

  1.) "<u>Def Jam's</u>" goal: of recording Rap music to specifically target a white, mainstream audience has now become a reality.

   - But there was new undercurrent in the New York City underground Rap scene…

    *… that was dealing with a completely different type of subject matter…

     a.)…and a return to the R&B musical tradition as it's main influence.

III. RAP FOCUSING ON THE MESSAGE (MESSAGE RAP)

  A.) <u>Earlier Generations of the 1960's</u>: joined rebellious organizations that were either progressive, militant, or non-violent.

   1.) Such organizations included the Southern Christian Leadership Conference (of Dr. King), The Black Panther Party, Spirit House Movers, and the Freedom Riders.

    - Each of these organizations attracted black youth into a viable, organized structure of resistance and political activism.

   2.) <u>1980's/90's</u>: Organizations that began in the 60's, no longer existed. The result: there were no organizations that could serve as outlets for black youths to get involved either politically or rebelliously.

    - <u>Message Rap</u>: a viable substitute but without the established organization of the aforementioned groups. Instead, they will share their message/cause as entertainers.

     * Rappers of this genre include: <u>Eric B. & Rakim</u>, <u>Sister Souljah</u>, <u>Public Enemy</u>, <u>A Tribe Called Quest</u>, <u>Lakim Shabazz</u>, etc. Although they represented a small segment of the overall rap domain, they also became highly influential to youths and rap artists alike.

      - <u>Rap</u>: the principle mode of expression for young African Americans insofar as their view of the world, a sense of order out of chaos, or the hardships of contemporary urban street-life. A genre where all subject matter is game.

   3.) <u>Message Rap Ingredients</u>: there basically three major types…

    - <u>Political Message</u>: dealing with a righteous, black youth rebellion.

     * Artists include: <u>Public Enemy</u>, <u>Kool Moe Dee</u>, <u>XClan</u>, <u>Ed O.G. & Da Bulldogs</u>, and the <u>Jungle Brothers</u>

    - <u>Islamic Nationalism</u>: mostly espousing Nation Of Islam mysticism and apocalyptic views with precise modes of living life.

* Artists include: <u>Lakim Shabazz</u>, <u>Poor Righteous Teachers</u>, <u>Eric B. & Rakim</u>, <u>Brand Nubian</u>, and <u>King Sun</u>.
- <u>Specific Message</u>: Violent urban life - expressions of gang warfare, misogyny, and interethnic [Black on Black] violence but with no acceptance of responsibility (i.e. rapper being nothing more than a product of his own environment).
* Artists include: <u>NWA</u>, <u>Ice T</u>, <u>Ice Cube</u>, <u>Schooly D</u>, <u>Geto Boys</u>, and <u>Compton's Most Wanted</u>.

B.) <u>Political Rap</u>: would turn Rap into a global force.

1.) <u>Public Enemy</u>: would bring political statement and social commentary back into Rap that had been missing since "The Message". Along with expressing agitated politics, they added militant characteristics (a la the Black Panther Party), high drama, and an arena rock-like essence. In the process, they made the world take Rap as a serious art form and a force to be reckoned with.

- An introduction of intellectualism into Hip Hop mixed with an outright rebellious attitude. Their productions sounded like chaos controlled within borders.
* <u>Style</u>: a new complexity to Rap music -- consisting of complex layerings of samples, sound bites, and rock elements over a driving funk groove which added a new intensity to Hip Hop. Or, as Nelson George wrote: "high intensity sound tapestries".

a.) Also included was an overt, rebellious message. The rock-essenced rebellious elements made Public Enemy's music attractive to young white audiences.

b.) <u>High Art</u>: a sort of "avant-garde" meets Rap music scenario with complex overlays of scratches, spoken word bites, and other samples cleverly juxtaposed by their production crew called: <u>The Bomb Squad</u>.
- In regard to Chuck D, rapping delivery was authoritative with a booming voice (which was influenced by sportscaster Marv Albert).

c.) "<u>Security of the First World</u>": PE's backup dancers dressed in full military regalia including battle fatigues, berets, combat boots, and plastic Uzi's -- reminiscent of the Black Panther Party of the late 60's.

- <u>Personnel</u>: <u>Chuck D</u> (b. Carlton Ridenhour, 8/1/60, New York, NY) and <u>Flavor Flav</u> (b. William Drayton, 3/1659, New York, NY): they were the two frontmen. Other members included: <u>Terminator X</u> (b. Norman Lee Rogers, 8/25/66), DJ and <u>Professor Griff</u> (b. Richard Griffen), Minister of Information.
* They signed with Def Jam Records in 1987.
- <u>Beginnings</u>: as a student at Adelphi University on Long Island, he reluctantly agreed to begin an entertainment career although he thought he was too old for it. At Adelphi, he hung out with <u>Hank Shocklee</u> and <u>Bill Stephney</u>.
* <u>Shocklee</u>: would create The Bomb Squad.
* <u>Stephney</u>: would become an executive for Def Jam Records.

a.) It was Chuck D's many conversations on politics and philosophy with Shocklee and Stephney that shaped his [Chuck D's] future activist Rap lyrics.
* <u>Chuck D</u>: recruited another friend, <u>William Drayton</u> (a.k.a. Flavor Flav) to be his sidekick. They considered themselves "prophets of rage".

a.) "<u>Yo! Bum Rush The Show</u>" (1987): their debut album released by Def Jam. At this time, they were known only in the New York Rap underground.

3.) Two of Public Enemy's Important Albums:

- "It Takes A Nation Of Millions To Hold Us Back" (1988): their breakthrough album establishing the primacy of political and social commentary back into Rap music.

    * An immediate success reaching #1 on the R&B charts which gave Public Enemy massive exposure.

    * Issues: dealing with drugs, poverty, black nationalism, and the prison system – Rap that had a social conscience.

        a.) "Night Of The Living Baseheads": expressing the need the to address the scourge of drugs destroying the black community.

        b.) "Rebel Without A Pause": a revolt against the establishment using the beats and rhymes as his weapons. Chuck D equating his rebel stance as that of the threatening artist.

Party For Your Right To Fight
Public Enemy

        c.) "Party For Your Right To Fight" (a takeoff on the Beastie Boys' title of their single: "Fight For Your Right To Party"): lyrics dealing with pro-black nationalism. Allusions to the Black Panther Party – citing the names of [Huey] Newton, [Eldridge] Cleaver, and [Bobby] Seale (…"the party of Newton, Cleaver, and Seale").

            - Another allusion: to Elijah Muhammad and the "Asiatic" black man – echoes of the mysticism and spiritual beliefs of the Nation Of Islam (of which Elijah Muhammad served as their prophet).

                * More detail on N.O.I. mysticism will be covered under "Islamic Rap"

            - Incidentally, this single – the last of the album -- ends with the words; "It takes a nation of millions to hold us back"

- "Fear Of A Black Planet" (1990): featuring "Fight The Power".

    * "Fight The Power": the refrain inspired by a mid 70's tune by the Isley Brothers called by the same name with the line: "We've got to fight the powers that be" (the same line Public Enemy uses).

Fight The Power
Public Enemy

        a.) Public Enemy's "Fight The Power" was also an epic video directed by Spike Lee.

    * NOTE: although MTV now had a show completely devoted to Rap music called "Yo! Raps" (started in 1988)…

        a.) They refused to show "Fight The Power".

            - Or for that matter, another genre of Rap video …

C.) Islamic Rap: represented by the "Five Percenters" (a.k.a. The Five Percent nation): an offshoot of the precepts introduced by the Nation Of Islam (NOI).

    1.) NOI (Nation Of Islam): founded in 1930 by W.D. Fard but elevated and brought into prominence by Elijah Muhammad, W.D. Fard's successor.

        - Doctrinal Ideology: that African Americans were descended from the original "Asiatic" black men. They were put into perpetual slavery and subservience under the white men created by the evil Yakub – who, according to NOI mysticism, created white people from the Asiatic blacks.

            * The whites were given complete dominion over the earth for 6000 years and when that period would end, an apocalyptic mother of all battles would ensue and the whites would be defeated and the Asiatic black man would be restored to inheriting his original world dominance. (This was supposed to have happened in 1914 but due to the need of attracting more converts – in the view of the NOI – a extended grace period was granted).

a.) NOI doctrine further holds that since all black men are descended from their "Asiatic" origins, they [black men] are considered to be gods.

- 1958: the NOI began the process of connecting with more mainstream, middle-class African Americans and modernizing its organization. As a result, the NOI adopted a more secularized stance (even though Elijah Muhammad was still its powerful, spiritual leader).

* There was a split between the spiritual and secular sides of the NOI where Malcolm X became NOI's secular spokesman.

2.) Clarence 13X (b. Clarence Jowars Smith): revolted against the secularism and the political hierarchal structure of the NOI in the early 60's and decided to begin his own NOI-influenced entity.

- RESULT: "The Five Percenters" (a.k.a. The Five Percent nation): a loose confederation of street-oriented black urbanites who embraced the original NOI spirituality/mysticism but without adhering to the NOI's strict, doctrinal, governing rules of living everyday life.

* Spiritual Goal: a commitment to the Islamic-oriented teachings of W.D. Fard and reinsurgence of "Asiatic" black male divinity (designated independently of the NOI hierarchy).

a.) The Five Percenters: no structural or hierarchal organization, no supreme leader, and no adherance to rule-oriented religious doctrine. Their membership consisted of a loose-knit group of street-oriented African Americans.

* Origin of the term ("Five Percenters"): W.D Fard's instructional manual entitled, "Lost Found Moslem Lesson No. 2" (1934). Note: the source of the following passage is an essay by Ernest Allen Jr. entitled *Making The Strong Survive: The Contours and Contradictions of Message Rap*. (from the book *Droppin' Science*... listed in the bibliography)

a.) Question #16: Who is the 5% on this poor part of the earth?

- Answer: They are the poor, righteous teachers... are all wise and know who the living god is and teach that the living god is the Son of Man, the supreme being, the black man of Asia; and teach freedom, justice, and equality to all human families...

* The Five Percenters' greatest communicative outlet: Rap.

a.) Rap Artists of the Five Percenters: Lakim Shabazz, Poor Righteous Teachers, Brand Nubian, King Sun, and the most notable: Eric B. & Rakim.

3.) Eric B. & Rakim: their style would become a significant influence to the rappers of the New York City renaissance of the mid 1990's. Reason: the emphasis of intricate rhyming and the poetry as the main focus instead of pop hooks and bottom-heavy funk grooves. The focus on words were superimposed over a repetitive loop that did not upstage the poetics.

- Eric B. (b. Eric Barrier, Nov. 8, 1965: Elmhurst, NY) DJ; Rakim Allah (b. William Griffin Jr., Jan. 28, 1968: Wyndanch, LI) Vocals. William Griffin Jr. changed his name to Rakim Allah after his Islamic conversion (at age 16).

* Background: Eric B. learned the trumpet and guitar as a child, from which built his musicianship skills. In high school, he discovered the Technics 1200 SL turntable (which changed his life). In time, he started hanging out with one of his greatest influences: producer Marley Marl.

a.) Marley Marl (b. Marlon Williams): influential in developing early New York City rap artists such as Big Daddy Kane, MC Shan, Biz Markie, and Roxanne Shanté.

- Marl's Stylistic Influence: Emphasis on words, scratchy sounds, the 808 Drum Machine, and a focus on a bopping, snare drum sampled backbeat with considerably less boom (than the massive funk grooves). These elements would be embraced by Eric B. & Rakim which in turn, would influence the NYC mid 90's renaissance.

- "Eric B. Is President" (1986): their debut single which ushered in sampling of James Brown clips into the Hip Hop arena (for which they were eventually sued).

> * It also opened the door for James Brown clips to be sampled on a massive scale by other artists -- thereby furthering James Brown's musical influence and legacy.

- "Paid In Full" (1987): their debut album released on the *4th & Broadway* label. Features intricate rhyming with Rakim's laid back vocal delivery and Eric B.'s Artistic DJ'ing.

Move The Crowd
Eric B. & Rakim

My Melody
Eric B. & Rakim

I Know You Got Soul
Eric B. & Rakim

> * Lyrics: dealing with Rakim boasting his mic prowess and more importantly, attesting his Islamic faith in singles such as *Move The Crowd* and *My Melody*.

> * DJ'ing: Eric B.'s turntable prowess and producing skills focused on repetitive grooves & loops with no pop melodic hooks. In addition, the beat samples are reminiscent of a conventional trap drum set with the back beat emphasis on a snare drum sample (as opposed to massive bass drum kicks and heavy bass lines).

>> a.) This in turn, allowed the rhyming/poetry to be spotlighted (in the foreground) without any distraction from the accompaniment – even in cases where the beats are emphatic as illustrated in *I Know You Got Soul*.

>>> - Their overall style of rapping, emphasis on intricate lyrics, DJ'ing, and production style helped set the tone for NYC's rap renaissance of the mid 90's.

- NOTE: After subsequent albums such as *Follow The Leader* (1998) and *Let the Rhythm Hit 'Em* (1990), they released their last album in 1992 entitled: *Don't Sweat The Technique*.

> * Some of the singles [in this album] take on a more metaphoric approach – using images of violent weapons as metaphors to symbolize the microphone. Case in point: *Pass The Hand Grenade* – the grenade serving as metaphor for Rakim's mic. In this context, the microphone is his lethal weapon of choice.

>> a.) In tracks such as *Know The Ledge*, tales of street violence and dominance over women hover on the surface…

>>> - The approached of these two examples were not new. In fact, the genesis came from an album of 1987 that first anticipated a style that would later be known as Gangsta Rap – a type of message rap depicting life from the tough, inner-city streets.

IV. RAP TAKES A NEW TURN BACK TO Its GHETTO ROOTS

A.) Boogie Down Productions: the harbinger of what would be known as "Gangsta Rap".

> 1.) Personnel: KRS One (b. Lawrence "Kris" Parker, 1966, Bronx) and Scott LaRock (b. Scott Sterling b.; 8/25/87, Bronx).

>> - Background: Parker grew up poor and was first introduced to Hip Hop by his mother's Rap records (including those of Grandmaster Flash). After leaving home at the age of 13, he lived on the streets.

>>> * His days were spent reading about religion and philosophy in the public library. At night, he'd rap in his homeless shelters. At the – The Franklin Armory Shelter, Parker had a counselor/social worker named Scott Sterling.

          a.) Both Parker and Sterling decided to collaborate and formed "Boogie Down Productions".

2.) "Criminal Minded" (1987): their debut album. Planted the seed of what would later become "Gangsta Rap".

9mm Goes Bang
Boogie Down Productions

- A concept album depicting the realities of crack-infested violence in the black inner city community.

    * Crack: a free-based, crystallized form of cocaine was mass-marketed in the inner city with enormous profits made by various, powerful street gangs. Violent "turf wars" erupted over prime locations to do business (among other things).

        a.) The language was direct over a dark, R&B influenced groove.

    * Boogie Down Productions (BDP): gained a notorious reputation due to the violent content of this album.

        a.) LaRock: intervening on behalf of a personal friend (who had offended a gang member), Scott LaRock was assassinated as his jeep was approaching the negotiating location on August 25, 1987.

            - A tragic anticipation of life mirroring art in the Hip Hop world that would spread on a wider scale later on.

B.) Background of the LA Street-Gang Culture.

1.) 1950's/60's: African American youth gangs emerged such as The Gladiators, Black Cobras, Boozies, Swamp Boys, etc.

    - August 1965: The LA Watts section rebellion inspired these inner-city youth [gang members] to join political organizations such as the US Organization and The Black Panther Party (BPP).

        * With the latter [BPP], their culture was reminiscent of the gangster mentality due to their militaristic stance. Especially, when it came to the advent of weaponry in the wake of the assassination of the BPP leadership in 1969.

        a.) This led to the revitalization of LA youth street gangs.

2.) Result of Gang Revitalization: Disenfranchisement due to becoming depoliticized (because of the demise of politically-oriented organizations).

    - Key Event: the emergence of The Crips. Founded by Raymond Washington who was greatly influenced by the Black Panther Party.

        * The Crack Era and Reaganism: In the mid 80's, The Crips and their major rivals, The Bloods, proliferated throughout the LA and, as a result, homicides grew at an unprecedented rate. This was due to two major factors:

            a.) Lack of jobs due to de-industrialization (where industries abandoned the LA inner city due -- in the view of many -- to Reagan-era economic policies).

            b.) The advent of Crack Cocaine, which translated into significant revenue (in the millions of dollars).

        * RESULT: A gang-influenced metaphysical view that differed completely from the viewpoint of affluent, middle-class, suburban Black-America. What mattered to Gang-Bangers? Respect and Turf the latter being the gauge of elevated social status.

            a.) Another Result: A cavalier attitude in regard to death and violence while simultaneously disavowing any individual responsibility.

C.) The Message of Gangsta Rap: inspired by the brutal day-to-day realities of inner city street life (at least on the surface). Below the surface, the use of extreme depictions of gang warfare and misogyny as metaphors for MC's showing off their bodaciousness. These extreme depictions served as a model for subject matter.

    1.) <u>Lyrics</u>: violent lyrics with metaphorical intentions rather then literal.

        - <u>Metaphors</u>: used to challenge other Rap competitors but from the microphone as opposed to actual violent encounters.

            * Violent metaphors are sometimes used boast or describe one's bodaciousness or superiority -- rather than the actual glorification of violence itself.

        - <u>In the case of the literal</u>: violence (not metaphorical) is depicted with humor and an exaggeration that exhibits a sense of unbelievably.

            * <u>Gross exaggeration</u>: used in competitions of virile masculinity (i.e. the "baddest motherfucker") -- their own art of wordsmithism but done in a raw, crude manner.

    2.) <u>Realism</u>: usually told in the first person giving loose descriptions from the standpoint of a self-described "<u>Street Reporter</u>".

        - From their perspective, [they see it] through the eyes of a criminal, a police brutality victim, one who lives in a ghetto, a gang member, or one who rules and dominates over women. And because of their detached "street reporter" status, they disavow any personal responsibility.

            * <u>Inspiration</u>: the virile, badass, assertive black heroes of the classic Blaxploitation movies of the 70's. (i.e. "Shaft, "Superfly", "Sweet Sweetback's Badass Song" -- legends of black inner city folklore).

    3..) <u>Social Commentary</u>: biting descriptions of the inner city plight of LA's black communities.

        - Poverty, unemployment, victimized by racism, viability of crack dealing enterprises, police brutality, and the notion that the "powers that be" have stacked the deck (so to speak) against them.

            * Blaming the white powers that make the money and resource-distribution decisions as well as the capitalist system itself -- the latter, encouraging an impoverished underclass.

                a.) Again, all told in the first person narrative -- on how those social inequalities adversely effect the black inner city community.

    4.) <u>Rebelliousness</u>: with a rock-inspired essence over a funk groove -- similar to the rock-inspired essences of <u>Run DMC</u>, <u>The Beastie Boys</u>, and <u>Public Enemy</u> (that would be appreciated by a white teenage segment of the mainstream).

        - <u>Especially white male teens</u>: who were looking for the rebelliousness of tough macho-ism inspired by the tales of everyday street life. While at the same time, romanticizing from afar without being directly engaged (thereby fulfilling their rebellious fantasies).

D.) "<u>Gangsta Rap</u>": West Coast Rap tales (told usually in the first person) of gang violence and misogyny.

    1.) <u>Ice T</u>: (b. Tracy Morrow, 2/16/58, Newark, NJ): the father of West Coast Gangsta Rap.

        - <u>Beginnings</u>: Born in New Jersey but moved to Los Angeles during his childhood. While attending Crenshaw High School, he joined a street gang and had a brief stint as a criminal. He briefly attended a junior college upon his high school graduation -- after which he spent four years in the military.

            * After his four years [in the military] were completed, he pursued his dream of becoming a Rapper.

                a.) <u>His first breakthrough</u>: appearing in a Hip Hop film called "Breakin".

        - "<u>Rhyme Pays</u>" (1987): his debut album.Also, the first West Coast Gangsta Rap album.

* Semi-biographical in nature (a sketch of his gang-related background) in which some subject matter was either inspired by personal experience (i.e. what he himself witnessed) or what he heard through the streets.

Squeeze The Trigger
Ice-T

a.) The debut of the use of subject matter pertaining to violence, crime, and misogyny in the West Coast arena.

- His argument: that he became the product of a brutal society that is: the dark, violent underside of LA street life.

- NOTE: although Ice T introduced the art of Gangsta Rap to the West Coast, it seemed that to a native LA audience, his East Coast origins diminished his credibility -- a harbinger of the West Coast/East Coast rivalry to come.

* As groundbreaking as Ice T's West Coast Gangsta Rap was, there would be another group that would take this genre to the extreme And, in the process of taking this genre to a new extreme, a new original sound will be achieved.

D.) NWA (Niggaz With Attitude): formed in 1986, would take art of Gangsta Rap to an entirely new dimension.

1.) Personnel: Ice Cube (b. O'Shea Jackson, 6/15/69/, LA): vocals; Eazy-E (b. Eric Wright, 9/7/63, Compton, CA; d. 5/26/95, LA): vocals; Dr. Dre (b. Andre Ramelle Young, 2/18/65, Compton, CA): producer; DJ Yella (b. Antoine Carraby, Compton, CA): DJ; the Arabian Prince (b. Michael Lezan, Compton, CA): vocals; replaced by MC Ren (b. Lorenzo Patterson, LA): vocals.

- NWA: would be the first to give Gangsta Rap a higher profile.

2.) "Straight Outta Compton" (1988): the album that gave NWA notoriety.

- Properties brought to the extreme which made this album unique and original:

Straight Outta Compton
NWA

* Exaggerated depictions of tough ghetto street life.
a.) More extreme than Ice T.
* Resistance against authority in a militant manner.
* Sexual violence (i.e. misogyny).
* So-called "underground Street reporting".
a.) From a highly biased point of view.
* RESULT: the most brutal lyrics in Gangsta Rap up to that time period (most extreme).

- West Coast Gangsta Rap standardized by NWA -- detailed street life narrations over heavy-duty funk grooves that were sampled.

* Sampled grooves from: Parliament/Funkadelic, Sly Stone, James Brown, and various other 70's Funk models -- especially from Parliament/Funkadelic.
a.) This style would expand rapidly throughout LA.

3.) They started their own independent labels.
- Eazy-E (a former drug dealer): started "Ruthless Records".
- Ice Cube (post NWA): "Street Knowledge Productions".
- Dr. Dre: "Death Row Records".

4.) Controversy: the single from "Straight Outta Compton" entitled, *Fuck Tha Police* – a gangsta rap staple with a story of gang-bangers having no hesitation of violence against police officers. In their view, the police are the enemy -- the epitome of oppression against African Americans who are marginalized by mainstream society – to be kept at bay and if necessary, kept behind bars.

- August 2, 1989: Milt Ahlerich, an assistant director of public relations for the FBI, released a statement to departments of law enforcement nationwide warning the *Fuck Tha Police* encourages disrespect and supports violence against police officers.

* In his words: "…recordings such as the one from NWA are both discouraging and degrading to the brave, dedicated police officers".

F___ Tha Police

a.) RESULT: police agencies refused to provide security for

NWA concerts and urged police departments to assist in canceling NWA performances.

5.) <u>NOTE</u>: not all rap music in the late 80's dealt with subjects revolving around violence, misogyny, gang warfare, social/political statements, and violence against the authorities.

- There was another type of rap brewing in the east coast that would unveil a completely different positive, humoristic message.

E.) <u>De La Soul</u> (formed in 1985, Amityville, NY): would present a completely different approach to Rap – one of humor and optimism. They were part of a group of alternative rap artists who dubbed themselves, "Native Tongues".

1.) Personnel: <u>Posdnous</u> (b. Kevin Mercer, 8/17/69, Bronx, NY): vocalist; <u>Trugoy The Dove</u> (b. David Jolicoeur, 9/21/68, Brooklyn, NY): vocalist; <u>Maseo</u> (b. Vincent Mason, 4/24/70, Brooklyn, NY): DJ.

- They were the first to <u>buck the dominant trend</u> of the macho-driven, self-absorbed, egocentric, crime & misogyny-based Rap music.

* Along with the trend of social commentary dealing with the plight of the black inner city.

Me Myself and I
De La Soul

a.) They replaced it with lyrics of whit, humor, optimism, and sometimes, thoughtful irreverence, with melodies that were at times, innocent and childlike.

b.) <u>Musically</u>: along with the type of melodies mentioned, they also bucked the common rap trend by <u>not</u> using hard, slamming Funk beats. Instead, they took a lighter, more laid-back beat approach.

- <u>RESULT</u>: they would become the first of the "alternative" rap groups under the Native Tongues umbrella that included Jungle Brothers and A Tribe Called Quest.

2.) <u>Background</u>: 3 friends from high school two of which, have pseudonyms of words spelt backwards.

- <u>Kevin Mercer</u>: as a high school DJ, was known as "Sound Sop".

* Spelt backwards: "<u>Posdnous</u>".The same with David Jolicoeur: "<u>Trugoy</u>" is yogurt (his favorite food) spelt backwards.

3.) "<u>3 Feet High And Rising</u>" (1989, released on the "Tommy Boy" label): their debut album consisting of 24 tracks: songs, skits, rap tunes, humor, and optimism.

- "<u>Eye Know</u>": samples of Steely Dan's "<u>Peg</u>" superimposed with a sample (whistling melody) from Otis Redding's "<u>Dock Of The Bay</u>".

Eye Know
De La Soul

* Rapping done in an easy-going, quasi-conversational manner (as opposed to the loud, in-your-face rapping with a macho stance as was prevalent at the time).

- <u>Sampling</u>: very liberal use of sampling that was carefree.

* These samples (i.e. clips of original music recorded by other artists) were used extensively without any regard for copyright violations.

a.) "<u>Rapper's Delight</u>" notwithstanding (for Sugar Hill Records was sued by <u>Nile Rodgers</u> and <u>Bernard Edwards</u> of "Chic" for copyright infringement of "Good Times" -- the borrowed groove for "Rapper's Delight")…

-…Rappers throughout the 80's sampled freely and without worry.

* <u>De La Soul</u>: took the liberty of taking samples from TV shows and very obscure, somewhat unknown records (many from their parents' collection) and using computerized technology to transpose musical samples from those records into a new key.

a.) Thereby creating a quilt of sound containing pastiches of various samples woven together (which Public Enemy also did – but in their own way different from De La Soul).

* "Transmitting From Mars": one of the tracks in "3 Feet High And Rising".

Transmitting From Mars
De La Soul

        a.) A French lesson record (complete with pops, scratches, crackles from the worn out vinyl record) superimposed over a transposed groove from a 1968 single entitled: "You Showed Me" by The Turtles. This marked the point where De La Soul started using samples of pre-recorded original music from outside of the black music arena.

            - NOTE: during this period, white artists who were sampled became outraged that clips of their music were being set to Rap music without their permission.

        b.) RESULT: Former members of The Turtles filed a copyright infringement lawsuit against De La Soul for $1,700,000. It was settled out of court for an undisclosed amount.

- RESULT: Rappers would become more hesitant or more cautious regarding the sampling of pre-recorded original material by other artists.

        * Instead of sound pastiches, sampling would become considerably simplified with only one sampled pop melody that was both previously well known and instant.

            a.) Artists in this vain included: MC Hammer sampling Rick James' "Super freak" and Puff Daddy sampling Diana Ross' "I'm Coming Up" -- pop melody hooks already well known in mainstream America thereby guaranteeing their hit success.

F.). Hip hop in the 90's: groundwork for a solid legacy beginning with the tentacles of former NWA members who would go on to have successful solo careers of their own (further solidifying the primacy of LA hip-hop in the early 90's).

        1.) Eazy-E: "Eazy Does It" (Ruthless/Priority: 1988)
                      "5150 Home 4 The Sick" (1992)
                      "It's On (Dr. Dre) 187um Killa": (1993)

                          * Combined total sales: about 5,000,000 copies at the time. "Ruthless": was Eazy-E's label and "Priority" was the distributor.

        2.) Dr. Dre: "The Chronic" (1992). Sold 3,000,000 copies.
                          * Released on the "Death Row/Interscope" Label.

        3.) MC Ren: "Kiss My Black Azz" (1992)
                          * Sold 1,000,000 copies.

        4.) Ice Cube: "AmeriKKKa's Most Wanted" (1990)
                      "Kill At Will (EP: 1900)
                      "Death Certificate" (1991)
                      "The Predator" (1992)
                      "Lethal Injection" (1994)
                      "Bootlegs and B-Sides" (1994)

                        * All told, combined sales of about 6,000,000 copies.

5.) Ice Cube: Joined NWA after graduating from college with a degree in drafting.

- Grew up in a strict, 2 parent, middle-class home in South Central, LA.

        * Him and Andre Young (Dr. Dre) met and began writing rap tunes and lyrics for Eazy-E/NWA.

            a.) Ice Cube's tenure with NWA ended due to a financial row with NWA's manager: Jerry Heller -- whom Ice Cube accused of withholding his [Cube's] royalties (eventually settled out of court).

- Solo Career: success with "AmeriKKKa's Most Wanted" (1990). Recorded in collaboration with his protégé crew: Da Lynch Mob.

* He also solicited Public Enemy's "Bomb Squad" to produce the album.

> a.) Used their [Bomb Squad's] production trademarks of complex, superimposed sampling tapestries bringing a sense of depth and substance to the music -- complete with sound bites and record scratches.

* RESULT: #19 on the pop charts and #6 on the R&B remaining platinum for three months.

- Ice Cube, The Lyricist: Possessed a gift not only for rhyming but also, as a poignant storyteller playing the role of a character (i.e. first person).

> * Example: In her essay entitled *"Kickin' Reality, Kickin' Ballistics: Gangsta Rap and Postindustrial Los Angeles"*, Robin D. G. Kelley uses "A Bird In The Hand" (from "Death Certificate": 1991) to illustrate Ice Cube's storytelling artistry.

A Bird In The Hand
Ice Cube

> > a.) Ice Cube: plays an unemployed, impoverished black man who repeatedly gets rejected for decent, mid-range paying jobs. He is a father who is desperate to provide for his newborn baby.

> > > - He reluctantly takes a low-paying McDonalds gig.

> > > > * With samples of screaming babies in the background, he thinks about the only model of a successful entrepreneur in his neighborhood: The Drug Dealer.

> > > - Although his financial conditions improve as a result of adopting the drug dealer model for himself, he is now haunted and threatened by the Police among other things.

> > b.) RESULT: a poignant example of an artist who was not only an adept lyricist, but also a gifted storyteller in a quasi self-made virtual movie where his words evoke stark, dramatic images that make one ponder.

> > > - This perhaps explains in part, Ice Cube's rapid adeptness at acting and movie making.

> > > > * By illustrating the relationship between dire living conditions and the effect they have on one's daily decisions.

> * Like in his NWA days, he also plays the role of the "street reporter" as well as biting social commentary especially against the Reagan/Bush era.

> > a.) "A bird in hand, is worth more than a Bush" from the song *Bird In The Hand*.

- Ice Cube, The Producer: he produced his protégé rap crew, Da Lynch Mob on their debut album "Guerrillas In The Mist".

> * Which went gold.

- Ice Cube, The Movie Maker: he wrote the script for "Friday" (1996) and directed "Players Club" (1998).

> * His debut acting gig was in a John Singleton film entitled: "Boyz In The Hood" (1991).

> > a.) RESULT: of all of the NWA alumni, Ice Cube became the most creative and artistically, the most multi-faceted (i.e. lyricist, songwriter (Hip Hop), actor, director, moviemaker). But it was another NWA alum, Dr. Dre who would go on to be the most gifted, influential *producer*.

6.) <u>Dr. Dre</u>: started writing with Ice Cube for Eazy-E's "Ruthless" label (which Eazy-E established with his drug dealing profits). In 1991, he [Dre] went solo and along with Marion "Suge" Knight, became an important part of "Death Row Records".

- <u>Marion "Sugar Bear" Knight</u> (b. Apr. 19, 1966, Compton, CA): former member of the Mob Piru Bloods and later. a star football player for UNLV. He also worked as a bodyguard for various celebrities. In 1991, along with attorney David Kenner, Knight founded Death Row Records. He teamed up with Interscope as his distributor and business ally (who gave him ownership of the master tapes – an unusual arrangement in the rap business).

* He immediately signed Dr. Dre – after threatening bodily harm to Eazy E forcing him [E] to release Dre from his Ruthless label contract.

a.) "Suge" Knight assembled a hefty roster for the Death Row label including artist such as: <u>Snoop Doggy Dogg</u>, <u>Kurupt</u>, <u>RBX</u>, <u>Jewell</u>, <u>Lady of Rage</u>, <u>Dat Nigga Daz</u>, and <u>The D.O.C.</u>

- <u>Death Row's Character</u>: the embracement, the selling of, and the embodiment of the LA urban gangsta legend. The star attractions who began their collaboration on Death Row -- Dr. Dre and Snoop Doggy Dogg (b. Calvin Broadus, 10/20/72, Long Beach, CA). – would become the face of this label's [gangland] embodiment.

* Their first collaboration was on a soundtrack entitled, *Deep Cover*. But it would on another project – namely a landmark album – that their collaboration would set the tone for rap music of the 90's.

- "<u>The Chronic</u>" (1992): went to #3 on the pop charts, #1 on the R&B, and went triple-platinum. The apex of the LA gangsta ethos that would inspire many emulators nationwide and popularize the G/Funk aesthetic.

* The album's hit single "<u>Nuthin' But A G-Thang</u>" reached #1 on the R&B, #8 on the pop charts, and had a hit video promoted by MTV (on which Dre introduced Snoop Doggy Dog to the mainstream public).

a.) The groove was sampled from a 70's funk tune called, *I Want'a Do Something Freaky To You* by Leon Haywood.

* Dre's production elements included:

a.) Lush, rich sound production

b.) Massive, heavy funk bass and choruses inspired by the sampling of Parliament/Funkadelic (a.k.a. P/Funk) – an aesthetic known as G/Funk (G for gangsta).

- Compare the chorus of Dre's *Let Me Ride* with a clip from P/Funk's *Mothership Connection* from 1976.

c.) Pop-driven synthesizer lines (another G/Funk staple).

d.) Continuity of extreme gangsta rap lyrics embodied by previous NWA albums such as *Straight Outta Compton* (1988) and *Efil4zaggin* (1991).

e.) Laid back West Coast character and shocking bad boy essences mixed together.

f.) <u>Vocal Variety</u>: voices of the Death Row roster in one album including: Snoop Doggy Dogg, RBX, Kurupt, Jewell, et al. – vocal contrasts giving the album more creative interest.

* RESULT: a very accessible G/Funk aesthetic that would not only sweep the mainstream by storm, but would also help inspire a new hip-hop rebirth emanating from the East Coast. What we'll see is a synthesis between the New York and LA traditions that will re-energize east coast rap.

Nuthin' But A G-Thang
Dr. Dre

I Want'a Do Something Freaky To You
Leon Haywood

Let Me Ride
Dr. Dre

Mothership Connection
Parliament/Funkadelic

V. THE NEW YORK HIP HOP RENNAISSANCE OF THE MID 1990'S
A.) Prelude: The Harbingers

1.) "The Message": Grandmaster Flash & The Furious Five. Echoing the frustrations of day-to-day life in the fast-paced, crime-ridden, impoverished inner-city ghetto of New York. The first harbinger to the "Message Rap" category.

2.) Public Enemy: avant-garde approach. Complex layerings of samples, spoken (media-derived) soundbites, and grooves.

- Making sensible control out of superimposed chaotic elements (capturing the essence of the New York City hustle and bustle).

3.) Rakim and Big Daddy Kane (among others): Deep. intense poetry rife with hidden meanings, no melodies, no pop hooks, no refrains/choruses, and no massive heavy-bass driven funk grooves.

- Definitely, an acquired taste where much time and effort had to be spent (repeated listenings) in order to fully appreciate.

B.) Answer to California Hip Hop: influence and response.

1.) Late 80's/early 90's: Rap has nationwide success from artists outside of New York such as 2 Live Crew (Miami), Geto Boys (Houston), Too Short (San Francisco), and NWA (LA/Compton). MC Hammer and Vanilla Ice were totally pop.

- Most influential album of the early 90's: "The Chronic" (1992) - Dr Dre's monumental classic.

* Listener-friendly with synth-driven lines that give particular passages pop, melodic focus; massive, bass-heavy, riff-driven funk grooves inspired by and [at times] directly sampling Parliament/Funkadelic (a.k.a. "G-Funk" = Gangsta + P/Funk); and pop tunesmithism with catchy choruses. In addition, lyrics with easy-to-follow storytelling displays of bodaciousness/sexual prowess.

a.) "The Chronic": made Gangsta-influenced rap a mainstream, nationwide phenomenon without sacrificing any street credibility or authenticity.

2.) New York City: The style of NYC renaissance artists will be a combination of elements derived from both West Coast Gangsta Rap (most notably, "The Chronic") and the NYC rap tradition from the mid 80's.

- From West Coast Gangsta rap: tales of gang warfare, misogyny, and tough NYC street life in the impoverished, crime-ridden inner city.

* In addition, NYC artists would also emulate the business/marketing acumen of West Coast rappers…

a.) …along with the concept of using synch-driven pop tunes and choruses (again, inspired by "The Chronic").

- From the NYC Rap: the tradition of intricate rhyming and wordplay continuing as the main focus.

* In the accompaniment: the continuity of repetitive loops with snare drum-driven samples accentuating the backbeat. In other words, no heavy bass grooves influenced by P/Funk.

a.) Although NYC rappers will begin using choruses, the avoidance of pop hooks for the most part, will be maintained.

- Additional Elements of the NYC Renaissance aesthetic: the use of skits (acting scenes with spoken dialog), samples of actual Kung Fu-derived film clips (presented in a Lo-Fi sound format), and the use of sampled musical clips of other artists.

C) Artists of NYC Hip Hop Renaissance To Be Covered: Wu-Tang Clan, Nas, and The Notorious B.I.G.

1.) Wu-Tang Clan: The first important group of MC's since NWA -- instrumental in spearheading the NYC Renaissance with elements of theatre, street rhymes, karate skits, and mass marketing. Among the first to blend both west coast and New York rap traditions together.

- Personnel (all of which were MC's): RZA/Prince Rakeem (b. Robert Diggs), GZA/Genius (b. Gary Grice), Ol' Dirty Bastard (b. Russell Jones), Inspectah Deck (b. Jason Hunter), Raekwon the Chef (b. Corey Woods), U-God (b.

Lamont Hawkins), <u>Ghostface Killah</u> (b. Dennis Coles), <u>Method Man</u> (b. Clifford Smith), and <u>Masta Killa</u> (b. Elgin Turner).

* They grew up in the tough, crime-ridden housing projects of Staten Island (which they refer to as The Shaolin).

- They reinvented the concept the concept of the rap group by presenting themselves as a collective of MC's/businessmen – they either collaborated together on an album or released their own albums individually.

* New York street rap meets west coast-influenced business acumen.

a.) <u>RZA</u> (Robert Diggs): the group's original founder and visionary who securing a recording contract for the group on Loud/RCA.

- The label, in the tradition of rap credibility, allowed the group and it's individual artists, complete creative freedom.

b.) Their works were more like [concept] album-lengthed cinematic soundtracks than a set of individual rap numbers.

- "<u>Enter The Wu-Tang (36 Chambers)</u>" (1993): their debut album – the result of synthesizing New York street rap (East Coast) with the gangsta rap ethos and business acumen made successful in LA (West Coast).

* The revitalization of New York City rap in a group format. Complete with cinematic skits and hardcore rap in a concept album format.

a.) <u>Introduction</u>: of some of NYC's future notable voices such as Method Man, Ol' Dirty Bastard, and Raekwon (among others)… would all have their own lucrative solo careers (an emulation of the NWA artists).

* Ingredients that would become standard in the NYC Renaissance:

a.) <u>Hardcore Gangsta Rap</u>: inspired by the west coast tradition.

b.) <u>Choruses/Refrains</u>: another west coast influence.

c.) <u>Skits</u>: New York influence (as illustrated in *Wu-Tang/7ᵗʰ Chamber*)

d.) <u>Intricate Rhyming and Wordplay</u>: NYC tradition.

e.) <u>Grooves</u>: Emphasis on the snappy, well-produced snare drum-driven backbeat (NYC tradition).

f.) <u>Repetitive Background Tune</u>: (West Coast): as illustrated in *C.R.E.A.M.*

g.) <u>Simple, Repetitive Loops</u>: NYC.

* A concept album complete with skits, cinematic Kung Fu sound samples (in a Lo-Fi format), and hardcore rap tunes. Example of a Kung Fu sample opens the track of *Shame On A N____a*.

a.) The sense of variety is furthered by the use by different MC's either within a rap single or as lead rappers in different singles (another West Coast influence initiated by "The Chronic").

a.) Different voice qualities give each tune different personalities furthering the consistent variety within a concept album narrative.

- <u>Case In Point</u>: the clip form *C.R.E.A.M.* begins with Method Man's voice (doing the chorus) and ends with Inspectah Deck rapping the next verse.

- NOTE: The precepts initiated by the Wu-Tang Clan – ushering in the NYC Renaissance -- would be influential to a host of other NYC street-rhyme artists to follow…

2.) <u>Nas</u> (b. Nasir Ben Olu Dara Jones, 1973, Brooklyn, NY): a reputation for transforming rap into an intricate art form from a poet's perspective which included

Shame On A N____a
Wu-Tang Clan

Wu-Tang/7ᵗʰ Chamber
Wu-Tang Clan

C.R.E.A.M.
Wu-Tang Clan

hidden meanings. His approach was one of integrity and authenticity (keeping it real) as opposed to commercial stardom.

- He signed with CBS Records in 1992. After collaborating with some of the best beat artists crafting his grooves (DJ Premiere and Q-Tip among others), his debut album, *Illmatic* (1994) was released. (It is worth noting that CBS Records, a major record label, granted Nas total artistic freedom).

* Consistent Formulaic Elements:

The Genesis
Nas

a.) Skits/Dialogue: in the opening track, *The Genesis*, a spoken dialogue (skit) takes place in a subway setting with the noise of the subway in the background.

N.Y. State Of Mind
Nas

b.) Focus on the words: intricate rhymes that speak to the realities of tough NYC street life (gangsta influence), while displaying poetic depth. *N.Y. State O f Mind* is an example.

c.) The Beat: focus on well-produced backbeat – mostly carrying a sampled snare drum sound (as opposed to the heavy-bass funk grooves of the West Coast style).

d.) Repetitive Loops: use of the same repetitive fragment to accompany the vocal line giving the rap poetry an unobscured focus.

Life's A Bitch
Nas

e.) Use of Chorus/Refrain: another NYC Renaissance-based consistency. In the example *Life's A Bitch*, at about the 19 second mark, the catchy section begins.

* Lyrics: contain picturesque, street-driven narratives and intricate poetry/rhyming – a continuity of NYC rap poetics in place since Eric B. & Rakim.

a.) NOTE: As celebrated as the integrity of this album was to the New York rap intelligencia, *Illmatic* never broke out into national mainstream market.

- It would take another artist to unleash the gangsta-influenced NYC street rap style into a national phenomenon…

3.) The Notorious B.I.G. (b. Christopher Wallace, May 21, 1972, Brooklyn, NY; d. May 9, 1997, Los Angeles, CA): would be the first NYC rapper of the 90's to crack the national hip-hop market (while maintaining the integrity of the NYC rap tradition). It would all end tragically on May 9, 1997 of an assassination in LA while riding in his motorcade from the Soul Train awards (where he appeared as a presenter) -- a tragic example of life imitating art.

- Bad Boy Entertainment: owned by Sean "Puffy" Combs signed B.I.G. to a recording contract.

Big Poppa
The Notorious B.I.G.

* "Big Poppa" (1995): B.I.G.'s first national hit. Emulation of the Dr. Dre ("The Chronic") structure that Sean Combs had carefully studied.

Let Me Ride
Dr. Dre

a.) Elements: pop-driven synth lines and in the chorus, sampling of an actual pop tune (in this case, The Isley Brothers' *Between The Sheets*) -- both elements along with a listener-friendly sound, were products of the Dr. Dre influence.

- In spite of pop-driven elements just mentioned, B.I.G. maintained his street credibility in part, due to his emulation of the pimp-driven, pornographic characteristics of San Francisco rapper, Too Short (b. Todd Shaw).

- "Ready To Die" (1995): the album that launched New York hip-hop back into the national mainstream stage. It also launched Sean "Puffy" Combs and his Bad Boy Entertainment into a powerful, viable business enterprise and creative force.

* Another synthesis of West Coast and New York rap traditions. Complete with skits, intricate street narratives (in this case, more accessible than the more deeper rhymes of the NYC tradition), use of choruses, pop tunes, and a bopping, snare-driven backbeat – mostly consistent with other artists of the New York Renaissance.

    a.) <u>Complete Narrative</u> (in a concept album format): about the life of the B.I.G. New York street character.

        1.) Opens with a skit entitled *Intro*, dramatizing the birth of the B.I.G. character. (Begins with a heartbeat fading in symbolizing the birth of a new life). Near the conclusion of the skit, a sample of Curtis Mayfield's *Superfly* appears (in a low-fi sound format).

        2.) <u>Street Narrative</u>: auto-biographical tales of criminality, violence, misogyny, and drug-driven street warfare as told by someone who had actually experienced it. *Gimme The Loot* is one example.

        3.) <u>Metaphor</u> (another West Coast influence): in *Ready To Die*, B.I.G. uses violent lyrics as metaphors to express his bodaciousness and superior rapping prowess (B.I.G.'s rapping style suggestive of an Ice Cube influence).

        4.) <u>Narrative Conclusion</u>: this concept album, beginning with a heartbeat introducing a new life concludes with the heartbeat gradually coming to a stop indicating the death of the main character (from a sampled, self-inflicted gunshot) in *Suicidal Thoughts*.

* "<u>Ready To Die</u>": reintroduced mainstream America to the essence, art, and reputation of New York City street rap. On the heels of this reintroduction, it's success opened the door for other pop-driven New York artists to flourish nationally such as Jay-Z and others.

D.) <u>Jay-Z</u> (b. Shawn Corey Carter, Dec. 4, 1970, Brooklyn, NY): the man who combined independent entrepreneurship with a highly successful rapping career – he would also become CEO of Def Jam Records. As a rapper, he transformed the art of the New York Rap Renaissance into pop and in the process, became its greatest success story.

    <u>Background</u>: as a child growing up in the Marcy Projects in Brooklyn, his first exposure to rap was a cipher – a group of people standing around in a circle clapping their hands in rhythm while the person in the middle [of the circle] was improvising rhymes. Jay Z was inspired enough that he thought he could do this (and that was his beginning). He started keeping a spiral notebook where he wrote rhymes every day – either at home or on the street. At the age of 13, he started selling crack cocaine where eventually, the bulk of his business was in Trenton, NJ (where he commuted from Brooklyn). It was during this time, that he developed his skills as a hustler, which would later bear fruit in his rapping career.

    <u>His First Serious Influence</u>: early New York rapper Big Daddy Kane and his album, *Long Live The Kane* (1988) – Shawn Carter's earliest inspiration of rap's possibility as a serious art. Watching him live was an important education -- his flamboyant shows included DJ Mister Cee and choreographed dancers Scoop & Scrap. His rhyming flow was skillful and awe-inspiring – he had a way of "condensing and stacking rhymes" with both speed and imagination.

Early Collaborators: he began practicing with his first collaborator: a kid who called himself "Jaz" and they'd practice together and make cassette recordings. He soon after, began engaging in rhyming battles on the streets of the Marcy Projects and developed a distinct voice.

Inspiration To Become A Rapper: as his rhyming skills were developing his initial ambition was to become a DJ, until he first heard Run DMC. They had a, slick hard-rapping style (unlike The Sugar Hill Gang) about the good life with fancy cars and champaign. In his view, Run DMC's style signaled the genesis of Rap finding a distinct voice – rough and forceful on the one hand, smooth and witty on the other. It was Run DMC that inspired Shawn Carter to become a rapper. His only criticism, was that their raps had little to do with the realities of life in the projects. What was missing [in his view] was the lure of the streets – the hustler.

> Rapping & Hustling: to him, they were one in the same although when he came of age, he was hustling first and rapping second. Due to his experience selling crack cocaine, he adopted the "hustler" essence into pursuing a career in rap. Hustling was a business that required vision, dedication, and above all, discipline. He would take that ethos with him into the hip-hop business -- it would also give him, his own unique story to tell.

Rakim: on the heels of his first ever recording session with Big Daddy Kane produced by Fresh Gordon, Jay-Z noticed a new rapping influence: Rakim (of Eric B. & Rakim). To him, Rakim was the apex of New York MC's. He was seen as a street poet, a street-wise intellectual, and someone who tapped into the spirit and captured the tone of everyday life [that Jay Z could relate to].

> NOTE: in a rap era defined by lyrics of partying, and party shouts, Rakim bucked the common trend by rhyming with a serious, real-life approach that tackled real-life situations in a highly intricate manner.

Gangland Rapping: on the heels of outsiders like Schoolly D (b. Jesse B. Weaver from Philadelphia, PA) and Ice T (b. Tracy Morrow from Los Angeles) rapping about gang-life was in. Boogie Down Productions (BDP) created a new standard in New York with their own rhymes about crack-fueled gang warfare, on their debut album: *Criminal Minded* (1987). When Jay-Z heard NWA's *Straight Outta Compton* (1988), he knew that gangland rapping went national. With Dr. Dre's *The Chronic* (1992), it was the first west coast album to be played everywhere in Brooklyn and it had all of the gangland earmarks: gangbanging, smoking weed, partying, etc.

> Perspective: It was in the face of this new gang-related rhyming onslaught, that Jay-Z would finally have his own story to tell. The goal of that story: the truth behind his life experiences. Whether it was hustling drugs on the street, boasting bodaciousness, or entertaining, in the end, the truth about the psychology behind the person/artist was vital – it was *his* story. In his view, the hustler and the rapper can be as one or go in their separate directions. Either way, rhyming was his way of *reporting* the story.

>> The "Hustler" Ethos: for him, the hustler story was a metaphor of *the* ultimate struggle for survival, which (he believed) defined everyone. Since it relates to everybody in one way or another, he found it necessary to present this metaphor as entertainment. With this approach, Jay-Z found credibility in synthesizing both art and entertainment together, which would eventually reach a wide, mainstream audience.

<u>Culmination of Rap Meets D.I.Y Ethos</u>: in summarizing the New York Rap Renaissance – <u>Wu Tang Clan</u> created the musical blueprint combining east coast and west coast rap elements together and became the first important rap group since NWA. <u>Nas</u> continued the New York tradition of intricate rhyming and laced with his own west coast/east coast synthesis in a one-man context with *Illmatic*. <u>Notorious B.I.G</u>. took this [Renaissance] blueprint with *Ready To Die* and gave it, its first nationwide success on Puffy's label, Bad boy Entertainment – thereby reestablishing the primacy of New York rap on a national scale. They were all accomplished as their own separate entities making separate contributions.

<u>Culmination</u>: Jay-Z would take these separate accomplishments of his predecessors (including Puffy) and combine them together – in other words, he was the culmination of all elements of the east coast/west coast synthesis [of the NY Rap Renaissance] combined into one:

- The street-gang, hustler narratives of Wu Tang and B.I.G.
- The New York tradition of intricate rhyming of Nas.
- Catchy, easily singable, easily memorable choruses along with catchy, repetitive loops (both New York Rap Renaissance staples).
- Massive funk grooves reminiscent of west coast rap (*not* a New York Renaissance staple).
- A steady flow of guest artists appearing on his albums giving a vibrant vocal variety (a practice made famous by Dr. Dre's *The Chronic*).
- The entrepreneurship of owning his own label (D.I.Y.) like Puffy did.
- The steady flow of his rapid, syllabic rapping style over a tight, metric groove (influential to Eminem).
- Skits (presented in both dialogue and musical approaches): either acted out in spoken dialogue or musically-driven skit-acting as illustrated between Jay-Z and Memphis Bleek in the song, *Coming of Age*.

Coming Of Age
Jay-Z

<u>NOTE</u>: in combining these elements, Jay-Z went further by transforming the New York Rap Renaissance blueprint into mainstream pop. As a result, he would have the most successful career of the New York artists from this period. In addition, he completed the transformation of reestablishing New York as rap music's epicenter (taking it away from LA once and for all).

<u>Roc-A-Fella</u>: his own label that he founded along with Kareem Burke and Damon Dash. In attempting to find a reliable distributor, Jay-Z had a meeting with Russell Simmons, co-owner and CEO of Def Jam Records. At first, Simmons suggested signing Jay-Z to the label but Jay Z wanted to cut out the middleman and become his own boss. In the end, Simmons agreed for Def Jam to be Roc-A-Fella Record's distributor.

<u>Dichotomy Of Commercialism</u>: Jay-Z's struggle between art and commerce – on the one hand, he wanted to create serious art but on the other, he wanted his raps played on mainstream radio, TV, and clubs.

<u>The Poetic Art</u>: dense, intricate rap lyrics with multiple meanings -- multi-layers of interpretation that he referred to as a "poet's mission… to make words do more than they normally do". In addition, within the realm of multiple meanings, rap had to carry a mystique, a mystery, with words that were somewhat deceptive (as opposed to being always literal) – even at the risk of being misunderstood.

<u>Artistic Choices</u>: he attempts to maintain his artistic integrity while targeting as wide an audience as possible. Some of his songs were crafted to attract wider audiences for a more instantaneous gratification (especially with catchy, tuneful choruses that were mostly sung) -- and other songs that were deeper, more complex, and more substantive.

In his view, the balance between serious and popular art was the key to crafting his albums.

> Collaborative Choices: were another key to crafting his album formats. In some ways similar to what Dr. Dre did in *The Chronic*, Jay-Z would also collaborate with other rap artists. But unlike Dr. Dre, he extended his collaborative horizons by working with other producers (and in many cases, in a singles format within an album – in fact, he would use several producers within an album). Some producers were more pop oriented such as Puff Daddy (b. Sean Combs) and Teddy Riley. Others were more rap-oriented such as Dr. Dre, Timbaland, Just Blaze, The Neptunes, and Kanye West.

> Rap Collaborative: within the Roc-A-Fella label, he had in-house collaborative rappers such as Memphis Bleek and female artist Amil. From outside the label, Notorious B.I.G., Mary J. Blige, Lil' Kim, Snoop Dogg, and Foxy Brown (the latter, featured in his debut album).

Brooklyn's Finest
Jay Z

Can't Knock The Hustle
Jay Z

Reasonable Doubt (1996): Jay-Z's debut album release, which established his approach to album-length variety -- vignettes chronicling drug hustling, home boy rivalries, crafty wordplay, and commercial success; the continuity of New York's tradition of intricate rhyming with the Renaissance element of catchy, pop choruses; and singles that are more pop-oriented and others that are deeper in meaning. To add to this variety, he has a number of guest artists: Notorious B.I.G. (*Brooklyn's Finest*), Mary J. Blige (*Can't Knock The Hustle*), Foxy Brown (*Ain't No Nigga*), Memphis Bleek (*Coming Of Age*), Big Jaz & Sauce Money (*Bring It On*), and Mecca (*Feelin' It*).

Ain't No N___a
Jay Z

Although *Reasonable Doubt* reached to #23 on the mainstream pop charts, Jay Z did immediately establish his credibility in the New York rap scene and eventually, the album would become a classic.

The City Is Mine
Jay Z

Streets Is Watching
Jay Z

In My Lifetime Vol. 1 (1997): his first top ten album (#3). Part of the reason for its popularity compared to his debut album, was his use of predominantly pop-crossover producers such as Teddy Riley and Puff Daddy. In addition, there were more pop hits than in his previous release: *The City Is Mine* (with a chorus arrangement of Glenn Frey's 1985 hit, *You Belong To the City*), *I Know What Girls Like* (featuring Puff Daddy and Lil' Kim), and *Sunshine* (featuring Babyface and Foxy Brown). But there were also hard-hitting tracks (again, pop vs. deeper songs) that kept the gangsta rap ethos intact such as *Streets Is Watching* and *Rap Game /Crack Game* as well as rapping a dialogue about ascendance from the streets to rapping success in *Real Niggazs* (featuring Too Short).

> In late 1998, there were a slew of successful New York rap artists who rose in notoriety like Lil' Kim and DMX among others. But with the release of his third album (on the heals of his two previous successes) *Vol. 2 Hard Knock Life*, Jay Z would rise to the very pinnacle of the New York rap scene and for all practical purposes, become this rap scene's one-man embodiment.

Vol. 2: Hard Knock Life (1998): the album that crowned Jay-Z, the undisputed rap king of New York by debuting at #1 on the mainstream pop charts thereby completing the process of transforming the New York Rap Renaissance style, into crossover pop.

Subject Matter: everything that young white Americans romanticize: fancy cars, dazzling women, a wealth of cash, and the rebellious gangsta element. There were more pop hits [in this album] than in any of his previous because, unlike his first two albums, he embraced pop conventions as opposed to bucking them.

Examples that charted in the top 20 include the title track: *Hard knock Life (Ghetto Anthem)* featuring the children's orphanage chorus from the Broadway musical "Annie"*; Cash, Money, Hoes* (featuring DMX); *Nigga What, Nigga Who (Originator '99)* featuring Big Jaz. In addition to guest artists are also included guest producers such as Kid Capri, Jermaine Dupri, and Timbaland (giving Jay-Z's sound a more R&B-oriented approach).

NOTE: two months following its release, Vol. 2: Hard Knock Life sold more than 2,000,000 copies (double-platinum) and earned Jay-Z a Grammy Award for best rap album of 1998.

E.) The State of West Coast Gangsta Rap (ca 1996) and Dr. Dre's Renaissance:
1.) Extinguishment of the Gangsta flame: in the wake of The Notorious B.I.G.'s assassination and Suge Knight's incarceration on a parole violation, Dr. Dre left Death Row Records and turned his full attention to his new business venture: Aftermath Entertainment. The Aftermath record label would be distributed by Interscope.
- Dre: released a compilation album that included himself along with other artists signed to his Aftermath label entitled: *Dr. Dre Presents...The Aftermath* (1996).
* It did not match the artistic level, success, and influential importance of *The Chronic* released four years earlier. What he needed, was a breakthrough artist. One that would not only crack the mainstream market, but would also directly connect with a young, white demographic. In other words, he needed a pop icon...
2.) Eminem (b. Marshall Bruce Mathers III, 10/17/74, St. Joseph, MO): the man who would put a "white face" on the black American art of Gangsta Rap, thereby exporting the genre into every home in white suburbia.
- Beginnings: at age 11, his mother (raising him and his half-brother as a single parent) moved the family to a black neighborhood on Detroit's East Side. After becoming the brunt of harassment by neighborhood kids, he won the friendship of some due to his talent for rhythmic rhyming (i.e. Rap).
* After dropping out of high school in the 9th grade, he began appearing on the local Hip Hop scene with his crew: "The Dirty Dozen".
a.) He competed in free-style competitions and became noted for his rapid-fire, staccato-styled delivery and a gift for rhyming.
- "The Slim Shady LP" (1998): the initial recording was made before Dr. Dre discovered him (originally released as an EP). After listening to an LA free-style rap radio show with an unknown Eminem doing his rapid-fire rhyming, Dr. Dre became immediately interested.
* He was impressed after listening to the "Slim Shady LP"
a.) So much so, he signed Eminem to his [Dre's] Aftermath label..
* With Dr. Dre serving as producer, the EP was expanded into a full-fledged album in 1999. It debuted at #3 on the pop charts, sold 3,000,000 copies, and won the Grammy Award for "Best Rap Album" (1999).
a.) It temporarily saved the "Aftermath" label.
- "The Marshall Mathers LP" (2000): most successful rap album since *The Chronic*. Complete with all of the elements of the West Coast/East Coast synthesis including: intricate rapid-fire rhymes, skits, gang-influenced violence & misogyny, skits, and pop hooks.
* In addition, he includes his own approach to twisted whit and derangement blurring the boundaries between what is real and

imaginary; what is funny and horrific; and storytelling as opposed to satire.

       a.) <u>Homáge to an Influence</u>: Eminem presents a quasi quote from one of his most important rap influences, <u>Rakim Allah</u> (b. William Griffith Jr.) in a track called, "The Way I Am".
         - Eminem derives his chorus from a line in Eric B. & Rakim's track from the *Paid In Full* Album, "As The Rhyme Goes On".

* <u>Staples consistent with the 90's rap tradition</u>:
       a.) <u>Skits</u>: in *Steve Berman*, the main character is expressing angst over having to distribute an offensive album that nobody wants. Sort of humoristic on one side, commentary on the other.
       b.) <u>Lyrics</u>: derangement depicted in an exaggerated manner blurring the line between believable and unbelievable (the exaggerated aspect, a West Coast gangsta staple dating back to Dre's NWA days).
         - *Kill You*, is an example of this highly exaggerated depiction of violence that is graphic yet absurd at the same time (again, blurring the boundaries).
       c.) <u>Chorus</u>: another 90's element used in the West/East hybrid where in this case, exemplified in *The Real Slim Shady*, catchy and easily memorable rap choruses accompanied with pop tunesmithism.
       d.) <u>Unique Rap Delivery</u>: rapid-fire, highly rhythmic, syllabic rap delivery that sets him apart form the rest. The words are articulated in fast, spoken rhythms as illustrated in *Bitch Please II*.

* The combined elements in the album translate into the last great rap success of the 20th century and the first of the new millennia.

- <u>RESULT</u>: Eminem, by putting a white face on the Gangsta Rap tradition, transported this genre into white teenage America on a massive scale and selling millions in the process fulfilling the same pattern set by Elvis, The Bee Gee's, Janis Joplin, et al.
       * From neglected, impoverished segments of society came styles of music (i.e. Rap, Blues, R&B, etc.) that eventually made their way into every white home in suburbia.

CHAPTER XII: REVIEW

List the three important elements that made the beginning of rap music possible (hint: two of those elements were from Jamaica):

    1.)

    2.)

    3.)

List three of the early Jamaican producers of the late 50's/early 60's:

    1.)

    2.)

    3.)

Who was the prominent of these producers and also, what was the name of his studio?

Who became the first original Jamaican DJ/Toaster?

What type of sound system did he use?

What was this toasting artist's original inspiration?

Name three other toasters from this period:

    1.)

    2.)

    3.)

Define the Dub:

What two things did the Dub accomplish?

    1.)

    2.)

Name the first original dub and the artists who recorded it:

Name the artist who further developed and popularized the Dub sound.

What was the Mixer and what impact did it have on the art of DJ'ing?

Who brought the Jamaican-influenced art of DJ'ing to the South Bronx?

What was his frustration as a break dancer in regard to the way Coxson-styled DJ's were playing records?

What became DJ Kool Herc's unique DJ'ing angle?

What was his credo?

Briefly describe "Break Spinning":

What did he create by expanding various instrumental breaks?

Briefly describe the "Merry-Go-Round" technique:

Name three instrumental break examples that Kool Herc pioneered:
1.)
2.)
3.)

What resulted from the use of these two techniques? In other words, what did DJ Kool Herc accomplish?

Who was the first American rapper? (Hint: he was Kool Herc's MC):

Name four elements that comprised Hip Hop culture:
1.)
2.)
3.)
4.)

Who founded Sugar Hill Records in 1979?

Name the first rap hit and the artists who recorded it:

What dubbed disco hit became the foundation for this [first rap hit's] single?

Name the first rap tune – and the artist who recorded it -- to reach gold:

In what vinyl format was this record was this record issued?

Who was the first white artist to make a serious attempt to execute the art of rap?

   Name the single:

What became the state of Rap music in the early 80s?

   Rap's association with disco needed a change. What was needed to make that change?

What was the significance of DJ Grandmaster Flash insofar as the art of DJ'ing was concerned?

   What was the main difference between Kool Herc's DJ'ing and Grandmaster Flash's?

List six of Grandmaster Flash's pioneering DJ'ing techniques:
   1.)
   2.)
   3.)
   4.)
   5.)
   6.)

Which technique – discovered by DJ Grand Wizard Theodore – did Grandmaster Flash standardized into Hip Hop?

Name the first example of a recorded track with a DJ mixing records in the studio.

List four reasons as to why "The Message" (1982) became the template that set the tone for black rap music for the 1980's and beyond:
   1.)
   2.)
   3.)
   4.)

In addition to Kool Herc and Grandmaster Flash, who was the other important pillar of the early Hip Hop period?

Name his groundbreaking single that ushered in the birth of "Electro-Funk".

Who founded Def Jam records?

What was the most important musical influence that Rick Rubin produced on rap records recorded by Def Jam?

What label was attached to the Run DMC's a raw, shout-like rapping style?

Name three elements that made up the original rapping/musical style of Run DMC:
    1.)
    2.)
    3.)

What was the significance of their debut album *RunDMC*?

What was the first black rap video was shown on MTV.

From the album *Raising Hell*, which black rap video was the first to be aggressively promoted by MTV?

Why?

What type of contract was RunDMC awarded following their performance of *My Addidas* at Madison Square Garden?

Name the first prominent white rap group:

Name their 1987 debut album:

What was their impact on rap in regard to mainstream appeal?

Who was the PMRC?

What resulted from their activism?

By 1987, what was the result of Def Jam's rock-oriented rap music – what did they accomplish?

Name three types of Message Rap, their brief meanings, and the artist of each type.
    1.) _____

        Artists:

    2.) _____

        Artists:

    3.) _____

        Artists:

Who was the most prominent of the political rap artists?

    What was their basic style?

    Name their breakthrough album, which established the primacy of political and social commentary back into rap music.

        Which single [from this album] makes allusions to the Black Panther Party, to Elijah Muhammad, and the "Asiatic" black man?

    List there other important album that was released in 1990.

Name the founder of The Five Percenters and briefly describe who the Five Percenters were.

    Name at least 5 rap artists among the Five Percenters.

        Among those artists, who was the most prominent?

List the reasons as to why the style of Eric B. & Rakim would become influential to the rappers of the New York City renaissance of the mid 1990's.

Which producer had the greatest early influence on Eric B.?

What was Eric B. & Rakim's debut album of 1987 that set the tone for NYC's rap renaissance?

What was Rakim's lyrical approach?

Describe the approach of Eric B.'s DJ'ing especially the character of the beat sampling.

Who was the first harbinger to what would later be known as gangsta rap?

Name their 1987 debut album:

What was the significance of this album? What type of album was it?

What was the result of gang revitalization in Los Angeles?

What was the result of the gang-influenced, metaphysical view?

What inspired the message of gangsta rap?

Lyrics:

Realism:

Social Commentary:

Rebelliousness:

Who was known as the father of west coast gangsta rap?

Name his 1987 debut album (hint: the first west coast gangsta rap album):

What type of subject matter did this album cover?

Name the group that brought the concept of gangsta rap to the extreme:

Name their 1988 debut album:

List four elements that made their debut album unique and original:
    1.)
    2.)
    3.)
    4.)

    List three influences for their heavy-duty funk grooves:
        1.)
        2.)
        3.)

Why did they use metaphors?

    What was their approach in regard to social commentary?

List the following four elements that make up De La Soul's originality:
    1.) Melodic Style:
    2.) Beat Style
    3.) Lyrics;
    4.) Rap Delivery Style:

    What genre of rap did De La Soul pioneer?

What resulted from the copyright infringement lawsuit imposed upon De La Soul that effected the way other rappers approached sampling?

Who – of the former NWA artists -- would have the most prolific solo artist career as a storyteller/lyricist and moviemaker (among other things)?

Of the NWA artists, which member became the most successful producer?

Name the two individuals who founded Death Row Records in 1991.

    Who was the first important artist (formerly of NWA) signed to the Death Row label?

        Name at least 5 other artists signed to this label.

    What was the characteristic of the Death Row label?

Which 1992 album – recorded on Death Row Records – not only popularized the G/Funk aesthetic but would also set the tone for rap music in the 90's.

List 6 elements of Dr. Dre's production style in "The Chronic".
    1.)
    2.)
    3.)
    4.)
    5.)
    6.)

What was G/Funk?

List 3 harbingers of the New York City Renaissance of the mid 1990's.
    1.)
    2.)
    3.)

Name the most influential album of the early 90's (that was released in 1992).

The style of NYC Renaissance artists had two combined major influences: West Coast Rap and the NYC Rap tradition…
    1.) List influences of west coast gangsta rap.

    2.) List influences of the NYC rap tradition.

    3.) List additional elements of the NYC renaissance aesthetic.

Who was the first important group of MC's since NWA?

    List 4 elements of their style.
        1.)
        2.)
        3.)
        4.)

    Which two traditions were they the first to synthesize together?

Name the debut album of the Wu-Tang Clan.

Who were the members of this group? (Please list all 9 of them)

List 7 ingredients of the Wu-Tang Clan's debut album that became standard in the NYC Renaissance.
    1.)
    2.)
    3.)
    4.)
    5.)
    6.)
    7.)

What was Nas' reputation in regard to rap?

What were his formulaic elements consistent with the NYC Renaissance aesthetic?
    1.)
    2.)
    3.)
    4.)
    5.)

Name Nas' landmark debut album of 1994.

    Briefly describe the lyrics:

What was the significance of The Notorious B.I.G.?

    What company and it's owner sign B.I.G. to a recording contract?

What was The Notorious B.I.G.'s first national hit?

    List 2 elements in this single that were influenced by Dr. Dre's "The Chronic".
        1.)
        2.)

Name The Notorious B.I.G.'s debut album of 1995.

What effect did this album have on the success of Sean "Puffy" Combs and his company?

What elements of the NYC rap tradition used on this album?

What was the subject of the complete narrative of this [concept] album?

Briefly describe 4 elements of the complete narrative about the life of this NYC street character.
1.) <u>Skit</u>:
2.) <u>Street Narrative</u>:
3.) <u>Metaphor</u>:
4.) <u>Narrative Conclusion</u>:

What was the significance of "Ready To Die"? In other words, what did it reintroduce?

Who became the New York Rap Renaissance's greatest success story?

Who was his first serious influence?

What possibility in Rap did this particular influence inspire?

Which rap group inspired Shawn Carter to become a rapper?

With regard to the rapper, Rakim, what was it about his rapping that Jay-Z could relate to?

What was the goal of Jay-Z's story?

What was the "Hustler" ethos a metaphor of?

Jay-Z became the culmination of his predecessors combined into one. Name 8 elements that he brought together.

1.)
2.)
3.)
4.)
5.)

6.)
7.)
8.)

In combining the aforesaid elements, what did Jay-Z transform the New York Rap Renaissance blueprint into?

Name Jay-Z's independent label.

Name some of the artists (from both inside and outside of the label) that he collaborated with.

Name Jay-Z's debut album from 1996.

Name at least 4 elements of his approach to album-length variety:
1.)
2.)
3.)
4.)

Name at least 3 elements (from this album) that maintain the continuity of New York's rap tradition.

Name Jay-Z's first top ten album from 1997.

Who were two pop-crossover producers in this album?

Name at least 3 pp hits from this album.

Name 2 of the more hard-hitting, deeper tracks within this album that kept the gangsta rap ethos intact.

Which album crowned Jay-Z as the undisputed rap king of New York?

What transformational process did this album complete for the New York Rap renaissance?

Name several subject matters in this album that young white Americans romanticized.

Unlike in his first two albums, what specific convention did he embrace? (as opposed to bucking it)

Name the artist who became the first prominent white gangsta rap artist.

Who was his producer?

Name his debut album of 1998.

Name the most successful rap album since "The Chronic".

What sort of boundaries did he blur? (there were 3 of them)

Which rapper was one of Eminem's most important influences?

In which one of his [Eminem's] tunes does he emulate this influence by presenting a quasi quote [from this influence]?

From which of this influence's song did he derive this quasi quote?

List Eminem's hip-hop staples that were consistent with the 90's rap tradition.
1.)
2.)
3.)
4.)

CHAPTER XIII: ELECTRONIC DANCE MUSIC
I. THE HARBINGERS

A.) The story begins in West Germany during the late 60's/early 70's during the European Psychedelic movement.

1.) Where extended improvisations dealt mostly with noise experimentation.

- As opposed to the more musically conventional extended improvisations taking place in San Francisco.

* To artists in Europe, the Psychedelic experience was more about becoming experimental…

a.) …by developing new sounds and new concepts involving the use of these new, unconventional sounds or noises.

* Two West German groups led the way in this avante garde cutting edge: "Can" and "Faust".

2.) Can: founded in 1968 in Cologne, West Germany.

- One of the first of the psychedelic, avante garde German rock (i.e. "Krautrock") bands.

* Musical Impressions: in the critically acclaimed album: "Tago Mago" (1971), snippets of electronic experimental sounds appear as background accompaniment in a conventional rock and roll song context.

a.) In The Foreground: lead guitar solos, studio-effected vocal lines displaying an "otherworldly"/quasi-echo sound with reverberation and some phase shifting.

b.) Drumbeat: also studio-effected with phase shifting, reverberation, and tape-deck echo (a harbinger of the "drum machine" sound to come).

- Metallic sounding.

- Personnel: Irmin Schmidt (keyboards), vocals; Michael Karoli (guitar, violin), Holger Czukay (bass, vocals, electronics), Jaki Liebezeit (drums, reeds, vocals), and Malcolm Mooney (vocals) replaced by vocalist Kenji "Damo" Suzuki.

* Influences: aspects of 20th century, avante garde art music (i.e. modern "classical") of composer Karlheinz Stockhausen for he was at the time, en vogue in the German "Art Music" world.

a.) Stockhausen was well known for his work on tape collages featuring noise experimentation.

- Schmidt and Czukay had previously studied under him.

* This "avante" art music influence was infused into a conventional rock and roll format that parallels The Velvet Underground (although the influences and resulting music were much different).

a.) "Can" featured extended improvisations, electronic textures, and angular rhythms.

- Using noise, synthesizers, and electronic textures.

- Influential: to post-psychedelic bands such as "Ash Ra Temple" and "Amon Duul".

* Also influential to artists of both experimental and ambient rock.

a.) As well as New Wave artists of the early 80's.

3.) Faust (formed in 1971 in Wumme, West Germany).

- Use of analog electronic soundscapes and collages that are sometimes phase shifted.

* Also using a "cut and paste" format where an experimental section is spontaneously followed by a starkly contrasting, conventional section.

a.) Example: from an electronic noise-scape section with no metric pulse to suddenly, a solo traditional-styled piano section with a beat.

- Sudden contrast is a very effective classical music tool that has been used for centuries.

     * <u>Example</u>: "Why Don't Eat Carrots" (audio example in Chapter VI).

* More symphonic-oriented than "Can" with a structurally extended (form) format in the context of longer lasting track durations.

     a.) Elements of "music concrete" (again, the Stockhausen influence being pervasive).

          - <u>Example</u>: Electronically manipulated sound that is somewhat repetitive in a track entitled: "<u>Meadow Meal</u>" from their debut album "Faust" (1971).

               * Produced by Uwe Nettlebeck.

- Other avante garde influences include standard electronic, analog art-music practices of <u>FM (frequency modulation)</u> which sounds like a trill; and <u>AM (amplitude modulation)</u> which sounds like vibrato.

     * The electronic noise/sound-scapes were usually in free-form fashion:

          a.) Static (non-pulsed), esoteric, and spontaneous.

     * Similar to "<u>Can</u>", they too use electronica elements as background accompaniment to conventional types of music performance (for example, a brass section) in the foreground.

          a.) <u>Concept</u>: a dichotomy – alternation between two worlds, conventional and experimental.

               - <u>Alternation</u>: by either superimposing the two worlds or by going from one directly to the other (back and forth).

     * <u>Faust</u>: made more extended use of 20th century art-music influences that did "Can".

          a.) Including their use of a contributor named <u>Tony Conrad</u>: minimalist composer and violinist.

               - who collaborated with LaMont Young's "<u>Dream Syndicate</u>" along with <u>John Cale</u> (later of The Velvet Underground).

4.) <u>NOTE</u>: Both "Can" and "Faust" rode on the cutting edge of German experimental, electronic music otherwise known as "Krautrock".

     - In addition to leaving on legacy with New Wave, experimental, post-psychedelic and ambient rock artists…

          a.)…they would also directly influence the next group that would transform the German electronic/experimental style into a completely new direction.

B.) <u>Kraftwerk</u> (formed 1970 in Düsseldorf, West Germany).

     1.) Personnel: <u>Rolf Hutten</u> (b. 1946, Krefeld, W. Ger.): vocals, Moog synthesizers, electronics, organ; <u>Florian Schneider-Esleben</u> (b. 1947, Dusseldorf): vocals, electronics, woodwinds; <u>Klaus Dinger</u>: drums; <u>Thomas Homann</u>: guitar, bass.

     - The genesis of the all-electronic, synthesizer, futuristic-sounding group that would directly influence all other artists of their ilk to follow.

     * <u>Style</u>: simple, catchy melodic focus with a minimalistic type of accompaniment.

          a.) <u>Sonorities</u>: totally electronic in the sense of the streamlining and simplification of electronic influences of "Can" and "Faust".

               - Over a synthetic drumbeat – the analog predecessor of the drum machine sound.

          b.) Tonal, accessible, simple and, because of the electronic sounds focused on the melody, the essence of a "futuristic" sound.

     2.) <u>Beginnings</u>: at the Düsseldorf Conservatory.

- Rolf Hutten and Florian Schneider-Esleben both studied classical and electronic composition when they met.
  * Together, they formed a studio called: "Kling-Klang".
    a.) Their first group, "Organization", recorded a debut single entitled: "Tone Flight"
      - Basically as mentioned, influenced by their contemporaries in the psychedelic "Krautrock" domain including Can and Faust.
        * Another noted German psychedelic group: Neu, would be founded by two former Kraftwerk members.
- Hutten and Schneider-Esleben: changed the group's name to "Kraftwerk" (meaning Power Plant).
  * They began using the electronic, mechanized timbres of the Moog synthesizer (first mass-produced analog synthesizer).
    a.) They refined and simplified the Krautrock, psychedelic style by creating simple melodies, atmospheric soundscapes, and hypnotic, minimalistic rhythm formulas over a synthetic drumbeat.
      - The simple, repetitive rhythm formulas allow for the electronic melodic and atmospheric colors to come out clearly...
        *...similar to that of a symphony orchestra doing music that's very direct – the instrumental colors jump out.
  * They went through many personnel changes but Hutten and Schneider-Esleben remained as the group's backbone.
3.) "Autobahn" (1975): their first US release.
  - An instant success reaching up to the top 5 in the US pop charts.
    * Released on the heels of the progressive rock boom of the early 70's.
      a.) Where the deep, symphonic sound of "art-rock" was in fashion...
        - ...along with the sophisticated musical tastes of the average rock listener hence, a ready audience in place to appreciate this type of sound influenced by the spirit of classical music.
  - Original version of the single ["Autobahn"] was 22 minutes.
    * As a single release, the duration was cut down considerably in order to get radio airplay.
      a.) It was the edited version that became a big hit.
  - Subject: an electronic soundscape that gives the listener, a visual impression of traveling on Germany's most famous highway.
4.) "Trans Europe Express" (1977): named after a train, this album would be the most influential to a very important artist to follow (more on this artist shortly).
  - Would also be influential on David Bowie's work on the "Low" (1977) album which he incidentally, recorded in Berlin.
    * "Trans Europe Express" – the single: is where the prototype drum machine sound becomes their standard.
      a.) This new drum beat standard anticipated the electronic, synthetic dance grooves of the early 1980's.
  - Concept Album: different tracks shared varied elements of the same repetitive, minimalistic material.
    * Which provided a common musical thread throughout the album.
      a.) For Example: similarities between "Europe Endless" and "Franz Schubert".
        - In Europe Endless, those title words are repeated

throughout practically the entire track.
> > > > * Sometimes electronically distorted, sometimes conventional (anticipating the same "Eurodisco" repeated words practice).
> > > > > a.) Same with the title track [Trans Europe Express].
> > > * "Metal On Metal": hypnotic "clang-bang" metal percussive repetitive theme over a groove with melodic elements from the title track (especially, the subordinate theme).
> > - "Trans Europe Express": contains two themes.
> > > * Main Theme: an ascending, stepwise motion melody.
> > > * Subordinate Theme: a simple, noodling type of melody that would be quoted later, in what would become the first "Electro-Funk" single in 1982 by a devoted follower of Kraftwerk (more on that later).
> > > > a.) Again, repeated vocal line, "Trans Europe Express" recorded in an electronically manipulated and distorted manner.
> > - RESULT: through "Trans Europe Express", Kraftwerk developed their most accessible music to date. To summarize:
> > > * Melodic, repetitive hooks.
> > > * Minimalistic, hypnotic, repetitive accompaniment riffs or melodic fragments that sound mechanized.
> > > * Electronically manipulated, distorted vocal lines.
> > > * Synthetic, bass drum heavy, percussive grooves emanating from an analog, synthesized drum set-up that anticipated the digital drum machine sound of the early 80's.
> > > > a.) RESULT: a style that was accessible, robotic, and above all, futuristic (was dubbed by some as "Robot Pop").

5.) Legacy: their legacy would directly inspire the development of both New Wave and Detroit Techno (the latter which will be covered shortly).
. > - Another important legacy of Kraftwerk, would be a direct inspiration on a new genre called: Electro-Funk.

II. THE ADVENT OF ELECTRONIC DANCE MUSIC

A.) DJ Afrika Bambaataa (b. Kevin Donovan, 4/10/60, Bronx, NY): his pseudonym was derived from a Zulu warrior film meaning: Affectionate Leader.

> 1.) Started out as a Lieutenant of a notorious street in the South Bronx called "The Black Spades".
> > - Upon quitting the gang, in 1974 he founded an organization called "Zulu Nation".
> > > * An organization consisting of DJs, break dancers, graffiti artists, and former gang members who would band together against crime and violence.
> > > > a.) Zulu Nation's Purpose: to mediate peaceful solutions to conflicts on the street between people.
> > > > > - Among its most famous alumni: DJ Afrika Islam.

2.) Along with DJ Kool Herc and DJ Grandmaster Flash, Bambaataa helped to create the founding musical force behind Hip Hop (they were the three founding fathers of the genre).
> > - Beginnings: in his teens, he was an avid record collector especially with rare, obscure recordings.
> > > * Though his musical foundation (i.e. obscure records) was similar to that of Kool Herc...
> > > > a.) He expanded the musical source range to genres such as African and Caribbean music and made them an integral part of the Hip Hop musical lexicon. (i.e. eclecticism).

- He also used musical sources from Europe.
　　　b.) RESULT: he became known as the "Master Of Records".
3.) 1977: he began organizing block parties and break dancing competitions; the latter, as an alternative to settling disputes through violence.
　　- He also became a virtuoso DJ in his own right and a popular one at that.
　　　　* His rapping inspiration was the Mohammed Ali (Cassius Clay) style of rapid, staccato rhyming.
　　- His early groups were: "The Jazzy 5" and "Soulsonic Force".
　　　　* They released records in the single, "12-inch' format.
　　　　* His debut single with Soulsonic Force: "Zulu Nation Throwdown".
　　-He usually performed with a live band up until, with Soulsonic Force….
　　　　* …he switched to high tech.
4.) "Planet Rock" (1982): his only true hit that would become one of the most important singles of all time.
　　- Produced by dance music expert and producer, Arthur Baker.
　　　　* He [Baker] would become an important force in the early development of electronic dance music.
　　- Inspiration: "Trans Europe Express" by Kraftwerk .
　　　　* Bambaataa: both played and heavily promoted this and other Kraftwerk albums at street parties.
　　　　　　a.) Albums such as "The Man Machine" (1978) and "Computer World" (1981).
　　- Direct Influences From "Trans Europe Express": the electronic music style that exhibits a futuristic sound.
　　　　* The synthetic drum sound now emanating from a digital drum machine.
　　　　　　a.) Quote of "Trans Europe Express's" subordinate theme (transposed at a faster tempo) directly from the original track.
　　　　　　　　- Becoming the main instrumental theme of "Planet Rock".
　　- Another Direct Kraftwerl Influence:
　　　　* The groove from Kraftwerk's "Numbers" from the album "Computer World" (1981)…
　　　　　　a.) …Inspired the groove in "Planet Rock"
　　- Idea: upon gaining an interest in the music of Kraftwerk, DJ Afrika Bambaataa asked the question that would lead to his originality: "Why isn't there any futuristic sound in black music?"
　　　　* By asking himself that question, he inevitably took the next step by implementing it.
　　　　　　a.) RESULT: a new musical style called: Electro-Funk.
　　　　　　　　- The template of what would become electronic dance music.
　　- "Planet Rock": by becoming the initial electronic dance music template, it set the in motion, a paradigm for the development of this genre that other artists would further advance.
　　　　* In this next case, a slightly different approach…

B.) New Order: rose out of the ashes of "Joy Division" and presented electronic dance music from a live-band, performance approach as opposed to DJing.
　　1.) As "Joy Division", they made a pact amongst themselves that if any member left the group, they would dispose of the Joy Division name.
　　　- May 18,1980: Ian Curtis (lead vocalist) of Joy Division committed suicide by hanging.
　　　　　* Out of the ashes of Curtis' death, they accomplished a rare feat that few rock groups in this position actually do:

a.) They successfully regrouped and in the process, completely reinvented themselves and their sound.

2.) RESULT: <u>New Order</u> (formed in 1980 in Manchester, ENG).

  - Personnel: <u>Bernard Sumner</u> (b. Bernard Dicken, 1/4/52): lead vocals, guitar; <u>Peter Hook</u> (b. 2/13/56, Salford, ENG): bass; <u>Steven Morris</u> (b. 10/18/57): drums; <u>Gillian Gilbert</u> (b. 1/27/61, Manchester, ENG): keyboards.

      * As with Joy Division, they avoided publicity.

        a.) Album covers did not have their photographs on them.

        b.) Their concerts were quiet, uneventful, low-key.

  - "<u>Ceremony</u>" (3/81): their debut single.

      * Originally, a Joy Division tune with the signature, dark melodic essence.

  - "<u>Movement</u>" (1981): their debut album.

      * Again, quite similar to the standard Joy Division sound.

        a.) They were starting to become written-off as a carbon-copy, regurgitated version of their former selves and were losing credibility in the process.

  - "<u>Everything's Gone Green</u>" their first single displaying a new artistic direction.

      * Influences: <u>Kraftwerk</u> and the "<u>electro-beat</u>" style. The latter, from the New York City underground dance clubs.

        a.) They utilized synthesizers and sequencers echoing the futuristic influences of Kraftwerk over a pumping dance beat (inspired by "electro-beat").

          - Resulting in their first underground hit.

  - "<u>Temptation</u>" (1982): a continuation of their new direction becoming another underground dance club hit.

3.) "<u>Blue Monday</u>" (1983): their breakthrough single.

  - Released as a "12-inch" with a record sleeve resembling a floppy disk displaying very minimal information.

      * <u>Style</u>: a fusion of Bernard Sumner's dark, cold, post-punk influenced vocalizing over drum machine beats and futuristic/sparse electronic sounds.

        a.) Different repetitions superimposed over one another creating an electronic dance music style in a live performance format.

          - Repetitions resulting from different instruments.

        b.) Produced by <u>Arthur Baker</u> (who also produced "Planet Rock").

          - The first of the Baker/New Order collaborations.

        c.) Their subsequent collaborations would include singles such as: "<u>Confusion</u>" and "<u>Thieves Like Us</u>".

  - Impact: "Blue Monday" was the single that established the "12-inch" as the new standard format in dance clubs all over America.

4.) <u>NOTE</u>: even though <u>Afrika Bambaataa</u> set the electronic dance music paradigm in motion with "Planet Rock", it was <u>New Order</u> who established it [Elec. Dance Music] as a new genre starting with "Blue Monday".

  - As innovative as this new style was, mainstream America had no idea that it existed for the only places one could hear it, was either in underground clubs or gay clubs (the latter, where cutting-edge dance music is always en vogue).

      * There would be one artist who would change that equation by introducing electronic dance music to the American mainstream.

C.) <u>Madonna</u> (b. Madonna Louise Ciccone, 8/16/58, Bay City, MI): one of the most media-savvy pop stars who always managed to maintain public attention due to her controversial nature.

  1.) <u>Impact</u>: the smashing of sexual boundaries, the challenging of moral norms, and the redefinition of the nature of eroticism in pop culture.

- She became the first woman in rock and roll to take full control of her career, her creative destinies, and her public image.
> * The latter she would constantly redefine. ·

2.) <u>Dance Background</u>: began studying dance at the age of 14.
- After graduating from high school, she attended the University of Michigan majoring in dance.
> * <u>1978</u>: she moved to New York City and studied for a brief period with the <u>Alvin Ailey Dance Troupe</u>.

3.) <u>Musical Background</u>: her first gig – a drummer in a band called "The Breakfast Club".
- She was also hired as a backup singer and dancer for <u>The Patrick Hernandez Review</u>.
> * He was a disco star who had one big hit: "<u>Born To Be Alive</u>".
- With former boyfriend <u>Steven Bray</u>, she started writing songs.
> * <u>Mark Kamins</u>: who DJ'd at a popular nightclub called "Dancetown", began playing her tapes.
>> a.) And subsequently, took her demo tape to <u>Sire Records</u>.
- <u>RESULT</u>: "Everybody" (1982): her first dance club hit.
> * Produced by Mark Kamins.
>> a.) "<u>Burning Up</u>"/ "<u>Physical Attraction</u>" her next dance club hits.
>>> - Released in a "12-inch" format and would reach #3 on the dance charts.
- <u>NOTE</u>: for these early releases, Sire Records avoided putting Madonna's photo on the record jacket because she sounded like a black singer and they didn't want to alienate their black audience.
> * The charade was dropped once MTV began aggressively promoting her.
>> a.) One of the first women to receive heavy promotion from MTV.
> * <u>MTV's Dirty Little Secret</u>: For its first few years, MTV refused to show videos by black artists.
>> a.) CBS Records, who owned a subsidiary called Epic Records had a black artist who was already well-known named <u>Michael Jackson</u>.
>>> - CBS Records gave MTV an ultimatum which resulted in MTV promoting its first black artist [Jackson].
>>>> * The album, *Thriller* (1983), made Michael Jackson into a pop superstar.

4.) "<u>Madonna</u>" (1983): her debut album made in collaboration with <u>DJ John "Jellybean" Benitez</u> (who produced the song "Holiday") and <u>DJ Mark Kamin</u> (who produced "Everybody"). The remaining tracks were produced by <u>Reggie Lucas</u>.
- This album set the standard for "dance-pop" that would remain in place for the next two decades.
> * <u>Style</u>: catchy, easily singable, memorable melodies over driving dance beats which were at that time, top of the line.
>> a.) <u>Heavily produced mixtures of</u>: multi synthesizers, electric & acoustic keyboards, electric bass guitar (on "Borderline" only), guitars, background vocals, and a drum machine programmer.
- <u>RESULT</u>: the new standard dance-pop idiom where the beat and instrumentation (especially synthesized bass and drums) blend together into one, intoxicating, almost hypnotic entity.

* Where serious musicianship limitations are marginalized to the point of being a non-factor (i.e. Madonna's vocally challenged singing sound).

    a.) <u>The Point</u>: beauty lies in the aggregate where put together, the sumptuous big picture is the focus.

      - Rather than the individual parts.

    b.) Madonna has shown that in dance-pop, a good voice or good musicianship for that matter, were not necessary.

      - Personality and overall nuance were the key.

- Her early hit singles including "<u>Holiday</u>", "<u>Lucky Star</u>", and "<u>Borderline</u>" would become sonic summaries of current electronic dance music practices condensed into a three-and-a-half-minute singles format.

    * Which became extremely accessible to a mainstream audience.

      a.) Her debut album reached to #8 on the pop charts.

5.) "<u>Like A Virgin</u>" (1984): the album that made her into an international pop icon.

- And began her legendary campaign of closely manipulating her image which would consistently change throughout her career.

    * <u>Nile Rodgers</u> formerly of the disco band "Chic" produced the album.

D.) <u>NOTE</u>: now that the dance-pop genre was firmly in place, other artists would come along and introduce their own versions this genre.

1.) <u>Prince</u>: (b. Prince Rogers Nelson, 6/4/58, Minneapolis, MN): son of a jazz band leader. His [Prince's] mother was a singer in that same jazz band.

    * Started learning music at the age of 7 beginning with the piano, then on to drums and guitar.

      a.) At age 18, he signed with <u>Warner Bros. Records</u>.

    * <u>Style</u>: a unique mixture of pop, rock, and funk performed with a respectable degree of musicianship.

      a.) He could sing, write, play, and produce.

        - As a performer, he was flamboyant and controversial.

          * His lyrics contained explicit sexual content.

      b.) <u>Musically</u> (beginning with his third album "Dirty Mind" in 1980): his style was a combination of the following specifics:

        - Rock guitar sounds slightly reminiscent of the 70's rock style.

        - <u>The Beat</u>: machine-like bass drum thud that is very dance friendly.

          * And reflects the 80's style drum beat sound.

        - Catchy, easily memorable pop tunesmith-ism.

          * Complete with sexually explicit lyrics.

        - <u>RESULT</u>: dance music that was written, recorded, and produced from a musician's perspective as opposed to machines or DJing.

          * Carrying a rock element that appealed to a mainstream audience.

III. THE RISE OF THE DJ AS SERIOUS ARTIST

A.) Two vacuums that led to Disco.

1.) <u>The Musical Vacuum</u>:

    - <u>Guitar-Driven Rock n Roll</u>: Had basically abandoned the dance beat.

      * Especially with the onset of country/folk rock the 70's.

        a.) Country/Folk rock received extensive airplay on listener-friendly FM radio stations.

2.) <u>The Club Vacuum</u>:

    - The demise of exclusive, private, chic, celebrity driven clubs.

      * <u>In Their Place</u>: Clubs devoted to the common person – the proletariat.

                a.) In addition, the demise of the exclusive clubs, opened the
                door for acceptance of everyone regardless of race, ethnicity,
                or sexual orientation.
      - RESULT: A new subculture would emerge that would be (at least in the
  beginning), small, underground, and primarily gay.
           * Another legacy of the Peace/Love ethos of the psychedelic era…
                a.) …of brotherhood and togetherness (i.e. an atmosphere of
                total acceptance of everyone).
           * Musical Byproduct: The Remix, The 12-Inch Single, and above all,
           The Club DJ.
                a.) The latter [DJ] being the most important legacy of the
                disco era.

B.) The Rise Of The Club DJ Artist: It all began with Francis Grasso (b. 1948, Brooklyn, NY;
d. 3/18/01 Brooklyn, NY): the father of the modern DJ'ing subculture.
      1.) Laid down the template – the new paradigm — that all modern DJ's would follow.
           - Old Paradigm: Club DJ's serviced the dancers by responding to the crowd.
              * They played what dancers wanted – record by record – and each
              record was displayed as a separate entity.
                a.) In this format, the DJ was seen as a substitute for a live
                band.
                    - Right down to the playing of slow tempo'd records
                    in order to give the bartenders some added business.
           - New Paradigm: The Club DJ takes command.
              * Although the modern club DJ spun records, his real instrument was
              the dance floor.
                a.) Goal: to keep the dance floor perpetually full and the party
                atmosphere alive throughout the entire night.
    2.) Key Technique. A non-stop array of records where one [record] would merge directly
  into the other exactly on the beat. In this context, the DJ creates an endless stream of
  music that would lead to various climactic moments.
           - To Francis Grasso, each single [record] was a small part of an overall whole;
           like movements in a magnum opus.
              * Through a continuous flow of music, Grasso could control the
              vibrancy and atmosphere of the dance floor.
                a.) Records: He concentrated on music that carried a funkier
                edge such as Motown, Southern Soul, Funk, etc.
  3.) Mixing Techniques: Techniques that Francis Grasso not only pioneered, but made an
  integral part of the modern DJ'ing creative arsenal. He used a two-turntable mixing
  system.
           - Beat Mix: Overlapping the conclusion of one record to the start of the next
           record without missing a beat (he focused on synchronization of the drum
           beats).
              * He only used the standard 45 rpm, 7 inch records that lasted an
              average of about three-and-a-half minutes.
                a.) Playing these records in such a manner required an
                enormous amount of skill (another Grasso legacy: all DJing
                would require skill).
           - Slip Cue: Applying a felt cloth in the exact shape and size of the turntable
           (known as a slipmat) to the surface of the turntable.
              * The record could be held (by one finger) without spinning over the
              rotating felt surface.
                a.) In this way, the held record is already cued to the precise
                first beat.
                    - Once he's ready to start that record, all he has to do
                    is let it go and it plays at exactly the precise moment.
                      * Right on the beat.

- <u>Extending A Record</u>: He extended a record on one turntable by switching to an identical record on the other turntable — exactly on the beat.
    * By going back and forth from one turntable to the next, he could extend a record's length indefinitely (thereby reinventing that record).
- <u>Phasing</u>: Taking two identical records and playing them simultaneously but with one of the records slightly delayed.
    * Producing a quasi echo effect.
        a.) He could also "blend" two different records together right on the beat.
            - <u>Example</u>: His blending trademark was in superimposing "I'm A Man" by Chicago over Led Zeppelin's "Whole Lotta Love".
- <u>RESULT</u>: The standardization of *mixing* records rather than just *playing* them.

4.) <u>His First Gig</u>: In 1968 at a club called "Salvation Too" replacing the club DJ named Terry Noel.
    - Terry Noel did not show up for his gig so Grasso filled in.
        * <u>His First Important Regular Gig</u>: "The Sanctuary" located in an old church on 407 West 43rd Street.
            a.) This was the venue where he honed in his DJing skills and inaugurated the club DJ as artist.
                - He was also a regular DJ at "The Haven".
            b.) It was at these clubs, where others would become inspired enough to emulate Grasso's work as a DJ artist.
    - His Disciples: <u>Steve D'Aquisto</u> and <u>Michael Cappello</u>.
        * They became Francis Grasso's first legacy by spreading the new DJ technique "Gospel" to various other clubs around New York City.
            a.) Along with their mentor, "The Big 3" would usher in the beginnings of what became known as the disco era.

C.) <u>The Rise Of Modern Clubbing</u>: The true disco ideal began with <u>David Mancuso</u> (b. 10/24/44, Utica, NY), the innovator of the modern disco clubbing scene.
    1.) He initially set the standards by which all clubs would follow.
        - The standards of great reproduced sounds systems, the essence of love & togetherness, and the liberating party atmosphere.
    2.) <u>Influences</u>:
        - <u>The Psychedelic Era</u>: Mancuso was a devoted follower of the psychedelic philosophy of Dr. Timothy Leary – the so-called "High Priest of LSD".
            * Leary also authored a "How-To" manual of properly experiencing an LSD trip called, "The Psychedelic Experience" (discussed in Chapter VI).
                a.) Inspired by "The Tibetan Book Of The Dead" and its three stages (or Bardos).
            * Mancuso regularly attended Leary's lectures and private parties at "The League For Spiritual Discovery".
                a.) These were very social events with offerings of music and food.
                    - This event had initially inspired Mancuso to emulate these gatherings at his own place that would become known as "The Loft".
            *<u>RESULT</u>: The psychedelic era legacy of peace and love found its way to the heart of New York City that would flourish on a much wider scale later on.
                a.) It became one of the inspirations for the all-inclusive disco ideal.
        - <u>Sister Alicia</u>: A Nun who worked at the orphanage where Mancuso had spent his early childhood.

* According to Mancuso, Sister Alicia had always found a reason to throw a party.

        a.) She played her records on a Victrola and had lots of balloons hovering around the room (which evoked a party atmosphere).

           - The idea of the benevolence of "throwing a party" would be highly influential later on.

3.) <u>The Loft</u>: Located on 647 Broadway. His home – a commercial loft – that also served as his "invitation-only" club where he would throw his own parties.

    - His first important gathering: "<u>Love Saves The Day</u>" (1970), the event that ushered in the genus of the modern dance-club culture (complete with plenty of balloons).

        * <u>Invited Guests</u>: Black and white, gay and straight blended together in an environment of total mutual acceptance.

           a.) <u>The Disco Ideal</u>: A sanctuary of the spirit of freedom, acceptance, inclusion, and love where everyone regardless of race, gender, or sexual orientation could be themselves in a comfortable, fun atmosphere.

              - The Loft: set the initial standard for that disco ideal.

4.) <u>State Of The Art Sound Reproduction</u>: Another standard set by The Loft.

    - Mancuso envisioned a unique, top of the line, sound experience to accompany his disco party ideals.

        * He collaborated with an engineer named <u>Alex Rosner</u> —- defense contractor by day, playing with sound systems (as a hobby) by night.

           a.) He initially engineered the first club standard, high fidelity stereo sound system.

              - He was also high influential in developing the first commercially mass-produced mixer: the 1971 "Buzak" (a device designed to synchronize two turntables).

                  * Rosner advised Louis Buzak on club-oriented dynamics that would make this mixer fit in.

              - RESULT: the first standard club mixer.

        * The speaker system was also state of the art for its absolute clarity.

           a.) Mancuso wanted clarity over volume.

              - Again, setting another disco standard.

5.) <u>Mancuso As DJ</u>: A somewhat mystical figure whose musical choices were designed to take guests through a spiritual, self-expressive journey (again, a psychedelic ethos).

    - He communicated musically, his vision of peace, love, and community.

        * He refused to mix records but rather, he'd play them in their entirety with pauses in between.

           a.) But yet, his control of the record sequence still electrified the party atmosphere experience.

        * His musical stages mirrored the Tibetan Book of The Dead model:

           a.) <u>Early Evening</u> (first stage): slow, mood-driven music that built up a momentum.

           b.) <u>Second Stage</u>: fast, electrifying sequences of records.

           c.) <u>Third Stage</u> (wee hours of the morning): slow, chill-out.

    - <u>Choice Of Records</u>: Songs whose words were positive but yet, had a funky, soulful, or rhythmic essence.

        * To quote Bill Brewster and Frank Broughton, "Love was the message".

        * Mancuso was also the first to standardize the Gamble & Huff "Philly Sound" into the disco record lexicon.

    - <u>Introduction of the Disco Concept</u>:

* It was within an article written by Vince Aletti (about The Loft) for *Rolling Stone* Magazine (1973) that first alerted mainstream America to the concept of what would become known as "disco".

6.) <u>Legacy</u>: The first commercial club to combine the legacies of Francis Grasso (mixing techniques) with David Mancuso (modern club culture) was a club called, "The Gallery".

- First opened on 22nd Street then moved to 172 Mercer Street.

* <u>Nicky Siano</u>: a David Mancuso protégé, was their legendary DJ.

- <u>NOTE</u>: From then on, the standard for disco had been established.

* RESULT: the advent of the discothèque boom.

a.) <u>Examples</u>: Reade Street, Galaxy 21, The Continental Baths, etc.

D.) <u>Note On The Disco Craze of The late 70's</u>: it marked the time when disco clubbing went mainstream.

1.) Along with this mainstream clubbing, the "disco ideal" of love and inclusiveness was no longer a factor.

- In its place, was unabashed, mass commercialism that was the complete antithesis of what true disco originally envisioned.

a.) It would mean that disco would once again, have to return to the underground in order to reclaim its venerated ideal status.

- This happened when the mainstream disco craze went out of fashion in the early 1980's.

2.) The demise of disco mania opened the door for disco's first important legacy: "House".

IV. NEW GENRES OF ELECTRONIC DANCE MUSIC: TECHNO, HOUSE, & AMBIENT HOUSE

A.) <u>Techno</u>: originated in Detroit, MI in the early to mid 80's.

1.) <u>Style</u>: a strictly mechanical emphasis where the computer is used in the electronic dance music domain for the first time.

- Whereas "House" music was connected to its disco roots (more on that later):

* <u>Techno</u>: was strictly electronically sequenced and not intended for mass, popular appeal.

a.) An avante garde type of genre that celebrated the essence of the machine as opposed to humanity.

2.) <u>Mixture of Influences</u>: electronic, synthetic driving beats of "<u>Electro-Funk</u>" (spearheaded as earlier mentioned by "Planet Rock") along with…

- The streamlined, melodic, minimalist, electronic-type futuristic sound of <u>Kraftwerk</u>.

* <u>In America</u>: it was strictly underground and intended for a small, select audience.

* <u>In England</u>: it became mainstream in the late 80's and spread quickly throughout Europe.

a.) Europeans in general were always more open to "avante garde" styles than mainstream Americans.

- <u>RESULT</u>: fast-paced, beat-driven music with a synthetic drum thud that was repetitive and relentless.

* That accompanied the refined, synthesized, and futuristic strains inspired by Kraftwerk.

3.) <u>The Catalysts</u>: "The Belleville Three": <u>Derrick May</u>, <u>Juan Atkins</u>, and <u>Kevin Saunderson</u> — the founding fathers of "Detroit Techno".

- <u>Derrick May</u> (b. 4/6/63, Detroit, MI): recorded some of the earliest techno tracks that many experts believe were the most original and influential.

* <u>Style</u>: streamlined, percussive-laden cascades of sound featuring string samples.

a.) He dubbed Detroit Techno as: "<u>Black Soul for the 80's</u>".

* "<u>Transmit</u>": his label. Especially when he went by the pseudonym of "<u>Rhythim Is Rhythim</u>" (1987-89).

a.) Some of his most notable works: "<u>Nude Photo</u>", "<u>Kaos</u>", and "<u>Strings Of Life</u>".

* <u>Influences</u>: Juan Atkins, a classmate of his at Belleville Junior High School, introduced May to the music of <u>Parliament/Funkadelic</u>, <u>Kraftwerk</u>, and an early 80's new wave pop star: <u>Gary Numan</u>.

   a.) He also took in interest in computerized synthesizers and the art of DJing.

      - He taught Kevin Saunderson the DJing art form.

   b.) Together with Saunderson and Juan Atkins, Derrick May helped establish a collective: "<u>Deep Space Soundworks</u>".

      - <u>Goal</u>: to get their music played at parties and clubs.

- <u>Juan Atkins</u> (b. 9/12/62, Detroit, MI): also recorded tracks that would set the standard and tone of what would become "Detroit Techno".

* <u>Style</u>: a futuristic sound molded with the influence of Parliament/Funkadelic and Kraftwerk's machine-like essence.

   a.) <u>His Aliases</u>: "Model 500", "Infiniti", and "Cybotron".

      - In "Cybotron", he collaborated with Rick Davis.

* <u>Influences</u>: the keyboard/synthesizer sounds of P/Funk.

   a.) <u>Ken Collier</u> and <u>The Electrifyin' Mojo</u> first introduced Atkins to an array of synthesizer bands such as:

      - <u>Kraftwerk</u>, <u>Telex</u>, <u>Gary Numan</u>, <u>The B-52's</u>, and <u>Prince</u>.

         * His new interest in these artists began in the late 70's.

   b.) He bought his first synthesizer: the <u>Korg MS 10</u>.

      - He recorded through a mixer onto cassette tapes.

         * The mixer was used for balance and over-dubbing between tracks.

      - He learned how to use the synthesizer from <u>Rick Davis</u>.

* "<u>Alleys Of Your Mind</u>" (1981): Cybotron's debut single on their own "Deep Space Records".

   a.) A molding of Funk-influenced grooves and futuristic electronic sounds that marked a new wave in black music that would eventually lead to Techno later on.

      -Heavily promoted by <u>The Electrifyin' Mojo</u> .

         * Which resulted in a local hit.

   b.) "<u>Enter</u>" (1982): their debut album.

      - Featuring "<u>Clear</u>": the single that would set the musical and structural foundation for the standard, machine-like sound to be forever associated with Techno.

         * A fusion of dance/techno pop and club music.

      - "<u>Alleys</u>…" set the essence, "<u>Enter</u>" set the structure.

* As "<u>Model 500</u>" (Juan Atkins going solo), he released as array of dance/techno singles between 1985 and 1989.

   a.) <u>His most influential period</u>: he molded his various influences together in a driving beat, futuristic sound, and easy-to-recognize melodies that were catchy.

      - <u>RESULT</u>: he would be dubbed "<u>The Godfather of Techno</u>".

   b.) His debut single as "Model 500": <u>No UFO's</u>.

      - One of his many singles that would pave the way in Techno's early development.

* Other singles included: "Night Drive",
"Interference", and "The Chase".
* The Music Institute: a downtown Detroit club founded by Atkins,
Derrick May, and another of the "Belleville Three": Kevin Saunderson.
- Kevin Saunderson (b. 9/5/64, Brooklyn, NY): made some of the most hard-
hitting, machine-like techno ever to come out of Detroit.
* An accomplished DJ who melded a thickly textured rhythmic
onslaught of various samples with synthetic percussive sounds
    a.) In most cases, a repetitive vocal chorus chanting in the
    background within the mix.
        - This vocal influence will further manifest itself into
        his machine-like sound on a wider scale (later on).
* KMS Records: his label founded in 1986.
    a.) He released his early singles through this label such as:
        - "Bounce Your Body To The Box" and "The
        Sound".
            * Recorded by Reese & Santonio.
        - "Triangle Of Love" recorded by Kreem.
    b.) KMS: also released Derrick May's earliest singles that
    were also influential to the early development of techno:
        - "Nude Photo" and "Strings Of Life".
* Inner City Productions (1988): his collaboration with a black female
singer named Paris Grey.
    a.) Purpose: to add a sense of more melodic focus that only a
    powerful, gospel-driven voice could give (no doubt influenced
    from his initial choral chanting arrangements).
        - "Big Fun" (1988): their debut single under the
        "Inner City" banner.
            * That, along with their second single "Good
            Life" became top ten its in the UK.
    b.) "Big Fun": their debut album released in 1989.
        - Techno's first, full-length album featuring their first
        two singles previously mentioned.
            * With vocal lines adding a more humanistic
            touch to an otherwise machine-driven sound.
4.) Techno: to summarize, introduced a new sound into the electronic dance music
domain.
    - A mechanized sound with synthetic, percussive thuds that are hard-driving and
    repetitive.
        * Members of "The Belleville Three" through their work and their
        "Music Institute" venue, would go on to influence techno's "second
        wave" artists such as:
            a.) Stacey Pullen, Kenny Larkin, Carl Craig, and Ritchie
            Hawtin (a.k.a. Plastikman).
    - A sound that celebrates the machine and the first of the electronic dance genres
    to make full use of computerized technology available at that time.
        * Emanating from the digital synthesizers of the early to mid 80's.
B.) "House": on the other hand, celebrates humanity.
    1.) Overview: rose out of the underground, post-disco dance club culture in the early
    80's.
        - But unlike Techno where influences were mostly synth-driven electronics…
            * "House": was primarily influenced by disco.
        - The Disco Legacy: during the height of disco mania, club DJs from the
        underground began making disco into a serious art form by inaugurating the
        club DJ as the new, virtuoso artist.

* A different type of DJ virtuosity than the ilk of Kool Herc or Grandmaster Flash.
>> a.) <u>The art of the club DJ</u>: extending parts of a dance mix recording – either the beginning, middle, or end — by "break spinning" these parts from two identical records superimposed over a heavy, bass drum sampled disco-influenced beat track.
>>> - In other words, the DJ making disco less pop-oriented and more crafty.
>>>> * Thereby reinventing an already existing dance tune.
>> b.) Superimposing the signature "House" beat.
>>> - A bass drum 4/4 pulse at about 125 beats per minute.
>>>> * That can string together an endless array of dance mixes into on continuous thread where all mixes are connected by that same beat throughout.
>>>>> - A hallmark of the club DJ as artist.
> - <u>Over The Beat Musical Style</u>: melodic focus with elements of synth-pop, soul music, Latin flavors, funk, rap, electronics, reggae (in dub form), folk guitars, and jazz elements.
>> * In other words: <u>Eclecticism</u>.
>>> a.) House mixes are usually instrumental but if there was any vocalizing involved…
>>>> -…it would most likely be a female voice.
> - <u>The Key</u>: eclecticism over a patented "House" beat where DJ's (as earlier mentioned) can string together a non-stop continuum of different dance mixes threaded seamlessly together by that beat…
>> *…which transformed the club DJ into legend.
>>> a.) One of those legendary pioneers was a DJ at a Chicago dance club called: "<u>The Warehouse</u>".
>>>> - Where the term "house" originated.

2.) <u>Frankie Knuckles</u> (b. Frank Warren Knuckles, Jr. 1/8/55, South Bronx, NY): the man who became known as "<u>The Godfather of House</u>".
> - Began DJing in New York spinning records during his middle teens in 1971.
>> * During the mid 70's, he began working at a well-known New York club called <u>The Gallery</u>.
>>> a.) He DJ'd alongside a childhood friend that would himself, become a legendary DJ: <u>Larry Levan</u>.
>>>> - They would later work together as DJs again in another club: The Continental Baths.
>>> b.) <u>Levan</u>: went on to establish his own club called The Soho Place.
>>>> - He suggested Frankie Knuckles to a group of businessmen eager to start a club in Chicago that they originally asked Levan to DJ in (Levan did not want to abandon his club).
>>>>> * The new Chicago club: <u>The Warehouse</u>.
> - <u>1977</u>: Knuckles moved to Chicago and began spinning records at The Warehouse and, in the process, introduced Chicagoans to the new art of New York DJ'ing.
>> * Initially, by playing <u>Salsoul</u> and <u>Philly International</u> records.
>>> a.) Whose musical trademarks were the funky dance beat, catchy melodies, and a glossy, symphonic string sound.

* <u>Vacuum</u>: in the early 80's, the death of mainstream disco stifled a once vibrant array of new disco record releases.

    a.) Mainstream labels were no longer releasing new disco tunes.

        - <u>Post Disco</u>: in some cases, saw the demise of upbeat, danceable club records.

            * Many of the post-disco records had slower tempos.

            * Other records, needed to be revamped, reenergized into something new (again, due to the lack of new records being released).

            * The solution: <u>Reediting</u>.

* <u>The Reedit</u>: Extending various sections of a dance record such as the opening, the middle break, or the conclusion.

    a.) In addition, new drum tracks were added along with completely new, eclectic sampled sounds.

        - Due to their complexity, these reedits were put on reel-to-reel tape and played on reel-to-reel tape machines in the club.

    b.) Both Frankie Knuckles and Erasmo Rivera did the reediting.

        - Ushering a new type of DJ as creative artist completely reinventing old dance records.

            * Hence, the music known as "<u>House</u>" was born.

        - <u>NOTE</u>: There was one other element necessary to complete its now conventional sound.

- <u>The Signature House Beat</u>:

    * <u>Jessie Saunders</u> (another prominent Chicago DJ): Started bringing a drum machine to the DJ booth.

    a.) He left the machine on the entire night playing the same exact beat: a heavy bass-drum kick-like sound at about 125 beats per minute.

        - Within the context of that constant beat, he would fade various dance records or dance mixes in and out without missing a beat.

            * In addition, fading different records in and out within this constant beat allowed the DJ to provide a non-stop stream of dance music for hours on end.

                In other words, the beat served as that musical thread seamlessly linking one record to the other.

    b.) <u>RESULT</u>: Disco records & remixes plus a constant drum machine beat became the now-conventional "House" sound.

        - A peppered-up, traditional funky soul.

            * The original "House" DJ's such as Frankie Knuckles and Ron Hardy went on to inspire other DJ's and producers in Chicago such as: <u>Marshall Jefferson</u>, <u>Larry Heard</u>, <u>Steve "Silk" Hurley</u>, and <u>Adonis</u>.

- <u>The Chicago "House" Explosion of the Mid 80's</u>: when Knuckles first started recording on the legendary, Chicago-based "<u>Wax Trax</u>" label (more on "Wax Trax" later).

    * Singles such as: "<u>Godfather</u>, "<u>Sacrifice</u>", "<u>Baby Wants To Ride</u>", "<u>Angel</u>", "<u>You Got The Love</u>", and "<u>Your Love</u>".

a.) He worked in collaboration with singer <u>Jamie Principle</u>.
- <u>1986</u>: Knuckles moved back to New York and started "<u>Def Mix Productions</u>" along with David Morales (another House music legend).
* <u>Focus</u>: producing House mixes of hits by some of the biggest pop stars in the business like:
a.) Michael Jackson, Chaka Khan, and Diana Ross.
- These versions notwithstanding, the mainstream was still unaware of the House sound. But that was about to change…
3.) "<u>Vogue</u>" (1990): would be the classic single that would introduce the sound of House music to the American mainstream.
- Once again, <u>Madonna</u> came out with an audio summary of the current state of electronic dance music (which focused on House) condensed into a three-and-a-half-minute, singles format.
* The famous MTV video also propelled this single displaying not only House elements, but also techno and electro-funk elements as well.
a.) It became one of THE most important singles of the 90's.
- Now that House has gone mainstream due in big part, to the popularity of "<u>Vogue</u>"…
* …the advent of the first sub-genre of House was about to unfold in the underground clubs…
a.) …which presented an entirely different take on the art of "House".
C.) <u>Creation of Ambient House</u> - <u>The Orb</u> (formed in 1988, London, ENG):
1.) Personnel: "<u>Dr.</u>" Alex Patterson (b. Duncan Robert Alexander Patterson, 10/15/59, London): sequencers, synthesizers, samplers; <u>Jimi Cauty</u> (b. James Cauty, 1956, Devon, ENG): guitar.
- Would develop later into a collective of different artists with Alex Patterson as the center.
* <u>The Orb</u>: would pioneer electronic dance music's first important sub-genre: <u>Ambient House</u>.
a.) <u>Ambient House</u>: a slower tempo'd House beat with music featuring tapestries of sample overlays, sustained dreamlike electronic sounds, string samples, spoken sound bites, and an overall mystic, atmospheric ambiance.
- Electronic dance music <u>made for listening</u> and chilling out in after-hours lounges after a night of dancing (a sort of "cool down" music).
* A digital styled "Music Concrete" over a throbbing beat.
2.) <u>Influences</u>: the ambient electronic sounds of <u>Brian Eno</u>, the <u>808 Drum Machine</u> (originally introduced by Run DMC), and the dubbing sound of <u>Reggae</u>.
- These were three of Alex Patterson's initial influences.
* <u>His main instruments</u>: sequencers, samplers, and synthesizers.
a.) Through these "instruments", Alex Patterson introduced an entirely new concept of DJing without turntables (replaced by computer technology).
- Which will set the structure for countless other DJ's to follow throughout the 90's and beyond.
b.) In addition, <u>The Orb</u> would set the foundation for development of electronic dance music (including various sub-genres) for the 90's.
- Their innovations still resonate today.
3.) <u>Beginnings</u>: Alex Patterson started out as a "roadie" for the band "Killer Joke' and became an A&R man for Brian Eno's label: "<u>EG</u>".

- As <u>The Orb</u>, Patterson first recorded under the "Orb's" banner in collaboration with Killer Joke band member <u>Jimi Cauty</u>.

* "<u>Tripping On Sunshine</u>" (1989): their debut release that would become a harbinger of things to come.

a.) Ambient Sound: first started resonating from this outfit.

- <u>Focus</u>: an ambient essence that would evolve into something more large scale where once again, as in dance-pop, the onus is on the overall, aggregate effect.

* As opposed to the individual parts.

- "<u>Kiss EP</u>" (1989): a 4-track EP emulating <u>Kiss-FM radio</u> out of New York City (including samples directly recorded from that station's broadcasts).

* It caught the attention of <u>DJ Paul Oakenfold</u> which led to the recruitment of Patterson (The Orb) to DJ at Oakenfold's club "<u>Heaven</u>" in the "Land of OZ" chill-out room.

a.) It was at this time that Patterson began adding a vast array of sounds into his ambient mixes such as:

- Sampled sounds from BBC nature shows, special effects, and sound bites from NASA space broadcasts.

* Woven together over a moderately tempo'd, pulsating beat.

4.) Patterson's breakthrough single: "<u>A Huge Evergrowing Pulsating Brain That Rules From The Centre of The Ultraworld</u>" (1989) – 22 minutes long.

- <u>Samples of</u>: chiming bells, Minnie Riperton's voice from her 70's hit tune "Lovin' You", a rainstorm, jet airplanes, roosters, ambient sustain, choral voice samples, and various electronic sounds.

* Over a hard-driving, slamming House beat.

a.) And a repetitive, catchy electronic melodic hook carrying an ethereal, mystic quality.

* <u>RESULT</u>: the first true ambient house single marking the beginning of a new genre (albeit with a conventionally tempo'd House beat).

a.) This was also the last Orb recording that <u>Jimi Cauty</u> was involved with.

- He went on to a similar outfit called: "<u>KLF</u>".

- <u>Kris "Thrash" Weston</u>: became Patterson's new collaborative partner.

5.) <u>RESULT</u>: The Orb's debut album entitled "<u>The Orb's Adventures Beyond The Ultraworld</u>" (1991).

- "<u>Little Fluffy Clouds</u>": a previously released single in collaboration with another Killer Joke member — <u>Youth</u> —first released in 1990.

* Featuring a melody originally composed by <u>Steve Reich</u> and samples of <u>Ricky Lee Jones</u> (famous for the 70's hit "Chucky's In Love") talking about her childhood days of living in the Arizona desert.

a.) She eventually filed suit and settled out of court.

* Accompanied by sampled chimes and electronics with heavy vibrato…

a.) …with various other samples including a tuba, car crash, and singing.

- Meshed with an ethereal, atmospheric essence and sustained, dreamlike quality.

* No pulsating beat added to the ethereal-styled atmospherics until 3:32 into the piece.

a.) A groove-heavy, sampled bass drum thud reminiscent of a House beat but in a slower, more moderate tempo.

- Hence, more ambient in nature.

* Setting the tempo that would be linked with "Ambient House" as a prime, stylistic feature.

6.) "Blue Room" (1992): another ambient single lasting 40 minutes.
- Complete with samples of nature including waterfalls, birds, etc. superimposed over sustained, atmospheric electronics.
* RESULT: the concept of "music concrete" meets electronica (more on the definition of "music concrete" a bit later).
- Very relaxing and listenable. A rhythmically static, sustained beginning that gradually sets into a groove (again, slower than conventional House).
* An atmospheric, dreamlike "soundscape" that became an Alex Patterson trademark with top-of-the-line production quality.

7.) Early 90's: The Orb's legendary mixes led them into the business of producing remix versions of earlier pop hits by artists: Erasure, Depeche Mode, Primal Scream, etc.
- Thereby reinventing the essence of these familiar hit singles and re-releasing them.
* Along with Frankie Knuckles, Alex Patterson set the "remix" trend in motion that would help define electronic dance music for the remainder of the 90's.
a.) But there was one other defining element that Alex Patterson [The Orb] inspired that would redefine 90's electronic dance music:
- The introduction of the sub-genre.

V. THE PROLIFERATION OF ELECTRONIC DANCE MUSIC SUB-GENRES

A.) In electronic dance music, The Orb first introduced the concept of the sub-genre thereby opening the door for both other sub-genres and completely new genres to come into existence.
1.) New sub-genres include: progressive house, acid house, ambient techno, etc.
- Insofar as new genres: Big Beat, Trance, Drum n' Bass.
* House and Techno were the original genres that paved the way.
a.) And proliferated throughout the 90's with House artists such as Basement Jaxx and Techno artists like Richie Hawtin.

B.) New Genres (all of which are DJ'd):
1.) Big Beat (a.k.a. "Rave n' Roll"): the most accessible form of early 21st century electronic dance music.
- Use of sequencers, samplers, and synthesizers consistent with the 90's foundation of DJing laid down by The Orb.
* Use of traditional pop song structures and pop music sensibilities resulting in pop-styled accessibility.
- Most prominent of the original Big Beat artists: The Chemical Brothers (formed 1992, Manchester, ENG).
* Personnel: Tim Rowlands (b. 1/11/71, Oxfordshire, ENG): producer; Ed Simons (b. 1/9/70, London): producer.
a.) They brought electronic dance music out of its experimental phase by making it straight-forward and more direct becoming the first to establish the Big Beat genre.
- In addition to the musical elements previously mentioned, there was one other element they would introduce into the electronic dance music mix: Rock (especially rock guitar samples).
* This Rock angle became their trademark.
- Another defining element in tune with electronic dance tradition: a hard-pumping, bass drum sample.
* Add to that, melodic dance music hooks,

electronics, Hip Hop influences, and catchy pop-styled tunes.
* They would include guest singers such as <u>Beth Orton</u>, <u>Tim Burgess</u> (of the UK Charlatans), and <u>Noel Gallagher</u> (of the band, Oasis).
    a.) "<u>Setting Sun</u>" (1997): features the voice of Noel Gallagher and also samples of the drum beat and veiled hook references to the Beatles' "<u>Tomorrow Never Knows</u>" (#1 in the UK pop charts).
        - "<u>Block Rockin' Beats</u>" from the album, "Dig Your Own Hole" (1997): became another of their #1 UK dance hits.
- Other Big Beat stars included <u>Fatboy Slim</u> and <u>Prodigy</u>.
* The two labels which spawned Big Beat were:
    a.) "<u>Skint</u>" (Brighton, ENG): home to Fatboy Slim and "<u>Wall Of Sound</u>" (London).
        - Of the two, <u>Skint</u> was the more innovative.

2.) <u>Trance</u>: derived from German techno of the early 90's.
- <u>Focus</u>:
    * Short, keyboard driven melodies (or melodic fragments) from the synthesizer that are endlessly repeated within a given track.
        a.) A nocturnally atmospheric, and ethereal characteristic.
        b.) Hypnotic, house beat.
        c.) Lots of reverberation.
    * <u>NOTE</u>: With all elements put together, this genre affects a dreamlike, trance-effect on the listener.
- <u>Initial Inspiration</u>: Detroit Techno, atmospheric elements of ambient music, and the melodic style of the group: New Order.
    * <u>Early Trance labels</u>: R&S Records (Ghent, Belgium) and Harthouse/ Eye Q Records (Frankfurt, GER).
        a.) <u>R&S</u>: laid down the early foundation for Trance with the following singles:
            - "<u>Energy Flash</u>" by Joey Beltran
            - "<u>The Rave Signal</u>" by CJ Bolland
                * Other artists included: <u>Sun Electric</u> and <u>Aphex Twin</u>.
- <u>Mid 90's</u>: interest in Trance began to dissipate but has since made a comeback beginning in the late 90's.
    * Subsequently becoming the most popular electronic dance music genre.
        - Surpassing the popularity of "House".
    * Trance would also start evolving a sub-genre of its own...
- <u>Progressive Trance</u>: a smoother, silkier, more streamlined trance sound.
    * Somewhat more hypnotic but less experimental than earlier, traditional trance.
        a.) Most notable DJs: <u>Paul Oakenfold</u>, <u>Sasha</u>, <u>Pete Tong</u>, and <u>Judge Jules</u>.
            - All of which hail from the UK.
        b.) Most notable DJs form the US: <u>Christopher Lawrence</u> and <u>Kimball Collins</u>.
- <u>NOTE</u>: TRANCE, BIG BEAT, HOUSE, and TECHNO can all be strung together seamlessly by the same type of beat (House) by a skilled DJ creating a non-stop, endless array of dance tunes derived from these different genres.
    * The same could not be said of the last genre to be focused on.

3.) <u>Drum n' Bass</u>: contains a considerably faster tempo. So much so, that a small, separate room is needed to play this type of electronic dance music (within the club as the other genres).

- <u>Inspirations</u>: elements of Reggae, Hip Hop, and early Techno.
  * Originated in the UK underground clubs.
    a.) In especially, the Techno and Rave scenes during the early 90's (was where this genre first developed).
- <u>Characteristics</u>: sped-up backbeats at about 165 beats per minute.
  * <u>Techno Influence</u>: Skittishly rapid percussive patterns.
    a.) That is, sampled percussive sounds.
  * <u>Reggae Influence</u>: A syncopated bass-drum sampled bassline reminiscent of reggae.
    a.) Churning beneath the rapid-tempo'd surface.
  * <u>Rap Influence</u>: Rapping is the vocal vehicle if words are used in the music.
  * <u>NOTE</u>: Both fast-tempo'd reggae-influenced backbeats and skittish, upper-register percussive sampled patterns…
    a.)…are sort of in the "push and pull" ("sort of" because it's sequenced rather than played on instruments)…
      -…with the slower, reggae-styled sampled bass guitar/bass drum elements.

- <u>DJ Krust</u>: one of the main innovators of this genre.
  * "<u>Coded Language</u>" (1999): the title track of the album (that bears the same name).
    a.) Complete with the signature musical properties previously mentioned.
      - Also, with DJ Krust rapping, he combines Hip Hop influences with this brand of electronic dance music.

C.) <u>Electronic Dance Music</u>: with its various developments throughout the 1980's and the 90's, E.D.M. has become a world-uniting type of musical language.
  1.) <u>Language</u>: could be in any spoken language because the emphasis, being on the danceable, aggregate sound…
    -…makes it pliable for any country or any culture to develop their own version…
      *…with musical properties familiar to the mainstream world (in any country)….
        a.) …becoming an international language in and of itself.
  2.) A "Planet Rock" that anyone, anywhere in the world could understand, emulate, and above all, dance to.
    - But as all-encompassing as it was, it wasn't the only electronic music game in town (so to speak)…
      -…there was one other.

CHAPTER XIII: REVIEW

Who was the artist who wrote and recorded the 1982 single, "Planet Rock"?

    Name the new genre that resulted because of this single.

    Who produced this single?

What type of music did "Planet Rock" set the blueprint for?

List two major influences of "Planet Rock":
    1.)
    2.)

In one word, how would you describe Kraftwerk's musical style?

List four elements that make up the originality of Kraftwerk:
    1.)
    2.)
    3.)
    4.)

Which Kraftwerk single – the title track of a 1977 album — had the most profound influence on "Planet Rock"? (Hint: they both share the same thematic material):

What was significant about New Order's approach to presenting/performing electronic dance music?

    How did it differ from DJ Afrika Bambaataa?

Name New Order's breakthrough single of 1983 and its vinyl record format:

    What became significance about this single in relation to a particular vinyl record format?

Who was New Order's producer? (Hint: the same one as DJ Afrika Bambaataa):

Who introduced Electronic Dance Music to the American mainstream?

What was her impact in relation to women place in pop culture? In other words, what did she redefine?

What was her impact in regard to redefining a woman's career in rock and roll?

Was she the first female artist that MTV aggressively promoted?

What was the musical result of her standard, dance-pop idiom?

Who became the first black artist that MTV aggressively promoted?

Name this artist's 1983 album that became the vehicle for that promotion:

What were the two vacuums that led to Disco?
1.)
2.)

What became the result of the club vacuum insofar as a psychedelic era legacy?

What became the musical byproduct?

Who became the first Club DJ as serious artist?

What was the old paradigm in regard to club DJ's?

What became the new paradigm?

In regard to the new paradigm, what became the club DJ's real instrument?

Name four of Francis Grasso's original techniques:
1.)
2.)
3.)
4.)

What standardization resulted from these techniques?

Where was Francis Grasso's first important gig where he honed in his DJing skills?

    Name two of his disciples:
        1.)
        2.)

    What new era did Grasso and his disciples usher in?

Which DJ became the innovator of the modern disco clubbing scene?

    List three standards that he had set by which all clubs would follow:
        1.)
        2.)
        3.)

Who was David Mancuso's psychedelic influence?

    What was "The League For Spiritual Discovery"?

    Name Mancuso's venue where he would emulate the "League" gatherings:

What important Sister Alicia influence would Mancuso adopt later on?

Name his first important gathering at The Loft:

    Who were the invited guests?

    What became the Disco Ideal as a result?

Name another standard set by The Loft in regard to the art of sound reproduction.

    Name the engineer that Mancuso collaborated with?

    This engineer was highly influential in developing the first commercially mass-produced item which would be very important for club DJs. What was that item?

In regard to the speaker system, what was Mancuso's main goal, which would set another standard for disco?

As a DJ, how did his musical stages mirror the Tibetan Book of The Dead model?
    1.)
    2.)

3.)

What important musical style did Mancuso standardize into the disco record lexicon?

When was mainstream America first alerted to the concept of what would become known as Disco?

List three elements that comprise the Techno style:
    1.)
    2.)
    3.)

Where did Techno originate:

    Name the three artists who originated this new genre:
        1.)
        2.)
        3.)

List two influences behind Techno's creation:
    1.)
    2.)

What was the overall character of Techno?

What electronic dance music genre came out of the underground, post-disco club culture in the early 80's?

    What was the art of the club DJ?

Describe the signature "House" beat:

    What five elements were superimposed over the House beat?
        1.)
        2.)
        3.)
        4.)
        5.)

Name two of the early legendary "House" DJ's:
      1.)
      2.)

      From where did the term, "House" originate?

What type of tempo did many post-disco records have?

      What was needed to revamp and reenergize these records into something new?

How would you define the reedit?

      What additional new elements were added along with the new drum tracks?

Name the DJ who added the signature house beat by bringing a drum machine to the DJ booth (he left that machine on for the entire night).

      Within the context of that constant beat, how would he manipulate various dance records?

What became electronic dance music's first important sub-genre?

      What group was the pioneer of that sub-genre?

What was the creative goal of ambient house insofar as electronic dance music?

What/who were Alex Patterson's three main influences?
      1.)
      2.)
      3.)

      What were Alex Patterson's three main instruments?
            1.)
            2.)
            3.)

List three elements that make up ambient house:
      1.) Musical Characteristics:
      2.) Textural (Tapestry) Characteristics:

3.) Tempos:

What was Alex Patterson's breakthrough single of 1989?

What concept of DJing did Alex Patterson standardize in the early 90's? (Hint: it was the concept of DJing *without* a certain thing):

List three elements of Big Beat:
      1.) Type of Influence:
      2.) Type of Structure:
      3.) Type of Sensibility:

List three initial inspirations (influences) for Trance:
      1.)
      2.)
      3.)

List four elements of Trance:
      1.) Type of Character:
      2.) Type of Melodic Treatment:
      3.) Type of Beat:
      4.) Signature Studio Technique (hint: the same technique used in garage band):

What were the three inspirations behind Drum n' Bass?
      1.)
      2.)
      3.)

List three elements of Drum n' Bass that make this genre unique:
      1.) Tempo:
      2.) Character of the Bass Line:
      3.) Type of Vocal Delivery:

Starting in the 1990's, what became the common denominator in writing, recording, and performing the five major genres of electronic dance music (i.e. house, techno, big beat, trance, drum n' bass)?

CHAPTER XIV: INDUSTRIAL – THE OTHER ELECTRONIC DANCE MUSIC

I. THE FUTURIST MOVEMENT

    A.) Originated in Italy around the turn of the 20th century as a "sociopolitical revolt against outworn institutions whose roots were seen to reside in the uncritical acceptance of the past".

        1.) The Initial Catalyst: <u>Filippo Tommaso Marinetti</u> (1876 - 1944). First wrote "The Founding Manifesto of Futurism" (1909). In it, he states:

            - "We will sing of the vibrant nightly fervor of arsenals and shipyards blazing with violent electric moons, greedy railway stations that devour smoke-plume serpents".

                * He was a poet whose "Manifesto of Futurist Poetry" was published in 1909.

                    a.) Other futurist manifestos on other artistic disciplines such as painting, sculpture, and music were published within the next three years.

            - <u>Ingredients of These Manifestos</u>: the thread between the different artistic disciplines that would transform them into a "Futurist" genre.

                * Reflective of the energies of urbanism, cacophony of the combination of machine-inspired noises, and the passion for speed in both travel and mechanized production.

                    a.) <u>Pratella</u> (1880-1955): in his "Technical Manifesto of Futurist Music" (1912), he suggested a new musical direction of <u>rhythmic irregularities</u>, <u>microtones</u>, and <u>atonality</u>.

        2.) The True Catalyst: <u>Luigi Russolo</u>. In his manifesto, "<u>The Art of Noise</u>" (1913) he wrote:

            - "Today, Noise triumphs and reigns supreme over the sensibilities of men".

                * A painter by trade, he goes on to say, "We must break out of the narrow circle of pure, musical sounds, and conquer the infinite variety of noise-sounds".

                    a.) As for his lack of musicianship, he defends his "musical" credibility in the following manner:

                        - "Unconcerned by my apparent incompetence, and convinced that all rights and possibilities open up to the daring, I have been able to initiate the great renewal of music by means of the Art of Noises".

            - RESULT: "<u>Intonarumori</u>" (Noise Intoners): Russolo's noise machine.

                * <u>Noises from these Intoners</u>: rumbles, roars, crashes, booms, splashes, snorts, hisses, whistles, crackles, buzzes, etc.

                    a.) <u>Percussion Noises</u>: on metal, wood, skin, stone, etc.

                    b.) <u>Noise from Animals and People</u>: shouts, screams, groans, howls, shrieks, sobs, etc.

                * The first Intoner concert: April 21, 1914 in Milan, Italy.

                    a.) <u>Russolo's works for that event</u>: "The Awakening of A City", "Luncheon On The Kursaal Terrace", and "Meeting Of The Automobiles and Airplanes".

                        - All works for Noise Intoners.

            - <u>Legacy</u>: Russolo's Noise Intoners were all destroyed in World War II.

                * No great, enduring works resulted from the initial decades of the Futurist Movement.

                    a.) The first great manifestation of this legacy would not occur until the early 1950's. It's name: <u>Electronic Music</u>.

    B.) <u>Electronic Music</u>: two genres — "Music Concrete" and Analog.

        1.) "<u>Music Concrete</u>": recording sounds of nature or of everyday life on to magnetic tape, then either manually or electronically manipulating the tape in order to produce original sounds.

            - <u>Catalyst</u>: the invention of the <u>Tape Recorder</u>.

                * It allowed the following manipulation of sound:

a.) Changing of speeds, ability to play a recorded sound backwards, and editing: the cutting, splicing, or pasting of recorded sound clips.

- Also filtering, mixing of sounds, and reverberation.

b.) In addition, volume-level control and tapeloops, the latter which gave a perpetual, repetitive ostinato.

- Pierre Schaeffer (b. 8/14/10): French composer, novelist, and acoustician.

* Working in a Paris radio station, he originated the idea of creating a musical tapestry of outside noises and random sounds.

a.) April 15, 1948: he formulated the theory of Music Concrete, which set the basic rules of assembling those sounds.

- With Magnetic Tape: acceleration & deceleration, changing of dynamic & pitch, and modification of instrumental timbres.

* All arranged in a collage of sound.

* "Etude aux chemins de fer" (1948): a three-minute work.

a.) A collage of railway train sounds.

* "Etude aux casseroles" (1948): collaging of sound of saucepans.

a.) Both this and the previously mentioned work were broadcast on a French radio program called: "Concert of Noises".

- "Concrete": direct manipulations of pure sound without the intricacies of a musical [written] score.

Poemé électronique
Edgard Varése

* Example: "Poemé électronique" by Edgard Varése.

a.) Written for the Phillips Pavilion for the 1958 World's Fair in Brussels, Belgium.

2.) Analog: the main instrument – The Oscillator.

- An electronic "instrument' that generates the following sounds:

* Sine Wave: a pure sound wave with no overtones.

* Sawtooth Wave: a sound with all overtones that has sort of a buzzsaw kind of sound.

* Square Wave: another distorted sounding wave.

* White Noise: a sound with no definite focus.

- The sound one hears when the TV picture goes out and displays a snowy picture.

Artikulation
György Ligeti

- Other studio tools to be developed:

* Band-Pass Filters: a device which controls both high and low cut-off frequencies (especially with white noise).

* Reverberation Chamber: a device which controls varying degrees of reverberation upon a recorded sound.

* NOTE: In the analog electronic music domain, all sounds are purely electronically generated (unlike Music Concrete).

- Karlheinz Stockhausen (b. 8/22/28, Modrath, W. GER): began his work on electronic music in Studio II at West German Radio in Cologne, W. GER.

* His first electronic piece: "Elektronische Studie I" (1953).

a.) Made entirely by Sine Wave sounds.

* "Elektronische Studie II" (1954): a multi-tapestry of sine wave synthesis with no filter or white noise.

a.) Only added element: a reverberation chamber.

b.) He also developed his own unique system of graphic notation to fit his electronic genre.

* These two works made Stockhausen a pioneer in the development of analog electronic music that, unlike music concrete…

a.) …was completely electronically generated.

3.) <u>NOTE</u>: in both Music Concrete and analog, the concept was to invent new sounds, to dispose of conventional structure, and to create a new musical spontaneity that could only be captured on magnetic recording tape.

- Thereby freeing a composer from the limitations of conventional instrumental performance…

*…and in the process, creating a music that reflects the modernity of a rising technological age.

a.) Exactly what the early futurists had in mind when they embarked on their manifestos.

- It would not be until the mid 70's, that concepts of the futurist movement would find their way into rock and roll.

C.) <u>Industrial Music</u>: an aggressive, highly abrasive mixture of rock and roll and electronic music presented in a free-formed manner.

1.) A blending of the avante garde and electronic experimentation reminiscent of the futurist legacy specifically, electronic composition of the 1950's.

- Music Concrete and Analog.

* In the case of the latter influence, white noise was especially used.

a.) Also, sequencers and synthesizers.

2.) As the genre evolved, avante garde influences gave way to pounding, relentless, jackhammer beats.

- Eventually transforming into a darker alternative to mainstream electronic dance music.

* Would bear a harsh, ominous essence that became its trademark.

a.) But also characteristic of mechanized, numbingly hypnotic, repetitive musical qualities.

- With lyrics dealing with alienation and dehumanization.

3.) It began with three early industrial groups…

- …whose trademark was as much about performance art as it was about the music.

II. THE FIRST GENERATION OF INDUSTRIAL ARTISTS: THROBBING GRISTLE, EINSTURZENDE NEUBAUTEN, & CABARET VOLTAIRE

A.) <u>Throbbing Gristle</u> (formed 1975, London, ENG): the first industrial band on record.

1.) Personnel: <u>Genesis P-Orridge</u> (b. Neil Megson): ringleader, vocals, electronic violin, bass; <u>Cosey Fanni Tutti</u>: cornet, guitar; <u>Peter "Sleazy" Christopherson</u>: trumpet, tape machines; <u>Chris Carter</u>: keyboards.

- <u>Genesis P-Orridge</u>: performance career began in Hull in 1969.

* He established a performance outfit called "COUM Transmissions" with <u>Cosey Fanni Tutti</u>.

a.) <u>Influences</u>: the Fluxus movement, punk rock, and performance art.

- They were initially unable to find a club performance space so they often performed on the streets.

- October, 1976: with the addition of Christopherson and Carter, COUM established "Pornography": an exhibit in London's "Institute of Contemporary Art".

* This was where they first performed as <u>Throbbing Gristle</u> doing "Music From The Death Factory".

a.) Because this particular exhibit consisted of a pile of used tampons and soiled diapers, it caused a major stir due to both it's offensive characteristic and...

-...the fact it was supported by taxpayer funding.

* Their usual early performances commenced with a punch clock, which ran for 60 minutes before power to the stage, was suddenly cut off.

2.) <u>Philosophy</u>: beginning as an experiment into what extent one could mutate and collage sound.

- To present complex, non-entertaining noises into a pop-music cultural situation.

* Fashion was the enemy.

- <u>Style</u>: antagonistic, abrasive, and aggressive.

* A cacophony of mechanized noises, extreme anti-music, tape loops, and aggressive beats.

a.) All properties one could find in the Futurist movement and it's electronic music legacy.

Hamburger Lady
Throbbing Gristle

- <u>Subject Matter</u>: death, mutilation, fascism, and human degradation.

* Examples: "<u>Hamburger Lady</u>": it's inspiration was based on a true story of burn-unit patient.

a.) "<u>Death Threats</u>": a compilation of murderous messages left on the group's answering machine.

* <u>Subject Matter Style</u>: bleak and distressing in both attitudes and observations.

3.) "<u>Industrial Records</u>": their own independent label.

- The "<u>Industrial</u>" term: meant as a criticism of the following:

* The recording industry's system of power control over the mainstream musical landscape.

* Their aversion to taking any artistic risks.

a.) Due to the dark, esoteric nature of their music, Throbbing Gristle understood that any chance at popular appeal would be nil.

- Which was exactly the reason they founded their own label

* The "Industrial" term was first coined by an original COUM member: <u>Monte Cazzaza</u>.

- <u>Throbbing Gristle</u>: proved that one could operate successfully at whatever they chose stylistically…

*…and reach an audience (however limited) and not compromise their artistic vision or principles.

a.) The result of having their own independent label.

4.) <u>Throbbing Gristle</u>: the inaugural industrial band was the first to incorporate the basic noise elements in a completely non-traditional manner reminiscent of the Futurist Movement of the early 20th Century…

Subhuman
Throbbing Gristle

-…into a rock and roll context.

* Using dark, mechanized-sounding, anti-social thematics in a free-form manner…

a.) Which resulted in an apocalyptic aura.

B.) <u>Einstürzende Neubauten</u> (formed April 1, 1980, West Berlin, GER): translates into "Collapsing New Buildings".

1.) <u>Specialization</u>: an avante garde, conceptual performance art collective.

- Personnel: <u>Blixa Bargeld</u> (b. Christian Emmerich, 1/12/59, Berlin, GER): vocals, guitar, percussion, bass; <u>N. U. Unruh</u> (Andrew Chudy, 6/9/57/ New York, NY): percussion, drums, vocals; <u>Beate Bartel</u>: percussion; <u>Gudrun Gut</u>: percussion.

* <u>Style</u>: another Futurist legacy with Dadaist influences making it's way this time, into the German rock domain.

a.) <u>Noises</u>: power tools and large metal industrial objects.
- The latter being beaten with chains, hammers, and pipes.

b.) <u>Howling Vocals</u>: giving a somewhat tribal, primitive flavor in conjunction to the metallic (literally metallic) sound.
- In some ways, like a modern, urbanized tribal music.

c.) <u>Instrumental</u>: distorted guitars, droning bass sounds, and aggressively thunderous, metallic percussion.

d.) "<u>FM Einheit</u>" (b. Frank Martin Strauss, 9/18/58): later joined the group and brought in the following "instruments":
- Power drills, jackhammers, amplified air-conditioning ducts, and giant industrial springs.

e.) <u>Musical Structure</u>: free-form.

- They started out performing in abandoned factories and junkyards.

* And performed on various objects associated with these venues.

a.) <u>RESULT</u>: their early signature sound was filled with the clang-bang of metal objects and tools played on other metal objects producing a sound reminiscent of an old factory machine.
- Hence, their music was the first to be associated in a purely musical manner with "Industrial" [factory-like] sounding characteristics.
* Whereas Throbbing Gristle's "Industrial" term was more of a protest symbol associated to their label).
a.) Which fused perfectly with Neubauten's style of tribal sounding, urbane primitivism.

2.) <u>Early Recordings</u>: German-issued singles and EP's (1980-83).
- Guttural, howling vocals with thunderous, bombastic metal percussion and bass drones.

* Later compiled in the album: "<u>Strategies Against Architecture: 1980-83</u>" (released in 1988).

3.) Two additional members would further impact the group's stylistic direction:
- <u>Alexander Hacke</u> (guitar) and <u>Mark Chung</u> (bass): on the one hand, expanded the group's musical scope.
* On the other (in the process), they seized considerable control over the group's noise elements.
a.) Thereby, both tightening and streamlining the group's musical sound.
* <u>RESULT</u>: they began the process to a more conventional sound for Einstürzende Neubauten.
a.) Which culminated in the album "<u>Tabula Rasa</u>" (1993).
- The title, meaning "clean slate" signified a new direction toward a more conventional, musical approach.

4.) <u>NOTE</u>: both <u>Throbbing Gristle</u> and early <u>Einstürzende Neubauten</u> were purely avante garde, experimental, dark, and basically free-form to a point of reaching a small, select cult of listeners.
- It was completely esoteric and out of reach from a mainstream perspective.
* As always in these cases, someone usually comes along to make a normally unpalatable sound become a bit more palatable.

C.) <u>Cabaret Voltaire</u> (formed in 1973, Sheffield, ENG): another of the early three important industrial bands of that genre's first generation.
1.) They started out as a clique of teenagers making tapes of noises just for kicks.

              - Soon after, there were only three members left but they gained access to <u>Sheffield Haddam University's Music Department</u>.

                      * They began experimenting with tape recorders, synthesizers, and other instruments of electronic nature.

      2.) Personnel: <u>Steven Mallinder</u>: vocals, bass, percussion; <u>Richard H. Kirk</u>: guitar, keyboards, wind instruments; <u>Christopher R. Watson</u>: tape machines, keyboards.

              - <u>Influences</u>: the ambient, electronic music style of <u>Brian Eno</u> and the <u>Dadaist Art Movement</u> of the early 20th century.

                      * "<u>Cabaret Voltaire</u>": named after a Dadaist club [Cabaret Voltaire] established by Hugo Ball in Zurich in 1917.

                            a.) <u>The Dadaist Movement</u> (1915-1922): a mixture of negativism and anti-art attitudes and proclamations.

                                - Emphasis on everyday objects presented in a way that deconstructs, distorts, and abstracts normal conventional artistic traditions.

                                      * <u>Purpose</u>: to challenge art's traditional aesthetic basis and in the process, make it meaningless.

                                - The movement originated in Zurich, Switzerland in the Cabaret Voltaire previously mentioned.

      3.) <u>Early Music of the Cabaret Voltaire Band</u>: harsh, abrasive, negative, distorted.

           - <u>Early 80's</u>: their sound began to develop into something more artistically mature.

                    * They incorporated both Middle-East influenced sounds and, most importantly:

Taxi Music
Cabaret Voltaire

                          a.) <u>A dance beat</u>: stringing together these disparate, experimental sounds in a way that made it easier for listeners outside of the industrial cult to appreciate.

          - <u>RESULT</u>: Cabaret Voltaire, added the dance beat to an esoteric, noise-ridden, experimental, Dadaist influenced rock and roll sound and in the process:

                    * Opened the door to industrial music's journey of eventual accessibility to a mainstream audience (it's not there yet, but they began the process).

                          a.) While also becoming the first to anticipate the industrial dance music of the next generation to come.

III. INDUSTRIAL MUSIC'S SECOND GENERATION: THE "COLD WAVE" GENRE

    A.) <u>Ministry</u> (formed 1981 in Chicago): the first to open the door of Industrial music to the awareness of the general American public by adding rock guitar influences [in this case Punk] into the industrial, electronic-influenced mix thereby creating the "Cold Wave" style.

      1.) Personnel: <u>Al Jourgenesen</u> (a.k.a. "Hypo Luxo", b. Allen Jourgensen, 10/9/58, Havana, Cuba): guitar, vocals; <u>Lamont Walton</u> (bass): replaced eventually by <u>Paul Barker</u> (a.k.a. "Hermes Pan", b. 2/8/50, Palo Alto, CA): bass; <u>Stevo</u> (drums): replaced eventually by <u>William Rieflin</u> (b. 9/30/60, Seattle, WA): drums; <u>Roland Barker</u> (b. 6/30/57/, Mountainview, CA): keyboards.

           - Originally, Al Jourgensen started out with a in new wave/synth-pop band called <u>Special Affect</u> (fronted by Groovie Man [Frank Nardiello] of the future industrial band: Thrill Kill Cult).

                    * Basically doing British new wave inspired synth-pop dance music.

      2.) <u>Al Jourgensen</u>: his influences in addition to the new wave/synth-pop sound.

           - <u>Late 70's</u>: inspired by the punk music of <u>The Ramones</u>.

                    * In Chicago: the music of Steve Albini with <u>Big Black</u>.

                        a.) Especially, with the aggressive shouting vocal style.

           - <u>1981</u>: he started Ministry and a series of singles and an EP on the Chicago-based <u>Wax Trax</u>! Label (founded in 1973 by Jim Nash and Danny Flesher).

                    * Ministry would become Wax Trax's first major recording success.

a.) At this label, Jourgensen's early style dealt with experimental electronic tracks with a driving dance beat.

- "Cold Life" (1981)" Ministry's first dance hit and the title track of their first EP.

* After a short stint on the Arista label (he was dropped from Arista due to creative disputes)…

a.) … there was a three-year hiatus.

3.) "Twitch" (1986): their first full-length album (recorded on the Sire label).

- At this stage, Jourgensen is now the sole member of Ministry.

* This album marked the beginning of a new direction in Jourgensen's artistic development.

a.) He begins utilizing his punk guitar influences.

4.) The "Aggro" (or "Cold Wave") sound: angry, shouted vocals (inspired by Steve Albini), electronic sampling with a pounding dancebeat (inspired by his early new wave influences), and an abrasive, aggressive thick wall of rock guitar sound (inspired by his punk influences).

- "The Land of Rape and Honey" (1988): the first album where the "aggro" sound becomes fully realized.

* Also, the beginning of Al Jourgensen's collaboration with Paul Barker.

a.) Style: intense, abrasive, and very repetitive.

- and a thick, pulsating dancebeat.

* "Stigmata": the opening track of the album.

a.) Features a thematic, abrasive sounding electric guitar hook that is heard throughout the song with an equally abrasive punk-guitar-noise wall of sound.

- With shouted vocals.

* "The Missing": rapid-tempo'd, highly repetitive, abrasive rock guitar hook that threads the entire song together.

* "You Know What You Are": makes use of electronic sampling with a pounding synthetic beat sans abrasive guitar noise.

a.) Again, with shouting, angry-sounding vocals.

- The title track of the album is similar in musical scope (i.e. more about electronic sampling/pounding beat than of aggressive guitars).

* This album marked the beginning of Jourgensen's collaborations with artists from other bands.

a.) On the album: Chris Connelly (from "Fini Tribe") and William Rieflin (who collaborated with KMFDM).

- On the album's tour: Trent Reznor (Nine Inch Nails), Nivek Ogre (Skinny Puppy), Daniel Yow (Jesus Lizard), Martin Atkins (Killer Joke & P.I.L.), as well as Connelly and Rieflin.

b.) These collaborations would inspire other Jourgensen side projects such as:

- The Revolting Cocks, Pigface, Acid Horse, and 1000 Homo DJ's.

* Jourgensen's side projects and collaborations with outside artists would inspire both of these practices to become the norm in the industrial music domain.

- "A Mind Is A Terrible Thing To Taste" (1989): added more toughness and vigor to the "aggro" sound thereby solidifying it's consistency.

5.) Another Jourgensen Impact: the recruitment of various European industrial artists to the Wax Trax! Label.

- <u>KMFDM</u> (Kein Mitleid fur die Mehrheit): translates to "No Sympathy for the Majority".

          * Formed 2/29/84 in Paris, France.

Spiritual House
KMFDM

          a.) Another of the industrial bands brandishing an emphasis on the punk rock influenced guitar metal sound mixed with sampling.

               - Headed by their only consistent member: <u>Sasha Konietzko</u>.

Vogue
KMFDM

- Jourgensen was also instrumental in bringing both <u>Front 242</u> (from Belgium) and <u>Front Line Assembly</u> (from Canada) into the Wax Trax! fold (more on these two bands shortly).

6.) By the late 80's, due in big part by Al Jourgensen's impact, Wax Trax's signature sound had evolved into a hybrid of the following sounds:

Neologic Spasm
Front Line Assembly

- <u>Disco</u>, <u>Punk</u>, <u>Electronic Music</u> (early 80's), <u>House</u>, and <u>Guitar Noise</u> (Punk derived).

      * By the early 90's, a derivative of this sound would become streamlined by another artist thereby making it palatable for a wider, mainstream audience.

B.) <u>Nine Inch Nails</u> (formed 1989; Cleveland, OH): responsible for bringing that streamlined "Cold Wave' style to the American mainstream.

1.) <u>Trent Reznor</u> (b. Michael Trent Reznor on May, 17, 1965; Mercer, PA): vocals, keyboards, guitar, bass, drums, and programming.

    - He writes, performs, arranges, and produces all of his material in the studio.

      * A one-man industrial session band.

        a.) He hires a full band for his tours.

    - <u>His musical stylistic focus</u>:

      * Writing with a pop-oriented melodic focus while utilizing conventional song structure in an "industrial" context.

        a.) He also added aggressive, cold wave influenced, electric guitar elements mixed with synth-laden electronics and sampling.

      * <u>Lyrically</u>: words of angst, alienation, and rage.

    - <u>RESULT</u>: Trent Reznor seized the cold wave "aggro" industrial sound, added pop melodic elements, traditional song structure, and angst-laden lyrics.

      * And in the process, by streamlining his influences, he made the industrial genre palatable for a wider, mainstream audience.

        a.) Thereby expanding industrial music's exposure.

      * In addition, he also adopted a sort of brooding, maverick-styled, self-absorbed persona.

2.) <u>Background</u>: began learning classical piano at the age of 5.

    - <u>In his teens</u>: he learned the tenor saxophone and tuba for his high school band. He also acted in high school musicals.

      * During this time, he was also playing in various garage bands.

        a.) One of his earliest primary rock influences was <u>Kiss</u>.

    - He attended Allegheny College to study music and computer technology.

      * He dropped out after one year in order to pursue music on a full-time basis.

3.) He moved to Cleveland with his friend and future drummer: <u>Chris Vrenna</u>.

    - Soon after, Reznor began taking an interest in the new industrial, cold wave sound that was just starting to flourish in the underground.

      * What attracted him to this music was:

        a.) The focus on computer technology mixed with aggressive metal guitars.

          - His initial Kiss influence meeting computers.

      * He would gig in various local Cleveland bands, work at a keyboard store, and work as a custodian at the "Right Track" recording studio.

a.) It was at "Right Track" where he taught himself the computer knowledge necessary to become a studio engineer.
- On off-hours, he began working on his own material.

4.) <u>1988</u>: Influences from the "cold wave" genre — <u>Ministry</u>, <u>Skinny Puppy</u>, and <u>Big Black</u> (the latter, though not industrial in style, was industrial in spirit) — would begin to show fruition in his debut album.
- "<u>Pretty Hate Machine</u>": released in 1989 on the TVT label (the label best known for jingles compilations).

Head Like A Hole
Nine Inch Nails

* Produced in collaboration with: <u>Flood</u> (Depeche Mode), <u>John Fryer</u> (Cocteau Twins), and <u>Adrian Sherwood</u> & <u>Chris LeBlanc</u>.
a.) <u>RESULT</u>: his first college radio hit: "<u>Head Like A Hole</u>".
- This single also resulted in an MTV video.

Sin
Nine Inch Nails

* <u>Another Result</u>: it introduced the style of industrial rock (i.e. cold wave) to the American mainstream audience.
a.) Albeit in a more musically streamlined manner.
- It became more mainstream accessible.

5.) <u>Nine Inch Nails</u>: gained a lot of exposure due in big part, by a three-year concert tour thereby acquiring a massive audience.
- In addition, they became the headline act on the first Lollapalooza tour in 1991.
* They also opened for Guns n' Roses' European tour.

6.) <u>TVT</u>: wanted to exercise more control over Reznor's artistic direction. In response Trent Reznor asked to be released from his contract which resulted in a long dispute with TVT.
- <u>Interscope Records</u>: not only agreed to co-release his next album, but they also gave him his own label entitled: <u>Nothing</u>.
* "<u>Broken</u>" EP (1992): debuted at #7 on the pop album charts.
a.) "<u>Wish</u>": a track from that EP, won a Grammy Award for best metal performance.
- Hence, his style now solidified in the mainstream rock domain.

7.) <u>Reznor</u>: in addition to introducing industrial rock to the masses, was also pushing the limits of decency in regard to his music videos.
- "<u>Happiness Is Slavery</u>": showing a man being sexually tortured and ground up by a machine.
* <u>MTV</u>: refused to show that video.
a.) Other NIN videos that MTV refused to show had snuff movie influences such as "<u>Down In It</u>" and "<u>Sin</u>" (both tracks from "Pretty Hate Machine").
- The FBI investigated Reznor for using actual snuff movie footage.

C.) Artists such as <u>Ministry</u>, <u>Skinny Puppy</u>, <u>KMFDM</u>, and <u>Nine Inch Nails</u> made up an important branch of an industrial music domain known as "cold wave" or "industrial rock".
1.) Complete with rock guitars mixed with synth-laden sounds and samples.
- There was however, another industrial domain that would have a completely different essence that would become the industrial rubric for the late 1990's and beyond….

IV. INDUSTRIAL DANCE: A.K.A. ELECTRONIC BODY MUSIC (EBM)

A.) <u>Early 90's</u>: a split occurs in the Industrial Dance music domain between the cold wave, electric guitar-based music (a la, Ministry, KMFDM, Nine Inch Nails among others) and music based more on pure electronics.
1.) The pure electronics branch would become the new rubric of Industrial starting in the early 90's.

- Characteristics:
    * Pounding, aggressive percussive beats.
    * Electronic sequences.
    * Sample-laden synthetic sounds.
    * Distorted vocals.
    * An overall dark essence of sound, mood, and character.

B.) The Harbingers: German Space music beginning with Tangerine Dream (among others) combined with the hard-hitting electronic disco sound of Giorgio Moroder, would comprise the initial influences on the artists who invented Electronic Body Music.

 1.) Tangerine Dream (formed in 1967, West Berlin, Germany): specialized in electronic music and among the first to use electronic sequencers in rock and roll.
  - Edgar Froese (b. 1946; Tilsit, East Prussia and founder of the group): began by studying art in West Berlin.
   * Initial influences: the Dadaist and Surrealist art movements.
    a.) Literary influences: Gertrude Stein, Walt Whitman, and Henry Miller.
   * He arranged a multi-media events at Salvador Dali's (his idol's) residence in Spain during the mid 60's.
    a.) This inspired him [Froese] to combine both his literary and artistic influences and apply them to music.
     - His first band: The Ones (a quasi R&B band).
      * Released only one single.
  - 1967: the original line-up for Tangerine Dream was formed.
   * Froese: guitar, keyboards, synthesizer; Kurt Herkenberg: bass; Lanse Hapshash: drums; Voker Hornbach: flute; Charlie Prince: winds.
    a.) By 1969: Klaus Schulze would become their new drummer and Conrad Schnitzler would be their new wind player.
  - Initial Musical Influences: Psychedelic rock of the Grateful Dead and The Jefferson Airplane.
   * 1970: they became increasingly attracted to wild, off-the-wall improvisations and eventually abandoned the conventional rock and roll setup of guitars and drums.
    a.) And replaced them almost completely with electronic keyboards and synthesizers.
    b.) The catalyst: the addition of Christopher Franke who initially replaced drummer Klaus Schulze and eventually…
     -…became the band's main sequencer artist.
    c.) RESULT: the creation of works bearing atmospherics, echoes, and drones instead of conventional songs.
   * "Electronic Meditation" (6/70): Their debut album and the first to introduce musical concepts of German Space music.
    a.) Sparse, electronic sound made up of tape manipulations originally by Shulze and Schnitzer.
     - And produced through various effects processors.
  - Early 70's: several electronic keyboards combined with the guitar work of Edgar Froese would be the group's new rubric.
   * Albums: "Alpha Centauri" (1971) and "Zeit" (1972) ushered in the concept of German space music to a full-fledged genre by pushing the stylistic envelope.
    a.) "Atem" (1973): the album that gave Tangerine Dream widespread notoriety out side of Europe.
     - Led to a five year contract with Richard Branson's Virgin Records label.
    b.) "Phaedra" (1974): their first attempt at a sound totally comprised of Moog synthesizers and sequencers.
     - Resulting in a hypnotic juggernaut of rhythm.

* Very minimalistic in nature akin to the avante garde minimalism (a la Terry Riley) of the early 1960's.

* Follow-up albums such as "Rubycon" (1975), "Richocet" and "Stratosphere" (1976)...

a.) Continued the electronic rubric set out by "Phaedra".

- Although "Stratosphere" featured a return to conventional instruments such as guitar and acoustic piano.

- Tangerine Dream: as the inventors of German space music would inspire other space music bands to follow such as:

* Ash Ra Temple (formed in 1970): by Manual Gottsching and Klaus Schulze (the latter formerly of Tangerine Dream). In 1973: Timothy Leary would be added to the group's lineup.

a.) Style: avante garde influences mixed with Psychedelic rock and electronics resulting in a genre called "Kosmiche Rock" (cosmic rock).

* In addition, the robotic electronic influence of Kraftwerk, who was covered in detail earlier in this chapter, was also an important influence on the band who invented EBM – "Front 242".

a.) However, before we get to them [Front 242], there is one other artist who was influential upon them that needs to be discussed.

2.) Giorgio Moroder (b. 4/26/40; Ortisei, Val Gardeno, Italy): the inventor of the "four on the floor" rhythmic technique.

- Musical Background: began playing guitar at the age of 16. Left school and home at 19 to play in what he said was, "a more or less dancing group".

* 1967: he settled in West Berlin and concentrated his efforts strictly as a songwriter.

a.) His first major hit: "Love To Love You Baby" (1975) which he wrote and produced for Donna Summer.

* 1979: he won his first Academy Award for the original movie score of "Midnight Express".

a.) 1984: his second Oscar (plus 2 Golden Globes) for the song, "What A Feeling" from the hit movie, "Flashdance".

- In which he stole a melody from composer Franz Schubert (1798-1828) to serve as the main melodic hook for the song.

b.) 1987: a third Oscar (plus a fourth Golden Globe) for the song entitled "Take My Breath Away" from the movie, "Top Gun".

- His Three Major Pop Periods:

* The Soft Disco Era (1975-77):

a.) Moroder's contribution to the Eurodisco genre (the genre was discussed in Chapter 10).

- Songs written and produced mostly for recording artists Donna Summer and Roberta Kelly.

* The Computer Disco Era (1977-79): where computer sequences were first applied to disco music.

a.) Very repetitive/synthetic sounding dance music with a sparse texture underlying the pop melodic voices of artists like Donna Summer.

- "I Feel Love" (1978): Eurodisco essence with electronic sequences.

- "Last Dance" (1978): which Moroder produced for the movie soundtrack "Thank God It's Friday".

     * <u>The Electro-Pop Era</u> (1980-85): the use of sequencers and synthesizers in a more straightforward pop idiom as opposed to disco.

          a.) Example: the soundtrack for the movie, <u>American Gigolo</u> (1980).

             - "<u>Call Me</u>": recorded by Blondie.

          b.) "<u>What A Feeling</u>" for the movie "Flashdance", is also included in this era.

- His style that influenced the beginning of Electronic Body Music.

     * <u>1975</u>: he started putting bass drums into disco songs that exhibited a hard-throbbing beat thereby marking the rhythm.

          a.) "<u>Four On The Floor</u>" (as he called it): using a powerful bass drum thud to exaggerate every beat in the measure (1,2,3,4/1,2,3,4/ etc.).

             - With this, Moroder introduced the deep, throbbing bass drum hits into disco that would directly influence the hammering bass drum beats of EBM later on.

             * <u>2 Examples</u>: from an album he both wrote and produced on "<u>Munich Machine</u>":

                a.) "Get On The Funk Train", "I Wanna Funk You Tonight".

Europe Endless
Kraftwerk

Metal On Metal
Kraftwerk

3.) <u>Summary</u>: the combination of electronic synth elements of German Space Music artists like <u>Tangerine Dream</u>, <u>Ash Ra Temple</u>, plus the robotic sequencing influences of <u>Kraftwerk</u> (as illustrated in tracks such as *Europe Endless* and *Metal On Metal*)…

     - …mixed with the hard-hammering bass drum disco sound of <u>Giorgio Moroder</u>…

          * All of the influences were in place for the new movement of Electronic Body Music to commence.

C.) <u>Front 242</u> (formed 10/81; Brussels, Belgium): the inventors of the EBM idiom.

    1.) A more electronic variant of the Industrial approach as opposed to the raging electric guitar essence of Ministry.

     - Personnel: originally consisted of two programmers – <u>Patrick Condenys</u> and <u>Dirk Bergen</u>.

          * To be later joined by lead vocalist <u>Jean-Luc De Meyer</u>.

          a.) Plus another programmer <u>Daniel Bressanutti</u> (a.k.a. David B. Prothese).

             - Eventually they were joined by percussionist <u>Richard 23</u> (b. Richard Jonckheere).

     - They began as a pure synthesizer band.

          * <u>1984</u>: a more aggressive sound featuring harder-pounding beats within a synth-driven format began to emerge.

          a.) De Meyer's vocals began sounding electronically distorted (a harbinger of things to come).

          * "<u>No Comment</u>" (1984): the album that spearheaded their emerging new sound.

    - <u>1987</u>: they were signed by Wax Trax! Records.

          * By that time, Wax Trax had already become known as the new exponent of the Industrial genre featuring a number of synth-driven, heavy-hitting Industrial bands.

    2.) <u>Geography</u> (1982): their debut album.

     - Featuring their debut single "<u>U-Men</u>": a synth-pop type of style reminiscent of the early 80's new wave electronics with the standard synthetic drum thud.

U-Men (lp mix)
Front 242

          * Echo-like speech vocalizing drenched in reverb.

          a.) Distant sounding – a unique feature that was not pop oriented.

- "Geography I": the title track.
Geography I
Front 242
                * More melodic focus with synthetic colors presented in a loose I, IV, V (blues influenced) format.
                      a.) Carrying their signature Euro flavored, reverb ladened speech-singing, in the background.
                          - With the synthesizers in the foreground.
- NOTE: with these two singles, Front 242 displayed a somewhat sparse, electronic texture somewhat reminiscent of the Bowie/Eno (Berlin sound) to a degree.

3.) No Comment (1984): took their initial synth-pop sound and added more hammering, hard-hitting, industrial sounding synthetic percussion tracks.
    - A early hallmark which would later be a defining feature of EBM.
        * With De Meyer's vocalizing sounding more menacing (another Front 242 trademark).

4.) Official Version (1987): the first of their two most important albums both recorded on the Wax Trax! Label.
    - Their first truly consistent album format.
        * "Masterhit": a thicker-textured synth sound displaying the following:

*Masterhit
(Parts I & II)*
Front 242

                a.) A consistent lush of harmonic color and adding a background of depth.
                b.) Sumptuous, heavy-hitting, hammering drum tracks that sounds both drum-like and synthetic.
                c.) Displaying an overall dark essence – consistent with all genres under the industrial umbrella.
                    - The vocals of De Meyer are more intoned/melodic but still with that sterile, menacing characteristic and Euro-style English pronunciation (sounding like it was coming from a metal chamber).
- This album was where the original sound of Electronic Body Music firmly took hold and melded all of it's musical properties into an entity that gave EBM a stylistic consistency.
        * Thereby turning it into a genre.

5.) Front By Front (1988): the second of the Wax Trax! Albums and arguably their greatest achievement.
    - More emphasis on song structure as opposed to their signature focus solely on the all-encompassing groove.
        * More melodic focus in addition to the thick harmonic texture supported by sustained, dark synthetic tones/colors…

*Until Death
(Us Do Part)*
Front 242

                a.) Reinforced with a heavy bassline giving the harmonic texture a solid foundation.
                b.) Some notable tracks that serve as prime examples are "Until Death (Us Do Part)", "Headhunter" (V3.0 & V1.0), and

Headhunter V. 3.0
Front 242

                "Never Stop!" (V1.0 & V1.1).
- This album marked the maturity of Electronic Body Music as both a template for other artists to emulate and, as a solid genre all it's own.

6.) By 1990: Front 242 became the first of the Wax Trax! Artists to go on to a mainstream label: Epic Records.
    - Marking the beginning of the Wax Trax! exodus of other artists to come.
        * The last to leave Wax Trax! (after the label filed for Chapter 11 bankruptcy protection) was KMFDM.

7.) NOTE: In regard to EBM, their would be others to come along that would give their own rendition of this new genre spearheaded by Front 242….

D.) Nitzer Ebb (formed 1982 in Chelmsford, Essex, England): the addition of punk elements into EBM.

    1.) Personnel: Douglas McCarthy: vocalist; Bon Harris: drummer; and David Gooday: keyboards.

- <u>Influences</u>: hardcore punk and the new emerging technology that was just becoming available.
  * <u>RESULT</u>: heavy-hitting, hammering synthetic drum beats/ percussion mixed with shouting style vocalization of hardcore punk but with a more militaristic twist.
- <u>Style</u>: a stripped-down, minimalistic, and abrasive type of EBM Industrial.
  * Just the <u>drum machine tracks</u> and <u>punk-influenced vocals</u> with little or no background color (i.e. sustained electronic timbres).
    a.) In essence, Nitzer Ebb, at least in their early phase, were like the "Run DMC" of the EBM Industrial music world (i.e. a stripped down, minimal approach).
      - Mixing punk rock elements with EBM.

2.) "<u>Isn't It Funny How Your Body Works</u>" (1985): their debut single, released on their own "Power Of Voice Communications" label (In 1986, they signed with the "Mute" label).

Let Your Body Learn
Nitzer Ebb

- <u>Phil Harding</u>: a producer, began working with Nitzer Ebb starting with this single (he would later become part of the group).
  * Mute Records singles by Nitzer Ebb: "<u>Murderous</u>" and "<u>Let Your Body Learn</u>" (both in early 1987).
    a.) Both would be included in their debut album: <u>That Total Age</u> (1987).

Join In The Chant
Nitzer Ebb

  * "<u>Joint The Chant</u>": another single from their debut album.
    a.) Produced by <u>Flood</u> who also produced Erasure, Nick Cave, and Nine Inch Nails (the latter on a limited basis).

Join In The Chant (metal mix)
Nitzer Ebb

      - Would become an underground dance hit and initially connect the group with more mainstream musical influences that would later on, impact their style.
- In a tour to support their debut album, Nitzer Ebb was the back up band for the <u>Depeche Mode</u> tour.
  * This exposure to Depeche Mode's brand of synth-pop would influence Nitzer Ebb's musical approach for their next album.

3.) <u>Showtime</u> (1990): where those pop influences and sensibilities combine with their earlier abrasive style.

Hold On
Nitzer Ebb

- <u>RESULT</u>: a more streamlined, less militaristic approach.
  * With a more harmonically sustained, electronic background color.
    a.) Which resulted in a more streamlined/accessible style.

E.) <u>Skinny Puppy</u> (formed 1983, Vancouver, BC): the band that would standardize EBM by conventionalizing the genre's various elements.
  1.) Background: <u>Kevin Crompton</u>: began playing in bands at the age of 13.
    - Some of his early bands were: The Fuck Brothers, Bastille, and Intelligent Youth.
      * His first significant band: <u>Image In Vogue</u> (4/29/81).
        a.) <u>Style</u>: early 80's synth-pop.
        b.) He eventually had the desire to branch out to something more experimental.
          - He felt that the current music he was involved with was too expressively and artistically limited.
    - <u>Experimentation</u>: he started with raw, intense, experimental sounds.
      * <u>Reason</u>: to observe how far he could stretch boundaries concerning the new technologies that became available (in the early 80's).
        a.) He discovered an arsenal of newfound, experimental sounds which were raw, intense, brutal, and distorted which resulted in a dark-colored foundation/essence.
          - They emanated from the synthesizer and became the blueprint for his new musical approach.

- <u>Attitude</u>: the more his awareness grew for these newfound sounds…
        *…the more contempt he harbored for conventional pop music.
            a.) Which he eventually refused to play.
- <u>Crompton</u> and fellow Image In Vogue bandmate <u>Joe Vizvary</u>…
        * Recorded singles under the name of Skinny Puppy that would be included in a 7 song cassette called "<u>Back and Forth</u>" (1984).
            a.) 35 out of the 50 high-speed dubbed copies were released.
2.) <u>Kevin Oglivie</u>: supposedly met Crompton at a party during the summer of 1983.
    - He became lead vocalist for Skinny Puppy.
        * Both he and Crompton had the desire for the esoteric and unconventional.
            a.) And a mutual contempt for conventional pop music.
        * They would both adopt pseudonyms:
            a.) For Kevin Ogilvie: "<u>Nivek Ogre</u>".
                - Translated as Kevin spelt backwards plus a slight shift of his last name bearing a menacing flavor.
            b.) For Kevin Crompton: "<u>cEvin Key</u>".
        * When Nivek Ogre joined the group, Skinny Puppy initially became his expressive outlet.
3.) <u>Skinny Puppy's Performance Philosophy</u>:
    - To shake up and rile the audience out of what they [Skinny Puppy] felt, was the audience's apathy and predictability.
        * <u>Inspiration</u>: they [Ogre and Key] were both horror film enthusiasts.
            a.) They would take the horror film concept – which included blood and gore – and transform it into performance art (with fake blood and vomit a standard feature).
                - Thereby imbuing a sense of theater in an EBM industrial music format.
                    * Mixed with brutal lyrics that were activist in nature brought oftentimes, to the extreme.
4.) <u>Nettwerk Records</u>: an independent label founded by Terry McBride (a friend of cEvin's).
    - "<u>Remission</u>" (1985): their debut album that would lay down the initial groundwork for their original style.
        * <u>Elements</u>:
            a.) Hypnotic synthetic drum patterns that were intoxicating by nature.
            b.) Rhythmically scattered, repetitive keyboard riffs.
            c.) Distorted vocals.
                - At times, also muffled.
        * <u>cEvin Key</u>: synthesizers, programming of synthetic drum tracks of both metallic and acoustic samples, tape manipulations, and vocals.
        * <u>Ogre</u>: lyrics, vocals, synthesizers, programming, and horns.
            a.) Other members included:
                - <u>Wilhelm Schroeder</u>: bass synthesizer.
                - <u>mr d. plevin</u>: fretless bass.
    - As their musical development progressed, they added more technological effects which further delineated their already unique sound.
5.) "<u>Mind, The Perpetual Intercourse</u>" (1986): their breakthrough album that solidified their forceful style.
    - This was <u>Dwayne Goettel's</u> debut with the group.
        * A classically trained keyboardist who brought an elevated sense of musicianship to the band.
    - The album itself, had more depth in an artistic sense.
        * Two singles would be initially released:

a.) "Dig It": later emulated by Trent Reznor (i.e. Nine Inch Nails) in the song "Down In It" from his Pretty Hate Machine album released in 1989..

b.) "Stairs and Flowers"

c.) A third single from the album, "Chainsaw", would be later released.

- RESULT: "Mind, The Perpetual Intercourse" greatly elevated Skinny Puppy's reputation in the industrial underground domain.

* On subsequent albums, Goettel would focus on sequencers, samplers, and synthesizers.

a.) Ogre: vocals, lyrics, objects, dramatics/theatrics, and torture/punishment plays.

b.) cEvin Key: synthesizers, guitar, drums, percussion, tape manipulations, and sampling (including radio & soundbite samples).

6.) "VIVIsectVI" (1988): their fifth album and next important release since "Mind,TPI".

- The first important industrial album on political commentary, anti-war issues, and animal experimentation.

* Purpose: to make audiences shockingly aware of these issues through their biting (and sometimes cryptic) lyrics and graphic stageshow/ theater presentation.

a.) This was where visual imagery (showing graphic depictions of these issues) became a regular part of their performance art approach.

- Musically: a more rhythmically and expressively aggressive sonic onslaught.

* Examples:

a.) "VX Gas Attack": dealing with chemical weapons.

b.) "Human Disease (S.K.U.M.M.)": destruction of the environment.

c.) "Testure": animal experimentation in labs.

7.) "Rabies" (1989): co-produced by Al Jourgensen (of Ministry).

- Due to Jourgensen's "Ministry" influence, this album contained more rock guitar-inspired influences.

* A continuation of their relentless, aggressive attacks solidified in "VIVIsectVI" complete with soundbite sampling

a.) Example: "Tin Omen" - an anti-war statement cloaked in raw, hidden-meaning poetics.

* The Album's Musical Angle: a back-to-basics, somewhat skeletal approach.

a.) …with a shouting, Jourgensen-inspired vocal style.

- "Warlock": their most revered single.

* Contained harmonic and melodic focus that gave the music an attractive, elegant, ethereal beauty.

a.) Featuring a sampled soundbite as one of the thematic elements: "Now, is the only thing that's real".

- Heard throughout the entire track.

b.) Contrasting the thematic soundbite:

- Distorted harmonic vocal treatment (which they transformed into a standardized, industrial music staple).

* RESULT: A mixture of esoteric elements superimposed over material designed to sound attractive and familiar.

a.) Almost, but not quite pop but nevertheless, their biggest underground industrial hit.

8.) "Too Dark Park" (1990): a considerably more experimental approach as opposed to their previous albums.

VX Gas Attack
Skinny Puppy

Human Disease (S.K.U.M.M.)
Skinny Puppy

Testure
Skinny Puppy

Warlock
Skinny Puppy

- This album brought a new complexity to the EBM industrial genre.
  * Complex layering of the following:

        a.) Spoken soundbites.
        b.) Synthetic drum and percussion samples.
           - As well as acoustic drums tracks.
        c.) Ethereal, sustained electronic soundscapes.
           - Either in the foreground or, as background harmonic support.
        d.) Panned effects on electronic sounds.
        e.) Electronic sound/noise collages.
        f.) Synthetic basslines.

- <u>Two Focal Points</u>: the glue that held these complexed, multi-track layerings together:
  * A hard-hitting, hammering, and hypnotic drum beat.
  * Distorted vocal lines.
          a.) The role of these elements as focal points are consistent throughout the entire album.

- <u>Stylistic Flavor</u>: an aggressive, "in-your-face" style that pulls no punches.
  * A complex sonic wall of sound that assaults the senses.
          a.) With brutal, harsh reality-based lyrics added in.

- <u>RESULT</u>: with "Too Dark Park", Skinny Puppy had brought the concept of industrial Electronic Body Music to it's logical artistic limit.
  * In expression, texture, concept, and complexity.
          a.) Thereby completing the development of EBM genre…
             - By which all who follow would emulate.

9.) <u>Aftermath</u>: band members (especially Ogre) went on to other outside projects namely:

    - <u>Pigface</u>, <u>Revolting Cocks</u> (both with Al Jourgensen), <u>Hilt</u>, <u>Legendary Pink Dots</u>, <u>Doubting Thomas</u>, and <u>Tear Garden</u>.

CHAPTER XIV: REVIEW

What was the initial concept of the Futurist Movement?

    Who wrote "The Founding Manifesto of Futurism" in 1909?

What did Pratella's "Technical Manifesto of Futurist Music" suggest in regard to a new music direction?

Who was the first *true* catalyst of the Futurist movement?

    Name his first manifesto of 1913.

    What instrument did he invent?

    List at least five noises that could be sounded on that instrument.
        1.)
        2.)
        3.)
        4.)
        5.)

What was the first great legacy of the Futurist Movement?

What is "Music Concréte"?

    What invention became the catalyst for Music Concréte?

    List at least four ways this invention allowed the manipulation of sound:
        1.)
        2.)
        3.)
        4.)

Who founded the theory of Music Concréte?

    How did he manipulate magnetic tape?

    Name two of his works:

What was meant by the term, "Concréte"?

What is Analog?

    Name its main instrument.

    List four different sounds that can be generated on that instrument:
        1.)
        2.)
        3.)
        4.)

What was the main difference between Music Concréte and analog?

What was Karlheinz Stockhausen's first electronic piece that was made entirely by sine waves?

Define "Industrial" music.

Name the first industrial band and their ringleader.

    What was their philosophy?

    What was their style?

    What was their subject matter?

    Name their record label.

What was the impact of Throbbing Gristle as the inaugural industrial band – what were they the first to incorporate?

    What thematics did they use to accomplish this and in what formal manner?

What was Einstürzende Neubauten's specialization?

    List at least 4 elements of their style:
        1.) Noises:
        2.) Howling Vocals:
        3.) Instrumental:

4.) FM Einheit – what "instruments" did he bring into the group?

5.) Musical Structure:

Where were their early performance venues?

What was the result of their sound from performing in these venues?

Insofar as their sound was concerned, why were they called "industrial"?

Name their first album, which was a compilation of their early singles released in 1988.

What type of instruments did the group, Cabaret Voltaire, begin experimenting with?

List two of their influences:
1.)
2.)

What was the Dadaist movement?

What was its purpose?

What were the characteristics of Cabaret Voltaire's early music?

What specific element did they use to effectively string together disparate experimental sounds that made it easier for listeners outside of the industrial cult to appreciate?

What was the result insofar as Cabaret Voltaire's artistic contribution?

What was the significance of Ministry – in other words, what were they the first to do?

List three of Al Jourgensen's musical influences:
1.)
2.)
3.)

How would you characterize Ministry's music after they signed with the Wax Trax! Label?

Name their first dance hit, which was also the title of their first EP.

Which album marked the beginning of Jourgensen's new artistic direction?

Describe the following elements of the "Aggro" sound of Ministry.
　　　　1.) Vocal Style:
　　　　2.) Sampling Style:
　　　　3.) Rock Guitar Style:

Name their first album that fully realized the agro sound.

　　　　What was the musical style of this album?

As a result of Jourgensen's collaborations with other artists, what would his additional side projects be?

Name at least 3 groups that Al Jourgensen recruited to the Wax Trax! label.
　　　　1.)
　　　　2.)
　　　　3.)

Like other industrial bands, what mixture of two elements was the emphasis of KMFDM's style?

By the late 80's, what was Wax Trax! Record's signature sound that was influenced in big part by Al Jourgensen? (List 5 elements)
　　　　1.)
　　　　2.)
　　　　3.)
　　　　4.)
　　　　5.)

What was the significance of Nine Inch Nails? In other words, what did he do with industrial music?

　　　　What was his musical stylistic focus?

What was his approach to lyrics?

What was one of his earliest primary rock influences?

Staring in 1988, what were his three "cold wave" influences?
    1.)
    2.)
    3.)

Name his debut album.

What was the significance of this album in regard to the mainstream?

Name at five characteristics of Electronic Body Music (EBM).
    1.)
    2.)
    3.)
    4.)
    5.)

Who were the three main harbingers of EBM?
    1.)
    2.)
    3.)

What influential rhythm technique did Giorgio Moroder invent?

List his three major pop periods:
    1.)
    2.)
    3.)

Who were the inventors of the EBM idiom?

Name four of their musical influences:
    1.)
    2.)
    3.)
    4.)

Name their debut album.

Name two of their most important albums recorded on the Wax Trax! label.
      1.)
      2.)

What musical element did Nitzer Ebb add to the EBM idiom?

    List 2 elements of their style:
      1.)
      2.)

Who standardized the EBM sound by conventionalizing the genre's various elements?

    What was their performance philosophy?

    What was the inspiration behind this philosophy?

Name their debut album recorded on the Nettwerk Label.

    List 3 musical elements attributed to the music of this album:
      1.)
      2.)
      3.)

What was the significance of the album, VIVIsectVI insofar as subject matter – what three subjects did they focus on?
    1.)
    2.)
    3.)

What was the musical angle behind the album "Rabies" recorded in 1989?

    Name the album's most revered single.

The album, "Too Dark Park" brought a new complexity to the EBM industrial genre with complexed layerings of various elements. Name 6 of them:
    1.)
    2.)
    3.)
    4.)
    5.)
    6.)

In the aftermath, band members of Skinny Puppy went on to other outside projects. Name at least 5:

    1.)

    2.)

    3.)

    4.)

    5.)

CHAPTER XV: THE HEAVY METAL JUGGERNAUT

I. PROLOGUE: The Disillusionment of the Psychedelic Era

    A.) The End Of An Era: the Psychedelic movement – an era built on the optimism of peace & love coupled with a rebellion against the status quo. This questioning and rebelling against established norms came in several forms: rebellion against the norms of traditional morality; rebellion against the draft in tandem with the Vietnam War; and experimentation with drugs (especially LSD). In practically all cases involving experimentation (i.e. with sex, drugs, etc.) followers were pushing the norms to the limit.

    1.) But there was an irony: as well intentioned as the peace/love ideal had become, the Psychedelic era ended on a number of violent, high-profiled tragic episodes between 1968 and 1971. These episodes played a significant role in destroying the pacifist idealism that defined the Love Generation:

        Dec. 6, 1969: the violent stabbing death of a spectator at Altamont (officially marking the end of the Psychedelic era).
        April 4, 1968: the assassination of Dr. Martin Luther King Jr.
        March 16, 1968: the My Lai massacre (Vietnam War) where US soldiers, under the command of Lt. William Calley, massacred an estimated 347-500 unarmed civilians.
        June 5, 1968: the assassination of Robert F. Kennedy who, as a presidential candidate, had just completed a victory speech (winning the California primary) at the Ambassador Hotel in LA.
        Aug. 5, 1968: the police killed 3 captains of the Black Panther Party: Little Tommy Lewis, Steve Bartholomew, and Robert Lawrence in the Watts section of Los Angeles.
        May 4, 1970: a National Guard unit at Kent State University (in Ohio) opened fire [with live ammunition] killing 4 students during an anti-war rally on the campus.
        August 8, 1969: the Charles Manson (i.e. the Manson Family) murders of Sharon Tate, Jay Sebring, Abigail Folger, and Wojciech Frykowski.
        Fall of 1970: the deaths of Jimi Hendrix (Sept. 18), Janis Joplin (Oct. 4), and on July 3, 1971, Jim Morrison.

    2.) With the demise of a disillusioned Love Generation in the early 1970's, a vacuum was set in place. There was a need for a new mood and a whole new vehicle of protest. It was through pragmatism rather than ideology that a new direction in rock 'n' roll – one that would fill in this vacuum – had begun. It had its roots in an industrial city in the British midlands and the musical emphasis would be metal-driven. Hence, the roots of heavy metal and its style of expressing protest would be born.

II. BLACK SABBATH: introducing the focused primacy of the loud, repeated, almighty guitar riff (as opposed to technical virtuosity). In the process, they created a simpler approach [than their blues revisionist predecessors) which scores of others would emulate. In doing so, they laid down the model of what would become known as heavy metal. In addition, they continued the rock 'n' roll tradition of writing protest songs but in this case, in a more dark, gloomy, macabre manner enveloped in a massive, all-riff fashion. This too would be emulated as part of the heavy metal model to come.

    A.) Beginnings: Ozzy Osbourne: hung an advertisement in the Ring way Music Store in Aston with the words, "OZZY ZIG NEEDS GIG". It went on to say that he was "an experienced front man" and "owns own PA system" (the latter was a must for singers during that time). For the record, he had no experience as a front man but listed it in order to gain credible responses.

1.) <u>Terence "Geezer" Butler</u>: answered the ad. He was a rhythm guitar player for an experimental, Pink Floyd-lightshow-type band called Rare Breed. At that time, psychedelic "Hippie" music was inundating the Birmingham area airwaves and Ozzy absolutely hated it. In his view, the hippie music of peace/love was gimmicky optimism that had no connection with the poor, depressed, working-class, grey, and smoggy environment of his native Aston.

> Geezer Butler, read books on ancient Greek warfare, Chinese poetry, and in time, books dealing with the occult – especially those of author Dennis Wheatley. He had a talent for writing lyrics that were intense, especially about wars, black magic, super heroes, etc. He and Osbourne decided to collaborate but the group was going nowhere. After the failure of Rare Breed, Ozzy was on the verge of quitting music altogether. But soon, another person would answer the OZZY ZIG ad: guitarist <u>Tony Iommi</u> and drummer <u>Bill Ward</u>.

2.) <u>Tony Iommi</u>: an apprentice sheet metal worker and welder who played in a blues band called, Mythology and before that, The Rocking Chevrolets (basically playing Chuck Berry, Bo Diddley, and Eddie Cochran covers). With Mythology, he covered blues revisionist artists like Buffalo Springfield, Jimi Hendrix, and John Mayall's Bluesbreakers. With his blues revisionist covers, he played them in a gritty, heavy manner.

> Another important influence was the Belgian jazz guitarist, Django Reinhardt: it was mostly for inspirational rather than stylistic reasons. Iommi had cut off the middle and ring finger tips of his right hand due to an industrial accident involving a sheet metal press. Since Iommi was left handed, this meant that his fret board fingers were affected. He was told [by his doctor] that he could never play again. Then one day, a fellow factory worker gave him an album by Django Reinhardt.

> Reinhardt had mastered the art of using only two fingers from his fret board hand (the others were burned off) proving that such a handicap could be overcome. Due to Reinhardt's example, Iommi took up the guitar again. He improvised homemade thimbles that enabled his injured fingers to effectively press the strings. He also loosened the strings, which made pressing the strings [on the fret board] easier.

3.) After the four of them – <u>Osbourne</u> (vocals), <u>Iommi</u> (guitar), <u>Butler</u> (now the bass player), and <u>Bill Ward</u> (on drums) – had decided to form a band, they named themselves the <u>Polka Tulk Blues Band</u> (after the talcum powder Ozzy's mother was using). They played what Osbourne described as "deep, heavy, Southern blues". They later changed their band name to <u>Earth</u>.

> <u>Late 1968</u>: Tony Iommi was writing his own, catchy electric guitar riffs that were quite heavy sounding and Geezer Butler was writing lyrics for them. But suddenly, Iommi had left that band for an opportunity to join Jethro Tull – a well-known, successful rock band with flutist Ian Anderson as front man. But after only four performances, Iommi left and returned to his previous group – he felt that he wanted pursue his own creative vision rather than someone else's (in this case, Anderson's).

> The Jethro Tull experience did teach him a valuable lesson – in order to be a successful band, you had to work hard and take yourselves seriously (for example, Jethro Tull used to practice for many hours a day for four days to prepare for one gig). Iommi declared to the band that in order to become successful, they had to adopt a highly disciplined, serious work ethic.

B.) <u>New Musical Direction</u>: it was Tony Iommi who introduced to the band, the idea of creating something that sounded "evil". They noticed how successful horror films were becoming just by watching long lines of people waiting to enter the local [movie] theatre. So, in Iommi's view, the group should focus on "scary" music instead of conventional blues. The result: *Black Sabbath*, the first single that marked this new direction.

1.) He improvised a catchy riff on the electric guitar based on a dissonant interval called the "tri-tone" (in Medieval times, it was banned by the Catholic church because they called in the "Devil's Interval"). Geezer Butler originated the idea of the title from an Italian horror film (titled *Black Sabbath*) directed by Mario Bava and starring Boris Karloff.

Black Sabbath
Black Sabbath

At this point, they were playing blues-oriented music with a Led Zeppelin-influenced heavy, amplitude-laden sound. Now, they were adding that dark, scary, macabre element to it. They would also change their name to one that would characterize this new sound. While gigging at a Hamburg, Germany club called The Star Club (where The Beatles once played in the early 60's), they had already changed their name to <u>Black Sabbath</u> (this was in 1969).

2.) <u>1970</u>: the year of their debut album, *Black Sabbath*. At this time, in addition to horror films, Geezer Butler's lyrics were being influenced by another source: the occult author, <u>Dennis Wheatley</u>. Evidently, with the popularity of horror films and the dark elements that accompanied it, the occult-ish, scary essence was in style.

Evil Woman
Black Sabbath

They signed with Vertigo Records, a subsidiary of Philips. Their debut recording, a cover song called *Evil Woman* (originally by The Crows). Their first recordings of original material would take place at Regent Sound Studios recording tracks that would make up their debut album. They worked with a producer named <u>Rodger Bain</u>.

They initially ran through their prepared material (in the studio) as if they were performing live. Then, after spending several hours double-tracking various guitar and vocal tracks, Black Sabbath embarked on a tour of Switzerland. After their return [from the tour], they were introduced to the finished product. The ideas for the scary, occult-ish characteristics and symbols [for the album] came from their manager and producer – the group members themselves had no input. The result: *Black Sabbath*. Their debut album that would reach #8 in the UK and #23 in the US.

3.) Their breakthrough album: *Paranoid*. The original intent was to call the album, *Warpiggers*. They then changed it to *War Pigs* after a song in which Geezer Butler wrote about the death, destruction, and doom inspired by the Vietnam War.

War Pigs
Black Sabbath

Paranoid
Black Sabbath

While recording at Island Record Studios (owned by Chris Blackwell of Bob Marley fame), they quickly wrote a song called *Paranoid* – it took about 20 minutes. It became their first original single to get radio airplay. Other noted tracks in the album included *Iron Man*, *Hand of Doom*, *Electric Funeral* and *War Pigs*. Eventually, the album named was changed to *Paranoid*.

*Children Of
The Grave*
Black Sabbath

<u>*Master of Reality*</u> (1971): for this album, Tony Iommi had detuned his guitar to loosen up the strings thereby making it easier for him to press the fret board – hence the heavier, thicker, fuzz-tone type of sound that became his trademark. Featuring an apocalyptic sense of foreboding with *Children of The Grave*, religious commentary with *After Forever*, and a celebration of cannabis called *Sweet Leaf*.

4.) <u>NOTE</u>: As previously mentioned, Black Sabbath laid down the initial groundwork [of heavy metal] that others would eventually emulate. What was now needed was to turn this focused, riff-driven entity into a full-fledged, artistic movement. But before that could happen, there were several additional elements that had to be introduced [by others] which were needed to complete the heavy metal musical structure.

C.) <u>Hard Rock</u>: in the wake of Black Sabbath, there were other bands that emphasized a loud melodic guitar focus that lacked the heaviness and riff-craft (that would become heavy metal staples). They did however, in their own separate ways, initiate various musical properties that, put together, would complete the [eventual] heavy metal puzzle.

1.) In addition to loud, riff-driven guitar focus [of heavy metal], other elements would include the following: an aggressive instrumental momentum; a harmonized twin-guitar format; high-registered, keening vocals; and lyrics of fantasy and mysticism (in addition to the protest lyric influence already discussed). Each of the following groups popularized these concepts separately (that would become part of the heavy metal genre).

Highway Star
Deep Purple

<u>Aggressive, Instrumental Momentum</u>: Under guitarist Ritchie Blackmore's leadership, the band, <u>Deep Purple</u> (formed in 1969) went from a progressive rock format, to a heavier, louder guitar-driven approach (with Jon Lord's, Hammond C3 organ as part of the melodic mix). In 1970, Blackmore wanted to emulate the aggressive instrumental, virtuoso approaches of The Jimi Hendrix Experience and Led Zeppelin. Their breakthrough album, *Machine Head* (1972), was where they honed-in this new approach. Their style was more melodically focused than riff focused (which led to substantial chart success and radio airplay).

The Boys Are Back In Town
Thin Lizzy

<u>Twin Guitar Harmonies</u>: Thin Lizzy (1970, Dublin, IRE) was the first rock band from Ireland to gain international recognition. They were the first to popularize twin guitar, harmonized approach with their only hit, *The Boys Are back In Town* from the album, *Jailbreak* (1976) – an homáge to regular, working class guys letting loose and blowing off steam.

Bohemian Rhapsody
Queen

<u>High-Registered, Keening Vocals</u>: the band, Queen (formed in 1971), featured an emphasis on showmanship and elevated vocal techniques of lead singer Freddie Mercury (b. Farroukh Bulsara, Sept. 5, 1946, d. Nov. 24, 1991), combined with the hard rock guitar credentials of Brian May. By 1975 with their album, *Night At The Opera*, Queen was presenting their own epic singles with Mercury's high-registered, lyric, vocals that were quasi-operatic in nature.

Man On The Silver Mountain
Rainbow

<u>Lyrics of Fantasy and Mysticism</u>: the band Rainbow, featured lead singer and lyricist Ronnie James Dio. Along with Ritchie Blackmore (formerly of Deep Purple), Dio recorded songs with lyrics of mystical fantasy as illustrated in the single, *Man On The Silver Mountain* from the album, *Ritchie Blackmore's Rainbow* (1975).

2.) The next step in the process, was to synthesize these aforesaid elements together and when that happens, the mosaic of the heavy metal format will be complete. Once again, the story begins in the industrial midlands city of Birmingham.

<u>III. THE NEW WAVE OF BRITISH HEAVY METAL (NWOBHM)</u>: where Heavy Metal found it's groove and became a bona fide, musical and cultural genre.

A.) <u>Judas Priest</u> (1969): the band that standardized the heavy metal model both musically and visually ushering in the New Wave of British Heavy Metal (NWOBHM). In addition (along with the band, Motörhead), they were the first of the NWOBHM bands to tour relentlessly throughout the US and in the process, introduced the sound of the NWOBHM to a mass US audience finding widespread commercial success.

1.) <u>Personnel</u>: <u>Kenneth "K.K." Downing</u> (b. Oct. 27, 1951, West Midlands, ENG): guitar. <u>Ian Hill</u> (b. Jan. 20,1962, West Midlands, ENG): bass. <u>Rob Halford</u> (b. Aug. 25, 1951, Birmingham, ENG): lead vocals. <u>Glenn Tipton</u> (b. Oct. 25, 1949, West Midlands, ENG): guitar. <u>John Hinch</u> (first of six consecutive drummers of the band).

2.) <u>Overview</u>: Judas Priest was not an innovator of the heavy metal concept – meaning high-registered vocal power, loud/distorted electric guitars delivering powerful melodic riffs, and thundering drumming sound -- but they were the first to present it as a distinct musical genre in and of itself. And, in the process, became the first model by which scores of aspiring heavy metal artists would emulate. In addition to the musical model, they initiated visual model -- the use of black, biker-styled leather outfits with metal studs. This too, would be a defining heavy metal trademark -- by way of fashion statement – that artists (and fans) would adopt for themselves.

3.) <u>Their Basic Formula</u>: the loud, riff-driven, twin-guitar attack of K.K. Downing and Glenn Tipton plus the powerful, keening, quasi-operatic sound of Rob Halford's voice. Their lyrics expressed social commentary from a mystical, apocalyptic, and dark, graphic approach. Touching upon subjects such as war, tyranny, rebellion, genocide, and working-class revolt against a rigged system. In addition, they employed rapid-rhythmed, high-registered, and melodically ornamented, lead guitar solos that others would copy ad infinitum. In essence, Judas Priest brought together, the disparate elements that preceded them – the loud, riff-driven gloom & doom of Black Sabbath; the twin guitar attack of Thin Lizzy; and the keening vocals of Ronnie James Dio – into one package thereby unleashing heavy metal as an official, unequivocal, stylistic entity.

4.) <u>Influences</u>: for <u>K.K. Downing</u>: the guitarists Jimi Hendrix, Eric Clapton, and John Mayall. For <u>Ian Hill</u> (bass): The Cream (heavy blues), Eric Clapton, John Mayall & The Bluesbreakers, and Fleetwood Mac. <u>Rob Halford's</u> inspiration: the desire to sing and perform beginning in his childhood. His first experience, the school choir and then later on school plays and other [school] musical productions. At 16, he quit school and entered the workforce employed at a large, local theatre. It was there, that he began connecting with other gay men and, for the first time, no longer felt like an outsider (which was how he felt in school). He would keep his sexual orientation out of the public eye until the mid 1980's.

5.) <u>Cultural Surround</u>: they hailed from Birmingham: the dark, bleak, smoke-ridden industrial city in the Midlands with surroundings that contributed to heavy metal's original essence. This was after all, where England's industrial revolution had originated and where the heavy metal process had begun with Black Sabbath. In the early 70's, their riff-driven, thickly textured, heavy sound was, in the words of Rob Halford, "…just a classic defining moment" (he was referring to the Black Sabbath song, *Paranoid*). In the late 60's, Birmingham youth were listening to the electrifying guitar work of Jimi Hendrix and the "heavy blues" of The Cream. The sounds that these artists put forth seemed to have reflected the noisy, industrial surround emanating from the factories.
> * <u>Local Musicianship</u>: within Birmingham in the late 60's, about 20 decently skilled musicians made up the main core (they saw music as a way out of their otherwise, pre-ordained, lower caste, working class way of life).

The Ripper
Judas Priest

Deceiver
Judas Priest

6.) <u>New Sound</u>: beginning with their breakthrough album of 1976, *Sad Wings of Destiny*, their main musical entities were established: <u>Rob Halford</u>: his accessible tunesmithism supported by a powerful voice – a combination of high-register keening, complimented by low-register edginess, and operatic quality. Examples from this album are excerpts from the singles: *The Ripper* and *Deceiver*.

The <u>Downing/Tipton</u> combination: their twin-guitar attack. In the track, *Victim Of Changes*, the twin guitars accompany Halford's voice with a repeated riff hovering underneath. In *between* sung verses, they unleash a powerful, thematic riff that serves as the main thematic foundation, which appears throughout the single which gives it [the single] a sense of accessible thematic unity.

<u>Guitar Solos</u>: for the most part, identified by rapid-rhythm melodic ornamentations in the mid to upper registers of the electric guitars (as illustrated in *Victim Of Changes*).

<u>Lyrics</u>: of gloom & doom plus apocalyptic-style of social commentary as illustrated in songs like *Tyrant*, *Deceiver* and *Genocide*. In *The Ripper*, Halford is playing the role of Jack The Ripper in the first person narrative giving out a stark warning to all would-be victims.

7.) <u>Continuity of The Blueprint</u>: the initial template laid out by Judas Priest would continue throughout the remainder of the 70's with albums such as *Sin After Sin* (1977), *Stained Glass* (1978), and *Hell Bent For Leather* (1978) – the latter ushering in their introduction of the black leather-clad, biker-styled attire which would be the defining fashion statement in the heavy metal tradition. In 1980, with the album *British Steel*, Judas Priest had truly honed in their heavy metal blueprint that others would emulate. Examples include the following:

<u>The Twin Guitar Combination</u>: in the track *Metal Gods*, the twin guitars establish the main thematic foundation – the repeated thematic riff – that gives the single a sense of overall coherence. The lyrics – inspired by Halford's enthusiasm for science fiction -- deal with an apocalyptic story of how machines in the form of robots are taking over and destroying humankind. It concludes with a sample of soldiers (Nazi style) marching in lock step. Another example, illustrated in *Rapid Fire*, is where the twin guitars lie underneath the vocal line and then in between vocal verses, unleash a powerful thematic riff. In addition, thundering, energetic drumming -- adding further aggressive momentum -- supports the entire single.

<u>Guitar Solos</u>: in the single entitled *Grinder*, an example of the heavy guitar solo style that Judas Priest made standard: mid to upper range with fast rhythmic ornamentation.

<u>Halford's Keening, Quasi-Operatic Sound</u>: at the conclusion of *Rapid Fire*, he unleashes a high-registered, shrieking sound that is operatic in character.

<u>NOTE</u>: each of the musical/lyric elements that were illustrated became the standard practice of the heavy metal genre that many others would emulate. In addition, *British Steel* would become their first album to reach Gold (500,000 copies sold) in the US. They made their first prominent videos from two songs: *Living After Midnight* and *Breakin' The Law*.

8.) *Screaming for Vengeance* (1982): the album that transformed Judas Priest into international icons. It sold over 2,000,000 copies (reaching double platinum) and gained significant radio airplay with their greatest hit, *You've Got Another Thing Comin'*. It was originally written and recorded quickly in order to fill the album (i.e. filler) and ironically, it turned out to be their biggest hit. They also included singles that dealt with normal subject matter such the track, *Electric Eye*, about a satellite which spies on everyone – sort of a take on the "Big Brother is watching you" scenario.

Victim Of Changes
Judas Priest

Victim Of Changes
Judas Priest

Metal Gods
Judas Priest

Rapid Fire
Judas Priest

Grinder
Judas Priest

Rapid Fire
Judas Priest

Living After Midnight
Judas Priest

Screaming for Vengeance
(guitar solos)

But of all the singles, the one in which they brought their attributes to the extreme is the title track, *Screaming for Vengeance*. One aspect: extremely fast, dual guitar solos – one solo follows with the other and then they both solo simultaneously playing the same rhythms in harmonization. Insofar as Rob Halford's shrieking, keening voice, he's at his most extreme in an operatic sense (there are examples of the guitar solos and extreme vocal renditions). They followed up with an album released in 1984 entitled, *Defenders of the Faith*.

> NOTE: Judas Priest initiated heavy metal and the NWOBHM as a genre in and of itself. The next step in the process was to standardize the elements of this new genre into bona fide trademarks that others could emulate, and, to solidify a heavy metal's distinct aesthetic identity.

B.) Iron Maiden (formed in 1976, London, ENG): If Judas Priest established the heavy metal model/musical style as a genre in and of itself (i.e. high-registered keening/vocalizing, twin-guitar attack, thundering drums, and the emphasis on the all-mighty electric guitar riff as primary focus), Iron Maiden solidified these elements as standard trademarks by which all heavy metal bands hereafter, would be compared. This in turn, made Iron Maiden one of the most influential artists of heavy metal.

> 1.) Original Line-up: Paul Di'Anno (b. May 17. 1959, London, ENG): lead vocals; Steve Harris (b. Mar. 12, 1957, London, ENG): bass, vocals; Dave Murray (b. Dec. 23, 1958, London, ENG): guitar; Doug Sampson: drums. In 1979, Tony Parson became the additional guitarist (starting their twin-guitar format). In 1980, Dennis Stratton (b. Nov. 9, 1954, London, ENG) replaced Tony Parson and Clive Burr, replaced Doug Sampson on the drums.

>> Classic Line-up: In addition to bassist Steve Harris, guitarist Dave Murray, and drummer Clive Burr; Adrian Smith (b. Feb. 27, 1957, London, ENG): guitar -- joined the band in 1980 replacing Dennis Stratton and Bruce "Air Raid Siren" Dickinson (b. Paul Bruce Dickinson, Aug. 7, 1958, Worksop, ENG): replaced Paul Di'Anno at lead vocals.

> 2.) Heavy Metal Elements: like Judas Priest, Iron Maiden would also have a twin-guitar format emphasizing the repeated riff attack. But, unlike Judas Priest, they present their type of riff-craft in an "all-riff" manner synchronizing vocals, bass, drums, and twin guitars in harmonic fashion together – making a thickly textured, heavier, harder sound [than their Birmingham predecessors]. Lyrics: In reference again to Judas Priest, they established lyrics precedent with the use of subject matter dealing with war, genocide, murderous thoughts, and apocalyptic elements. Iron Maiden would standardize those properties as well by not only using similar subject content, but also transcending them with the following examples: a first person account of a murder witness that gets accused of the crime and goes on the run (*Murders In The Rue Morgue*); an imaginary witness account of an episode form the Book of Revelations (*The Number of The Beast*); and a Gothic invasion of the Vikings invading and pillaging the Saxons (*Invaders*).

>> Lead Guitar Solos: a flurry of fast notes with melodic lines reminiscent of ornamentation with repeated clusters of notes at rapid speeds (mostly in the upper register) -- again, a precedent established by Judas Priest, which Iron Maiden would standardize into heavy metal that scores of others would emulate.

> 3.) The Growth of the Heavy Metal Scene in London: it was the result of a do-it-yourself (DIY) ethos in regard to small independent labels such as *Ebony*, *Neat*, and *Heavy Metal*. Forward-thinking enthusiasts and London-area bands founded these labels. The advantage of small labels (as opposed to mid-sized or major labels): they could survive by selling in small quantities anywhere from 1000 to 2000 copies. As a result, they

established a recording foundation that transformed obscure bar bands into recording artists and in the process, set the heavy metal movement in motion.

Once the movement got underway, well known, established British weekly publications such as *Sounds* and *New Music Express (NME),* began writing about these groups such as Raven, Def Leopard, and Tygers of Pan Tang (among others) for their considerable readership. It was Geoff Barton, a writer for *Sounds*, who was the first to coin (and popularize) the term, "New Wave Of British Heavy Metal" (NWOBHM).

4.) Among the bands that rose to the top of this burgeoning London scene was Iron Maiden. -- founded in 1976 by bass player/songwriter Steve Harris and guitarist Dave Murray. Their original line-up took shape when guitarist Tony Parson, drummer Doug Sampson, and vocalist Paul Di'Anno joined the group. They, like other bands, gigged constantly within the London-area nightclub circuit. After several personnel changes and performing to an ever-widening club circuit, Iron Maiden performed to a sold-out house at the famous Marquee Club in London on October of 1979, which drew the attention of the EMI label. A month later, they were signed to EMI/Capitol Records.

Sanctuary
Iron Maiden

Iron Maiden
Iron Maiden

Phantom of the Opera
Iron Maiden

Debut Album: *Iron Maiden* (1980: released on the Capitol label. The simple, direct, and rapid tempo'd influence of punk (along with Di'Anno's rough, gritty vocalizing) can be heard in tracks such as *Sanctuary* and *Iron Maiden*. More advanced influences that suggest a more progressive rock influence – especially when it came to more sophisticated riff-craft that transcended punk – can be heard on *Phantom of The Opera*. These riffs carried a more advanced melodic shape [than punk] and greater harmonic density presented in an epic, seven minute single complete with sectional outer forms reminiscent of progressive rock.

In addition to the fusion of punk and high-minded progressive rock influences, the initial Judas Priest model – lyrics of macabre, violence, war, etc. plus the twin-guitar attack [in an "all-riff" format] – was another part of what made Iron Maiden the new model by which others would follow. Theirs was a style that was advanced beyond punk, but more streamlined than progressive rock (using intricate, repeated riff action as opposed to instrumental complexity).

Wrathchild
Iron Maiden

Murders In The Rue Morgue
Iron Maiden

5.) *Killers* (1981): their second album showing the unification of influences alchemized into an all-riff, original sound. It also had a more harder, heavier sound [than their debut album]. Examples of their honed-in sound are the songs, *Wrathchild* and *Murders In The Rue Morgue*. This album also marks the debut of Guitarist Adrian Smith (replacement for George Stratton) setting in place, the long, twin guitar collaboration of Murray and Smith. This was their first album to crack the US market reaching to #60 on the charts and selling 200,000 copies. This was also the last Iron Maiden album with Paul Di'Anno as lead vocalist (due to chronic alcohol problems).

6.) *Number Of The Beast* (1982): where Bruce Dickinson makes his debut as lead vocalist completing Iron Maiden's classic line-up which would transform them into international metal icons. Dickinson's voice had a more shrieking, high-registered, quasi-operatic sound [reminiscent of the Rob Halford/Judas Priest model] in comparison to his predecessor. In addition, the vocal power of Dickinson could hold it's own over the thickly textured, twin-guitar riffing and the rhythmically vibrant bass lines and thundering drums – the ultimate "all-riff" approach adding a new musical language to heavy metal.

The Number Of
The Beast
Iron Maiden

The Number Of
The Beast
(guitar solo)
Iron Maiden

The Prisoner
Iron Maiden

Example: *The Number Of The Beast* – a first-person account [in the future] witnessing an event from the Book of Revelations (Chapter VIII, v. 18). Steve Harris opens the single by reading the actual biblical verses. Musically, there are two examples presented that illustrate Iron Maiden's elevation to superior songcraft: the powerful all-riff attack highlighted by Bruce Dickinson's vocals and the rapid-rhythm guitar solo in mostly the upper register (again, a take from the Judas Priest model). *The Prisoner* is another musical illustration.

The Number Of The Beast album became Iron Maiden's first major success in America, which transformed them and the heavy metal juggernaut into a worldwide, global force.

C.) 1980: the year that the NWOBHM hit it's stride and went into high gear. You may recall, that this was the year Judas Priest released their landmark album, *British Steel* and it was also the year of Iron Maiden's self-titled debut album. We also saw the solidification of the NWOBHM model laid down by Judas Priest that would be standardized by Iron Maiden. In regard to additional landmark albums, 1980 saw the release of *Wheels of Steel* by a group called Saxon (formed in 1977, Barnsley, ENG).

1.) Background: originally called Son Of A Bitch in 1976 founded by guitarist Graham Oliver and bass player Steven Dawson -- vocalist Biff Byford, guitarist Paul Quinn, and drummer Peter Gill later joined them. They began, like their contemporaries, on the club and concert circuit (the latter as a warm-up act). Their first break, was when Peter Hilton of EMI Records saw their performance at the Civic Hall in Barnsley which he had reviewed positively. He encouraged them to send a demo tape to Claude Carrere, owner of the French-based Carrere Records and in 1979, Saxon signed [with Carrere].

Stallion Of
The Highway
Saxon

Saxon (1979): their debut album. Although they had a notable single from this album, *Stallion Of The Highway* (the first of their biker anthems), which did well on the UK "Powerhouse" charts, their style was more hard rock and lightweight than true heavy metal. They toured that year as the warm-up act for Motörhead's nationwide UK tour, which gained them wider exposure.

Wheels of Steel
Saxon

Motorcycle Man
Saxon

Wheels Of Steel (1980): their breakthrough album that transformed them into a bona fide, heavy metal outfit. The trademarks of the NWOBHM are here including a harder, heavier, and metallic twin guitar attack with high-flying vocals and hammering drums. Landmark tracks of this new direction include the title track, *Motorcycle Man*, and *Machine Gun*. They released two follow up albums that were an integral part of the NWOBHM force: *Strong Arm of the Law* (1980) and *Denim and Leather* (1981).

Machine Gun
Saxon

2.) NOTE: There were several elements that each of the NWOBHM artists [mentioned earlier] had shared. First of all, the musical properties (i.e. twin-guitar attack, high-flying, shrieking vocals, a hard/heavy sound, etc.), Secondly, the biker/black leather look initiated by Judas Priest. And finally, their influence upon a new genre [of heavy metal] that would begin on the west coast of the US: Thrash Metal. But in addition to Judas Priest, Iron Maiden, Saxon, etc., there was one other influential group (also to Thrash Metal) that would do things differently. Instead of a twin-guitar model, they used only one – but with arguably more loudness and massive speed. Instead of high-registered, accomplished vocals, their vocal sound was rough, low-to-mid registered, node-ridden, gritty. In addition, they added something new to the NWOBHM scene: lots and lots of attitude. The name of that band was Motörhead.

D.) Motörhead (formed in 1975): the band that added blazing speed, grit, and attitude into heavy metal along with the outlaw, biker-trash image. Their influence upon heavy metal's development is paramount. A year before punk officially began, they were already mixing metal with the fast and furiously aggressive style [of punk] that would eventually, become influential to the advent of Thrash Metal.

1.) Personnel: <u>Lemmy</u> (b. Ian Fraser Kilmister, Dec. 24, 1945, Stoke-on-Trent, West Midlands, ENG): bass, vocals; <u>Phil "Philthy Animal" Taylor</u> (b. Sept. 21, 1954, Chesterfield, ENG): drums; <u>Edward "Fast Eddie" Clarke</u> (b. Oct. 5, 1950, Twickenham, London, ENG): guitar. Although there were many personnel changes (with Lemmy as the only consistent mainstay), the band members listed above were the most prominent (i.e. the "classic" lineup).

2.) <u>Background</u>: During his childhood, Lemmy idolized artists such as, Little Richard, Buddy Holly, and Eddie Cochran. The latter two [Holly and Cochran] inspired him to take up the guitar in 1957. It was Eddie Cochran though, who represented the true, self made artist – for Cochran {in Lemmy's view] was the first to write and produce his own material (an inspiration that would manifest itself later on in his career). He once wrote that after seeing TV rock shows: *Oh Boy* and *6-5 Special*, he was "driven to be a guitar slinger".

3.) <u>Manchester</u>: he moved there in the early 60's and became caught up in the rock 'n' roll cultural surround. He was in a number of different bands including The Rainmakers and <u>The Motown Sect</u> – a group he would be associated with for three years. They were an R&B band that played no Motown covers (but used the Motown name because of it's popularity which led to more gigs). They wore long hair and striped t-shirts and played covers of blues-revisionist bands like The Yardbirds and R&B artists such as James Brown and Chuck Berry.

4.) His next band was <u>The Rocking Vicars</u> (1965-1967), a cover band that played loud and fast. Although they didn't write any original material, they did have the distinction of being the first British band to play behind the Iron Curtain in Yugoslavia. After brief stints as a roadie for Jimi Hendrix's second UK tour (Nov. 14 – Dec. 5, 1967), and as a member of the band, Opal butterfly, Lemmy joined the group, Hawkwind.

5.) <u>Lemmy's Hawkwind Tenure</u>: since Hawkwind did not have an opening for a guitarist but did have a vacancy in bass, Lemmy joined in and began his bass-playing career (he had never played the bass before). In addition, inspired by the confidence instilled in him from the band's leader, Dave Brock, Lemmy began writing his own songs. His first experience at being a lead vocalist was on the recording, *Silver Machine*, recorded in 1971 that incidentally, reached #2 on the UK pop charts (their only big hit).

Space Is Deep
Hawkwind

<u>Hawkwind's Style</u>: that of an "art-based" band as opposed to a hippie-type, peace/love operation. The band stood mostly in the shadows (in the darkness) while an extravagant lightshow was flashing overhead. Their use of multi-media consisted of movie screens (18 of them) displaying film-clips of animation, war footage, political scenes, and melting oil (among other things). There was also a set of dancers onstage doing slithering type of contortions in the midst of loud, space-like music. Some of "space sounds" were made by advanced instruments such as a mellotron, ring modulator, and audio generator.

Motörhead
Hawkwind

After spending four years with Hawkwind, which included four US tours, and four albums, Lemmy was sacked from the band following his arrest at the Canadian border for drug possession (charges were later dismissed). The last song he had written for Hawkwind, was a song entitled *Motörhead* (from the 1974 album, *Warrior on the Edge of Time*) – it would be the name of his new band.

6.) <u>Motörhead</u>: Lemmy had originally intended to call his new band, Bastard but at behest of his manager, Doug Smith, he [Lemmy] changed the name to Motörhead (which in addition to being the last song he wrote for Hawkwind, it was also an American term for speedfreak [of which he was]). He wanted to have a band that was like an MC5 type (MC5 were underground heroes at the time and they had a fast, brash, aggressive guitar sound). In addition, he would use elements of Little Richard and Hawkwind. In his view, they [Motörhead] were nothing but a blues band playing at breakneck, massive speeds. Their debut performance was at The Roundhouse in London on July 20, 1975.

> <u>Recording Contract</u>: after being voted as "Best Worst band in the world", they were signed with United Artists in 1975. They recorded their first album called *On Parole*, but United Artists refused to release it (they would release it four years later). In 1977, they were joined by guitarist Eddie Clarke who played electric guitar at rapid speeds (hence the nickname "Fast Eddie") and with Phil "Philthy Animal" Taylor on drums, Motörhead's "classic lineup" was in place.

> <u>Their Debut Album</u> (their first *released* album): *Motörhead* (1977). They recorded thirteen songs but only eight of them made it on the album. Re-recorded material from *On Parole* (including "Lost Johnny" and "Born to Lose") and re-recorded material from Hawkwind's *Warrior on the Edge of Time* album ("Motörhead" and "The Watcher") were included. In addition, there were two originals: "White Line Fever" and "Keep Us On The Road".

> <u>Overkill</u> (1979): recorded on the Bronze label, were recordings of songs that they have been performing live already. These songs were primarily rapid-tempo'd which further cemented their "fast and furious" reputation. After recording the album *Bomber* later that year (which introduced the famous "Bomber" lighting rig), They released their breakthrough album entitled, *Ace of Spades*.

7.) <u>Ace of Spades</u> (1980): in Lemmy's words, this album was, "…the ultimate record for that particular line-up of Motörhead". It was also their official American debut. In addition, *Ace of Spades* sealed its reputation as the loudest, meanest, and dirtiest album to date. Already a huge concert draw in the UK, the album's success in America was a testament to Motorhead's growing cult following among metalheads in the US. It further built up their denim-clad, outlaw type of image by posing as gunslingers on the cover and using gambling and cowboy/western motifs as metaphor.

> <u>*Ace of Spades*</u> (title track): setting the tone for the album's lyrics with gambling metaphors expressing the philosophy that the chase is better than the catch (incidentally, the eleventh track in the album is named, *The Chase is Better Than The Catch*). Western metaphors are used as well with words like "…the dead man's hand again". The title track also sets the musical tone [for the entire album] with a fast & furiously rapid tempo, gritty vocalizing, and an in your face, heavy metal onslaught – all Motörhead artistic staples.

> <u>*The Hammer*</u>: another example of a nasty, fast, furious, and gritty sound that hardcore punks would eventually relate to (more on that later).

> <u>NOTE</u>: *Ace of Spades* was the album that transformed Motörhead from cult obscurity to a big American following once the heavy metal juggernaut hit the mainstream in the early 1980's. They accomplished this in big part by their relentless touring (one of which was with Alice Cooper, Judas Priest, and Metal Church), and, their inroads into the LA punk scene.

8.) <u>Motörhead's Relation to Punk</u>: In 1977, Lemmy had direct connections with the London underground punk scene and for a brief period, jammed alongside a punk band known as The Damned (he also gave Sid Vicious some of his first bass lessons). During the 80's, hardcore punks began showing respect for Motörhead among other NWOBHM bands. This growing respect was culminated in 1985 when they crossed over to the LA hardcore punk scene by sharing the same bill with a hardcore punk band: The Cro-Mags.

> In addition to this Punk crossover, there was another influence that Motörhead would inspire among the LA scene – as was previously mentioned, the advent of a fast and furious style that would be forever known, as Thrash Metal.

III.THE WEST COAST SCENE AND THE RISE OF THRASH METAL

A.) <u>Prologue: The Rise of the West Coast Metal Underground</u>

1.) <u>The Growing Network of Tape Trading</u>: throughout the LA and San Francisco areas, underground [cassette] tape trading inner circles were sprouting up in the late 1970's. Disillusioned by the glam [metal] bands, these metal enthusiasts were looking for something honest -- especially heavier and faster – that could be found within the NWOBHM bands. With the exception of Judas Priest and Motörhead (both of whom toured throughout the US), these bands had limited financial resources due to their association with small record labels. As a result, they only toured throughout the UK.

> - Their only exposure on the West Coast [prior to tape trading] were British heavy metal fanzines such as *Kerrang!* and *Sounds*. It would be soon after, that west coast fans would get to hear these groups by either trading cassette tapes or going to the few outlets that carried rare import records.

2.) <u>Brian Slagel</u>: was one of those veteran tape traders and import record hunters who had an immense enthusiasm for British heavy metal. It began in the parking lot of the Capitol Records offices in Hollywood. He started making connections with record shop owners and tape traders who shared his passion for metal (such as AC/DC, Kiss, etc.). As his passion for NWOBHM bands grew, he and a friend named John Kornarens, began hanging out with another heavy metal fanatic named Lars Ulrich. Together, the three of them traveled from one record store to the next hunting for imports. And because of their extensive tape and record collections, their knowledge of the repertoire grew considerably (this was typical of many west coast, tape trading inner circles).

> - When the European metal press began covering the growing LA scene, Brian Slagel (with help from Kornarens), founded his own fanzine, *New Heavy Metal Revue*. One of his inspirations [to establish this magazine] was his job as import record buyer for Oz Records store (which gave him the inside track on the latest imports). He also decided to produce a compilation album of local LA metal bands such as Mötley Crüe and Ratt (among others). As a result, he founded an independent label called *Metal Blade*. It was on this compilation album that Metallica's first recording would be featured.

B.) <u>Metallica</u> (formed in 1981): the worldwide purveyors of the Thrash Metal "House Style".

1.) Original Line-up: <u>James Alan Hetfield</u> (b. Aug. 3, 1963, Los Angeles, CA): guitar, vocals; <u>Dave Mustaine</u> (b. Sep. 13, 1961, La Mesa, CA): lead guitar; <u>Ron McGovney</u> (b. Nov. 2,1963, Los Angeles, CA): bass; <u>Lars Ulrich</u> (b. Dec. 26,1963, Gentofte, DEN): drums. Later on, <u>Clifford Lee Burton</u> (b. Feb. 10.1962, d. Sept. 27, 1986): bass, replaced

Ron McGovney in 1982 and <u>Kirk Hammett</u> (b. Nov. 18, 1962, San Francisco, CA): guitar, replaced Dave Musitaine in 1983. After Cliff Burton's death, <u>Jason Newsted</u> (b. Mar. 4, 1963, Battle Creek, MI) became the new bass player, and <u>Rob Trujillo</u> (b. Oct. 2, 1964, LA) later replaced him in 2003.

2.) <u>Background</u>: James Hetfield and Ron McGovney, guitarists who both shared an enthusiasm for the bands, Kiss and Aerosmith, formed the first of several bands (they would be associated with) called Obsession --- they basically did Led Zeppelin, Deep Purple, Thin Lizzy, and Black Sabbath covers. After a short stint as Phantom Lord, they became <u>Leather Charm</u> doing covers of heavier bands such as Quiet Riot The Scorpions, and Iron Maiden. They wrote several original songs including *Hit The Lights*.

- <u>Lars Ulrich</u>: grew up in privilege -- his father was a world-class professional tennis player. As Lars' fledgling tennis ambitions ran a fowl (he couldn't compete with his LA counterparts), he turned his passion (and ambition) to music. He especially preferred the heaviest metal varieties such as Diamond Head and Motörhead (he actually hung out with Sean Harris of Diamond Head for a few months and followed Motörhead on tour). On April of 1981, Ulrich answered an ad to audition for Leather Charm but was turned down.

- <u>Reunion</u>: a year later, Ulrich befriended Ron Quintana, a writer, record collector, and radio Dee Jay who was in the process of naming his new fanzine either *Metal Mania* or *Metallica* and asked Ulrich which name was the best fit. In response, Ulrich suggested *Metal Mania* while keeping the latter name for a new band that he had not yet formed. Another friend, Brian Slagel, owner of the *Metal Blade* label alerted Ulrich of his plan to produce a heavy metal compilation and left a slot open for his band [Ulrich's]. He contacted James Hetfield to put together a band [for this recording], and the song, at Ulrich's suggestion, would be *Hit The Lights*.

At the time, Hetfield's influences evolved into the heavy, raw, and rapid-riffing ethos of the NWOBHM bands. For their debut recording, James, Ron, and Lars recruited guitarist Lloyd Grant (who played for this one recording only). Even though the recording was hastily produced and finished at the last minute (so to speak), *Hit The Lights* was included in Slagel's compilation *Metal Massacre* released on June 14, 1982. It was after this recording that a new guitarist, <u>Dave Mustaine</u>, joined the band after answering a want ad in *Recycle*.

3.) <u>Debut Performance</u>: March 14, 1982 at the Radio City venue in Anaheim, CA. In addition, to *Hit The Lights* (their opening song), they performed four Diamond Head covers and covers of Blitzkrieg, Savage, and Sweet Savage. By May 25th, Metallica's set consisted of one-half covers and one-half originals. The originals included *Metal Militia*, *Jump In The Fire*, and *Motorbreath* (all of which would be included in their debut album, *Kill 'Em All*).

4.) <u>Influences</u>: according to Dave Mustaine, <u>Diamond Head</u> was a primary influence (Ulrich was also a Diamond Head devotee). He along with Hetfield would listen to their [Diamond Head] records. In addition, they listened to Motörhead, Mercyful Fate, Raven, and Angel Witch. In 1984, Ron Quintana once said that Metallica [in their early days] sounded "like a revved-up Motörhead (hence, the emphasis on speed). This [Motörhead] influence would be furthered by Mustaine's replacement, <u>Kirk Hammett</u> -- a former lead guitarist for the band Exodus. Their initial influences were the NWOBHM groups especially with the rapid-speeds of Motörhead.

Am I Evil?
Diamond Head

5.) <u>The Birth of the Metallica Legend</u>: *No Life 'Til Leather* (1982), a demo tape that changed the rules of heavy metal. Before *No Life 'Til Leather* (a.k.a. *NLTL*) was released,

Motörhead was the benchmark for speed metal (but was still considered blues influenced). To those who first heard this seminal demo [*NLTL*], it was the fastest and heaviest metal heard yet and was devoid of blues influences (unlike their NWOBHM counterparts). By transcending the Motörhead speed/heaviness model, Metallica basically re-wrote the heavy metal script and in the process, inspired many artists to form their own bands intending to emulate the rapid speeds and heaviness of *NLTL*. But they not only played the fastest and heaviest, they also executed their playing with absolute precision – in other words, they were tight (which again, set them apart from the Motörhead model).

Hit The Lights
Metallica

- <u>Elements</u>: bright, speedy, highly energized style that transcended conventional tunesmithism. There was slight distortion but it did not obscure the electric guitar's harmonies. James Hetfield's voice was higher than baritone (but not soaring like Rob Halford) and lightly gritty (not as much as Lemmy). Mustaine's guitar solos were wild and super-charged. The result was an American version of Diamond Head that transcended the NWOBHM style taken further. The demo consisted of current original songs that the group had been performing up to this point. One of the more noted singles was *Hit The Lights*. Others included *Motorbreath*, *Seek & Destroy*, *Jump In The Fire*, and *Metal Militia*.

- Released as a cassette tape, *NLTL* was a popular commodity in the underground LA and San Francisco tape-trading network. With fans duplicating this cassette thousands of times over (via their own dubbing machines), tape trading became a unique distribution/promotional system. This helped spread the popularity of *NLTL* and established Metallica's reputation – both inside and outside of the LA and San Francisco scenes. It was during this time, that metal fans began coining a new stylistic term known as Thrash Metal....

6.) <u>Thrash Metal</u>: a product of accident rather than design. Jeff Dunn (a.k.a. Mantas) and his band <u>Venom</u> (formed 1978, Newcastle-upon-Tyne, ENG), decided one day – in a serendipitous moment – to play fast (at rapid speed) and the result was the first "thrash" song, *The Witching Hour*. The defining element was when their drummer Tony Bray played a double-speed pattern on the snare drum (reminiscent of hardcore punk).

The Witching Hour
Venom

- <u>Elements of Thrash</u>: in addition to rapid drumming speeds, rapidly picked single string riffs (palm-muted) and two-string power chords were added. NOTE: because the rapid tempos were too fast, full chords [using all six strings] could not be executed except in slower tempos.

- <u>Benchmark</u>: it wasn't until the release of Venom's *Welcome To Hell* album of 1981, that the notion of "faster is better" came into play. The main subject matter: Satanism – it was intended for shocking audiences and rebellious expression and not devil worship. Venom's influences included heavy metal bands like <u>Black Sabbath</u>, <u>Judas Priest</u>, and <u>Motörhead</u>. They also brandished a punk attitude.

- <u>NOTE</u>: in addition to Motörhead, Venom would set the standard for extreme speed metal that west coast bands like Exodus (from San Francisco) and Slayer (from LA) would adopt. Metallica also adopted this speed metal approach and, in the NWOBHM tradition, wrote lyrics of commentary and social protest instead of Satanism. In fact, if Venom released the first thrash metal album, Metallica would release the first *big selling* thrash album...

7.) *Kill 'Em All* (1983): Metallica's debut album and their first release on vinyl. It was also the debut of two new band members: <u>Cliff Burton</u> on the bass (replacing McGovney) and <u>Kirk Hammett</u> on lead guitar (replacing Dave Mustaine). Almost identical to *NLTL*, *Kill 'Em All (a.k.a. KEA)* was executed at a higher skill level thereby, setting a new standard of rhythmic precision, power, and dexterity to the west coast, heavy metal ethos. The result was a combination of intricate riffing of NWOBHM bands (especially Diamond Head) with the fierce, rapid-tempo'd onslaught of Motörhead and hardcore punk. An excerpt from song *Whiplash*, serve s as an example.

Whiplash
Metallica

- They re-recorded the songs from *NLTL* (including *Hit The Lights*) and in one case, completely rewrote a song (*Mechanix* was rewritten as *The Four Horsemen*). It was at this point that the tone was set for their later LP's with that heavy, machine-like sound and precision. *KEA* was released on the *Megaforce* label (who also released *NLTL*) owned by their manger, John "Johnny Z" Zazula.

8.) <u>*Ride The Lightning*</u> (1984): album that marked the progression of Metallica to a more mature level of songwriting craftsmanship. In addition, this album set the tone for their remaining albums in terms of artistry. The tracks were more highly structured and rhythmically precise than in *KEA*. They even included an acoustic guitar ballad furthering their artistic boundaries. The album was recorded in Copenhagen, Denmark under producer Flemming Rasmussen at his Sweet Silence Studio.

Fight Fire With Fire
Metallica

- <u>Lyrics</u>: continuing the tradition established by the NWOBHM bands, the lyrics [in *RTL*] speak to social commentary and responsibility. In examples such as <u>*Fight Fire With Fire*</u>, they speak against the deterrent nuclear policy of "Mutually Assured Destruction" (MAD) adopted by the US and USSR.

Ride The Lightning
Metallica

* Referring to the electric chair, the <u>*Ride The Lightning*</u> title track is a protest against capital punishment as seen through the eyes of one strapped to the chair [on the verge of his execution] – just waiting in horror for the executioner to flick the switch.

For Whom The Bell Tolls
Metallica

* <u>*For Whom The Bell Tolls*</u>,: a narrative account of a young soldier fighting in a grey, smoke–filled battlefield. The soldier is on the brink death for the whims of the powerful (who deem the soldier's life as expendable). The chorus of this anti-war song is a paraphrase of the Hemingway story.

- <u>Setting Of A New Standard</u>: although their initial influences came from the NWOBHM, Metallica created a sound that was so unique, it marked a clean break [from the NWOBHM] and in the process achieved an originality by setting a new standard in thrash metal (and *RTL* was the key to setting that new standard). This standard was solidified with their next album *Master Of Puppets* (1986) – their debut on Elektra Records (by now, a major record label) and their first album to reach gold (500,00 copies sold). This success gave testament to the growth in their popularity – even though they had no radio airplay and no videos appearances on MTV.

Master Of Puppets
Metallica

* <u>NOTE</u>: If *RTL* set the new standard, *Master Of Puppets* solidified their new standard of the west coast, Thrash Metal, "house style" – a style that would be emulated by many others. But there would be those who would add their own unique stamps on this "house style". And although there were many who made their own artistic contributions, two in particular made particularly significant ones. As a result, they stood out from the rest and thereby warrant further discussion – one was called <u>Megadeth</u> (Dave Mustaine's next band) and the other, the

band that would bring attitude into west coast Thrash Metal – they were known as <u>Slayer</u>…

C.) <u>Megadeth</u> (formed in 1983, Los Angeles, CA): Dave Mustaine's new band that he formed in wake of his dismissal from Metallica. Musically, he would take the high-speed, thrash metal model of his former band and add instrumental virtuosity, more intensity, and faster, blinding speeds.

1.) Personnel: <u>Dave Mustaine</u> (b. Sept. 13, 1961, La Mesa, CA): guitar, vocals; <u>David Ellefson</u> (b. Nov. 12, 1964, Jackson, MN): bass; <u>Chris Poland</u> (b. Dec. 1, 1957, Dunkirk, NY): lead guitar; <u>Gars Samuelson</u> (b. Feb. 18, 1958, Dunkirk, NY, d. July 14, 1999, Orange City, FL): drums. Eventually, <u>Jeff Young</u> (b. Mar. 31, 1962, Ann Arbor, MI) replaced Chris Poland on lead guitar and <u>Chuck Behler</u> (b. June 13, 1965, Livonia, MI) replaced Samuelson on the drums. Although there would be additional line-up changes, Mustaine and Ellefson were the only original members to record on every Megadeth album.

2.) <u>Background</u>: because of his excessive alcohol abuse and resulting combative behavior (that was increasingly difficult to tolerate), Metallica sacked Mustaine in 1983 and replaced him with Kirk Hammett. In response, Mustaine wanted revenge and endeavored to create a new band that would "out metal" his former colleagues. The result was Fallen Angel (in reference to his falling from grace), which he changed to Megadeth – a name that is reminiscent of ballistic killer missiles rather than the darkness of the occult.

- Their early line-up was a revolving door of different rhythm guitarists, which included Kerry King (of another important thrash band, Slayer) whose tenure lasted only a couple of days. In fact, Mustaine taught King various techniques of advanced guitar playing that King would use to the fullest in the music of Slayer.

3.) <u>Musical Influences</u>: for Dave Mustaine, the NWOBHM bands that pioneered cyclical patterns of riffs as the central theme. Among the more specific early influences: <u>Diamond Head</u> and <u>Mercyful Fate</u>.

4.) <u>Virtuosity</u>: once he settled on guitarist Chris Poland and drummer Gar Samuelson, the band's artistic direction was set. Poland and Samuelson both came from a jazz musical background – at one point, they engaged in jazz-fusion rock. Their jazz backgrounds translated into instrumental virtuosity, which became a hallmark of Megadeth's sound. In addition to the rapid speeds and emotional extremes of thrash metal, they included advanced technical skill at lead guitar and drums -- a brutal combination of thrash metal and jazz-influenced virtuosity. In the example, *Rattlehead*, Chris Poland is heard at solo guitar.

Rattlehead
Megadeth

5.) <u>Debut Album</u>: *Killing Is My Business…and Business Is Good!* (1985): released on the independent label, Combat Records. This marks their beginning where lightning speed and technically skilled chops combine. Lyrically, the album deals with the subject matter of death and damnation in various contexts such as war ("Chosen Ones"), misogyny ("These Boots" – a takeoff on a Nancy Sinatra hit from the 60's), and the threat of a sniper speaking in the first person ("Killing Is My Business…and Business Is Good!").

Killing Is My Business… …and Business Is Good!
Megadeth

6.) *Peace Sells…But Who's Buying?* (1986): their first album on a major label, Capitol Records. Lyrically, a typical [thrash metal] viewpoint: preoccupations of the evil within ranging from a homicidal man ("Good Mourning/Black Friday") to elements of the occult ("Bad Omen") to a Russian Roulette metaphor ("My Last Words") and fear ("Wake Up Dead").

Wake Up Dead
Megadeth

7.) *Rust In Peace* (1990): with a sobered-up Mustaine (who did the 12-step program) is joined by a new line-up of lead guitar virtuoso Marty Friedman and Nick Menza on the drums. Most critics contend that this album was their best artistic effort – with rhythmically and technically complex thrash epics that he and Friedman execute with absolute precision. The result is more about the music than the lyrics although Mustaine does delve in anti-war protest in songs such as *Hangar 18*.

D.) Slayer (formed in 1982, Los Angeles, CA): another product of the LA thrash metal scene that would bring the concept of thrash metal to the absolute extreme. If Metallica was about precision and Megadeth about lead guitar virtuosity, Slayer was about brutality.

1.) Personnel: Tom Araya (b. June 6, 1961, Chile): bass, vocals; Jeff Hanneman (b. Jan. 31, 1964, LA): guitar; Kerry King (b. June 3, 1963, Huntington Park, CA): guitar; Dave Lombardo (b. Feb. 16, 1965): drums – he would later be replaced by Paul Bostaph (b. March 4, 1965, Hayward, CA).

2.) Influences: for Kerry King, early influences were Judas Priest and other NWOBHM bands especially Iron Maiden (with their emphasis on heavy guitar riffs). After he and another NWOBHM enthusiast, Jeff Hanneman began collaborating, they did Judas Priest and Iron Maiden covers but Hanneman was also interested in the rapid speeds of hardcore punk. Drummer Dave Lombardo soon joined them after answering a want ad in a local newspaper, *The Recycler*. When bass player and [metal] vocal extraordinaire, Tom Araya joined the band, their original line-up was complete.

- Style: a mixture of unpolished, edgy guitar riffing (á la Iron Maiden) with ultra rapid tempos influenced by hardcore punk. Unlike Metallica's polished precision that was devoid of punk, Slayer maintained a punk influence that was peppered with malicious satanic lyrics (at least in their early career).

3.) Debut Performance: October 31, 1981 at South Park Gate Auditorium but their next performance Huntington Park High School was more indicative with covers ranging from Van Halen to heavier bands such as UFO and Iron Maiden. Soon after, they began wearing thick facial make-up influenced by King Diamond (of Mercyful Fate) and Kerry King wore a self-made, nail-studded, leather wristband. They also developed a makeshift light show comprised of some stolen lighting material (they would eventually drop the make-up after metal fans viciously harassed them [about it] during a performance in San Francisco).

4.) Turning Point: the influence of Venom: the first purveyors of thrash metal from Newcastle-upon-Tyne, ENG. Venom played extremely fast and yelled out gravelly, guttural lyrics of satanism. At the time [of their influence on Slayer], they had just released their second album, *Black Metal*. As a result, their influence was extensive, profound, and instantaneous. They [Slayer] immediately applied the Venom template to their own songs – especially with the nasty speeds and satanic lyrics – they [Venom] were a huge influence.

- Artistic Vision: the Venom influence tied everything together: the metal influences of Kerry King (i.e. heavy guitar riffing) and the punk influences of Jeff Hanneman (i.e. punk speed and aggression). Gradually, the tempo got faster and faster as exemplified by Dave Lombardo's rapid, snare drum patterns (these rapid snare patterns were the hallmark of extreme, thrash metal).

5.) Debut Recording: *Aggressive Defender*, which appeared on *Metal Massacre III*, Brain Slagel's compilation on his Metal Blade label. In fact, *Aggressive Defender* became the opening track due to its rapid speed, fast riffing, speedy snare drum patterns, and Tom Ayala's barked vocals. The speed and outright aggression made it stand out from the remaining songs of the album. It also became Slayer's template for their future original songs.

- <u>Crossover Appeal</u>: while Metallica was establishing their thrash metal credentials in San Francisco, Slayer remained in LA and built their own reputation. Eventually, due to their hardcore punk speeds, they crossed over and attracted a punk audience. In 1983, they were the first metal band to unite both punk and metal fans together under one show.

6.) <u>Debut Album</u>: *Show No Mercy* (1983): recorded on Brian Slagel's *Metal Blade* label which became the label's biggest success up to this point. Musically, its an extension of the *Aggressive Defender* template and the manifestation of their NWOBHM influences presented in a punk-derived thrash metal approach (i.e. a synthesis of punk speeds/metal riffing equaling high-speed thrash). These influences included <u>Mercyful Fate</u> (featuring King Diamond), <u>Iron Maiden</u>, and <u>Judas Priest</u> -- the [album's] duration is only 35 minutes.

- Examples: *Metal Storm*: the kinetic riffing of Iron Maiden (a long time influence for Slayer). Although there were other songs throughout the album reminiscent of their influence, *Metal Storm* is a typical example. *Crionics*: featuring the Judas Priest, Rob Halford vocal influence that can be heard in the high-registered, wailing vocals of Tom Araya. For the Mercyful Fate influence, a song called *The Antichrist* is the riffing influence [of Mercyful Fate] presented at lightning fast speed.

- <u>NOTE</u>: their second album, *Hell Awaits*, was similar to *SNM* although the lyrics are more dark and nihilistic manifesting that Venom and King Diamond (of Mercyful Fate) influences. The dark, blurry production quality was also similar due to the limited resources of the Metal Blade label. With their next album, which would be their landmark, a new clear production quality on a major record label would be unveiled...

7.) *Reign In Blood* (1986): considered by Lars Ulrich (drummer of Metallica) as the greatest thrash metal album ever. It was with this album – only 28 minutes in length -- that Slayer brought the concept of thrash metal to the extreme. In the mid 80's, while other bands were engaged in lyrics of social commentary and other thoughtful insights, Slayer was using extreme lyrics of mutilation, corruption, and dismemberment (and considerably less on satanism). In addition, their trademark elements of speed and ugliness were pushed to the extreme – which included guitar solos that bordered on atonality – their most brutal statement yet.

- <u>Clarity</u>: their extremes notwithstanding, it was also their most professionally produced album ripe with a clean sound. Gone was the reverb-laden murkiness of their previous releases and in, was the clarity of each instrument. The reason: they signed with Def Jam Records under producer <u>Rick Rubin</u>. Def Jam had vast financial resources (that afforded them great studio and production personnel) compared with the low-budget operations of Metal Blade. As a result, this new clarity was key in highlighting all of the band's visceral strengths.

- <u>Lyrics</u>: extreme, sick, and controversial.

* *Angel Of Death*: opens the album with a crisp, fresh sound that was immediate – the distortion notwithstanding, the initial guitar riff stands out cleanly. The lyrics dealt with Dr. Joseph Mengele, the notorious Nazi criminal at the Auschwitz concentration camp. This single drew scores of protesters and the controversy followed the band for a long

Piece By Piece
Slayer

Necrophobic
Slayer

period after its release.

       * *Piece By Piece*: the first truly "gore metal" single depicting graphic images of human dismemberment.

       * *Necrophobic*: the speediest tempo recorded)up to this point). The lyrics describe someone who is so frightened to die, that he presents a list of different ways to make it happen like strangulation, mutilation, etc.

    - Distribution: after CBS Records, Def Jam's distributor refused to release this record due to the controversial lyrics, Geffen Records (another major label) agreed to distribute it instead. As a result, the legend of this album and the extreme approach of Slayer, would be born.

8.) NOTE: in comparison to Metallica and Megadeth, Slayer was not only transforming thrash metal to an utmost brutal extreme, they were also part of a process. This process involved the next new wave in heavy metal. Slayer didn't know it yet, but they would be one of he first anticipators and inspirations of a new genre that would become forever known, as Death Metal – a derivative of the Black Metal style.

IV. THE PHENOMENA KNOWN AS BLACK METAL

A.) Definition of Black Metal: NWOBHM influences synthesized with rapid speeds inspired by hardcore punk plus, lyrics dealing with evil/satanic subject matter and performers displaying occult-driven imagery.

1.) There were three black metal bands that were most influential to the LA thrash scene and later on, to the second wave of black metal known as Scandinavian/Viking Black Metal. These bands were: Venom, Mercyful Fate, and Bathory.

B.) Venom (formed in 1979, Newcastle-upon-Tyne, ENG): the undisputed innovators of thrash metal and progenitors of the power, black, and death metal aesthetics. They originally called themselves "Guillotine" before changing their name to Venom in 1979.

Angel Dust
Venom

1.) Personnel: Jeff "Mantas" Dunn: guitar; Conrad "Cronos" Lant: bass, vocals; and Tony "Abaddon" Bray: drums. They synthesized the following influences: the occultist imagery of Black Sabbath, the amplitude & attitude of Motörhead, the face-painting & pyrotechnics of Kiss, the speed of hardcore punk, and the black leather/studs of Judas Priest.

2.) Beginnings; when they first began rehearsing their first song *The Witching Hour*, there was no pre-conceived notion of rapid speeds. In one serendipitous moment, they just decided to play fast thereby creating the first thrash metal song. It all culminated in the drummer's use of a double-speed, galloping snare drum pattern for the first time (this would be one of *the* defining elements in thrash metal).

The Witching Hour
Venom

    - In addition, raw riffing on the guitar; low, gravelly roars from the vocalist "Cronos"; and a low budget, rough production quality with the instruments blurring into one another (adding a sense of grit to the sound) that carried an aggressive, menacing effect. In time, *The Witching Hour* became highly influential which led to many covers -- the most famous of which, was by the LA , Slayer (who was highly influenced by Venom).

3.) <u>Venom</u>: eventually became influential to scores of other bands who attempted to both emulate and outdo them in the thrash and occult lyrics/image departments. Some of these bands were: <u>Bulldozer</u> (Italy), <u>Sepultura</u> (Brazil), <u>Bathory</u> (Sweden), <u>Hellhammer/Celtic Frost</u> (Switzerland), and <u>Mayhem</u> (who introduced Norway to the world of black metal).

4.) <u>Debut Album</u>: *Welcome To Hell* (1981) – the album that introduced that thrash metal blueprint which led to the inspiration -- especially to underground bands in LA -- that "faster is better". In fact, it was through this album, that writer Martin Popoff believes, that, "…in their own hapless and stupid way (sic), they invented thrash, speed, and black metal". Their follow-up album of 1982 was entitled, *Black Metal* (where the term of "black metal" had originated).

C.) <u>Mercyful Fate</u>: another of the highly influential metal bands of the 1980's. Due to the powerful, thickly textured guitar riffing – and the dark, horror-laden theatrics of King Diamond, they paved the way for the development of death metal, black metal, and any other obscure dark-metal-derivative styles to come.

1.) <u>Personnel</u>: <u>King Diamond</u> (b. Kim Bendix Peterson, June 14, 1956, Copenhagen, DK): vocals; <u>Hank Sherman</u>: guitar ; <u>Michael Denner</u> (b. Nov. 5, 1958, DK): guitar; <u>Timi Hansen</u>: bass; and <u>Kim Ruzz</u>: drums.

- <u>Trademark Style</u>: huge, massive guitar riffs of the Hank Sherman/Michael Denner duo supporting the wide-ranged, extreme vocality of King Diamond. He pioneered the gravelly, sinister vocal style of death metal but complemented it high-registered, operatic shrieks that transcended Rob Halford's abilities. In other words, he rose and fell from high operatic falsettos to angst-driven, guttural growls.

- <u>Examples</u>: from their debut album *Melissa* (1983), *Curse Of The Pharaohs* illustrate the heavy riffing and *Into The Coven* illustrates King Diamond's extended vocal range.

2.) <u>King Diamond's Persona</u>: his shock/horror approach was influenced by attending a concert of Alice Cooper's *Welcome To My Nightmare Tour* in Copenhagen. He felt that Cooper's facial make-up transformed him into something "unreal" (which eventually, he would adopt in his own satanic-like manner). He [Diamond] shocked audiences by wearing thick, pasty facial make-up that made him look evil and demonic. He also used stage props to further his persona such as a microphone stand that was cross-shaped with human bone replicas.

- His occult fascination began with his previous band called Black Rose: it was meant as a vehicle of revolt against social constraints. He brought this shock-for-shock's-sake ethos to Mercyful Fate and although he adopted this evil, demonic persona, he did not ascribe to the Church of Satan In America (founded by the late Anton McVey). Instead, he used it strictly for shock value.

3.) <u>Debut Album</u>: *Melissa* (1983), immediately embraced by metal underground as a classic – first in Europe and later, in Los Angeles. It was originally distributed in Europe on Cees Wessel's *Roadrunner* label (out of The Netherlands). When Brian Slagel's *Megaforce* label was licensed to distribute the album in the US, it arrived at a point where there was no "one style" to classify the combination of power metal, heavy metal, and black metal (which together, would become known as thrash metal). In LA, this album was a favorite among ardent tape traders. It was the darkest, sinister album up to that point.

- Among the artists they would influence: Dave Mustaine & James Hetfield (of early Metallica), Motörhead, Venom, Diamond Head, and Slayer (among others). They would also become influential to the Scandinavian Black Metal bands to come.

4.) <u>Don't Break The Oath</u> (1984): their second album and landmark, proto black metal masterpiece as illustrated by a single [from this album], *A Dangerous Meeting*. Soon after this album's release the tension between King Diamond and the rest of the band reached a breaking point. Evidently, the band had negative feelings of King Diamond's constant use of evil/occult imagery and as a result, they broke up. King Diamond would go on and have a successful solo career of his own.

A Dangerous Meeting
Mercyful Fate

D.) <u>Bathory</u>: founded by lead vocalist, artistic visionary, and frontman, <u>Quarthon</u> (b. Tomas Börje Forsberg, Feb. 17, 1966, Hägersten, Stockholm, SWE, d. June 3, 2004, Hässelby, Stockholm, SWE).

1.) <u>Background</u>: they were for the most part, the work/vision of one man who dubbed himself <u>Quarthon</u>. They were from a small suburb in Sweden, which accounts for their obscurity and lack of initial widespread exposure. Artistically, they were more about a concept than skilled, convincing musicianship.

- <u>The Concept</u>: an obsession for everything relating to Satanism and the occult. This obsession bordered on the extreme with imageries such as inverted crosses, pentagrams, and the ubiquitous goat's head emblem. In the early 1990's they would become the godfathers of the second wave of black metal -- Scandinavian Black Metal.

2.) <u>Influences</u>: primary musical influences were punk and the NWOBHM bands. The initial influence which drove him to the occult imagery direction: Hammer horror movies. He would later, reach an influential awareness: when Quarthon first heard Venom in 1984 (about 3 months after Bathory's debut album release), he realized that there was a movement happening on the outside. This inspired him and his band to spread their tentacles.

- Musically, they became the embodiment of unskilled, amateurism in a punk-influenced, death metal format – the very antithesis highly skilled virtuosity. They represented ideas and concepts rather than skill and precision. Their style has been described as either heavy metal, black metal, or death metal. In fact, it was Quarthon who claimed to have originated the term "death metal" (Jeff Bacerra of the group Possessed, also laid claim to inventing the term).

Massacre
Bathory

3.) Following their first two albums: *Bathory* (1984) and *The Return* (1985), they released their most noted album, *Under the Sign Of The Black Mark* in 1987: a primitive, punkish, and unskilled aggressive sound suggestive of rank amateurism where Quarthon has a demonically constricted, gravel-like tone (reminiscent of an angry Beavis from MTV's "Beavis & Butthead" cartoon of he 1990's).

- In the end, it was occult imagery and mystique that mattered more than skill and in the eyes of some, Bathory was a sub-par copy of Venom. But in spite of their limitations, Bathory did become an important influence on the wave of extreme metal even though they had no radio airplay and no fanzine coverage. As a result, the wider world would not become aware of them until much later. But in Scandinavia, their influence (upon a new style of metal) would be quicker and more significant. Along with groups like Venom, Celtic Frost, and Possessed, Bathory would be influential to the advent of a new style known, as Norwegian Black Metal.

Equimanthorn
Bathory

E.) <u>Death Metal</u>: *the first wave* of heavy metal centered around the NWOBHM bands, *the second wave* was spearheaded (for the most part) by the west coast thrash metal bands. But by the time of the early 1990's, a metal musical vacuum appeared. Thrash metal kingpins such as Metallica were adopting less edgy sounds and in the process, went mainstream. As a result, there was a lack of an extreme approach to metal. There was however, a new underground emerging, which gave rise to a new sound proving that there was still a demographic hungry for all things extreme. The most extreme of which would Death Metal: *the third wave* in heavy metal's artistic evolution. <u>Definition</u>: a more extreme version of black metal where a higher degree of instrumental skill and rapid, lightning speeds are required -- the focusing on gore-driven and satanic lyrics are emphasized. <u>The genesis</u>: a combination of black metal and "grindcore".

1.) <u>Grindcore</u> is defined as a warp-speed derivative of "metalcore" (metal + hardcore punk) with a wall of distortion at ultimate blinding speeds. As a result, the guitar riffs sound like blurry wall of ferocity (as opposed to precision) with hammering, pulverizing snare drum blast beats – the vocals spew out growling, guttural indecipherable words. In addition, there is no conventional song structure but rather, a massive sonic onslaught (with song durations of 30 seconds or less).

Siege Of Power
Napalm Death

- <u>Napalm Death</u> (formed in 1982, Birmingham, ENG): the first grindcore band on record who raised the bar to new extremes of sonic, skull-splitting intensity. They disposed of all conventions including melody, clarity, and anything resembling mainstream likeability. Instead, they presented an extreme assault of distorted sonic fury where riffs were indiscernible and song durations were microscopically brief. They executed this distorted ferocity with a two-stringed guitar connected to a distortion box in front of a wall of amps. Their lyrics delivered extreme, political commentary.

- *Scum* (1987): their debut album that set the new, grindcore standard – it was released on the Earache label. There were 28 singles on the album whose durations ranged from 16 seconds (the briefest) to 2:38 (the longest). This album exuded extreme explosive energy and all out cacophony to the utmost extreme.

2.) <u>Death Metal's First Harbinger</u>: <u>Possessed</u> (formed in 1983, San Francisco, CA). Originally inspired by Slayer's *Show No Mercy* album of 1984. They were characterized with a raw, brutal approach that unveiled a gory/satanic obsession in their lyrics – they would be influential to scores of other like-minded [future Death Metal] bands to come.

- *Metal Massacre IV*: their first appearance on an album which led to their signing with Combat Records.

Death Metal
Possessed

- <u>Debut Album</u>: *Seven Churches* (1985): the album that anticipated the concept of death metal [for the first time] and in the process became the first death metal album proto-type. Lead vocalist/bassist <u>Jeff Becerra</u> introduced the practice of growling, guttural, and indecipherable lyrics that became a death metal trade-mark. With Slayer as their greatest influence, Possessed brought in a new level of absolute, thrash-driven brutality.

3.) <u>Tampa, FL</u>: Death Metal's first American scene to where scores of [death metal] bands throughout the US had gravitated. <u>Morrisound Studios</u>: owned by Scott Burns where he and his staff produced and engineered local death metal albums. Local Bands included <u>Death</u>, <u>Deicide</u>, <u>Morbid Angel</u>, <u>Obituary</u>, and <u>Hellwitch</u> (among others). Their style was technically demanding in terms of physical endurance mixed with surprisingly elevated artistic sensibilities that channeled their unholy, satanic spirit into instrumental proficiency.

Mutilation
Death

- <u>Death</u> (formed in 1983, Long Island, NY): took brutally aggressive speed metal and morbid lyrics into new, elevated depths at a time when Metallica and Slayer were progressing to decreased tempos and more subtlety. They pioneered the death metal style by which future bands such as Cannibal Corpse would earn their stripes (so to speak).

> * They were also acknowledged as the <u>first death metal band</u> and their vocalist/guitarist <u>Chuck Shuldiner</u> became death metal's founding father. For their debut album, *Scream Bloody Gore* (1987), he played every instrument except the drums and used Slayer's *Reign in Blood* album as a model. <u>Precedent</u>: advanced technical skill that increased significantly with each subsequent album.

Lunatic Of God's Creation
Deicide

- <u>Deicide</u> (formed in 1987): another of the significant bands from Tampa's death metal scene. Their main characteristic: taking their gory and satanic views to an exaggerated, diabolical extreme (as well as all other forms of blasphemy). They received severe criticism for their lyrics that favored the practice of animal sacrifice. The backlash was so intense, that during a concert in Stockholm, SWE, they were forced to abandon stage when a bomb was discovered underneath.

> * <u>Glen Benton</u> (bass/vocals): seemed to have practiced what he preached by branding an inverted cross on his forehead. Their debut album: *Deicide* (released on the Roadrunner label in 1990).

Vengeance Is Mine
Morbid Angel

- <u>Morbid Angel</u> (formed in 1984, Tampa, FL): another of the Tampa bands that stood in the line of succession to Slayer and Venom and took these influences to a new extreme level and made their own contributions to death metal's extreme development. <u>Trey Azagthoth</u> (b. George Emmanuel III, March 26, 1965): founder of Morbid Angel executed his lead guitar skills with complex tap fingerings, wailing sounds, and extensive use of the Wah-Wah pedal – he also experimented with synthesizers. His skills were symbolic of the technical demands that Tampa-based death metal had established.

> * <u>Debut Album</u>: *Altars Of Madness* (released on the Earache label in 1989) – a confident, menacing sound that exuded an elevated sense of skill thereby standardizing the higher skill level tradition in the death metal genre. In the early 90's, they signed with Giant Records and hired Metallica's producer Flemming Rasmussen to record their *Covenant* album of 1993.

4.) <u>New Wave Of Signings</u>: in the early 1990's, major labels were signing death metal bands giving testament to their growing influence beyond cloistered inner circles. Examples: <u>Cannibal Corpse</u> signed with Warner Bros.; <u>Sepultura</u> (from Brazil) signed with Epic Records (a subsidiary of CBS Records); <u>Carcass</u>, <u>Cathedral</u>, <u>Napalm Death</u>, and <u>The Entombed</u> (Sweden) signed with the Sony/Columbia conglomerate.

> - NOTE: the death metal scene in the US was not the only scene that became a product of black metal influences such Venom, Mercyful Fate, and Bathory. There was another scene brewing way up in the northern tundra of Scandinavia. It was known as Norwegian Black Metal.

F.) <u>Norwegian Black Metal (*NBM*)</u>: the transfer of the metal power from the sunny beach sides of Tampa, to the dark, cold winters of Scandinavia. It was there, that the speed and experimentation of the metal fringe would regroup with extreme, primal passion.

1.) <u>Definition</u>: the concoction of death metal into a simpler, more direct, and highly concentrated form – it was all about *feeling* (as opposed to instrumental virtuosity). Norwegian Black Metal (*NBM*) disposed of the chaotic, warp-speed onslaught on the senses (in many cases) and replaced it with slower tempos, orchestral angst synth-driven fugues, and choral arrangements. Although there are still rapid tempos being used, they were not as exclusive as they were in death metal. In a word, *NBM* had more flexibility. There will be three different examples of *NBM* artists: <u>Mayhem</u> (who established the *NBM* blueprint), <u>Emperor</u> (who opened up that blueprint to outside, eclectic influences), and <u>Immortal</u> (who standardized the *NBM* blueprint and maintained its tradition).

2.) <u>Mayhem</u> (formed in 1985): the godfathers of *NBM* and the first of the *NBM* bands to have a significant impact in their native country's underground scene. Perhaps no other band has been overshadowed by their notorious off-stage activities as them. Founded in 1985 by guitarist <u>Øystein "Euronymous" Aarseth</u>, they first achieved prominence in the underground, Norwegian scene.

Buried By Time And Dust
Mayhem

     - <u>Debut Album</u>: *Deathcrush* (1987) – mainly a death metal type of album but in time, they developed a more aggressive, violent form of metal that, once refined, would become known as Norwegian Black Metal.

     - <u>*De Mysteriis Dom Sathanas*</u> (1993): regarded as one of the most influential *NBM* albums of all time. The music is high-octaned speed and furious with unintelligible vocal line that can churn one's stomach. This album, released after Euronymous' death, is their most readily available album in the US.

     - <u>Tragedies</u>: there were two deaths of band members: in 1991, lead vocalist <u>Per Yngve</u> (a.k.a. "Death"), committed suicide by repeatedly slitting his wrists and firing a shotgun to his head and bassist <u>Varg Vikernes</u> – who had been setting church fires (some say as a publicity stunt), murdered Euronymous by stabbing him 23 times. Vikernes, who is still serving time in prison, has since adopted the white supremacist philosophy and is currently doing a one-man synthesizer project (on a prison-approved synthesizer) called <u>Burzum</u>.

3.) <u>Emperor</u> (formed in 1992, Notodden, Norway): founded by guitarist/bassist <u>Ihsahn</u> (b. Vegard Sverre Tveitan, Oct. 10, 1975) and guitarist/drummer <u>Samoth</u> (b. Tomas Thromdosæter Haugen, June 9,1974). Unlike Mayhem, whose notorious "extracurricular" activities drew more attention than their music, Emperor was just the opposite. Their approach to *NBM* would achieve critical acclaim due to their creative innovations that set a new standard to the genre. If Mayhem established an anti-social ethos to *NBM*, Emperor's eclecticism provided a new level of artistry.

     - <u>Eclecticism</u>: in addition to maintaining satanic/occultist credentials and the use of rapid speeds (basic to black metal), Emperor employed slower/moderate tempos, elements of Norwegian folk music, and the use of synthesizers thereby opening up [*NBM*] to outside, eclectic sources. In regard to their lyrics, they added nostalgic Viking imagery and pagan worship of nature -- both an indelible part of Norway's pre-Christian era.

The Burning Shadows Of Silence
Emperor

     - <u>Debut Album</u>: *In The Nightside Eclipse* (1994): the quintessential album that expanded *NBM's* artistic and emotional range. It was here that – in addition to their black metal ferocity -- a new eclectic approach was unveiled with dark, depressing moodiness, Viking/pagan imagery, and ominous synthesizer arrangements. They recorded it in the Memorial Hall of Edvard Grieg which gave the recording a grander, larger-than-life sound.

- <u>Criminality</u>: like Mayhem, Emperor's members would have their own run-ins with the law -- drummer <u>Faust</u> (b. Bård G. Eithun, Apr. 21, 1974), who was found guilty and imprisoned for murder; <u>Samoth</u> was convicted of church arson; and <u>Tchort</u> (b. Terje Vik Schei, June, 1974), tried on assault charges. But unlike Mayhem, they miraculously bounced back, regrouped, and in the process, reestablished their careers and artistic credentials.

4.) <u>Immortal</u> (formed in 1989, Bergen, Norway): the consummate *NBM* band that standardized the genre's trademarks as opposed to expanding its horizons (as Emperor did). They added mystique by using only their pseudonyms and painting their faces in "Kiss" makeup (white base with black touches) giving themselves a deathly, evil, corpse-like visage. Founded by guitarist/vocalist <u>Demonaz Doom Occulta</u> (b. Harald Nævdal, July 6. 1970) and guitarist/vocalist/bassist <u>Abbath Doom Occulta</u> (b. Olve Eikemo, Sept. 13, 1973) – the latter formerly of the band, Old Funeral (featuring former Mayhem member and future jailbird Varg Vikernas).

- <u>Blashyrkh</u>: their fictional Nordic kingdom, from where demonic entities and apocalyptic Viking battles would emanate. Their first notable album: *Pure Holocaust* (1993). This album was key to the maintenance of tradition, artistic integrity, and advanced skill of *NBM* especially with an emphasis on Viking/Nordic subject matter.

5.) <u>A Word On Church Arsons</u>: the rise of the *NBM* scene paralleled with the 1,000[th] anniversary of Christianity's forced arrival in Norway. Two pagan kings – <u>Olaf I Tryggvason</u> (ca 995 AD) and <u>Olaf II Haraldsson</u> (ca 1015 AD) – violently imposed Christianity upon Norway's coastal region and in the process, expedited the Viking era's demise along with their pagan/natured traditional worship.

- In protest, fanatical *NBM* followers launched their own campaign of religious destruction. They burnt down historic churches that were built during the Olaf I/Olaf II era. In other words, they were out to destroy the symbols – the actual historical embodiments – of an era that, in their view, brutally suppressed Viking culture. The [*NBM* follower's] crusade: a restoration of Viking tradition and pagan/nature worship as the mainstream religion of Norway.

- <u>Fantoftkirke</u>: a 12th century wooden church with carved, spiraling, mystical staves pointing upward toward the heavens. During the pre-dawn hours of June 6, 1992, this historic site was burnt to the ground -- the first such arson case. Other churches that were also destroyed included: <u>Ullandhaug Bedehaus Church</u>, <u>Hauketo og Prinsdal Church</u>, <u>Holmenkollen Chapel</u>, and <u>Skjold Church</u>. Each of them were of extreme historical, and antiquity value that dated from the aforesaid historical era, previously mentioned.

CHAPTER XV: REVIEW

1.) Name at least five episodes that played a significant role in destroying the defining pacifist ideals of the Love Generation.

      1.)

      2.)

      3.)

      4.)

      5.)

      With the demise of a disillusioned Love Generation in the early 1970's, a vacuum was set in place. What was needed to fill in this vacuum? (In other words, what was here a need for?)

2.) Who laid down the model of what would become known as heavy metal?

      As opposed to technical virtuosity, what was the focused primary element that they introduced? (It would become a hallmark of the heavy metal genre.)

      What rock 'n' roll tradition did they continue to write in albeit, in a darker, gloomy, macabre manner?

3.) Name the four original members of Black Sabbath.

4.) Name three of Tony Iommi's blues revisionist influences:

      1.)

      2.)

      3.)

      Why was the Belgian guitarist, Django Reinhardt, an inspirational influence on Tony Iommi?

5.) In Tony Iommi's view, what was Black Sabbath's new musical direction (instead of conventional blues) that he introduced?

6.) Name their debut album of 1970.

      What was geezer Butler's lyrics influence for this album?

7.) Name their breakthrough album.

      What single from this album was a protest song against the death and destruction of the Vietnam war?

8.) In the *Master Of Reality* album of 1971, how did Tony Iommi achieve a heavier, thicker, fuzz-tone type of sound that became his trademark?

      Why did he use this technique?

      Name a song from this album that featured an apocalyptic sense of foeboding.

9.) What were the four separate elements of hard rock that would come together to complete the heavy metal puzzle? Also, name the artist associated with each element.

     1.)

          - Artist:

     2.)

          - Artist:

     3.)

          - Artist:

     4.)

          - Artist:

10.) Which band from Birmingham, standardized the heavy metal model in terms of both musically and visually? (In other words, who was the first to combine all of the hard rock elements together?)

    What new musical movement did they usher in?

    What was their basic formula in regard to the following elements?
        1.) Guitar Approach:
        2.) Vocal Approach:
        3.) Lyrics (Subject Matter):
        4.) Guitar Solo Approach:

    List the musical influences of the following artists:
        1.) K.K. Downing:
        2.) Ian Hill:
        3.) Rob Halford:

11.) Name Judas Priest's breakthrough album of 1976 where their main musical entities were established.

    What type of defining fashion statement did they usher into heavy metal that many other [heavy metal] artists would emulate? Also, name the 1978 album that ushered it in.

    Name their 1980 album where they truly honed in their heavy metal blueprint that others would emulate.

    Name the 1982 album that transformed them into international icons.

12.) If Judas Priest established the heavy metal model as a genre in and of itself, who solidified it as a standard trademark by which all heavy metal bands hereafter, would be compared?

    Which heavy metal elements (established by Judas Priest) did they [Iron Maiden] adopt in terms of the following:
        1.) Guitar Approach:
        2.) Lyrics (subject matter):
        3.) Lead Guitar Solos:
        4.) Vocal Approach:

13.) Who was the first to coin the term, "New Wave Of British Heavy Metal" (NWOBHM)? What magazine did he write for?

14.) For their debut album, *Iron Maiden* (1980), there were two main influences:
    1.) The simple, direct, rapid tempo'd influence of _____.

2.) The more advanced influences that suggest _____.

Result: their style was more advanced than _____ but more streamlined than _____.

15.) Which 1981 Iron Maiden album showed the unification of influences alchemized into an all-riff, original sound? (It also introduced what would be, the long, twin-guitar collaboration of Dave Murray and Adrian Smith.)

16.) Name the album that marked the debut of lead singer Bruce Dickinson which completed Iron Maiden's classic line-up. It also transformed them into international icons.

How did Bruce Dickinson's vocal style differ from his predecessor, Paul Di'Anno (that was reminiscent of the Rob Halford model)?

17.) Name Saxon's breakthrough album of 1980.

What trademarks of the NWOBHM were in this album in regard to the following?
1.) Guitar Approach:
2.) Vocal Approach:
3.) Drumming Approach:

What sort of look (reminiscent of NWOBHM established by Judas Priest) did they adopt?

18.) Along with their outlaw, biker-trash image, what were several aspects that Motörhead added into heavy metal?

A year before punk officially began, they were already mixing metal and _____.

What would this combination eventually become influential to?

19.) List the members of Motörhead's "classic" line-up.

20.) With which group did Lemmy first began playing bass?

Which single [with this group] marked his first experience at being a lead vocalist?

What was the last song he wrote for this band?

21.) What type of band did Lemmy have in mind when he first started Motörhead? (Hint: the band in question were underground heroes at the time due to their fast, harsh, aggressive guitar sound.)

Who were two other additional influences?
1.)
2.)

In his view, they [Motörhead] were nothing but a blues band with a unique approach. What was that unique approach that set them apart from the rest? (Hint: it had to do with tempo.)

22.) With the album *Overkill* (1979), what type of reputation did their songs further cement?

23.) What was Motörhead's 1980 breakthrough album? It was also their official American debut.

What type of reputation did this album seal?

What type of image did this album build up?

What type of motifs and metaphors were used?

What was impact of this album in terms of their American audience? (In other words, how did this album transform their notoriety in America?)

24.) With regard to Motörhead's relation to punk, which punk band did Lemmy jam alongside with?

In the 1980's, to which punk scene did Motörhead cross over? (Name the city.)

25.) What practice familiarized the metal underground people of San Francisco and LA, with the NWOBHM bands? (In other words, what did they trade?)

Name Brian Slagel's fanzine.

Name Brian Slagel's independent record label.

26.) Who were the first purveyors of the thrash metal "house style"?

Name their debut single.

Which 1982 compilation album did this single appear on?

27. According to Dave Mustaine, who was Metallica's primary influence?

Name four additional influences:
        1.)
        2.)
        3.)
        4.)

28.) Name the 1982 demo tape by Metallica that changed the rules of heavy metal.

To those who first heard this seminal demo tape, what did they notice? (Hint: it set them apart from the Motörhead model.)

29.) What was the first "thrash" song and the band who recorded it?

30.) What were the three elements of rapid tempo'd thrash metal?
        1.)
        2.)
        3.)

31.) Name three of Venom's heavy metal influences.
        1.)
        2.)
        3.)

32.) Name Metallica's debut album of 1983.

        Because it was executed at a higher skill level, what three new standards did it [their debut album] set for the west coast heavy metal ethos?
                1.)
                2.)
                3.)

33.) Which 1984 album marked the progression of Metallica to a more mature level of songwriting craftsmanship? It also set the tone for their remaining albums in terms of artistry.

        Who was the producer for this album?

        Continuing in the tradition of the NWOBHM, what constituted Metallica's lyric content?

                List three song examples:
                        1.)
                        2.)
                        3.)

        How did this album set a new standard in relation to the NWOBHM?

34.) If *Ride The Lightning* set the new standard, which 1984 album solidified the new standard of the west coast thrash metal "house style"? (It would be emulated by many others.)

35.) Name the band that Dave Mustaine formed in the wake of his dismissal form Metallica.

        Musically, what would Mustaine add to the high-speed, thrash metal model of his former band? There were three things:
                1.)
                2.)
                3.)

36.) What were the two specific early influences for Dave Mustaine?
        1.)
        2.)

37.) What became the hallmark of Megadeth's sound? It was due to the jazz backgrounds of guitarist Chris Poland and drummer Gar Samuelson.

38.) What was Megadeth's debut album of 1985 that marked the beginning where lightning speed technically skilled chops had combined?

What was their first album released on a major record label?

39.) If Metallica was about precision, and Megadeth was about instrumental virtuosity, what was [the band] Slayer all about?

40.) Who were Kerry King's early influences and why was Iron Maiden so influential?

What was Jeff Hanneman's main influence in regard to rapid speed?

What was Slayer's resulting style?

41.) What specific influence marked the turning point for Slayer with nasty speeds and satanic lyrics?

What three elements did this specific influence tie together with the following Slayer members?
1.) Kerry King:
2.) Jeff Hanneman:
3.) Dave Lombardo:

42.) Name Slayer's debut recording and the compilation album in which it appeared.

43.) In 1983, Slayer united two types of fans in one show. Who were the two fan types?
1.)
2.)

44.) What was Slayer's debut album of 1983 on Brian Slagel's *Metal Blade* label?

What two elements were synthesized [in this album]?
1.)
2.)

Name three specific influences for this album:
1.)
2.)
3.)

45.) Which Slayer album of 1986 brought the concept of thrash metal to the extreme?

Name the label that recorded this album:

Name the album's producer:

How did this album's produced sound compare to their previous releases on the *Metal Blade* label?

What was this album's lyric content?

What was the first truly "gore metal" single?

46.) What new genre would [the band] Slayer be one of the first anticipators and inspirations for? (Hint: it would be the next new wave of heavy metal.)

47.) What is definition of Black Metal?

48.) There were 3 black metal bands who were most influential to both the LA thrash metal scene and the second wave of black metal known as Scandinavian Black Metal. Who were they?
    1.)
    2.)
    3.)

49.) Who were the undisputed innovators of thrash metal and progenitors of the power, black, and death metal aesthetics?

    Who were some of the bands that Venom were influential to? They would try to emulate and outdo them [Venom] in thrash and occult lyrics/image departments. Name five of them:
        1.)
        2.)
        3.)
        4.)
        5.)

50.) There were two elements of Mercyful Fate that made them highly influential to metal bands of the 1980's. What were they?
    1.)
    2.)

    What types of metal did they pave the way for?

51.) What was Mercyful Fate's trademark style?

    What were the 2 components of King Diamond's voice? (Hint: one of them had to do with the Rob Halford component.)

52.) Who influenced King Diamond's shock/horror approach?

    Why did he use an occult approach? In other words, what was his occult approach meant as a vehicle of?

53.) Name Mercyful Fate's debut album of 1983.

54.) Name at least 6 metal artists that Mercyful Fate would be influential to:
    1.)
    2.)
    3.)
    4.)
    5.)
    6.)

What type of Scandinavian would they be influential to?

55.) Name Mercyful Fate's second album which was a landmark, proto black metal masterpiece.

56.) Who founded the Swedish group, Bathory? (use stage name.)

Artistically, they were more about a concept (rather than skilled musicianship). What was that concept?

What new type of metal would Bathory become the godfathers of?

57.) What were Bathory's primary musical influences?

What initial influence drove Quarthon to the occult imagery direction?

58.) What was Bathory's most noted album of 1987?

59.) What is the definition of Death Metal?

What was the genesis of death metal? It was a combination of two things:
1.)
2.)

60.) Describe Grindcore.

61.) Who was the first grindcore band?

This band disposed of all conventions. What were those conventions?

Instead, what did they present?

Name their debut album of 1987.

62.) Who was death metal's first harbinger?

What Slayer album originally inspired them?

How were they characterized?

From their debut album *Seven Churches* (1985), what type vocal practice did Jeff Becerra introduce that would become a death metal [vocal] trademark?

63.) Where was death metal's first American scene?

Name the studio and it's owner who produced local death metal albums.

Name at least 5 local death metal bands [from this scene]:
1.)
2.)
3.)
4.)
5.)

How would describe the style of these bands? In other words, at what level was their technical skill?

64.) Who was acknowledged as the first death metal band?

Who was death metal's founding father?

What was this band's precedent?

65.) What was Deicide's main characteristic?

66.) Who was Morbid Angel's founder and lead guitarist?

List some of the elements of his guitar skills:

What other instrument did he experiment with?

67.) The death metal scene [in the US] was not the only scene that was a product of black metal influences such as Venom, Mercyful Fate, and Bathory. There was another scene brewing. What was it?

68.) What is the definition of Norwegian Black metal?

As opposed to instrumental virtuosity, what was *NBM* (Norwegian Black Metal) all about?

What did *NBM* replace the chaotic, warp-speed onslaught with?

In a word, what did *NBM* have that death metal did not?

69.) What was the significance of the following three *NBM* groups?
1.) Mayhem:
2.) Emperor:
3.) Immortal:

70.) Who were the godfathers of *NBM* and the first of the *NBM* bands to have a significant impact in their native country's underground scene?

Which 1983 album is regarded as one of the most influential *NBM* albums of all time?

71.) Unlike Mayhem, whose notorious "extracurricular" activities drew more attention than their music, Emperor was just the opposite. How did they [Emperor] set a new standard to the *NBM* genre? If Mayhem established the anti-social ethos of *NBM*, what did Emperor provide as a new level of artistry?

        What were some of the elements they employed that opened up *NBM* to eclectic, outside sources? There were three things:
            1.)
            2.)
            3.)

72.) Who was the band that standardized the *NBM* genre's trademarks as opposed to expanding it's horizons (as Emperor did)?

        How did they add mystique?

        What was the name of their fictional Nordic kingdom where demonic entities and Viking battles would emanate?

73.) Why did fanatical NBM followers launch their own campaigns of religious destruction (by burning 10th century churches)? What were they protesting?

Discography

CHAPTER I: ROCK 'n' ROLL'S FIRST GOLDEN AGE

<u>Frank Sinatra</u>. *Songs For Swingin' Lovers!* Capitol 72434 96226 2 3: 1998.
    "I've Got You Under My Skin"

Roots n' Blues: The Respective 1925-1950. Sony C4K 47911: 1992.
    "Dixie Cannonball" – <u>Gene Autry</u>

<u>Louis Jordan</u>. *The Best of Louis Jordan: The Millennium Collection*. MCA 088 112 065-2: 1989.
    "Saturday Night Fish Fry"

<u>Fats Domino</u>. *My Blue Heaven: The Best of Fats Domino, Volume 1*. EMI CDP-7-92808-2: 1990.
    "The Fat Man"
    "Ain't That A Shame"
    "Blueberry Hill"
    "I'm Walkin' "

<u>Little Richard</u>. *Little Richard: The Greatest Hits 16*. Bescal CD-31: 1986.
    "Good Golly Miss Molly"
    "Tutti Frutti"
    "Lucille"

The Sun Records Collection. Rhino R2 71780: 1994.
    Disk 1: "Rocket 88" – <u>Jackie Brensten and His Delta Cats</u>
             "Moanin' At Midnight" – <u>The Howlin' Wolf</u>
             "Mystery Train" – <u>Little Junior's Blue Flames</u>
    Disk 2: "Blue Suede Shoes" – <u>Carl Perkins</u>
             "Dixie Fried" – <u>Carl Perkins</u>
    Disk 3: "Matchbox" – Carl Perkins
             "Crazy Arms"– <u>Jerry Lee Lewis</u>
             "Whole Lot Of Shakin' Going On" – <u>Jerry lee Lewis</u>
             "Great Balls of Fire" – <u>Jerry Lee Lewis</u>
             "High School Confidential" – <u>Jerry Lee Lewis</u>

<u>Bill Monroe</u>. *Blue Moon Of Kentucky*. Sony Music Special Products, A 16652: 1993.
    "Blue Moon Of Kentucky"

<u>Elvis Presley</u>. *Elvis, The King of Rock n' Roll: The Complete 50's Masters*. BMG/RCA 07863 66050-2: 1992.
    Disk 1: "Harbor Lights"
             "My Happiness"
             "That's Alright"
             "I Love You Because"
             "Blue Moon Of Kentucky"
             "Mystery Train"
             "Baby Let's Play House"
             "Good Rockin' Tonight"
    Disk 2: "I Want You, I Need You, I Love You"
             "Don't Be Cruel"

Chess Blues. MCA CHD4-9340: 1992.
    Disk 3: "Got My Mojo Working" – <u>Muddy Waters</u>

John Lee Hooker. *John Lee Hooker: The Definitive Collection*. HIP-O/UM 80006127-02: 2000.
    "Boogie Chillen"
    "Walkin' The Boogie (Alternate Take)"

Bo Diddley. *Bo Diddley The Chess Box*. CHESS/MCA Records CHD2-19502: 1990.
    "Bo Diddley"
    "Pretty Thing"
    "Say Man"

Chuck Berry. *The Best of Chuck Berry: The Millennium Collection*. MCA MACD-11944: 1989.
    "Maybelline"
    "School Day"
    "Johnny B. Goode"

20 Super Hits: At The Hop. 50's Rock-n-Roll. Volume One. Dominion 3701-3: 1997.
    "Tiger" – Fabian

CHAPTER II: 1958 TO FEBRUARY 7, 1964

20 Super Hits: Tell It Like It Is – 60's Soul. Dominion 3735-3: 1997.
    "Baby Workout" – Jackie Wilson

Sam Cooke. The Best Of Sam Cooke. BMG/RCA 3863-2-R: 1988.
    "Wonderful World"

20 Super Hits: Tossin' & Turnin' – 60's Rock-n-Roll. Dominion 3711-3: 1997.
    "Goin' Out Of My Head" – Little Anthony & The Imperials
    "Remember (Walkin' In The Sand)" – The Shangri-Las

The Ultimate History of Rock n' Roll Collection: Chapter Five – Girl Group Sound. Dominion 3805-2: 1997.
    "Then He Kissed Me" – The Crystals
    "Will You Love Me Tomorrow" – The Shirelles
    "Leader of The Pack" – The Shangri-Las
    "Chapel of Love" – The Dixie Cups
    "He's So Fine" – The Chiffons

Blues Masters: The Essential Blues Collection – Volume3: Texas Blues. Rhino Records R2 71123: 1992.
    "Hound Dog" – Willie Mae "Big Mama" Thornton

The Isley Brothers. *Isley Brothers 60's Greatest Hits and Rare Classics*. Motown Records 3746354832: 1991.
    "Twist & Shout"

20 Super Hits: At The Hop. 50's Rock-n-Roll. Volume One. Dominion 3701-3: 1997.
    "Kansas City" – Wilbert Harrison

The Coasters. *The Very Best Of The Coasters*. Atlantic/Rhino R2 71597: 1994.
    "Smokey Joe's Café"
    "Searchin' "
    "Young Blood"
    "Yakety Yak"
    "Along Came Jones"

Ben E. King. *The Very Best of Ben E. King*. Rhino R2 72970: 1998.
    "There Goes My Baby"
    "This Magic Moment"
    "Spanish Harlem"
    "Stand By Me"

Listen: Fourth Brief Edition – Joseph Kerman. Worth Publishers & Sony Music A6B 26259: 1995.
    Disk 4: "Prelude: Tristan und Isolde" – Richard Wagner

Phil Spector. *Back To Mono (1958-1969)*. Phil Spector Records/Abkco 7118-2: 1991.
    Disk 1:   "To Know Him Is to Love Him" – The Teddy Bears
           "Corrine, Corrina" – Ray Peterson
           "I Know How You Love Me" – The Paris Sisters
           "He's A Rebel" – The Crystals
           "Da Doo Ron Ron" – The Crystals

The Ronettes. *The Best of The Ronettes: Phil Spector Hits*. ABKCO/Phil Spector Records 72122: 1992.
    "Be My Baby"

The Righteous Brothers. *The Very Best Of The Righteous Brothers: Unchained Melody*. Polygram P2-47248: 1990.
    "You've Lost That Lovin' Feelin' "
    "(You're My) Soul and Inspiration"

Dick Dale. *King Of The Surf Guitar: The Best of Dick Dale & His Del-Tones*. Rhino R2 75756: 1989.
    "Misirlou"
    "The Wedge"

The Four Freshmen. *The Four Freshmen Greatest Hits: All Original Recordings*. Curb Records D2-77612: 1993.
    "Day by Day"
    "Charmaine"

The Beach Boys. *The Beach Boys: Endless Summer*. Capitol CDP 746467 2: 1974.
    "Surfer Girl"
    "Surfin' USA"
    "In My Room"
    "Don't Worry Baby"

CHAPTER III: THE BIG SPREAD – BOB DYLAN AND THE BEATLES

Country Legends: The Bristol Sessions – Volume 1. BMG Heritage 07863 65131 2: 2002.
    "Single Girl, Married Girl" – The Carter Family

Woody Guthrie. *Woody Guthrie Sings Folk Songs with Leadbelly, Cisco Houston, Sonny Terry, Bess Hawes*. Smithsonian/Folkways SF CD 40007. 1989.
    "Oregon Trail"
    "Dirty Overhalls"
    "The Boll Weevil"

Bob Dylan. *Bob Dylan*. CBS Records CK 94239: 1962/Sony BMG: 2005.
    "Talkin' New York"
    "Song To Woody"

Peter, Paul, & Mary. *The Best of Peter, Paul, & Mary: (Ten) Years Together*. Warner Bros. 3105-2: 1970.
        "Blowin' In The Wind"
        "If I Had A Hammer (The Hammer Song)"

The Byrds. *The Byrds: The Original Singles 1965-1967*. CBS Records CK 37335: 1980.
        "Mr. Tambourine Man"

Bob Dylan. *Highway 61 Revisited*. CBS Records CK 1989: 1965.
        "Just Like Tom Thumb's Blues"

Bob Dylan. *Bob Dylan's Greatest Hits*. CBS Records CK 9463: 1967.
        "Blowin' In The Wind"
        "The Times They Are A-Changin' "
        "Like A Rolling Stone"
        "Mr. Tambourine Man"
        "Subterranean Homesick Blues"

Bob Dylan. *Bob Dylan Live 1966: The Bootleg Series Volume 4 – The "Royal Albert Hall" Concert*. CBS C2K 65759: 1998
        Disk 2:   "Just Like Tom Thumb's Blues"
                "Like A Rolling Stone"

Lonnie Donegan. "Does Your Chewing Gum Loose Its Flavor"?

The Beatles. *The Beatles Anthology: Volume 1*. Apple/Capitol CDP 7243 8 34445 2 6: 1995.
        Disk 1:   "My Bonnie" (Tony Sheridan, vocals)
                "Love Me Do"
                "Please, Please Me"
                "From Me To You"
        Disk 2:   "She Loves You"
                 "I Wanna Hold Your Hand"
                "A Hard Days Night"

The Everly Brothers. *The Everly Brothers: 15 Classic Hits From The Early Days Of Rock 'n' Roll*. The Essential Artist Collection, Rhino Records OPCD-8190M: 2007.
        "Wake Up Little Susie"

The Beatles. *Help!*. EMI/Capitol CDP 46439 2: 1965.
        "Help!"
        "You've Got To Hide Your Love Away"
        "Ticket To Ride"
        "Yesterday"

The Beatles. *Rubber Soul*. EMI/Capitol CDP 7 46440 2: 1965.
        "Norwegian Wood (This Bird Has Flown)"
        "The Word"
        "I'm Looking Through You"
        "Run For Your Life"

The Beatles. *Revolver*. EMI/Capitol CDP 7 46441 2: 1966.
        "Taxman"
        "Eleanor Rigby"
        "I'm Only Sleeping"
        "Love You To"
        "Doctor Robert"
        "Tomorrow Never Knows"

CHAPTER IV : A TALE OF TWO AND A HALF CITIES

ADZIDO Pan African Dance Ensemble. *Traditional Songs and Dances from Africa.* ARC Music Productions EUCD 1415: 1997.
      IVORY COAST: "Tematei/Zaouli"
      BOTSWANA: "Setapa"
      UGANDA: "Bakisimba/Nankasa"

Georgia Sea Island Songs. New World Records 80278-2 DIDX 01172: 1977.
      "Kneebone" – Joe Armstrong, leader with Group A
      "Read 'Em, John" – John Davis, leader with Group A
      "Beulah Land" – John Davis, leader with Group C

Classic African American Gospel from Smithsonian Folkways. Smithsonian Folkways Recordings SFW CD 40194, 2008.
      "Oh Lord, I'm So Glad I Got Good Religion" – Starlight Gospel Singers
      "I Heard The Voice of Jesus Say" – Bishop Bowen and the Combined Gospel Choirs

Ray Charles. *The Best of Ray Charles: The Atlantic Years.* Atlantic/Rhino R2 711722: 1994.
      "I've Got A Woman"
      "Hallelujah I Love Her So"
      "Swanee River Rock (Talkin' 'Bout That River)"

Sam Cooke. *The Best of Sam Cooke.* BMG/RCA 3863-2-R: 1988.
      "You Send Me"

A Tribute to Berry Gordy: The Music, The Magic, The Memories of Motown. Motown Records 31453-0436-2: 1995.
      "Lonely Teardrops" – Jackie Wilson
      "Money (That's What I Want)" – Barrett Strong

Motown Legends: Volume II. Motown/Polygram Special Markets 314 520 283-2: 1994.
      "Please Mr. Postman" – The Marvelettes

The Temptations. *The Temptations: The Ultimate Collection.* Motown Records 31453-0562-2: 1997.
      "The Way You Do The Things You Do"
      "Ain't Too Proud To Beg"

Motown Legends: Volume 1. Motown/Excelsior 440 060 1186: 1994.
      "Shop Around" – Smokey Robinson & The Miracles
      "My Guy" – Mary Wells
      "Come See About Me" – Diana Ross & The Supremes
      "You Keep Me Hangin' On" - Diana Ross & The Supremes
      "Ain't That Peculiar" – Marvin Gaye

The Jackson 5. *Jackson 5: The Ultimate Collection.* Motown Records 314530558-2: 1996.
      "I Want You Back"
      "ABC"

60's Soul: Try A Little Tenderness. Flashback/Rhino R2 72657: 1997.
      "Green Onions" – Booker T. & The MG's
      "Hold On! I'm Comin' " – Sam & Dave
      "In The Midnight Hour" - Wilson Pickett

Otis Redding. *The Ultimate Otis Redding*. Warner Special Products 9-27608-2: 1986.
  "These Arms Of Mine"
  "Try A Little Tenderness"   (3:48)

20 Super Hits: Tell It Like It Is – 60's Soul. Dominion 3735-3: 1997.
  "When A Man Loves A Woman" – Percy Sledge

Arthur Alexander. *The Ultimate Arthur Alexander*. Razor & Tie RE 2014: 1993.
  "You Better Move On"

Wilson Pickett. *The Very Best of Wilson Pickett*. Rhino R2 71212: 1993.
  "Land Of 1000 Dances"
  "Mustang Sally"

Aretha Franklin. *The Very Best of Aretha Franklin: The 60's*. Atlantic/ Rhino R2 71598: 1994.
  "I Never Loved A Man (The Way I Love You)"
  "Do Right Woman – Do Right Man"

James Brown. *20 All Time Greatest Hits*. Polydor 314 511 326-2: 1991.
  "Say It Loud (I'm Black And I'm Proud)"

Al Green. *Call Me*. Hi Records/The Right Stuff 7243-8-28538-2-4: 1994.
  "Here I Am (Come And Take Me)"
  "You Ought To Be With Me"

CHAPTER V: BRITISH BLUES REVISIONISM

Roots N' Blues: The Retrospective. Columbia/Legacy C4K 47911: 1992.
  Disk 1: "Empty Bed Blues" – Elizabeth Johnson
  Disk 2: "Jersey Hill Blues" – Charlie Patton

Son House. *Martin Scorsese Presents The Blues: Son House*. Columbia/Legacy CK 90485: 2003.
  "My Black Mama, Part 1"

Robert Johnson. *Cross Road Blues*. New Sound 2000 PVCD 711:1997.
  "Cross Road Blues"

Chess Blues. MCA/Chess CHD4-9340: 1992.
  Disk 1 "I Can't Be Satisfied" – Muddy Waters
     "I Feel Like Going Home" – Muddy Waters
  Disk 3: "Smokestack Lightnin' " – Howlin' Wolf
     "29 Ways" – Willie Dixon
     "Keep It To Yourself" – Sonny Boy Williamson
     "So Many Roads, So Many Trains" – Otis Rush
  Disk 4: "First Time I Met the Blues" – Buddy Guy

Elmore James & John Brim. *Whose Muddy Shoes*. MCA CHD-9114: 1991.
  "The Sun Is Shining" – Elmore James
  "Tool Bag Boogie" – Elmore James

Blues Masters: The Essential Blues Collection – Volume 2: Postwar Chicago Blues. Rhino R2 71122: 1992.
  "Bright Lights Big City" – Jimmy Reed

The Best of The Blues: Original Artists. Excelsior EXB 2-2068: 1997.
    "Boom Boom" – <u>John Lee Hooker</u>

<u>The Animals</u>. *The Animals: Original Hits.* Disky BA 860072: 1995.
    "The House of The Rising Sun"
    "Boom Boom"

<u>Eric Clapton</u>. *Eric Clapton Crossroads.* Polydor 835 268-2: 1988.
    Disk 1: "Boom Boom" – <u>The Yardbirds</u>
             "For Your Love" – <u>The Yardbirds</u>
             "Got To Hurry" – <u>The Yardbirds</u>
             "Have You Ever Loved A Woman" – <u>John Mayall's Bluesbreakers</u>
             "Strange Brew" – <u>The Cream</u>
    Disk 2: "Crossroads" – <u>The Cream</u>

Blues Masters: The Essential Blues Collection – Volume3: Texas Blues. Rhino Records R2 71123: 1992.
    "The Stumble" – <u>Freddy King</u>

<u>Woody Guthrie</u>. *Woody Guthrie Sings Folk Songs with Leadbelly, Cisco Houston, Sonny Terry, Bess Hawes.* Smithsonian/Folkways SF CD 40007. 1989.
    "The Rising Sun Blues"

<u>Bob Dylan</u>. *Bob Dylan.* CBS Records CK 94239: 1962/Sony BMG: 2005.
    "House Of The Rising Sun"

<u>The Rolling Stones</u>. *Forty Licks.* ABKCO/Virgin 724381 337820: 2002.
    Disk 1: "(I Can't Get No) Satisfaction"
             "The Last Time"
             "Not Fade Away"
             "It's All Over Now"

<u>The Rolling Stones</u>. *Aftermath.* ABKCO 74762: 1986.
    "Paint It Black"
    "Under My Thumb"

<u>The Rolling Stones</u>. *Beggars Banquet.* ABKCO 75392: 1986.
    "No Expectations"
    "Street Fighting Man"

<u>The Rolling Stones</u>. *Let It Bleed.* ABKCO NCD 4 80042: 1986.
    "Country Honk"
    "Live With Me"

<u>The Rolling Stones</u>. *Sticky Fingers.* Virgin Records 7243-8-39525-2-6: 1971.
    "Sway"
    "Can't You Hear Me Knocking"

<u>The Rolling Stones</u>. *Exile On Main Street.* Virgin Records 7243-6-39524-2-7: 1972.
    "Torn And Frayed"
    "Stop Breaking Down"

<u>The Yardbirds</u>. *Roger The Engineer.* Warner Bros. 9 45734-2: 1998.
    "Lost Woman"
    "The Nazz Are Blue"

Albert King. *Blues Masters: The Essential Blues Collection – The Very Best of Albert King.* Rhino R2 75703: 1999.
    "Answer To The Laundromat Blues"

Jimi Hendrix. *The Jimi Hendrix Experience: Are You Experienced.* MCA MCAD-11602: 1997.
    "Manic Depression"
    "Fire"
Led Zeppelin. *Led Zeppelin II.* Atlantic 82633-2: 1994.
    "Whole Lotta Love"
    "Heartbreaker"

Led Zeppelin. *Led Zeppelin IV.* Atlantic 82638-2: 1971.
    "The Battle of Evermore"
    "When The Levee Breaks"

Led Zeppelin. *Houses Of The Holy.* Atlantic 82639-2: 1973.
    "The Ocean"

Black Sabbath. *Master Of Reality.* Warner Bros. 2562-2: 1971.
    "After Forever"

CHAPTER IV: PSYCHEDELIA – THE OTHER BLUES REVISIONISM

HP Lovecraft. *Two Classic Albums by HP Lovecraft.* Universal Music CCM-139-2 314542821-2: 2000.
    "At The Mountains of Madness"

Garage Band Classics. Simitar 55362: 1998.
    "Shape Of Things To Come" – Max Frost & The Troopers

Blue Cheer. *Outsideinside.* Polygram 314514683-2: 1968.
    "The Hunter"

The Beatles. *Sgt. Peppers Lonely Hearts Club Band.* EMI/Capitol CDP 7 46442 2: 1967.
    "Within You Without You"

György Ligeti. *György Ligeti: Continuum/ Zehn Stücke für Bläserquintett/ Artikulation/ Glissandi/ Etüden für Orgel/ Volumina.* WERGO WER 61061-50: 1998.
    "Artikulation"
    "Glissandi"

The 13th Floor Elevators. *The Psychedelic Sounds of The 13th Floor Elevators.* Collectables Records COL-CD-0550: 1993.
    "You're Gonna Miss Me"

John Coltrane. *Live At The Village Vanguard? The Master Takes.* Impulse! IMPD-251: 1997.
    "India"

The Byrds. *The Byrds: The Original Singles 1965-1967.* Columbia CK 37335: 1980.
    "Eight Miles High"

The Beatles. *Revolver.* EMI/Capitol CDP 7 46441 2: 1966.
    "Tomorrow Never Knows"

The Jefferson Airplane. *The Best Of Jefferson Airplane.* BMG/RCA 66197-2: 1993.
    "White Rabbit"
    "Somebody To Love"

Janis Joplin. *Janis.* Columbia/Legacy C3K 65409: 1993.
    Disk 1: "Ball And Chain"

Janis Joplin. *Janis Joplin's Greatest Hits.* Columbia CK 32168: 1973.
    "Try (Just A Little Bit Harder)"
    "Cry Baby"

The Grateful Dead. *So Many Roads (1965 – 1995).* Grateful Dead Records/Arista GDCD 4066: 1999.
    Disk 1: "Can't Come Down"
             "On The Road Again"
             "Dark Star"
    Disk 3: "Eyes Of The World"

The Beach Boys. *Pet Sounds.* Capitol 72435-21241-2-1: 1999.
    "Wouldn't It Be Nice"
    "God Only Knows"
    "Sloop John B."
    "I Just Wasn't Meant For These Times"

Faust. *Faust.* Polydor POCP-2404: 1971.
    "Why Don't You Eat Carrots"

Pink Floyd. *The Piper At The Gates Of Dawn.* EMI 50999-503919-2-9: 2007.
    Disk 2: "Astronomy Domine"
             "Interstellar Overdrive"
             "Lucifer Sam"
             "Pow R. Toc H."
             "Scarecrow"
    Disk 3: "Arnold Layne"
             "See Emily Play"

Woodstock: Music from The Original Soundtrack and More. Atlantic Records SD 500-2: 1970.
    Disk 1: "I-Feel-Like-I'm-Fixin'-To-Die Rag" – Country Joe McDonald
    Disk 2: "I'm Going Home" – Ten Years After

Gram Parsons. *Sacred Hearts, Fallen Angels: The Gram Parsons Anthology.* Rhino R2 76780: 2001.
    Disk 1: "Luxury Liner"
             "Hickory Wind"
             "Christine's Tune (Devil In Disguise)"
             "Do Right Woman"
    Disk 2: "Streets Of Baltimore"

The Grateful Dead. *Skeletons From The Closet.* Warner Bros. 2764-2: 1974.
    "Uncle John's Band"

CHAPTER VIIa AND VIIb: ANTAGONIZATIONS: PROTO PUNKS AND GLAM

Garage Band Classics. Simitar 55362: 1998.
    "Dirty Water" – The Standells

The Sun Records Collection. Rhino R2 71780: 1994. (Complete)
    "Rock 'N' Roll Ruby" – <u>Warren Smith</u>

<u>Terry Riley</u>. *In C*. Materiali Sonori 7178: 1998.
    "In C"

<u>Small Faces</u>. *The Autumn Stone*. Charly Records SNIP 404CD: 2003.
    "Whacha Gonna Do About It"

<u>The Velvet Underground</u>. *The Velvet Underground: Peel Slowly And See*. Polydor 31452 7077-2 (Disk 1), 31452 7070-2 (Disk 2): 1995.
        Disk 1: *The Velvet Underground and Nico*.
                "Sunday Morning"
                "I'm Waiting For The man"
                "Venus In Furs"
                "All Tomorrow's Parties"
                "Heroin"
                "The Black Angel's Death Song"
      Disk 2: *White Light White Heat*
                " I Heard Her Call My Name"

<u>Love</u>. *Forever Changes*. Elektra Traditions/Rhino R2 76717: 1987, 2001.
    "A House Is Not A Motel"

<u>The Doors</u>. *The Doors*. Elektra/Asylum E2 60345: 1985.
        Disk 1: "Break On Through"
                  "Light My Fire"
        Disk 2: "The End"

<u>The Stooges</u>. *The Stooges*. Elektra 74051-2: 1988.
    "1969"
    "I Wanna Be Your Dog"

<u>The Stooges</u>. *Fun House*. Elektra 74071-2: 1970.
    "Down On The Street"
    "TV Eye"
    "l.a. Blues"

<u>The MC5</u>. *Kick Out The Jams*. Elektra 9 60894-2: 1969.
    "Ramblin' Rose"
    "Borderline"

<u>Alice Cooper</u>. *Killer*. Warner Bros. 2567-2: 1971.
    "Under My Wheels"

<u>T-Rex</u>. The Slider. Mercury Records 534355: 1997.
    "Baby Boomerang"

<u>Roxy Music</u>. *Roxy Music*. Virgin Records 7243 8 47447 2 4: 1972.
    "Re-make/Re-model"

<u>Roxy Music</u>. *For Your Pleasure*. Virgin Records 7243 8 47449 2 2: 1973.
    "Editions of You"
    "In Every Dream Home a Heartache"

<u>Roxy Music</u>. *Country Life*. Virgin Records 7243 8 47453 2 5: 1974.
    "The Thrill Of It All"

Anthony Newley. *The Best of Anthony Newley*. Decca 882 961-2: 2004.
    "What Kind Of Fool Am I?"

David Bowie. *London Boy*. Spectrum Music 551 706-2: 1995.
    "Space Oddity" (Original Version)
    "When I Live My Dream"
    "Love You Till Tuesday"
    "The London Boys"

David Bowie. *Hunky Dory*. Virgin Records 724 3 521899 0 8: 1999.
    "Changes"
    "Life On Mars?"
    "Oh! You Pretty Things"

David Bowie. *The Best Of David Bowie 1969/1974*. Virgin Records 7243 8 21849 2 8: 1997.
    "Space Oddity" (Revised Version, 1972)

David Bowie. *The Rise And Fall Of Ziggy Stardust And The Spiders From Mars*. Virgin Records 7243 521900 0 3: 1999.
    "Ziggy Stardust"
    "Suffragette City"

Lou Reed. *Transformer*. BMG/RCA 44541-2: 1997.
    "Vicious"
    "Walk On The Wild Side"

David Bowie. *Aladdin Sane*. Virgin Records 7243 521902 0 1: 1999.
    "Time"
    "Watch That Man"
    "The Gene Genie"

David Bowie. *Diamond Dogs*. Virgin Records 7243 521904 0 9: 1999.
    "Rebel, Rebel"
    "1984"

David Bowie. *The Best Of David Bowie 1974/1979*. Virgin Records 7243 494300 0 6: 1998.
    "Golden Years"
    "Fame"
    "Young Americans"
    "TVC 15"
    "Heroes"
    "Boys Keep Swinging"

David Bowie. *Low*. Virgin Records 7243 521907 0 6: 1999.
    "Always Crashing In The Same Car"
    "Warszawa"
    "Weeping Wall"
    "Subterraneans"

CHAPTER VIII: PUNK PROPER

King Crimson. *In The Court Of The Crimson King*. Virgin Records 0 1704 65102 2 4: 1999.
    "Epitaph"

Emerson, Lake, & Palmer. *Brain Salad Surgery*. Rhino R2 72459:1996.
    "Toccata"

The Modern Lovers. *The Modern Lovers*. Rhino R2 70091: 1986.
    "Roadrunner"
    "Pablo Picasso"

The New York Dolls. *New York Dolls*. Mercury/Polygram 832 752-2: 1973.
    "Personality Crisis"
    "Trash"

Television. *Marquee Moon*. Elektra/Asylum 1098-2: 1977.
    "Friction"

Garage Band Classics. Simitar 55362: 1998.
    "Pushin' Too Hard" – The Seeds
Nuggets Volume 1: A Classic Collection from the Psychedelic Sixties. Rhino Records. R2 75892: 1986.
    "Little Girl" – The Syndicate of Sound

Patti Smith. *Horses*. Arista 07822-18827-2: 1996.
    "Gloria"
    "Kimberly"
    "Land: Horses"

Pere Ubu. *The Modern Dance*. DGC DGCD-25206: 1998.
    "Street Waves

Pere Ubu. *Terminal Tower: An Archival Collection, Nonlp Singles & B Sides 1975-1980*. DGC DGCD-25207: 1998.
    "30 Seconds Over Tokyo"
    "Final Solution"

Pere Ubu. *Dub Housing*. Thirsty Ear thi 57069-2: 1978.
    "Dub Housing"

The Ramones. *All The Stuff (And More): Volume Two*. Sire/Warner Bros. 26618-2: 1991.
    "I'm Against It"
    "I Wanna Be Sedated"
    "Go Mental"
    "Bad Brain"

Small Faces. *The Autumn Stone*. Charly Records SNIP 404CD: 2003.
    "Whacha Gonna Do About It"

The Sex Pistols. *Never Mind The Bollocks: Here's The Sex Pistols*. Warner Bros. 3147-2: 1977.
    "God Save The Queen"
    "Anarchy In The UK"
    "Pretty Vacant"

The Clash. *The Singles*. Columbia/Sony 468946 2: 1982.
    "White Riot"
    "White Man In Hammersmith Palais"

Don Drummond. *Don Drummond Greatest Hits*. Jet Set Records 44 414-2: 1989.
    "Feeling Fine"

Laurel Aitken. *Jamaican Ska: Laurel Aitken: The Blue Beat Years.* Moon/Ska Records MR061 CD: 1985.
  "Rudi Wedding"
  "Little Sheila"

Jackie Mittoo. *The Keyboard Legend: Jackie Mittoo.* Sonic Sounds Jamaica SON CD 0073.
  "Hot Milk"

Bob Marley & The Wailers. *The Wailers: Reggae Greats.* Island Records D 102297 (162-539 796-2): 1984.
  "Concrete Jungle"
  "Get Up Stand Up"
  "Baby We've Got A Date (Rock It Baby)"
  "Small Axe"

Bob Marley and The Wailers. *Catch A Fire.* Island/Tuff Gong 314 548 803-2: 2001. (Complete)
  "Slave Driver"
  "Stir It Up"

Bob Marley and The Wailers. *Gold.* Tuff Gong/Island Def Jam Music Group B0004008-02: 2005.
  Disk 1: "Trenchtown Rock" (Live)

Public Image Limited (P.I.L.). *Second Edition.* Warner Bros. 3288-2: 1979.
  "The Suit"
The Police. *The Police.* A&M Records B009080-02: 2007.
  Disk 1: "Roxanne"

The Police. *Ghost In The Machine.* A&M Records CD-3730 DIDZ-10070: 1981.
  "Spirits In The Material World"
  "Hungry For You (j aurais toujours faim de toi)"
  "Too Much Information"

CHAPTER IX: BRITISH POST PUNK

The Buzzcocks. *Singles Going Steady.* AAD Records X2-13153: 1979.
  "What Do I Get?"

24 Hour Party People: Music From The Motion Picture. Warner Strategic Marketing/ Warner Music Group 0 8122-78136-2 8: 2002.
  "Transmission" – Joy Division

Joy Division. *Unknown Pleasures.* Factory/QWEST 9 25840-2: 1979.
  "Disorder"
  "I Remember Nothing"

Joy Division. *Closer.* Factory/QWEST 25841: 1989.
  "Eternal"

The Fall. *Live At The Witch Trials.* COG Sinister COGVP1 38CD: 2002.
  "Industrial Estate"
  "Underground Medicin"
  "Bingo Master"

The Smiths. *Singles.* Reprise 4532-2: 1995.
  "Hand in Glove"
  "How Soon Is Now?"

Public Image Ltd. *Public Image: First Issue*. Virgin Records 0777 7 87475 2 9: 1978.
    "Public Image"
    "Fodderstompf"

Public Image Ltd. *Second Edition*. Warner Bros. 3288-2: 1979.
    "Swan Lake"
    "Memories"
    "Careering"

Public Image Ltd. *The Flowers Of Romance*. Warner Bros. 3536-2: 1981.
    "Flowers of Romance"
    "Under The House"

Scritti Politti. *Early*. Rough Trade RTA30054-2: 2004.
    "Skank Bloc Bologna"
    "Messthetics"
    "The 'Sweetest Girl' "

Scritti Politti. *Cupid & Psyche 85*. Warner Bros. 9 25302-2: 1985.
    "Wood Beez (Pray Like Aretha Franklin)"
    "Perfect Way"
    "The Word Girl"

ABC. *The Lexicon of Love*. Universal Distribution 5382502: 2002.
    "Tears Are Not Enough"
    "Poison Arrow"
    "The Love of Love"
    "All of My Heart"

ABC. *Beauty Stab*. Polygram 536397: 1998.
    "That Was Then But This Is Now"

Orange Juice. *You Can't Hide Your Love Forever*. Universal Distribution POCP-2613: 1998.
    "Falling and Laughing"

Orange Juice. *Rip It Up*. Polydor 5399812: 1998.
    "Rip It Up"

Bauhaus. *Bauhaus Crackle*. Beggars Banquet Records BEGL 2018 CD: 1998.
    "Bela Legosi's Dead"
    "A Kick I The Eye (Alternate Version)"
    "The Passion of Lovers"

Siouxsie & The Banshees. Once Upon a Time: The Singles. Hip-O 8315422:2009.
    "Hong Kong Garden"

Siouxsie & The Banshees. *The Scream*. Polydor 9843511: 2007.
    "Suburban Relapse"

Siouxsie & The Banshees. *Juju*. Polydor 8390052: 1995.
    "Spellbound"
    "Halloween"
    "Voodoo Dolly"

The Birthday Party. *Prayer On Fire*. WEA 20014: 2008.
    "Zoo Music Girl"

The Birthday Party. Junkyard. Ad Music Ltd. 20033: 2008.
    "Big Jesus Trash-Can"
    "Release The Bats"

Killing Joke. *Killing Joke*. Slowburn 68632: 2007.
    "Wardance"

Killing Joke. *What's THIS For…!* EMI 58: 1989.
    "Follow The Leaders"

The Cure. *Staring At The Sea – The Singles*. Elektra/Asylum 9 60477-2: 1986.
    "Killing An Arab"
    "Boys Don't Cry"
    "A Forest"
    "Charlotte Sometimes"
    "Close To Me"

Tubeway Army. *Tubeway Army*. Blanco y Negro Records BBL 4CD: 1998.
    "My Shadow In Vain"

Tubeway Army. *Replicas*. Blanco y Negro Records 80007: 1998.
    "Are Friends Electric?"
    "Praying To The Aliens"

Gary Numan. *The Pleasure Principle*.
    "Cars"

Gary Numan. *Teleekon*. Blanco y Negro Records BBL 19CD:1998.
    "We Are Glass"

Ultravox. *Ultravox!* Hip-O IMCD 324: 2009.
    "I Want To Be A Machine"

Ultravox. *Vienna*. EMI Music Distribution 5255230: 2006.
    "Vienna"

Visage. *Visage*. Universal International 800029: 2002.
    "Fade To Grey"

Visage. *The Anvil*. One Way Records OW 34518: 1997.
    "The Damned Don't Cry"

The Human League. *Dare!* Virgin Records VJCP-68634: 2004.
    "The Sound of the Crowd"
    "Don't You Want Me"

The Human League. *The Very Best of The Human League*. Virgin 592391: 2003.
    "(Keep Feeling) Fascination"

Dead Boys. *Young, Loud, and Snotty*. Sire/Warner Bros. 9 26981-2: 1992.
"Sonic Reducer"

Bad Brains. *Banned in D.C.: Bad Brains Greatest Riffs*. Caroline REC CAR 83049-2: 2003.
"Pay To Cum"

Twenty Years of Dischord: 50 Bands. Dischord DIS 125: 2002.
Disk 1: "Get Up and Go" – The Teen Idles
"Public Defender" – State Of Alert
"Drink Deep" – Rites Of Spring

Minor Threat. *Complete Discography*. Dischord 40: 1989.
"Filler"
"Straight Edge"

Black Flag. *Black Flag: The First Four Years*. SST CD 021: 1983.
"Nervous Breakdown"
"Jealous Again"
"Clocked In"
"Louie Louie"
"Damaged 1"

Dead Kennedys. *Fresh Fruit for Rotting Vegetables*. Cleopatra Records CLP 1198-2: 2002.
"California Über Alles"
"Holiday In Cambodia"

Fugazi. *Repeater*. Dischord 45: 2005.
"Turnover"
"Blueprint"

Sunny Day Real Estate. *Diary*. Sub Pop sp 246b: 1993.
"In Circles"

James Brown. *20 All Time Greatest Hits*. Polydor 314 511 326-2: 1991.
"Super Bad, Pts. 1&2"

No New York: Island Records/Polygram ONCO-002: 1978.
"Dish It Out" – James Chance & The Contortions
"I Woke Up Dreaming" – Teenage Jesus and The Jerks
"Tunnel" – Mars
"Helen Forsdale" - Mars
"Lionel" – DNA

Glenn Branca. *The Ascension*. Acute Records ACT002: 2003.
"Structure"

Sonic Youth. *Screaming Fields Of Sonic Love*. DGC DGCD-24809: 1995.
"Inhuman"
"Death Valley 69"

Sonic Youth. *Evol*. DGC DGCD-24513: 1986.
"Tom Violence"
"Shadow Of A Doubt"

Sonic Youth. *Sister*. DGC DGCD-24514: 1987.
    "(I Got A) Catholic Block"
    "Tuff Gnarl"

Sonic Youth. *Daydream Nation*. DGC DGCMD-24515: 1988.
    "Teen Age Riot"

Hüsker Dü. *Metal Circus*. SST. SST 020CD: 1987.
    "Real World"
    "It's Not Funny Any More"

Hüsker Dü. *Zen Arcade*. SST Records SST CD 027: 1984.
    "Turn On The News"
    "Pink Turns To Blue"

Hüsker Dü. *New Day Rising*. SST Records SST CD 031:1985.
    "Girl Who Lives On Heaven Hill"
    "Celebrated Summer"

Hüsker Dü. *Flip Your Wig*. SST Records SST-CD-055: 1985.
    "Makes No Sense At All"

Hüsker Dü. *Candy Apple Grey*. Warner Bros. 7599253852: 1987.
    "Hardly Getting Over It"

Pixies. *Come On Pilgrim*. Elektra/4AD 961296-2. 1992.
    "Isla De Encanta"

Pixies. *Surfer Rosa*. Elektra/4AD 961295-2: 1992.
    "Gigantic"
    "Something Against You"
    "Broken Face"
    "Where Is My Mind"
    "Tony's Theme"

Green River. *Dry As A Bone/Rehab Doll*. Sub Pop SP11b: 1990.
    "Forever Means"

The Melvins *Gluey Porch Treatments*. Ipecac Recordings IPC 12: 1999.
    "Echo/Don't Piece Me"

Mudhoney. *Superfuzz Bigmuff Plus Early Singles*. Sub Pop SP 21b: 1990.
    "Touch Me I'm Sick"

Mudhoney. *Every Good Boy Deserves Fudge*. Sub Pop SP 105b: 1991.
    "Let It Slide"
    "Good Enough"

Butthole Surfers. *Locust Abortion Technician*. Touch and Go Records T&GLP#19CD: 1987.
    "Human Cannonball"

Nirvana. *Bleach*. Sub Pop SP34b: 1989.
    "Floyd The Barber"
    "Love Buzz"

Nirvana. *Nevermind.* DGC DGCD-21425: 1991.
    "In Bloom"

Nirvana. *In Utero.* DGC DGCD 24607: 1993.
    "Scentless Apprentice"
    "Heart-Shaped Box"

CHAPTER XI: POST SOUL AND FUNK'S DEVELOPMENT

The Ultimate History Of Rock n' Roll Collection: Chapter Two – R&B Greats. Dominion 3802-2: 1997.
    "Let's Go, Let's Go, Let's Go" – Hank Ballard

The 5 Royales. *Sing For You.* King Records/Highland Music. Inc. KCD-616: 1987.
    "Your Only Love"

James Brown. *20 All Time Greatest Hits.* Polydor 314 511 326-2: 1991.
    "Get Up (I Feel Like Being A) Sex Machine, Pt. 1"
    "Papa's Got A Brand New Bag, Pt. 1"
    "Try Me"
    "Night Train"
    "Cold Sweat, Pt. 1"
    "Please, Please, Please"

James Brown. *Roots Of A Revolution.* Polydor 817304: 1995.
    "That Dood It"
    "(Do The) Mashed Potatoes"

Sly & The Family Stone. *Sly & The Family Stone: Greatest Hits.* Epic EK 30325.
    "Dance To The Music"
    "Thank You (Falettinme Be Mice Elf Agin)"

The Temptations. *The Temptations: The Ultimate Collection.* Motown Records 31453-0562-2: 1997.
    "Ball Of Confusion (That's What The World Is Today)"
    "Papa Was A Rollin' Stone"

Donny Hathaway. *A Donny Hathaway Collection.* Atlantic 7 82092-2: 1990.
    "The Ghetto"

Marvin Gaye. *What's Going On.* Motown Records 314530883-2: 1998.
    "What's Going On"
    "What's Happening Brother"
    "Mercy Mercy Me (The Ecology)"

Parliament/Funkadelic. *P. Funk; Uncut Funk… The Bomb: Parliaments Greatest Hits.* Casablanca/
Polygram 822 637-2: 1984.
    "Give Up The Funk"
    "Flashlight"

Earth, Wind, & Fire. *Greatest Hits.* Columbia/Legacy CK 65779: 1998.
    "Getaway"

The O'Jays. *The O'Jays Super Hits.* Epic Associated/Legacy ZK 65445: 1998.
    "Love Train"
    "Back Stabbers"

Harold Melvin & The Blue Notes. *Harold Melvin & The Blue Notes: All Their Greatest Hits!* Philadelphia International ZK 34232: 1987.
        "The Love I Lost"
        "If You Don't Know Me By Now"

Pure Funk. Polygram TV 314 558 299-2: 1998.
        "Jungle Boogie" – Kool & The Gang
        "Kung Fu Fighting" – Carl Douglas

Love Is The Message: The Best Of MFSB. Legacy Epic Associated ZK 66689: 1986.
        "T.S.O.P (The Sound Of Philadelphia)"

Silver Convention. *Get Up and Boogie with Silver Convention: Their Greatest Hits.* Music Club 358:1999.
        "Fly Robin Fly"

Donna Summer. *Donna Summer: Gold.* Hip-O/Mercury B0002719-02: 2005.
        Disk 1: "I Feel Love"

The Bee Gee's. *Bee Gee's, Their Greatest Hits: The Record.* UTV Records 314 589 400-2 BK02: 2001.
        Disk 1: "New York Mining Disaster 1941"
             "How Can You Mend A Broken Heart"
             "Jive Talkin' "
             "Nights On Broadway"
             "You Should Be Dancing"

Saturday Night Fever: The Original Movie Soundtrack. Polydor 42282 5389 2: 1995.
        "More Than A Woman" – The Bee Gee's
        "A Fifth Of Beethoven" – Walter Murphy

The Rolling Stones. *Some Girls.* Virgin Records 7243-8-39526-2 5: 1978.
        "Miss You"

The Grateful Dead. *Grateful Dead: Shakedown Street.* Arista ARCD 8228: 1978.
        "Shakedown Street"

CHAPTER XII: HIP HOP

Studio One DJ's: The Original. Soul Jazz Records SJR CD 58: 2002.
        "More Scorcha" – Count Machuki

Dub Sampler (Compilation): 2005/2006.
        "Ghetto Dub" – King Tubby

Michael Viner. *Michael Viner's Incredible Bongo Band: Bongo Rock.* Mr. Bongo Records MRBCD 043: 2006.
        "Apache"

Babe Ruth. *First Base/Amar Caballero.* BGO Records BGOCD 382: 1998.
        "The Mexican"

The Perfect Beats: New York Electro Hip Hop & Underground Dance Classics 1980-1985/ Volume 1. Timber!/Tommy Boy TRCD 1196: 1998.
        "The Mexican" – John "Jellybean" Benitez

Pure Funk. Polygram TV 314 558 299-2: 1998.
        "Good Times" – <u>Chic</u>

The Sugar Hill Records Story. Rhino R2 72449:1997
        Disk 1: "Rapper's Delight" – <u>The Sugar Hill Gang</u>
        Disk 2: "Adventures of Grandmaster Flash On The Wheels of Steel" – <u>Grandmaster Flash</u>
                "Apache" – <u>The Sugar Hill Gang</u>
        Disk 3: "The Message" – <u>Grandmaster Flash and The Furious Five</u>

<u>Kurtis Blow</u>. *The Best of Kurtis Blow.* Mercury 314 522 456-2: 1994.
        "The Breaks"
        "Christmas Rappin' "

<u>Blondie</u>. *The Best of Blondie.* Chrysalis F2 21337 DIDX 71: 1984.
        "Rapture"

<u>Afrika Bambaataa & The Soulsonic Force</u>. *Don't Stop… Planet Rock: The Remix EP.* Tommy Boy TBCD 1052: 1992.
        "Planet Rock: Original Vocal Version"

<u>Run DMC</u>. *Run DMC.* Arista/Legacy 82876695602: 2005.
        "Rock Box"

<u>Run DMC</u>. *King Of Rock.* Profile/Arista 07822-16407-2: 1999.
        "King Of Rock"

<u>Aerosmith</u>. *Aerosmtih's Greatest Hits.* Columbia CK 57367: 1993.
        "Walk This Way"

<u>Run DMC</u>. *Raising Hell.* Profile/Arista 07822-16408-2: 1999.
        "My Adidas"
        "Walk This Way"

<u>The Beastie Boys</u>. *Licensed To Ill.* Def Jam 527351: 1995.
        "Fight For Your Right"
        "No Sleep Till Brooklyn"

<u>Boogie Down Productions</u>. *Criminal Minded.* B Boy Records BB4787: 1997.
        "9mm Goes Bang"

<u>Public Enemy</u>. *It Takes A Nation Of Millions To Hold Us Back.* Def Jam 314 527 358-2: 1988, 1987.
        "Party For Your Right To Fight"

<u>Public Enemy</u>. *Fear Of A Black Planet.* Def Jam P2-23446: 1990.
        "Fight The Power"

<u>Eric B. & Rakim</u>. *Paid In Full.* The Island Def Jam Music Group B00044323-02: 2005.
        "My Melody"
        "I Know You Got Soul"
        "Move The Crowd"
        "As The Rhythm Goes On"

<u>Ice-T</u>. *Rhyme Pays.* Sire 25602: 1990.
        "Squeeze The Trigger"

N.W.A. *Straight Outta Compton.* Ruthless/Priority Records CDL57102: 1988.
    "Straight Outta Compton"
    "Fuck Tha Police"

De La Soul. *3 Feet High and Rising.* Tommy Boy TBCD 1019: 1989.
    "Transmitting From Mars"
    "Eye Know"
    "Me Myself and I"

Ice Cube. *Death Certificate.* Priority CDL-57155: 1991.
    "A Bird in the Hand"

Dr. Dre. *The Chronic.* Death Row Records DRR 63000-2: 1992, 2001.
    "Nuthin' But A G Thang"
    "Let Me Ride"

Old School Jams: Gold. Hip-O B0008207-02: 2007.
    Disk 2: "I Want'a Do Something Freaky To You" – Leon Haywood

Parliament/Funkadelic. *P. Funk; Uncut Funk… The Bomb: Parliaments Greatest Hits.* Casablanca/
Polygram 822 637-2: 1984.
    "Mothership Connection"

Wu-Tang Clan. *Enter The Wu-Tang (36 Chambers).* RCA 66336-2: 1993.
    "Shame On A Nigga"
    "Wu-Tang/7th Chamber"
    "C.R.E.A.M."

Nas. *Illmatic.* Columbia CK 57684: 1994.
    "The Genesis"
    "N.Y. State Of Mind"
    "Life's A Bitch"

The Notorious B.I.G. *Ready To Die.* Bad Boy Records 94567-2: 2004.
    "Intro"
    "Gimme The Loot"
    "Ready To Die"
    "Big Poppa"

Run DMC. *Run DMC.* Arista/Legacy 82876695602: 2005.
    "Sucker M.C.'s"

Jay-Z. *Reasonable Doubt.* Roc-A-Fella/Priority Records LLC P2 50040: 1996.
    "Can't Knock The Hustle"
    "Brooklyn's Finest" (featuring Notorious B.I.G.)
    "Ain't No Nigga" (featuring Foxy Brown)
    "Coming Of Age" (featuring Memphis Bleek)

Jay-Z. *In My Lifetime, vol.1.* Roc-A-Fella Records/Def Jam Music Group 314 536 392-2: 1997.
    "The City Is Mine" (featuring Blackstreet)
    "Streets Is Watching"

Jay-Z. *Vol.2… Hard Knock Life.* Roc-A-Fella/Def Jam Music Group 314 558 902-2: 1998.
    "Hard Knock Life (Ghetto Anthem)"
    "Can I Get A …" (featuring Amil (of Major Coins) & Ja Rule)

Enimen. *The Marshall Mathers LP.* Aftermath/Interscope Records 069490629-2: 2000.
      "Kill You"
      "Steve Berman (Skit)"
      "The Way I Am"
      "The Real Slim Shady"
      "Bitch Please II"

CHAPTER XIII: ELECTRONIC DANCE MUSIC

Faust. *Faust.* Polydor POCP-2404: 1971.
      "Meadow Meal"

Kraftwerk. *Trans-Europe Express.* Capitol CDP 0777 7 46473 2 8: 1977.
      "Europe Endless"
      "Metal On Metal"
      "Trans-Europe Express"

The Perfect Beats: New York Electro Hip Hop & Underground Dance Classics 1980-1985/ Volume 1. Timber!/Tommy Boy TRCD 1196: 1998.
      "Numbers" – Kraftwerk
      "Don't Make Me Wait" – Peech Boys
      "A Little Bit Of Jazz" – Rick Straker Band

Afrika Bambaataa & The Soulsonic Force. *Don't Stop… Planet Rock: The Remix EP.* Tommy Boy TBCD 1052: 1992.
      "Planet Rock: Original Vocal Version"
      "Planet Rock: Classic Mix" – Elektric Music

New Order. *(The Best Of) New Order.* QWEST/Warner Bros. 945794-2: 1990.
      "Blue Monday"

Madonna. *The Immaculate Collection.* Sire/Warner Bros. 9 26440-2: 1990.
      "Lucky Star"
      "Vogue"

Madonna. *Madonna.* Sire/Warner Bros. 9 23867-2: 1983.
      "Everybody"

Michael Jackson. *Thriller.* Epic EK 38112: 1982.
      "Thriller"

Prince. *The Hits 2.* Warner Bros./Paisley Park 9 45435-2: 1993.
      "I Wanna Be Your Lover"
      "Kiss"

Juan Atkins. *Wax Trax! Master Mix: Volume 1.* Wax Trax! Records TVT-7254-2: 1998.
      "Nude Photo" – Rhythim Is Rhythim (featuring Derrick May)

Frankie Knuckles. *Beyond The Mix.* Virgin Records 91618-2: 1991.
      "Godfather"
      "Sacrifice"

Basement Jaxx. *Remedy.* Astralwerks ASW 6270-2. 0 1704 66270 2 3: 1999.
    "Rendez-Vu"
    "Red Alert"

The Orb. *U.F. Off: The Best Of The Orb.* Island Records CDD 8078524 599 2: 1998.
    "A Huge Evergrowing Pulsating Brain That Rules From The Centre Of The Ultraworld"
    "Little Fluffy Clouds"
    "Blue Room"

The Chemical Brothers. *Dig Your Own Hole.* Astralwerks ASW 6180: 1997.
    "Block Rockin' Beats"
    "Setting Sun"

Richie Hawtin. *Decks, EFX, & 909.* Novamute minus4Cd: 1999.
    "Orange/Minus 1"

Krust. *Coded Language.* Mercury 314 546 687-2: 1999.
    "Coded Language" (featuring Saul Williams)

Sasha. *Airdrawndagger.* BMG UK & Ireland Ltd. 67728 547252:: 2002.
    "Bloodlock"

CHAPTER XIV: INDUSTRIAL – THE OTHER ELECTRONIC DANCE MUSIC

Listen: Third Brief Edition – Joseph Kerman. Worth Publishers & Sony Music A6B 26259: 1995.
    Disk 4: "Poemé électronique – Edgard Varése

György Ligeti. *György Ligeti: Continuum/ Zehn Stücke für Bläserquintett/ Artikulation/ Glissandi/ Etüden für Orgel/ Volumina.* WERGO WER 61061-50: 1998.
    "Artikulation"

Throbbing Gristle. *Throbbing Gristle's Greatest Hits: Entertainment Through Pain.* Mute Records 9 61001-2: 1990.
    "Hamburger Lady"
    "Subhuman"

Einstürzende Neubauten. *Strategies Against Architecture.* Mute Records 61677-2: 1994.
    "Tanz Debil" *(with metal drumkit, record player)*
    "Draußen ist feindlich" *(with amplified spring, glass)*
    "Krieg In Den Städten" *(with tools, metal plates, scratching metals)*

Cabaret Voltaire. *Hai!* Mute Records 9 61091-2: 1991.
    "Taxi Music"

Ministry. *Land Of Rape And Honey.* Sire 9 25798-2: 1988.
    "The Missing"
    "Stigmata"
    "You Know What You Are"

KMFDM. *Money.* Wax Trax! Records WAX CD 7177: 1992.
    "Vogue"
    "Spiritual House"

Nine Inch Nails. *Pretty Hate Machine.* TVT Records 2610-2: 1989.
    "Head Like A Hole"
    "Sin"

Front Line Assembly. *Hard Wired.* Metropolis Records MET 015: 1995.
    "Neologic Spasm"

Tangerine Dream. *Stratosfear.* Virgin Records V2-91010: 1976.
    "3 AM At The Border Of The Marsh From Okefenekee"

Donna Summer. *Donna Summer: Gold.* Hip-O/Mercury B0002719-02: 2005.
    Disk 1: "Spring Affair" (single version)
           "I Feel Love"

Kraftwerk. *Trans-Europe Express.* Capitol CDP 0777 7 46473 2 8: 1977.
    "Europe Endless"
    "Metal On Metal"

Front 242. *Back Catalogue.* Wax Trax! Records WAX CD 033: 1987.
    "U-Men (lp mix)"
    "Geography I"

Front 242. *Official Version.* Epic EK 52405: 1992.
    "Masterhit (Parts I & II)"

Front 242. *Front By Front.* Epic EK 52406: 1992.
    "Until Death (Do Us Part)"
    "Headhunter V. 3.0"

Nitzer Ebb. *That Total Age.* Geffen Records 9 24155-2: 1987.
    "Let Your Body Learn"
    "Join In The Chant"
    "Join In The Chant (metal mix)"

Nitzer Ebb. *Showtime.* Geffen Records 9 24284-2: 1990.
    "Hold On"

Skinny Puppy. *VIVIsectVI.* Nettwerk Records 0 6700 30024-2: 1988.
    "VX Gas Attack"
    "Human Disease (S.K.U.M.M.)"
    "Testure"

Skinny Puppy. *Rabies.* Nettwerk Records 0 6700 30040 2 2: 1989.
    "Warlock"

Skinny Puppy. *Too Dark Park.* Nettwerk Records 0 6700 30207 2 5:1990.
    "Convulsions"
    "Tormentor"
    "Nature's Revenge"

Revolting Cocks. *Beers, Steers, & Queers.* Wax Trax! Records TVT 7063: 1990.
    "Stainless Steel Providers"

CHAPTER XV: THE HEAVY METAL JUGGERNAUT

Black Sabbath. *The Original Black Sabbath: Symptom Of The Universe 1970-1978.* Warner Bros./Rhino
R2 73772: 2002.

Disk 1: "Black Sabbath"
"Evil Woman"
"War Pigs"
"Paranoid"
"Children Of The Grave"

Deep Purple. *Machine Head*. JVC Compact Disks 64310/11: 2008.
"Highway Star"

Thin Lizzy. *Jailbreak*. Vertigo Records UICY-9232: 2002.
"The Boys Are Back In Town"

Queen. *A Night at the Opera.* Parlophone 3384782: 2005.
"Bohemian Rhapsody"

Rainbow. *Ritchie Blackmore's Rainbow*. Universal Polygram 9190: 2006.
"Man On The Silver Mountain"

Judas Priest. *Sad Wings of Destiny*. Koch Records KOC-CD-8067: 2000.
"The Ripper"
"Deceiver"
"Victim Of Changes"

Judas Priest. *British Steel*. Columbia Legacy CK 85752: 2001.
"Metal Gods"
"Rapid Fire"
"Grinder"
"Living After Midnight"

Judas Priest. *Screaming For Vengeance*. CK 85435: 2001.
"Screaming For Vengeance"

Iron Maiden. *Iron Maiden*. Sony Music Distribution 86051: 2002.
"Sanctuary"
"Iron Maiden"
"Phantom Of The Opera"

Iron Maiden. *Killers*. Sanctuary 86209: 1998.
"Wrathchild"
"Murders In The Rue Morgue"

Iron Maiden. *The Number Of The Beast*. Capital CDP 7 46364 2: 1982.
"The Number Of The Beast"
"The Prisoner"

Saxon. *Saxon*. EMI Music Distribution 6944432: 2009.
"Stallions of the Highway"

Saxon. *Wheels Of Steel*. EMI Music Distribution 6944452: 2009.
"Wheels of Steel"
"Motorcycle Man"
"Machine Gun"
Hawkwind. *Doremi Fasol Latido*. EMI Music Distribution 5300312: 2001.
"Space Is Deep"

Hawkwind. *Warrior On The Edge Of Time*. Red Fox Records RFM011: 2005.
"Motorhead"

Motörhead. *Motörhead*. Big Beat Records 021:2007.
    "Motorhead"

Motörhead. *Overkill*. BMG 37960: 2007.
    "Overkill"

Motörhead. *Ace Of Spades*. Metal-In Records 00076 85206-2: 2001.
    "Ace Of Spades"
    "The Hammer"

Diamond Head. *Lightning To The Nations (The White Album)*. Castle Music Ltd. CMRCD-239: 2001.
    "Am I Evil"

Venom. *Welcome To Hell*. Metal-Is Records 73003: 2006.
    "Witching Hour"
    "Angel Dust"

Venom. *Black Metal*. Neat Records 288482: 2004.
    "Black Metal"

Metallica. *Kill 'Em All*. Elektra Records 60766-2: 1995.
    "Hit The Lights"
    "Whiplash"

Metallica. *Ride The Lightning*. Elektra 9 60396-2: 1984.
    "Fight Fire With Fire"
    "Ride The Lightning"
    "For Whom The Bell Tolls"

Metallica. *Master Of Puppets*. Elektra 9 60439-2: 1986.
    "Master Of Puppets"

Megadeth. *Killing Is My Business...And Business Is Good*. Loud Records 9046-2: 2003.
    "Rattlehead"
    "Killing Is My Business...And Business Is Good"

Megadeth. *Peace Sells...But Who's Buying?* Capitol 72435 986244-2-2: 2004.
    "Wake Up Dead"

Megadeth. *Rust In Peace*. Capitol 72435 98619-2-0: 2004.
    "Hangar 18"

Slayer. *Show No Mercy*. Metal Blade 3984140320: 2004.
    "Metal Storm/Face The Slayer"
    "Crionics"
    "The Antichrist"

Slayer. *Hell Awaits*. Metal Blade 3984140310: 2004.
    "Necrophobic"

Slayer. *Reign In Blood*. Universal Distribution 586796: 2002.
    "Aggressive Perfector'
    "Angel of Death"
    "Piece By Piece"

Mercyful Fate. *Don't Break The Oath*. Roadrunner RR-9835-2: 1997.
    "Desecration of Souls"
    "A Dangerous Meeting"

Mercyful Fate. *Melissa*. Roadrunner 81165: 2005.
    "Curse of the Pharaohs"
    "Into The Coven""

Bathory. *Under The Sign: The Sign of the Black Mark*. Black Mark 6663: 1999.
    "Massacre"
    "Equimanthorn"

Napalm Death. *SCUM*. Earache MOSH 3666CD: 2006.
    "Siege of Power"

Possessed. *Seven Churches*. Combat 1769-2: 1999.
    "Death Metal"

Death. *Scream Bloody Gore*. Combat 81464: 1987.
    "Mutilation"

Deicide. *Deicide*. Roadrunner 25059: 2008.
    "Lunatic of God's Creation"

Morbid Angel. *Covenant*. Giant Records 9 24504-2: 1999.
    "Vengeance Is Mine"

Mayhem. *De Mysteriis Dom Sathanas*. Century Media Records 7767-2: 1994.
    "Buried By Time And Dust"

Emperor. *In The Nightside Eclipse*. Candlelight CDL0101CD: 2001.
    "The Burning Shadows of Silence"
    "I Am The Black Wizards"

Immortal. *Pure Holocaust*. Osmos Productions OPCD 2093: 1993.
    "A Sign For The Norse Hordes To Ride"

Bibliography

Ambrose, Joe. *Gimme Danger: The Story of Iggy Pop*. London: Omnibus Press, 2004.

Azerrad, Michael. *Come As You Are: The Story of Nirvana*. New York: Broadway Books, 2001.

_____. *Our Band Could Be Your Life: Scenes from the American Indie Underground 1981-1991*. New York: Little, Brown and Company, 2001.

Barkley, Elizabeth. *Crossroads: Popular Music in America*. Upper Saddle River, NJ: Prentice Hall, 2003.

Blake, Mark, ed. *Punk: The Whole Story*. London: Mojo Magazine/Dorling Kindersley, 2006.

Bowe, Brian J. *Judas Priest: Metal Gods*. Berkeley Heights, NJ: Enslow Publishers Inc., 2009.

Brewster, Bill and Frank Broughton. *Last Night A DJ Saved My Life: The History of the Disc Jockey*. New York: Grove Press, 2000.

Brown, James with Bruce Tucker. *James Brown: The Godfather Of Soul*. New York: Thunder's Mouth Press, 1997.

Brown, Mick. *Tearing Down The Wall Of Sound: The Rise and Fall of Phil Spector*. New York: Alfred A. Knopf, 2007.

Bukszpan, Daniel. *The Encyclöpedia öf Heavy Metal*. New York: Sterling Publishing Company, 2003.

Covach, John. *What's That Sound? An Introduction to Rock and Its History*. New York: W.W. Norton, 2006.

Cray, Ed. *Ramblin' Man: The Life and Times of Woody Guthrie*. New York: W.W. Norton, 2004.

Christe, Ian. *Sound of the Beast: The Complete Headbanging History of Heavy Metal*. New York: Harper Entertainment/Harper Collins Publishers, 2004.

Davies, Hunter. *The Beatles: Second Revised Edition*. New York: W.W. Norton, 1996.

Dylan, Bob. *Chronicles: Volume One*. New York: Simon & Schuster, 2004.

Escott, Colin with Martin Hawkins. *Good Rockin' Tonight: Sun Records and the Birth of Rock n' Roll*. New York: St. Martin's Press, 1991.

Farley, Christopher John. *Before The Legend: The Rise of Bob Marley*. New York: Harper Collins, 2006.

Frank, Josh with Caryn Franz. *Fool The World: The Oral History of a Band Called Pixies*. New York: St. Martin's Griffin, 2008.

Gendron, Benard. *Between Montmartre and The Mudd Club: Popular Music and the Avant-Garde*. Chicago: University of Chicago Press, 2002.

George, Nelson. *Hip Hop America*. New York: Penguin Books, 1998.

_____. *The Death of Rhythm & Blues*. New York: Plume, 1988.

George-Warren, Holly and Patricia Romanowski, editors, Jon Pareles, consulting ed., *The Rolling Stone Encyclopedia of Rock & Roll: Third Edition*. New York: Fireside, 2001.

George-Warren, Holly, ed. *Rolling Stone Book Of The Beats: The Beat Generation and American Culture*. New York: Hyperion/Rolling Stone Press, 1999.

Graff, Gary with Daniel Durchholz, ed. *Music Hound Rock: The Essential Album Guide*. Detroit: Visible Ink Press, 1999.

Guralnick, Peter. *Last Train To Memphis: The Rise of Elvis Presley*. Boston: Back Bay Books, 1994.

Hermes, Will and Sia Michel, ed. *SPIN: 20 Years of Alternative Music: Original Writing on Rock, Hip-Hop, Techno, and Beyond*. New York: Three Rivers Press, 2005.

Hopkins, Jerry and Danny Sugarman. *No One Here Gets Out Alive: The Biography of Jim Morrison*. New York: Haku Olelo, Inc./Grand Central Publishing, 1980.

Jay-Z. *Decoded*. New York: Spiegel & Grau, 2010.

Kilmister, Lemmy with Janiss Garza. *White Line Fever: The Autobiography*. New York: Kensington Publishing Corporation, 2002.

Kugelberg, Johan, ed. *True Norwegian Black Metal: We Turn In The Night Consumed By Fire. 3rd Edition*. Brooklyn: Powerhouse Books, dist., 2009.

Light, Alan, ed. *The Vibe History of Hip Hop*. New York: Three Rivers Press, 1999.

Lydon, John with Keith and Kent Zimmerman. *Rotten: No Irish, No Blacks, No Dogs*. New York: Picador, 1994.

McIver, Joel. *Justice For All: The Truth About Metallica*. London: Omnibus Press, 2009.

_____. *The Bloody Reign of Slayer*. London: Omnibus Press, 2008.

Morrow, "Cousin Brucie" with Rich Maloof. *Doo Wop: The Music, The Times, The Era*. New York: Sterling Publishing Co., 2007.

Osbourne, Ozzy. *I Am Ozzy*. New York: Grand Central Publishing, 2009.

Palmer, Robert. *Rock and Roll: An Unruly History*. New York: Harmony Books, 1995.

Perkins, William Eric, ed. *Droppin' Science: Critical Essays on Rap Music and Hip Hop Culture*. Philadelphia: Temple University Press, 1996.

Posner, Gerald. *Motown*. New York: Random House, 2002.

Reynolds, Simon. *Rip It Up and Start Again: Postpunk 1978-1984*. London: Penguin Books, 2006.

Richards, Keith. *Life*. New York: Little Brown and Company, 2010.

Sanford, Christopher. *Kurt Cobain*. Cambridge, MA: Da Capo Press, 1995.

Santelli, Robert. *The Bob Dylan Scrapbook: 1956-1966*. New York: Simon & Schuster, 2005.

Smith, Patti. *Just Kids*. New York: HarperCollins Publishers, 2010.

Spitz, Bob. *The Beatles: The Biography*. New York: Back Bay Books/Little Brown and Company, 2005.

Spitz, Marc. *Bowie: A Biography*. New York: Crown Publishers, 2009.

Walker, Michael. *Laurel Canyon: The Inside Story of Rock and Roll's Legendary Neighborhood*. New York: Faber & Faber, 2006.

Wall, Nick. *When Giants Walked The Earth: A Biography of Led Zeppelin*. New York: St. Martin's Griffin Press, 2008.

Watkins, Glenn. *Soundings: Music in the Twentieth Century*. New York: Schirmer Books, 1988.

MEDIA/INTERNET

Basvarnozel, Skinny Wiki. *Skinny Puppy: History*. www.skinny-puppy.net. 2007.

Branca, Glenn. *Glenn Branca Biography*. www.glennbranca.com/bio.html. 2003

Crib, Martin. *Andy Warhol: Biography*. www.warholfoundation.com. New York: 2002.

Deane, Elizabeth, exec. producer. *Rock & Roll: Episodes 1 – 10*. WGBH Educational Foundation and the BBC, 1996.

Empire: Zeen -- A Writers Cookbook. www.empirezeen.com/spotlight/bau/bau-bio.htm

Erlewine, Stephen Thomas, et al. *All Music Guide*. www.Allmusic.com, Ann Arbor, MI: All Media Guide, 2006.

Geerlinck, Jan. *History of Rap and Hip Hop*. Antwerp: www.Jahsonic.com, 1996.

Grimes, William. *Harold Norse: Beat poet had explored gay identity*. www.nytimes.com. June 14, 2009.

Harrison, Andrew. *Green Gartside: The Brainiest Man in Pop (Besides Brian Eno)*. www.Guardian.co.uk. London: 2011.

The History of the Black Panther Party (BPP). www.hartford-hwp.com/archives, 1999.

Industrial Machine Muzik: The Internal Revolution. www.noizeemuzic.tripod.com, 2001.

Iron Maiden. www.ironmaiden.com, 2009.

Landemaine, Olivier. *The Velvet Underground Web Page*. http://members.aol.com/olandem/vu.html. 2008.

Moss, Robert F., ed. *The Raymond Chandler Web Site: Criticism & Scholarship*. http://home.comcast.net/~mossrobert. 2007.

Merriman, C. D. *William Blake*. www.online-literature.com/blake/. Jalic, Inc.: 2006.

Ogg, Alex and David Upshal. *DJ Kool Herc*. London: Channel 4 Books, 1999.

Pareles, John. *College Radio, New Outlet for the Newest Music*. www.nytimes.com . New York: 1987.

Saxon. www.saxon747.com, 2009.

Shepard, Melissa. Arthur Rimbaud (1854-1891): The Impact of a Child Poet On Modern Poetry. www.empirezeen.com.

Weber, Bruce. Alan Livingston, at 91: helped to reshape American pop culture with The Beatles, Bozo. www.nytimes.com. March 22, 2009.

Wicks, Robert. *Stanford Encyclopedia of Philosophy: Friedrich Nietzche*. http://plato.stanford.edu/entries/nietzche/#NieinfUpo20tCenTho, Palo Alto, CA: 2007.

Wilson, Greg, essayist. *David Mancuso: The Art Of Deejaying Without Deejaying*. www.TheLoftNYC.com, 2003.

Zaretsky, Eli. *Obituaries/Profiles: Norman O. Brown, 1913-2002*. www.radicalphilosophy.com. Middlesex University, London: 2003.

LINER NOTES

Fricke, David, essayist. *The Velvet Underground: Peel Slowly and See, 5 CD Set.* Polydor 31452 7887-2.

Harris, Emmylou and Holly George-Warren, et al. *Sacred Hearts, Fallen Angels: The Gram Parsons Anthology (Insert Booklet).* Rhino Records R2 76780, 2001.

MacKaye, Ian, Jeff Nelson and Henry Rollins. *20 Years of Dischord 1980-2000 Anniversary Compilation: 134 page book.* Washington DC: Dischord, DIS 125.

McKaie, Andy. *Bo Diddley, The Chess Box: Bo Diddley on Bo Diddley (from the 24 Page Booklet).* Universal City, CA: Chess/MCA Records, CHD2-19502.

Palmer, Robert. *Bo Diddley, The Chess Box: Bo Diddley, The Overview (from the 24 Page Booklet).* Universal City, CA: Chess/MCA Records, CHD2-19502.

Pooley, Eric and Mikal Gilmore, et al. *Grateful Dead: So Many Roads (1965-1995).* Grateful Dead Records/Arista GCCD 4066, 1999.

Terrell, Tom. *Eric B. & Rakim: Paid In Full (Liner Notes).* The Island Def Jam Music Group B00044323-02: 2005.